Advances in

ARCHAEOLOGICAL
METHOD AND THEORY

Volume 7

Advisory Board

Advances in
ARCHAEOLOGICAL
METHOD AND THEORY

Volume 7

Edited by
MICHAEL B. SCHIFFER

Department of Anthropology
University of Arizona
Tucson, Arizona

1984

ACADEMIC PRESS, INC.
Harcourt Brace Jovanovich, Publishers
Orlando   San Diego   San Francisco   New York   London
Toronto   Montreal   Sydney   Tokyo   São Paulo

ACADEMIC PRESS, INC.
Orlando, Florida 32887

United Kingdom Edition published by
ACADEMIC PRESS, INC. (LONDON) LTD.
24/28 Oval Road, London NW1 7DX

ISSN: 0162-8003

ISBN: 0-12-003107-8

PRINTED IN THE UNITED STATES OF AMERICA

84 85 86 87   9 8 7 6 5 4 3 2 1

Contents

v

3 The Nature of Organization of Intrasite Archaeological Records and Spatial Analytic Approaches to Their Investigation
CHRISTOPHER CARR

4 Discovering Sites Unseen
FRANCIS P. McMANAMON

5 Remote Sensing Applications in Archaeology
JAMES I. EBERT

6 Geomagnetic Dating Methods in Archaeology
DANIEL WOLFMAN

Contributors

Numbers in parentheses indicate the pages on which the authors' contributions begin.

Christopher Carr (103), Institute for Quantitative Archaeology, Department of Anthropology, University of Arkansas, Fayetteville, Arkansas 72701

Margaret W. Conkey (1), Department of Anthropology, State University of New York, Binghamton, New York 13901

James I. Ebert (293), Branch of Remote Sensing, National Park Service, Albuquerque, New Mexico 87125

Gary Feinman (39), Department of Anthropology, University of Wisconsin, Madison, Wisconsin 53706

Francis P. McManamon (223), Division of Cultural Resources, North Atlantic Regional Office, National Park Service, Boston, Massachusetts 02109

Jill Neitzel (39), Department of Anthropology, Arizona State University, Tempe, Arizona 85287

Janet Spector (1), Departments of Anthropology and Women's Studies, University of Minnesota, Minneapolis, Minnesota 55455

Daniel Wolfman (363), Arkansas Archeological Survey, Arkansas Tech University, Russellville, Arkansas 72801

Contents of Previous Volumes

Volume 1

Volume 2

Volume 3

Volume 4

Volume 5

Volume 6

Advances in
ARCHAEOLOGICAL
METHOD AND THEORY

Volume 7

Archaeology
and the Study of Gender

MARGARET W. CONKEY
JANET D. SPECTOR

INTRODUCTION

A serious challenge to the function of archaeology in contemporary society has
been raised with the assertion that a largely unrecognized rationale for archaeology is the empirical substantiation of national mythology (Leone 1973:129). This
use of archaeology reinforces values of which we are not always aware. As
archaeologists, we "can properly be accused of being acolytes . . . to our culture," unaware of what we have been doing, and whom we serve (Leone
1973:132). Although Leone has offered a fundamental insight with respect to the
relationship of archaeology to a *national* mythology, we show how archaeology
similarly provides substantiation for a particular *gender* mythology. That is, the
following review of archaeology and the study of gender should make it clear
how archaeology has substantiated a set of culture-specific beliefs about the
meaning of masculine and feminine, about the capabilities of men and women,
about their power relations, and about their appropriate roles in society.

We argue that archaeology, like other traditional disciplines viewed through
the lens of feminist criticism, has been neither objective nor inclusive on the
subject of gender. Furthermore, because archaeologists lack an explicit frame-

1

work for conceptualizing and researching gender and—more widely—social roles, we have drawn upon a framework that is implicit and rooted in our own contemporary experience. Thus, we must formulate not only an explicit theory of human social action (see Hodder 1982a, 1982b, 1982c) but also, as part of this, an explicit framework for the archaeological study of gender. This framework must begin with theories and terms that are gender inclusive, not gender specific. As Minnich cogently argues, it is more radical than it appears to develop gender inclusive theories and terms, given that our intellectual tradition is based on a fundamental conceptual error. *Man* and *mankind* are not general, but exclusive; they are partial, and so is the scholarship about *man* and *mankind* (Minnich 1982:7).

The role of archaeology in substantiating contemporary gender ideology is complicated. There is virtually no systematic work on the archaeological study of gender. There are no publications in the field with titles like "Methods for Examining Gender through the Archaeological Record"; or "Gender Arrangements and Site Formation Processes"; or "Gender Arrangements and the Emergence of Food Production"; or, more generally, "Gender Structures and Culture Change." We know of no archaeological work in which an author explicitly claims that we can *know* about gender in the past as observed through the archaeological record who then proceeds to demonstrate that knowledge, or to describe *how* we can know.

This does not mean that archaeologists have not said anything about gender structures or gender behavior in past human life. In spite of the absence of serious methodological or theoretical discourse on the subject, the archaeological literature is not silent on the subject of gender. Rather, it is permeated with assumptions, assertions, and statements of "fact" about gender. This is a serious problem.

We have two major purposes in this review of archaeology and the study of gender. First, we critically evaluate and make explicit some of the messages archaeologists convey about gender in their work. These messages exemplify how archaeology functions to provide "empirical" substantiation or justification for contemporary gender ideology. We illustrate that archaeologists, consciously or not, are propagating culturally particular ideas about gender in their interpretations and reconstructions of the past. This aspect of archaeological interpretation not only undermines the plausibility of our reconstructions of the past but also has serious political and educational implications.

Second, we discuss some of the recent literature on gender by feminist scholars within and outside anthropology. Here we suggest a variety of questions and research problems about gender that might be approached by archaeologists, even by those employing currently accepted methods of analysis. We hope that the feminist critique of archaeology will contribute new ways of thinking about what we do and what we can know about social life in the past. Most important, we hope to bring the subject of gender into the domain of archaeological discourse. In so doing, we hope to call into question the role of archaeology in supporting gender mythology.

A FEMINIST CRITIQUE OF ARCHAEOLOGY

Androcentrism in Anthropology

The phenomenon of gender bias in scholarship is by no means unique to archaeology or anthropology but rather is a feature of our entire intellectual tradition (see Minnich 1982). To some extent, the male-centered or *androcentric* bias in archaeology reflects the dependence upon, if not the actual "tyranny" of, the ethnographic record in structuring archaeological work (Wobst 1978). Archaeologists draw heavily on the research of anthropologists and rely upon their ethnographic descriptions as the basis for understanding cultural diversity and regularities. Whether ethnographically derived models are formulated to be tested by archaeological data, or ethnographic interpretations are invoked as analogies or parallels to "explain" archaeological data, all the limitations—the theoretical and methodological biases and problems of the anthropology that generated the ethnographic interpretations and data—are inherited by the archaeologist. Although archaeologists are generally cautious about simplistic ethnographic analogies, this has not been true with regard to the subject of gender. Furthermore, archaeologists cannot be excused for drawing upon gender-biased ethnography and anthropology (Milton 1978) if only because there has been a substantial restructuring of the gender paradigms in ethnography that archaeologists have neither participated in nor drawn upon, either in ignorance or by choice.

In the past decade feminist scholars in sociocultural anthropology have defined and demonstrated pervasive and multifaceted gender bias in anthropological research and studies of cross-cultural life (see Milton 1978; Rogers 1978; Rohrlich-Leavitt *et al.* 1975; Rosaldo and Lamphere 1974a). There is general agreement about the basic dimensions of the problem and the educational and political ramifications of this kind of bias. Just as the scholarly use of racial stereotypes essentially perpetuates racism given the role of academic research in the enculturation process (i.e., the use of our work in the whole educational system), the uncritical use of gender stereotypes in our scholarship perpetuates and supports sexism and gender asymmetry. If our descriptions and interpretations of life in other cultures simply reiterate our own assumptions about gender, we undermine efforts toward explicating cultural diversity or commonalities (one widely accepted goal of anthropology), while at the same time justifying our own gender ideology.

Androcentrism takes several different forms in anthropology. One principal feature is the imposition of ethnocentric assumptions about the nature, roles, and social significance of males and females derived from our own culture on the analysis of other groups. Researchers presume certain ''essential'' or ''natural'' gender characteristics. Males are typically portrayed as stronger, more aggressive, dominant, more active, and in general more important than females. Females, in contrast, are presented as weak, passive, and dependent. Given this picture of universal gender dichotomies, it is not surprising to find that many anthropologists directly or indirectly assume biological determinants for gender differences and for the asymmetrical relations between males and females. Biological differences are seen as structuring and, in the case of females, limiting social roles and social position (see Sacks 1979).

A second feature of androcentrism in anthropology is, in part, derived from the first. Many researchers, both male and female, who work with the gender assumptions presented above, place more credence in the views of male informants than in those of females (see E. Ardener 1975). The male perspective is taken to be representative of the culture, whereas the female view is typically portrayed as peripheral to the norm or somehow exceptional or idiosyncratic. In the male-centered view of culture, women are often described primarily in terms of their *lack* of male characteristics. They do not do certain things that men do or they do not hold certain beliefs or participate in certain social networks that men do. Women in many ethnographies are described relative to men or primarily in terms of their relationships to men, for example, as sisters, wives, and mothers.

The emphasis on the native male view of culture is associated with the fact that until recently most ethnographers were men and had greater access to male than to female informants. This contributes to another dimension of androcentrism. Most anthropologists have been western, white, and middle- or upper-class men, and their own position within a race, class, and gender system has shaped their perspective on research, particularly in the selection of research problems. An emphasis on topics like leadership, power, warfare, exchange of women, rights of inheritance, and notions of property—to name a few—can all be cited as issues of special interest to males in particular historic contexts and sociopolitical structures (Sacks 1976; Van Allen 1972). The research problems that have been emphasized are not inherently more important than others nor are they necessarily relevant in many of the cultural contexts examined. They do reflect the perspective of the dominant gender, race, and class of the researchers. The fact that some women have learned this perspective and conduct their research from its vantage point does not deny the sources of the perspective, or that such a perspective has been perpetuated over and above the specific, dynamic contexts of social action among the peoples being studied.

Despite the intensive discussion and dissection of gender bias in sociocultural anthropology and ethnography (e.g., Friedl 1975; Schuck 1974; Slocum 1975), this has barely surfaced as a methodological or theoretical concern in archeaology. It has been said that, in general, a "paradigm lag" characterizes the development of archaeology within the broader discipline of anthropology (Leone 1972). This view is at least partially confirmed by the striking contrast between the rising scholarly interest in gender dynamics in ethnology and the virtual absence of attention to this subject in contemporary anthropological archaeology. The point at hand, however, is that although archaeologists have not participated in the discourse about gender, they have not remained silent on the subject of gender.

Androcentrism in Archaeology: Some Illustrations

All the androcentric problems outlined above are found in archaeological work, but in archaeology the problems are in some ways even more insidious than in sociocultural anthropology. Most archaeologists would agree that "we must resist the temptation to project too much of ourselves into the past" (Isaac 1978a:104), and that we "cannot assume the same or even similar organization of adaptive behavior" among past societies (Binford 1972:288). It is precisely because of the intellectual obstacles involved in reconstructing characteristics of social life in the past that so many contemporary archaeologists seek more rigorous methods of analysis.

There has been no rigor in the archaeological analysis of gender. Although archaeologists often make assertions and suggestions about gender arrangements in the past, these are often by-products of the consideration of other archaeological topics or they are so implicit as to be excluded from the attempts of archaeologists to confirm and validate their inferences about past human life. The sources that archaeologists draw upon to derive their implicit notions about past gender arrangements are rarely made explicit. As some case studies discussed here show, it is probable that most derive from androcentric ethnographies or from the researchers' own unexamined, culture-bound assumptions about gender. That is, they do not draw upon nor create a body of theory of social life, or of gender arrangements.

When archaeologists employ a set of stereotypic assumptions about gender, how it is structured, and what it means—what might be called a gender *paradigm*—a temporal continuity of these features is implied. Even when this paradigm is "merely" a cultural backdrop for the discussion of other archaeological subjects (e.g., what an artifact was used for), there is a strongly presentist flavor to archaeological inquiry (Butterfield 1965; Stocking 1965); *presentist* in the sense that the past is viewed with the intent of elucidating features that can be linked with the present. The implicit suggestion of a cultural continuity in gender arrangements from the earliest hominids into the present has two important implications. First, it is part of and contributes to a wider research strategy that emphasizes continuities in many aspects of hominid behavior and evolution (see Pilbeam 1981). Second, the presentist stance forcefully suggests that contemporary gender dynamics are built into the species through unspecified evolutionary processes. Although most American archeologists research human life after the establishment of modern *Homo sapiens,* these archaeologists inherit a picture of human social life and gender structures that appear to have been established for several million years.

One other important implication of the implicit, presentist gender paradigm is what can be called the *false notion of objectivity.* Archaeologists appear to be objective about what we can know about the past. They are quick to point out that ''we have no idea how prehistoric human groups were socially partitioned'' (Binford and Binford 1968b:70). Yet in the very same article, we read about casually made stone tools that indicate presumed occupation by women engaged in plant processing. It has been said that ''as long as we do not correct for the imbalance created by the durability of bone as compared with that of plant residues, studies of human evolution will always have a male bias'' (Isaac 1978a:102). Thus female roles and activities are not only distinct from but less visible than those of their male associates, despite the fact that we do not know how adaptive behavior was organized.

We argue that the archaeological ''invisibility'' of females is more the result of a false notion of objectivity and of the gender paradigms archaeologists employ than of an inherent invisibility of such data. The differential preservation of bones compared to plant remains is *not* the problem, only a diversion. One can claim that female-related data in the archaeological record are invisible only if one makes some clearly questionable assumptions, such as the existence of an exclusive sexual division of labor. It is ironic that a central feature of much contemporary archaeology has been that most of the past is knowable, if only we ask the right questions (Binford 1972:86). But questions that would elucidate prehistoric gender behavior or organization are rarely asked.

It is important to see how these general notions on androcentrism in archaeology can actually be substantiated in particular archaeological studies. Our review of selected archaeological literature is not meant to be exhaustive. Instead we have chosen to discuss those works that exemplify particular problems of androcentrism, that highlight the kinds of gender imagery conveyed in archaeological studies, and that illustrate some of the ways in which those images are conveyed by authors. Our survey includes literature representing archaeological approaches to the entire temporal span of human existence from the emergence of the earliest hominid populations to ethnoarchaological research among contemporary gatherer–hunters.

Perhaps the most obvious case of androcentricism in archaeology both in conceptualization and mode of presentation occurs in the reconstructions of earliest hominid life. Feminist scholars, drawn to this literature in their search for origins of contemporary sex roles and gender hierarchy, have critically evaluated the Man-the-Hunter model of human evolution and have found it permeated with gender bias (see Dahlberg 1981; Martin and Voorhies 1975; Morgan 1972; Slocum 1975; Tanner 1981; Tanner and Zihlman 1976; Zihlman 1978, 1981).

The Man-the-Hunter model was crystallized by Washburn and Lancaster (1968), elaborated by Laughlin (1968), and was subsequently popularized by numerous writers. This model includes a set of assumptions about males and females—their activities, their capabilities, their relations to one another, their social position and value relative to one another, and their contributions to human evolution—that epitomize the problems of androcentrism. In essence, the gender system presented in the model bears a striking resemblance to contemporary gender stereotypes. In spite of recent revisions of the Man-the-Hunter model as part of the human evolutionary scenario (e.g., Isaac 1978a; Lovejoy 1981), the revised gender arrangements are not substantively different from those first presented by Washburn and Lancaster (see Zihlman 1982 for a review). Thus, among ourselves, to students enrolled in our introductory classes, and to the lay public (e.g., Johanson and Edey 1981), we present a picture of continuity in gender arrangements and ideology from early humans to the present, a continuity that suggests an inevitability, if not the immutability of this sphere of social life.

We consider the Man-the-Hunter model here for several reasons. First, as has been noted above, the gender arrangements assumed to characterize the earliest human populations often serve as a baseline for archaeologists working with fully *sapiens* populations. Second, as a scholarly issue, the deconstruction of the model has been under consideration for a decade. We ought to be able to learn from this in our application of more critical thinking to other reconstructions of prehistory. Third, given that the Man-the-Hunter scenario is one with which most archaeologists are familiar, we can use it not merely as a particular instance of androcentrism but also as an example that, in fact, embodies most of the major issues to be considered in a review of archaeology and the study of gender.

These major issues include: (1) the prevalence of gender-specific models that result in gender-exclusive rather than gender-inclusive reconstructions of past human behavior; (2) the common assumption of a relatively rigid sexual division of labor that results in the sex linking of activities with one sex or the other, which in archaeology is often compounded by assuming sex linkages artifactually (e.g., projectile points as male, ceramics as female); and (3) the differential values placed on the different (and usually sex-linked) activities, such that there is a prevailing overemphasis on those activities or roles presumed to be male associated.

There is also another issue that is not—as are the above three issues—androcentrism or a component of male bias, and this issue is perhaps the most important archaeological issue lurking behind this review. What we find lacking in the Man-the-Hunter model is an explicit theory of human social life and, by implication, the lack of a specific paradigm for the study of gender. Without such theory it is precisely in the attempts to reconstruct prehistoric social life that culturally derived (from our own culture), implicit notions about gender serve as the basis for reconstruction. The study of early hominid social life is one of the more obvious domains of archaeological research in which the lack of archaeological theory for elucidating past human life—including, but not limited to, gender structures—is most glaring.

The gender bias in Man-the-Hunter formulations of hominid evolution is apparent on several levels of analysis. On the surface there is the frequent problem of using *man* and *human* interchangeably when, in fact, the authors are referring to males. Washburn and Lancaster state that "human hunting, if done by males, is based on a division of labor and is a social and technical adaptation quite different from that of other mammals" (Washburn and Lancaster 1968:293). Having established the gender-specific nature of human hunting, they go on to suggest that "the biology, psychology and customs that separate us from the apes—all these we owe to the hunters of time past" (1968:303). The gender-specific character of the model is even further exemplified in the discussion of the relationships between human psychology and hunting in which Washburn and Lancaster report: "the extent to which the biological bases for killing have been incorporated into human psychology may be measured by the ease with which boys can be interested in hunting, fishing, fighting and games of war" (1968:300).

All the statements quoted imply an empirical basis that masks the biases of the model. We are provided little detail on the sources for their reconstructions of early human social life, particularly the strict sexual division of labor. Washburn and Lancaster claim that "in a very real sense our intellect, interests, emotions and basic social life—all are evolutionary products of the success of the hunting adaptation" (1968:293). What accompanies that adaptation is not only a strict division of labor but also a clear asymmetry in the contributions of males and females. There is no explanation as to how the strict sexual division of labor evolved in early hominids (but cf. Lovejoy 1981), nor any supporting data for assuming differential contributions of males and females in the areas of group protection or provisioning. Females are allegedly restricted by their biological characteristics associated with pregnancy, lactation, and childbirth, and circumscribed—almost immobilized—by their presumed roles in childcare. That pregnancy, childbirth, or nursing are disabilities and that childrearing is a full-time, exclusively female activity are not universal ideas. These are culturally specific beliefs and comprise a cultural ideology that has been reflected onto our earliest ancestors.

The fact that Washburn and Lancaster emphasize presumed male activities (e.g., hunting, warfare, sexual competition over females) as critical variables to explain hominid evolution speaks more to the perspective of the researchers than to the reality of prehistoric life. There have been challenges to the argument that hunting by males set the course for human evolution, including brain expansion and sociocultural elaboration, but these have only led to a replacement of that argument by more subtle but still androcentric versions. The "homebase," "central place foraging," and "food-sharing" hypothesis (see Lee 1980a for an early formulation of this hypothesis; Isaac 1978a, 1978b, 1982) that now replaces male hunting as central to the success and biobehavioral divergence of the hominid line remains based not only on the assumption of a strict sexual division of labor, but, to many proponents, on an accompanying set of assumptions including limited female mobility and a differential value of gender-associated activities and foodstuffs. The sexual division of labor is envisioned as the means by which food carrying and the delayed consumption of resources could develop. These behaviors in turn allowed for the food sharing that makes the human career distinctive (Isaac 1978a; Lancaster 1978).

The selective pressures for the primordial hominid sexual division of labor—and hence for the foundation adaptation of human life—are attributed to increasingly encumbered females, monogamous pair-bonding and the nuclear family, and even more rigidly to the provisioning of females and young by increasingly skillful and daring australopithecine hunters (Johanson and Edey 1981; Lovejoy 1981; Pfeiffer 1980).

Although plausible alternative behaviors that also may have led to regular food sharing have been presented by feminist anthropologists (see Tanner 1981; Tanner and Zihlman 1976; Zihlman 1978), the basic features of the Man-the-Hunter model persist in anthropology and the alternatives have been ignored or dismissed (Isaac 1978a). Although the homebase and food-sharing model of early hominid life has come under serious attack recently (Binford 1981), its promoters (e.g., Isaac 1982) continue to direct their methodological energies (e.g., Bunn 1981) toward confirmation of hunting and meat processing as central to early hominid lifeways, rather than toward restructuring the questions asked of the archaeological record (but see Potts 1982 for some modifications).

Feminist critiques of early hominid studies should raise the question of the universality of the sexual division of labor (see Cucchiari 1981). Although the division between the sexes in human life may well be an "elementary structure" (LaFontaine 1978:7–8), the degree to which a division of labor along sex lines exists in any culture is varied, dynamic, and closely interrelated with the social relations of production. A division of labor between males and females should not be assumed but rather be considered a problem or a feature of social structure to be explained (Beechy 1978; Hartman 1975; Hochschild 1973). However, with the "documentation" of a sexual division of labor back in the Plio-Pleistocene, researchers working with archaeologically more recent human groups tend to assume its existence without reflection. In fact, analysis of archaeological work focused on human groups in the more recent past shows that the gender systems presented are suspiciously like those discussed in the context of hominization.

We present here an analysis of five widely cited archaeological studies. These were intentionally selected because there was reason to believe, given their problem orientation, that the subject of gender might be explicitly addressed (see Kennedy 1979). Studies by Winters, Hill, Longacre, and Deetz, published in the Binfords' classic collection, *New Perspectives in Archeology*, (1968a), all attempt to consider aspects of social life as reflected or manifested in the archeological record. Yellen's ethnoarchaeological study of the !Kung San, published almost a decade after the other studies (1977), also was selected for review, in part because the researcher based his report on direct observation of a living population reducing the potential for bias of the "ethnographer-as-middleman." Yellen's work was conducted in a climate of increased interest in gender and heightened awareness of the problems of androcentrism in anthropology. Finally, Yellen's study seemed likely to be more accurate and comprehensive on the subject of gender than other earlier works because of the substantial body of literature about sex roles among the !Kung San that could supplement Yellen's own observations (e.g., Draper 1975; Draper and Cashdan 1974; Howell 1977; Lee 1976, 1980b; Yellen and Harpending 1972). We thought Yellen's work might reveal new perspectives in the archaeological treatment of gender.

All these examples of anthropological archaeology suffer from serious interpretive biases. Though each study has its own particular constellation of problems, there are some general patterns of androcentrism that can be summarized. First, there is a persistent and consistent linkage of certain activities with each sex, combined with a failure on the part of investigators to provide any supporting data to justify such associations. This problem is exacerbated by the presumption of linkages between artifact types and each sex; for example, projectile points are associated with men, pots with women. This kind of reasoning implies a rigid, cross-culturally similar system of sexual division of labor in the past. It also imposes rigidity in interpretations of archaeological assemblages that produces simplistic inferences about social life in prehistoric societies. In short, researchers bring to their work preconceived notions about what each sex ought to do, and these notions serve to structure the way artifacts are interpreted. This circular reasoning surely fails to conform to the rigorous methodological standards advocated by most contemporary archaeologists.

A second general feature revealed in our examination is the differential treatment of males and females in archaeological reporting. The descriptions of male activities are more detailed, and are portrayed more actively and more frequently than female-associated activities. There is asymmetry in the visibility, energy levels, accomplishments, and contributions of the sexes. The very language used to describe or refer to males and females differs to the disadvantage of women. For example, there is a striking absence of the word *activity* used with reference to women, though the phrase *male activity* or some version of that phrase is common. Finally, passive verb forms are typically used for females in contrast to the use of active forms for males. Sex bias then is both reflected and realized by the language of archaeology.

In looking more specifically at these studies, detailed aspects of androcentrism are revealed. Howard Winters's work on mortuary materials illustrates how preconceived notions about gender arrangements can confuse, in fact contort, archaeological interpretations. Winters's approach to mortuary materials, like similar work conducted by others, has been criticized for resting on the simplistic and passive assumption that "status and role differences in life are reflected in treatment at death" (see Pader 1982; Parker-Pearson 1982). But even allowing that assumption, which is basic to Winters's inferences, it has been applied differentially to males and females.

For example, when grinding pestles are found with females in burial contexts, they are interpreted as reflecting the grinding and food-processing activities of women. When such items are found associated with males, however, they suggest to Winters that the men must have manufactured these artifacts (for their women?) or utilized them as hammerstones in pursuing other (less feminine?) tasks. The same kind of reasoning is applied in the interpretation of trade goods. When found with males, Winters infers that this indicates men controlled trading activities. But when found with women, the association suggests only that women possessed such items, not that they participated in trade.

Winters's discussion of the meaning of atlatls when found in association with male and female burials is especially problematic. Atlatl components are found rather commonly with female burials. Winters offers several possible explanations: they may have been purely ceremonial inclusions; they may have been related to the transfer of a corporate estate; the Indian Knoll culture may have included a "platoon of Amazons or a succession of Boadicceas defending the Green River" (Winters 1968:206); or, finally, the women may have hunted. "But at the moment, all that can be concluded is that the roles of females overlapped those of males in some way, leading to the . . . association with the former of a weapon that one would expect *a priori* to be a symbol of male activities" (Winters 1968:207). The androcentric problem here is precisely the a priori expectations about what males and females did; what materials they manufactured, used, or exchanged; and what the archaeological association of materials with either sex might mean.

The work of Hill, Longacre, and Deetz (all Ph.D. theses presented in summary form in Binford and Binford 1968a) present other, less blatant aspects of androcentrism in archaeology. None of these studies was explicitly concerned with sex roles, although one could say that the archaeological visibility of women was potentially enhanced, given the methodological focus on the role of potters, who were presumed to be female, as a way to document matrilocal residence patterns. The attention to women was in a sense a by-product of archaeologists' efforts to do social anthropology (see Conkey 1977) working with archaeological materials that happened to be linked with a female activity. Unfortunately, these studies do not demonstrate any serious understanding of the complexities of gender arrangements although their concerns with the archaeological expression of social phenomena such as postmarriage residence patterns would seem to demand such knowledge. Although Deetz, Hill, and Longacre depend on ethnographic data to formulate and test hypotheses, they underutilize these resources as a basis for understanding gender arrangements.

There have been numerous critiques of these "paradigm-setting" studies, but few have considered issues related to gender arrangements. Schiffer has shown some of the methodological weaknesses of these studies in terms of assumptions about site formation processes (1976:22–25), assumptions that include aspects of gender arrangements and how these social phenomena are expressed archaeologically. All the studies presume prior knowledge about who made and used ceramics, the transmission of ceramic design and manufacturing techniques, and about the cultural and spatial contexts of pottery use. None of the studies viewed the ceramics and their makers as active participants in the wider cultural system; rather, the patterning of creamic variability was seen as reflecting social processes to the archaeological observer.

The work of Hill, Longacre, and Deetz has the potential to raise important issues about possible female networks, female roles as keepers or transmitters of a symbolic repertoire, or females as socializers. None of these topics is explored. Nor is any consideration given to the role and power of these female potters, given that ceramics might have significance in group boundary-maintenance processes (Washburn 1977) or in extradomestic exchange systems (Plog 1980). Instead, their studies show serious differential treatment of men and women, highlighting the contributions and activities of males while minimizing those of females. Women are portrayed as performing a very limited number of exclusively domestic tasks—they make pots, and cook and process food. Men, in contrast, carry out a broad range of activities in a variety of cultural domains: weave textiles, use clubhouses, make decisions of public concern, and perform ritual, craft, and manufacturing activities (Hill 1968:117–119).

Some of the criticisms of Longacre, Hill, and Deetz can be attributed to the time at which their work was conducted. Feminist anthropology was not a force in the field and in fact most researchers at the time could be faulted for androcentric bias. But these are some of the founding treatises of the "new archaeology" and they, like much of the research of the following decade, set the tone for the anthropological archaeology that is, at best, weak on the social theory demanded for the solution of anthropological problems (see Aberle 1968).

The analysis of Yellen's work reveals the persistence of bias well into the 1970s. The differential treatment of men and women in this study is particularly striking because the archaeologist was in the role of observer–reporter and not dependent on limited ethnographic information. Yellen had direct access to information on both male and female activity patterns but his approach parallels that of Winters, Deetz, Longacre, and Hill in peripheralizing women and emphasizing men. This practice in "living" archaeology confirms the suspicions of E.

Ardener (1972, 1975) and others who suggest that researchers are more attracted to the models and behaviors of native males regardless of the particular features of the society studied.

Although Yellen acknowledges and reports (1977:62–63) the importance of female gathering among the !Kung (it constitutes 60–80% of their diet as reported by Lee 1965, 1968), he finds that "in practice it is much easier to talk to the men because each day is in some way unique and stands out in the hunter's mind. Asking women where they went produces much less detailed and reliable information" (1977:62–63). Yellen does not acknowledge that this may be a problem of the relationship between the male observer and female informant. As Kennedy suggests, "rather than think that the San women wander out of camp, gather food in the Kalahari, and find their way back home again, having no clear recollection of what they did or where they had been, it may be safer to conclude that the San women are reluctant to give detailed accounts of their activities to strange men" (Kennedy 1979:12). This argument is supported by the amount of detailed and reliable subsistence data collected by female anthropologists from !Kung women (e.g., Draper 1975), including the fact that these women often collect information while out gathering that may be critical in determining the success of male hunters with whom they share this information (Allison Brooks, personal communication, 1977; Heinz 1978).

Even when the contributions and activities of women are observable, as in the case of Yellen's research, the visibility of women is obscured by the mode of reporting. It is interesting to note, for example, that Yellen never identifies women by name in his narrative of events although he frequently does so for men. The women are referred to only in terms of their relationships to men—as someone's spouse or as a member of some specific male's family—or ambiguously and anonymously as part of the "women." Named male individuals hunt, cooperate, follow, lead, butcher, and carry, whereas unspecified women "set out to gather," "spread out" and "maintain voice contact." Unspecified by name, women appear to be mere adjuncts in group movements, leaving the impression that they have no instrumental role in decisions or actions regarding such movements. As Kennedy states, "If we are constantly presented with a picture of men who move about with nameless, faceless families in tow, we will use that picture when we evaluate the archeological record" (Kennedy 1979:14–15).

Although our review of archaeological literature is by no means exhaustive, we would argue that it does represent common themes in terms of the treatment of gender as a subject matter. In general, the contributions, activities, perceptions, and perspectives of females are trivialized, stereotyped, or simply ignored. Regardless of the temporal or cultural contexts examined, we are presented with the same imagery of males, of females, and of sexual asymmetry (male dominance and female subordination). Men are portrayed as more active, more important, and more responsible for group maintenance and protection than are women. Women are typically presented as confined to a domestic sphere where their activities and mobility patterns are allegedly restricted by their roles as mothers and wives. Archaeological research, in content and mode of presentation, has been androcentric. Fortunately, a large body of feminist literature and research on gender is now available to undermine this kind of bias and, more important, to serve as a basis for developing explicitly archaeological approaches to the study of gender.

TOWARD AN ARCHAEOLOGICAL APPROACH TO THE STUDY OF GENDER

The past decade has witnessed the publication of literally hundreds of books and articles in the area of gender studies. Feminist scholars in sociocultural anthropology have played a major role in this discourse (see review articles by Quinn 1977; Lamphere 1977; Rapp 1979; and Atkinson 1982). Although there are no published works attempting to define archaeological approaches to gender, there are publications written by nonarchaeologists within and outside anthropology that explore the origins and evolution of sex roles and gender hierarchy (see Dahlberg 1981; Rorhlich-Leavitt 1977; Slocum 1975; Tanner 1981; Tanner and Zihlman 1976 for examples within anthropology. See Davis 1971; Diner 1973; Morgan 1972; and Reed 1975 for examples in popular literature). Martin and Voorhies's (1975) book is unique in having been authored by archaeologists. Most of the authors contributing to these volumes are unfamiliar with current approaches to archaeological data, inference, or argument, but their work does reflect the enormous interest in evolutionary perspectives on gender as well as the paucity of work by researchers with training in contemporary archaeological methods or theory.

Ethnographic studies now demonstrate complexity and cross-cultural variability in gender arrangements in living societies. These newly formulated examinations focusing on the expression and meaning of gender can serve as the basis for more detailed analysis of the possible material mainifestations of various dimensions of gender arrangements, a first and crucial step toward developing methods for interpreting the archaeological record.

Assuming that we will be able to establish some meaningful correlations between the material and nonmaterial aspects of gender systems, we may then be in a methodological position to use the archaeological record to examine long-term evolutionary patterns and processes concerning gender. Ultimately, this line of research could lead to major theoretical contributions explaining the emergence and development of aspects of gender arrangements and the conditions that contribute to diversity and commonalities in those arrangements as observed through time and across space. At the same time, this kind of research will lead

Jones 1979; Murphy and Murphy 1974; Strathern 1972; Weiner 1976. Also see review articles above for additional ethnographic sources).

Approaches in feminist anthropology fall into three major categories: feminist critiques of androcentrism in the discipline; studies that can aptly be described as ''the anthropology of women''; and work in feminist theory focused either on issues related to sexual asymmetry or on the relationships between gender systems and other facets of social life. In some ways, these categories reflect the chronological development of feminist anthropology from critique to theory building, although the field is still very dynamic, and all three types of studies continue to influence and strengthen the others. Each kind of study is potentially important in working toward archaeological approaches to the subject of gender and is briefly summarized here.

The earliest work in feminist anthropology identified and described male bias in the field. Stimulated by the rising interest in gender arrangements that accompanied the contemporary women's movement, anthropologists reviewed traditional studies in the discipline to learn about the lives of women in other times and places or to consider more generally the treatment of women as subject matter in anthropological work. Previous sections of this chapter discussed the findings of feminist critics in terms of androcentrism in anthropology and these need not be repeated here. The result of the early critiques was to introduce the subject of women as legitimate, interesting, and important in anthropological inquiry. Subsequent and deeper critiques of the field challenge many of the concepts and theories employed by anthropologists, arguing that attention to sex roles and cultural concepts of gender profoundly and essentially alters our analyses and will ultimately transform present understandings of human life (see Atkinson 1982:249).

In response to the feminist critiques of anthropology, numerous researchers in recent years have initiated new ethnographic studies or reanalyses of previous works in efforts to highlight the roles and contributions of women in specific cultures and to examine female participation and influence in various institutions or domains of social life (e.g., Weiner 1976). Studies in the anthropology of women seek to understand commonalities and diversity in women's lives—interculturally and intraculturally—and to examine women's spheres of power and influence. Studies in the anthropology of women essentially reinvestigate human life with females at the center of analysis (see Murphy and Murphy 1974; Rogers 1975; and Rohrlich-Leavitt 1977).

These studies have been particularly useful in revealing the enormous range of activities undertaken by women when viewed cross culturally, challenging stereotypic notions common in anthropology that suggest limitations in female roles or task performance. They further call into question basic anthropological understandings of specific cultures previously examined through the lens of male informants and male observer–analysts (see Rohrlich-Leavitt 1977; Slocum

1975; Weiner 1976; and Zihlman 1981). In all cases these female-centered studies have introduced new and appropriate variables into the analysis of human life.

The third and perhaps the most important area of feminist anthropology focuses on gender theory. Much of the thereotical discourse in the field centers on debates about the universality and expression of sexual asymmetry. The issues were initially presented in what has become a classic in feminist anthropology, *Women, Culture and Society,* edited by Michelle Rosaldo and Louise Lamphere (1974a). The contributors in this volume generally take as given "that all contemporary societies are to some extent male-dominated and although the degree and expression of female subordination vary greatly, sexual asymmetry is presently a universal fact of human social life" (Rosaldo and Lamphere 1974b:3).

The articles in this collection represent the first serious attempts in contemporary anthropology to consider the constellation of factors—economic, social, and ideological—that structure relations between the sexes and, more specifically, determine the social position of females in society. The working assumption of most of the authors in the volume is that there exist distinct gender-linked realms or social spheres: the public–male and the domestic–female. Although many researchers, including those who contributed to *Women, Culture and Society* have come to abandon this conceptualization, or at least its universality, Rosaldo summarized the perspective as follows (Rosaldo 1980:397):

> Our . . . argument was, in essence, that in all human societies sexual asymmetry might be seen to correspond to a rough institutional division between domestic and public spheres of activity, the one built around reproduction, affective, and familial bonds, and particularly constraining to women; the other, providing for collectivity, jural order, and social cooperation, organized primarily by men. The domestic/public division as it appeared in any given society was not a necessary, but an "intelligible" product of the mutual accommodation of human history and human biology. . . . From these observations, we argued, one could then trace the roots of a pervasive gender inequality.

Women, Culture and Society provoked a tremendous response and stimulated serious debates about the presumed universality of sexual asymmetry and the most appropriate methods and frameworks for studying female status (see Lamphere 1977 for a review of these debates). Many argued that the universality of sexual asymmetry assumed by the authors was more apparent than real and that this idea reflected the continuation of androcentric analyses despite the feminist consciousness of the authors. The critics suggested that the appearance of universal female subordination was rooted in the very categories of analysis used by ethnographers, particularly the public–domestic dichotomy. Many researchers, including Rosaldo (1980), have raised serious questions about the applicability of this dichotomy to small-scale or prestate societies.

The structural opposition inherent in the public–private notion and the gender linkages associated with it may be appropriate in describing western, industrial, suburban societies but it distorts the structure and character of gender relations in many other groups. In fact, all too often the division into public and domestic spheres merely describes presumed male and female domains regardless of the specific spatial or social context of their activities and behaviors. The analytical consequences of a *contrast* between a familial sphere and a political–jural sphere (following Fortes 1969) are not only linked to modern western ideology (Nash and Leacock 1977), but also are "incompatible with the study of [human] relationships" and of their articulation (Rosaldo 1980:407, citing O'Laughlin 1977; see also Caplan and Burja 1979). There is now systematic critique of research priorities (see Yanagisako 1979) and core concepts in the discipline of anthropology, concepts and vocabularies (see also Schuck 1974) that have been taken as givens and appear on the surface to be "neutral" and "value free:" *social structure, public–domestic, formal–informal.* The point of this criticism is to pull such concepts apart, trace them back to their origins and evaluate their utility in theory building (Spector n.d.). Archaeologists have only to gain from this kind of theory building.

Although debates continue concerning the universality of female subordination and appropriate methods for measuring the status of women cross culturally, most current feminist research in anthropology has moved away from discussion of gender universals and focuses more on variability. Whyte's overview (1978), *The Status of Women in Preindustrialized Societies,* Liebowitz's (1978) examination of the wide range of family structures in human and nonhuman primate societies, and numerous studies examining the complexities of understanding issues of power, status, and influence within one society or cross culturally (see Quinn 1977) mark a departure in feminist anthropology from "our analytical tradition [that] has preserved the 19th century division into inherently gendered spheres" (Rosaldo 1980:407). Extremely variable contexts and forms of gender-linked organization, status, and behaviors have been demonstrated.

Questions now center on examination of the factors that seem to influence the nature of relations between men and women, the circumstances in which women and men exert power and influence, and the ways that gender arrangements affect or structure group responses to various conditions in their social or natural environments.

Recent work emphasizing the relationships between gender organization and culture change are especially relevant to archaeology and in some respects the approaches taken overlap with the problem-orientation of archaeologists. Several important contributions have been made in the study of colonization and culture contact. These demonstrate the differential impact that these processes have on the roles, activities, and experiences of both men and women (e.g., Bossen 1975; Draper 1975; Etienne and Leacock 1980; Helms 1976; Klein 1976; Leacock 1975; Matthiasson 1976). In certain situations of culture change, gender organization and gender-linked roles are certain not only to be affected but may well structure and set the basis for the new configuration of roles and social organization, from the extractive–productive tasks through the cosmological and ideological realms. Myers (1978) has shown how a period of population decline and demographic anxiety channeled early Israelite women into domestic and reproductive ''niches'' to meet the crisis, and how this limited role was elaborated and made rigid despite demographic recovery by late biblical times. Silverblatt's study (1978) shows how the very roles and rankings of females in the early Inca state became the means whereby they were later subordinated and excluded first within the Inca Empire and, more extensively, with the Spanish Conquest. Rothenberg (1976) has shown how the ''conservatism'' of the subsistence strategies of Seneca women after European contact is, in fact, a deliberate and adaptive response to the exigencies of the contact situation.

Other studies of special interest to archaeologists concern the formation of pristine states. These studies generally do not approach the subject through analysis of the archaeological record but are more concerned with processes of state formation as a major reorganization of human social structures, including gender relations. Reiter, for example, criticizes the archaeological systems approach to state formation, arguing that the framework has not brought enough attention to the contexts in which political formations change (Reiter 1978). She suggests that the domain of kinship deserves careful consideration, for it is probably precisely within this domain that dramatic tensions occurred; with the rise of the state, it is kinship-based societies that are being transformed (Reiter 1978:13). The suppression of the kinship base that is so powerful an organizer of social relations in prestate societies undoubtedly triggered important changes in gender status or gender relations (see Sacks 1979).

Reiter argues that ''we should expect to find variations within state making (and unmaking) societies over time, and between such societies, rather than one simple pattern'' (Reiter 1978:13). The examination of such variability can only be done through the analysis of the contexts of change and the formulation of specific research questions. In this kind of research approach aspects of gender will be illuminated rather than obscured, as is often the case with the broad focus and general scale of analysis typical of archaeological systems studies. Reiter suggests that those approaches that derive models from ethnographic or ethnohistoric accounts have the most potential for refining the archaeological resolution of state formation questions.

In suggesting new approaches to the study of state formation, Reiter reviews existing literature in archaeology and sociocultural anthropology that she believes can contribute to the ''contextualization'' of changes, studies including those that emphasize: the politics of kinship (e.g., Adams 1966; Gailey 1976;

Ortner 1976; Silverblatt 1978); changing content and roles of cosmologies (e.g., Adams 1966; Eliade 1960; Flannery and Marcus 1976; Nash 1978; Willey 1971); intensification of warfare (e.g., McNamara and Wemple 1973; Muller 1977; Pomeroy 1974; but see also Harris and Divale 1976); and trade (e.g., Adams 1974; Kohl 1975; Mintz 1971; Rohrlich-Leavitt 1977). Within any of these topic areas, questions about gender can and should be formulated to enhance our understanding of state formation. Feminist researchers argue that in studying the rise of the state it is likely that one can learn a great deal about the reorganization of gender behavior (e.g., Muller 1977; Nash 1978). The converse is also true. The examination of gender relations, roles, and ideologies must be included in any comprehensive attempts to explain the rise of the state.

This last point is important in articulating the intersection of interests in feminist anthropology and archaeology. Most of the questions about culture process raised by contemporary archaeologists have a gender component or dimension: site functions; site uses; subsistence systems that are, of course, based on task-differentiation; inter- and intrasite spatial phenomena; settlement systems; the power and role of material culture; mechanisms of integration and cultural solidarity; extradomestic trade and exchange systems; and, above all, the course of culture change.

Archaeology and Building Critical Theory

The task before us in developing archaeological approaches to gender is similar to other theoretical and methodological challenges posed in the field in recent years. Most contemporary archaeologists would agree that our knowledge of the past is not necessarily limited by the fragmentary nature of our data but rather by our epistemologies (Wylie 1981) and by our methods for analyzing the archaeological record. Working from this optimistic perspective, archaeologists in recent years have initiated studies into a wide range of issues and questions to increase our understanding of social life and cultural processes in the past. Examples include renewed interest in the role of the individual (Hill and Gunn 1977); increasing concern with site-formation processes (Binford 1980; Schiffer 1976); household-level or other studies of smaller social units (Flannery and Winter 1976; Wilk and Rathje 1982); emphasis on more structural perspectives (Deetz 1977; Hodder 1982b; Lechtman 1976; Wylie 1982); and more sophisticated and explicit realization of the role and power of symbolic forms, rituals, and cosmologies in past human life (Fritz 1978; Hodder 1982c; Isbell 1976; Leone 1982). Most of these are directly related to the inquiry into prehistoric gender behavior, organization, and ideology, and we advocate the explicit addition of the subject of gender arrangements and ideology to this growing list of concerns of contemporary archaeology. However, the success of any of these new approaches in explaining any aspect of prehistoric life or in accounting for the archaeological record is dependent upon critical theory-building and the development of appropriate epistemologies (Wylie 1981, 1982).

Critical theory-building, simplistically, involves the recognition that one generation's gain is the next generation's problem (Rapp 1982). Although the archaeology of at least the past two decades has advocated the pursuit of culture process and prehistoric social organization (Binford and Sabloff 1982; Flannery 1967; Longacre 1963; Sabloff and Willey 1980), there have been trends associated with this pursuit that have inhibited the archaeological study of gender. This pursuit of culture process is precisely one context within which we might have expected a series of questions into the transformation of cultural forms, including those associated with gender roles and organizations. However, as we have seen, these questions have not been raised. Before we turn to a more positive approach to archaeology and the study of gender it is relevant to consider, albeit briefly, why such gender-related questions have not been raised, why archaeologists have been ignorant of the bulk of feminist research of the 1970s, and why social *action* of most sorts has been absent from archaeological theory and interpretation. Only one major theme of archaeological theory is discussed, but this is clearly this generation's problem despite the significant contributions made by archaeological practitioners of the 1970s and earlier.

Few would disagree that one dominant theme of archaeology has been the systems perspective. Ever since Flannery's classic polarization of archaeology into culture history versus culture process and his advocacy of a systems perspective (Flannery 1967), many researchers have become preoccupied with the analysis of subsystems that interact to compromise the total cultural system to be studied. Binford and Sabloff (1982:139) are still advocating the replacement of the normative paradigm with the preferred systems paradigm.

The systems approach per se does not preclude attention to gender structures or dynamics but the research priorities that have resulted tend to focus on such broad processes and in such functional perspective that the sources of change or the roles of individuals, small groups, or even the role of choice have rarely been considered. Although the systems approach has produced useful analyses of resource-procurement systems, seasonality, scheduling, and other general features of subsystems, the actors who procured resources and made decisions about the allocation of their time and labor have somehow become invisible, if not irrelevant and subservient to the system of which they are a part. This preoccupation with the system(s) behind the Indian and the artifact (after Flannery 1967) is not unique to archaeology, and there are insightful critiques of how this perspective on humans as biotic components in information-processing systems has both dominated research in the social and biological sciences and structured our own concepts of ourselves (Haraway 1979, 1983).

There are a number of other problems with a systems approach in archaeology, particularly for the study of gender. Archaeology has become characterized by fragmented studies of the various subsystems—subsistence, settlement, and so forth—and each has essentially become its own subdiscipline of archaeology with its own vocabulary, cross-cultural analyses, and studies of each across time and space. Instead of doing the culture history of different taxonomic units, many contemporary archaeologists do the culture history of different subsystems.

Another problem with the systems approach as practiced in archaeology is the methodological problem of scale. There is a disjunction between the nature of the archaeological data we have to work with and the very broad processes that are examined within the systems perspective. The archaeological remains that we have on hand are the by-products of so much sociocultural behavior that we have not even begun to find a way to read all or even most of the behavior from the data. Given "the dense load of cultural information that every artifact bears" (Kintigh 1978), we should not be surprised at the relative lack of success we have had in answering broad questions that lack requisite specificity. Furthermore, the scale of analysis of the systems approach that focuses on changes within certain subsystems tends to preclude contextualizing the study of change. Thus, the systems approach promotes an ahistoric archaeology: the *contexts* in which social and political formations change are not brought into focus.

Finally, the systems approach of the past decade has relegated the material culture of past human societies—that which comprises the bulk of the archaeological record—to a passive role in human life. Burial treatment *reflects* status, or the numbers and distributions of ovens or wells *imply* certain household sizes or residential systems.

However, both ethnographically and archaeologically the distributions of such artifacts and features as wells, ovens, or pots can be looked at as layouts or structural features that may have not only promoted or channeled interaction and information exchange among the users, whether male, female, or unknown, but also actually defined social action (Braithwaite 1982). Hodder (1983), for example, has shown how women in western Europe negotiated social positions by the use of decorated pottery during the fourth to fifth millennia B.C. Architectural features may also be viewed as potential media through which social action may be defined; there is Carpenter's study (1980) on Islamic house structures of the fifteenth century with room arrangements that are more and less sex-linked in usage, and there is the implication of how rooftop connections in an Iranian village structure patterns of information exchange and female social action (Jacobs 1979).

Just as E. Ardener (1975) has argued that there are other models of society to be obtained, models other than those deriving from the functional approaches to ethnography, there are other models of prehistoric life (e.g., Davis 1978) to be developed than those based on a systemic and functional archaeology. Ardener suggests that these other models for ethnography may best be approached by means of studies of symbolic and ritual behaviors, and certainly these aspects of prehistoric life have been seriously neglected in the past decades. Archaeologists have yet to realize the power of the understanding that the essence of human— and, hence, cultural—life is that it is both material and symbolic simultaneously. We submit that archaeologists must rethink their slavish adoption of the systems perspective and develop a working concept of culture that includes attention to the centrality of symbolic behavior. This is particularly the case if archaeologists want to contribute to the study of gender, and, more broadly, if archaeologists are going to develop an adequate theory of human social and cultural life that must lie behind our research and interpretations. We address some of these broader issues of critical theory-building in the final section of this review, within a discussion of just one possible approach to the archaeology of gender.

An Analytical Framework for the Archaeology of Gender

One most promising general approach to the archaeology of gender is an ethnoarchaeological or ethnohistorical one. The power of the ethnoarchaeological approach in archaeological theory-building has been shown within a variety of theoretical stances (compare Kramer 1979 with Hodder 1982c). Various statements by practioners of ethnoarchaeology (e.g., Binford 1980:5; Deetz 1972:115) emphasize that this domain of research has great potential to aid in the construction of models that we need to link the material and nonmaterial world. However, employing ethnoarchaeological approaches in the case of gender is complicated by the pervasiveness and persistence of androcentrism (as shown in the case of Yellen 1977), and, as discussed above, by the theoretical and epistemological preferences that have inhibited attention to gender.

Our first task in undertaking an ethnoarchaeological approach to gender must be the reconceptualization of gender dynamics. This is one reason why we can only gain from a thorough comprehension of contemporary feminist research in anthropology. Certainly the foundation must be a theory of social life that explicitly acknowledges the parameters and variations in gender arrangements, the possible material manifestations of those arrangements, and above all the ways in which material culture (and other archaeologically accessible data, such as spatial patternings) actively structure (and restructure) not only gender arrangements but many other sociocultural phenomena.

We illustrate here how a new set of terms for some very basic subjects of archaeological inquiry can, when based on a reconceptualization of gender dynamics, yield immediate methodological implications for the archaeology of gender. Janet Spector (1981, 1982) has designed an analytical framework that can be used either to organize observations of gender behaviors and materials among living groups or to reanalyze information about gender available in existing primary or secondary written sources. This is called a *task-differentiation* framework, and it is proposed as a new way to think about and research what is usually considered "activities." This task-differentiation framework focuses on the material parameters of gender arrangements, reduces the possibility of androcentric bias, and overall is more sensitive to and allows for variable and changing configurations of human division of labor. We hope that with sufficient cross-cultural application of the framework we can gain more reliable knowledge about variations in gender arrangements, the factors explaining observed variations, and how such variability might be expressed in the archaeological record. Although the task-differentiation framework is still in the formative stages of development and has been applied only in limited cultural contexts utilizing existing written accounts (see Spector 1981, 1982), it is presented here as an illustration of one kind of approach to the archaeology of gender.

The task-differentiation framework highlights dimensions of male and female activity patterns. The assumption underlying this orientation is that what people do—how they are socially, temporally, and materially organized—is achieved by and hence directly related to the types and structure of sites and their "contents" that are the archaeological record. The framework focuses attention on four interrelated aspects of task performance: the social, temporal, spatial, and material dimensions of each task undertaken by any given group.

To use the framework, one first identifies the tasks performed by people in a given cultural setting—tasks associated with resource procurement and processing; those associated with the physical maintenance of the group, including construction and repair of buildings, facilities, and the manufacture of material goods; and tasks associated with social maintenance of the group, that is, those tasks associated with reproduction, ritual life, health, and inter- and intragroup relations. These categories are not meant to be exhaustive, but such a list should imply a far more comprehensive conception of tasks. Too often, studies of activity patterns or division of labor limit attention to tasks directly associated with subsistence or technology.

Once tasks have been identified, one describes the other parameters of task performance. The *social dimension* of task differentiation identifies the sex, age, number, and relationships (age groups, kin groups, nonkin groups) of task performers. At any one time, who performs the task? How are people organized, scheduled, and interacting in the context of the specific task being examined? Do people work in groups? individually? at the same time and place as others performing the same task? Attention to questions of this type on a task-by-task basis begins to suggest the possibilities of intra- and cross-cultural variability. There are clearly many alternative ways to organize people to perform the same task and each alternative has implications in terms of the task system as a whole, and for the social dynamics. The social dimensions of task performance should be described as precisely as possible rather than using generalizing concepts (e.g., *communal, individual, group*) that may mask important details of task organization.

The next aspect of task differentiation to be described is the *temporal dimension*. For each task identified, one inventories the frequency and duration of task performance. It is important to consider when (seasonally, at what time of the month, day, etc.) the task is performed and how long it takes each time it is performed. These are essentially questions about scheduling and the tempo of people's lives and, again, there is clearly a considerable range of possibilities along this dimension of task differentiation.

The *spatial dimension* of task differentiation identifies where each task is performed within the context of particular site types (depending on the specific subsistence–settlement system being examined). Attention is drawn to tasks that may be spatially discrete in contrast to others that may be performed in various locations. Some tasks always take place within a dwelling or proximate to certain stationary facilities. Other tasks are less restrictive in a spatial sense. Again this dimension of task differentiation has implications in terms of understanding variability in gender systems—for example, differences in the mobility patterns and use of space by men and women within and between cultures—and in terms of understanding possible relationships between gender arrangements and archaeological site formation processes and site structure (see Kent 1980 for a cogent critique of our predetermined notions on these relationships).

Finally, the task-differentiation framework directs attention to the material dimensions of activity patterns. For each task identified, one indicates all the materials associated with task performance. Materials, facilities, and structures are produced, utilized, transformed in the course of use, and left behind as by-products of task performances. One further examines how materials are used by task performers. Are pieces of equipment shared, or individually owned or used? Are some materials that are produced during task performance consistently removed from the location of use? Are there other patternings and structures of materials? It is in this area of investigation that we might begin to learn in a systematic way about similarities and differences between males and females in terms of their use of and knowledge about certain materials, artifact types, and contexts. This is particularly the case if one assumes that the material patternings we observe are brought into existence by cultural classifications and (implicit) cultural knowledge of the makers and users. The picture is clearly more complicated and dynamic than simply identifying one set of tools with males and another with females.

The task-differentiation approach enables those archaeologists interested in gender to consider a number of related questions, some centered on furthering our general understanding of gender as a basic and fundamentally important aspect of human life and other questions more specifically related to the archaeological expression of gender arrangements. In the first case, the approach provides a detailed and quantifiable means of examining and comparing the activity configurations of males and females. Each gender can be separated for analytical purposes to study gender-specific features of the task-differentiation system, including aspects of scheduling, mobility patterns, knowledge of the environment, and resource utilization patterns of men and women. These are all subjects referred to in traditional archaeological studies and treated androcentrically.

Because the framework is cross-culturally applicable, it also allows archaeological researchers to compare groups in different ecological, economic, or social contexts to understand better the expression and sources of variations in gender arrangements. Ultimately, with enough studies of this type, we may begin to approach the archaeological record with sufficient understanding to interpret assemblages in terms of gender. The task framework does begin to illustrate the ways that gender organization and material culture patterning are interactive; these ways are far more complex and variable than previously appreciated.

Finally, the task-differentiation framework allows us to frame research questions that should contribute to the mandatory construction of gender theory. For example, the approach specifies a range of questions to be asked in culture change studies. In cases where we can document the introduction of new elements of technology, we can "model" out the possible differential impact on men and women, given the previously existing task system. Whose labor patterns are likely to be altered? whose mobility patterns affected? whose scheduling patterns?

The task-differentiation framework obviously does not encompass all aspects of gender. Most important, the whole area of the relations between material culture and gender ideology awaits serious investigation (but look for Moore, in press). However, the relevance of such a framework for the archaeology of gender should be clear. At present, the framework involves a methodology of modeling. Certain constraints or attributes (e.g., the spatial dimension of task differentiation) are specified for the construction and testing of paramorphic models (Wylie 1981). These models are built on the basis of better-known contemporary ethnographic or historic contexts, and they are built to represent past cultural contexts, or at least to represent the generative processes that led to the material (and other) output of these contexts. The data of the archaeological record that one is investigating acquire significance as evidence (for gender arrangements or task differentiation) only in relation to the "models of context" that, in this case, the task-differentiation framework can construct (Wylie 1981).

SOME CONCLUSIONS

We are still far from being able to interpret with confidence the archaeological record in terms of gender, and the same can be said for many other features of prehistoric life. Although gender is information that has not regularly and reliably been recovered by archaeologists who lack a theoretical and methodological framework to do so, statements on gender have not been absent in archaeological interpretation. As we have shown, the so-called methodological barriers (the archaeological problem of women; cf. Hayden 1977) have not kept many archaeologists from covert inclusion of assumptions about roles and relationships, nor have these barriers prompted archaeologists to draw upon an increasingly rich literature on human gender. This literature embodies theoretical reconceptualizations, new vocabularies, and a set of research questions immediately relevant to archaeologists.

We are not advocating that archaeologists abandon their currently preferred research objectives and replace them with those that elucidate gender organization, although we do believe that the methodological and theoretical restructuring that this would entail would lead to a much more compelling archaeology. We are not demanding that archaeology try to elucidate whether a male or a female made a certain tool or performed a certain task, nor that archaeologists who have attempted to do so (e.g., Winters 1968) must now empirically support or test their notions.

One thing we *are* saying is that there are certain assumptions about these behaviors that underlie archaeological research and it is these assumptions that must be evaluated and reworked in light of recent feminist research. The organization of gender behavior relates to and is intimately a part of most other aspects of past cultural systems in which archaeologists have always been interested. Archaeologists will have to understand gender dynamics at some level if we are to continue to pursue some research objectives that we have set out for ourselves: site functions and uses; subsistence systems that are, of course, based on task differentiation; inter- and intrasite spatial phenomena; the power and role of material culture; mechanisms of cultural solidarity and integration; extradomestic trade and exchange system; and, above all, the course of culture change.

We hope that our discussion of how archaeologists have perpetuated gender stereotypes stimulates further discussion among archaeologists about appropriate methods for studying gender and about the theoretical implications of including gender in our examination of other archaeological research questions. We hope that this review will stimulate more critical awareness of the role of archaeologists in employing and perpetuating gender stereotypes and androcentric perspectives. We hope also that archaeologists can realize how the roots of the barriers to elucidating past gender arrangements and ideology lie in two related domains. On the one hand, the roots lie more in the sociopolitical contexts of archaeological research than in our inherent abilities to interpret the archaeological record and the past. On the other hand, it will be difficult to do archaeology other than that elicited by contemporary sociopolitical contexts without (1) a critical theory-building that questions aspects of epistemology (e.g., empiricism) and sociocultural theory (e.g., the primacy of systems), and (2) the development of methods appropriate to the actualization of research goals. In order to begin these latter tasks we must question the rationale and role of archaeology, and this has implications for more than the archaeology of gender.

ACKNOWLEDGMENTS

This chapter has been several years in the making and it has been difficult to keep up with and include the more recent literature. The completion of the chapter has been challenged by the fact that we two authors have never met, and it is truly the product of correspondence and telephone calls; we are grateful to Mike Schiffer for getting us together, and it has been a powerful experience in collaboration. Our particular thanks go to the reviewers whose insightful and critical comments have helped immeasurably, if not changed the chapter: Diane Gifford, Joan Smith, Adrienne Zihlman, Randy McGuire, Mike Schiffer, Susan Geiger, Sara Evans, Naomi Scheman, and several anonymous reviewers whose often strong criticisms did not go without serious consideration. We appreciate the fine detective work done by Mary Kennedy in her honors paper research for Janet Spector that elucidated some of the archaeological case studies of androcentrism discussed in the text. We are particularly grateful to the burgeoning literature of feminist anthropology, and various spokespersons whose demand for restructuring anthropological inquiry have been articulate and compelling. We thank Carole Vance and Rayna Rapp for an opportunity for one of us (Conkey) to present a short version of this chapter as a paper at the 1982 American Anthropological Association meetings. We are sincerely grateful to unflagging typists Peg Roe, Liz Newton, and Karen Wright, as well as to the Department of Anthropology at the State University of New York-Binghamton for support services.

REFERENCES

Aberle, D.
>   1968   Comments, in discussion. In *New perspectives in archaeology,* edited by S. R. Binford and L. R. Binford. Chicago: Aldine Press. Pp. 353–359.

Adams, R. McC.
>   1966   *The evolution of urban society.* Chicago: Aldine.
>   1974   Anthropological perspectives on trade. *Current Anthropology* **15**(3):239–258.

Ardener, E.
>   1972   Belief and the problem of women. In *The interpretation of ritual: essays in honor of A. I. Richards,* edited by J. S. LaFontaine. London, Tavistock. Pp. 135–158.
>   1975   Belief and the problem of women. The problem revisited. In *Perceiving women,* edited by Shirley Ardener. New York: John Wiley and Sons. Pp. 1–28.

Ardener, S. (editor)
>   1975   *Perceiving women.* New York: John Wiley and Sons.

Atkinson, J.
>   1982   Review essay: anthropology, *Signs,* **8**(2):236–258.

Beechy, V.
>   1978   Women and production: a critical analysis of some sociological theories of women's work. In *Feminism and materialism,* edited by Annette Kohn and Ann-Marie Wolpe. London: Routledge and Kegan Paul. Pp. 155–197.

Binford, L. R.
>   1972   Archaeological Perspectives. In *An archaeological perspective,* New York: Academic Press. Pp. 78–104.

1980   Willow smoke and dogs' tails: hunter–gatherer settlement systems and archaeological site formation. *American Antiquity.* **45**(1):4–20.

1981   *Bones: ancient men and modern myths.* New York: Academic Press.

Binford, S. R. and L. R. Binford

1968a   *New perspectives in archaeology.* Chicago: Aldine.

1968b   Stone tools and human behavior. *Scientific American* **220** 70–84.

Binford, L. and J. Sabloff

1982   Paradigms, systematics and archaeology. *Journal of Anthropological Research* **38:**137–153

Bledsoe, C.

1980   *Women and marriage in Kpelle society.* Stanford, California: Stanford University Press.

Boserup, E.

1970   *Women's role in economic development.* New York: St. Martin's Press.

Bossen, L.

1975   Women in modernizing societies. *American Ethnologist* **2:**587–601.

Braithwaite, M.

1982   Decoration as ritual symbol: a theoretical proposal and an ethnographic study in southern Sudan. In *Symbolic and structural archaeology,* edited by I. Hodder. Cambridge: Cambridge University Press. Pp. 80–88.

Bunn, H.

1981   Archaeological evidence for meat-eating by Plio Pleistocene hominids from Koobi Fora and Olduvai Gorge. *Nature,* **291:**574–576.

Butterfield, H.

1965   *The Whig interpretation of history.* New York: Norton.

Caplan, P. and J. M. Burja (editors)

1979   *Women united, women divided: comparative studies of ten contemporary cultures.* Bloomington, Indiana: Indiana University Press.

Carpenter, D.

1980   A structural analysis of vernacular architecture. The degree of privatization and its functional implications. B. A. honors thesis, Department of Anthropology, State University of New York, Binghamton, New York.

Chiñas, B.

1973   *The Isthmus Zapotecs: women's roles in cultural context.* New York: Holt, Rinehart, and Winston.

Conkey, M. W.

1977   By chance: the role of archaeology in contributing to a reinterpretation of human culture. Paper presented at Annual Meetings, American Anthropological Association, Houston, Texas.

Cucchiari, S.

1981   ''The gender revolution and the transition from bisexual horde to patrilocal band: the origins of gender hierarchy,'' in *Sexual meanings,* edited by S. Ortner and H. Whitehead. Cambridge, England: Cambridge University Press. Pp. 31–79.

Dahlberg, F. (editor)

1981   *Woman the gatherer.* New Haven: Yale University Press.

Davis, E. G.

1971   *The first sex.* New York: Putnam.

Davis, E. (editor)

1978   *The ancient Californians: Rancholabrean hunters of the Mojave Lakes country.* Los Angeles: Natural History Museum of Los Angeles County, Social Sciences Series 29.

Deetz, James
  1968   The inference of residence and descent rules from archaeological data. In *New perspectives in archaeology*, edited by S. R. Binford and L. R. Binford, Chicago: Aldine. Pp. 41–48.
  1972   "Archaeology as a social science", in *Contemporary archaeology*, edited by M. P. Leone. Carbondale, Illinois: Southern Illinois University Press. Pp. 108–117.
  1977   *In small things forgotten. The archaeology of early American life*. New York: Doubleday Anchor.

Diner, H.
  1973   *Mothers and amazons. The first feminine history of culture*. New York: Doubleday Anchor.

Draper, P.
  1975   !Kung women: contrasts in sexual egalitarianism in foraging and sedentary contexts. In *Toward an anthropology of women*, edited by R. R. Reiter. New York: Monthly Review Press. Pp. 77–109.

Draper, P. and E. Cashdan
  1974   The impact of sedentism on !Kung socialization. Paper presented at Annual Meetings of the American Anthropological Association, Mexico City.

Dwyer, D.
  1978   *Images and self-images: male and female in Morocco. New York:* Columbia University Press.

Eliade, M.
  1960   Structures and changes in the history of religions. In *City invincible*, edited by K. Kraeling and R. Adams. Chicago: University of Chicago Press. Pp. 361–366.

Etienne, M. and E. Leacock
  1980   *Women and colonization: anthropological perspectives*. New York: Praeger.

Flannery, K. V.
  1967   Culture-history vs. culture-process. Review of *An introduction to American archaeology: North and Middle America* (vol. 1) by Gordon R. Willey. *Scientific American*, **3**:399–426.

Flannery, K. V. and J. Marcus
  1976   Formative Oaxaca and the Zapotec cosmos. *American Scientist* **64**:374–383.

Flannery, K. V. and M. C. Winter
  1976   Analyzing household activities. In *The early Mesoamerican village.* edited by K. Flannery, New York: Academic Press. Pp. 34–44.

Fortes, M.
  1969   *Kinship and the social order*. Chicago: Aldine.

Friedl, E.
  1975   *Women and men*. New York: Holt, Rinehart and Winston.

Fritz, J. M.
  1978   Paleopsychology today: ideational systems and human adaptation in prehistory. In *Social archaeology: beyond subsistence and dating.* edited by C. Redman *et al*. New York: Academic Press. Pp. 37–57.

Gailey, C.
  1976   The origin of the state in Tonga. Gender hierarchy and class formation. Paper presented at American Anthropological Association meetings, Washington, D.C.

Goodale, J.
  1971   *Tiwi wives: a study of the women of Melville Island, North Australia*. Seattle, Washington: University of Washington Press.

Haraway, D.
  1979   Sex, mind, and profit: from human engineering to sociobiology. *Radical History Review* **20**:206–237.
  1982   Signs of dominance. *Studies in History of Biology* **6**:129–219.
Harris, M. and W. T. Divale
  1976   Population, warfare, and the male supremacist complex. *American Anthropologist,* **78**:521–538.
Hartman, H.
  1975   Capitalism, partriarchy, and job segregation by sex. *Signs: Journal of Women in Culture and Society.* **1** (3, Part 2): 137–169.
Hayden, B.
  1977   Stone tool functions in the Western Desert. In *Stone tools as cultural markers: change, evolution and complexity,* edited by R. V. S. Wright. New Jersey: Humanities Press, Inc. Pp. 178–188.
Heinz, H. J.
  1978   *Namkwa: life among the Bushmen.* London: Cape Publishers.
Helms, M. W.
  1976   Domestic organization in Eastern Central America: The San Blas Cuna, Miskito, and Black Carib compared. *W. Canadian Journal of Anthropology* **VI** (3):133–163. Special issue: *Cross-sex relations: native peoples,* edited by P. A. McCormack.
Hill, J. N.
  1968   Broken K Pueblo: patterns of form and function. In *New perspectives in archaeology,* edited by S. R. Binford and L. R. Binford. Chicago: Aldine. Pp. 103–142.
Hill, J. and J. Gunn
  1977   *The individual in prehistory.* New York: Academic Press.
Hochschild, A.
  1973   A review of sex role research. *American Journal of Sociology* **78**(4) 1011–1025.
Hodder, I.
  1982a   Theoretical archaeology: a reactionary view. In *Symbolic and structural archaeology,* edited by I. Hodder. Cambridge, England: Cambridge University Press. Pp. 1–16.
  1982b   (editor) *Symbolic and structural archaeology.* Cambridge, England: Cambridge University Press.
  1982c   *Symbols in action. Ethnoarchaeological studies of material culture* Cambridge, England: Cambridge University Press.
Hodder, I.
  1983   Burials, houses, women and men in the European Neolithic. In *Ideology and social change,* edited by D. Miller and C. Tilley. Cambridge, England: Cambridge University Press.
Howell, N.
  1979   *Demography of the Dobe !Kung.* New York: Academic Press.
Hughes-Jones, C.
  1979   *From the Milk river: spatial and temporal processes in Northwest Amazonia.* Cambridge, England: Cambridge University Press.
Isaac, G. Ll.
  1978a   The food-sharing behavior of protohuman hominids. *Scientific American,* **238**(4):90–108.
  1978b   "Food sharing and human evolution: archaeological evidence from the Plio-Pleistocene of South Africa." *Journal of Anthropological Research* **34**:311–325.

1982   Bones in contention: competing explanations for the juxtaposition of Early Pleistocene artifacts and faunal remains. Paper presented at 4th International Archaeozoology Congress, London.

Isbell, W.
1976   Cosmological order expressed in prehistoric ceremonial centers. *Actes du XLII Congres International des Americanistes.* **IV**:269–297.

Jacobs, L.
1979   Tell-i-Nun: archaeological implications of a village in transition. In *Ethnoarchaeology,* edited by C. Kramer. New York: Columbia University Press. Pp. 176–191.

Johanson, D. and M. Edey
1981   *Lucy: the beginnings of humankind.* New York: Simon and Schuster.

Kennedy, M. C.
1979   Status, role, and gender: Preconceptions in archaeology. Manuscript, Department of Anthropology, University of Minnesota, Minneapolis.

Kent, S.
1980   Search and what shall ye find: a holistic model of activity area use. Paper presented at annual meetings, Society for American Archaeology. Philadelphia, Pennsylvania.

Kessler, S. and W. MacKenna
1978   *Gender: an ethnomethodological approach.* New York: John Wiley & Sons.

Kintigh, K.
1978   A study in the archaeological inference of aspects of social interaction from stylistic artifact variation. Preliminary paper. Department of Anthropology, Ann Arbor: University of Michigan.

Kohl, P.
1975   The archaeology of trade. *Dialectical Anthropology* **1**:43–50.

Klein, L.
1976   ''She's one of us, you know''—the public life of Tlingit women: traditional, historical, and contemporary perspectives. In *Western Canadian Journal of Anthropology,* **VI,** (3):164–183. Special issue: *Cross-sex relations: Native Peoples,* edited by P. A. McCormack.

Kramer, C.
1979   Introduction. In *Ethnoarchaeology. Implications of ethnography for archaeology,* edited by C. Kramer. New York: Columbia University Press. Pp. 1–20.

LaFontaine, J. S.
1978   Introduction in *Sex and age as principles of social differentiation.* ASA Monograph 17, New York: Academic Press. Pp. 3–20.

Lamphere, L.
1977   Review essay: anthropology. *Signs, Journal of Women in Culture and Society* **2**(3):612–627.

Lancaster, J. B.
1978   Caring and sharing in human evolution. *Human Behavior,* **1**(2):82–89.

Laughlin, W. S.
1968   Hunting: An integrating biobehavior system and its evolutionary importance. In *Man the hunter,* edited by R. Lee and I. Devore. Chicago: Adline. Pp. 304–320.

Leacock, E. B.
1973   Introduction. In *The origin of the family, private property and the state,* by F. Engels, New York: International Publishers.
1975   Class, commodity, and the status of women. In *Women cross-culturally: change and challenge,* edited by R. Rohrlich-Leavitt. The Hague: Mouton. Pp. 601–616.

1977   Women in egalitarian societies. In *Becoming visible. Women in European History*, edited by R. Bridenthal and C. Koonz. Boston: Houghton-Mifflin. Pp. 11–35.

1978   Women's status and egalitarian society: implications for social evolution. *Current Anthropology* **19** (2):247–254.

Lee, R. B.

1965   Subsistence ecology of !Kung bushmen. Unpublished Ph.D. dissertation, Department of Anthropology, University of California, Berkeley.

1968   What hunters do for a living, or how to make out on scarce resources. In *Man the hunter*, edited by R. B. Lee and I. DeVore. Chicago: Aldine. Pp. 30–48.

1976   !Kung spatial organization: an ecological and historical perspective. In *Kalahari hunter–gatherers*, edited by R. B. Lee and I. DeVore. Cambridge, Massachusetts: Harvard University Press. Pp. 74–97.

1980a   The hand-to-mouth existence: a note on the origin of human economy. Appendix in *The !Kung San* Cambridge: Cambridge University Press (originally 1968). Pp. 489–494.

1980b   *The !Kung San. Men, women, and work in a foraging society*. Cambridge: Cambridge University Press.

Lechtman, H.

1976   Style in technology—some early thoughts. In *Material culture. Style, organization, and dynamics of technology*, edited by H. Lechtman and R. Merrill. Proceedings of American Ethnological Society, 1975. St. Paul: West Publishing. Pp. 3–20.

Leone, M. P.

1972   Issues in anthropological archaeology. In *Contemporary archeology*, edited by M. Leone. Carbondale, Illinois: Southern Illinois University Press. Pp. 14–27.

1973   ''Archaeology as the science of technology: Mormon town plans and fences.'' In *Research and theory in current archeology*, edited by C. L. Redman. New York: John Wiley & Sons. Pp. 125–150.

1982   Some opinions about recovering mind. *American Antiquity* **47**(4):742–760.

Liebowtiz, L.

1978   *Males, females, families*. North Scituate, Mass: Duxbury Press.

Longacre, W. A.

1963   Archeology as anthropology: a case study. Ph.D. dissertation, Department of Anthropology, University of Chicago.

1968   Some aspects of prehistoric society in east-central Arizona. In *New perspectives in archeology*, edited by S. R. Binford and L. R. Binford. Chicago: Aldine. Pp. 89–102.

Lovejoy, C. O.

1981   The origin of man. *Science* **211**, (4480):341–350.

MacCormack, C. and M. Strathern (editors)

1980   *Nature, culture and gender*. Cambridge: Cambridge University Press.

Martin, M. K. and B. Voorhies

1975   *Female of the species*. New York: Columbia University Press.

Matthiasson, C. (editor)

1974   *Many sisters: women in cross-cultural perspective*. New York: Free Press.

Matthiasson, J.

1976   ''Northern Baffin Island women in three cultural periods. In *Western Canadian Journal of Anthropology*, **VI**, (3):201–212. Special Issue: *Cross-sex relations: native peoples*, edited by P. A. McCormack.

McNamara, J. and S. Wemple

1973   The power of women through the family in medieval Europe: 500–1100. *Feminist Studies* **I**(3–4):126–141.

Milton, K.
    1978   Male bias in anthropology. *Man* (n. s.) 14:40–54.
Minnich, E.
    1982   "A devastating conceptual error: how can we *not* be feminist scholars?" *Change Magazine* **14**(3):7–9.
Mintz, S.
    1971   Men, women and trade. *Comparative Studies in Society and History,* 13(3):247–269.
Moore, H. (editor)
    in   *Women, archaeology and material culture.* Cambridge: Cambridge University Press.
    press
Morgan, E.
    1972   *The Descent of Woman.* New York: Stein and Day.
Muller, V.
    1977   The formation of the state and the oppression of women: A case study in England and Wales. *Radical Review of Political Economy* **9**:7–21.
Murphy, Y. and R. Murphy
    1974   *Women of the forest.* New York: Columbia University Press.
Myers, C.
    1978   The roots of restriction: women in early Israel. *Biblical Archeologist* **41**(3):91–103.
Nash, J.
    1978   The Aztecs and the ideology of male dominance. *Signs: Journal of Women in Culture and Society,* **4**(2):349–362.
Nash, J. and E. Leacock
    1977   Ideologies of sex: archetypes and stereotypes. *Annals of the New York Academy of Science,* **285**:618–645.
Ortner, S. B.
    1976   The virigin and the state. *Michigan papers in anthropology* **2**
Ortner, S. B. and H. Whitehead
    1981a   *Sexual meanings: the cultural construction of gender and sexuality.* Cambridge: Cambridge University Press.
    1981b   "Introduction: accounting for sexual meanings," in *Sexual meanings.* Cambridge: Cambridge University Press.
Pader, E.
    1982   Symbolism, social relations and the interpretation of mortuary remains. *British Archeological Reports,* International Series, 130.
Parker-Pearson, M.
    1982   Mortuary practices, society and ideology: an ethnoarcheological study. In *symbolic and structural archaeology,* edited by I. Hodder. Cambridge: Cambridge University Press: 99–114.
Pfeiffer, J.
    1980   Current research casts new light on human origins. *Smithsonian* **11**(3):91–103.
Pilbeam, D.
    1981   Major trends in human evolution, in *Current argument on early man,* edited by L-K. Königsson. New York and Oxford: Pergamon Press.
Plog, S.
    1980   *Stylistic variation of prehistoric ceramics: design analysis in the American southwest.* New York: Cambridge University Press.
Pomeroy, S.
    1974   *Goddesses, whores, wives and slaves: women in classical antiquity.* New York: Schocken.

Potts, R.
  1982   Caches, campsites and other ideas about earliest archaeological sites. Paper presented
          at Symposium, Origins of Culture: John Hopkins University Medical School, Bal-
          timore, Maryland.
Quinn, N.
  1977   Anthropological studies on women's status. *Annual Review of Anthropology,*
          6:181–225. Palo Alto: Annual Reviews, Inc.
Rapp, R.
  1979   Review essay: anthropology. *Signs: Journal of Women in Culture and Society,*
          4(3):497–513.
  1982   Introduction to Worlds in collision: the impact of feminist scholarship in anthropology.
          A Symposium presented at the 1982 annual meetings, American Anthropological
          Association, Washington, D.C.
Reed, E.
  1975   *Women's evolution.* From matriarchal clan to patriarchal family. New York: Path-
          finder Press.
Reiter, R. R.
  1975   *Toward an anthropology of women.* New York: Monthly Review Press.
  1978   The search for origins: unraveling the threads of gender hierarchy. *Critique of An-
          thropology,* **3**(9–10):5–24.
Rogers, S. C.
  1975   Female forms of power and the myth of male dominance: a model of female/male
          interaction in peasant society. *American Ethnologist,* **2**(4):727–755.
  1978   "Women's place: a critical review of anthropological theory," *Comparative Studies in
          Society and History* **20**(1):123–162.
Rohrlich-Leavitt, R. (editor)
  1975   *Women cross-culturally: change and challenge.* The Hague: Mouton.
Rohrlich-Leavitt, R.
  1977   Women in transition: Crete and Sumer. In *Becoming visible.* Women in European
          History, edited by R. Bridenthal and C. Koonz. Boston: Houghton-Mifflin Co. Pp.
          36–59.
Rohrlich-Leavitt, R., B. Sykes, and E. Weatherford
  1975   Aboriginal women: male and female anthropological perspectives. In *Toward an an-
          thropology of women,* edited by R. R. Reiter. New York: Monthly Review Press. Pp.
          110–126.
Rosaldo, M. Z.
  1980   The use and abuse of anthropology: reflections on feminism and cross-cultural under-
          standing. *Signs: Journal of Women in Culture and Society,* **5**(3):389–417.
Rosaldo, M. Z. and L. Lamphere (editors)
  1974a   *Woman, culture, and society.* Stanford, California: Stanford University Press.
  1974b   Introduction to *Woman, culture and society.* Stanford, California: Stanford University
          Press. Pp. 1–16.
Rothenberg, D.
  1976   Erosion of power—an economic basis for the selective conservatism of Seneca women
          in the 19th century. In *Western Canadian Journal of Anthropology,* **VI,** (3). Special
          issue: *cross-sex relations: native peoples,* edited by P. McCormack: 106–122.
Sabloff, J. and G. Willey
  1980   *A history of American archaeology,* (2d ed.) San Francisco: W. H. Freeman & Co.
Sacks, K.
  1976   State bias and women's status. *American Anthropologist,* **78**(3):565–569.

1979   *Sisters and wives: the past and future of sexual equality.* Westport, Connecticut: Greenwood Press.
Sanday, P. R.
    1981   *Female power and male dominance: On the origins of sexual inequality.* Cambridge: Cambridge University Press.
Schiffer, M. B.
    1976   *Behavioral archeology.* New York: Academic Press.
Schlegel, A. (editor)
    1977   *Sexual stratification: a cross-cultural view.* New York: Columbia Press.
Schuck, V.
    1974   A symposium: masculine blinders in the social sciences. *Social Science Quarterly* **55**(3):563–585.
Silverblatt, I.
    1978   Andean women in the Inca empire. Feminist Studies, **4**:37–61.
Slocum, S.
    1975   Woman the gatherer: male bias in anthropology. In *Toward an anthropology of women,* edited by R. R. Reiter. New York: Monthly Review Press. Pp. 36–50.
Spector, J. D.
    n.d.   On building a feminist base in anthropology. Manuscript on file, Department of Anthropology, University of Minnesota, Minneapolis, Minnesota.
    1981   Male/female task differentiation: A framework for integrating historical and archeological materials in the study of gender and colonization. Paper presented at the 5th Berkshire Conference on the History of Women, Vassar College, Poughkeepsie, New York.
    1982   Male/female task differentiation among the Hidatza: toward the development of an archeological approach to the study of gender. In *The hidden half: studies of native plains women,* edited by P. Albers and B. Medicine. Washington, D.C.: University Press of America.
Stocking, G.
    1965   On the limits of 'presentism' and 'historicism' in the historiography of the behavioral sciences. *Journal of the History of the Behavioral Sciences.* **1**:211–218.
Strathern, M.
    1972   *Women in between: female roles in a male world: Mount Hagen, New Guinea.* London: Seminar Press.
Tanner, N.
    1981   *On becoming human.* Cambridge: Cambridge University Press.
Tanner, N. and A. Zihlman
    1976   Women in evolution. Part I. Innovation and selection in human origins. In *Signs: Journal of Women in Culture and Society:* **1**(3):104–119.
Van Allen, J.
    1972   Sitting on a man: colonialism and the lost political institutions of Igbo women. *Canadian Journal of African Studies* **6**:165–181.
Wallman, S.
    1976   Difference, differentiation, discrimination. *New Community: Journal of the community Relations Commission,* **V** (1–2).
Washburn, D. K.
    1977   *A symmetry analysis of upper Gila area ceramic design.* Peabody Museum Papers, **68.** Cambridge, Massachusetts:Harvard University Press.
Washburn, S. and C. S. Lancaster
    1968   The evolution of hunting. In *Man the hunter,* edited by R. Lee and I. DeVore. Chicago: Aldine. Pp. 293–303.

Weiner, A.
1976   *Women of value, men of renown.* Austin: University of Texas Press.
Whyte, M. K.
1978   *The status of women in preindustrialized societies.* Princeton, N.J.: Princeton University Press.
Wilk, R. and W. Rathje (editors)
1982   *Archaeology of the household:* building a prehistory of domestic life. A Special issue of *American Behavioral Scientist,* **25**(6):611–724.
Willey, G.
1971   "Commentary on: 'The emergence of civilization in the Maya Lowlands'." In *Observations on the emergence of civilization in MesoAmerica,* edited by R. Heizer. Contributions of the University of California Archaeological Research Facility (Berkeley), No. 11:97–109.
Winters, H.
1968   Value systems and trade cycles of the late archaic in the Midwest. In *New perspectives in archeology,* edited by S. R. Binford and L. R. Binford. Chicago: Aldine. Pp. 175–222.
Wobst, H. M.
1978   The archaeo-ethnology of hunter–gatherers, or the tyranny of the ethnographic record in archaeology. *American Antiquity,* **43**:303–309.
Wylie, M. A.
1981   Positivism and the new archeology. Unpublished Ph.D. dissertation, Department of Philosophy, State University of New York, Binghamton.
1982   Epistemological issues raised by a structural archaeology. In *Symbolic and structural archaeology,* edited by I. Hodder. Cambridge: Cambridge University Press. Pp. 39–56.
Yanagisako, S.
1979   Family and household: the analysis of domestic groups. *Annual Review of Anthropology,* **8**:161–205.
Yellen, J.
1977   *Archaeological approaches to the present.* New York: Academic Press.
Yellen, J. and H. Harpending
1972   Hunter-gatherer populations and archaeological inference. *World Archaeology* **4**(2):244–253.
Zihlman, A.
1978   Women in evolution, part II: subsistence and social organization in early hominids. *Signs: Journal of Women in Culture and Society,* **4**(1):4–20.
1981   Women as shapers of the human adaptation. In *Woman the gatherer,* edited by F. Dahlberg. New Haven, Connecticut: Yale University Press. Pp. 75–102.
1982   Whatever happened to woman-the-gatherer? Paper presented at annual meetings, American Anthropological Association, Washington, D.C.

Too Many Types:
An Overview of Sedentary
Prestate Societies
in the Americas

GARY FEINMAN
JILL NEITZEL

INTRODUCTION

Over the past 40 years anthropological studies of culture change have centered on the origins of agriculture and the rise of the state. Recently, social scientists have recognized that if the development of hierarchical governments, marketing systems, and social stratification is to be explicated, then the evolution of pre-state forms of social differentiation and political leadership must be understood. As a consequence, there has been an increasing interest in societies that are organizationally intermediate between mobile hunter–gatherers and bureaucratic states.

In this chapter we focus on ethnographic and ethnohistoric information from the New World to examine prestate sedentary societies. Preliminary conclusions concerning the range of variability in this sample of cases are presented. In

ADVANCES IN ARCHAEOLOGICAL
METHOD AND THEORY, VOL. 7

addition, suggestions for a less typological approach to the study of long-term change are offered.

PRESTATE SEDENTARY SOCIETIES: THE CLASSIFICATION PROBLEM

The definition of an intermediate form of organizational complexity has been in the anthropological literature for more than a century (e.g., Morgan 1963). In this section several of the classificatory schemes that have been used to describe prestate sedentary societies are reviewed along with the impact that these schemes have had on current studies in both archaeology and ethnography. In general, we argue that despite the considerable attention that has been given to ordering middle-range societies, our understanding of both variation and change in them remains inadequate.

Anthropologists studying prestate sedentary societies have continually vacillated between defining a general stage in cultural evolution and identifying subtypes to interpret variability (Table 2.1). Because several overviews (Carneiro 1981; Dunnell 1980; Harris 1968) have been completed recently, a detailed historical reconstruction of these different approaches is not necessary here. However, it is important to note that a diversity of societal attributes has been used to define the different stages and subtypes that comprise each of these typological schemes.

Morgan (1963) proposed anthropology's first general evolutionary scheme, dividing world societies into the three stages of savagery, barbarism, and civilization. Each of Morgan's stages was based on a particular means of food procurement with technological innovations used to subdivide these categories further. Different social, economic, and political institutions were presumed to parallel each subsistence mode (Leacock 1963; Voget 1975:294).

Following decades of field study and several regional overviews (Oberg 1955; Steward 1946–1950; Steward and Faron 1959), a second developmental scheme was outlined by Service (1962). Adopting White's (1959) general evolutionary approach, Service identified four societal types: bands, tribes, chiefdoms, and states. These divisions were quite similar to the four categories of South American societies that had been defined previously by Steward in the *Handbook of South American Indians* (Harris 1968:675; Steward 1949a). However, unlike Steward, Service incorporated into his scheme the general tripartite typology of economic relations that had been proposed by Polanyi (1957). For Service, societies that were intermediate between hunting–gathering bands and states were subdivided into a tribal stage associated with Polanyi's reciprocal mode and more complex chiefdoms that were defined by redistribution.

An alternative evolutionary scheme based on social stratification and class

TABLE 2.1

Organizational Subtypes of Prestate Sedentary Societies

Steward (1949a)	Oberg (1955)	Steward and Faron (1959)	Morgan (1963)	Service (1962)	Fried (1960, 1967)	Goldman (1970)	Sahlins (1958)	Renfrew (1974)	Taylor (1975)	Steponaitis (1978)	Sanders and Webster (1978)
Circum-Caribbean societies	Politically organised chiefdoms	Theocratic chiefdoms / Militaristic chiefdoms	Upper Barbarism	Chiefdoms	Stratified	Stratified	1	Individualizing chiefdoms	Paramountcies	Complex chiefdoms	Chiefdoms and stratified societies
							2A	Group-Oriented chiefdoms	Ranked chieftaincies	Simple chiefdoms	
						Open	2B				
	Segmented tribes	Topical Forest chiefdoms	Middle Barbarism		Rank	Traditional	3		Non-ranked chieftaincies		Tribes
Tropical Forest societies			Lower Barbarism	Tribes			Big Man societies				
	Homogeneous tribes										

distinctions was proposed by Fried (1960, 1967). Fried, like Service (1962), divided world societies into four categories. However, although both he and Service identified states as the most complex form, no simple equivalencies could be drawn between the first three types in the two schemes. For example, Fried's ranked and stratified societal types cross-cut Service's chiefdom concept. Thus, even in these general stage sequences, the selection of different diagnostic attributes resulted in a variety of idealized forms.

Whereas the definitions of middle-range societies proposed by Morgan (1963), Service (1962), and Fried (1967) were general and theoretically based, alternative subdivisions were produced through more detailed, area-specific data analyses. Variation in intermediate-level societies has been recognized in 40 years of research conducted in Polynesia (Goldman 1970; Sahlins 1958), South and Central America (Helms 1979; Oberg 1955; Steward 1949a; Steward and Faron 1959), sub-Saharan Africa (Taylor 1975), and prehistoric Europe (Renfrew 1974). These differences have been recognized in both quantitative (Taylor 1975) and nonquantitative analyses of ethnographic, historical (Helms 1979), and archaeological (Renfrew 1974) data. Subtypes have been defined using a variety of diagnostic attributes including environmental, organizational, and historical factors (Table 2.1).

In Polynesia, the region on which Service's (1962) definition of the ideal chiefdom was based, two comparative studies focusing on different diagnostic criteria yielded two distinct subdivisive schemes (Goldman 1970; Sahlins 1958). Whereas Sahlins defined four societal modes using environment, redistribution, and stratification as his key factors, Goldman identified only three based on variation in political authority and succession. Although there is a correspondence between the schemes in the relative complexity assigned to individual cases (Helms 1976:29), discrepancies exist in the specific societies that comprise comparable subtypes. For example, the four societies defined as Sahlins's (1958:11–12) second-most-stratified category (IIA) are distributed across all three of Goldman's types. Alternatively, the seven societies in Goldman's (1970:21) *traditional* type fall into three of Sahlins's modes (Table 2.2). Similar disagreements concerning the subdivisions of middle-range societies characterize typological studies that have been conducted in both South America (Oberg 1955; Steward 1949a; Steward and Faron 1959) and Africa (Fortes and Evans-Pritchard 1940; Horton 1976; Richards 1978; Southall 1965; Stevenson 1968; Taylor 1975; Vansina 1962; Vengroff 1976).

Despite the continued emphasis on the construction of typologies in both general and area-specific studies, relatively little consensus has been achieved concerning the nature of middle-range societies. Major unresolved issues include: (1) which attributes should be used to subdivide intermediate-level societies; (2) how exactly these societies should be subdivided, if at all; (3) what is the range of variability that characterizes these societies; and (4) what processes

TABLE 2.2

Comparison of Sahlins's and Goldman's Classification of Polynesian Chiefdoms

Goldman[a]	Sahlins[b]			
	3	2B	2A	1
Traditional	Pukapuka Ontong Java Tokelau	Tikopia Futuna	Uvea	
Open		Marquesas	Mangaia Easter Island	Samoa
Stratified			Mangareva	Hawaii Tonga Tahiti

[a] 1970:21.
[b] 1958:11–12.

are involved in their development and change. The solution to these issues lies not in rearranging, contracting (Fried 1975; Service 1975), or expanding the typological schemes. Instead, alternative approaches focusing on societal variation and change are necessary (e.g., Blanton *et al.* 1981; Butzer 1980; Dunnell 1980; Kohl 1978; Wenke 1981; Yoffee 1979).

Service's (1962) chiefdom category, the most-often-utilized model of middle-range societies, can be used to illustrate some of the problems inherent in the typological approach. To Service (1962:144), *chiefdoms* were "redistributional societies with a permanent central agency of coordination." The development of chiefdoms was viewed as a functional response to economic specialization that resulted from environmental diversity (Service 1962:145). Consequently, the economic role of redistribution was interpreted both as diagnostic of chiefdoms and as causally significant in their formation.

Service's (1962) chiefdom model was based largely on Sahlins's (1958) description of redistribution in Polynesian societies. Yet, a recent reinterpretation of Hawaiian chiefdoms has disputed the central role that Sahlins gave to this activity (Earle 1977, 1978). Earle has challenged the notion that environmental diversity between subunits required a single node of exchange. Thus, he has argued that the position of the chief in food distribution was not essential to the integration of society but rather occurred infrequently in response to disasters. Earle found that chiefly exchange often involved status goods that were used to create alliances and mobilize support to increase the chief's powers. Chiefs did not disperse all that they collected and thus had greater access to economic resources. Earle's reanalysis weakens previous arguments concerning the purely integrative or functional role of chiefs (see also Finney 1966; Gilman 1981).

Studies in other areas have supported Earle's (1977, 1978) reanalysis of the role of redistribution. In both Africa (Taylor 1975) and Panama (Helms 1979), chiefs were found to have had little importance in local exchange but rather functioned as adjudicators, long-distance traders, and conveyors of secret knowledge. As in Hawaii, chiefs in Panama acted to mobilize their own power by collecting tribute rather than to benefit society as a whole (Helms 1979). Thus, although these studies do not deny redistribution as one function of chiefs, they certainly cast doubt on the causal and core role that Service (1962) gave to that activity.

Questions concerning the universality of redistribution raise serious doubts with Service's (1962) model of chiefdom development. If chiefs were not always redistributors, then the transition from a reciprocal to a redistributive economy cannot be a general cause for the evolution of chiefdoms. Yet, in recent anthropological theory (Harris 1980; Service 1962, 1975), chiefdoms have been linked so closely to redistribution that, without this activity, no general feature of these societies remains as clearly diagnostic. In more specific areal studies variation in population size (Taylor 1975), rules of succession (Goldman 1970; Helms 1980), degrees of stratification (Sahlins 1958), and chiefly functions (Taylor 1975) have been used to define subtypes of chiefdoms; but these attributes have not been demonstrated to have either cross-cultural or processual relevance. More important, these variables have not been shown to have general utility for distinguishing chiefdoms from other levels of societal complexity.

This discussion of redistribution suggests an important limitation inherent in the typological approach. That is, the occurrence of a single attribute is assumed to evidence the presence of the entire constellation of characteristics used to define the type (Blanton *et al.* 1981; Leach 1973; Sawyer and Levine 1966; Skinner 1977). The acceptance of such a relationship between attributes results in the adoption of an as-yet-undemonstrated steplike view of change (Graves *et al.* 1969; Plog 1973, 1977a, 1979; Udy 1965). The futility of this approach is suggested by the continual redefinition of key attributes and the formulation of new societal types in the anthropological literature. This repeated classification has not significantly increased our understanding of either the degree of variation that characterizes middle-range societies or the processes of change that led to their development (Granovetter 1979:511; Plog and Upham 1979; Tainter 1978).

Clearly, organizational and demographic differences exist between world societies. This is supported by the statistical associations that have been found between specific attributes (Carneiro 1962, 1967; Ember 1963; Naroll 1956). However, when more limited comparisons are made within more narrowly defined societal categories, these relationships do not necessarily hold. For example, Johnson (1982) has shown that although a strong relationship exists between population and organizational complexity when comparisons are made on a broad scale, this correlation is weakened considerably when the analysis is limited to societies within narrower population parameters. Thus, conclusions

drawn from investigations of the entire range of world societies do not necessarily apply in more limited comparisons. However, recent analyses of early
states (Claessen and Skalnik 1978) and hunting–gathering bands (Binford 1980)
have begun to enhance our interpretations of the relationships between attributes
in these more restricted contexts. A similar fine-grained focus is employed in this
chapter to examine the nature of the relationships between specified attributes in
prestate sedentary societies.

PROBLEM ORIENTATION AND DATA SELECTION

Comparative analyses are necessary to understand prestate sedentary societies.
Ideally, such research should focus on long-term change in specific societal
attributes at a regional scale. Unfortunately, few studies of such broad spatial and
temporal scope are available for comparative purposes. Yet because prior cross-
cultural investigations have merely contrasted middle-range societies with simpler and more complex forms, we argue that a synchronoic cross-cultural analysis can still be productive. This approach allows us to assess which attributes, if
any, are shared by societies that are intermediate between hunting–gathering
bands and states.

In this chapter we focus on the characteristics of middle-range societies and
the relationships between attributes for two reasons. First, we want to assess the
nature and extent of variability of ethnographically and ethnohistorically known
prestate sedentary societies. Second, we want to evaluate the implications of this
diversity for archaeological research.

We arbitrarily limit our examination of prestate sedentary societies to the New
World for several reasons. First, general schemes of sociopolitical development
have made only limited use of cases from the western hemisphere. Consequently, we examine the data from this area and see how it compares to the
previously proposed models. Second, intermediate-level societies in the Americas are found in a wide range of topographic, climatic, and vegetation zones,
providing a good sample for comparative purposes. Finally, the wealth of ethnographic and ethnohistoric information on middle-range societies prohibits us
from examining all cases and necessitates the selection of a smaller sample.
Although we realize that our focus on the New World omits a number of important cases, this study should provide a clearer picture of middle-range societies
than prior syntheses that have relied so heavily on Polynesia. Because islands are
small, bounded, and biogeographically distinctive (Evans 1973; Pianka 1974),
the societies that developed in Polynesia must have faced a rather atypical set of
problems. Thus, these societies seem poorly suited for theoretical generalizations
concerning sociopolitical organization.

In this analysis the sample includes societies that are neither mobile hunter–gatherers nor bureaucratic states. Because the distinction between mobile and sedentary populations is not a simple dichotomy, we formulate an operational criterion for selecting sedentary societies. Cases were chosen when at least a segment of the population continuously occupied a settlement for minimally three seasons during several successive years. The sample is drawn from Central and South America, the Caribbean, and a number of regions in North America, including the Northeast, the Southeast, the Southwest, the Northwest Coast, and California.

In this investigation, ethnographic and ethnohistoric materials are used because, in general, they contain more complete descriptions of societal organization and regional demography than archaeological studies. To expand the scope of the analysis, we rely heavily on compilations of information such as the handbooks of North and South American Indians (Heizer and Sturtevant 1978; Ortiz and Sturtevant 1979; Steward 1946–1950; Trigger and Sturtevant 1978). These sources have the advantage of providing comparable information in a standardized format. Supplemental references are also used for most cases (Appendix 1). Generally, the utilized information pertains to the early contact period because later societies were affected by depopulation and often were incorporated into European colonial systems. The study also does not include the petty states that existed in parts of Postclassic Mesoamerica at the time of conquest. Although these polities usually lacked multitiered administrative bureaucracies, their highly developed social class systems, incorporation into large-scale market networks, and dense regional populations (Appel 1982; Brumfiel 1983; Kowalewski 1976; Miles 1957; Spores 1967, 1974) seem to distinguish them from the societies examined in this investigation.

Because we rely on ethnographic and ethnohistoric data from the New World, we are concerned with several potential difficulties. The most serious problem involves the representativeness of our sample, given the effects of European contact. Admittedly, the examined societies were affected by early European intrusions into the New World. Yet change in response to external relations also took place during the precontact period. Even though the eventual consequences were extreme, the selective forces operating on societies in the early contact period may not have been qualitatively different from those that were present previously (cf. Plog 1977b:262). Any attempt to generalize about societies must recognize that change is constantly occurring and that to assume the existence of a static equilibrium prior to European intervention is unrealistic (cf. Schrire 1980). Additionally, restricting the sample to only those societies that lacked external connections with other differentially organized populations would limit the analysis to few, if any, cases (cf. Lee and Devore 1968:3).

In compiling the material for this investigation, a series of more technical problems also have to be addressed. Because the ethnographic accounts did not always record the same kinds and amounts of information, we have to rely on a different sample of cases for each analytical issue that was examined. Often data are not available on a specific topic for a particular society. When these omissions occur, the case is simply eliminated from the specific analysis in question. Exceptions to this procedure are made in the investigation of two variables. We consider it significant when some leadership functions are mentioned whereas others are excluded because rarely did researchers record the activities that leaders did not perform. Similarly, we think it is relevant when certain status markers associated with leaders are identified whereas others are not. However, given the substantial number of cases examined, the results of this study should not be affected significantly by inconsistencies present in the data.

DATA ANALYSIS AND INTERPRETATION

This investigation focuses on the set of attributes that has been used to characterize and subdivide middle-range societies. We have selected those social, political, economic, and demographic factors that are considered directly relevant to archaeological as well as ethnographic research (Peebles and Kus 1977). As discussed previously, one key attribute has been the specific duties or functions of leaders. Since the seminal work of Sahlins (1958) and Service (1962), redistribution has been used as the diagnostic feature for one form of intermediate societies. Though the generality of this task has been challenged (Earle 1977, 1978), no recent study has examined whether there is any function that characterizes leadership cross culturally in middle-range societies. Using our sample of cases, we assess the relative importance of the chief's role as redistributor as compared to a series of other functions that have been noted in more specific areal studies (Earle 1977, 1978; Helms 1979; Taylor 1975).

A second important variable is the nature and extent of social differentiation. Though Service (1962) asserted that the position of the chief was social in nature with no long-term economic or political advantages, both Sahlins (1958) and Fried (1967) have argued that social stratification is an important aspect of interpersonal relations in at least some prestate sedentary societies (see also Sanders and Webster 1978). In order to examine the role of social differentiation we consider variation in patterns of succession and the physical manifestations of different status categories.

A third examined property is the structure and complexity of the political organization of middle-range societies. Recent general approaches to political development have contrasted chiefdoms, one form of intermediate-level society, with simpler and more complex organizational types by the numbers of levels in the decision-making hierarchy (Flannery 1972; Johnson 1973, n.d.). Following Service (1962), Johnson (1973:4–12) defined *tribes* and *chiefdoms* as two stages of prestate sedentary societies characterized by one and two administrative tiers, respectively. Steponaitis (1978:420) has defined societies with one level of decision-making as *simple chiefdoms*, although his description of these societies differs little from the tribal or big-man stage. In contrast to Johnson, Steponaitis has argued that *complex chiefdoms* can have political hierarchies with two or three tiers. Using our sample, we examine these contradictory expectations and evaluate the utility of this approach for defining different degrees of sociopolitical complexity.

A set of demographic variables also is investigated. Although previous researchers have suggested that total population and maximal community size vary with increasing organizational complexity (Forge 1972; Fried 1967; Service 1962; Steward 1949b), the expected ranges of these variables have rarely been defined empirically for middle-range societies (cf. Baker and Sanders 1972; Sanders and Price 1968). This analysis evaluates whether specific demographic patterns could be associated with intermediate-level societies. Because Steponaitis (1978) has proposed a model of settlement distribution in complex chiefdoms, we also examine the spatial arrangement of communities in our sample to assess his expectation.

Finally, we examine the interrelationships between these variables. This is important because ethnographic and archaeological studies have tended to rely on one or two key attributes to infer the presence of all characteristics that have traditionally been associated with middle-range societies. The goal of this investigation is to go beyond this kind of classificatory work (Grebinger 1973; Peebles

TABLE 2.3

Functions of Leaders in Central and South America

	Subsistence	Ambassadorial affairs	Warfare	Administer village tasks	Host visitors	Control trade	Ceremonies
Carib	X	—	—	—	—	—	—
Mapuche–Huilliche	—	X	X	—	—	—	—
Camayura	—	X	—	X	X	—	—
Bacairi	—	—	—	X	X	X	—
Paressi	—	—	X	X	X	—	X
Manasi	X	—	X	—	—	—	X
Mojo	X	—	X	—	—	—	X
Sherente	—	X	—	—	X	—	X
Chiriguano	X	—	X	X	—	—	—
Hispaniola Arawak	—	X	X	X	X	—	X
Cuna	—	—	X	—	—	X	X
	4	4	7	5	5	2	6

and Kus 1977; Renfrew 1973) and define both the variability and the nature of the patterning evident in New World prestate sedentary societies.

Functions of Leaders

Positions of leadership are defined in each of the prestate sedentary societies that is examined. Information concerning the specific duties of these leaders was recorded for 63 cases. A cross-cultural examination of these function was undertaken to evaluate traditional anthropological conceptions of leadership in middle-range societies (Service 1962).

In the analysis the cases are grouped for organizational purposes into three broad geographic regions. The largest sample, 34 cases, was collected from the western United States. In addition, data were obtained on 18 groups from the eastern United States and 11 from Central and South America. The role of leaders is found to encompass a broad set of tasks. Initially these activities were divided into 18 specific categories so that the relative importance of various duties could be evaluated (Tables 2.3–2.5). More general categories were defined and utilized in subsequent analyses.

Leaders are involved in a range of economic activities. In our initial, more specific tabulations, these duties included the distribution of goods, storage, tribute collection, the organization of feasts, and support of the poor. These functions were intentionally not lumped under the rubric of redistribution. Al-

Punish wrongdoers	Settle disputes	Village meetings	Guardian of morals	Feasts	Store information	Distribution of goods	Storage	Total
—	—	—	—	—	—	—	—	1
—	—	—	—	—	—	—	—	2
—	—	—	—	—	—	—	—	3
—	—	—	—	—	—	—	—	3
—	—	—	—	—	—	—	—	4
X	—	—	—	—	—	—	—	4
X	X	—	—	—	—	—	—	5
X	X	X	X	—	—	—	—	7
X	X	—	—	X	X	—	—	7
—	—	—	—	X	—	X	X	8
X	X	=	X	=	X	=	X	8
5	4	1	2	2	2	1	2	11 cases

TABLE 2.4

Functions of Leaders in Eastern North America

	Ambassadorial affairs	Village meetings	Control trade	Tribute	Ceremonies	Host visitors	Warfare	Feasts
Santa Lucia	X	—	—	—	—	—	—	—
Nottoway–Meherrin	X	—	—	—	—	—	—	—
Western Abenaki	—	X	—	—	—	—	—	—
Virginia Algonkians[a]	—	—	X	X	—	—	—	—
Cherokee	—	X	—	—	X	—	—	—
Iroquois	X	X	—	—	—	X	—	—
Cusabo	—	—	—	—	—	X	X	X
Choctaw	X	—	—	—	X	—	X	—
Calusa	—	—	—	—	X	—	X	—
Guale	X	—	—	X	—	—	X	X
Timucua	X	—	—	X	X	—	X	—
Narragansett	—	—	—	X	—	—	X	—
Natchez	—	—	—	—	X	—	—	—
Delaware	X	X	X	—	X	X	X	—
Hasinai	—	X	—	—	X	X	X	X
Powhatan	X	—	X	X	X	X	—	X
Huron	X	X	X	X	X	—	X	X
Creek	X	X	—	—	X	X	X	X
	10	7	4	6	10	6	10	6

though each of these activities may be part of the process of redistribution, the presence of any of these tasks alone or in concert does not necessarily imply the operation of this process. For example, whereas feasts may provide a means of redistributing goods, the organization of feasts does not necessarily indicate that a redistributive economy is at work.

In addition to these economic duties, leaders perform a diversity of other tasks. Ideological activities include the sponsoring of ceremonies and the guarding of public morals. Administrative tasks encompass leading public meetings, appointing officials, and supervising community chores such as construction. Leaders also organize subsistence activities, including the allocation of resource zones and the scheduling of food procurement. Judicial responsibilities involve the adjudication of disputes and the punishment of wrongdoers. Another important task is the storage of information concerning territorial boundaries and genealogical histories.

Leaders also act to link their constituents with other populations. They control trade, declare war, make alliances, and host guests. Although these latter duties are primarily externally directed, they are clearly related to such internal activities as feasts and ceremonies.

Settle dis-putes	Punish wrongdoers	Subsis-tence	Provide for poor	Admin-ister vil-lage tasks	Distribution of goods	Appoint officials	Storage	Store infor-mation	Total
—	—	—	—	—	—	—	—	—	1
—	—	—	—	—	—	—	—	—	1
—	—	—	—	—	—	—	—	—	1
—	—	—	—	—	—	—	—	—	2
—	—	—	—	—	—	—	—	—	2
—	—	—	—	—	—	—	—	—	3
—	—	—	—	—	—	—	—	—	3
—	—	—	—	—	—	—	—	—	3
X	—	—	—	—	—	—	—	—	3
—	—	—	—	—	—	—	—	—	4
—	X	—	—	—	—	—	—	—	5
—	X	X	X	—	—	—	—	—	5
—	X	—	—	X	X	X	—	—	5
X	X	—	—	X	—	—	—	—	9
X	X	—	—	X	X	—	—	—	9
—	X	—	—	—	—	X	X	—	9
X	—	—	—	X	—	—	—	X	10
X	—	—	—	X	X	—	X	—	10
5	6	1	1	5	3	2	2	1	18 cases

a Excluding Powhatan.

In each of the three study areas, variation is noted in the total number of functions that different leaders perform. Yet although leaders in each area carry out the same basic range of activities (see Wirsing 1973), some regional distinctions are observed in the relative frequencies of different tasks (Tables 2.6 and 2.7). For example, whereas roughly two-thirds of the Central and South American leaders act in war-related matters, approximately one-half of the leaders in the eastern United States and one-third in the west are described as having military duties. It is also interesting to note that in cases in which leaders carry out three tasks or less, the same task did not occur most frequently in each region (Tables 2.3–2.5).

In order to examine variability in the activities of leaders who performed different numbers of functions, we have pooled our cases into a single sample (Tables 2.6 and 2.7). Societies in which leaders are listed as having one to three, four to seven, and more than eight functions are then compared. Certain tasks such as the distribution of goods, centralized storage, support of the poor, the appointment of officials, punishment of wrongdoers, and storage of information are never recorded among leaders with three or fewer functions. Alternatively,

TABLE 2.5

Functions of Leaders in Western North America

	Tribute	Warfare	Guardian of morals	Ceremonies	Feasts	Administer village tasks	Settle disputes	Subsistence	Ambassadorial affairs
Obispeno Chumash	X	—	—	—	—	—	—	—	—
Klamath	—	X	X	—	—	—	—	—	—
Bella Coola	—	—	—	X	X	—	—	—	—
Coast Miwok	—	—	X	—	—	X	—	—	—
Luiseno	—	X	—	X	—	—	—	—	—
Salinan	X	—	—	—	—	—	X	—	—
Serrano	—	—	—	X	—	—	—	X	—
Cupeno	—	—	—	—	—	X	X	—	X
Shasta	—	—	X	—	—	—	X	—	X
Yana	X	—	—	X	—	—	—	—	—
Tipai–Ipai/Diegueno	—	X	—	—	—	X	—	—	—
Wintu	X	—	—	X	—	—	—	—	X
Hopi	—	—	—	X	—	—	X	—	X
Atsugewi	X	—	X	—	X	—	X	—	—
Barbareno Chumash	X	X	—	X	—	—	—	X	—
Yurok	—	—	—	X	X	—	X	—	—
Wappo	—	X	—	X	—	X	—	—	X
Maidu	X	X	—	X	—	—	—	X	X
Nisenan	—	—	—	X	X	—	X	X	—
Patwin	—	—	—	X	—	X	—	—	X
Costanoan	X	X	X	X	—	—	—	—	—
Chimariko	X	X	—	—	X	—	X	X	—
Zuni	—	—	—	X	—	—	—	X	X
Gabrielino	X	X	X	X	X	—	X	—	X
Nootka	X	X	—	X	X	—	—	X	X
Salish	—	—	—	X	X	—	X	X	X
Cahuilla	X	X	—	X	X	—	X	X	—
E. & S.E. Pomo	—	—	X	X	X	X	X	X	X
Nomlaki	—	—	X	X	X	X	X	X	X
W. & N.E. Pomo	—	—	X	X	X	—	—	—	X
Eastern Miwok	—	X	X	X	X	X	X	X	X
Southern Kwakiutl	X	—	—	X	X	X	—	X	X
Yuki	—	X	X	X	X	X	X	X	X
Yokut & W. Mano	—	—	—	X	X	X	X	X	X
	13	13	11	25	16	11	16	15	18

20–40% of these individuals are described as leading ceremonies, making alliances, and conducting war.

In the sample with four to seven functions, all but two of the recorded tasks (control trade, storage) are present in at least one case. However, different functions occur more frequently than others (Table 2.7). In three-fourths of the cases leaders are noted as having ceremonial responsibilities, whereas more than half of these individuals have military duties and organize subsistence activities. In general, leaders with more than eight functions perform the recorded tasks

Village meetings	Punish wrongdoers	Host visitors	Distribution of goods	Store information	Provide for poor	Appoint officials	Storage	Control trade	Total
—	—	—	—	—	—	—	—	—	1
—	—	—	—	—	—	—	—	—	2
—	—	—	—	—	—	—	—	—	2
—	—	—	—	—	—	—	—	—	2
—	—	—	—	—	—	—	—	—	2
—	—	—	—	—	—	—	—	—	2
—	—	—	—	—	—	—	—	—	2
—	—	—	—	—	—	—	—	—	3
—	—	—	—	—	—	—	—	—	3
X	—	—	—	—	—	—	—	—	3
X	X	—	—	—	—	—	—	—	4
—	X	—	—	—	—	—	—	—	4
—	—	X	—	—	—	—	—	—	4
—	—	—	X	—	—	—	—	—	5
—	—	X	—	—	—	—	—	—	5
—	—	X	—	X	—	—	—	—	5
—	—	X	—	X	—	—	—	—	6
—	—	X	—	—	—	—	—	—	6
X	—	—	—	—	X	—	—	—	6
—	—	X	—	X	X	—	—	—	6
—	—	X	—	X	X	—	—	—	7
—	—	X	—	—	X	—	—	—	7
X	—	X	—	X	—	X	—	—	7
—	—	—	—	—	—	—	—	—	7
—	—	—	X	—	—	—	—	—	7
X	X	—	—	—	X	—	—	—	8
—	—	—	—	X	—	—	X	—	8
—	—	X	—	—	—	—	—	X	9
—	—	—	X	—	—	—	—	X	9
X	—	X	X	—	X	—	—	X	9
—	X	X	—	—	—	—	—	—	10
—	—	X	X	—	—	—	X	X	10
—	X	X	—	—	X	—	—	X	12
X	X	X	X	X	X	—	—	X	13
7	6	15	6	7	8	1	2	6	34 cases

with greater frequency. The most marked increases are noted in the relative proportion of leaders who lead feasts, preside over meetings, distribute goods, store food, control trade, and negotiate alliances.

To assess the validity of the observed patterning, we repeated the preceding analysis by grouping functionally related tasks into 10 more-general categories (Table 2.8). Leaders with few functions primarily perform intervillage, ideological, administrative, judicial, and military tasks. Redistributive activities are less important in these cases. In addition, leaders with few functions can perform all

TABLE 2.6

Comparison of Leadership Functions by Region

	Ceremonies	Settle disputes	Warfare	Ambassadorial affairs	Subsistence	Feasts	Administer village tasks	Tribute
Western North America ($n = 34$)	25	16	13	18	15	16	11	13
Eastern North America ($n = 18$)	10	5	10	10	1	6	5	6
Central and South America ($n = 11$)	6	4	7	4	4	2	5	0

TABLE 2.7

Comparison of Functions among Leaders Performing Different Numbers of Tasks

Total number of tasks	Ceremonies	Settle disputes	Warfare	Ambassadorial affairs	Subsistence	Feasts	Administer village tasks	Tribute
1–3 ($n = 28$)	7	4	6	8	2	2	4	4
4–7 ($n = 24$)	18	9	15	11	10	8	6	11
8–13 ($n = 16$)	16	12	9	13	8	14	11	4

TABLE 2.8

Comparison of General Functions among Leaders Performing Different Numbers of Tasks

Total number of general tasks	Subsistence	Redistribution[a]	Feasts	Ideological[b]
1–3 ($n = 25$)	2	4	2	11
4–6 ($n = 26$)	10	17	10	22
7–9 ($n = 12$)	8	10	12	12

[a] Redistribution = distribute resources, provide for poor, tribute, storage.
[b] Ideological = ceremonies, guardian of morals.
[c] Judicial = settle disputes, punish wrongdoers.
[d] Administrative = administer village tasks, village meetings, appoint officials.
[e] Intertribal affairs = ambassadorial affairs, host visitors.

Host visitors	Punish wrongdoers	Distribution of goods	Guardian of morals	Control trade	Village meetings	Provide for poor	Store information	Storage	Appoint officials
15	6	6	11	6	7	8	7	2	1
6	6	3	0	4	7	1	1	2	2
5	5	1	2	2	0	0	2	2	0

Host visitors	Punish wrongdoers	Distribution of goods	Guardian of morals	Control trade	Village meetings	Provide for poor	Store information	Storage	Appoint officials
4	0	0	3	2	4	0	0	0	0
11	9	3	4	0	4	5	6	0	2
11	8	7	6	10	7	4	4	6	1

Judicial[c]	Administrative[d]	Store information	Warfare	Control trade	Intertribal affairs[e]
6	9	0	6	2	11
15	11	7	17	3	18
11	11	3	6	7	11

but one (store information) of the entire range of duties, and no single activity is present in even half of these cases.

In societies in which leaders have four to six of these general functions, the importance of redistributive activities increases markedly. Yet roughly comparable increases also occur in the relative importance of several other tasks (Table 2.8). Most of the leaders who perform more than six general functions fulfill the entire range of duties. However, only ideological tasks and the leading of feasts are undertaken in each of these cases.

In summary, positions of leadership are identified in all our cases of middle-range societies. However, the number of activities associated with particular leaders is found to be quite variable. For analytical purposes, we define a set of leaders as *weak* if they perform fewer than four of the specific functions. *Strong* leaders are identified as those individuals who perform at least eight tasks. Because a range of activities is recorded for weak leaders, one cannot predict the specific duties that are carried out in each case. In addition to performing a greater number of these same tasks, strong leaders also carry out six activities that are not observed among our sample of weak leaders.

Based on these investigations, redistribution is clearly not the central function of leadership in sedentary prestate societies. Weak leaders only ocassionally redistribute; and although the importance of redistribution increases among strong leaders, this activity is not shared by all of them. In fact, an examination of Table 2.8 reveals that among leaders who perform greater numbers of general functions, other tasks show comparable increases in importance and are more commonly observed than redistribution. It should be noted that in this more general analysis, *redistribution* refers to a diverse set of activities (Table 2.8). If by *redistribution* one implies merely the distribution of food and other goods by leaders (Table 2.7), then the relative importance of this task is diminished further (cf. Peebles and Kus 1977).

The observed increase in the incidence of redistributive activities among more powerful leaders may reflect one strategy used by these individuals to increase their access to goods. In this regard, it is significant that the control of external trade is also a more important activity for strong as opposed to weak leaders. Thus, the greater control over goods through redistribution and trade that characterizes more powerful leaders tentatively seems to support current definitions of redistribution as a largely self-serving activity (Earle 1977, 1978; Flannery 1972:423; Gilman 1981; Helms 1979; Moseley and Wallerstein 1978:274–275).

Status Differentiation

The nature and extent of status differentiation in prestate sedentary societies has been the subject of continous debate. Whereas Service (1962) has argued that leaders in his tribal and chiefdom categories retain no long-term economic advantage, Fried (1967) has used the existence of such advantages to contrast his ranked and stratified societal types. Although the definition of *stratification* is controversial (Cancian 1976), few would deny that the concept embodies two principles: (1) differential access to wealth, resources, and social position (Fried 1967), and (2) the inheritance of the rights to these benefits (Eisenstadt 1971:61–63). In this section we examine the physical manifestations of wealth and social position that accrue to individuals of special rank. Later we discuss the differential inheritance of these perogatives.

Information is recorded on the trappings of status in 51 societies. For comparative purposes, our sample is restricted to those cases for which data on other sociopolitical variables is also available. The sample includes 13 cases from Central and South America, 23 societies from western North America, and 15 groups from the eastern United States (Table 2.9).

Nine markers of chiefly status are recorded (Table 2.9). Special residence and dress are observed most frequently. Houses of leaders are distinguished from other domiciles by their size, decoration, construction materials, interior furniture, and location. Variation in residential architecture ranges from the Carib whose leaders lived in slightly larger houses (Bennett 1949:16; Rouse 1948a) to the Natchez whose leaders resided on high mounds in very large houses that were ornamented in special ways and that had distinctive furniture (Spencer *et al.* 1965:412; Swanton 1946). Leaders are also distinguished by special dress that includes various kinds of ornaments, regalia, tatoos, body paint, and insignia of office.

Marital patterns and treatment at death also serve to differentiate leaders from the rest of the population. In over one-third of our cases leaders are described as having more than one spouse. At death, special mortuary practices involve the construction of distinctive tombs or the inclusion of additional individuals or large quantities of grave goods with the corpse.

In 17 cases chiefs are treated with obeisance. This behavior entails such actions as being carried on a litter, being approached only with special etiquette, and being addressed by a prestigious title. In a small number of cases, leaders are also provided with services by their followers, have servants or slaves, eat different food, or speak in a special language.

In our sample of cases, leaders are distinguished by one to as many as eight attributes marking their higher position (Table 2.9). Although all these attributes involve costs, some are more expensive than others. Based on these costs, we suggest that high status does entail at least minimal economic consequences that are present in each case but to a variable degree. The continuous rather than steplike frequency-distribution of the total number of status markers per case suggests that no clear societal modes can be identified within our sample of prestate sedentary societies. Contrary to Fried (1967), no clear distinction can be seen in our cases between *ranked* and *stratified* societies.

TABLE 2.9

Status Markers of Leaders

	Special houses	Multiple wives	Special dress	Special burials	Obeisance	Services	Servants/ slaves	Special food	Special language	Total
Carib	X	—	—	—	—	—	—	—	—	1
Cherokee	X	—	—	—	—	—	—	—	—	1
Hasinai	X	—	—	—	—	—	—	—	—	1
Eastern Abenaki	X	—	—	—	—	—	—	—	—	1
Maidu	X	—	—	—	—	—	—	—	—	1
Obispeno Chumash	—	X	—	—	—	—	—	—	—	1
Costanoan	—	X	—	—	—	—	—	—	—	1
Tolowa	—	X	—	—	—	—	—	—	—	1
Mojo	—	X	—	—	—	—	—	—	—	1
Nomlaki	—	—	X	—	—	—	—	—	—	1
Wappo	—	—	X	—	—	—	—	—	—	1
Chiriguano	—	—	X	—	—	—	—	—	—	1
Salish	—	—	X	—	—	—	—	—	—	1
Tuscarora	—	—	—	X	—	—	—	—	—	1
Choctaw	—	—	—	X	—	—	—	—	—	1
Chickasaw	—	—	—	—	X	—	—	—	—	1
Iroquois	—	—	—	—	X	—	—	—	—	1
Hopi	—	—	—	—	—	X	—	—	—	1
Timucua	X	—	—	—	X	—	—	—	—	2
Nanticoke	X	—	X	—	—	—	—	—	—	2
Paressi	X	—	—	—	—	X	—	—	—	2
Klamath	—	X	—	—	—	—	X	—	—	2
Nisenan	—	X	—	—	—	X	—	—	—	2
Patwin	—	X	—	—	—	X	—	—	—	2

Distribution table of traits by group.

Group	23	20	23	16	17	14	7	6	5	Cases
Yana	x	x	—	—	—	x	—	—	—	2
Paria	x	x	—	—	—	—	—	—	—	2
Barbareno Chumash	x	x	x	—	—	—	—	—	—	2
Sherente	x	—	x	x	—	—	—	—	—	2
Caquetio	x	—	x	x	—	—	—	—	—	2
Camayura	x	—	x	x	—	—	—	—	—	2
Huron	x	—	—	—	—	—	—	—	—	2
Zuni	x	—	—	x	x	x	—	—	—	2
Pomo	—	x	x	x	x	x	—	—	—	3
Yokut–W. Mano	x	x	x	—	—	x	—	—	x	3
Eastern Miwok	x	x	x	—	x	—	—	—	—	3
Tocobaga	x	—	—	—	—	—	x	—	—	3
Delaware	—	—	x	x	—	—	—	—	—	3
Creek	—	x	x	x	—	—	—	—	—	3
Aruacay	x	x	x	—	x	x	—	x	x	4
Gabrielino	x	x	x	x	x	x	—	x	—	4
Bella Coola	x	x	—	—	x	—	—	—	—	4
Lile	x	—	x	x	—	—	x	x	x	4
Yurok	—	x	—	x	—	x	—	—	—	4
Yuki	x	x	x	—	x	x	—	—	x	5
S. Kwakiutl	x	x	x	x	x	x	x	x	x	5
Manasi	x	x	—	x	x	—	—	x	—	5
Hispaniola Arawak	x	x	x	x	x	—	x	x	—	6
Powhatan	x	x	x	x	x	—	x	—	—	6
Natchez	x	x	x	x	x	x	x	x	x	7
Nootka	x	x	x	x	x	—	x	—	—	7
Cuna	x	x	x	x	x	x	x	—	x	8
	X/23	X/20	X/23	X/16	X/17	X/14	X/7	X/6	X/5	51 cases

A correlation ($V = .40$) was found between the gradation in the trappings of status and the number of duties performed by leaders (Table 2.10). This moderate relationship supports Gregory Johnson's (1978:103) argument that leaders who execute a greater number of tasks require relatively more training and support, and thus are liable to be more clearly distinguished from the remainder of society. However, the relationship between status differentiation and leadership functions does not hold in all cases. Although there is only one society (Bella Coola) in which highly differentiated leaders performed few functions,

TABLE 2.10

Comparison of Status Markers and Leadership Functions[a]

Functions	Status markers	
	1–3	4–8
1–3	Carib Abenaki Obispeno Chumash Cherokee Iroquois Klamath Camayura Yana Choctaw	Bella Coola
4–7	Hopi Mojo Wappo Maidu Chiriguano Costanoan Paressi Timucua Barbareno Chumash Nisenan Patwin Sherente Zuni	Yurok Gabrielino Manasi Natchez Nootka
8–13	Salish Hasinai Nomlaki Pomo Huron Delaware Creek Eastern Miwok Yokut–Western Mano	Southern Kwakiutl Yuki Hispaniola Arawak Powhatan Cuna

[a] Gamma (V) = .40 (gamma measures the correlation between number of status markers and number of leadership functions).

there are several cases in which leaders who execute many tasks have few status trappings.

Considerable variability also is observed in the ways in which leadership positions are transferred from one generation to the next (see also Goody 1966). The relative importance of heredity and achievement differs across cases. This variability ranges from the achievement of leadership roles based solely on personal qualifications to strict rules of familial succession. No clear-cut distinctions between different modes of succession are found; instead, a continous pattern of variability is observed. In only seven cases (Bacairi, Cusabo, Sherente, Maidu, Northern Pomo, Tolowa, and Yuki) is leadership described as based solely on achievement. The low frequency of this successsionary pattern is not totally unexpected since even in several Melanesian big-man societies the transference of leadership has been noted as having an ascriptive component (Meggitt 1973:194; Read 1959:427; Strathern 1971:210–211).

Whereas purely achieved leadership positions are rare, inflexible hereditary systems based solely on prescribed rules are not found at all. Considerable variability is observed in the nature and the relative importance of genealogical ties. In some cases, leadership is based largely on achievement, although it tends to follow certain familial lines (e.g., Carib [Rouse 1948a:555], Eastern Abenaki [Snow 1978:140]). However, in most societies leadership roles are largely inherited, yet the succession of the new chief is subject to the approval of his constitutents on the basis of his personal qualifications. Although the specific details vary, this basic pattern has been reported in such cases as the Powhatan (Turner 1976:99), Huron (Trigger 1969:69), Gabrielino (Bean and Smith 1978a:544), Atsugewi (Garth 1978:237), and Costanoan (Levy 1978a:487).

In a relatively small number of cases a set of hereditary rules for succession is followed. In these societies, strict specifications are made to keep the chiefly title within a single bloodline; however personal qualities still have a role. Helms (1976, 1979, 1980) has thoroughly detailed this kind of system for ancient Panama where individual character became more important as the genealogical distance between a leader and his successor increased.

Thus, as with the markers of status, the succession of leadership positions in middle-range societies is extremely variable. Contrary to the traditional typological approaches (Carneiro 1981; Fried 1976; Service 1962), the patterning found in these two attributes is not modal. A more continuous distribution is observed in the numbers of status markers and in the relative importance of achievement and ascription in succession. Despite flexibility in the systems of succession, leadership positions and their associated status markings and privileges tend to remain in specific familial lines. Considering the costs involved in supporting these partially inherited status positions, it would seem that economic advantages associated with leadership also are retained through time by certain population segments. Consequently, social distinctions with economic implications are found in most of our societies but to varying degrees; it seems more productive to discuss social differentiation as a continuous variable (Cancian 1976; Fallers 1973; Sahlins 1958:1–2; Tumin 1967:12–18) rather than as a set of traits that are either present or absent (Fried 1967; Plotnicov and Tuden 1970).

Levels of Political Decision-Making

In order to evaluate the utility of using levels of political decision-making to define specific societal types, we examine administrative complexity. Information was collected on the number of organizational tiers present in 59 societies. However, problems were encountered due to temporal and spatial variability in the number of levels that operate in particular contexts. Data were gathered for 29 groups from western North America, 20 cases from eastern North America, and 10 societies from Central and South America.

Cases are assigned to five categories on the basis of ethnographic descriptions. The least hierarchical groups have only a village chief or lineage headman. In certain cases these units are temporarily linked (e.g., during warfare) into larger concentrations. Thus, these latter cases are characterized by either one or two levels of decision-making, depending on the situational context. The largest number of societies have two administrative tiers. These levels are usually composed of a village leader and a superior tribal or district chief. Cases that are classified as having two or three levels are administered by both village and district chiefs, with districts occasionally joined into a larger organizational unit. Several societies have three discrete decision-making levels with district chiefs consolidated under a single paramount leader.

In several cases discrepancies are recorded in the observations made by different researchers. As a result these societies are placed in multiple categories (Table 2.11). A number of interrelated factors seem to have been responsible for these duplicate placements. In several societies, changes in administrative complexity occurred over time. For other cases, the discrepancies seem more the consequence of differences in the scale of observation. The causes of the reported disagreements are difficult to determine in some situations, although many seem to have been related to periodic confederations.

Differences are observed among the three study areas. All but one of the Central and South American societies have organizational structures that extend beyond the village level. Three distinct tiers are described for the Arawak and Cuna, whereas only two levels are noted for the other seven groups. No duplicate classifications or evidence of occasional confederations are encountered for this region.

The societies from the eastern United States cross-cut the entire range of political complexity (Table 2.11). Duplicate categorization occurs in four cases.

TABLE 2.11

Administrative Levels in Prestate Sedentary Societies

1 (lineage head or village chief)	1–2 (village chief and occasional confederation)	2 (village and tribal or district chief)	2–3 (village chief, district chief, and occasional confederation)	3 (village chief, district chief, and paramount chief)
Tocobaga	Tuscarora	Natchez	Choctaw[a]	Cherokee
Nottoway–Meherrin	Hasinai	Chickasaw	Creek	Choctaw[a]
Nomlaki[a]	Choptanks[a]	Timucua	Guale[a]	Powhatan
Lake Miwok[a]	Delaware[a]	Guale[a]	Iroquois	Nootka
Tolowa	Eastern Abenaki	Delaware[a]	Huron	Hispaniola Arawak
Atsugewi	Atsugewi[a]	Nanticoke[a,b]	Wabanaki	Cuna
Chumash[a]	Chumash[a]	Accomac	Pomo[a]	
Gabrielino[a]	Yana[a]	Salinan[a]	Miwok[a]	
Coast Miwok[a]	Foothill Yokut	Eastern Miwok[a]	Patwin[a]	
Nisenan	Nomlaki[a]	Yokut	Shasta[a]	
Maidu	Diegueno/Tipai-Ipai[a]	Costanoan	Gabrielino[a]	
Cupeno		Patwin[a]	Diegueno/Tipai-Ipai[a]	
Cahuilla		Central Pomo[a]	Salinan[a]	
Yana[a]		Shasta[a]	Klamath	
Salish		S. Kwakiutl[a]	S. Kwakiutl[a]	
Hopi		Yuki		
Sherente		Manasi		
		Caquetio		
		Paria		
		Aruacay		
		Lile		
		Tupinamba		
		Paressi		

[a] Cases for which conflicting information was recorded.
[b] Includes Choptanks.

For the Delaware, Guale, and Choctaw, disagreement over the permanence of the uppermost decision-making level accounts for the discrepancies. The Choptank case is more complicated because their alliance at times is included within the much larger Nanticoke Confederacy (Feest 1978a).

In the western United States the duplicate classifications are all the result of occasional confederations. Some of these alliances apparently joined together polities that have both one and two levels of decision-making (e.g., Pomo, Miwok). Only the Nootka are found to have three permanent organizational levels.

Comparisons are made between administrative complexity and the two previously examined variables. When functions of leaders are compared with levels of decision-making (Table 2.12), only a weak relationship is observed ($V = .19$). However, a strong correlation ($V = .95$) is found between the extent of

TABLE 2.12

Comparison of Administrative Levels and Leadership Functions[a]

Functions	Levels		
	1–1.5	2–2.5	3
1–3	Nottoway–Meherrin Cupeno Yana	Salinan Klamath Shasta Iroquois	Cherokee
4–7	Hopi Atsugewi Chumash Nisenan Maidu Sherente	Guale Manasi Paressi Natchez Timucua Patwin Costanoan	Nootka
8+	Cahuilla Salish Nomlaki Hasinai	Pomo Miwok S. Kwakiutl Creek Huron Yuki Yokut	Hispaniola Arawak Cuna Powhatan

[a] Cases that overlapped levels were excluded. Gamma (V) = .19 (gamma measures the correlation between administrative level and number of leadership functions).

the political hierarchy and the degree of status differentiation (Table 2.13). Though cases that have few status markers exhibit the entire range of political complexity, those leaders that rule as district or paramount chiefs are markedly differentiated from the rest of the population.

In summary, four observations concerning political complexity are apparent. First, the largest number of cases have two decision-making levels, although considerable variation is present. Second, flexibility in administrative complexity is described for many of the sample cases even though the relevant observations often cover periods of only short duration. Societies with both one and two decision-making levels are periodically confederated depending on specific circumstances. Third, regional differences are apparent in the relative organizational complexity of prestate sedentary polities. Finally, the degree of status differentiation is found to be strongly associated with the number of administrative levels in our sample of middle-range societies.

The general patterning of the data supports Johnson's (1973) contention that prestate sedentary societies have from one to two levels of decision-making. However, several cases conform to Steponaitis's (1978) expectation that complex chiefdoms may have more than two administrative tiers. The utility of

TABLE 2.13

Comparison of Administrative Levels and Status Markers[a]

	Levels		
Status markers	1–1.5	2–2.5	3
1–3	Nomlaki	Chickasaw	Cherokee
	Tolowa	Costanoan	
	Maidu	Paressi	
	Salish	Timucua	
	Hopi	Nanticoke	
	Chumash	Patwin	
	Nisenan	Caquetio	
	Sherente	Paria	
	Yana	Miwok	
	Tocobaga	Yokut	
	Tuscarora	Aruacay	
	Hasinai	Iroquois	
	E. Abenaki	Huron	
		Pomo	
		Klamath	
		Creek	
4+		Lile	Powhatan
		Yuki	Hispaniola
		Manasi	Arawak
		S. Kwakiutl	Nootka
		Natchez	Cuna

[a] Cases that overlapped levels categories were excluded. Gamma (V) = .95 (gamma measures the correlation between administrative level and number of status markers).

defining political stages simply in accordance with the number of organizational levels is therefore brought into question by these more complex societies as well as by the observed patterns of regional variation and situational complexity.

Settlement Patterns

Previous studies have associated sedentary, prestate societies with specific settlement patterns (Steponaitis 1978) and demographic ranges (Ember 1963; Naroll 1956; Naroll and Margolis 1974; Tatje and Naroll 1970). Steponaitis (1978) has proposed a model for complex chiefdom settlement organization in which he suggests that the paramount leader should be found in the largest settlement at the center of the political domain and that secondary sites and villages should be clustered around this primary location (see also Sears 1968).

Given the nature of the ethnographic record, a systematic evaluation of Steponaitis's (1978) model is not possible. Information on settlement pattern is available for only a few cases, and the data are not always as explicit as desired.

In several cases, such as the Creek (Cotterill 1954:8) and Nisenan (Wilson and Towne 1978:388), the proposed expectations are supported because the largest settlements were located at the center of the territory and were surrounded by smaller villages. However, although the capital settlement was centrally located among the Powhatan, the chief lived in territory that was recently incorporated by the expanding chiefdom (Turner 1976:111, 129, 139).

Marked exceptions to Steponaitis's (1978) model are found in a roughly equal number of cases. The largest settlements in certain regions were located at the edges of their territories. Among the Hasinai (Wyckoff and Baugh 1980:246) and the Conibo and Cocama (DeBoer 1981), the most populous settlements were situated at the periphery of their respective domains, perhaps as a response to intertribal relations. Trade is mentioned as the explanation for the location of the Western Timucua chief at the eastern edge of his territory (Milanich 1978:71). The major centers of the Maliseet–Passamaquoddy (Erickson 1978:124), Tapajo (Meggers 1971:133), and Barbareno Chumash (King 1975:174–175) were located at the mouths of rivers and along the coast to take advantage of both trading opportunities and coastal resources. Although in some cases these patterns may be attributed to the effects of European trade and contact, this does not seem to be true for the Cocama and Conibo, who were observed very early in the contact period (DeBoer 1981). In addition, similar patterns have been found archaeologically (Smith and Kowalewski n.d.). Based on this small sample, Steponaitis's model appears to hold for only some middle-range societies. However, these cases cannot be organizationally distinguished from those for which the model does not apply.

Although a general relationship between increasing societal complexity and larger settlements has often been noted (Carneiro 1967; Childe 1950; Naroll 1956; Tatje and Naroll 1970), only a few investigators have attempted to define specific maximal community populations for particular levels of sociopolitical organization (e.g., Forge 1972). In order to assess whether distinct settlement-size ranges could be identified for sedentary prestate societies, we recorded for 21 cases the numbers of inhabitants living in the largest settlement (Figure 2.1). For seven of these groups, the maximal community population has to be expressed as a range, because multiple estimates are present in the literature. The population of these largest settlements varies between 164 for the Obispeno Chumash (Greenwood 1978:521) and an upper limit of 4000 for the Huron (Trigger 1963:91). The variation between these extremes is relatively continuous and no clear, discrete modes are discerned. However, regional differences are observed. Whereas the largest communities in western North America contain fewer than 2000 people, the range of maximal community size is variable in the other two areas, extending from 300 to as much as 4000 in eastern North America and from 200 to 3000 for Central and South America.

To facilitate a comparison of maximal community sizes with other variables,

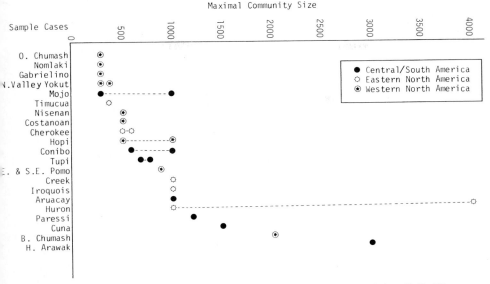

Figure 2.1. Maximal community sizes found in prestate sedentary societies. Dotted lines indicate specified ranges.

the sample cases are subdivided into three categories. These divisions are defined by slight discontinuities that are noted when the data are plotted (Figure 2.1). The three divisions are used for analytic, comparative purposes and should not be interpreted as discrete, inflexible categories.

A strong correlation ($V = 1.00$) is found between maximal community size and the number of status markers. Leaders in societies with relatively small primary centers have few trappings of high position (Table 2.14). However, in cases in which maximal community size is large, leaders have a variable number of status markers. The absence of societies having small primary centers and highly differentiated leaders suggests that marked differences in status should be expected only when community size becomes too large to permit daily face-to-face interactions among the populace (Binford 1962; Forge 1972:371–375).

Only moderate correlations (Tables 2.15 and 2.16) are found when maximal community size is examined in relation to the functions of leaders ($V = .46$) and the numbers of levels in the political hierarchy ($V = .47$). Thus, not only are maximal community sizes continously distributed, but correlations of varying strength are found when comparisons are made with other attributes. The complexity of these relationships suggests that although certain correlations do exist, no single attribute can be used to predict the values of all the rest.

Total population size has been an important criterion for defining stages of

TABLE 2.14

Comparison of Status Markers and Maximal Community Size[a]

Maximal community size	Status markers	
	1–3	4+
100–400	Obispeno Chumash Nomlaki Timucua Gabrielino	
500–1000	Cherokee Nisenan Creek Iroquois Hopi Mojo	
1200+	Barbareno Chumash Paressi Huron	Hispaniola Arawak Cuna

[a] Mean values used for cases with population ranges. Gamma (V) = 1.00 (gamma measures the correlation between number of status markers and maximal community size).

sociopolitical complexity (Fried 1967; Service 1962; Steward 1949b), although the demographic ranges associated with different organization stages have rarely been specified (cf. Baker and Sanders 1972:163; Sanders and Price 1968:85). Information was collected on 70 prestate sedentary societies to identify the variability in total population and to examine the relationship between increasing demographic size and other variables. Four cases were obtained from Central and

TABLE 2.15

Comparison of Leadership Functions and Maximal Community Size[a]

Maximal community size	Functions		
	1–3	4–7	8–13
100–400	Obispeno Chumash	Gabrielino Timucua	Nomlaki
500–1000	Cherokee Iroquois	Mojo Nisenan Costanoan Hopi	Eastern and South- eastern Pomo Creek
1200+		Paressi Barbareno Chumash	Huron Cuna Hispaniola Arawak

[a] Mean values used for cases with population ranges. Gamma (V) = .46 (gamma measures the correlation between the number of leadership functions and maximal community size).

TABLE 2.16

Comparison of Administrative Levels and Maximal Community Size[a]

Maximal community size	Levels		
	1–1.5	2–2.5	3
100–400	Obispeno Chumash	Timucua	
500–1000	Hopi	Costanoan	Cherokee
	Nisenan	Aruacay	
		Creek	
		Iroquois	
1200+	Barbareno Chumash	Huron	Cuna
			Hispaniola Arawak

[a] Cases that overlapped levels categories are excluded; mean values are used for cases with population ranges. Gamma (V) = .47 (gamma measures the correlation between administrative level and maximal community size).

South America, 26 from the eastern United States, and 40 from western North America. Because inconsistent estimates are frequent in the literature, total population is reported as a range for roughly half the cases (Figure 2.2). The disparate values provided in such a large number of cases seem to be the consequence of two factors. First, observations made at different analytical scales result in variable population estimates. Second, the organizational fluidity of middle-range societies apparently leads observers to make accurate but diverse estimates at different times (Sahlins 1968:20–27; Service 1962:152). The discrepancies are greatest and most frequent for societies with the largest populations.

Total systemic populations are found to vary in continuous fashion, with the minimum demographic estimates ranging from 200 to 22,000. Maximum estimates did not exceed 31,000 except for the Hispaniola Arawak, who at Spanish Conquest were reported to have had as many as 100,000 to 6 million people under the domain of a single paramount chief (Rouse 1948b:522).

Although distinct modes are not obvious, we divide the range of total population sizes into three categories for analytic purposes (Figure 2.2). Cases are grouped into those with 4000 individuals or less, those between 4001 and 13,000, and those with more than 13,000. Mean population values are used to place societies for which we have demographic ranges into one of the three categories. Areal differences are observed among the three regions, with cases from western North America tending to have smaller populations (Table 2.17).

A relatively strong relationship (V = .83) is observed when a comparison is made between total population and administrative levels (Table 2.18). As population increases, so does the number of tiers in the decision-making hierarchy. No large populations are found that have fewer than two political levels; and no small groups are present that have three administrative tiers. These results sup-

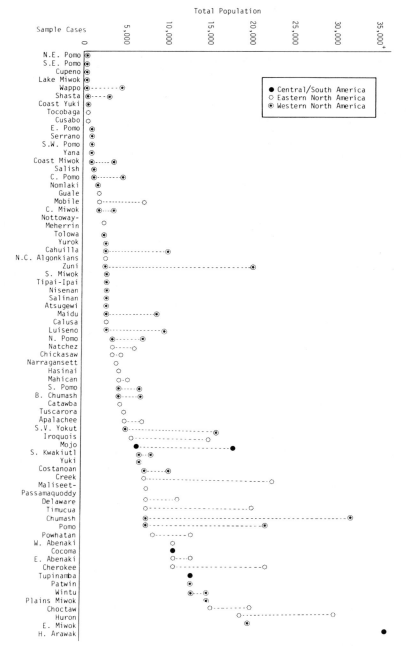

Figure 2.2. Total populations found in prestate sedentary societies. Dotted lines indicate specified ranges.

TABLE 2.17

Regional Comparison of Total Population

Total population	Area				
	Eastern North America		Western North America		Central and South America
0–4000	Tocobaga Cusabo Guale Calusa Chickasaw Narragansett N.C. Algonkians Nottoway–Meherrin		NE Pomo SE Pomo Cupeno Lake Miwok Wappo Shasta Coast Yuki East Pomo Atsugewi Yana Nomlaki Nisenan	SW Pomo Serrano Coast Miwok Central Pomo Central Miwok Tolowa South Miwok Tipai–Ipai Salish Yurok Salinan	
4001–13,000	Mobile Natchez Hasinai Mahican Catawba Apalachee Maliseet–Passama- quoddy	Delaware Powhatan W. Abenaki E. Abenaki Iroquois	Cahuilla Zuni Maidu N. Pomo S. Pomo Luiseno B. Chumash	S. Valley Yokut S. Kwakiutl Yuki Costanoan Patwin Wintu	Mojo Cocoma Tupinamba
13,001+	Creek Timucua Cherokee Choctaw Huron		Chumash Plains Miwok East Miwok Pomo		Hispaniola Arawak

port the general expectation that organizational differentiation should correlate with greater population size (Blau 1970, 1977; G. Johnson 1978). Weaker correlations are found when total population is compared to the numbers of functions performed by leaders ($V = .44$) and the degree of status differentiation ($V = .05$) (Tables 2.19 and 2.20).

A final characteristic of settlement patterns that is examined is the numbers of districts encompassed under a leader's jurisdiction. Because data are available for just a few cases, only subjective observations can be made. Leaders who rule five or more administrative units generally perform a greater range of functions (Table 2.21). When the numbers of districts ruled by a leader and the degree of status differentiation (Table 2.22) are compared, there are no cases of highly differentiated leaders ruling few districts or leaders with few status markers administering more than seven districts. Thus, the number of organizational units

TABLE 2.18

Comparison of Administrative Levels and Total Population[a]

Total population	Levels		
	1–1.5	2–2.5	3
0–4000	Tocobaga	Chickasaw	
	Salish	Guale	
	Nomlaki	Salinan	
	Yana	C. Pomo	
	Tolowa	Shasta	
	Coast Miwok		
	Nisenan		
	Cupeno		
	Lake Miwok		
	Atsugewi		
	Nottoway–Meherrin		
4001–13,000	Maidu	Natchez	Powhatan
	Cahuilla	Patwin	
	Barbareno Chumash	Yuki	
		Costanoan	
		Tupinamba	
		Iroquois	
		S. Kwakiutl	
13,001+		Timucua	Cherokee
		Creek	Hispaniola Arawak
		Pomo	
		E. Miwok	
		Huron	

[a] Mean values used for cases with population ranges. Gamma (V) = .83 (gamma measures the correlation between administrative level and total population).

may be a more significant factor than total population size in determining the degree of social differentiation in middle-range societies (G. Johnson 1978, 1982).

Archaeological Implications

The results of this study have important implications for archaeological analyses of sociopolitical organization. The continuous distribution of each examined attribute and the complexity of the relationships among them indicate that serious inadequacies characterize the typological approach to societal diversity. Archaeological analyses have focused primarily on the classification of specific societies into ideal organizational types. In addition, archaeologists have tended to use one or two key attributes to infer the presence of all characteristics traditionally associated with particular types (Grebinger 1973; Peebles and Kus 1977; Renfrew 1973). By doing this, the opportunity to recognize the full range of

TABLE 2.19

Comparison of Leadership Functions and Total Population[a]

Total population	Functions		
	1–3	4–7	8–13
0–4000	Cusabo	Guale	Salish
	Calusa	Narragansett	E. and S.E. Pomo
	Central Miwok	Tipai–Ipai	Nomlaki
	Salinan	Atsugewi	W. and N.E. Pomo
	Serrano	Yurok	
	Cupeno	Wappo	
	Nottoway–Meherrin	Nisenan	
	Yana		
4001–13,000	Luiseno	Natchez	Hasinai
	Abenaki	Maidu	Cahuilla
	Iroquois	Zuni	Delaware
		Mojo	Powhatan
		Wintu	S. Kwakiutl
		Barbareno Chumash	Yuki
		Patwin	S.V. Yokut
		Costanoan	
13,001 +	Cherokee	Timucua	Creek
	Choctaw		Pomo
			Hispaniola Arawak
			Huron
			E. Miwok

[a] Mean values used for cases with population ranges. Gamma (V) = .44 (gamma measures the correlation between the number of leadership functions and total population).

variability that existed prehistorically has been precluded (Blanton *et al.* 1981; Hill 1977; Kehoe 1981; Plog and Upham 1979:1–3; Tainter 1978).

In the analysis of leadership duties, no single function is found to characterize every society in the sample. Not only do the kinds of tasks vary in different cases, but so do the number of duties performed by each leader. Consequently, it would be difficult to predict which specific tasks are performed by leaders in any particular case. Archaeologists finding evidence of middle-range societal complexity certainly should not infer the presence of redistribution (Peebles and Kus 1977), because this is a relatively rare task. Nor should the absence of archaeological evidence for redistribution be interpreted as particularly meaningful in a more general sense.

As in the analysis of functions, the examination of status differentiation indicates that chiefs are characterized by variable kinds and quantities of status markers. Once again, variability is found to be continuous, thus suggesting that archaeologists should not expect to find a clear dichotomy between stratified and

TABLE 2.20

Comparison of Status Markers and Total Population[a]

Total population	Status markers	
	1–3	4 +
0–4000	Tocobaga Nisenan Yana Tolowa Nomlaki Wappo Salish Chickasaw	Yurok
4001–13,000	Delaware Zuni Patwin Barbareno Chumash Maidu Hasinai E. Abenaki Costanoan Mojo Tuscarora Iroquois	Natchez Powhatan Yuki S. Kwakiutl
13,001 +	Creek E. Miwok Timucua Pomo Huron Cherokee Choctaw	Hispaniola Arawak

[a] Mean values used for cases with population ranges. Gamma (V) = .05 (gamma measures the correlation between the number of status markers and total population).

TABLE 2.21

Comparison of Leadership Functions and Administered Districts

Administered districts	Chiefly functions									
	1	2	3	4	5	6	7	8	9	10
2–3		Cherokee	Choctaw							Creek
5–7								Arawak	Pomo	E. Miwok
7+								Cuna	Powhatan	

TABLE 2.22

Comparison of Status Markers and Administered Districts

Administered districts	Chiefly status markers									
	1	2	3	4	5	6	7	8	9	10
2–3		Choctaw	Creek							
		Cherokee								
5–7		Iroquois	Eastern			Arawak				
			Miwok							
7+						Powhatan		Cuna		

unstratified societies. Rather, social differentiation might be more productively examined as varying by degree. Measurements could be taken along a set of organizational axes. Residential patterns, chiefly dress, and mortuary practices may be the most productive indicators of social differentiation for archaeologists. However, the results of this investigation suggest that several considerations should be taken into account when studying these variables.

One of the most frequently reported means of differentiating leaders is by the size, construction, and location of their houses. These attributes are generally observable when residential architecture is found in the archaeological record and have already been used to infer social differences (Cordy 1981; Lightfoot and Feinman 1982; Whalen 1976; Wilcox and Shenk 1977; Wilcox et al. 1981). Analyses, however, should not only concentrate on variation in house size or the placement of domiciles on mounded platforms but should also consider differences in the specific materials of construction (Helms 1979:9; Swanton 1946:409), exterior and interior ornamentation (Brasser 1978:198; Goddard 1978:219; Helms 1979:9; Spencer et al. 1965:410; Steward and Faron 1959:249), household furniture (Levy 1978:410; Spencer et al. 1965:412; Steward and Faron 1959:249; Wyckoff and Baugh 1980:247), and the location of residences within neighborhoods (Pilling 1978:141; Suttles 1958:498–499).

Although chiefly dress and burial practices are frequently occurring markers of social differentiation, the physical manifestations of these activities leave remains of varying utility for archaeologists. Many of the insignia and more durable markers of leaders are observable in the prehistoric record. Yet, archaeologists rarely find items of clothing, feathers, and other ephemeral types of personal ornamentation, such as tatoos, body painting, and hair styles (see Feest 1978b:260; Goldschmidt 1951:385; Helms 1979:16; Hudson 1976:203; Oberg 1953:50; Speck 1907:114; Spencer et al. 1965:412, 424; Swanton 1946:477, 151; Turner 1976:103–105).

Mortuary remains also provide a valuable means for examining status differences (Brown 1971; King 1978; Rothschild 1979; Saxe 1970; Tainter 1977,

1978; Tainter and Cordy 1977). Leaders not only are buried with large quantities and special kinds of grave goods, but they also are interred in special tombs (Swanton 1946:718–719) and at distinctive locations (Spencer *et al.* 1965:417). Although these practices usually leave archaeological remains, some leaders receive special funerary treatments of a sort that would not be visible in the prehistoric record. At death, their bodies are hung from trees (Drucker 1951:147), burned, and/or eaten (Rouse 1948a:559; Steward 1949a:721; see also Tainter 1978:108–109).

Thus, although leaders are generally differentiated during life by their dress and at death by their mortuary treatment, the absence of evidence of these differences in the archaeological record is not necessarily sufficient to conclude that social distinctions are not present. In addition, no single type of archaeological remains should be interpreted as the sole diagnostic indicator of a specific stage or degree of societal complexity. It is suggested that archaeologists study social differences along a broad range of analytical attributes for two reasons. First, certain activities may not leave easily interpretable prehistoric remains. Second, social distinctions are frequently marked in diverse ways along a number of different dimensions (Table 2.9). The full range and complexity of social differentiation can be revealed only if the set of activities that distinguish leaders are examined concurrently (Tainter 1980).

Prestate sedentary societies are found to have from one to three administrative levels that can vary in relation to situational contexts. Although it would therefore seem inappropriate to use specific numbers of organizational tiers to define particular typological stages, this variable is still a good indicator of political complexity. In this analysis the extent of the decision-making hierarchy is correlated with the degree of social differentiation, maximal community size, and total population. Consequently, this is an important variable for archaeological research. Yet, to operationalize it, we need alternative architectural and artifactual measures of administrative organization (R. E. W. Adams 1981; Blanton *et al.* 1981; Flannery and Marcus 1976; G. Johnson 1973; Lightfoot 1981; Smith 1978a:497). As Johnson (n.d.) has previsouly argued, the numbers of political levels may not clearly correspond with the number of modal divisions in settlement-size distributions.

The empirical range of total systemic population derived from this cross-cultural analysis corresponds rather closely to the figures proposed by other researchers (Baker and Sanders 1972; Sanders and Price 1968). However, whereas other researchers suggest a bimodal pattern for prestate sedentary societies, we find the distribution of total population as well as maximal community size to be more continous. As in the analysis of administrative levels, larger populations are generally associated with increasing organizational complexity along other dimensions. Yet the broad range of the population figures and the absence of discrete modes would seem to limit the utility of these demographic variables as indicators of particular societal types.

In summary, we have demonstrated several important weaknesses with the use of simple typological schemes to account for societal variation. The complex interrelationships found among variables suggest that increasing complexity along one societal dimension may or may not imply similar variation along other dimensions. Consequently, it may be counterproductive to use specific archaeological correlates to infer the presence of a series of attributes that have been used to characterize a particular organizational stage (Tainter 1978:115). Instead, researchers should study change and variation along a set of societal dimensions concurrently. A similar multivariate approach has been advocated by Skinner (1977:5) for the comparative study of the organization and principal functions of cities. This strategy would enable archaeologists to understand the nature of the relationships among key variables and to compare societal complexity in a less-typological manner.

CONCLUSIONS

In this analysis of New World prestate sedentary societies, considerable variability was found for each examined attribute. This diversity was continuous rather than discrete and no clear societal modes or subtypes were readily apparent. In addition, relationships of varying strength were found between the different organizational characteristics.

The strongest correlations were found when the degree of status differentiation was compared with variability in maximal community size and levels in the political hierarchy. Status differences also appeared to be related to the number of districts within a leader's domain. These relationships are particularly interesting given the lack of correlation between the number of status markers and total population. Thus, the extent of social differentiation seems to depend less on the number of people in a society than on its organizational divisions (G. Johnson 1982). Nevertheless, both demographic variables (total population and maximal community-size) were moderately correlated with the number of administrative levels.

The number of functions performed by leaders showed a moderate correlation with the degree of status differentiation and both demographic variables. That is, in our sample, the number of leadership functions tended to increase with total population and the size of the largest center. Leaders carrying out more tasks also seemed to be more markedly differentiated from the rest of the population. However, only a weak relationship was found between administrative complexity and chiefly tasks. Thus, leaders at the top of more hierarchical political systems did not necessarily perform a wider range of activities. This weak relationship may be the consequence of the fact that leaders in more hierarchical organizations are concerned primarily with the coordination of responsibilities that have been delegated to their subordinates.

An understanding of the diversity found in this sample of societies cannot be achieved by simply grouping them into one or two broad evolutionary types. No simple modal patterns were present. Instead the observed variation was multidimensional and continuous. No single value for any attribute characterized each case nor could the state of a particular variable be used to predict the values of all other attributes. Because each variable represents a specific organizational dimension, it would be a mistake to focus on any one attribute as a general indicator of societal complexity.

In the past, archaeologists have achieved only limited success in gaining understanding of sociopolitical variability and change in prestate sedentary societies. Most analyses have simply reified the ethnographically defined types by using one or two indicator variables to classify societies into these general categories (Tainter 1978:115). Many archaeologists have recognized that these modes do not account for the considerable variability observed in prehistoric middle-range societies (Flannery 1976; Greber 1979; Griffin 1979:278–279; Smith 1978b; Upham 1980). However, most alternative theoretical approaches (Renfrew 1973) have generally adopted the strategy of a number of ethnographers (Goldman 1970; Taylor 1975) and have simply subdivided these broad categories into more precise subtypes. Yet given the continuous and complex nature of societal variability, further refinement of the typological approach would seem to have at best limited utility. The construction of additional synchronic typologies would neither allow us to explain the diversity of prestate sedentary societies nor enable us to explicate the different causal processes involved in their development.

The results of this cross-cultural, synchronic analysis have demonstrated some of the variability and relational patterning present in middle-range societies. It is unlikely that the complexity of this patterning would change even if more complete ethnographic and ethnohistoric data were available. The different associational patterns found to characterize the relationships between societal variables deserve further investigation. However, more detailed cross-cultural studies that encompass additional areas and examine a wider set of variables cannot alone clarify this issue. Synchronic studies can only demonstrate correlations and cannot reveal the historical or causal processes responsible for societal variation (Dunnell 1980:84–85; Kohl 1981:96; Plog 1974).

Long-term, processual analyses are necessary. Such studies must be regional in scope and examine change along a whole range of organizational dimensions (Schiffer 1979:359). Analyses should consider three sets of dynamic relationships: those between regional populations, those between different social segments within a population; and those between a population and its physical environment. Only if diachronic, contextual studies are undertaken in different regions will social scientists be able to understand the causal processes and sequences of change that are responsible for societal variability.

APPENDIX 1: SAMPLE CASES

Case	Source
Central and South America	
Aruacay	Kirchoff (1948)
	Steward (1948:22; 1949a:718)
	Steward and Faron (1959:241–245)
Bacairi	Oberg (1953:73)
Camayura	Meggers (1971:44–55)
	Oberg (1953:40–51)
Caqueito	Steward (1948:21; 1949a:721)
	Steward and Faron (1959:241–243)
Carib	Bennett (1949:16)
	Rouse (1948a)
	Steward (1948:25)
Chiriguano	Lowie (1949)
	Metraux (1948d)
Cocoma	DeBoer (1981)
Conibo	DeBoer (1981)
Cuna	Helms (1976, 1979, 1980)
	Lothrop (1937)
	Lowie (1949)
	Schwerin (1973)
	Stout (1947:78–80; 1948)
	Steward (1948:28; 1949a:718, 721)
	Steward and Faron (1959:224–227)
Hispaniola Arawak	Rouse (1948b)
	Sauer (1966)
	Schwerin (1973)
	Steward (1948:23–24; 1949a:718, 721)
	Steward and Faron (1959:246–249)
Lile	Hernandez de Alba (1948:302–307)
	Steward and Faron (1959:217–218)
Manasi	Metraux (1948b:388–392)
	Steward (1949a:729)
	Steward and Faron (1959:252–253, 259–261)
Mapuche–Huilliche	Cooper (1946)
	Steward (1949a:712–713)
Mojo	Lowie (1949)
	Metraux (1948b:408–424)
	Steward (1949a:729)
	Steward and Faron (1959:252–256)
Paressi	Metraux (1948c)
	Steward (1949a:729)
	Steward and Faron (1959:252–253, 257–258)
Paria	Kirchoff (1948)
	Steward and Faron (1959:244)
Sherente	Lowie (1949)
	Nimendaju (1942)
Tapajo	Meggers (1971:133)
Tupi	Steward (1949a:700)
Tupinamba	Metraux (1948a)

(continued)

APPENDIX 1 *Continued*

Case	Source
Eastern North America	
Accomac	Feest (1978a:240–241)
Apalachee	Swanton (1946:91, 598, Map 3)
Calusa	Swanton (1946:102, 648, Map 3)
Catawba	Hudson (1970)
	Swanton (1946:102)
Cherokee	Corkran (1962)
	Cotterill (1954:5)
	Fogelson (1977)
	Gearing (1962)
	Mooney (1975)
	Service (1975:140–148)
	Swanton (1946:114, 654, Map 3)
	Wahrhaftig and Lukens-Wahrhaftig (1977:228)
	Woodward (1963)
Chickasaw	Cotterill (1954:7)
	Gibson (1971)
	Swanton (1946:118, 387–389, 598, 653, Map 3)
Choctaw	Cotterill (1954:6)
	Debo (1934)
	Swanton (1918, 1946:123, 653, 718–719, Map 3)
Choptanks	Feest (1978a:241–242)
Creeks	Corkran (1967)
	Cotterill (1954:8)
	Green (1979)
	Hudson (1976)
	Opler (1952)
	Speck (1907, 1915:492)
	Spencer, Jennings *et al.* (1965:419–432)
	Swanton (1946:378–381, 386–420, Map 3)
Cusabo	Swanton (1946:Map 3)
Delaware	Goddard (1978)
	Herman (1950)
	Newcomb (1956)
	Speck (1915:492)
	Thurman (1975)
	Weslager (1972)
Eastern Abenaki	Snow (1976, 1978, 1980)
Guale	Larson (1978:120–140)
	Swanton (1946:Map 3)
Hasinai	Swanton (1946:99, Map 3)
	Wyckoff and Baugh (1980)
Huron	Heidenreich (1978)
	Tooker (1964)
	Trigger (1962, 1963, 1969, 1970, 1976)
Iroquois	Fenton (1940, 1978)
	Morgan (1928)
	Speck (1915:492; 1945)
	Tooker (1970)
	Trigger (1962, 1963, 1969)
	Tuck (1971)

(continued)

APPENDIX 1 *Continued*

Case	Source
Mahican	Brasser (1978)
	Snow (1980)
Maliseet–Passamaquoddy	Erickson (1978)
	Snow (1980)
Mobile	Swanton (1946:150, 652, Map 3)
Nanticoke	Feest (1978a)
Narragansett	Simmons (1978)
Natchez	Albrecht (1946)
	Brain (1971)
	Fischer (1964:59)
	Hudson (1976)
	MacLeod (1926)
	Spencer, Jennings *et al.* (1965:409–410)
	Swanton (1946:161, 378–381, 516, 600, 629–650, 779, Map 3)
	White *et al.* (1971)
North Carolina Algonkians	Feest (1978c)
Nottoway–Meherrin	Binford (1967)
	Boyce (1978)
	Swanton (1946:149, Map 3)
Powhatan	Feest (1978b)
	Mooney (1907)
	Swanton (1946:175, 378–379, 415, 477, 643–648, 718–719, 730, Map 3)
Santa Lucia	Swanton (1946:765)
Timucua	Deagan (1978)
	Milanich (1978)
	Swanton (1946:201, 378–381, 405, 648, Map 3)
Tocobaga	Bullen (1978)
	Swanton (1946:195, 718–719)
Tuscarora	Boyce (1975, 1978)
	Swanton (1946:510, 718–719)
Virginia Algonkians	Feest (1978b)
Wabanaki	Erickson (1978:131)
	Speck (1915)
Western Abenaki	Day (1978)
	Snow (1978)
Western North America	
Atsugewi	Garth (1978)
	Heizer and Elsasser (1980:18)
	Kroeber (1925)
Barbareno Chumash	Grant (1978a, 1978b)
Bella Coola	McIlwraith (1948)
Cahuilla	Bean (1978a)
	Heizer and Elsasser (1980:19)
	Hooper (1920)
	Kroeber (1908, 1925)
	Phillips (1975)
	Strong (1929:36–182)
Central Miwok	Heizer and Elsasser (1980:86)

(continued)

APPENDIX 1 *Continued*

Case	Source
Central Pomo	Heizer and Elsasser (1980:86)
	McLendon and Oswalt (1978)
Chimariko	Heizer and Elsasser (1980:18)
	Kroeber (1925)
	Silver (1978a)
Chumash	Bean (1978b:675)
	Heizer and Elsasser (1980:18)
	King (1975)
Coast Miwok	Heizer and Elsasser (1980:14)
	Kelly (1978)
Coast Yuki	Heizer and Elsasser (1980:21, 86)
Costanoan	Heizer and Elsasser (1980:16)
	Kroeber (1925)
	Levy (1978a)
Cupeno	Bean and Smith (1978b)
	Heizer and Elsasser (1980:19)
	Kroeber (1925)
	Strong (1929:183–273)
Eastern Miwok	Levy (1978b)
Eastern Pomo	Heizer and Elsasser (1980:86)
Eastern and Southeastern Pomo	McLendon and Lowy (1978)
Foothill Yokuts	Spier (1978)
Gabrielino	Bean (1978b:675)
	Bean and Smith (1978a)
	Heizer and Elsasser (1980:19)
	Kroeber (1925)
Hopi	Brew (1979)
	Bolton (1930)
	Dorsey and Voth (1901)
	Eggan (1950)
	Hammond and Rey (1928, 1940, 1953, 1966)
	Schroeder (1979)
Klamath	Spier (1930)
	Stern (1965)
Lake Miwok	Heizer and Elsasser (1980:15)
Luiseno	Bean and Shipek (1978)
	Heizer and Elsasser (1980:19)
	Kroeber (1925)
	Phillips (1975)
	Strong (1929:274–328)
Maidu	Heizer and Elsasser (1980:15)
	Kroeber (1925)
	Riddell (1978)
Miwok	Bean (1978b:675)
	Kroeber (1925)
Nisenan	Wilson and Towne (1978)
Nomlaki	Goldschmidt (1948, 1951, 1978)
Nootka	Drucker (1939, 1951)
	Goddard (1972)
	Ruddell (1973)

(continued)

APPENDIX 1 *Continued*

Case	Source
Northeastern Pomo	Bean and Theodoratus (1978)
Northern Pomo	Heizer and Elsasser (1980:86)
	McLendon and Oswalt (1978)
Northern Valley Yokuts	Wallace (1978a)
Obispeno Chumash	Greenwood (1978)
Patwin	Bean (1978b:675)
	Kroeber (1932)
	McClellan (1953)
	Johnson, P. J. (1978)
Plains Miwok	Heizer and Elsasser (1980:86)
Pomo	Bean (1978b:675)
	Gifford (1926)
	Heizer and Elsasser (1980:18)
	Kroeber (1925)
	Loeb (1926)
	McLendon and Oswalt (1978)
Salinan	Bean (1978b:675)
	Heizer and Elsasser (1980:18)
	Hester (1978)
	Kroeber (1925)
	Mason (1912)
Salish	Barnett (1955)
	Ray (1933)
Serrano	Bean and Smith (1978a)
	Heizer and Elsasser (1980:19)
	Kroeber (1925)
	Strong (1929:5–35)
Shasta	Bean (1978b:675)
	Heizer and Elsasser (1980:19)
	Holt (1946)
	Kroeber (1925)
	Silver (1978b)
Southern Kwakiutl	Adams, W. (1981)
	Boas (1966)
	Codere (1957, 1961)
	Drucker (1939, 1955)
	Leland and Mitchell (1975)
	Piddocke (1965)
	Ringel (1979)
	Rohner and Rohner (1970)
	Ruyle (1973)
	Weinberg (1965)
Southern Miwok	Heizer and Elsasser (1980:86)
Southeastern Pomo	Heizer and Elsasser (1980:86)
Southern Pomo	Bean and Theodoratus (1978)
Southwestern Pomo	Heizer and Elsasser (1980:86)
Southern Valley Yokuts	Heizer and Elsasser (1980:86)
	Wallace (1978b)
Tipai–Ipai	Bean (1978b:675)
	Heizer and Elsasser (1980:18)
	Kroeber (1925)
	Luomala (1978)

(continued)

APPENDIX 1 *Continued*

Case	Source
Tolowa	Gould (1978)
	Heizer and Elsasser (1980:12, 86)
Wappo	Driver (1936)
	Heizer and Elsasser (1980:22, 86)
	Kroeber (1925)
	McClellan (1953)
	Sawyer (1978)
Western and Northeastern Pomo	Bean and Theodoratus (1978)
Wintu	Goldschmidt (1948)
	Kroeber (1925)
	LaPena (1978)
Yana	Heizer and Elsasser (1980:18)
	Johnson, J. J. (1978)
	Kroeber (1925)
	Sapir and Spier (1946)
Yokuts	Heizer and Elsasser (1980:3, 15)
	Kroeber (1925)
Yokuts and Western Mono	Gayton (1930, 1945, 1948)
Yuki	Foster (1944)
	Heizer and Elsasser (1980:18, 20, 86)
	Kroeber (1925)
	Miller (1978)
Yurok	Heizer and Elsasser (1980:11, 86)
	Kroeber (1925)
	Pilling (1978)
Zuni	Bolton (1949)
	Bunzel (1932)
	Eggan (1950)
	Hammond and Rey (1928, 1940, 1953, 1966)
	Ladd (1979)
	Schroeder (1979)
	Stevenson (1904)
	Woodbury (1979)

ACKNOWLEDGEMENTS

The authors thank Michael B. Schiffer for providing the impetus to write this chapter. He also made many useful comments on the initial draft. In addition, we acknowledge Gary Brown, Gregory A. Johnson, Kent G. Lightfoot, Steadman Upham, and the anonymous reviewers for their constructive suggestions. The ideas expressed here have developed out of discussions that the authors have had over the past few years with Richard E. Blanton, Warren DeBoer, Jeffrey Hantman, Stephen A. Kowalewski, Linda Nicholas, Barbara Stark, and David Wilcox. Dawn M. Poli assisted with the typing and organization of the manuscript. The authors, of course, take full responsibility for the interpretations and conclusions presented.

REFERENCES

Adams, R. E. W.
  1981 Settlement patterns in the central Yucatan and southern Campeche regions. In *Lowland Maya settlement patterns,* edited by W. Ashmore. Albuquerque: University of New Mexico Press. Pp. 211–257.

Adams, W.
  1981 Recent ethnology of the Northwest Coast. *Annual Review of Anthropology* **10:**361–392.

Albrecht, A. C.
  1946 Indian–French relations at Natchez. *American Anthropologist* **48**(3):321–354.

Appel, J. A.
  1982 A summary of the ethnohistoric information relevant to the interpretation of Late Postclassic settlement pattern data, the central and Valle Grande survey zones. In Monte Alban's hinterland, Part 1, The Prehispanic settlement patterns of the central and southern parts of the Valley of Oaxaca, Mexico, by R. Blanton, S. Kowalewski, G. Feinman, and J. Appel. *Museum of Anthropology, University of Michigan, Memoirs* 15.

Baker, P. T., and W. T. Sanders
  1972 Demographic studies in anthropology. *Annual Review of Anthropology* **1:**151–178.

Barnett, H. G.
  1955 *The Coast Salish of British Columbia.* Eugene: University of Oregon Press.

Bean, L. J.
  1978a Cahuilla. In *Handbook of North American Indians,* Vol. 5, *California,* edited by R. F. Heizer and W. C. Sturtevant. Washington, D.C.: Smithsonian Institution. Pp. 575–587.
  1978b Social organization. In *Handbook of North American Indians,* Vol. 5, *California,* edited by R. F. Heizer and W. C. Sturtevant. Washington, D.C.: Smithsonian Institution. Pp. 673–682.

Bean, L. J., and F. C. Shipek
  1978 Luiseno. In *Handbook of North American Indians,* Vol. 5, *California,* edited by R. F. Heizer and W. C. Sturtevant. Washington, D.C.: Smithsonian Institution. Pp. 550–563.

Bean, L. J. and C. R. Smith
  1978a Gabrielino. In *Handbook of North American Indians,* Vol. 5, *California,* edited by R. F. Heizer and W. C. Sturtevant. Washington D.C.: Smithsonian Institution. Pp. 538–549.
  1978b Cupeno. In *Handbook of North American Indians,* Vol. 5, *California,* edited by R. F. Heizer and W. C. Sturtevant. Washington, D.C.: Smithsonian Institution. Pp. 588–591.
  1978c Serrano. In *Handbook of North American Indians,* Vol. 5, *California,* edited by R. F. Heizer and W. C. Sturtevant. Washington, D.C.: Smithsonian Institution. Pp. 570–574.

Bean, L. J. and D. Theodoratus
  1978 Western Pomo and northeastern Pomo. In *Handbook of North American Indians,* Vol. 5, *California,* edited by R. F. Heizer and W. C. Sturtevant. Washington, D.C.: Smithsonian Institution. Pp. 289–305.

Bennett, W. C.
  1949   Habitations. In *The Comparative Ethnology of South American Indians, Handbook of South American Indians,* Vol. 5, edited by J. H. Steward. *Bureau of American Ethnology Bulletin* **143**:1–20.
Binford, L. R.
  1962   Archaeology as anthropology. *American Antiquity* **28**(2):217–225.
  1967   An ethnohistory of the Nottoway, Meherrin and Weancock Indians of southeastern Virginia. *Ethnohistory* **14**:(3–4):104–218.
  1980   Willow smoke and dogstails: hunter–gatherer settlement systems and archaeological site formation. *American Antiquity* **45**(1):4–20.
Blanton, R., S. Kowalewski, G. Feinman and J. Appel
  1981   *Ancient Mesoamerica: a comparison of change in three regions.* New York: Cambridge University Press.
Blau, P. M.
  1970   A formal theory of differentiation in organizations. *American Sociological Review* **35**(2):201–218.
  1977   *Inequality and heterogeneity: a primitive theory of social structure.* New York: The Free Press.
Boas, F. (edited by H. Codere)
  1966   *Kwakiutl ethnography.* Chicago: University of Chicago Press.
Bolton, H. E.
  1930   *Spanish exploration in the Southwest 1542–1706.* New York: Scribner's Sons.
  1949   *Coronado: Knight of Pueblo and Plains.* Albuquerque: University of New Mexico Press.
Boyce, D. W.
  1975   Did a Tuscarora confederacy exist? In *Four centuries of southern Indians,* edited by C. M. Hudson. Athens: University of Georgia Press. Pp. 18–45.
  1978   Iroquoian tribes of the Virginia–North Carolina coastal plain. In *Handbook of North American Indians,* Vol. 15, *Northeast,* edited by B. G. Trigger and W. C. Sturtevant. Washington, D.C.: Smithsonian Institution. Pp. 282–289.
Brain, J. P.
  1971   The Natchez "paradox". *Ethnology* **10**(2):215–222.
Brasser, T. J.
  1978   The Mahican. In *Handbook of North American Indians,* Vol. 15, *Northeast,* edited by B. G. Trigger and W. C. Sturtevant. Washington, D.C.: Smithsonian Institution. Pp. 198–212.
Brew, J. O.
  1979   Hopi prehistory and history to 1850. In *Handbook of North American Indians,* Vol. 9, *Southwest,* edited by A. Ortiz and W. C. Sturtevant. Washington, D.C.: Smithsonian Institution. Pp. 514–523.
Brown, J. A. (editor)
  1971   Approaches to the social dimensions of mortuary practices. *Society for American Archaeology Memoirs* 25.
Brumfiel, E. M.
  1983   Aztec state making: ecology, structure and the origin of the state. *American Anthropologist* 85(2):261–284.
Bullen, R. P.
  1978   Tocobaga Indians and the Safety Harbor culture. In *Tacahale: essays on the Indians of Florida and southeastern Georgia during the historic period,* edited by J. M. Milanich and S. Proctor. Gainesville: University Presses of Florida. Pp. 50–58.

Bunzel, R. L.
    1932   Introduction to Zuni ceremonialism. *Bureau of American Ethnology Annual Report* 47.
Butzer, K. W.
    1980   Civilizations: organisms or systems? *American Scientist* **68**(5):517–523.
Cancian, F.
    1976   Social stratification. *Annual Review of Anthropology* **5**:227–248.
Carneiro, R. L.
    1962   Scale analysis as an instrument for the study of cultural evolution. *Southwestern Journal of Anthropology* **18**(2):149–169.
    1967   On the relationship between size of population and complexity of social organization in human societies. *Southwestern Journal of Anthropology* **23**(3):234–243.
    1981   The chiefdom: precursor of the state. In *The transition to statehood in the New World*, edited by G. D. Jones and R. R. Kautz. Cambridge: Cambridge University Press. Pp. 37–79.
Childe, V. G.
    1950   The urban revolution. *Town Planning Review* **21**(1): 3–17.
Claessen, H. J. M. and P. Skalnik (editors)
    1978   *The early state*. The Hague: Mouton Publishers.
Codere, H.
    1957   Kwakiutl society: rank without class. *American Anthropologist* **59**(3):473–486.
    1961   Kwakiutl. In *Perspectives in American Indian culture change*, edited by Edward H. Spicer. Chicago: University of Chicago Press. Pp. 431–515.
Cooper, J. M.
    1946   The Araucanians. In *The Andean Civilizations, Handbook of South American Indians*, Vol. 2, edited by J. H. Steward. *Bureau of American Ethnology Bulletin* **143**:687–766.
Cordy, R. H.
    1981   *A study of prehistoric social change: the development of complex societies in the Hawaiian Islands*. New York: Academic Press.
Corkran, D. H.
    1962   *The Cherokee frontier: conflict and survival, 1740–62*. Norman: The University of Oklahoma Press.
    1967   *The Creek Frontier, 1540–1783*. Norman: University of Oklahoma Press.
Cotterill, R. S.
    1954   *The southern Indians: the story of the civilized tribes before removal*. Norman: University of Oklahoma Press.
Day, G. M.
    1978   Western Abenaki. In *Handbook of North American Indians*, Vol. 15, *Northeast*, edited by B. G. Trigger and W. C. Sturtevant. Washington, D.C.: Smithsonian Institution. Pp. 148–159.
Deagan, K. A.
    1978   Cultures in transition: fusion and assimilation among the eastern Timucua. In *Tacahale: essays on the Indians of Florida and southern Georgia during the historic period*, edited by J. Milanich and S. Proctor. Gainesville: University Presses of Florida. Pp. 89–119.
Debo, A.
    1934   *The rise and fall of the Choctaw republic*. Norman: University of Oklahoma Press.
DeBoer, W. R.
    1981   Buffer zones in the cultural ecology of aboriginal Amazonia: an ethnohistorical approach. *American Antiquity* **46**(2):364–377.

Dorsey, A. and H. R. Voth
    1901   The Oraibi Soyal ceremony. *Field Museum Publication* 55, *Anthropological Series* **3**(1).

Driver, E. H.
    1936   Wappo ethnography. *University of California Publications in American Archaeology and Ethnology* **36**(3):179–220.

Drucker, P.
    1939   Rank, wealth, and kinship in Northwest Coast society. *American Anthropologist* **41**(1):55–65.
    1951   The northern and central Nootkan tribes. *Bureau of American Ethnology Bulletin* 144.
    1955   *Indians of the Northwest Coast.* Garden City: The Natural History Press.

Dunnell, R. C.
    1980   Evolutionary theory and archaeology. In *Advances in archaeological method and theory* Vol. 3, edited by M. B. Schiffer. New York: Academic Press. Pp. 35–99.

Earle, T. K.
    1977   A reappraisal of redistribution: complex Hawaiian chiefdoms. In *Exchange systems in prehistory,* edited by T. K. Earle and J. E. Ericson. New York: Academic Press. Pp. 213–229.
    1978   Economic and social organization of a complex chiefdom: the Halelea District, Kaua'i, Hawaii. University of Michigan, *Museum of Anthropology, Anthropological Papers* 63.

Eggan, F.
    1950   *Social organization of the Western Pueblos.* Chicago: University of Chicago Press.

Eisenstadt, S. N.
    1971   *Social differentiation and stratification.* Glenview: Scott, Foresman and Co.

Ember, M.
    1963   The relationship between economic and political development in nonindustrialized societies. *Ethnology* **2**(2):228–248.

Erickson, V. O.
    1978   Maliseet–Passamaquoddy. In *Handbook of North American Indians,* Vol. 15, *Northeast,* edited by B. G. Trigger and W. C. Sturtevant. Washington, D.C.: Smithsonian Institution. Pp. 123–136.

Evans, J. D.
    1973   Islands as laboratories for the study of culture process. In *The explanation of culture change,* edited by C. Renfrew. Pittsburgh: University of Pittsburgh Press. Pp. 517–520.

Fallers, L. A.
    1973   *Inequality: social stratification reconsidered.* Chicago: University of Chicago Press.

Feest, C. F.
    1978a   Nanticoke and neighboring tribes. In *Handbook of North American Indians,* Vol. 15, *Northeast,* edited by B. G. Trigger and W. C. Sturtevant. Washington, D.C.: Smithsonian Institution. Pp. 240–252.
    1978b   Virginia Algonquians. In *Handbook of North American Indians,* Vol. 15, *Northeast,* edited by B. G. Trigger and W. C. Sturtevant. Washington, D.C.: Smithsonian Institution. Pp. 253–270.
    1978c   North Carolina Algonquians. In *Handbook of North American Indians,* Vol. 15, *Northeast,* edited by B. G. Trigger and W. C. Sturtevant. Washington, D.C.: Smithsonian Institution. Pp. 271–281.

Fenton, W. N.
  1940 Problems arising from the historic northeastern position of the Iroquois. *Smithsonian Miscellaneous Collections* **100**:159–251.
  1978 Northern Iroquoian culture patterns. In *Handbook of North American Indians*, Vol. 15, *Northeast*, edited by B. G. Trigger and W. C. Sturtevant. Washington, D.C.: Smithsonian Institution, Pp. 296–321.
Finney, B.
  1966 Resource distribution and social structure in Tahiti. *Ethnology* **5**(1)80–86.
Fischer, J. L.
  1964 Solutions for the Natchez paradox. *Ethnology* **3**(1)53–65.
Flannery, K. V.
  1972 The cultural evolution of civilization. *Annual Review of Ecology and Systematics* **3**:399–426.
Flannery, K. V. (editor)
  1976 *The early Mesoamerican village.* New York: Academic Press.
Flannery, K. V. and J. Marcus
  1976 Evolution of the public building in Formative Oaxaca. In *Cultural change and continuity: essays in honor of James Bennett Griffin*, edited by C. Cleland. New York: Academic Press. Pp. 205–221.
Fogelson, R. D.
  1977 Cherokee notions of power. In *The anthropology of power*, edited by R. D. Fogelson and R. N. Adams. New York: Academic Press. Pp. 185–194.
Forge, A.
  1972 Normative factors in the settlement size of Neolithic cultivators (New Guinea). In *Man, settlement, and urbanism*, edited by P. J. Ucko, R. Tringham, and G. W. Dimbleby. London: Gerald Duckworth. Pp. 363–376.
Fortes, M. and E. E. Evans-Pritchard
  1940 *African political systems.* London: Oxford.
Foster, G.M.
  1944 A summary of Yuki culture. *University of California Anthroplogical Records* **5**(3):155–244.
Fried, M. H.
  1960 On the evolution of social stratification and the state. In *Culture in history*, edited by S. Diamond. New York: Columbia University Press. Pp. 713–731.
  1967 *The evolution of political society: an essay in political anthropology.* New York: Random House.
  1975 *The notion of tribe.* Menlo Park: Cummings.
Garth, T. E.
  1978 Atsugewi. In *Handbook of North American Indians*, Vol. 5, *California*, edited by R. F. Heizer and W. C. Sturtevant. Washington, D.C.: Smithsonian Institution. Pp. 236–248.
Gayton, A. H.
  1930 Yokuts–Mono chiefs and shamans. *University of California Publications in American Archaeology and Ethnology* **24**(8):361–420.
  1945 Yokuts and western Mono social organization. *American Anthropologist* **47**(3):409–426.
  1948 Yokuts and western Mono ethnography. *University of California Anthropological Records* **10**(1–2):1–302.

Gearing, F.
   1962   Priests and warriors: social structures for Cherokee politics in the 18th century. *Memoirs of the American Anthropological Association* 93.
Gibson, A. M.
   1971   *The Chickasaws*. Norman: University of Oklahoma Press.
Gifford, E. W.
   1926   Clear Lake Pomo society. *University of California Publications in American Archaeology and Ethnology* **18**(2):287–390.
Gilman, A.
   1981   The development of social stratification in Bronze Age Europe. *Current anthropology* **22**(1):1–23.
Goddard, I.
   1972   *Indians of the Northwest Coast*. New York: Cooper Square Publishers.
   1978   Delaware. In *Handbook of North American Indians*, Vol. 15, *Northeast*, edited by B. G. Trigger and W. C. Sturtevant. Washington, D.C.: Smithsonian Institution. Pp. 213–239.
Goldman, I.
   1970   *Ancient Polynesian society*. Chicago: The University of Chicago Press.
Goldschmidt, W.
   1948   Social organization in native California and the origins of clans. *American Anthropologist* **50**(3):444–456.
   1951   Nomlaki ethnography. *University of California Publications in American Archaeology and Ethnology* **42**:303–443.
   1978   Nomlaki. In *Handbook of North American Indians*, Vol. 5, *California*, edited by R. F. Heizer and W. C. Sturtevant. Washington, D.C.: Smithsonian Institution. Pp. 341–349.
Goody, J.
   1966   Introduction. In *Succession to high office*, edited by J. Goody. London: Cambridge University Press, Pp. 1–56.
Gould, R. A.
   1978   Tolowa. In *Handbook of North American Indians*, Vol. 5, *California*, edited by R. F. Heizer and W. C. Sturtevant. Washington, D.C.: Smithsonian Institution. Pp. 128–136.
Granovetter, M.
   1979   The idea of ''advancement'' in theories of social evolution and development. *American Journal of Sociology* **85**(3):489–515.
Grant C.
   1978a   Chumash: introduction. In *Handbook of North American Indians*, Vol. 5, *California*, edited by R. F. Heizer and W. C. Sturtevant. Washington, D.C.: Smithsonian Institution. Pp. 505–508.
   1978b   Eastern coastal Chumash. In *Handbook of North American Indians*, Vol. 5, *California*. edited by R. F. Heizer and W. C. Sturtevant. Washington, D.C.: Smithsonian Institution. Pp. 509–519.
Graves, T. D., N. B. Graves and M. J. Kobrin
   1969   Historical inferences from Guttman scales: the return of age-area magic? *Current Anthropology* **10**(4):317–338.
Greber, N.
   1979   Variations in social structure of Ohio Hopewell Peoples. *Mid-Continental Journal of Archaeology* **4**(1):36–78.

Grebinger, P.
  1973   Prehistoric social organization in Chaco Canyon, New Mexico: an alternative recon-
          struction. *The Kiva* **39**(1):3–23.
Green, M. D.
  1979   *The Creeks: a critical bibliography.* Bloomington: Indiana University Press.
Greenwood, R. S.
  1978   Obispeno and Purisimeno Chumash. In *Handbook of North American Indians*, Vol. 5,
          California, edited by R. F. Heizer and W. C. Sturtevant. Washington, D.C.: Smithso-
          nian Institution. Pp. 520–523.
Griffin, J. B.
  1979   An overview of the Chillicothe Hopewell Conference. In *Hopewell Archaeology: the
          Chillicothe conference,* edited by D. S. Brose and N. Greber. Kent: Kent State Univer-
          sity Press. Pp. 266–279.
Hammond, G. P. and A. Rey
  1928   *Obregon's history of 16th century explorations in western Arizona.* Los Angeles:
          Western Publishing Company.
  1940   *Narratives of the Coronado Expedition 1540–1542.* Albuquerque: University of New
          Mexico Press.
  1953   *Don Juan de Onate, colonizer of New Mexico 1595–1628.* Albuquerque: University of
          New Mexico Press.
  1966   *The rediscovery of New Mexico 1580–1594.* Albuquerque: Univeristy of New Mexico
          Press.
Harris, M.
  1968   *The rise of anthropological theory.* New York: Thomas Y. Crowell.
  1980   *Cultural materialism: the struggle for a science of culture.* New York: Vintage Books.
Heidenreich, C. B.
  1978   Huron. In *Handbook of North American Indians*, Vol. 15, *Northeast,* edited by B. G.
          Trigger and W. C. Sturtevant. Washington, D.C.: Smithsonian Institution. Pp.
          368–388.
Heizer, R. F. and A. B. Elsasser
  1980   *The natural world of the California Indians.* Berkeley: University of California Press.
Heizer, R. F. and W. C. Sturtevant (editors)
  1978   *Handbook of North American Indians,* Vol. 8, *California,* Washington, D.C.:
          Smithsonian Institution.
Helms, M. W.
  1976   Competition, power and succession to office in Pre-Columbian Panama. In *Frontier
          adaptations in lower Central America,* edited M. W. Helms and F. O. Loveland.
          Philadelphia: ISHI. Pp. 25–35.
  1979   *Ancient Panama: chiefs in search of power.* Austin: University of Texas Press.
  1980   Succession to high office in Pre-Columbian, Circum-Caribbean chiefdoms. *Man*
          15(4):718–731.
Herman, M. W.
  1950   A reconstruction of aboriginal Delaware culture from contemporary sources. *Kroeber
          Anthropological Society Papers* **1**(1):45–77.
Hernandez de Alba, G.
  1948   Sub-Andean tribes of the Cauca Valley. In *The Circum-Caribbean Tribes, Handbook
          of South American Indians* Vol. 4, edited by J. H. Steward. *Bureau of American
          Ethnology Bulletin* **143**:297–328.

Hester, T. R.
  1978   Salinan. In *Handbook of North American Indians,* Vol. 5, *California,* edited by R. F. Heizer and W. C. Sturtevant. Washington, D.C.: Smithsonian Institution. Pp. 500–504.

Hill, J. N.
  1977   Introduction. In *Explanation of prehistoric change,* edited by J. N. Hill. Albuquerque: University of New Mexico Press. Pp. 1–16.

Holt, C.
  1946   Shasta ethnography. *University of California Anthropological Records* 3(4):299–349.

Hooper, L.
  1920   The Cahuilla Indians. *University of California Publications in American Archaeology and Ethnology* 16(3):315–380.

Horton, R.
  1976   Stateless societies in the history of western Africa. In *History of West Africa* Vol. 1, edited by J. F. A. Ajayi and M. Crowder. New York: Columbia University Press. Pp. 72–113.

Hudson, C. M.
  1970   The Catawba nation. *University of Georgia Monographs* 18.
  1976   *The southeastern Indians.* Knoxville: University of Tennessee Press.

Johnson, G. A.
  1973   Local exchange and early state development in southwestern Iran. University of Michigan, *Museum of Anthropology Anthropological Papers* 51.
  1978   Information sources and the development of decision-making organizations. In *Social archaeology: beyond subsistence and dating,* edited by C. L. Redman *et al.* New York: Academic Press. Pp. 87–112.
  1982   Organizational structure and scalar stress. In *Theory and explanation in archaeology: the Southampton conference,* edited by C. Renfrew, M. J. Rowlands, and B. Abbott Segraves. New York: Academic Press. Pp. 389–421.
  n.d.   The changing organization of Uruk administration on the Susiana Plain. In *Archaeological perspectives on Iran: from prehistory to the Islamic Conquest,* edited by F. Hole. Albuquerque: University of New Mexico Press.

Johnson, J. J.
  1978   Yana. In *Handbook of North American Indians,* Vol. 5, *California,* edited by R. F. Heizer and W. C. Sturtevant. Washington, D.C.: Smithsonian Institution. Pp. 361–369.

Johnson, P. J.
  1978   Patwin. In *Handbook of North American Indians,* Vol. 5, *California,* edited by R. F. Heizer and W. C. Sturtevant. Washington, D.C.: Smithsonian Institution. Pp. 350–360.

Kehoe, A. B.
  1981   Bands, tribes, chiefdoms, states: Is Service serviceable? Paper presented at the 46th Annual Meeting of the Society for American Archaeology, San Diego.

Kelly, I.
  1978   Coast Miwok. In *Handbook of North American Indians,* Vol. 5, *California,* edited by R. F. Heizer and W. C. Sturtevant. Washington, D.C.: Smithsonian Institution. Pp. 414–425.

King. C.
  1975   The names and locations of historic Chumash villages. *The Journal of California Anthropology* 2(2):171–179.

King, T. F.
  1978 Don't that beat the band? Non-egalitarian political organization in prehistoric central California. In *Social archaeology: beyond subsistence and dating,* edited by C. L. Redman *et al.* New York: Academic Press. Pp. 225–247.

Kirchoff, P.
  1948 The tribes of the Orinoco River. In *The Circum-Caribbean Tribes, Handbook of South American Indians,* Vol. 4, edited by J. H. Steward. *Bureau of American Ethnology Bulletin* **143**:481–493.

Kohl, P. L.
  1978 The balance of trade in southwestern Asia in the third millennium (B.C.). *Current Anthropology* **19**(3):463–492.
  1981 Materialist approaches in prehistory. *Annual Review of Anthropology* **10**:89–118.

Kowalewski, S. A.
  1976 Prehispanic settlement patterns of the central part of the Valley of Oaxaca, Mexico. Unpublished Ph.D. dissertation, Department of Anthropology, University of Arizona, Tucson, Arizona.

Kroeber, A. L.
  1908 Ethnography of the Cahuilla Indians. *University of California Publications in American Archaeology and Ethnology* **8**(2):29–68.
  1925 Handbook of Indians of California. *Bureau of American Ethnology Bulletin* 78.
  1932 The Patwin and their neighbors. *University of California Publications in American Archaeology and Ethnology* **29**(4):253–423.

Ladd, E. J.
  1979 Zuni economy. In *Handbook of North American Indians,* Vol. 9, *Southwest,* edited by A. Ortiz and W. C. Sturtevant. Washington, D.C.: Smithsonian Institution. Pp. 492–498.

LaPena, F. R.
  1978 Wintu. In *Handbook of North American Indians,* Vol. 5, *California,* edited by R. F. Heizer and W. C. Sturtevant. Washington, D.C.: Smithsonian Institution. Pp. 324–340.

Larson, L .H.
  1978 Historic Guale Indians of the Georgia Coast and the impact of the Spanish mission effort. In *Tacahale: essays on the Indians of Florida and southern Georgia during the historic period,* edited by J. Milanich and S. Proctor. Gainesville: University Presses of Florida. Pp. 120–140.

Leach, E.
  1973 Concluding address. In *The explanation of culture change,* edited by C. Renfrew. Pittsburgh: University of Pittsburgh Press. Pp. 761–771.

Leacock, E.
  1963 Introduction. In *Ancient society,* by L. H. Morgan, New York: World Publishing. Pp. i–xx.

Lee, R. B. and I. Devore
  1968 Problems in the study of hunters and gatherers. In *Man the hunter,* edited by R. B. Lee and I. Devore. Chicago: Aldine. Pp. 3–12.

Leland, D. and D. H. Mitchell
  1975 Some correlates of local group rank among the Southern Kwakiutl. *Ethnology* **14**(4):325–346.

Levy, R.
  1978a Costanoan. In *Handbook of North American Indians,* Vol. 5, *California,* edited by R. F. Heizer and W. C. Sturtevant. Washington, D.C.: Smithsonian Institution. Pp. 485–495.

1978b Eastern Miwok. In *Handbook of North American Indians,* Vol. 5, *California,* edited by R. F. Heizer and W. C. Sturtevant. Washington, D.C.: Smithsonian Institution. Pp. 398–413.

Lightfoot, K. G.
1981 Prehistoric political development in the Little Colorado region, east-central Arizona. Unpublished Ph.D. dissertation, Department of Anthropology, Arizona State University, Tempe, Arizona.

Lightfoot, K. G. and G. M. Feinman
1982 Social differentiation and leadership development in pithouse villages in the Mogollon region of the American Southwest. *American Antiquity* **47**(1):64–86.

Loeb, E. M.
1926 Pomo folkways. *University of California Publications in American Archaeology and Ethnology* **19**(2):149–404.

Lothrop, S. K.
1937 Cocle, an archaeological study of Central Panama, Part I. *Memoirs of the Peabody Museum of Archaeology and Ethnology* 7.

Lowie, R. H.
1949 Social and political organization of the tropical forest and marginal tribes. In *The Comparative Ethnology of South American Indians, Handbook of the South American Indians,* Vol. 5, edited by J. H. Steward. *Bureau of American Ethnology Bulletin* **143**:313–350.

Luomala, K.
1978 Tipai and Ipai. In *Handbook of North American Indians,* Vol. 5, *California,* edited by R. F. Heizer and W. C. Sturtevant. Washington, D.C.: Smithsonian Institution. Pp. 592–609.

MacLeod, W. C.
1926 On Natchez cultural origins. *American Anthropologist* **28**(2):409–413.

Mason, J. A.
1912 The ethnology of the Salinan Indians. *University of California Publications in American Archaeology and Ethnology* **10**:97–240.

McClellan, C.
1953 Ethnography of the Wappo and Patwin. In *The archaeology of the Napa region,* edited by Robert F. Heizer. *University of California Anthropological Records* **12**(6):233–241.

McIlwraith, T. F.
1948 *The Bella Coola Indians.* Toronto: University of Toronto Press.

McLendon, S. and M. J. Lowy
1978 Eastern Pomo and southeastern Pomo. In *Handbook of North American Indians,* Vol. 5, *California,* edited by R. F. Heizer and W. C. Sturtevant. Washington, D.C.: Smithsonian Institution. Pp. 306–323.

McLendon, S. and R. L. Oswalt
1978 Pomo: introduction. In *Handbook of North American Indians,* Vol. 5, *California,* edited by R. F. Heizer and W. C. Sturtevant. Washington, D.C.: Smithsonian Institution. Pp. 274–288.

Meggers, B. J.
1971 *Amazonia: man and culture in a counterfeit paradise.* Chicago: Aldine-Atherton.

Meggitt, M. J.
1973 The pattern of leadership among the Mae-Enga of New Guinea. In *Politics in New Guinea,* edited by R. M. Berndt and P. Lawrence. Seattle: University of Washington Press. Pp. 191–206.

Metraux, A.
1948a   The Tupinamba. In *The Tropical Forest Tribes, Handbook of South American Indians,* Vol. 3, edited by J. H. Steward. *Bureau of American Ethnology Bulletin* **148**:95–134.
1948b   Tribes of eastern Bolivia and the Madeira headwaters. In *The Tropical Forest Tribes, Handbook of South American Indians,* Vol. 3, edited by J. H. Steward. *Bureau of American Ethnology Bulletin* **143**:381–454.
1948c   The tribes of Mato Grasso and eastern Bolivia. In *The tropical Forest Tribes, Handbook of South American Indians,* Vol. 3, edited by J. H. Steward. *Bureau of American Ethnology Bulletin* **143**:349–360.
1948d   Tribes of the eastern slopes of the Bolivian Andes. In *The Tropical Forest Tribes, Handbook of South American Indians* Vol. 3, edited by J. H. Steward. *Bureau of American Ethnology Bulletin* **143**:465–485.
Milanich, J. T.
1978   The western Timucua: patterns of acculturation and change. In *Tacahale: essays on the Indians of Florida and southeastern Georgia during the historic period,* edited by J. Milanich and S. Proctor. Gainesville: University Presses of Florida. Pp. 59–88.
Miles, S. W.
1957   The sixteenth-century Pokom-Maya: a documentary analysis of social structure and archaeological setting. *American Philosophical Society, Transactions* **47**(4).
Miller, V. P.
1978   Yuki, Huchnom, and Coast Yuki. In *Handbook of North American Indians,* Vol. 5, *California,* edited by R. F. Heizer and W. C. Sturtevant. Washington, D.C.: Smithsonian Institution. Pp. 249–255.
Mooney, J.
1907   The Powhatan confederacy, past and present. *American Anthropologist* **9**(1):129–152.
1975   *Historical Sketch of the Cherokee.* Chicago: Aldine.
Morgan, L. H.
1928   Government and institutions of the Iroquois. *Researches and Transactions of the New York Archaeological Association* **7**(1).
1963   *Ancient society,* edited by E. Leacock. New York: World Publishing, (orig. 1851)
Moseley, K. P. and I. Wallerstein
1978   Precapitalist social structures. *Annual Review of Sociology* **4**:259–290.
Naroll, R.
1956   A preliminary index of social development. *American Anthropologist* **58**(4):687–715.
Naroll, R. and E. Margolis
1974   Maximum settlement size: a compilation. *Behavior Science Research* **9**(4):319–326.
Newcomb, W. W.
1956   The culture and acculturation of the Delaware Indians. University of Michigan, *Museum of Anthropology Anthropological Papers* 10.
Nimendaju, C. (translated by R. H. Lowie)
1942   The Sherente. *Publications of the Frederick Webb Hodge Anniversary Publication Fund* 4.
Oberg, K.
1953   Indian tribes and northern tribes of Mato Grosso, Brazil. *Smithsonian Institution Institute of Social Anthropology Publication* 15.
1955   Types of social structure among the lowland tribes of South and Central America. *American Anthropologist* **57**(3):472–487.
Opler, M. E.
1952   The Creek ''town'' and the problem of Creek Indian political reorganization. In *Human problems in technological change,* edited E. H. Spicer. New York: Russell Sage Foundation. Pp. 165–180.

Ortiz, A. and W. C. Sturtevant (editors)
    1979   *Handbook of North American Indians,* Vol. 9, *Southwest,* Washington, D.C.: Smithsonian Institution.
Peebles, C. S. and S. M. Kus
    1977   Some archaeological correlates of ranked societies. *American Antiquity* **42**(3):421–448.
Phillips, G. H.
    1975   *Chiefs and challengers.* Berkeley: University of California Press.
Pianka, E. R.
    1974   *Evolutionary ecology.* New York: Harper and Row. Pp. 253–278.
Piddocke, S.
    1965   The potlatch system of the Southern Kwakiutl: a new perspective. *Southwestern Journal of Anthropology* **21**(3):244–64.
Pilling, A. R.
    1978   Yurok. In *Handbook of North American Indians,* Vol. 5, *California,* edited by R. F. Heizer and W. C. Sturtevant. Washington, D.C.: Smithsonian Institution. Pp. 137–154.
Plog, F. T.
    1973   Diachronic anthropology. In *Research and theory in current anthropology,* edited by C. L. Redman. New York: John Wiley and sons.
    1974   *The study of prehistoric change.* New York: Academic Press.
    1977a   Explaining change. In *The explanation of prehistoric change,* edited by J. N. Hill. Albuquerque: University of New Mexico Press. Pp. 17–57.
    1977b   Systems theory and simulation: the case of Hawaiian warfare and redistribution. In *Explanations of prehistoric change,* edited by J. N. Hill. Albuquerque: University of New Mexico Press. Pp. 259–270.
    1979   Alternative models of prehistoric change. In *Transformations: mathematical approaches in culture change,* edited by C. Renfrew and K. L. Cooke. New York: Academic Press. Pp. 221–236.
Plog, F. T. and S. Upham
    1979   The analysis of prehistoric political organization. Paper presented at the 101st Annual Meeting of the American Ethnological Society, Vancouver, British Columbia.
Plotnicov, L. and A. Tuden
    1970   Introduction. In *Essays in comparative social stratification,* edited by L. Plotnicov and A. Tuden. Pittsburgh: University of Pittsburgh Press. Pp. 3–25.
Polanyi, K.
    1957   The economy as instituted process. In *Trade and market in the early empires,* edited by K. Polanyi, C. M. Armstrong, and H. W. Pearson. Chicago: Henry Regnery. Pp. 243–270.
Ray, V. F.
    1933   *The Sanpoil and Nespelemi: Salishan peoples of northeastern Washington.* Seattle: University of Washington Press.
Read, K. E.
    1959   Leadership and consensus in a New Guinea society. *American Anthropologist* **61**(3):425–436.
Renfrew, C.
    1973   Monuments, mobilization and social organization in Neolithic Wessex. In *The explanation of culture change: models in prehistory,* edited by C. Renfrew. Pittsburgh: University of Pittsburgh Press. Pp. 539–558.
    1974   Beyond a subsistence economy: the evolution of social organization in prehistoric

Europe. In *Reconstructing complex societies,* edited by C. B. Moore. Cambridge: American Schools of Oriental Research, Pp. 69–85.

Richards, P.
    1978   Farming systems, settlement and state formation: the Nigerian evidence. In *Social organization and settlement,* edited by D. Green, C. Haselgrove and M. Spriggs. Pp. 477–509. *British Archaeological Reports, Series Supplement* 47.

Riddell, F. A.
    1978   Maidu and Kankow. In *Handbook of North American Indians,* Vol. 5, *California,* edited by R. F. Heizer and W. C. Sturtevant. Washington, D.C.: Smithsonian Institution, Pp. 370–386.

Ringel, G.
    1979   The Kwakiutl potlatch: history, economics, and symbols. *Ethnohistory* **26**(4):347–362.

Rohner, R. P. and E. C. Rohner
    1970   *The Kwakiutl: Indians of British Columbia.* New York: Holt, Rinehart and Winston.

Rothschild, N. A.
    1979   Mortuary behavior and social organization at Indian Knoll and Dickson Mounds. *American Antiquity* **44**(4):658–675.

Rouse, I.
    1948a   The Carib. In *The Circum-Caribbean Tribes, Handbook of South American Indians,* Vol. 4, edited by J. H. Steward. *Bureau of American Ethnology Bulletin* **143**:547–565.
    1948b   The Arawak. In *The Circum-Caribbean Tribes, Handbook of South American Indians,* Vol. 4, edited by J. H. Steward. *Bureau of American Ethnology Bulletin* **143**:507–546.

Ruddell, R.
    1973   Chiefs and commoners: nature's balance and the good life among the Nootka. In *Cultural ecology: readings on the Canadian Indians and Eskimos,* edited by Bruce Cox. Toronto: McClelland and Stewart. Pp. 254–268.

Ruyle, E.
    1973   Slavery, surplus and incipient stratification on the Northwest Coast: the ethnoenergetics of an incipient stratification system. *Current Anthropology* **14**(5):603–17.

Sahlins, M. D.
    1958   *Social stratification in Polynesia.* Seattle: University of Washington Press.
    1968   *Tribesmen.* Englewood Cliffs: Prentice-Hall.

Sanders, W. T. and B. J. Price
    1968   *Mesoamerica: the evolution of a civilization.* New York: Random House.

Sanders, W. T. and D. L. Webster
    1978   Unilinealism, multilinealism and the evolution of complex societies. In *Social archaeology: beyond subsistence and dating,* edited by C. L. Redman *et al.* New York: Academic Press. Pp. 249–302.

Sapir, E. and L. Spier
    1946   Notes on the culture of the Yana. *University of California Anthropological Records* **3**(3):239–298.

Sauer, C. O.
    1966   *The early Spanish main.* Berkeley: University of California Press. Pp. 37–69.

Sawyer, J. O.
    1978   Wappo. In *Handbook of North American Indians,* Vol. 5), *California,* edited by R. F. Heizer and W. C. Sturtevant. Washington, D.C.: Smithsonian Institution. Pp. 256–263.

Sawyer, J. and R. A. Levine
  1966   Cultural dimensions: a factor analysis of the world ethnographic sample. *American Anthropologist* **68**(3):708–731.
Saxe, A. A.
  1970   *Social dimensions of mortuary practices.* Ph.D. dissertation, Department of Anthropology, University of Michigan. University Microfilms; Ann Arbor.
Schiffer, M. B.
  1979   A preliminary consideration of behavioral change. In *Transformations: mathematical approaches to culture change,* edited by C. Renfrew and K. L. Cooke. New York: Academic Press. Pp. 353–368.
Schrire, C.
  1980   An inquiry into the evolutionary status and apparent identity of San hunter–gatherers. *Human Ecology* **8**(1):9–32.
Schroeder, A. H.
  1979   Pueblos abandoned in historic times. In *Handbook of North American Indians,* Vol. 9, *Southwest,* edited by A. Ortiz and W. C. Sturtevant. Washington D.C.: Smithsonian Institution. Pp. 236–254.
Schwerin, K. H.
  1973   The anthropological antecedents: caciques, cacicazgas, and caciquismo. In *The Caciques,* edited by R. Kern. Albuquerque: University of New Mexico Press. Pp. 5–17.
Sears, W.
  1968   The state and settlement patterns in the New World. In *Settlement archaeology,* edited by K. C. Chang. Palo Alto: National Press Books. Pp. 134–153.
Service, E. R.
  1962   *Primitive social organization.* New York: Random House.
  1975   *Origins of the state and civilization: the process of cultural evolution.* New York: W. W. Norton.
Silver, S.
  1978a   Chimariko. In *Handbook of North American Indians,* Vol. 5, *California,* edited by R.F. Heizer and W. C. Sturtevant. Washington, D.C.: Smithsonian Institution. Pp. 205–210.
  1978b   Shastan peoples. In *Handbook of North American Indians,* Vol. 5, *Calfornia,* edited by R. F. Heizer and W. C. Sturtevant. Washington, D.C.: Smithsonian Institution. Pp. 211–224.
Simmons, W. S.
  1978   Naragansett. In *Handbook of North American Indians,* Vol. 15, *Northeast,* edited by B. G. Trigger and W. C. Sturtevant. Washington, D.C.: Smithsonian Institution. Pp. 190–197.
Skinner, G. W.
  1977   Introduction: urban development in imperial China. In *The city in late Imperial China,* edited by G. W. Skinner. Stanford: Stanford University Press. Pp. 3–31.
Smith, B.
  1978a   Variation in Mississippian settlement patterns. In *Mississippian settlement patterns,* edited by B. Smith. New York: Academic Press. Pp. 479–502.
Smith, B. (editor)
  1978b   *Mississippian settlement patterns.* New York: Academic Press.
Smith, M. T. and S. A. Kowalewski
  Ms   Tentative identification for a prehistoric "province" in piedmont Georgia. Manuscript in the files of the author, Department of Anthropology, University of Georgia, Athens, Georgia.

Snow, D. R.
1976 The ethnohistoric baseline of the Eastern Abenaki. *Ethnohistory* **23**(3):291–306.
1978 Eastern Abenaki. In *Handbook of North American Indians,* Vol. 15, *Northeast,* edited by B. G. Trigger and W. C. Sturtevant. Washington, D.C.: Smithsonian Institution. Pp. 137–147.
1980 *The archaeology of New England,* New York: Academic Press.
Southall, A. W.
1965 A critique of the typology of states and political systems. In *Political systems and the distribution of power,* edited by Michael Banton. London: Tavistock. Pp. 113–140.
Speck, F. G.
1907 The Creek Indians of Taskigi town. *Memoirs of the American Anthropological Association* **2** (Part 2):99–164.
1915 The eastern Algonkian Wabanaki Confederacy. *American Anthropologist* **17**(3):492–508.
1945 The Iroquois: a study in cultural evolution. *Cranbrook Institute of Science* 23.
Spencer, R. F., J. D. Jennings *et al.*
1965 *The native Americans.* New York: Harper and Row.
Spier, R. F. G.
1978 Foothill Yokuts. In *Handbook of North American Indians,* Vol. 5, *California,* edited by R. F. Heizer and W. C. Sturtevant. Washington, D.C.: Smithsonian Institution. Pp. 471–484.
Spier, L.
1930 Klamath ethnography. *University of California Publications in American Archaeology and Ethnology* 30.
Spores, R.
1967 *The Mixtec kings and their people.* Norman: University of Oklahoma Press.
1974 Marital alliances in the political integration of Mixtec kingdoms. *American Anthropologist* **76**(2):297–311.
Steponaitis, V. P.
1978 Location theory and complex chiefdoms: a Mississippian example. In *Mississippian settlement patterns,* edited by B. Smith. New York: Academic Press. Pp. 417–453.
Stern, T.
1965 *The Klamath tribe.* Seattle: University of Washington Press.
Stevenson, M. C.
1904 The Zuni Indians. *Bureau of American Ethnology Annual Report* 23.
Stevenson, R.
1968 *Population and political systems in tropical Africa.* New York: Columbia University Press.
Steward, J. H.
1948 The Circum-Caribbean tribes: an introduction. In *The Circum-Caribbean Tribes, Handbook of South American Indians,* Vol. 4, edited by J. H. Steward. *Bureau of American Ethnology Bulletin* **143**:1–42.
1949a South American cultures: an interpretative summary. In *The Comparative Ethnology of South American Indians, Handbook of South American Indians,* Vol. 5, edited by J. H. Steward. *Bureau of American Ethnology Bulletin* **143**:669–772.
1949b Cultural causality and law: a trial formulation of early civilization. *American Anthropologist* **51**(1):1–27.
Steward, J. H. (editor)
1946– Handbook of South American Indians. *Bureau of American Ethnology Bulletin* 143.
1950

Steward, J. H. and L. C. Faron
    1959   *Native peoples of South America.* New York: McGraw-Hill.
Stout, D. B.
    1947   San Blas Cuna acculturation: an introduction. *Viking Fund Publications in Anthropology* 9.
    1948   The Cuna. In *The Circum-Caribbean Tribes, Handbook of South American Indians,* Vol. 4, edited by J. H. Steward. *Bureau of American Ethnology Bulletin* **143**:257–268.
Strathern, A.
    1971   *The Rope of Moka, big-men and ceremonial exchange in Mount Hagen, New Guinea.* London: Cambridge University Press.
Strong, W. D.
    1929   Aboriginal society in southern California. *University of California Publications in American Archaeology and Ethnology* 26.
Suttles, W.
    1958   Private knowledge, morality, and social classes among the Coast Salish. *American Anthropologist* **60**(3):497–507.
Swanton, J. R.
    1918   An early account of the Choctaw Indians. *Memoirs of the American Anthropological Association* 5.
    1946   The Indians of the southeastern United States. *Bureau of American Ethnology Bulletin* 137.
Tainter, J. A.
    1977   Woodland social change in West-Central Illinois. *Mid-Continental Journal of Archaeology* **2**(1):67–99.
    1978   Mortuary practices and the study of prehistoric social systems. In *Advances in archaeological method and theory* (Vol. 1), edited by M. B. Schiffer. New York: Academic Press. Pp. 105–139.
    1980   Behavior and status in a Middle Woodland mortuary population from the Illinois Valley. *American Antiquity* **45**(2):308–313.
Tainter, J. A. and R. H. Cordy
    1977   An archaeological analysis of social ranking and residence groups in prehistoric Hawaii. *World Archaeology* **9**(1):95–112.
Tatje, T. and R. Naroll
    1970   Two measures of societal complexity. In *A Handbook of method in cultural anthropology,* edited by R. Naroll and R. Cohen. Garden City: Natural History Press. Pp. 766–833.
Taylor, D.
    1975   Some locational aspects of middle-range hierarchical societies. Unpublished Ph.D. dissertation, Department of Anthropology, The City University of New York, New York, New York.
Thurman, M. D.
    1975   Delaware social organization. In *A Delaware Indian symposium,* edited by H. C. Kraft. *Pennsylvania Historical and Museum Commission Anthropological Series* **4**:111–134.
Tooker, E.
    1964   An ethnography of the Huron Indians, 1615–1649. *Bureau of American Ethnology Bulletin* 190.
    1970   Northern Iroquoian socio-political organization. *American Anthropologist* **72**(1):90–97.

Trigger, B. G.
  1962   Trade and tribal warfare on the St. Lawrence in the sixteenth century. *Ethnohistory* **9**(3):240–256.
  1963   Settlement as an aspect of Iroquian adaptation at the time of contact. *American Anthropologist* **65**(1):86–101.
  1969   *The Huron farmers of the north.* New York: Holt. Rinehart, and Winston.
  1976   *The children of Aataentsic: a history of the Huron people to 1660.* Montreal: McGill–Queen's University Press.
Trigger, B. G. and W. C. Sturtevant (editors)
  1978   *Handbook of North American Indians,* Vol. 15, *Northeast,* Washington, D.C.: Smithsonian Institution.
Tuck, J. A.
  1971   The Iroquois confederacy. *Scientific American* **224**(2):32–42.
Tumin, M. M.
  1967   *Social stratification: the forms and functions of inequality.* Englewood Cliffs: Prentice-Hall.
Turner, E. R.
  1976   An archaeological and ethnohistorical study on the evolution of rank societies in the Virginia coastal plains. Unpublished Ph.D. dissertation, Department of Anthropology, Pennsylvania State University, University Park, Pennsylvania.
Udy, S.
  1965   Dynamic inferences from static data. *American Journal of Sociology* **70**(5):625–627.
Upham, S.
  1980   Political continuity and change in the Plateau Southwest. Unpublished Ph.D. dissertation, Department of Anthropology, Arizona State University, Tempe, Arizona.
Vansina, J.
  1962   A comparison of African kingdoms. *Africa* **32**(4):324–335.
Vengroff, R.
  1976   Population density and state formation in Africa. *African Studies Review* **19**(1):67–74.
Voget, F. W.
  1975   *A history of ethnology.* Holt, Rinehart, and Winston, New York.
Wahrhaftig, A. L. and J. Lakens-Wahrhaftig
  1977   The thrice powerless: Cherokee Indians in Oklahoma. In *The anthropology of power,* edited by R. D. Fogelson and R. N. Adams. New York: Academic Press. Pp. 225–236.
Wallace, W. J.
  1978a Northern Valley Yokuts. In *Handbook of North American Indians,* Vol. 5, *California,* edited by R. F. Heizer and W. C. Sturtevant. Washington, D.C.: Smithsonian Institution. Pp. 462–470.
  1978b Southern Valley Yokuts. In *Handbook of North American Indians,* Vol. 5, *California,* edited by R. F. Heizer and W. C. Sturtevant. Washington, D.C.: Smithsonian Institution. Pp. 448–461.
Weinberg, D.
  1965   Models of Southern Kwakiutl social organization. *General Systems* 10:169–181.
Wenke, R. J.
  1981   Explaining the evolution of cultural complexity: a review. In *Advances in archaeological method and theory* Vol. 4, edited by M. B. Schiffer. New York: Academic Press. Pp. 79–127.
Weslager, C. A.
  1972   *The Delaware Indians: a history.* New Brunswick: Rutgers University Press.

Whalen, M. E.
    1976   Zoning within an Early Formative community in the Valley of Oaxaca. In *The early Mesoamerican village,* edited by K. V. Flannery. New York: Academic Press. Pp. 75–79.
White, D. R.*et al.*
    1971   Natchez class and rank reconsidered. *Ethnology* **10**(4):369–388.
White, L.
    1959   *The evolution of culture.* New York: McGraw-Hill.
Wilcox, D. R., T. R. McGuire and C. Sternberg
    1981   Snaketown revisited. *Arizona State Museum Archaeological Series* 155.
Wilcox D. R. and L. O. Shenk
    1977   The architecture of the Casa Grande and its interpretation. *Arizona State Museum Archaeological Series* 115.
Wilson, N. L. and A. H. Towne
    1978   Nisenan. In *Handbook of North American Indians,* Vol. 5, *California,* edited by R. F. Heizer and W. C. Sturtevant. Washington, D.C.: Smithsonian Institution. Pp. 387–397.
Wirsing, R.
    1973   Political power and information: a cross–cultural study. *American Anthropologist* **75**(1):153–170.
Woodbury, R. B.
    1979   Zuni prehistory and history to 1850. In *Handbook of North American Indians,* Vol. 9, *Southwest,* edited by A. Ortiz and W. C. Sturtevant. Washington, D.C.: Smithsonian Institution. Pp. 467–473.
Woodward, G. S.
    1963   *The Cherokees.* Norman: University of Oklahoma Press.
Wyckoff, D. G. and T. G. Baugh
    1980   Early historic Hasinai elites: a model for the material culture of governing elites. *Mid-Continental Journal of Archaeology* **5**(2):225–288.
Yoffee, N.
    1979   The decline and rise of Mesopotamian civilization: an ethnoarchaeological perspective on the evolution of social complexity. *American Antiquity* **44**(1):5–35.

The Nature of Organization of Intrasite Archaeological Records and Spatial Analytic Approaches to Their Investigation

CHRISTOPHER CARR

INTRODUCTION

In the past 10 years, major advances have been made in the analysis and behavioral interpretation of spatial patterning within archaeological sites. Two areas of growth are apparent. First, a number of quantitative methods that allow the discovery of spatial patterning among entities have been introduced to archaeology, permitting more sophisticated analysis of the arrangement of artifacts within sites and more precise definition of tool kits and activity areas. These techniques, derived largely from the field of mathematical ecology (Greig-Smith 1964; Pielou 1969, 1977), include: the Poisson method of detecting spatial clustering of items (Kershaw 1964), dimensional analysis of variance and covariance used in conjunction with correlation analysis (Greig-Smith 1952b; Whallon 1973), several nearest neighbor approaches (Clark and Evans 1954; Morisita 1959; Whallon 1974), and segregation analysis (Pielou 1961; Peebles

---

ADVANCES IN ARCHAEOLOGICAL
METHOD AND THEORY, VOL. 7

1971) used in conjunction with clustering algorithms. Additionally, correlation analysis followed by principal components analysis has been employed (Speth and Johnson 1976; Schiffer 1975c). Both Price (1975) and Brose and Scarry (1976) have summarized the methods, as well as some of the assumptions of some of these techniques within the context of examples. Price has illustrated how the techniques may be integrated into a multistep analytic design.

The second area of growth in intrasite spatial analysis consists of studies of archaeological formation processes, including behavioral and natural processes of formation and disturbance (Ascher 1968; Binford 1976; Gifford 1978, 1981; Gould 1971, 1978; O'Connell 1977, 1979; Schiffer 1972, 1973, 1975a, 1975c, 1976; Schiffer and Rathje 1973; Wood and Johnson 1978; Yellen 1974, 1977). Ethnoarchaeological, experimental, and formal-deductive approaches have been taken. These studies are useful because they document the kinds and distributions of archaeological remains that different activities and formation processes can generate under variable conditions, thereby helping the archaeologist to bridge the interpretive gap between the archaeological record and past behavior.

Up to now, these two approaches to describing and interpreting intrasite archaeological variability have proceeded relatively independently of each other. The precise impact of archaeological formation processes on the organization of artifacts within sites as they are mapped from the behavioral domain into the archaeological record has not generally been expressed with quantitative measures of spatial patterning. Inversely, mathematical techniques for analyzing intrasite artifact distributions have not commonly been evaluated for the appropriateness of their data requirements, given the structure of intrasite archaeological remains and the nature of the processes responsible for them. Exceptions include: (1) Speth and Johnson's (1974) delineation of several expected patterns of correlation between tool-type counts, given different depositional processes and spatial distributions of activity; (2) Schiffer's (1975c) study of the capability of correlation and factor analysis in identifying tool kits as the deposition of tools from distinct activity areas becomes more focal; and (3) Whallon's (1979, 1984) design of the new strategy, unconstrained clustering, to define activity areas.

It is clear, however, that a wedding of these two approaches to intrasite analysis is both desirable and necessary. For any quantitative analysis and interpretation of complex data to be accurate, the relationships of logical contingency existing between a predictive hypothesis (or law or model), its test implications, the technique chosen for analysis, and the data must be *logically consistent* ones. A test implication of an hypothesis must be expressed in mathematical terms reflecting the techniques to be used in analysis, to be fully operational and concordant with the hypothesis. Also, the techniques one chooses for analysis should make only those assumptions that are congruent with the expectable and empirical structure of one's data (Carr 1981, 1984b). For intrasite spatial analysis, these requirements translate as follows. (1) Given an hypothesis of the kinds of activities that occurred at a site, test implications stating the expectable spatial patterning of artifacts and derived with the aid of principles of formation of the archaeological record should be expressed in mathematical terms reflecting the analytical method to be used; Also, (2) the mathematical techniques one chooses to analyze the spatial arrangement of artifacts within a site should make only those assumptions that are logically concordant with the expectable structure of the data, as determined by the nature of the hypothesized activities and the formation processes that mapped them into spatial configurations of artifacts. To the extent that the empirical structure of remains is known, the technique also should be consistent, in its data requirements, with that structure. Only if these conditions of spatial analysis are met can one be confident of the logical consistency of one's analysis and the accuracy of one's quantitative results and conclusions.

This chapter is concerned with both aspects of a unified approach to intrasite spatial analysis. The nature of the organization of archaeological records within sites, as determined and impacted by human behavior, archaeological formation processes, and archaeological recovery techniques, is expressed as a partially mathematical model. Common techniques of spatial analysis are summarized and evaluated for the consistency of their assumptions with the proposed model. Alternative approaches to spatial analysis having designs more consistent with the proposed model—some new, others previously available but not applied in archaeology—then are described.

In evaluating analytical techniques against the model of intrasite archaeological records, the most conservative position possible has been taken. The model is generalized, encompassing the effects of a large number of behavioral processes and archaeological formation processes. It is assumed that (1) any or all of these effects may be present within a specific site of study, limiting which techniques are appropriate for analysis; (2) it may not be possible to determine which constraining effects are present within a site; and (3) consequently, spatial analytic techniques should be able to cope with all these constraining effects. Very robust, widely applicable techniques are considered preferable to more limited methods.

In practice, however, it is possible to determine to a certain degree what formation processes have occurred at a site (e.g., Schiffer 1973, 1975b). This is especially true where historic documentation is available but is becoming much more feasible for prehistoric sites, as well (Binford 1978; Schiffer 1982). Under these conditions, techniques that have certain limitations and that have been evaluated here as generally inappropriate may actually be useful. Also, it is possible to use multiple, restricted approaches to spatial analysis—different techniques in different known circumstances; one generalized technique need not always be preferable.

Whether or not the processes responsible for an archaeological record and its specific organization can be determined prior to spatial analysis, the discussions presented here on possible incongruencies between data and technique, their causes, and their effects on analysis should be helpful to archaeologists. First, they provide the archaeologist an awareness of those characteristics of intrasite data that *should* be investigated before a technique of analysis is chosen. It is the archaeologist's responsibility to try to determine what constraining effects of formation processes are and might be represented in the data, prior to analysis (Schiffer 1982), and to choose an appropriate technique in light of this knowledge. Second, when the nature of the data is clear, the discussions form a basis for choosing the one technique among the considered alternatives that *certainly* is most appropriate to the prevailing conditions. When the nature of the data remain impossible to specify, the discussions suggest which techniques are most robust and most *likely* to be appropriate.

THEORETICAL AND OPERATIONAL GOALS OF INTRASITE SPATIAL ANALYSIS

Goals

Intrasite spatial analysis has several goals, at both the *inferential* level, concerned with the reconstruction and explanation of past behaviors and activities (nonobservables), and the *operational* level, concerned with relationships between archaeological observables. At the inferential level, intrasite spatial analysis is undertaken for two reasons:

1. to define the spatial limits of *activity areas,* and
2. to define the organization of artifact types into *tool kits.*

(Appropriate use and definition of these terms are discussed later.) These two basic classes of information may be used to reconstruct the kinds, frequencies, and spatial organization of activities that occurred within a community, which in turn may be used to infer the seasons of occupation of the site, site function, community population, group composition, patterns of household interaction, community kinship and social organization, and many other behavioral and ecological phenomena.

At the operational level of analysis, intrasite spatial analysis seeks to answer four questions (after Whallon 1973):

1. Are the artifacts of each recognized functional type randomly scattered over space, aggregated into clusters, or systematically aligned?
2. If the artifacts of a given type cluster, what are the spatial limits of clusters of that type?

3. Whether or not the artifacts of given types are clustered, randomly scattered, or systematically aligned (see pages 107–108), do artifacts of different types tend to be similarly arranged such that, for example, their frequencies covary or their presence states associate over space?
4. If the artifacts of several types both cluster *and* are co-arranged, what are the spatial limits of multitype clusters?

The first, second, and fourth operational questions reflect concern at the inferential level in defining activity areas. The third question is posed in response to interest, at the inferential level, in defining tool kits.

The Appropriateness of Contingency Relations between Some of the Operational Goals of Spatial Analysis

In the past, the several operations of spatial analysis have been seen as *sequential* steps of analysis. When using grid-cell methods, it has been suggested (Whallon 1973:266) that analysis proceed from assessment of the form of arrangement of single types to assessment of the degree of co-arrangement of different types. When using nearest neighbor methods, the preferred sequence (Whallon 1974; Price 1975) has been to proceed from evaluation of the form of arrangement of single types to definition of clusters and finally to assessment of the degree of co-arrangement of artifact types. The manner of operation at later stages of analysis has been envisioned as contingent upon the results of earlier stages, either *algorithmically* or of *logical necessity*. For example, calculation of the degree of association between pairs of artifact types using Whallon's (1974) nearest neighbor approaches is *algorithmically* contingent upon (can only occur after) definition of the limits of single-type clusters. Definition of single-type clusters having statistical significance, using Whallon's nearest-neighbor approaches, is seen as *logically* contingent upon (should only occur after) determination of whether an artifact type significantly clusters, using the nearest neighbor statistic.

Not all the contingency relations implied by or stated as part of this "step-wise" approach to spatial analysis are necessary or desirable (Hietala and Stevens 1977:539). In particular, those operations concerned with the definition of tool kits are not logically contingent upon those concerned with the definition of activity areas, and vice versa. They probably should not be made algorithmically contingent upon each other, either.

As a case in point, consider the *logical* contingency expressed in the view that only those classes of artifacts showing significant trends toward clustering should be analyzed for their degree of co-arrangement (Whallon 1974). This perspective seems to have its basis in the following arguement: Only when artifacts are distributed among spatially nonoverlapping activity areas, apparent as artifact clusters, will types that belong to the same tool kit by detectable by patterns of covariation or association between them. This contingency need not be true (Hietala and Stevens 1977:539–540). Consider an activity that is not tied, operationally, to spatially permanent facilities and that generates several forms of debris, expediently. If the activity is performed numerous times, randomly over space, the several kinds of artifacts will each have random spatial arrangements, but the artifact types will covary in their frequencies over space. Flint knapping and whittling within hunter–gatherer camps can produce such artifact arrangements. Likewise, systematically aligned artifact types can covary or co-occur. Curated, domestic tools stored within the confines of houses having a regular arrangement over space would exemplify this pattern. Thus, investigation of patterns of co-arrangement of multiple artifact types should not be envisioned as logically contingent upon evaluation of the form of arrangement of individual artifact types. Nor should procedures of spatial analysis express this contingency as stepwise algorithmic dependency. (Currently used techniques do not.)

Similarly, the *algorithmic* contingency between definition of the limits of artifact clusters and assessment of the co-arrangement of artifact types, when using nearest neighbor methods (Whallon 1974), is undesirable. This stepwise procedure prohibits artifact types that do not cluster from being assessed for their degree of co-arrangement with each other and with those that do cluster. Methods of intrasite spatial analysis should not require this contingency.

Appropriateness of the Goal of Assessing the Form of Arrangement of Artifacts

Recently, the appropriateness of two of the four operational goals of intrasite spatial analysis just enumerated has been questioned. Whallon (1979, in press) has argued that assessment of the nature of the spatial distributions of artifact types (random, clustered, or aligned) is meaningless, given that results depend entirely on the size of the area chosen for analysis (when using the nearest neighbor statistic) or the size grid cells (when using the Poisson method). I disagree with his conclusion.

It is true that an assessment of the form of spatial arrangement of entities using the nearest neighbor statistic does depend on the size of the area chosen for analysis. Figure 3.1 illustrates this. Hsu and Tiedemann (1968; Pinder 1979: Figure 2) have demonstrated that if 10 regularly spaced points occupying a unit area are framed in increasingly larger areas, the nearest neighbor statistic will drop from values suggesting systematic alignment of points to values implying their random distribution, and finally to values implying their clustered distribution. It also is true that an assessment of the form of arrangement of items over space using grid-cell counts and the Poisson method depends on the scale of the grid laid over the distribution (Greig-Smith 1961). However, the existence of

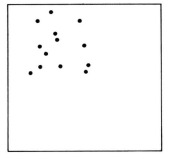

Figure 3.1. Whether a spatial arrangement of entities appears random or clustered to the human eye, and whether a nearest neighbor statistic indicating randomness or clustering is calculated, depends on the size of the area chosen for analysis.

such functional relationships between the size of frame units chosen for analysis and the estimate of arrangement obtained does *not* imply that assessment of the form of spatial arrangement of items with the nearest neighbor or Poisson methods is always a meaningless endeavor. Not all analyzable areas or grid-cell sizes are equally meaningful from a behavioral perspective, and not all possible results are important.

For an assessment of the spatial arrangement of artifacts to be meaningful using the nearest neighbor statistic, it is only necessary that the analyzed area be a "natural" unit having *meaning in terms of past behavior,* and have *clear boundaries* (Getis 1964:394–395). These conditions often can be met. For example, an archaeological site, as a whole, is a natural unit with behavioral significance. An estimate of the degree of clustering or random dispersion of artifacts within a whole site has behavioral meaning; it suggests the degree to which the site as *the* unit of analysis is internally differentiated into multiple use-areas. This condition of a site is important to know, for if it can be shown that artifacts within a site do cluster significantly, then further attempts to define the boundaries of clusters become justifiable. Sites, as wholes, also often meet the requirement of nearest neighbor analysis that the area to be examined have clear boundaries. The boundaries of sites often are delimited by a drop in the density of artifacts at a given high rate or to some minimal level of background noise.

Subareas of a site, which are delimited by some behaviorally significant archaeological criterion, also may be analyzed with the nearest neighbor statistic so as to produce meaningful results. An area of clustering of facilities or the interior of a house, for example, might be assessed for the form of arrangement of artifacts within it. In contrast, a block excavation within a site, having areal limits that are somewhat arbitrary and not meaningful in terms of past behavior, does not constitute a valid area of analysis using the nearest neighbor statistic. The interitem distances used to estimate the degree of clustering or dispersion of artifacts within a block are not assessed relative to the dimensions of a meaningful area.

Statements made by Clark and Evans (1954:450) in general terms, and reiterated by Pinder *et al.* (1979:433) for intrasite cases, imply that nearest-neighbor analysis of arbitrary units, such as block excavations within sites, is justifiable. These authors suggest that to avoid bias in the nearest neighbor statistic, the area of analysis should lie "*well within* the total area covered" by the distribution of items of interest (e.g., within a site). This strategy, however, clearly is inappropriate for artifact distributions. Artifact scatters often have multiple forms of arrangement, hierarchically organized. For example, within a random, low-density scatter of artifacts there may be high-density concentrations, themselves composed of artifacts that are randomly scattered. The form of arrangement of artifacts found within a block excavation will depend on its size and placement, and the particular level of the organizational hierarchy unveiled. Meaningful estimates of the form of arrangement of items within a block will be found only when its boundaries and areal extent correspond with the boundaries and extent of some natural, behaviorally meaningful, portion of the site.

Using the Poisson method, assessments of the form of arrangement of artifacts within a site are less clearly meaingful, and Whallon's skepticism of the method seems justifiable. The size of grid cells to be used for analysis *can* be chosen in reference to an expectable, meaningful scale of patterning, to reduce the arbitrariness of results. However, often factors that can lead to the arbitrariness of results, such as uncontrolled lack of correspondence between shape or orientation of grid cells and the shapes or orientations of artifact clusters, are less easily remedied (pages 143–144).

Appropriateness of the Goal of Searching for Site-Wide Patterns of Co-Arrangement of Artifact Types

Whallon (1979, in press) has implied, though never stated directly, that the search for site-wide organization of activities into depositional sets—including activity sets, storage sets, and discard sets—is meaningless. His technique of unconstrained clustering is designed explicitly (1979:4; in press) to avoid the assessment of site-wide relationships between artifact types, and focuses on patterns of internal association or covariation of artifacts within clusters.

The motive behind Whallon's efforts to avoid examination of site-wide relationships among artifact types is his observation that the same set of artifact types may show different patterns of covariation or association (positive, null, negative) in different portions of a site. From this fact he draws the conclusion that depositional sets as site-wide phenomena do not exist and need not be searched for. This conclusion, however, is not the only one that can be inferred and is not necessarily correct. Variable covariation and association of artifacts over a site also might indicate the incapability of correlation and simple association to accurately measure the strength of relationships between artifact types and to define site-wide depositional sets that really do exist (see pages 161–170, 172–175, and 191–199).

The view taken in this chapter is that site-wide depositional sets and activity sets often do exist but in forms that are *polythetic* rather than monothetic in organization, and *overlapping* rather than nonoverlapping in organization (terms defined on pages 113–121). Under these conditions, correlation and simple association are not accurate measures of the strength of the relationships between types. Thus, Whallon's empirical results can be explained by an incompatibility between the analytical techniques he used (correlation, simple association) and the structure of archaeological data.

Ethnography, ethnoarchaeology, and experimental approaches to the study of tool manufacture and use suggest that certain kinds of tools do tend to be used together, repeatedly, constituting tool kits (see Table 3.1) (Cook 1976; Winters 1969). It is not necessary that archaeologists give up the search for such site-wide entities. Rather, it is only necessary that they realize that tool kits and depositional sets often are polythetic and overlapping in structure and that the mathe-

TABLE 3.1

Examples of Preservable Tool and Debris Types Often Used or Produced Together (Activity Sets) While Performing Some Specific Task

Artifact types used/produced together	Activity	Reference
Mauls, decortication debris	Quarrying and preforming chert	Crabtree (1940, 1967), Ellis (1940)
Decortication flakes, large hammerstones	Primary knapping	
Hard-hammer secondary flakes, hammerstones	Secondary knapping	
Pressure flakes, pressure flakers	Pressure flaking	
Edge-worn cobbles, prismatic cores, blades	Manufacturing blades	Crabtree and Swanson (1968)
Abraders, pressure flaker, pressure flakes	Roughening platforms while knapping	Crabtree (1972:7), Speth (1972)

(continued)

TABLE 3.1 *Continued*

Artifact types used–produced together	Activity	Reference
Abraders, drills, saws, notches, spurs, knives, scrapers	Working wood, bone	Cook (1973)
Saws, flake knives	Notching arrow shafts	Sollerberger (1969:238–239)
Gouges, chisels	Carving concavities such as wooden bowls	Waugh (1916:58)
Burned abraders, fire-cracked rock, hearth-liner	Straightening wooden shafts	Mason (1899)
Mauls, grooved axes	Felling or girdling trees; obtaining fire wood, slabs of wood, and bark	Waugh (1916)
Mauls, cobble anvils, knives	Pounding bark into cloth and cutting it	McCarthy (1967:51), Waugh (1916:61)
Spurs, antler debris	Working antler	Clark and Thompson (1954)
Spurs, pigment	Painting grooves in arrow shafts	Winters (1969:54)
Red ochre; mortar and pestle, or mano and metate	Grinding red pigment for paint	Battle (1922), Moorehead (1912)
Abraders, hide scrapers	Defleshing and thinning hides	Mason (1889:560, 572–573, 1899:78–79)
Hammerstones, hide scrapers	Dressing hides	Mason (1895:53)
Red ochre, hide scrapers	Coloring hides while dressing them	Mason (1889)
Denticulates, cobble anvil	Extracting plant fibers from stems and leaves to make cordage and textiles	Osborne (1965:47–48)
Spurs or drills, bone needles	Sewing	de Heinzelin (1962:29), Mason (1899), Nero (1957), Winters (1969)
Hammerstones, metates	Roughening and refurbishing grinding surface of metate	
Manos, metates	Grinding seeds; pounding large seeds, dried roots, bulbs, fruits, meat	Kraybill (1977), Riddell and Pritchard (1971), Driver (1961:93), Miles (1973:44), Wheat (1972:117)
Manos, nuttingstones	Cracking nuts	Battle (1922), Swanton (1946), Waugh (1916:123)
Hammerstones or mauls, unburnt bone, knives	Butchering	Wheat (1972)
Hammerstones or mauls, crushed bone	Extracting marrow, tallow	Mason (1895:28), Leechman (1951), Peale (1871), Wheat (1972:113)
Bone, pottery, fire-cracked rock, hearth liner	Boiling bone to soften it prior to working	Semenov (1964:159)
Pottery, fire-cracked rock, hearth liner	Boiling materials	Carr (1979:346)
Burned bone, fire-cracked rock, hearth liner, ash	Roasting meat over fire, feeding fire to cook	
Tempering material, water-smoothed pebble	Manufacturing pots	Swanton (1946:243, 529)

matical techniques used to search for depositional sets must be modified and made concordant with this structure. This conclusion was foreshadowed 15 years ago, when David Clarke (1968) introduced the concept of polythetic organization to the archaeological community (Thomas and Bettinger 1973).

A MODEL OF THE NATURE OF ORGANIZATION OF INTRASITE ARCHAEOLOGICAL RECORDS

The mathematical techniques that one chooses to search for spatial patterns among artifacts within a site in order to define depositional areas or depositional sets implies (or should imply, if one is interested in logical consistency during analysis) one's conception of the nature of organization of the archaeological record, the nature of the processes by which it was formed, and what one expects to find with the search technique. This section describes a model of the form of organization of intrasite archaeological records, in relation to which previously used techniques of spatial analysis can be assessed for their logical consistency, and new techniques can be proposed. The model was formulated in light of the new understanding of activity organization within sites and archaeological formation processes that has been reached over the course of the 1970s through ethnoarchaeological, experimental, and formal-deductive studies (see page 104). In as much as this research focuses largely on mobile to semisedentary populations, the model is biased toward processes pertinent to these groups.

The model has two primary components. One describes the organizational characteristics of archaeological "tool kits" in set-theoretic terms and enumerates some of the behavioral processes and archaeological formation processes by which the structural features of tool kits are generated. The second describes the characteristics of archaeological "activity areas" and some of the behaviors responsible for them. The first component is a product of my own efforts (Carr 1977, 1979, 1981), whereas the second was developed largely by Whallon (1979), with some additions by me (Carr 1979, 1981). The model pertains primarily to patterns of artifact deposition and distribution, but might be qualified to include patterns of facility manufacture and distribution.

Definitions: Activity Sets, Depositional Sets, Activity Areas, and Depositional Areas

Verbal models should use terms that are defined precisely. It is appropriate, then, to define the terms *activity set* and *activity area*—the entities an archaeologist hopes to reconstruct through spatial analysis.

In the archaeological literature, the term, activity set, is used to refer to two distinct phenomena: (1) those artifact types that repeatedly are used or produced together by the occupants of a site during the behavioral past; and (2) those artifact types that repeatedly aggregate in the archaeological record when it is excavated. Likewise, the term, activity area, has two referents: (1) the location at which an activity was performed in a site, during the behavioral past; and (2) the location where tools or debris indicating past activity aggregate within a site, at the time of excavation.

To avoid ambiguities, it is best if entities in the behavioral past are distinguished from entities in the archaeological present. The sets of tool types used repeatedly in the past to perform a particular task and the resulting debris may be called an *activity set.* The area in which the work occurred may be called an *activity area.* In contrast, the tool and debris types that repeatedly are found together in the archaeological record today may be termed, in the broadest sense (see page 115), *depositional sets,* and the areas in which they cluster, *depositional areas.* Activity sets and activity areas may be said to belong to a *behavioral domain*—the set of all phenomena that might possibly have occurred in the behavioral past. Depositional sets and depositional areas may be said to belong to an *archaeological domain*—the set of phenomena that might possibly occur in the archaeological record of the present. The terms *behavioral domain* and *archaeological domain* are equivalent to the terms *systemic context* and *archaeological context* defined by Schiffer (1972) and Reid (1973) but are introduced to bridge the former pair with mathematical set theory (see page 117).

This distinction of activity sets from depositional sets and activity areas from depositional areas is necessary because they—as all analogous phenomena in the behavioral and archaeological domains—may differ internally in their defining attributes and organization, externally in their relations with entities of like or different kind, and finally in their behavioral meanings.

Consider the differences between activity sets and depositional sets, activity areas and depositional areas, in their behavioral meaning. In the behavioral domain, tools and debris that associate are those actually produced and/or used together. In the archaeological domain, the tools and debris found together could represent a number of behavioral phenomena. They might represent all the tools and debris produced and used together in one kind of task by the previous occupants of the site and deposited in their locations of use. They also might include only a portion of the artifacts, if some were saved for use in other activities at a latter time. Such associations are called *primary refuse* (Schiffer 1972, 1975a). An association also could represent tools and debris that were thrown away together in a formalized dumping location. Associations of this kind have been called *secondary refuse* (Schiffer 1972, 1975a). Other possible kinds of artifact aggregations include: items stored together as a cache for later use—a special kind of primary refuse—or items used in a number of independent tasks that occurred at different times but happened to *overlap* spatially. An association of artifacts also might reflect a particular *social context* rather than some common task in which the artifacts were used (Yellen 1974:204, 207). For example, among the Alyawara Aborigines (O'Connell 1979), the Western Desert Aborigines (Gould 1971) and the !Kung Bushmen (Yellen 1974), a large group of activities occur within the context of the family around the hearth. The remains from such activities overlay each other and are mixed within a single area. Co-occurrences between different artifact types in this situation reflect the common social context in which they were used, rather than use in a common activity.

Adding further complexity, an aggregation of artifacts may not reflect past human behavioral processes at all, but rather, postdepositional processes of natural origin or contemporary human origin. Fluvial transport, solifluction, rodent activity, and contemporary farming are examples of such processes (Wood and Johnson 1978).

Similarly, an *area* in which several kinds of tools and debris cluster together on an archaeological site does not necessarily correspond to an "activity area" in the behavioral domain. Other possibilities include: a trash dump; a storage area; an area of social gathering where multiple activities were performed; or simply the common final resting place of the artifacts, each having been removed and transported from different primary depositional contexts by geological or other natural processes. An area of artifact aggregation also might represent any combination of these possibilities.

Thus, it is misleading to call all repeated associations of given artifact types in the archaeological record activity sets, and all locations of artifact aggregation in the archaeological record activity areas. The behavioral meanings of these terms, referring to phenomena in the behavioral domain, are too restrictive; they do not reflect the full range of archaeological phenomena that a depositional set or depositional area may represent. Similarly, it will be shown in the next section that activity sets and activity areas differ in their internal organizational and external relational properties from depositional sets and depositional areas. Consequently, depositional sets and depositional areas in the archaeological domain must be distinguished from activity sets and activity areas in the behavioral domain.

To refer in a precise way to the *multiple kinds* of depositional sets and depositional areas that may occur in the archaeological record, at the same time distinguishing them from activity sets and activity areas, a hierarchy of terms may be used (Figure 3.2). The terms within different levels of the hierarchy vary in their specificity as to the nature of the associations or aggregations. At the most general level, the terms *depositional set* and *depositional area* may be used to describe associations of artifact types and locations of artifact aggregation, without specifying the processes by which the associations and aggregations were generated. Behavioral, geological, biological, or agricultural processes might be responsible for them. If natural environmental or agricultural disturbances do not

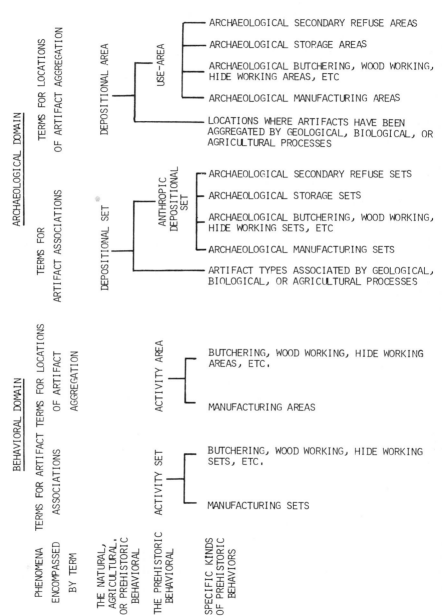

Figure 3.2. Terms for referring to artifact associations and locations of artifact aggregation in the behavioral and archaeological domains.

appear to have generated the associations and aggregations, and past behavioral processes appear responsible, more specific terms may be used. The term, *use-area*, may be applied to the locations, implying that they were used in the past for artifact manufacture, use, storage, or disposal, but not specifying which of these. The term, *anthropic depositional set,* can be used for the set of artifacts that repeatedly were manufactured, used, stored, or disposed of together. These midrange terms are of greatest importance to this chapter. Finally, at the most specific level of designation, associated artifact types might be termed *archaeological manufacturing sets, archaeological butchering sets, archaeological wood-working sets, archaeological storage sets, archaeological refuse sets,* etc. The corresponding locations of artifact aggregation would be *archaeological manufacturing areas, archaeological butchering areas,* etc.

The Polythetic, Overlapping Character of Activity Sets and Depositional Sets

Depositional sets and depositional areas of the archaeological present may be similar to or different from activity sets and activity areas in the behavioral past, not only in their meaning, but also in their organizational and relational properties. This section and the next two explore these similarities and differences.

Given the distinction between depositional sets and activity sets and between an archaeological domain and a behavioral domain, it is possible to view depositional sets as alterations of activity sets, with archaeological formation and disturbance processes linking the two. A depositional set may be thought of as a mathematical set, the organization of which is the end product of structural transformations (archaeological formation and disturbance processes) operating upon a previously structured set (activity sets organized by human behavior). In set theoretic terms, activity sets in a behavioral *domain* may be pictured as being *mapped* into depositional sets in an archaeological domain (or more precisely, *range*) through the operation of various *mapping relations* (Ammerman and Feldman 1974). Importantly, the organization of activity sets and depositional sets, and the nature of the change in organization as one is transformed into the other, also can be described in set theoretic terms.

In set theory, an organization of entities can be described using four basic concepts: (1) *sets*—groups of entities; (2) *members* or *elements of sets*—the entities that are grouped together; (3) *attributes*—the character states that the entities possess; and (4) the *list of attributes* that the entities in a set must share in part or completely to belong to the set. To apply these concepts to the behavioral and archaeological domains for the purpose of describing the organization of activity sets and depositional sets and the organizational transformations linking them, it is necessary to focus on sets of *events* and the sets of *deposits* generated by them, rather than on sets of artifact types (activity sets, depositional sets, tool kits). Suppose a group of past events at a site can be classified into several kinds, according to the functional types of artifacts they involved. The several events (entities) that are of one kind comprise a *set*; they always or often entailed certain common artifact types (attributes). The several artifact types that were used in common comprise a *list of attributes* defining the set, or what has been termed here an "activity set." Similarly, suppose that the archaeological deposits within a site can be classified into several kinds, according to the functional types of artifacts they contain. The several deposits (entities) of one kind comprise a set; they always or often contain certain artifact types (attributes). The several artifact types held in common or tending to be held in common by the deposits comprise a *list of attributes,* or what has been termed a "depositional set," here.

It is unfortunate that the term, activity set, occurs in the archaeological litera-ture, for in set-theoretic terms, within the framework presented here, an activity set is a *list of attributes* required for membership in a set (of events) rather than a set, itself. Similarly, a depositional set is not a mathematical set, but rather is a list of attributes required for membership in a set (of deposits). Because the term, activity set, is cemented in the archaeological literature and depositional sets are analogous to them, I will continue to use these archaeological terms along with the mathematical ones.

Sets, and by extension, the list of attributes that characterize their members, may be described as *overlapping* or *nonoverlapping* in nature, and *monothetic* or *polythetic* in nature. Different sets are said to be overlapping when their members *share* some of the character states required of them (partially or completely) for admittance into their respective sets. Different sets are said to be nonoverlapping when the members do not have in common any of the character states required of them for admittance to their sets (Jardine and Sibson 1968; Sneath and Sokal 1973:207–208). In the behavioral domain, two different functional categories of events—different sets of events—which are defined by the artifact types used in them, would be considered overlapping sets if some of the defining artifact types were shared by the sets. The sets of events would be nonoverlapping if none of the artifact types defining them were shared by the sets. In the archaeological domain, two different functional classes of archaeological deposits—two differ-ent sets of deposits—would be considered overlapping if some of the artifact types defining the sets were the same. The different sets of deposits would be nonoverlapping if none of the artifact types defining them were the same (see Table 3.2).

Likewise, by extension, different lists of attributes required partially or com-pletely of the members of different sets may be termed overlapping if some of the attributes in the lists are the same. They may be termed nonoverlapping if none of the attributes in the lists are the same. Two activity "sets" (two different lists of artifact types that always or often were entailed in the events falling in two

TABLE 3.2

Examples of Monothetic, Polythetic, Overlapping, and Non-overlapping Sets of Archaeological Deposits

A Monothetic Set of Archaeological Deposits
Set 1. Member 1: deposit 1 with artifact types (attributes) A, B, C, D
       Member 2: deposit 2 with artifact types (attributes) A, B, C, D
       Member 3: deposit 3 with artifact types (attributes) A, B, C, D
       Member 4: deposit 4 with artifact types (attributes) A, B, C, D

Two Monothetic Sets of Archaeological Deposits That are Nonoverlapping
Set 1. Member 1: deposit 1 with artifact types (attributes) A, B, C, D
       Member 2: deposit 2 with artifact types (attributes) A, B, C, D
       Member 3: deposit 3 with artifact types (attributes) A, B, C, D
       Member 4: deposit 4 with artifact types (attributes) A, B, C, D

Set 2. Member 1: deposit 5 with artifact types (attributes) E, F, G
       Member 2: deposit 6 with artifact types (attributes) E, F, G
       Member 3: deposit 7 with artifact types (attributes) E, F, G

No artifact type (attribute) is shared by the members of both Set 1 and Set 2, making them nonoverlapping in nature.

Two Monothetic Sets of Archaeological Deposits That are Overlapping
Set 1. Member 1: deposit 1 with artifact types (attributes) A, B, C, D
       Member 2: deposit 2 with artifact types (attributes) A, B, C, D
       Member 3: deposit 3 with artifact types (attributes) A, B, C, D
       Member 4: deposit 4 with artifact types (attributes) A, B, C, D

Set 2. Member 1: deposit 5 with artifact types (attributes) D, E, F
       Member 2: deposit 6 with artifact types (attributes) D, E, F
       Member 3: deposit 7 with artifact types (attributes) D, E, F

Artifact type D is shared as an attribute of the members of both Set 1 and Set 2, making them overlapping in nature.

A Polythetic Set of Archaeological Deposits
Set 1. Member 1: deposit 1 with artifact types (attributes) A, B, C, D
       Member 2: deposit 2 with artifact types (attributes) A, B, C
       Member 3: deposit 3 with artifact types (attributes)   B, C, D
       Member 4: deposit 4 with artifact type (attribute)   A
       Member 5: deposit 5 with artifact types (attributes) A,   C, D

Two Polythetic Sets of Archaeological Deposits That Are Overlapping
Set 1. Member 1: deposit 1 with artifact types (attributes) A, B, C, D
       Member 2: deposit 2 with artifact types (attributes) A, B, C
       Member 3: deposit 3 with artifact types (attributes)   B, C, D
       Member 4: deposit 4 with artifact types (attributes) A
       Member 5: deposit 5 with artifact types (attributes) A,   C, D

Set 2. Member 1: deposit 6 with artifact types (attributes) D, E, F
       Member 2: deposit 7 with artifact types (attributes)   E, F
       Member 3: deposit 8 with artifact types (attributes) D, E
       Member 4: deposit 9 with artifact types (attributes) D,   F

different sets) would be considered overlapping if some of the artifact types comprising each activity set were the same. Two depositional "sets" (two different lists of artifact types that always or often are found among members of two different sets of deposits) would be considered overlapping if some of the artifact types comprising each depositional set were the same. The depositional sets would be considered nonoverlapping if none of the artifact types comprising each depositional set were the same (Table 3.2).

Set theoreticians use the adjectives, overlapping, nonoverlapping, monothetic, and polythetic, to describe only sets, not attribute lists. In this chapter, the use of these adjectives is extended to attribute lists, such as activity "sets" and depositional "sets," in accordance with the different use of the term, set, in the archaeological literature.

The distinction between overlapping and nonoverlapping sets and attribute lists refers to the *external* organization of sets. The distinction between monothetic and polythetic sets, and between monothetic and polythetic attribute lists, refers to the *internal* organization of sets. In a monothetic set, the elements of the set all share the same character states; all character states are essential to group membership. In a polythetic set, the elements share a large number of character states, but no single state is essential to group membership (Sneath and Sokal 1973:21; Clarke 1968:37). In the behavioral domain, a functional set of events defined by the artifact types used in them would be monothetic if all the events used the same artifact types. The set of events would be polythetic if the events used a similar but not identical array of artifact types, and no one artifact type was essential to the occurrence of the events. In the archaeological domain, a set of functionally similar deposits would be monothetic if each deposit encompassed the same artifact types. The set of deposits would be polythetic if they shared many artifact types in common, but no single artifact type were essential to the deposits' character.

By extension, if *all* the attributes possessed by the members of a set as a whole are also possessed by each member, the list of attributes may be said to be *monothetic*, or more precisely, *monothetically distributed* among members of the set. If *most* of the attributes possessed by the members of a set are shared in common by them, but no one attribute is required for membership in the set, then the list of attributes may be said to be *polythetic*, or *polythetically distributed* among members of the set. An activity "set" (the list of artifact types characterizing a set of events) would be monothetically distributed among the events if all the artifact types in the activity "set" were used in each of the events. An activity "set" would be polythetically distributed among the events if the events involved in common most of the artifact types in the activity "set," but no one artifact type were used in all the events. A depositional "set" (the list of artifact types characterizing a set of deposits) would be monothetically distributed among the set of deposits if all the artifact types in the depositional "set" were contained in each of the deposits. A depositional "set" would be polythetically distributed among a set of deposits if the deposits held in common most of the artifact types in the depositional "set," but no one artifact type were required of a deposit to be a member of the set of deposits (Table 3.2).

Polythetic sets can vary in the degree to which their members share attributes; one set may be *more polythetic* than another. By "more polythetic," I mean that the percentage of attributes shared by a given percentage of the members of a set is less, or that the percentage of members sharing a given percentage of the attributes is less. A polythetic set of archaeological deposits would be more polythetic than the set of events that generated them if a given percentage of the deposits shared a lower percentage of the artifact types characterizing them as a set compared to those shared by the same given percentage of events. Likewise, the set of archaeological deposits would be more polythetic if the percentage of its members sharing a given percentage of artifact types were less than the percentage of events sharing the same given percentage of artifact types.

Processes Responsible for the Polythetic, Overlapping Organization of Activity Sets and Depositional Sets

Activity sets and depositional sets may be either monothetic or polythetic, nonoverlapping or overlapping, in organization. It is suggested, however, that in most circumstances, at least some of the activity sets used on a site and some of the depositional sets formed at a site are polythetic and overlapping. It also is suggested that, in many cases, depositional sets tend to be more polythetic than the activity sets from which they are derived. These generalizations are supported in this section.

The overlapping organization of some activity sets in the behavioral domain results from at least two factors. First, single-type tools (tools having one kind of functional edge) may have multiple purposes and may be used in combination with several different sets of tools. Prismatic blades, for example, may be used to whittle wood, butcher animals, or shave the scalp (Crabtree 1968). Table 7.1 clearly shows the extensive degree to which tools may have multiple purposes, and thus, may participate in different activities and activity sets. This fact has previously been emphasized by Cook (1976). Second, a single item may have multiple functional edges used in different activities, all the functional edges of which spatially coincide when the item is used in any one of the activities. For example, a Swiss army knife has knife blades, a can opener, a cork screw, a fingernail file, and other functional edges. As a result of the compound nature of the item, by physical constraint but not functional requirement, all the activity sets in which any one of the functional edges participates must share the Swiss army knife as a whole item and all the functional edges (individual tools) comprising it.

The polythetic organization of some activity sets results from the fact that several alternative tool types may be used to accomplish the same ends. For example, the Nunamiut Eskimo use both saws and knives to cut meat (Binford 1976). In any particular butchering event, one or the other of these tools might be used, but not necessarily both. A set of Nunamiut butchering events would be defined by all the tool types (attribute list) usually used to butcher animals, but only some of the events would involve saws and only some would involve knives.

The polythetic, overlapping organization of depositional sets results in part from their derivation from activity sets having a polythetic, overlapping structure. The *more* polythetic nature of depositional sets than activity sets derives from a number of additional factors involving behavioral processes, processes of formation and disturbance of the archaeological record, and processes of recovery and analysis (Binford 1976; Schiffer 1972, 1973a,b, 1975a,c, 1976, 1977, 1982).

Factor 1: Time of deposition of artifacts within their life-histories. The artifact types comprising an activity set in the behavioral domain may enter the archaeological domain as subsets, separated in different locations of their manufacture, use, storage, or discard.

Factor 2: Size-sorting of artifact classes. Artifact types of different size classes, belonging to the same activity set, may be discarded in different locations upon fulfillment of their use. Large items will tend to be discarded in convenient, out-of-the-way, secondary trash deposits, whereas smaller items may be discarded or lost anywhere (McKellar 1973).

Factor 3: Curation and differential wear and breakage rates of artifact classes. If the artifact types within an activity set are *curated*—that is, removed from one use-area for reuse at another later in time (Binford 1976)—and if the activity is not performed repeatedly in the same use-areas, differential wear rates and breakage rates may lead to different subsets of the activity set being deposited in the different locales. The degree to which the artifact types within an activity set are curated and not always deposited with each other depends on the labor invested in manufacturing them, their cultural importance, the ease with which they can be moved, the distance to the next site to be occupied in the annual round of the community, the availability of the types (or the raw materials from which they can be made) at the next site, whether abandonment of the current site is planned, and the degree of mobility of the community (Schiffer 1972:160, Lange and Rydberg 1972:430; Joslin–Jeske 1981). The number of classes of tools curated by a social group tends to increase with the residential stability of that social group (Binford 1976:42).

The great impact that curation can have on the organization of the archaeological record is illustrated by Binford's (1976) work among the Nunamiut Eskimo.

Binford recorded the number and kinds of items that were taken by the Nunamiut on 47 logistics trips away from their base camps. Of the 647 trip-items carried, 99 were totally consumed in the course of their use, most of these being food items. The remaining

five hundred and forty-eight (548) of the trip-items carried were visible in that there were tangible by-products from their use or no destruction occurred during their use. Of these items, fifty-three, or only 9.67 percent of the total visible items were not returned to the village. . . . Of these fifty-three (53) trip-items, thirty-six (36) are items which are disposable byproducts in the context of their use, including the peanut butter jar, sardine can. . . . Of the remaining eighteen (18) items not returned to the village, fourteen (14) or 26.3% of the total were cached in the field for future use. Of the remaining four items, three were unintentionally lost on the trail and *only one was discarded, broken at the location where it was used.* This is not, however, the only item broken during the course of the forty-seven trips. Twelve additional items were broken, but returned to the village for repair [1976: 334–335].

Factor 4: The multipurpose nature of tool types. The multipurpose nature of some tool types, which in the behavioral and archaeological domains is responsible for the overlapping organization of activity sets and depositional sets, also is responsible for the polythetic organization of depositional sets. A multipurpose tool can be deposited with the members of only one of the activity sets in which it participates.

Factor 5: The compound nature of tool types. In a similar manner, a compound tool having several different functional edges and used in several different activities, such as a Swiss army knife, not only will make the activity sets and depositional sets to which it belongs overlapping, but also will make the depositional sets polythetic. A multifunctional compound tool can be deposited with the members of only one of the activity sets in which it participates.

Factor 6: Recycling of artifacts. The polythetic organization of depositional sets may be caused by the reworking of an artifact of one type, that has been used or produced in one activity and that belongs to one activity set, into a different type used in another activity ("recycling" in Schiffer's terminology). The reworked artifact will be deposited with the members of only the last activity set in which it participated.

Factor 7: Mining of artifacts. When a site is abandoned over an extended period of time, useful or valuable material items in the abandoned area may be "mined" (another form of recycling) by the residual occupants and reused for the same or different purposes in other areas of the site. This behavior creates deposits in the abandoned area that form polythetic sets. Similarly, but on a smaller scale, Reid (1973) has noted that as households expand and contract in size over time and new rooms or huts are built and abandoned, the abandoned ones may be mined for materials by the members of the household. Also, as a site shifts gradually in location without loss of membership to the social group, previously occupied areas may be mined of tools and debris for use in the newly occupied part of the site (Ascher 1968). The artifacts mined are not always tools; debris items and junk also may be picked up. Some debris items are recycled immediately, but some are cached as raw material to be used at a later time and might never be reused (James O'Connell, personal communication 1977).

A site also may be mined of materials after its total abandonment by either prehistoric individuals or contemporary artifact collectors (Schiffer 1977:26). This behavior may cause items to be missing from deposits where they normally would occur, some artifact types being picked up more heavily than others.

The methods of data collection and analysis used by the archaeologist may artifically cause recovered depositional sets to appear polythetic in organization. Factors 8 through 11, below, are of this artificial nature.

Factor 8: Incomplete recovery of artifacts. When recovery of artifacts is not complete, as is the case with surface survey data or when screening is not used during excavation, depositional sets will be polythetic (Collins 1975; Schiffer 1977:26).

Factor 9: Classification of artifacts using other than functional attributes. When tool and debris classifications are based on stylistic rather than functional attributes, functionally equivalent items belonging to the same activity set may be classified into separate types, causing depositional sets to appear more polythetic. This is the case when classic lithic tool typologies are used, in which attention is given to flake shape and size and to retouch patterns (e.g., Balout 1967; Bordes 1961, 1968; de Heinzelin 1962; Tixier 1963) rather than to more functional attributes, such as the angle, shape, and wear of the working edge of the tool (e.g., Ahler 1971; Keeley 1977; Odell 1977; Odell and Odell–Vereecken 1980; Wilmsen 1970).

Factor 10: Overly divisive artifact classification. An overly divisive typology also will yield polythetic depositional sets. Care must be taken not to overclassify artifacts, particularly with the assemblages of mobile populations who apparently are more opportunistic about the tools they use to accomplish tasks. As Gould *et al.* have pointed out:

> [It would be] a mistake to overclassify the ethnographic adzes (i.e., scrapers) of the Western Desert Aborigines. Ethnographic observations over an extended period of time and in a variety of situations lead, instead, to an appreciation of the casualness and opportunism of present day Aborigine stone chipping. To these people, the primary aim is to perform a task involving either cutting (of sinew, flesh, vegetable fibers, etc.) or scraping (of wood) with little interest in the shape of the tool except for the angle of the working edge relative to the particular task involved [1971:154].

James O'Connell (personal communication, 1977) estimates that there are only about 10 functional types of artifacts in Alyawara assemblages—a quite small number compared to the elaborateness of some supposedly functional typologies of tools of mobile groups that archaeologists have designed. Binford and Binford's (1966:251) list of 40 tool types used in examining the Mousterian of Levallois facies would be an example of an overly divisive tool typology.

Factor 11: Misclassification of artifacts. Finally, misclassification of artifacts will cause certain classes of artifacts to appear missing from the deposits where they are expected to occur, producing depositional sets with a greater degree of polythetic organization than would otherwise be the case.

In summary, a consideration of human behavior, the organization of artifacts in the behavioral domain, the processes by which that organization is transformed when mapped into the archaeological record, and archaeological recovery and typological techniques suggest that some artifact types are likely to be distributed polythetically among activity sets and depositional sets, and that some activity sets and depositional sets are overlapping in nature. Additionally, depositional sets tend to be more polythetic than the activity sets from which they were derived. These facts must be taken into consideration when designing spatial analytic techniques that search for depositional sets and use-areas and when interpreting the results of applying those techniques.

Characteristics of Activity Areas and Use-Areas

In this section, I will not try to specify the nature of *all* depositional areas. In particular, I will not discuss the nature of areas of artifact occurrence resulting solely from natural or agricultural transport processes (e.g., fluvial transport, landscaping). This would require a treatment of geomorphological, sedimentological, and agricultural taphonomic processes that would be too broad in scope for this chapter (e.g., Behrensmeyer 1975; Gifford 1978; Hill 1975; Saunders 1977; Shipman 1981; Voorhies 1969a,b). Instead, I will discuss the nature of only use-areas—those areas of artifact occurrence that result from primary or secondary refuse deposition by *past human agents,* with *incomplete* postdepositional disturbance. Areas of artifact manufacture, use (e.g., butchering and cooking areas), storage, and disposal are of concern.

The characteristics of use-areas, like those of anthropic depositional sets, may be seen as the end product of structural transformations (archaeological formation and disturbance processes) operating on previous structure in the behavioral domain. To define the nature of use-areas, therefore, it is necessary to specify first the characteristics of the entities from which they are derived—activity areas.

Characteristics of Activity Areas

Whallon (1979) has specified four characteristics of activity areas that one must take into account when designing spatial analytic techniques that search for use-areas. Activity areas vary greatly in their size, shape, artifact densities, and artifact compositions. To these characteristics may be added the following. Activity areas are not necessarily high-density clusters of artifacts in a background of lower densities of artifacts; they may be areas of low-artifact density surrounded by zones of higher artifact density. Activity areas may vary in the degree to which they are internally homogeneous in their artifact densities. They may differ in the degree to which they are internally homogeneous in their artifact composition. The borders of activity areas may vary in their crispness. Finally, activities and activity areas within a site may be hierarchically organized, with more localized areas of activity (general or special purpose) aggregating and forming broader zones of activity.

A large number of behavioral processes are responsible for these characteristics of activity areas. Some may be enumerated, in the order of the characteristics they determine.

Factors Affecting the Size, Shape, and Artifact Density of Activity Areas.

Factor 1. Different kinds of activities may produce different amounts of debris, creating different densities of artifacts within the areas where these activities are performed. For example, secondary butchering (requiring only a few flake knives), hide dressing (requiring only a few scrapers, knives, and organic materials), and weaving all produce very little preservable refuse compared to activities such as primary butchering, shelling mollusks, flint knapping, or pottery manufacture.

Factor 2. Different kinds of activities may require different amounts and shapes of space, producing activity areas of different sizes and shapes. Hide dressing, for example, requires more room than whittling wood or knapping flint. In Alyawara Aborigine base camps hides are worked away from the huts, where space is more abundant and they can be laid out without interferring with the space requirements of other activities (O'Connell 1979, personal communication 1977). At the Crane site, a Middle Woodland base camp in Illinois, tools used to work hides were found to have larger nearest neighbor distances than did artifacts used for or produced by butchering meat, boiling meat, hulling nuts, grinding seeds, and sewing/basket-making (Carr 1977). The different space requirements of different kinds of activities also have been noted on a grander scale by Binford (1972). Binford suggests that the functions of sites and the activities performed at them may change directionally over time in response to directional changes in the amount of space available at the site for use. For example, the functions of a cave site may change as it becomes filled with debris and provides less utilizable space.

Factor 3. The degree to which an activity (a) requires much space and time, (b) produces much debris, and (c) creates obnoxious byproducts, such as smoke or animal residues that attract vermin or carnivores, may determine where it is performed within a community. The placement of an activity, in turn, may constrain the size, shape, and artifact density of the area in which it is performed. Activities that require large amounts of space or that are obnoxious often are performed away from residential locations or at the periphery of the base camps or mobile to semimobile peoples. There, space is not so limited and valuable as in the central portion of camp, and the activities may be performed without interfering with other events; they also are of less annoyance at a distance. In the periphery where more work space is available, debris from the activities may tend to be spread more widely and randomly. Also, activity areas may be shifted laterally to avoid debris buildup within them, rather than cleaned. The result is work areas that are larger, are more amorphous in shape, and contain a lower density of debris than might be expected from the rate of refuse production of the activities. In contrast, centrally located activities (e.g., knapping, sewing, food preparation) may occupy smaller areas in which debris tends to concentrate. More commonly, all the central activities may be performed in one large, multipurpose activity area that is within easy access of residences and is cleaned periodically and between activities of different kinds. The action of cleaning the area will cause it to have a low density of items of all sizes, except those that are very small. Centrally located activity areas will tend to be well defined in shape, as a result of their location where space is limited and allocated with care.

Activity areas in the base camps of !Kung Bushmen (Yellen 1974) and Alyawara Aborigine (O'Connell 1977, 1979; personal communication, 1977) follow the pattern of location, size, shape, and artifact density just described. For example, stretching hides (a long-term activity that requires much space) and repairing cars (a messy activity) occur at the periphery of Alyawara camps. In Bushman camps, stretching hides and roasting meat (messy activities) occur peripherally. In Ainu base camps, skinning, skin decomposition, drying fresh meats, and fish processing are done away from the house (Watanabe 1972:Figure 4). Archaeologically, at the Boston Ledges Rock Shelter (Brose and Scarry 1976), tools for scraping hides and butchering animals occurred peripheral to hearth-oriented activities. At the Hatchery West site (Binford et al. 1970), shallow earth ovens that were used in preparing animal products and that would have produced obnoxious odors were placed away from the houses. At the Crane site (Carr 1977), hide dressing, pottery manufacture, rough working of wood, butchering, and possibly drying of meat occurred with greater frequency away from the central, residential portion of the site, whereas chert knapping, nut processing, seed grinding, and sewing/basket-making occurred in the central, residential portions of the site in a multipurpose work area. The centrally located activities were performed in a constrained area, whereas the peripheral activities were widely scattered.

Factor 4. Different kinds of activity areas may be used repeatedly for different lengths of time. In addition to causing differences in the amount of refuse generated by the activities per episode of use, this behavior will cause the density of artifacts within the areas, and perhaps their size, to vary from area to area. The period of time over which an activity area is used in turn can depend upon a number of factors. (*a*) If an activity produces obnoxious organic refuse, it probably will be relocated periodically to avoid distasteful and unhealthy conditions in the area of work. (*b*) If an activity requires the use of a permanent facility as well as work space, and if the facility represents an investment of labor and time, the activity area probably will be cleaned rather than relocated to avoid the interference of refuse, and will be used for a long time. (*c*) Activities that can occur under cover or indoors during rainy or cold seasons will tend to be repeated in the same protected location for a length of time dependent upon the length of the harsh season and the use-life of the protecting structure. (*d*) As before, the length of time over which an activity occurs in the same area can depend on whether it is located peripherally in a site, where space is less constrained and periodic relocation of the activity is possible, or more centrally in the site, where space is at a premium and relocation is less feasible. (*e*) Dumping stations may be used for variable lengths of time, depending on: whether they remain close to work areas that shift in space over time; the amount of space allocated for growth of the dump before it interferes spatially with neighboring activity areas; or the time at which the refuse begins to produce a stench.

Factors Affecting the Artifact Composition of Activity Areas.   The composition of activity areas of the same function can vary as a result of at least three factors.

Factor 1. The factors that cause an activity set to be polythetic may cause different locations of the same activity to encompass different subsets of the activity set used. In some locations of an activity, some combinations of tool and debris types may be used or produced, whereas in other locations of the same activity, other combinations of tool and debris types may be used or produced, all of which comprise one activity set.

Factor 2. The composition of activity areas of the same function may vary according to their durations of use. This relationship, between composition and duration of use, can arise from either of two circumstances: one pertaining to the different *combinations* of artifact types (subsets of an activity set) that are *used or produced* in an activity area at different times, and the other pertaining to the different *probabilities of discard* of the artifact types in an activity set. (1) Given an activity with a polythetic activity set, as the number of times the activity is performed at an area increases, the variety of *combinations* of artifact types used or produced in the area and the variety of artifact types deposited there will increase. Eventually, most or all of the artifact types within the activity set will be deposited at the location, provided it is not cleaned regularly. Thus, different activity areas of the same kind may encompass different numbers of artifact types that more or less represent the complete activity set of which they are a part, as a function of the life spans of the areas and the *number of different subsets* of the activity set used or produced at each of them. (2) Not all of the artifacts and artifact types used in or produced by any single occurrence of an activity are necessarily deposited expediently at the location of activity. The probability of deposition of each artifact class involved in one activity occurrence depends on its rate of breakage and the suite of factors governing its rate of curation (see pages 122–123). An activity area used only a few times may bear only a few of the artifact types used or produced at it—those with high rates of breakage or wear and low curation rates. The deposited artifacts will be a subset of those used at the location (which in turn may be a subset of the activity set to which they belong, as in Circumstance 1). As the length of time over which the location is used increases, the probability that artifact types with longer life spans and greater curation rates will be deposited at it will increase, provided the area is not cleaned regularly. Thus, different activity areas of the same kind may encompass different numbers of artifact types that more or less represent the complete activity set to which they belong, as a function of the life span of the areas and the relative probabilities of discard of the artifact types. Longer-used activity areas of the same function will tend to be more similar in their artifact compositions.

These circumstances pertain equally to activity areas used for work and those used for refuse deposition. Storage areas, however, do not show the time-dependent alternations in artifact composition just discussed.

Factors Affecting the Artifact Density of Activity Areas Compared to Their Surroundings. Activity areas may be zones of low artifact density within a background of higher artifact density, as well as high density clusters of artifacts. This pattern relates to the fact that activity areas may be cleaned and swept. The swept refuse may be deposited around the activity area, emphasizing the locally low relative artifact density in the area of work, or it may not.

Several factors determine whether an activity area is cleaned. First is the degree to which space in the vicinity of the area is limited. If space is limited and the activity area cannot be moved, upon becoming cluttered, to a new, clean area, it will be cleaned for reuse. This logic is exemplified in Alyawara and Bushman camps; activity areas next to residences, where space is at a premium, are cleaned, whereas work areas around the periphery of the camps are moved laterally. Space can be limited because the site population is high or because the ground available for habitation is constrained (as in a rock shelter or house). A second determinant of whether an activity area is cleaned is the degree to which the area, itself, is valued. An area may be the prefered location of an activity because it includes a permanent facility that is not easily rebuilt elsewhere, or because of intrinsic reasons (it has a pleasant view; it is shaded or protected from the wind; etc.). Finally, the degree to which the refuse generated in the activity area is messy or unhealthy determines whether an activity area is cleaned.

Factors Affecting Internal Variation in the Artifact Densities and Compositions of Activity Areas. The degree of homogeneity of an activity area in its artifact densities and compositions depends on several factors. For primary refuse deposits, these factors include: whether use-space is limited, whether the activity area of concern is swept for reuse, and whether the activity is tied to a permanent facility. When an activity occurs in a portion of a site where space is abundant, debris can be scattered widely, producing a large, amorphous activity area with internally variable artifact density and artifact composition. Under conditions of space restriction and some other circumstances (above), on the other hand, an activity area may be swept for reuse, leaving within it a scatter of artifacts that is uniformly low in density and relatively homogenized in artifact type composition by the sweeping action. Also, an activity that requires, in part, the use of a permanent facility may produce a scatter of artifacts that has higher densities of artifacts, or more artifacts of specific kinds, in the immediate vicinity of the facility.

For secondary refuse deposits, internal density and composition depend on how the area of primary deposition (source of refuse) was cleaned, how refuse was transported to the dumping location, and the transportability of the refuse (dependent on the sizes, weights, and shapes of the refuse items). For example, if a refuse dump is generated from the sweepings of an adjacent work area, and if all items of refuse of different kinds are similarly transportable, the dump may be fairly homogeneous in artifact composition as a result of the randomizing action of the broom. Homogeneity in composition will decrease as variability in the transportability of artifacts by class becomes more pronounced and sorting of artifacts by type occurs. Similarly, the dump's internal pattern of artifact density will depend on the degree of variation in the transportability of refuse items. If the work area is cleaned by collecting refuse in containers that are filled and dumped many times, rather than by sweeping, the dump may exhibit a more heterogeneous artifact density and composition.

A Factor Affecting the Crispness of the Borders of Activity Areas. This attribute of an activity area depends particularly on how constrained space is. Where space is abundant, work areas and refuse areas can be expected to have "fuzzy" borders characterized by a slow gradient of change in artifact density. This results from the broadcasting of refuse from the core of the work space outward, and a lack of concern for where the refuse is deposited. Artifact scatters from space-consuming, time-consuming, or messy activities performed at the peripheries of sites, as those in Bushman and Alyawara camps, can be expected to show this pattern. Where space is limited, activity areas—whether work, storage, or refuse areas—can be expected to have better monitored, imposed borders.

Factors Affecting the Hierarchical Clustering of Activity Areas. Activity areas within a site, and the artifacts composing them, often are arranged in a hierarchically clustered form, rather than a random one (Figure 3.4). For example, a community might be arranged into two groups of residences, each with multiple households that, in turn, have multiple activity areas around them. Artifact distributions would parallel this structure, ignoring the effects of secondary depositional processes. Within the wide, low-density scatter of artifacts defining the site (community) would occur two broad zones of moderate, average artifact density (residential groups), themselves composed of multiple zones of high artifact density (residences) that could be subdivided into areas of varying artifact density (activity areas of different kinds). The hierarchical arrangement of activities and activity areas within a site may derive from the social segementation and organization of the occupants, the different degrees to which different kinds of activities are contingent upon each other, and site topography, among other things.

Characteristics of Use-Areas

Use-areas, as transformations of activity areas, may have all the variable characteristics of activity areas as just described, plus an additional one. Use-areas of similar or different function may *overlap spatially*. The overlapping nature of use-areas may result from either *accidental* or *planned* overlapping of activity areas within a site over time. Accidental overlapping of activity areas may occur, for example, when a base camp is annually reoccupied by the same local group but the camp is set up in a slightly different arrangement each year. The "homogeneous" middens of many Late Archaic sites in the Eastern United States exemplify the results of this process. Planned spatial overlap of activity areas may occur when work space within a community is limited. For example, valued work space around the hearths and huts of Bushman and Alyawara camps is used for multiple purposes, with different kinds of activities scheduled at different times (Yellen 1974; O'Connell 1977, 1979).

Use-areas may vary more than activity areas in the characteristics they share as a result of the broader range of factors affecting use-areas.

Factor 1. Variation in the degree of spatial overlap of use-areas within a site may increase the range of variation in their other characteristics. A greater degree of overlap among use-areas may cause them to have higher artifact densities, more internal variation in artifact density, less distinct borders, and a more diversified artifact composition than they would have otherwise.

Factor 2. When an activity occurs in a portion of a site where space is unconstrained, its location may shift gradually over time, from its original position where primary refuse has built up, to adjacent, cleaner zones. This process will create a composite use-area that is larger, more amorphous, and less distinct in its boundaries than the numerous activity areas that generated it.

Factor 3. Numerous postdepositional processes of disturbance in the archaeological domain (Schiffer 1976; Wood and Johnson 1978) may alter the characteristics of activity areas, producing use-areas of modified size, shape, average artifact density, overall artifact composition, degree of internal variation of artifact density and composition, and border definition. The operation of these factors differentially over space may cause variability among and within use-areas in these attributes to be greater than that of the activity areas from which they are derived.

Most postdepositional processes have the effect of disordering artifact patterning in the archaeological record—increasing the entropy of the archaeological record (Ascher 1968). They make use-areas larger, more amorphous, lower in artifact density, more homogeneous in their internal artifact density, less distinct in their boundaries, and more similar (or at least skewed) in artifact composition. Examples of such processes include: (1) trampling of abandoned use-areas by residents of the site or contemporary artifact collectors (Ascher 1968; Gifford 1978); (2) systematic mining of abandoned use-areas by residents of a site or contemporary artifact collectors (Ascher 1968); (3) plowing and other farming operations (Roper 1976; Trubowitz 1981; Lewarch and O'Brien 1981); and (4) a variety of natural pedoturbations of biological and geological cause, such as the burrowing actions of mammals, insects, and earthworms (Stein 1983); tree falls; soil creep; solifluction; cryoturbations and aquaturbations (Wood and Johnson 1978). Some postdepositional disturbance processes, however, may increase the degree of patterning of artifact disturbances, but toward natural arrangements. Examples include the burrowing actions of earthworms, which can produce novel arrangements of surficial debris (Ascher 1968); freeze–thaw cycles, which produce "patterned ground" (surface stone aggregations in the shapes of rings, polygons, or stripes) or stone pavements; expansion–contraction cycles in vertisols, which form "linear gilgai"; precipitation of salt crystals in the soil, followed by cracking the soil, producing patterned ground; and soil creep, which may result in the accumulation of heavier or denser objects downslope (Wood and Johnson 1978). Finally, some postdepositional processes may simply truncate use-areas, altering only their size and shape. Examples include the scooping up of archaeological deposits by site occupants to build earthworks and mounds (Schiffer 1977:25), modern landscaping, and intensive localized fluvial disturbance.

In summary, activity areas, as the products of many different behavioral processes, may be highly variable in their size, shape, and many other basic characteristics. Use-areas, being derived from activity areas and operated on by additional archaeological formation and disturbance processes, may be even more variable. Mathematical techniques used to search for use-areas within archaeological data consequently must not assume that they are similar in nature, if the methods are to be concordant with the structure of the archaeological record.

A REVIEW OF PREVIOUSLY USED SPATIAL ANALYTIC TECHNIQUES AND EVALUATION OF THEIR APPROPRIATENESS FOR INTRASITE ANALYSIS

Introduction

Despite the advances made in recent years in techniques for quantitatively analyzing spatial arrangements of artifacts within archaeological sites, satisfaction with these techniques and their results has been limited (Whallon 1979). In general, the results of such analyses have told archaeologists less about the arrangement of artifacts within sites than have their own perceptions of the data and their own mental capabilities to discover and understand patterns within the data. As a consequence, quantitative spatial analysis of intrasite patterning has not become the standard approach in archaeology that once seemed probable.

There is good reason for this state of affairs. The techniques of spatial analysis currently available to the archaeologist do not have assumptions that are logically consistent with: (1) the organization of archaeological remains, and (2) the patterns of human behavior and the archaeological formation processes responsible for that organization, as modeled here.

This section briefly describes the mathematical techniques that currently are available to archaeologists for intrasite spatial analysis, cites more detailed explanations and examples of use of the techniques, and evaluates the methods for their logical consistency with the structure of intrasite archaeological records, as modeled. The techniques to be discussed are shown in Table 3.3, along with their manner of concatenation into several alternative approaches for meeting the several operational goals of intrasite spatial analysis. Table 3.4 summarizes, for quick reference, the unwarranted assumptions that the techniques make about the spatial structure of artifacts within archaeological sites, and by implication, the nature of human behavior, archaeological formation processes, and archaeological recovery techniques.

Methods for Assessing Whether Artifacts Cluster in Space

Definitions and Qualifications

A study area with scattered artifacts minimally has two global attributes that are important to the archaeologist: (1) the average *density* of artifacts within it, and (2) the *form of arrangement* of artifacts within it—clustered, random, or

TABLE 3.3

Alternative Routes of Spatial Analysis Using Different Sets of Techniques

Question	Previously used approaches[a]			New, more appropriate approaches[a]		
	Approach 1 (grid-cell counts)	Approach 2 (grid-cell counts)	Approach 3 (point locations of items)	Approach 4 (point locations of items or grid-cell counts)	Approach 5 (point locations of items preferable)	Approach 6 (grid-cell counts)
Artifacts randomly scattered?	Poisson method of assessing if random scatter	Dimensional analysis of variance or Morisita's Index	First-order nearest neighbor statistics	Bypass, "not considered relevant" by Whallon (1979)	Nth-order nearest neighbor statistics or point-to-item distance statistics	Luton and Braun's contiguity method
Spatial limits of clusters, defining "activity areas"?	No attempt to define	No attempt to define	Whallon's "radius approach"	Whallon's "unconstrained clustering"	Carr's modifications, 1 or 2, of Whallon's "radius approach"	Contiguity– anomaly method
Artifact types co-vary/co-occur, defining "tool kits"?	Correlation of artifact type counts within excavation/survey grid units, over *whole site*, followed by factor analysis, cluster analysis, matrix ordering, or *MDSCAL*	Correlation of blocked data, *over whole site*, followed by factor analysis, cluster analysis, matrix ordering, or *MDSCAL*	Pielou's segregation analysis, *over whole site*, or Whallon's "radius approach" *over whole site*	Correlation or association of artifact type counts *within clusters* after they are defined. Avoidance of defining site-wide "tool kits"	Carr's "polythetic association" *over whole site*	Appropriate index of co-arrangement yet to be designed

[a] The form of data required is given in parentheses under each approach.

systematically spaced—independent of density (Pielou 1977:124). For clustered arrangements of artifacts, the degree of clustering (form) is a function of both the *intensity* and *grain* of patterning of artifacts (Pielou 1977:155) and whether clusters themselves cluster hierarchically in a *nested* or *unnested* fashion. The intensity of a clustered pattern is the extent to which clusters and sparse areas differ in their density. An intense pattern is characterized by very high density clusters and very low density interstitial spaces. The grain of a clustered arrangement refers to the size of clusters and sparse areas. A coarse-grained arrangement has very large clusters widely spaced, whereas a fine-grained arrangement has small, closely spaced clusters. All clustered arrangements are hierarchical (compared to arrangements that are uniformly random or aligned throughout) in that they exhibit minimally two levels or organization: arrangement of items within clusters, and the spacing of clusters with respect to each other (Figure 3.3). Additional hierarchical levels may take the form of nested or unnested clusters of clusters (Figure 3.4).

A large number of techniques are available in the ecological literature for assessing the form of arrangement of items over space, most of which are summarized and evaluated by Greig-Smith (1964:54–111) and Pielou (1969:124–165). The various techniques allow assessment of arrangement in either or both of two ways. (1) They may provide an *index* of the degree of aggregation or dispersion of items over space (e.g., the variance:mean ratio) that may be compared between areal units (statistically or not), giving a *relative* assessment of arrangement. (2) They may provide a statistical test measuring the significance of the deviation of an observed index value for a scatter of items from that expected for a random arrangement of items of the same number and density, giving an *absolute* assessment of form of arrangement. Applied archae-

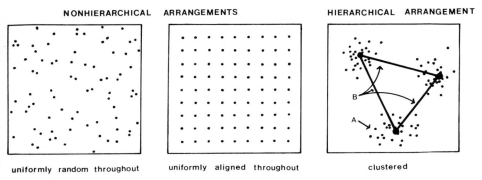

NONHIERARCHICAL ARRANGEMENTS   HIERARCHICAL ARRANGEMENT

uniformly random throughout   uniformly aligned throughout   clustered

Figure 3.3. Clustered arrangements are hierarchical compared to arrangements that are uniformly random or aligned throughout. Clustered arrangements exhibit two levels of arrangement: (A) arrangements of items within clusters and (B) the spacing of clusters with respect to each other.

TABLE 3.4

Unwarranted Assumptions Made by Spatial Analytic Techniques Currently Used by Archaeologists Regarding the Nature of Formation/Organization of the Archaeological Record

Unwarranted assumptions	Poisson method	Dimensional analysis of variance	Morisita's Index	First-order nearest neighbor statistics	Correlation analysis	Association analysis
			Technique			
Assessment of co-arrangement is contingent upon delimiting clusters.						
Activity sets are always monothetic.					X	X
Members of activity sets are deposited expediently in their locations of use.					X	X
Artifact types in the same activity set are deposited in pairs in all locations of their deposition.						
Artifact types in the same activity set are deposited in similar proportions in all locations of their deposition.					X	
Artifact types in the same activity set are deposited together in unspecified numbers in all locations of their deposition.						X
Artifacts are not disturbed by polythetic-causing, postdepositional processes.					X	X
Artifact types are completely recovered and correctly classified to function.					X	X
Activity areas were used an extended, approximately equal period of time.					X	X
Activity sets are always nonoverlapping.					X	X
Use-areas are of similar size.	X	X	X		X	X
Use-areas are of similar shape.	X	X	X		X	X
Use-areas, if oblong, have the same orientation.	X	X	X		X	X
Use-areas are spaced systematically.	X	X	X		X	X
Use-areas are of similar density.						
Use-areas have the same number of artifacts.						
Use-areas are internally homogeneous in artifact density.						
Use-areas are internally homogeneous in artifact composition.						
Use-areas have crisp borders.						
Use-areas do not overlap spatially.						
Use-areas are always high-density clusters of artifacts in a background of lower artifact densities.						
Use-areas are never hierarchically arranged.	X			X		
Sites are of square or rectangular shape.		X	X			

Segregation analysis	Whalon's overlapping clustering approach	Whalon's radius approach	Nth-Order nearest neighbor statistics	Pielou's point-to-item distance statistics	Luton and Braun's contiguity method	Polythetic association	Modified radius approach I	Modified radius approach II	Contiguity–anomaly method	Unconstrained clustering
X	X									X
x	x									x
x	x									
										X
X	X									X
x	x									X
	X									X
X	X									
					X					
					X					
					X					
		X								
			X							
	X	X								
	X						X			X
									X	
										X
	X	X				X	X	X		

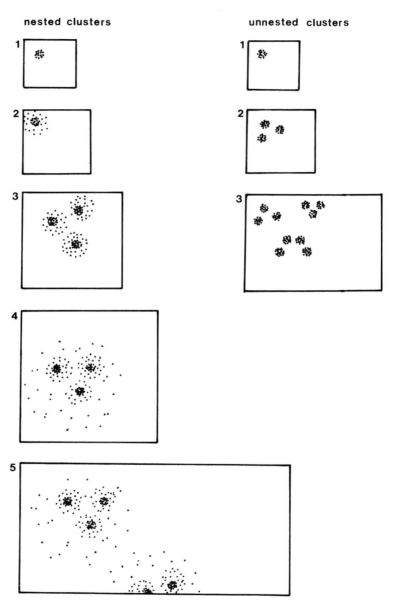

Figure 3.4. Clusters, themselves, may cluster in either nested or unnested patterns.

ologically, the former approach allows comparison of the arrangement of items within different use-areas or sites directly to each other, whereas the latter allows an absolute evaluation of arrangement within single study units.

Archaeologists most frequently have used four methods to assess the form of arrangement of artifact scatters. These are listed in Table 3.5, along with: their sensitivity to the various aspects of arrangement form just described, whether they provide relative or absolute measures of arrangement, and the kind of data they require (grid-cell counts or point locations of items).

The usefulness of these or any of the available techniques for assessing the form of arrangement of artifacts within a study area depends on the nature of the data and the information sought. When average artifact densities within a study area are high, in many circumstances the pattern of arrangement may be clear on visual inspection, and no rigorous testing may be necessary. At lower average densities, however, the same arrangement may become more difficult to evaluate for its form, as a result of the loss of potential contrast between high-density and low-density areas (Kershaw 1964:106). Quantitative assistance then is required for evaluation. Also, visual inspection may not allow one to determine the scale(s) of patterning within an artifact scatter and the form of patterning at different scales, whereas quantitative approaches can provide such information.

Finally, it must be stressed that for all the available techniques evaluating form of arrangement, meaningful results can be obtained only if the study area approximates a behaviorally significant unit, such as a site at large or an activity area (see pages 109–110). In all cases, form of arrangement is evaluated *relative* to the size and shape of the analytical frame; widely differing assessments may be obtained for the same scatter of items framed differently.

TABLE 3.5

Characteristics of Archaeologically Used Techniques for Evaluating the Form of Arrangement of Items

Technique	Aspect of form of arrangement to which sensitive	Relative or absolute measures of arrangement provided	Form of data required
Poisson methods	Intensity	Relative, absolute	Grid counts
Dimensional analysis of variance	Intensity, grain, hierarchy	Absolute	Grid counts
Morisita's method	Intensity, grain, hierarchy	Relative, absolute	Grid counts
First-order nearest neighbor analysis	Intensity	Relative, absolute	Point location of items

The Poisson Method

The oldest quantitative method for detecting nonrandomness in the arrangement of items within a study area is the Poisson method. It was first used by the plant geographer, Svedberg (1922), and since has been evaluated by several plant ecologists (Greig-Smith 1964:57–63; Pielou 1977:124–126, 144). Archaeologically, the approach has been suggested for use by Whallon (1973) and has been applied in several contexts (Dacey 1973; Brose and Scarry 1976; Hodder and Orton 1976:35).

Good descriptions of the method with example calculations are provided by Kershaw (1964) and Greig-Smith (1964:61–62), so only a minimal presentation is required here. The approach is based on the fact that when a random arrangement of items is overlaid with a grid of quadrats of sufficiently small size such that the chance of occurrence of an item in a quadrat is very small (Greig–Smith 1964:57–58; see below), the frequency distribution of number of cells with n items will approximate a Poisson distribution,

$$P_n = \frac{\bar{X}^n \exp(-\bar{x})}{n!} \tag{3.1}$$

where $\bar{X}$ is the average number of items per cell and P_n is the probability of finding n items in a cell. The expected number of cells, E, having n items, can be found by multiplying P_n by the total number of cells, N, in the study area.

Given this fact, it is possible to use the variance:mean ratio of the frequency distribution of number of cells with n items, for a scatter, as an index of its form of arrangement (Pielou 1977:125). A Poisson distribution has a variance equal to its mean, and a variance:mean ratio equal to 1. A random arrangement of items, therefore, will produce a variance:mean ratio similar to 1. A clustered arrangement will define a larger variance:mean ratio, whereas a more aligned arrangement will be characterized by a lower value.

The degree to which two study areas differ relative to each other in the form of arrangement of items within them may be tested statistically by a procedure described by David and Moore (1954; Pielou 1977:125–126; Greig–Smith 1964:65–66). If two study areas have the same number of items n, variances s_1^2 and s_2^2, and means $\bar{X}_1$ and $\bar{X}_2$, the statistic

$$w = -\frac{1}{2} \ln\left(\frac{s_1^2/\bar{X}_1}{s_2^2/\bar{X}_2}\right) \tag{3.2}$$

will lie outside the range of $\pm 2.5/\sqrt{n-1}$ if the variance:mean ratios of the two populations differ significantly at the 5% level. This test has seldom, if ever, been used in an archaeological context.

Evaluation of a study area on an absolute scale for the degree to which items within it depart from a random arrangement can be tested by two methods. First, a Student's t-test may be calculated under the null hypothesis that the observed histogram of number of cells with n items has a Poisson distribution and a variance:mean ratio of 1 (VMR test). The statistic

$$t = \frac{(\text{observed } S_x^2/\bar{X}) - 1}{\sqrt{2/(N - 1)}} \qquad (3.3)$$

may be compared to t tables using a one-sided test with a significance level of α and degrees of freedom equal to $N - 1$, where N is the number of quadrats. The observed t statistic will be greater than $t_{(1-\alpha)}$ (df) if the arrangement is significantly aggregated and less than $-t_{(1-\alpha)}$ (df) if the arrangement is significantly dispersed.

The second method of absolute evaluation is a χ^2 test of the goodness of fit of the observed histogram of number of cells with n items to a Poisson distribution with the same mean number of items per cell. The expected number of cells, E, with n items is determined with Equation 3.1 and compared to the observed, O, so as to allow the calculation of a χ^2 statistic

$$\chi^2 - \text{stat} = \sum_{i=1}^{c} \frac{(O - E)^2}{E} \qquad (3.4)$$

where c is the number of histogram classes compared. It is appropriate to compare only those histogram classes for which five or more cells with n counts are expected. For classes with lower expectations (usually in only the right tail of the distribution), the pooling of expected counts and the pooling of observed counts is required (Greig-Smith 1964:69). The χ^2-stat then may be compared to values in a χ^2 table ($\chi^2_{(1-\alpha)}$(df)) for a given significance level, α, and with $c - 2$ degrees of freedom. Values larger than those found in the table will indicate significant departure of the observed arrangement from the expected random one, but without specifying whether it tends to be clustered or aligned.

The Poisson approach to evaluating item arrangement has a number of technical problems and problems of concordance with the archaeological record. Let us begin with the technical problems.

Problem 1. The χ^2 test may vary in its accuracy, depending on the mean number of items per quadrat. When this figure is low, the expected number of quadrats having certain large numbers of items per grid cell may be less than 5, and the counts of quadrats (expected and observed) for these classes may have to be lumped to perform the χ^2 test. Lumping reduces the accuracy of the χ^2 test because it reduces the effect of the individual classes of quadrats with *high* numbers of items on the χ^2 statistic; it is these classes with many items per cell (as well as those with few items per cell) that are most likely to express deviations between expected and observed frequencies when an arrangement of items is nonrandom (Greig-Smith 1964:68). As a result, a clearly nonrandom arrangement of items may be found not to differ significantly from a random one. Greig-Smith (1964:68–69) gives an example of this.

Problem 2. The VMR test may not give accurate results, depending on the shape of the observed distribution of number of cells with n items. Many distributions that are shaped differently from the Poisson and suggest departure from random arrangement can have variances equal to their means and produce test results suggesting randomness. Evans (1952) provides one possible example.

Problem 3. The VMR test may behave inaccurately when the average density of items per cell is very low, "presumably because the distribution of deviations of the variance of a Poisson distribution from its mean is too strongly skewed" (Jones 1955, 1956).

As a result of these three technical problems, the χ^2 test and VMR test may produce contradictory results. Either one may detect nonrandomness when the other fails (Greig-Smith 1952a,b). When the average density of items per cell is great and the χ^2 test is accurate, however, the χ^2 test is to be preferred over the VMR test, because it *directly* assesses distribution shape.

Problem 4. The Poisson approach, in general, involves a loss of information that may lead to inaccurate results. It assesses the *frequency* distribution of cells having given numbers of items, rather than the *spatial arrangement* of cells having given numbers of items. A set of grid-cell counts having a Poisson distribution may be arranged in space such that high count cells and low count cells mingle randomly, or segregate so as to form a clustered distribution (Pielou 1977:135, 144; see Hietala and Stevens 1977 for an illustrated example). Consequently, although it is true that all random arrangements of items, when overlaid with a grid of sufficiently small cells, will yield a Poisson distribution of number of cells with *n* items, it is not true that such a Poisson distribution always indicates a random arrangement of items among grid cells. Thus, the results of a Poisson test suggesting random arrangement must be verified visually, with consequent loss of rigor.

The Poisson approach requires a number of assumptions about the nature of the archaeological record that need not be true (Table 3.4).

Problem 5. The Poisson approach assumes that the chance of occurrence of an item within a quadrat is very small, and that the density of items within a quadrat is much lower than the maximum possible density (Greig-Smith 1964:57). If the average density of items per quadrat approaches the maximum possible, then the expected frequency distribution of number of cells with *n* items, for a random arrangement of items, will approximate a binomial distribution rather than a Poisson, and the Poisson method cannot be used. The Poisson approach, therefore, can be applied to investigate the form of arrangement of only those artifact classes having low volumetric densities compared to their maximum possible volumetric densities. For example, the approach could not be used to assess the form of arrangement of pottery sherd counts among grid cells within a secondary pottery refuse dump, where pottery comprised a moderate to high percentage of the dump's volume.

A number of constraining assumptions about the archaeological record are made by the Poisson method, resulting from its operation on grid count data. These constraints it shares with many techniques that attempt to assess form of arrangement with grid count data.

Problem 6. It is assumed that if a scatter of items is arranged in a nonrandom way, the mesh of the grid corresponds to the dominant, behaviorally meaningful scale of variability in item density. For a clustered arrangement, it is assumed that the size of grid cells approximates the size of clusters. For an aligned arrangement, the cells should be larger (preferably several times larger) than the approximately equidistant interval between items. If this condition is not met, the Poisson approach may assess the form of arrangement of items different from that of its dominant, behaviorally significant arrangement.

For any one arrangement of items, the Poisson method produces different results with grids of different mesh (Greig-Smith 1952b, 1964:56–57). When applied to a clustered arrangement, the Poisson approach will suggest first a random arrangement, then a contagious one, and finally a uniform arrangement, as the grid mesh is increased from very small (compared to the size of clusters and density of items), through the size of clusters, to a mesh much larger than clusters (Kershaw 1964:104). When grid cells approximate the size of clusters and clusters center within them, grid cell counts will be either very high or very low, resulting in a distribution of "number of cells having n items" with a large variance compared to its mean (Figure 3.5a). Reducing the mesh of the grid reduces the counts of cells in the high density areas disproportionally compared to those in the low (reduces the contrast between high-density and low-density areas) so as to produce a frequency distribution with fewer outliers, more cells having moderate to low counts, and a more Poisson-like shape (Figure 3.5b). Increasing the mesh of the grid greater than the maximum scale of clustering, such that each cell includes a number of clusters, equalizes the number of items found among cells such that their frequency distribution again deviates from a Poisson shape, but in the direction of alignment (Figure 3.5c). In a similar manner, for an arrangement of items tending to be aligned, detection of nonrandomness becomes easier as the mesh of the grid is increased and local stochastic variation is averaged out geographically (Greig-Smith 1964:57).

Problems 7–9. It is assumed that if a scatter of items has a clustered arrangement, clusters are the *shape* of the grid cells, are *centered* within grid cells, and if oblong, are *oriented* in the direction of the grid; that is, the clustered arrangement must conform to the shape, placement, and orientation of the grid. If any one of these conditions is not true, even though grid mesh is chosen carefully to correspond to the size (area) of clusters, the items in a cluster will be subdivided

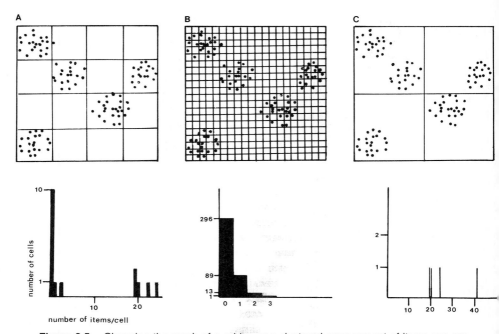

Figure 3.5. Changing the mesh of a grid over a clustered arrangement of items can produce frequency distributions of "number of cells with *N* items," suggesting the items' (A) clustered arrangement, (B) random arrangement, or (C) alignment. The frequency distribution for the fine mesh grid is equivalent to a Poisson distribution with an average density of .3 items/cell, *N* = 104.

among several grid cells and the cluster will not stand out as readily as an outlier in the histogram of number of cells with *n* items (Figure 3.6).

Problems 10–13. By logical extension of the constraints that clusters of items in a scatter must have the same size, shape, placement, and orientation as grid cells, they must be similar to *each other* in these regards.

Problem 14. Finally, the Poisson approach allows evaluation of the form of arrangement of items at only one scale: that of the grid. It ignores the possibility that artifact scatters may have multiple levels of organization at different spatial scales, with different forms of arrangement at each scale.

Dimensional Analysis of Variance

Dimensional analysis of variance (DAV) was designed by plant ecologists to eliminate some of the problems and ambiguity involved in the Poisson method. The founding concept and rationale for the approach are attributable to Greig-Smith (1952b), with extensions by Kershaw (1957, 1964), and particularly, Thompson, (1958) who provides tests of significance. Excellent descriptions of

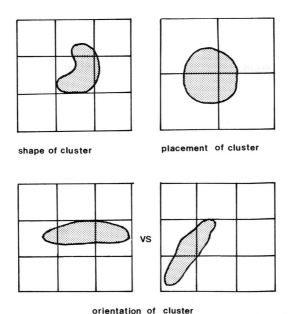

shape of cluster   placement of cluster

orientation of cluster

Figure 3.6.   When clusters are the size (area) of grid cells yet do not correspond to cells in their shape, placement, or orientation, their items become subdivided among multiple cells, and they do not stand out as readily as an outlier in a histogram of number of cells with *N* items.

the technique are given by Greig-Smith (1961, 1964), Kershaw (1964), Pielou 1977:140–144), and Whallon (1973).

The method was introduced to archaeology by Whallon (1973). It has been applied in this field in only a few instances (Whallon 1973; Paynter *et al.* 1974; Price 1975; Brose and Scarry 1976; Wandsnider and Binford 1982), largely for the purpose of assessing the technique, rather than in the course of normal research.

From an archaeological perspective, the goal of DAV is to assess the form of arrangement of artifacts within a study area using multiple grid systems with cells of differing sizes, shapes, and orientations, in order to find that grid system for which clustering of artifacts is most significant. This grid system is taken to represent an organization of the data that concords most with the organization of depositional areas within space: counts of artifacts within its grid cells are taken to approximate counts of artifacts within *behaviorally significant clusters*, rather than within arbitrarily sized grid units. Only when gridded data are organized in this manner does correlation analysis between artifact types produce meaningful results (see pages 166–170).

Dimensional analysis of variance aims at assessing the form of arrangement of items within a study area on an absolute scale, rather than relative to the arrangement of items in other areas. This is achieved in the following manner. Counts within the cells of some original grid system are summed into counts within square or rectangular blocks of 2, 4, 8, . . . , 2^j, . . . , T adjacent cells, where T is the total number of cells in the study area. The total variance in counts of items among the original grid cells then is partitioned (Greig-Smith 1961:696), using the usual analysis of variance procedure, into variances derived from the differences in counts between original cells with blocks of size 2, differences in counts between blocks of size 2 within blocks of size 4, etc. If N_i is the number of items found in block i, then the sums of squares pertinent to variation at the scale of blocks with 2^j cells, that is, to the differences in counts between blocks of scale 2^j cells within blocks of scale 2^{j+1} cells, is

$$S_j = \frac{1}{2^j} \sum_{i=1}^{T/2^j} N_i^2 - \frac{1}{2^{j+1}} \sum_{i=1}^{T/2^{j+1}} N_i^2 \tag{3.5}$$

Dividing this quantity by its degrees of freedom, $T/2^j$, yields the sought difference of variances (Kershaw 1964:107), and dividing again by the mean number of items per original grid cell defines a variance:mean ratio (Greig-Smith 1964:86; Mead 1974:297). (Whallon [(1974:272)] makes the latter division by the mean number of items per block of size 2^j cells, which is inappropriate [Greig-Smith, personal communication, 1983].) The notation used here parallels that provided by Pielou (1977:140–141) but applies the symbols of Whallon (1973:271). Differences in the equations presented here from those of Whallon stem from this change and from his ambiguous use of the letter j for two parameters.

To determine the scale(s) at which potentially significant clustering of artifacts occurs, a plot is made of the observed variance:mean ratios against block size. If artifacts are perfectly randomly arranged within the study area, the variance:mean ratios will equal 1 at all block sizes, as in the Poisson approach (Greig-Smith 1964:86). A negative deviation from this value indicates a tendency toward uniform alignment at the block size of the deviation, whereas a positive one indicates a tendency toward clustering at the corresponding block size.

For a clustered arrangement, the height of a peak in the graph indicates the *intensity* of clusters having a scale corresponding to the block size of the peak, comparable to that of other peaks in the graph (Greig-Smith 1961:698). The measure can not, however, be used to compare the intensity of clustering within different study areas overlain with grids of the same mesh yet having different mean numbers of items per original grid cell. For this purpose, a measure proposed by Hill (1973:227) may be used:

$$I_{jk} = (V_{jk} - m_k)/m_k^2 \tag{3.6}$$

where I_{jk} is the intensity of the clustered pattern in study area k using blocks of size 2^j cells, V_{jk} is the variance in number of items among the blocks in area k, as calculated above, and m_k is the mean number of items per original grid cell in area k.

Additional information in a plot of variance:mean ratios against block size pertains to the spread of a peak over a number of block sizes. This indicates the *range* of *sizes* of clusters (Greig-Smith 1961:698–699) of one hierarchical level or multiple levels. If a trend in artifact density occurs over the site, within which there is clustering, the graph of variance:mean ratio against block size will exhibit a steady rise at larger block sizes that may mask patterning at some scales. To avoid this circumstance, it is necessary to make the spatial arrangement stationary in mean density (Greig-Smith 1961:700), using any of a number of methods (e.g., trend surface analysis, spatial filtering).

To test statistically whether a spatial arrangement, as a whole, departs from random expectation, considering all scales of arrangement, confidence intervals for the variance:mean ratios at various block sizes can be constructed and overlain on the graph of ratios vs. block sizes. Deviation of one or more peaks beyond the intervals indicates nonrandom tendancies. Confidence intervals of 95% are provided in tables by Greig-Smith (1961, 1964). Intervals having other significance levels can be constructed using the method of Thompson (1958). It is based on the fact that for a random arrangement, having a Poisson distribution with unit variance, the sums of squares calculated in equation 3.5 have an approximately χ^2 distribution with 2^j degrees of freedom, and the sought variances a $\chi^2/2^j$ distribution.

The confidence interval approach of Greig-Smith and Thompson has the disadvantage that it does not allow the testing of individual peaks in the graph for nonrandomness at scales of several block sizes. Only the distribution as a whole can be assessed (Mead 1974:298), a point that Whallon (1973:275) mistakens. To test for nonrandomness at each block size, Mead (1974:298–302) provides three alternative approaches, all based on whether the counts of items in blocks partition or combine randomly within the nested hierarchy of blocks.

The above analysis is performed on each artifact type separately to determine how its form of arrangement varies with scale and to assess the scale of clusters, if they occur. To define depositional sets, correlation analysis between artifact types can be performed, with grid-cell counts grouped at that block size exhibiting significant clustering for the greatest number of artifacts (Whallon 1973).

Use of the grouped cell counts to calculate correlation coefficients among artifact types, though common practice in archaeological applications, is not the most preferable approach to defining correlations among types. The resulting coefficients will necessarily reflect the covariation of types not only at the scale of blocking, but also at all larger scales. To obtain measures of correlation among types pertaining to only the scale of interest, dimensional analysis of covariance procedures (Kershaw 1960, 1961) may be used. The procedures require the determination of the dimensional partitioned variances of counts of each type ($S_j/(T/2^j)$) among cells and blocks of various sizes, as in DAV, plus the partitioned variances of the *combined* counts of each pair of types. The correlation between any two types, A and B, at each scale of blocking and attributable to covariation at that scale, alone, then can be determined as

$$r_j = \frac{V_{AJ+BJ} - V_{AJ} - V_{BJ}}{2/V_{AJ}V_{BJ}} \tag{3.7}$$

where r_j is the sought correlation at the scale of blocks with 2^j cells, V_{AJ} and V_{BJ} are the partitioned variances of counts of types A and B at that scale, and V_{AJ+BJ} is the partitioned variance of the combined counts of types A and B at that scale.

The mathematical procedures of dimensional analysis of variance and covariance can be applied to transect as well as two-dimensional grid data, to find the simple average linear dimensions of clusters in some one direction (Kershaw 1957; Greig-Smith 1961:696, 1964:87). Quadrats along the transect are expanded into blocks in the same way as the two dimensional situation, but with the potential for blocks to be any multiple of the original quadrats in size rather than simply multiples of two (Hill 1973:228). Multiple, parallel transects, dispersed or contiguous, may be used. In the latter case, two dimensional gridded data are envisioned as a series of transects, with grid expansion restricted to one dimension. The procedure may be repeated, expanding in the second dimension of the grid.

Dimensional analysis of variance circumvents only some of the problems mentioned previously as being inherent to the variance:mean ratio approach to evaluating form of arrangement, for it is similar to a series of concatentated VMR tests. Most of the technical problems encumbered by the VMR test, including dependence of the accuracy of results on the shape of the observed distribution, inaccuracy at very low item densities, and assessment of the frequency distribution rather than spatial arrangement of items among grid cells (Problems 2–4, above), also plague DAV to the same degree. DAV is limited equally by the archaeological requirement that artifact classes have low volumetric densities (Problem 5, above).

The method offers some improvements over the VMR test in its requirements of several aspects of the organization of the archaeological record, but these are only partial (see Table 3.4).

Problems 6 and 10, above. The method only partially circumvents the erroneous assumption that all clusters are of one specified scale, equivalent to the mesh of the grid. (1) It is constraining in requiring the size of clusters, if they exist, to be some multiple of two times the original grid mesh if two dimensional grid methods are used, or any multiple if transect methods are used (Hill 1973:228). If the sizes of clusters fall in between the required multiples of the original grid, the block sizes at which significant clustering is found will be larger than the actual scales of clustering (Figure 3.7). (2) It also is preferable if the sizes of clusters are distributed modally over the block sizes investigated, rather than continuously, so that one or a few scales of significant clustering can be found. This is not strictly a *requirement* of the technique, however; if clusters range continuously in size, the graph of variance:mean ratios against block sizes will indicate this circumstance accurately.

Problems 7 and 11, above. To a minimum extent, limitation on the shape of clusters by the VMR test is lifted in DAV. Clusters need not approximate squares. However, it still is assumed, if two dimensional grid methods are used, that clusters tend to be rectangular with lengths equal to or twice their width and that all clusters of one type are the same shape. Similar restrictions hold if transect methods are used, only the length of the clusters may be any multiple of their width. To the extent that these restrictions are not true, significant clustering will be found at block sizes larger than the areas of clusters (Figure 3.7).

Problems 8 and 12, above. When clusters are not centered in grid cells and their counts are partitioned among multiple cells, DAV will correctly detect clustering whereas the VMR test may not. The scale at which clustering is

shape of cluster   orientation of cluster   placement of cluster

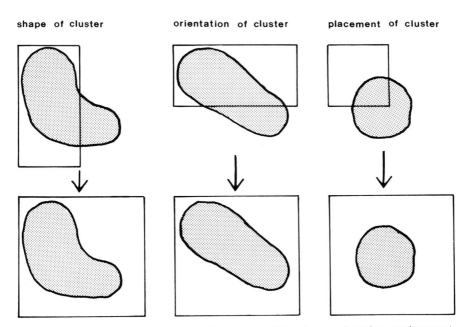

Figure 3.7. Discordance between a grid system and the shape, orientation, or placement of artifacts will cause clustering to be found at erroneously large block sizes when dimensional analysis of variance is applied.

indicated, however, will be erroneously large by *at least* 2–4 times that which would be found if the clusters were centered within cells using two-dimensional grid methods. Using transect methods, the determined scale of clustering will be 2 times the true scale.

Problems 9 and 13, above. A minimal allowance is made in DAV for differences in the orientation of clusters compared to that of the grid. When grid cells are grouped into blocks, some of which are rectangular (blocks of 2, 8, and 32 cells), rectangles may be oriented horizontally or vertically. Two analyses can be done per artifact type, one lumping cells horizontally, the other vertically. Those analyses providing graphs of variance: mean ratio against block size with the clearest peaks then are used to determine the scale(s) of clustering of artifacts. Although this procedure allows some flexibility in the orientation of clusters, it is still quite constraining: orientation can be in only two directions, determined a priori by and corresponding with the alignment of the grid, and all clusters must have a similar orientation. If this is not true, significant clustering will be found at scales one to several block sizes larger than the size of clusters (Figure 3.7). A similar problem holds when transect methods are applied to two dimensional gridded data, only clustering may be found at scales intermediate between the length and width of clusters.

Problem 14, above. The primary improvement of DAV over the VMR test is that it allows multiple scales to be investigated for the form of arrangement of items, thereby acknowledging that clusters may be organized into multilevel hierarchies. Again, however, the scales that can be investigated are limited.

Dimensional analysis of variance involves a number of *additional* problems that do not encumber the VMR test, most of which are technical in nature.

Additional Problem 1. The mesh of the original grid has a strong effect on the scale at which patterning is detected. This is so for two reasons. (1) The minimum size of cluster that can be detected effectively by the technique is twice the size of the original grid (Kershaw 1957). (2) As block sizes increase geometrically, so do *differences* in the mesh of grids derived from different original grid systems.

Additional Problem 2. The degree of precision with which the scale of clustering can be specified decreases geometrically as the size of clusters increases. This results from the doubling of block sizes at each step of the analysis. Thus, for example, a peak in the graph of variance:mean ratio versus block size at block size 2 would indicate clusters of 1–4 units in size, whereas a peak at block size 16 would indicate a much wider potential range of cluster sizes, 8–32 units.

Additional Problem 3. Accuracy of analysis—specifically, the estimates of variance—decreases as block size increases. This results from halving the degrees of freedom (numbers of blocks) with each step (Pielou 1977:142). Consequently, at larger block sizes, confidence intervals must be much wider, and peaks indicative of clustering may be assessed insignificant.

Additional Problem 4. The graph of variance:mean ratios against block size often has a sawtoothed shape, making assessment of the significance of peaks unreliable. This noise results from alternating between blocks having square and those having rectangular shapes. Oblong blocks consistently give lower mean squares than do square blocks (Pielou 1977:142). All of these problems, save 1a, are less encumbering or do not occur when using transect methods of analysis. In this case, blocks can be any multiple of the original grid mesh and the grid is expanded in only one direction.

Additional Problem 5. Dimensional analysis of variance also is discordant with the organization of the archaeological record in one way that the VMR test is not. DAV requires a square or rectangular study area. Most behaviorally significant archaeological units (e.g., sites, portions of sites used for broad classes of activities) are not of this shape. Technically, it is possible to achieve analysis by "filling out" a natural area with extra grid cells of zero counts until the required shape is obtained. This, however, may cause patterning to appear at erroneous block sizes (Price 1975:211).

Morisita's Method

Dimensional analysis of variance represents the first attempt made by plant ecologists (Greig-Smith 1952b) to cope with the problems of the VMR and χ^2 tests in assessing the form of arrangement of items over space. Excluding Mead's test of significance, however, DAV is still a Poisson-based approach, having many of the difficulties of that approach. More recent advances not utilizing the Poisson distribution but following the dimensional strategy of DAV include Morisita's method (Morisita 1959, 1962; Stiteler and Patil 1971) and Goodall's method (Goodall 1974; Pielou 1977:142). Of these, only the former has been applied archaeologically (Price 1975; Brose and Scarry 1976).

Archaeological literature does not explain the mathematical basis of Morisita's method. This is done here so that the potential of the method for archaeological applications then may be evaluated. Following Pielou's (1977:139) discussion, Morisita's method is based on Simpson's (1949) measure of diversity. If each cell of a grid is imagined to be of a different nature, having items of different kinds, then the probability of choosing at random (without replacement) two items of the same kind (from the same cell) is

$$\delta_0 = \frac{\sum_{i=1}^{q} x_i(x_i - 1)}{N(N - 1)} \qquad (3.8)$$

where x_i is the number of items in cell i, there being q cells and N items in total. If items are aggregated in only a few cells, and the diversity of kinds of items is low, the probability, δ_0, of obtaining two items of the same kind will be high. If items are dispersed uniformly among cells and there is great diversity in the kinds of items, δ_0 will be low.

To obtain an index relating the observed δ_0 to its expected value given a random level of diversity (random arrangement of items among grid cells), it is noted that for such an arrangement, the probability of selecting one individual from a given quadrat is $1/q$ and two individuals from the same quadrat is $1/q^2$. The expected value for the probability δ, then, summing over all q cells, is $\delta_e = q(1/q^2) = 1/q$. Morisita's Index, relating the degree of observed aggregation or dispersion to that expected for a random distribution is defined as

$$I_{\delta_q} = \frac{\delta_0}{\delta_e} \tag{3.9}$$

$$= \frac{\sum_{i=1}^{q} x_i(x_i - 1)}{N(N - 1)} \Big/ (1/q) \tag{3.10}$$

$$= q \left[\frac{\sum_{i=1}^{q} x_i(x_i - 1)}{N(N - 1)} \right] \tag{3.11}$$

This index constitutes a relative measure for comparing arrangement between study units having the same area and examined with the same mesh grid. It takes the value 1 for a random arrangement of items. It ranges from greater than 1 to q (the number of cells/study area) for more aggregated arrangements, and from 1 to 0 for more dispersed arrangements.

Using the strategy of dimensional analysis of variance, Morisita's Index may be calculated for blocks of 2, 4, 8, . . . 2^j . . T adjacent grid cells. A graph of I_{δ_q} against block size will have a shape characteristic of the form of arrangement of items (Figure 3.8). If the plot indicates clustering of items, it is possible to determine the scale of clusters and whether multiple levels of clustering occur by plotting a graph of $I_{\delta_{(2j)}}/I_{\delta_{(2j+1)}}$ against block size 2^{j+1} (Morisita 1959:230), or preferably 2^j (Price 1975:210). The ratio of $I_{\delta_{(2j)}}/I_{\delta_{(2j+1)}}$ will indicate changes in the slope of the graph of I_{δ_q} against block size, some of which pinpoint the scale of clusters. Using a plot of the ratio rather than I_{δ_q} is preferable for two reasons. First, it emphasizes more clearly the block size at which clustering occurs. Second, $I_{\delta_{(2j)}}$ varies as a function of the number of blocks considered as well as form of arrangement; the effect of the former can be approximately factored out

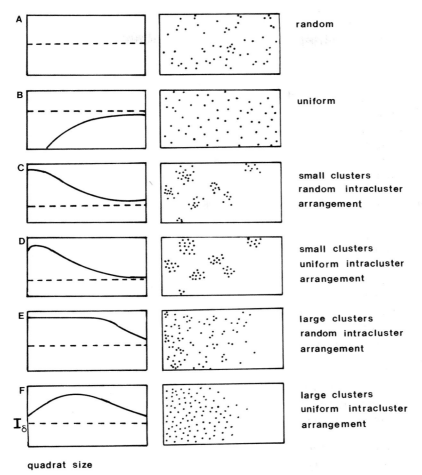

quadrat size

Figure 3.8. Variation in Morisita's Index with quadrat size for item-scatters of several arrangements.

by dividing $I_{\delta_{(2j)}}$ by $I_{\delta_{(2j+1)}}$. A plot of this form can be interpreted like one made with DAV, with peaks identifying potential scales of clustering.

An absolute assessment of the degree of deviation of an arrangement of items at a given block size from a random arrangement may be made using an F test. The statistic

$$F - \text{stat} = \frac{I_{\delta_{(2j)}} (N - 1) + 2^j - N}{2^j - 1} \qquad (3.12)$$

will have an $F (q - 1, \infty)$ distribution if items are arranged randomly (Morisita 1959:221). For a chosen level of significance, α, a value of F − stat greater than $F_{(1-\alpha)} (q - 1, \infty)$ will indicate significant aggregation, and a value less than $F_{(\alpha)}$ $(q - 1, \infty)$ will indicate significant alignment. This F test of Morisita's Index is equivalent to the χ^2/df test used by Brose and Scarry (1976:189).

Morista's method offers some, but hardly a complete improvement over DAV. The measure of relative assessment of arrangement, because it is not founded on the Poisson distribution, is not hampered with most of the technical problems of DAV and the VMR test associated with the Poisson strategy (Problems 2 and 3, page 142). One exception is that it assesses the distribution of counts (variability in counts) among grid cells rather than the spatial arrangement of counts. As a consequence, some clustered arrangements can erroneously be identified as random. Morisita's absolute test of the arrangement of items, on the other hand, is not as free of technical constraints as is his relative method. The test is simply a restatement of the VMR test in terms of Morisita's Index (Stiteler and Patil 1971:446). It is encumbered with all of the technical problems of that test (problems 2–4, page 142). Additionally, all the technical problems and erroneous assumptions about the nature of the archaeological record specific to DAV, related to expanding the mesh of a two dimensional grid, encumber Morisita's approach (see Table 3.4 and pages 148–151).

Empirically, the results of Morisita's method have been compared to those of DAV for at least two archaeological data sets (Price 1975; Brose and Scarry 1976). In both instances, the methods produced comparable results. Price (1975:211), however, notes that in plots of the two measures of aggregation against block size, when multiple scales of clustering are apparent, Morisita's measure emphasizes the significance of clustering at the lower scales, whereas DAV exaggerates the significance of clustering at the larger scales.

First-Order Nearest Neighbor Statistics

When the point locations of artifacts within a site are known, rather than simply their counts in grid cells, it is possible to assess their form of arrangement using nearest neighbor statistics. The nearest neighbor statistics were developed by plant geographers to assess community patterning (Clark and Evans 1954; Thompson 1956; Pielou 1959, 1960) and more recently have been applied by geographers to problems of locational analysis (e.g., Getis 1964; Haggett 1965; Pinder 1971). In archaeology, they have been used primarily for the analysis of regional site distributions (Adams and Nissen 1972; Earle 1976; Hodder 1972; Hodder and Hassal 1971; Hodder and Orton 1976; Plog 1974; Washburn 1974; Zubrow 1971). They have been applied less frequently to artifact distributions within sites (Brose and Scarry 1976; Graybill 1976; Price 1975; Trubowitz 1978; Whallon 1974).

Nearest neighbor analysis begins with a *finite* plane of unrestricted area A, unrestricted shape, and scattered with N items to be assessed for the form of their arrangement *relative to the size of their framing area*. The scatter of items is characterized by its density, d, within the framing area,

$$d = N/A, \tag{3.12}$$

and by the average distance $\bar{r}_0$, between nearest neighbor items within the plane,

$$\bar{r}_0 = \frac{\sum_{i=1}^{N} r_i}{N}, \tag{3.13}$$

where r_i is the distance from each item to its nearest neighbor.

The form of arrangement of items over the plane is assessed by comparing the *empirical* average nearest neighbor distance between items to the average distance between nearest neighbor items expectable if an *infinite* number of items were scattered at the same density in a random pattern over an *infinite* plane. The expected average nearest neighbor distance, $\bar{r}_e$, between items is calculated by

$$\bar{r}_e = 1/(2\sqrt{d}) \tag{3.14}$$

The comparison between the observed and expected average nearest neighbor distances is given by the *nearest neighbor statistic, R,* where

$$R = \frac{\bar{r}_0}{\bar{r}_e}. \tag{3.15}$$

R will be approximately equal to 1 if items are scattered randomly across the whole framing area. If they tend to cluster within the frame, the nearest neighbor statistic will tend toward its minimum possible value, 0, for a perfectly clustered arrangement. As items become more evenly spaced (systematically aligned), R will tend toward its maximum value 2.149, for a perfectly aligned arrangement.

The statistical significance of deviations of the arrangement of a scatter of items from a random scatter may be determined by calculating the following test statistic,

$$C - \text{stat} = \frac{\bar{r}_0 - \bar{r}_e}{\sigma_{\bar{r}_e}} \tag{3.16}$$

where

$$\sigma_{\bar{r}_e} = .26136/\sqrt{Nd} \tag{3.17}$$

A value of $C - \text{stat}$ less than $-z_{(1-\alpha)}$ will indicate significant clustering at the α level of significance, whereas a value greater than $z_{(1-\alpha)}$ will indicate significant alignment. The tests of significance should be one-sided, as given, if the direction of departure from randomness is of concern (most instances). If not, then a two-sided test should be used.

This test for deviations from randomness requires the assumption that nearest neighbor distances are distributed normally when items are scattered randomly. This is true only for large N, greater than 100. For random scatters with fewer items, nearest neighbor distances are positively skewed, resembling a Pearson's type III distribution. Thus, when N is less than 100 items, test statistic values should be compared to Pearson's III distribution rather than to normal tables (Clark and Evans 1954:448) (The opposite condition is mistakenly stated by Whallon 1974:19).

A preferred alternative for measuring the significance of departure of an arrangement of items from a random pattern is the χ^2 test (Dacey 1963; Whallon 1974). For the test statistic

$$\chi^2 - \text{stat} = 2\pi d \sum_{i=1}^{N} r_i^2 \tag{3.18}$$

a value less than $\chi^2_{(\alpha)}(\text{df})$ indicates significant clustering at the α level of significance, whereas a value greater than $\chi^2_{(1-\alpha)}(\text{df})$ indicates significant alignment. The appropriate degrees of freedom are $2N$. If the number of items within the scatter is greater than 15, the χ^2 statistic can be converted to a standard normal variate

$$S - \text{stat} = \sqrt{2\chi^2 - \text{stat}} - \sqrt{2(2N) - 1} \tag{3.19}$$

and the new statistic can be compared to normal tables. A value of $S - \text{stat}$ less than $-z_{(1-\alpha)}$ indicates significant clustering at the α level of significance, whereas a value greater than $z_{(1-\alpha)}$ indicates significant alignment. Whallon (1974) found the χ^2 test of significance more conservative in assessing spatial distributions as clustered than the Clark and Evans statistics for one archaeological application.

When applied to scatters of items of a finite number, including artifact distributions, the nearest neighbor statistics just outlined provide biased assessments of item arrangement. The bias can result from two problems: a *framing problem*, which can be circumvented by appropriate application of the technique, and a *boundary problem* inherent in the statistics.

The framing problem refers to the fact that the value of the nearest neighbor statistic determined for a scatter of items varies greatly with the size of the area within which it is framed. If a scatter of items is systematically arranged, R can range from values suggesting clustering (when a frame much larger than the scatter is used), through values indicating randomness (when a somewhat oversized frame is used), to values indicating systematic alignment (when the frame is the size of the scatter or smaller) (Hsu and Tiedemann 1968). If the scatter of items exhibits a random arrangement, R can range from values suggesting clustering (for an oversized frame) through values indicating randomness (for a frame coincident with or smaller than the cluster).

Previously, several authors (Clark and Evans 1954:450; Pinder *et al.* 1979: 435) have suggested that the framing problem can be circumvented by placing the analytical frame ''well within'' the scatter of items to be evaluated. Additionally, the frame would have to be large enough to encompass several clusters, should the distribution be a clustered one, or a number of items (as many as possible), should the distribution be random or aligned, to ensure an adequate sample of the arrangement. Clearly, however, this approach is appropriate only when the scatter of items is *uniformly* clustered, random, or aligned throughout, as opposed to *hierarchically* arranged, with different or similar forms of arrangement at different geographic scales (see Figure 3.3). Only if the scatter is similarly arranged throughout will any *one* frame of one large size, placed anywhere within the scatter and sampling only a portion of its arrangement, always accurately assess the nature of the scatter.

In many archaeological circumstances, this is not the case, and the solution to the framing problem offered by Clark and Evans and Pinder *et al.* is not appropriate. Activity areas and artifact scatters may be hierarchically arranged, with different forms of arrangement at different hierarchical levels (see pages 130–131; Figure 3.4). Under these conditions, the results of a nearest neighbor analysis will vary with the size and placement of the frame.

The only universally applicable solution to the framing problem is to ensure that the area of interest is behaviorally meaningful and that the boundary of the analytical frame coincides with the boundary of that area. Only under this condition will the form of arrangement of items be assessed relative to an area of meaningful scale and will all local arrangements within the scatter contribute to the estimate of its overall arrangement.

The boundary problem results from a discordance between assumptions and operations used in deriving the nearest neighbor statistics, regardless of how the scatter to be analyzed is framed. The expected average nearest neighbor distance, $\bar{r}_e$, is calculated for an *infinite* number of items postulated to occur over a plane of *infinite* expanse, including the study area, at a density equal to item density inside the study area. The postulated items inside the study area have extant counterparts. Those outside the study area and near its border may or may not have extant counterparts, depending, respectively, on whether the analytical frame lies within the scatter of items being investigated, or whether it coincides with or is larger than the scatter. In contrast, the observed average nearest neighbor distance, $\bar{r}_0$, is calculated for a finite number of extant items within the *finite* area of the study unit, alone, irrespective of postulated items outside the study area. Thus, in calculating $\bar{r}_0$, the boundary of the study area severs some theoretical connections between real items just inside the area and their postulated nearest neighbors outside the area (with or without real counterparts). The theoretical, severed connections may or may not have extant counterparts, depending on the size of the frame relative to that of the scatter of items. As a result of such severed connections, for those items inside the area having nearest neighbors (extant or theoretical) outside it, the distance (r_i) found to their nearest neighbors within the area will be greater than the distance to their true nearest neighbors outside the area. The average observed nearest neighbor distance for items within the area will be inflated, as will the nearest neighbor statistic, R. This will bias against the detection of clustered arrangements.

This boundary effect will increase with: (1) a decrease in the number of items within the area of analysis (particularly as N drops below 100 for square or circular areas), or (2) an increase in the circumference of the boundary of the analytical frame compared to the area enclosed (as in the case of rectangles or amorphous frames compared to square or circular ones). With either condition, the proportion of interitem connections that are severed between nearest neighbors by the boundary will increase.

Pinder *et al.* (1979) and McNutt (1981) explain the boundary problem in terms that assume the area of analysis occurs within the scatter of interest and that all severed connections are existing ones. The problem, however, also occurs when the area of analysis includes the scatter of interest completely, and the severed connections are theoretically postulated ones. The problem results from the discrepancy between the theoretically infinite scatter of items assumed to calculate $\bar{r}_e$ and the finite scatter of items used to calculate r_0, rather than whether extant connections, per se, are severed.

Several solutions have been offered to the boundary problem since the time of its original definition by Clark and Evans (1954). Each diminishes the problem, regardless of whether the study area lies within or surrounds the scatter of interest and whether the severed connections have real counterparts or not. Dacey (1963:505) suggests using in analysis only those items within the study area that are located more than a specified distance from its boundary and that could not possibly have severed connections with nearest neighbors. This approach overcorrects for the boundary effect, producing a deflated R. Hodder and Orton (1976:41) approximately offset the effect of severed connections by surrounding the study area with randomly placed points at the same density as items within it and allowing the points to serve as nearest neighbors to items within the study area. The analysis must be repeated a number of times, with different random placements of points, to obtain an estimate of the expected value and range of potentially accurate results.

The approach of Pinder *et al.* (1979) allows a much closer estimation of the nearest neighbor statistic and the significance of its departure from values indicating randomness than the two solutions just cited. These authors have derived empirical constants for modifying the values of $\bar{r}_e$, R, and $\sigma_{\bar{r}_e}$ to compensate for the boundary effect. The approach is highly constrained, however, in requiring that the frame of analysis be square. The framing errors introduced by this requirement, when the natural area of interest is of some other shape, may offset in magnitude the accuracy gained in circumventing the boundary problem.

The most preferable solution to the boundary problem—being most precise, least constrained by assumptions, and based on mathematical theory—is that formulated by McNutt (1981). McNutt has deduced, from geometric considerations, equations specifying the number of items within a study area that can be expected to have severed connections. This figure may be used to determine *finite-corrected* values for d and $\bar{r}_e$, which may then, therefore, be compared to $\bar{r}_0$ (a finite-based statistic) with logical consistency in calculating R.

For rectangular study areas, the expected number of items, N_0, having severed connections with nearest neighbors is

$$N_0 = \frac{(s_x + s_y)\sqrt{N - 1}}{3\sqrt{A}} - \frac{1}{12}. \qquad (3.20)$$

where s_x and s_y are the lengths of the sides of the study area, N is the number of items within it, and A is its area. Analogous formulae are given for equilateral triangles, other triangles, and circular study areas. A finite corrected density then can be calculated using the formula

$$d = \frac{N - 1 - N_0}{A}. \qquad (3.21)$$

This value may be used with Equations 3.14 and 3.15 to determine an unbiased nearest neighbor statistic.

The formulae given by McNutt for determining N_0 for study areas of given shapes are not nearly as important as the equations provided by him for determining N_0 for *components* of such shapes: linear borders (equation 7), 90° corners (equation 13), 60° corners (equation 32), and circular arcs of a specified sweep (equation 40 multiplied by the proportional sweep of the arc compared to that of a full circle). These may be used in combination to approximate N_0 and finite corrected values for d and $\bar{r}_e$, for polygons of many complex shapes.

The array of analyzable, geometric study areas could be increased significantly, and particularly to the archaeologist's advantage, if an equation determining N_0 for 270° corners were available (the obtuse angle *inside* the study area). This, with the equations for linear borders and 90° corners, would allow the definition of accurate nearest neighbor statistics for complexly shaped areas approximately represented by an aggregate of squares. An important archaeological application would be to a behaviorally meaningful area approximately represented by a group of excavated units.

McNutt does not say whether his approach to correcting the nearest neighbor statistic can also be used to correct the values of $\sigma_{\bar{r}_e}$, which is underestimated by Equation 3.17 (Ebdon 1976; Pinder *et al.* 1979). Presumably, d in this equation can be calculated with Equation 3.21 and N can be reduced by 1 and N_0 to yield an accurate estimate of $\sigma_{\bar{r}_e}$. This possiblity needs to be researched.

Nearest neighbor analysis is a highly unconstrained approach to assessing the form of arrangement of artifacts within a study area (Table 3.4). As such, it has several distinct advantages over dimensional analysis of variance and Morisita's method. The nearest neighbor statistics make no assumptions about the size, shape, relative placement, or orientation of clusters of artifacts that might occur within the area of analysis. Clusters of artifacts can vary freely in these attributes without inhibiting their detection. Also, the statistics do not limit analysis, as do dimensional analytic techniques, to square or rectangular areas. An area of any shape can be analyzed, *so long as the area coincides with the boundaries of a behaviorally meaningful unit and includes all artifacts of potential meaning for that area.*

In other ways, nearest neighbor analysis is less informative or logically less consistent with the organization of intrasite archaeological records than is DAV or Morisita's method. First, nearest neighbor analysis allows evaluation of only the intensity (significance, relative density) of clustering of artifacts within a study area, not the grain (size and spacing) of artifact clusters. Dimensional analysis of variance and Morisita's method allow assessment of both. This limitation may be corrected by extending nearest neighbor procedures to include the assessment of nth-order nearest neighbor distances (see pages 183–188).

Second, artifact distributions within sites sometimes may exhibit multiple scales of clustering hierarchically organized (see pages 130–131 and Figure 3.4). Dimensional analytic methods assume that such hierarchical organization is possible and allow the significance of clustering of artifacts at multiple scales of potential clustering to be evaluated. Nearest neighbor analysis, on the other hand, assumes that the form of arrangement of items is nonhierarchically random or aligned, or if clustered, seeks evaluation of form of arrangement at only one scale—the smallest scale of potential clustering. It focuses on distances between nearest neighbor items (within clusters), and ignores distances between the centroids of aggregates of items (Figure 3.3).

This bias of first-order nearest neighbor analysis may cause misleading as well as incomplete results to be obtained. For example, suppose artifacts are distributed across a site in reflexive pairs (pairs of items both closer to each other than to other items) or in clusters of several items, as a result of artifact breakage, but the pairs or clusters themselves are distributed randomly (a hierarchical arrangement). From an interpretive standpoint concerned with the spatial organization of past activities or refuse deposits, the random arrangement of the pairs/clusters of artifacts is more important than the clustering of the individual subportions of broken items. A first-order nearest neighbor analysis of such a distribution, however, would focus on interitem patterning, finding significant clustering of the artifacts and leaving undetected the higher-level pattern of arrangement of clusters. This situation was found to be a problem by Brose and Scarry (1976) in their spatial analysis of one site. To circumvent this problem, either nth-order nearest neighbor statistics (Thompson 1956) or point-to-items statistics (Pielou 1959) may be used (see pages 183–190).

Methods for Assessing Whether Artifact Types are Co-Arranged

General Approach of the Methods

Most analytic approaches that attempt to define site-wide depositional sets involve two steps. First, the degree of co-arrangement of *pairs* of artifact types is expressed with any of a number of statistics, such as a correlation coefficient or an average nearest neighbor distance. Then, a matrix of the coefficients for all possible pairs of artifact types is subjected to a higher level pattern-searching algorithm to reveal groups of one to multiple artifact types that are more similar to each other in their spatial arrangement than they are to artifact types in other groups. The many varieties of factor analysis (Christensen and Read 1977; Davis 1973; Rummel 1970), cluster analysis (Anderberg 1973; Hartigan 1975; Sneath and Sokal 1973), multidimensional scaling (Kimbell *et al.* 1972; Kruskal and Wish 1978), and matrix ordering (Cowgill 1972; Craytor and Johnson 1968; Hole and Shaw 1967; Marquardt 1978) can be used for this purpose. In this section, the appropriateness of only the pairwise coefficients of co-arrangement to intrasite spatial analysis will be discussed.

Correlation Analysis of Grid-Cell and Block Counts

The degree of co-arrangement of artifact types within a site can be expressed with several coefficients—on nominal, ordinal, or ratio scales of measurement—when artifact locations are recorded as counts per grid cell. These coefficients include Pearson's correlation coefficient, Kendall's and Spearman's rho (rank correlation coefficients; Kendall 1948), and a variety of similarity coefficients, such as the simple matching, Jaccard, and indices of Dice and Bray (Cole 1949; Sneath and Sokal 1973). There also is choice in the frequencies of artifacts to be manipulated—those found within the original grid cells used to record the data or those within larger blocks of grid cells derived from dimensional analytic techniques.

Plant ecologists have discussed at length the relative appropriateness of the different coefficients, of working at different scales of measurement, and of using blocked or unblocked data of different spatial scales (Cole 1949; Greig-

Smith 1961, 1964; Kershaw 1964; Pielou 1969). Archaeologists have shown concern for the effect of grid cell and block size on the pattern of co-arrangement found in analysis (Hodder and Orton 1976; Whallon 1973), but generally have not appreciated the relative merits of using the different coefficients and scales of measurement in spatial analysis. Most intrasite spatial analyses using cell count data have proceeded directly on raw ratio-scale counts using the most common measure of relationship, Pearson's *r*, without considering if evaluation on that scale, using that coefficient, is justifiable in light of the characteristics of depositional sets and use-areas.

One important exception is Hietala and Stevens's (1977:540–543) discrimination of three degrees of strength in spatial relationships that may occur between artifact types (uniform, strong, weak), which correspond to ratio, ordinal, and nominal scale relationships. The significance of the different kinds of relationships in terms of behavior or archaeological formation processes, however, is not discussed. A second exception is Speth and Johnson's (1976) postulations of the impact of various kinds of depositional patterns on correlations among artifact types.

The following two sections, on correlation and association, question the validity of using these common measures of relationship in searching for depositional sets. They lay the foundation for the introduction of an alternative method (see pages 191–199).

The correlation coefficient has been used with original grid-cell counts to define depositional sets in many intrasite studies. Examples include: Brown and Freeman's (1964) pioneering application of the technique to differentiate the functions of Pueblo rooms, and works by Anderson and Shutler (1977), Freeman and Butzer (1966), Goodyear (1974), Hill (1970), Kay (1980), and Schiffer (1976). Correlation of blocked cell frequencies of artifacts has been used less commonly (e.g., Brose and Scarry 1976; Price 1975; Whallon 1973).

Pearson's correlation coefficient applied to grid-cell or block counts of artifact types, or any measure of covariation so applied, are poor indicators of the degree of co-arrangement of artifact types in most archaeological circumstances (Table 3.4). For these measures to accurately reflect co-arrangement, several characteristics of activity sets, depositional sets, and use-areas, which are inconsistent with their nature, must be true.

Condition 1. Most problematic, the activity sets sought must have been *monothetic*. At every location where a task was performed, the same artifact types must have been used. More restrictive, the artifact types used together must always have been used in similar proportions (such that their frequencies covary).

Condition 2. The artifacts must have been deposited *expediently* at their locations of use.

Condition 3. The deposited artifacts must have *remained* in their approximate locations of deposition until the time of excavation, without the polythetic-causing effects of postdepositional disturbance processes.

Condition 4. The artifact types must have been recovered completely and classified as to their function correctly.

Only if these four conditions are true will *depositional* sets by monothetic, will like use-areas have the same sets of artifact types present in them, and will the proportions of artifact types within like use-areas be similar, regardless of the duration of use of use-areas, such that measures of covariation accurately define the depositional sets.

The inverse of these conditions, more typical of the archaeological record and its formation and disturbance, will cause depositional sets to be polythetic. The proportions of artifacts of different types belonging to the same depositional set and found within use-areas of similar kind will vary among them. Covariation and correlations between the types over the several use-areas, consequently, will be weakened, inadequately measuring their co-arrangement and membership in one depositional set. For example, if an activity set were polythetic in organization, different subsets of it will have been used during different occurrences of the activity at different locations, producing like use-areas differing in the kinds and combinations of artifact types they encompass and thus, the proportions of artifact types within them. If artifacts were not deposited expediently at the locations of their use, but rather, in accord with when they *happened* to break at the locations and *happened* to be no longer repairable with efficiency, then again, different kinds of artifact types will have been deposited in different areas of use, and proportions of artifact types among like areas will vary greatly. If postdepositional disturbance processes were operative, if artifact recovery was incomplete, or if artifact classification was inaccurate, causing depositional sets to be more polythetic or appear to be more polythetic than they would be otherwise, like use-areas will have become more variable in the kinds of artifact types present in them and the proportions of artifact types within them.

Condition 5. When measures of covariation are used to define co-arrangements, the requirement that artifacts were deposited expediently may be relaxed, if another requirement is made in its place: that all activity areas were used an *extended, approximately equal period of time.* If an activity was performed numerous times at a location, if the activity set used was monothetic, and if no archaeological formation processes that cause depositional sets to be polythetic other than differential artifact breakage and curation rates operated, then the relative frequencies of artifact types deposited in that location will have stabilized over time to constant values approaching the ratios of the discard rates of those types. For a number of locations of this kind, correlation will be 'an appropriate measure of the strength of the relationship between the various artifact types. However, conditions 1, 3, and 4, above, would still have to be true. For example, if the number or intensity of polythetic-causing processes involved in the formation and disturbance of the deposits were increased and randomness in the net accumulation of the artifact types at different locations were introduced, the tendency of the locations to have the types in the same relative frequencies approaching the ratios of their discard rates over time would decrease. This would weaken correlations between artifact types in the same depositional sets. The appropriateness of correlation as a measure of the strength of relationship between artifact types would decrease.

The inadequacy of covariation as a measure of co-arrangement of artifact types, with respect to its requirements that activity sets and depositional sets be monothetic, can be illustrated in the following way. Suppose two artifact types exhibit perfect positive covariation in their grid-cell frequencies within a site, defining a monothetic depositional set. If the counts of one of the artifact types in some cells are reduced to zero (Table 3.6), grossly simulating the effect of polythetic-causing processes of formation of the archaeological record, the strength of correlation found between the two artifact types will be attenuated. The rate of attenuation will tend to be a linear function of the percentage of grid cells having frequencies reduced to zero for the one artifact type (a function of the degree of polytheticness introduced into the depositional set), if frequencies are reduced to zero at random. For a 10% increase in the number of cells with a

TABLE 3.6

Simulating Monothetic and Polythetic Depositional Set Organization[a]

Grid-cell observation number	Frequency of artifact type A	Frequency of artifact type B	Modified frequency of artifact type B
1	1	1	1
2	2	2	0
3	3	3	3
4	4	4	4
5	5	5	0
.	.	.	.
.	.	.	.
.	.	.	.
95	95	95	95
96	96	96	96
97	97	97	97
98	98	98	0
99	99	99	0
100	100	100	100

[a] In Columns 2 and 3, two artifact types, A and B, show perfect correlation in their grid-cell frequencies within a site, defining a monothetic set, AB. In Column 4, the frequencies of artifact type B in some grid cells have been modified to grossly simulate the polythetic organization of depositional set AB. The two artifact types show less than perfect correlation in their grid-cell frequencies within the site, as a result of this modification.

zero count, the correlation coefficient will decrease approximately .1 units (Whallon, personal communication, 1976).

In real archaeological data, the effect of polythetic organization of depositional sets on cell counts is not as clear as that simulated. Artifact type counts are not necessarily reduced to *zero* in affected cells, but rather, are reduced by a *percentage* of the number of items expected to occur in them under the assumption of monothetic organization of depositional sets. The percentage varies from cell to cell, as the number and intensity of polythetic-causing factors that produced the effect varied spatially. As a consequence of the nonsystematic nature of the disturbing variation, screening methods bringing concordance between data structure and technique, including identification of the affected cells and removal of them from analysis or correcting their counts, become difficult to operationalize.

Condition 6. Measures of covariation will accurately assess the degree of co-arrangement of artifact types belonging to multiple depositional sets only when the depositional sets and activity sets from which they are derived are non-overlapping. Suppose an activity set is monothetic and expediently deposited, producing a monothetic depositional set. If none of the artifact types within the activity set are shared with other activity sets, each artifact type will be used and deposited at each location of activity in the same proportions. The correlations between the artifact types within the set will equal $+1$. If one of the artifact types within the set is shared with a second set used in different locations from the first, the shared artifact type will be deposited more widely than the other members of either the first or second set (Figure 3.9). At the various locations at which the shared type is deposited, the artifact types with which it co-occurs, and their proportions, will vary. Consequently, the correlation of the shared type and the other members of either of the activity sets to which it belongs will be less than 1. For example, in Figure 3.9, artifact type X is shared by two activity sets (XO, XAB). The ratio of artifact type counts X:O would be 1:1 in all locations, and the correlation between types X and O would be 1, if type X were not a member of activity set XAB. Because it is, however, the ratio of artifact type counts X:O varies between 1:0 (where X occurs with members of activity set XAB) and 1:1 (where X occurs with members of activity set XO). The correlation between types X and O, consequently, is less than 1. This effect of overlap among activity sets and depositional sets has been noted previously by Speth and Johnson (1976).

Condition 7. Spatial overlap of activity areas and use-areas does not affect the accuracy of correlation and other measures of covariation as measures of co-arrangement of artifact types. As the debris generated from multiple kinds of activities overlap more and more, the identity of the separate activity sets becomes less pronounced in the matrix of correlation coefficients, which becomes dominated by strong positives between members of different activity sets as well

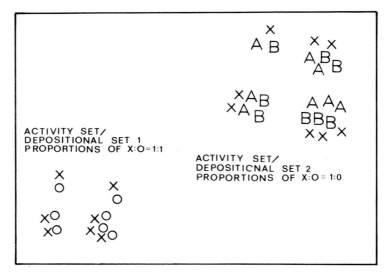

Figure 3.9. When an artifact type is shared by two activity sets, the kinds of artifacts and their proportions, deposited where the shared type was used, will vary.

as members of the same activity sets. This is as would be expected (assuming activity sets are monothetic and nonoverlapping).

The response of the correlation coefficient to spatial intermingling of artifact types from separate activity sets obviously does not facilitate the detection of depositional sets that reflect activity sets. This, however, is not to be expected of the technique. No analytic method can find sets of artifacts that initially were manufactured, used, or stored separately *after* they have become spatially intermixed to a large extent (Schiffer 1975c).

The inability of Pearson's *r* and other measures of covariation to accurately describe the degree of co-arrangement of artifact types and their organization into polythetic, overlapping depositional sets, as a result of the inadequacies of the measure mentioned previously, is suggested by recent findings by Whallon (1979, in press). Whallon found that across the occupation floor of a hunter–gatherer camp, from locale to locale, patterns of correlation among artifact types varied. This is precisely what would be expected if the degree of polytheticness and degree of overlapping of activity sets and depositional sets varied over space, and if different use-areas were used for different lengths of time.

Additional problems in using correlation analysis to define the degree of co-arrangement of artifact types stem from the use of grid-cell counts (or block counts when concatenated with DAV or Morisita's method.

Condition 8. The use of grid cells of one size requires that all artifact clusters, the same or different in kind, be the same size—that of the cells—if correlation analysis is to be accurate. When grid cells or blocks are larger than clusters and may encompass clusters of different kinds, the correlations between artifact types belonging to *different* depositional sets (and clusters) may become *greater* than the correlations would be if cells of the size of the clusters were used (Figure 3.10). There will be no effect upon correlations between artifact types in the same depositional sets (clusters). The net result will be a decrease in the distinctness of depositional sets in the matrix of correlation coefficients. When cells are smaller than clusters, the correlations between types belonging to different depositional sets (and clusters) will not be affected. The correlations between artifact types belonging to the same depositional set may increase, stay the same, or decrease, depending on the degree and pattern of internal homogeneity of clusters, and where cells fall within the clusters encompassing them (Figure 3.11). Kershaw (1964:112) illustrates such changing patterns of correlation among clustered items of different types using ecological data.

Application of dimensional analysis of variance or Morisita's method with

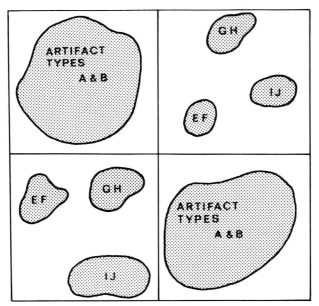

Figure 3.10. Block sizes are larger than clusters of artifacts forming depositional sets EF, GH, and IJ. Correlations between these artifact types, within different depositional sets, (E versus G, H, I, J; F versus G, H, I, J; G versus E, F, I, J; H versus E, F, I, J; I versus E, F, G, H; J versus E, F, G, H) will be inflated because items of kinds belonging to different depositional sets are lumped in the same blocks. Correlations between artifact types within the same depositional sets (E versus F, G versus H, I versus J) will not be affected by the larger block sizes.

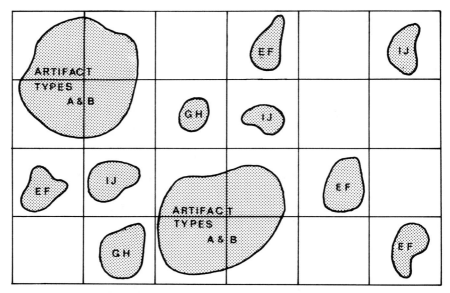

Figure 3.11. Block sizes are smaller than clusters of artifacts forming depositional set AB. Correlations between these two artifact types, within the same depositional set, may be inflated, accurate, or deflated, depending on the pattern of variation in artifact composition within clusters and where blocks fall within them.

grid expansion in two dimensions, allowing counts per arbitrarily sized grid cells to be grouped into counts per blocks approximating the scale of natural clusters, may lessen these problems, but usually will not totally circumvent them for two reasons. (1) Because the sizes of blocks in dimensional analytic techniques are *doubled* at each stage of analysis, the degree of precision with which grid cells can be scaled to clusters decreases geometrically as the size of clusters increases. Correlations between pairs of artifact types will be biased in the manner just described to the extent that they occur in clusters that are large and do not correspond in size to some multiple of the mesh of the original grid. (2) Artifacts of the same or different types may exhibit significant clustering at different scales. However, in dimensional analytic methods, only one block size, usually that at which most artifact types show significant clustering (Whallon 1973), can be used to perform the correlation analysis between all pairs of types. As a consequence, those pairs of artifact types exhibiting clustering at scales other than the chosen block size will have biased correlations.

Condition 9. Square grid cells or square or rectangular blocks, which are taken to represent one cluster or one void each, are at best crude approximations of the shapes and orientations of such natural areas. Correlations between artifact types will be biased to the extent that this is not true. When artifact types of several depositional sets form clusters that weave in and out of grid cells (Figure 3.12), correlations among types within different sets will be increased above those that would be found if the borders of clusters and cells corresponded. This results from the lumping of artifacts from different depositional sets in the same cells. Correlations among artifact types within the same depositional sets may be slightly augmented, unaltered, or slightly deflated, compared to those that would be found if the borders of clusters and grid cells corresponded, depending on the degree and pattern of internal homogeneity of the clusters. The net effect of both of these kinds of bias will be a decrease in the distinctness of depositional sets within the correlation matrix.

Condition 10. Use of gridded (unblocked or blocked) data assumes that clusters are spaced systematically with respect to each other and the grid, such that their centers fall in the centers of grid cells and each cluster occurs within only one cell. (a) If clusters, instead, fall between several grid cells (Figure 3.6), correlations between artifact types in the same depositional set may be inflated, remain the same, or be deflated, depending on the degree of internal homogeneity of clusters. Correlations between types in different sets will not be affected as long as clusters of different kinds do not fall in the same cells, as a result of off-centering. (b) If dimensional analytic techniques are applied to data where grid

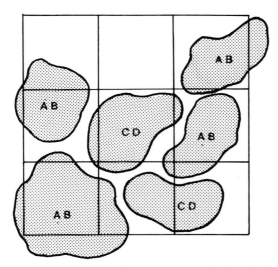

Figure 3.12. The borders of clusters do not correspond to the borders of blocks. The correlation between artifact types in different depositional sets (A versus C, D; B versus C, D) will be inflated above those that would be found if borders of clusters and blocks corresponded. As a result of the lumping of artifacts from different depositional sets in the same blocks, correlations between artifact types within the same depositional sets (A versus B; C versus D) will be only slightly affected.

and cluster spacings do not correspond, significant clustering will be found at block sizes one or more units larger than the scale of clusters (see pages 149–150). When counts are grouped at this oversized scale (Figure 3.13), correlations among types belonging to different depositional sets may be increased, whereas those among types in the same depositional sets will be unaffected. The net effect may be a decrease in the distinctness of depositional sets within the correlation matrix.

Association Analysis of Grid Cell and Block Counts

At the nominal scale of measurement, where counts of artifact types per grid cell have been reduced to presence/absence states, or dichotomized high-count/low-count states using some count threshold, patterns of association and co-arrangement among artifact types may be investigated by three means. In the realm of statistical tests, the χ^2 test of independence, using a contingency table of the form shown in Table 3.7, may be applied to original grid-cell counts or blocked data. The χ^2 statistic, with Yate's continuity correction,

$$\chi^2 - \text{stat} = \frac{(|ad - bc| - n/2)^2 n}{(a + b)(a + c)(b + d)(c + d)} \tag{3.22}$$

where a, b, c, and d are the cell values of the contingency table, can be compared to the values of the χ^2 distribution with 1 degree of freedom to test the null hypothesis of independent arrangement of dichotomized observations. A value of $\chi^2 - \text{stat}$ greater than $\chi^2_{(1-\alpha)}$ (1) indicates significant spatial association or segregation of the pair of artifact types at the α level. To use this test, the

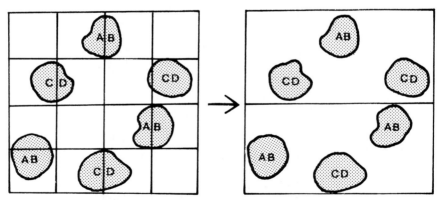

Figure 3.13. If dimensional analytic techniques are applied to data where grid and cluster spacings do not correspond, significant clustering will be found at block sizes larger than the scale of clustering. Grouping of counts of artifact types from different depositional sets within the same blocks at this oversized scale will cause correlations among types in different sets to increase, whereas those among types in the same set will be unaffected.

TABLE 3.7

Contingency Table for Generating the χ^2 Statistic, Testing Whether Artifact Types Associate

	Artifact type Y		Row
	+	−	totals
+ Artifact type X	A NUMBER OF GRID CELLS WITH BOTH TYPES PRESENT	B NUMBER OF GRID CELLS WITH TYPE X PRESENT AND TYPE Y ABSENT	A + B
−	C NUMBER OF GRID CELLS WITH TYPE X ABSENT AND TYPE Y PRESENT	D NUMBER OF GRID CELLS WITH BOTH TYPES ABSENT	C + D
Column totals	A + C	B + D	N

expected value of counts in the *a, b, c,* and *d* cells must all be greater than 5, requiring minimally 20 grid cells for analysis. If the number of observations are fewer, a χ^2 test of independence based on information statistics (Kullback *et al.* 1962) or the hypergeometric distribution (Lieberman and Owen 1961) may be used.

The χ^2 test of independence was applied in spatial analysis originally by plant geographers (Cole 1949; Pielou 1969) and geographers (Dacey 1968). More recently, it has been applied to archaeological data by Dacey (1973), and Dekin (1976:84); and by Hietala and Stevens (1977), who employed the hypergeometric distribution. Dichotomized high-count/low-count states were used rather than presence/absence states by Dacey and by Hietala and Stevens, the former using the mean of cell counts and the latter, the median of cell counts, as the dichotomizing threshold for each artifact type.

The χ^2 test allows arrangements of *pairs* of artifact types to be tested for their independence but does not provide a way for defining depositional sets composed of only one through many artifact types. To define depositional sets, an additional step must be taken, using the second or third approach now discussed.

Cook (1976) has drawn upon the ideas of formal analysis (e.g., Brown 1971; Peebles 1971; Saxe 1970) and has developed a means for defining depositional sets using Venn diagrams as the particular "artificial language" (Gardin 1965) selected for analysis. A table of dichotomized states for each variable (artifact type) over a number of cases (grid cells) is used formally to construct Venn diagrams depicting a series of sets of tools that repeatedly co-occur and that may be overlapping. The method was applied by Cook to the regional analysis of tool kits distributed among sites but also is applicable to intrasite analysis. The method is not powerful, in that it requires mental pattern recognition processes to construct the Venn diagrams rather than mathematical algorithms that can focus on complex data patterning.

A third approach to spatial analysis with nominal data, allowing the definition of depositional sets, involves measuring the degree of co-arrangement of artifact types with a "similarity coefficient" and then grouping types into depositional sets on the basis of their similarity, using cluster analysis, multidimensional scaling, or matrix ordering. Analysis begins with the construction of a contingency table of the form used in χ^2 analysis (Table 3.7) for each possible pair of artifact types, based on dichotomized grid-cell or block counts. Using the values of the cells within each table, a "similarity coefficient" is calculated for each pair of artifact types, summarizing their degree of co-arrangement. The simple matching coefficient, Jaccard coefficient, indices of Dice and Bray, and others (Sneath and Sokal 1973) are among the most commonly used for this purpose. The various coefficients differ in the weights they attach to the a, b, c, and d cells of a contingency table. For intrasite spatial analysis, where many grid cells or blocks may lack all but a few artifact types and may have absent–absent paired states for many pairs of types, a coefficient that omits consideration of negative matches is desirable (Cole 1949; Sneath and Sokal 1973:131). The rationale for this is the same as that for screening double-zero cells from analysis in correlation analysis (Speth and Johnson 1976): one is concerned with the degree of similar placement of locations where artifact types occur as opposed to locations where they do not. The Jaccard similarity coefficient accomplishes this requirement

$$J_{xy} = \frac{a}{a + b + c} \tag{3.23}$$

where a, b, and c are the values of the a, b, and c cells in the contingency table for artifact types x and y.

The techniques of association analysis just described are somewhat more consistent with the organization of intrasite archaeological records than is correlation analysis. It was noted in the previous section that if an activity is performed numerous times at several locations, if the activity set used is monothetic, and if no archaeological formation processes causing depositional sets to be polythetic (other than differential breakage and discard rates) operate, then the relative frequencies of the artifact types accumulated at those locations will stabilize over time to constant proportions approaching the ratios of the discard rates of those types. Only under these constraints will correlation analysis accurately measure the strength of relationship between the types in the activity set and depositional set. With association analysis, some of these rigorous requirements can be relaxed. Archaeological formation processes that cause depositional sets to be polythetic (see pages 122–125) can operate on artifact types having moderate to high discard rates and spatial densities. When such processes operate on plentifully deposited artifact types, the relative frequencies of such types in different use-areas of like function may not approach constant proportions, but *their presence/absence states will tend toward occurrence*. Artifact types in the same activity set and depositional set will tend to co-occur repeatedly and associate over a number of use-areas of similar function. Thus, *assessment of co-arrangement of artifact types on the nominal scale of measurement is more appropriate than assessment on the ratio scale*.

Cook (1973:28) has emphasized this point:

> While the absolute and relative frequencies of occurrence of artifact types at an archaeological site [or within subareas of that site] are important facts to record, it does not follow that such facts are *ipso facto* relevant to the solution of the problem at hand [definition of activity sets as manifested in depositional sets].

The conditions required of the archaeological record in order to apply association analysis and obtain accurate definition of patterns of co-arrangement of artifact types, nonetheless, are still rigorous, making it less appropriate than some other techniques (Table 3.4).

Condition 1. As is true of correlation analysis, association analysis requires that activity sets in the behavioral domain were monothetic. Only if this is true can depositional sets be monothetic, with all artifact types used together always occurring together archaeologically. If an activity set and the depositional set derived from it are polythetic, lower associations between artifact types within the same depositional set will be found than if it were monothetic.

Condition 2. If activity areas were not used over extended periods of time, association analysis also requires that artifacts were deposited expediently in their locations of use, such that artifact types used together always occur together archaeologically. If this is not the case, the effects of differential breakage rates and curation rates and other formation processes will cause different subsets of the activity set to be deposited at different locations of its use. The associations found between the artifact types within the generated, polythetic depositional set thus will be lower than would occur if the artifacts had been deposited expediently. If activity areas were used for a long duration, however, expedient deposition need not have occurred. Despite the effects of processes causing depositional sets to be polythetic, the presence/absence states of all types in the same depositional set will tend toward occurrence in all locations of use and deposition of the types, as just described.

Condition 3. At least one representative of each artifact type used and deposited in a use-area must have remained there. Whereas *any* amount of postdepositional disturbance (e.g., mining) of a use-area will distort the *proportions* of artifact types within it, affecting correlations among types across areas, a fair amount of disturbance of a use-area can occur without affecting the pattern of presence/absence states within it and associations among types across areas. The amount of postdepositional disturbance that is possible without altering patterns of association will be inversely related to the density of the least frequent artifact types within the use-areas.

Condition 4. The duration of use of depositional areas need not have been long, if the activity sets used within them were monothetically organized and if artifact deposition was expedient; otherwise, depositional areas must have been used for some duration, such that the presence/absence states of all artifact types within the depositional set used in the areas stabilize at presence.

Condition 5. Depositional sets and the activity sets from which they were derived must have been nonoverlapping in organization. The rationale for this requirement is the same as that given for correlation analysis (page 165, Condition 6).

Condition 6. Spatial discreteness of activity areas is not required for association analysis to depict accurately the degree of co-arrangement of artifact types, as described for correlation analysis (pages 165–166, Condition 7).

As with correlation analysis, association analysis is plagued with the problems of analysis of grid-cell counts or block counts.

Conditions 7 and 8. Clusters must be similar to each other and to the cells or blocks used to calculate associations in their sizes and shapes (usually square or rectangular).

Condition 9. Clusters must be systematically spaced so they can be encompassed within single blocks.

Condition 10. If oblong, clusters must be oriented in the direction of the grid. The effects of deviations of the archaeological record from these last four conditions on the magnitude of similarity/association found between artifact types within the same or different depositional sets are analogous to those cited for correlation analysis (see pages 166–169).

Unlike correlation analysis, association analysis runs into operational difficulties when the artifact types to be analyzed have ubiquitous distributions within which spatial patterning of high-count cells is evident. Patterning evident in the arrangement of high-count/low-count cells for each given ubiquitous type deserves investigation for its degree of co-arrangement with high-count/low-count patterns of other ubiquitously distributed types and with the presence/absence patterns of more sparcely distributed types. To do so, it is necessary to dichotomize the cell counts of ubiquitously distributed artifact types into two states, high count and low count (thereafter treated as ''presence'' and ''absence'' states), using site-wide or local threshold count values. Problematically, different thresholds chosen to dichotomize the cell counts of a ubiquitously distributed artifact type may yield different arrangements of cells with ''presence'' and ''absence'' states, producing different patterns of association between it and other types. Dichotomizing thresholds consequently must be chosen with great care, in

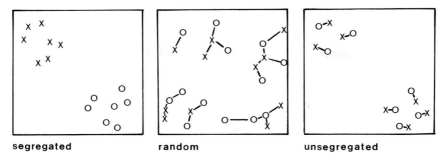

Figure 3.14. Segregated, random, and unsegregated spatial arrangements of two artifact types, X and O.

awareness of their *behavioral* significance. Some mathematical methods and logical criteria for defining thresholds will be discussed later (pages 200–201, 204–206).

Segregation Analysis

Techniques for determining the degree of co-arrangement of artifact types that operate on point locations have been used much less frequently than techniques operating on grid-cell counts. Two point location approaches that have been applied to archaeological data are segregation analysis and Whallon's "overlapping cluster approach."

Segregation analysis (Pielou 1964; Price 1975) measures the degree to which items spatially pair with others of their own class, *segregating* themselves from items of some second class; pair with items of the second class, such that the two classes associate and are *unsegregated*; or pair as often with items of their own class as with those of the second, such that the two classes randomly intermingle (Figure 3.14). To quantify these possible relationships, a tabulation is made of the number of items of each type that have as nearest neighbors items of the same type and the opposite type (Table 3.8). The *a, b, c,* and *d* cells of the resultant contingency table then can be used to calculate an index of segregation *S*.

TABLE 3.8

Contingency Table Used in Calculating Pielou's Segregation Statistic, *S*

		Base item		
		Type 1	Type 2	
Reference item	Type 1	A	B	A + B
(nearest neighbor)	Type 2	C	D	C + D
		A + C	B + D	N

$$S = 1 - \frac{b + c}{N(wz + xy)} \qquad (3.24)$$

where

$$w = \frac{a + c}{N} \qquad y = \frac{a + b}{N}$$

$$x = \frac{b + d}{N} \qquad z = \frac{c + d}{N}$$

S will take the value -1 if items of the two types are completely unsegregated, pairing only with items of the opposite type. It will be zero if items of the two types randomly intermingle and pair with each other, and $+1$ if they are completely segregated, pairing only with like items.

Price (1975) extends the method by redefining S as an index of association

$$A = 1 - S \qquad (3.25)$$

such that the value 1 is taken by A when two artifact types are positively associated (unsegregated), and the value -1 when they are completely negatively associated (segregated). A matrix of A coefficients for all possible couples of artifact types then is treated as a similarity matrix and subjected to a clustering algorithm, in order to define a hierarchy of types tending to associate or segregate (depositional sets).

Segregation analysis has a number of severe problems, both in what it assumes about the nature of the archaeological record and in how association and segregation are measured. In its assumptions about the organization of archaeological records (Table 3.4), segregation analysis is more stringent than correlation and association analysis. It requires that couples of artifact types belonging to the same archaeological activity set be deposited together *in pairs,* one for one, in equal numbers. For this to occur, several circumstances must pertain. (1) Activity sets must have been monothetic. (2) Activity sets must have been non-overlapping. (3) Artifacts must have been deposited expediently at their locations of use. (4) Artifact types in the same activity set must have had the same discard rates. (5) Artifacts must not have been disturbed by postdepositional processes before excavation. (6) Artifacts must have been completely recovered and accurately classified to type. Additionally, the technique assumes (7) the non-hierarchical patterning of artifact aggregations; it examines spatial relationships between artifact types at only the smallest scale, between nearest neighbors.

When applied to archaeological circumstances where the discard rates of artifact types in the same activity sets are unequal and depositional sets are polythetic, segregation analysis will produce questionable results. The maximum value that possibly can be taken by the A statistic will be attenuated by an uncontrollable amount, depending on the degree to which artifact types in the same depositional sets occur in *unequal* numbers (Pielou 1964:259), and thus, have unequal discard rates and are polythetically distributed. Figure 3.15 illustrates the attenuation that may occur, causing artifact types that are completely, though polythetically, associated (unsegregated) to be characterized as randomly interspersed to mildly segregated.

Segregation analysis also is encumbered because it uses as its measure of association and segregation *relative* nearest neighbor distances rather than *absolute* nearest neighbor distances. Two artifact types are judged more or less associated on the basis of how often they are nearest neighbors to items of the same kind *relative to* how often they are nearest neighbors to items of the opposite kind, rather than on the basis of their geographic proximity to each other. This has two consequences. First, it represents a loss of information, a reduction of ratio-scale point-location data with known geographic distances between items to ordinal-scale relative location data (e.g., A's are closer to B's than B's are to other B's). This information loss may lead to erroneous conclusions about the degree of association of artifact types. Consider Figure 3.16. Two different pairs of artifact types, X and O, and A and B, are compared for their degrees of co-arrangement. It is clear that types X and O are highly associated, occurring together repeatedly in the same clusters and being *close in proximity*. Artifact types A and B, on the other hand, are distant from each other and unassociated. Nevertheless, segregation analysis would characterize Types A and B more associated with types X and O, because on a relative scale, A's are closer to B's than A's are to A's and B's are to B's, whereas X's segregate to

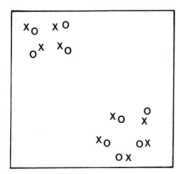
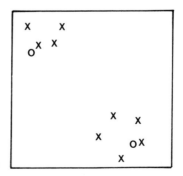

monothetic activity set and
archaeological activity set

equal rates of discard

A = +1

polythetic archaeological
activity set

unequal rates of discard

A = −.222

Figure 3.15. Segregation analysis assumes the monothetic organization of activity sets and archaeological activity sets, and equal discard rates for artifact types belonging to the same activity set. If this is not so, the maximum value possibly taken by the A statistic will be attenuated.

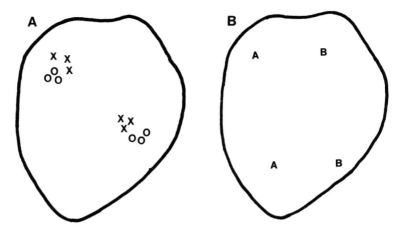

Figure 3.16. Artifact type pairs X–O, and A–B, are shown distributed on the same site. Whether pair X–O or pair A–B is judged more associated depends on whether a relative or absolute measure of proximity is used.

themselves and O's segregate to themselves within clusters. Thus, measures of coarrangement of artifact types using the relative placement of types, including the segregation statistic, may be misleading; measures of the absolute geographic proximity of items of different types are preferable (see pages 191–199). The activities that occurred on an archaeological site were performed in absolute space, not relative space.

The second consequence of using relative rather than absolute nearest neighbor distances as the measure of co-arrangement in segregation analysis is that comparability of the measure between *different couples* of types is precluded. This is so because the standard against which association of two types is assessed—the degree of association of the types with themselves—is relative and varies from one couple of types to another. For example, the degree of co-arrangement of items of two types, A and B, is judged relative to the degree to which items of type A pair with themselves and items of type B pair with themselves. Similarly, the degree of co-arrangement of items of two other types, C and D, is judged relative to the degree to which items of type C pair with themselves and items of type D pair with themselves. Comparison of the two assessments of co-arrangement is meaningless because they are based on different standards of association.

As a result of this noncomparability of multiple segregation indices (or Price's aggregation indices) to each other, it is inappropriate to apply any higher level grouping algorithm (e.g., cluster analysis, matrix ordering) to a matrix of such coefficients to define multitype depositional sets, as Price (1975) has done. Such algorithms assume the comparability of the coefficients. Although segregation analysis is poorly suited to the definition of depositional sets, the method and its problems do suggest a productive approach, to be described later (see pages 194–199).

Whallon's Overlapping Cluster Approach

The overlapping cluster approach to defining the degree of co-arrangement of artifact types, using the point locations of items, was developed by Whallon (1974). It is one of the few spatial analytic techniques currently available that has been devised by an archaeologist for archaeological purposes rather than borrowed from geography or quantitative ecology. It has been applied to several sites (Brose and Scarry 1976; Hietala and Larson 1980; Price 1975; Whallon 1974).

The method is algorithmically contingent upon defining the boundaries of single-type clusters. This usually is done with Whallon's radius approach (next section) but not out of logical necessity. It is desirable, then, to evaluate the requirements of these two steps separately for their concordance with the nature of the archaeological record.

The overlapping cluster approach measures the degree of similar arrangement of two artifact types, using either of two criteria. These are: (1) the amount of area shared in zones of overlap of single-type clusters having different artifact types, compared to the total union of their areas or (2) the number of items shared in zones of overlap of single-type clusters having different artifact types, compared to the total number of items in the clusters. If the area or number of items in the zones of overlap and nonoverlap are tabulated in the a, b, and c cells of a fourfold contingency table similar to that used in association analysis (Table 3.7), then a coefficient of the degree of similar arrangement of types can be calculated by

$$I = \frac{100a}{a + b + c} \qquad (3.26)$$

The index varies from 0 for complete segregation of the two types to 100 for complete spatial overlap of the two types.

The method is somewhat more concordant with the nature of organization of intrasite archaeological records than are correlation and association analysis using grid cell counts (Table 3.4). No assumptions are made about the size or shape of clusters. The approach, however, still is stringent in that it requires that activity sets and depositional sets be monothetic and nonoverlapping, that artifacts be expediently deposited in their locations of use or that such location be reused often, and that artifacts not be disturbed by postdepositional processes. Only if these conditions are met will items of two different artifact types in the same activity set always occupy similar areas, maximizing the coefficient of similarity.

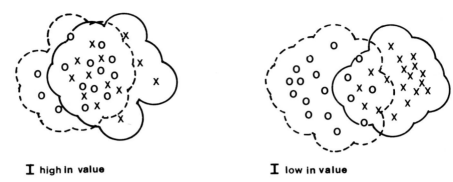

I high in value I low in value

Figure 3.17. Different patterns of inhomogeneity in the density of items of two types *within* a depositional area can produce different values of Whallon's item-based measure of co-arrangement, *I*.

The measure of co-arrangement using number of items shared by clusters of different kinds is more constraining than the measure using the amount of area shared. The former requires the additional condition that artifacts within single-type clusters and multitype depositional areas be homogeneously distributed in density and by extension, that depositional areas be internally homogeneous in composition and not hierarchically nested. Figure 3.17 illustrates this requirement.

Finally, Whallon's overlapping cluster approach has the drawback that determination of the degree of co-arrangement of artifact types is contingent upon the definition of single-type depositional areas. This contingency is undesirable because it limits the assessment of co-arrangement of artifact types to those exhibiting clustered patterns rather than allowing evaluation of relationships between types having any spatial pattern.

Methods for Delimiting Spatial Clusters of Artifacts

A number of standard map techniques (Davis 1973) can be used to define the spatial limits of clusters of artifacts of one type when data are in the form of densities observed over a regular grid (counts per grid cell) or item point locations that can be converted to this form. These methods include simple contouring, trend surface analysis, spatial filtering, and in certain situations, Fourier analysis (Carr 1982, 1983, 1984a). A detailed examination of these methods is beyond the scope of this chapter, although one use of spatial filtering is discussed later (see pages 204–206). It can be mentioned, however, that in using gridded data of a particular scale, all the techniques constrain the form of patterning that may be found, as a function of the chosen grid interval (Greig–Smith 1964). The techniques also require approximate homogeneity in the density of artifacts within depositional areas to define depositional areas with internal spatial continuity.

Whallon's Radius Approach

A method for delimiting clusters of artifacts of one type using item point location data directly has been devised by Whallon (1974) and applied in several circumstances (Whallon 1974; Price 1975; Brose and Scarry 1976). The method operates on the frequency distribution of nearest neighbor distances between items. The mean and standard deviation of these observations are determined, along with a "cutoff" distance of 1.65 standard deviations above the mean. Those nearest neighbor distances smaller than the cut-off threshold will represent 95% of all distances that join items separated by a potentially significant, small distance indicative of clustering, under one assumption. It is assumed that clustered patterns have unimodal, approximately normal distributions of nearest neighbor distances (Whallon 1974:23).

Next, items having nearest neighbors at distances less than the cutoff threshold are joined to define the limits of clusters. Linkage can be done in two ways. First, significantly close neighbors can be joined by lines, producing an area of minimal extent with ragged edges (Figure 3.18A). Second, circles of a radius equivalent to the cutoff threshold can be drawn around items, such that their intersecting arcs delimit an area of maximal extent with a smoother, more pleasing outline (Figure 3.18B).

Whallon's method for delimiting clusters was introduced as a "rough outline of an approach" this problem, rather than a finalized technique (Whallon 1974:23). The method has several limitations, but is a solid beginning and can be reworked into more reasonable approaches (see pages 202–206).

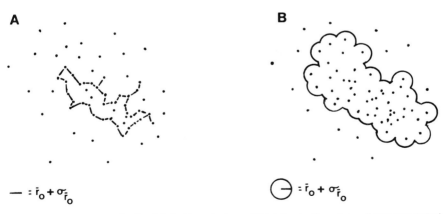

A

$- : \bar{r}_0 + \sigma_{\bar{r}_0}$

B

$\ominus : \bar{r}_0 + \sigma_{\bar{r}_0}$

Figure 3.18. Two methods of delimiting clusters: (A) joining by lines those items separated by less than the cutoff distance $\bar{r}_0 + \sigma_{\bar{r}_0}$ and (B) circumscribing items by circles with a radius equal to the cutoff distance $\bar{r}_0 + \sigma_{\bar{r}_0}$.

The primary difficulty with the method is that it assumes the nearest neighbor distances of a clustered arrangement to be unimodal and approximately normal (Pearson's Type III distribution) in order to define an appropriate cutoff threshold. This may be true for an individual cluster, and it may also be true for multiple clusters in a scatter all having approximately the same average density and grading off in density at their broders at a similar rate. It is possible, however, for a distribution of nearest neighbor distances to be multimodal, different modes representing clusters of different average density or subportions of clusters of different densities. It also is possible for the distribution to approach a square fuction, if clusters are numerous and each varies in density over a wide range (personal observation). A hierarchical nested clustered arrangement may yield a distribution similar to an inverse function, extremely skewed to the right. The cutoff thresholds defined for these nonnormal distributions will be more or less meaningful, varying with the form of the distribution. For example, for a multimodal distribution indicating multiple clusters of differing density, obviously one threshold should be defined for each mode and different thresholds applied in delimiting different clusters, rather than defining a single threshold for the total distribution to be applied to all the clusters (see page 205). Likewise, should a distribution of nearest neighbor distances have a long tail with a few outliers, indicating scattered isolated items, these items should be eliminated from analysis to prevent the calculation of an unduly large $\bar{r}_0$ and $\sigma_{\bar{r}_0}$ and a large cutoff threshold. The latter will result in most items in the scatter being joined into one massive cluster.

Thus, as outlined by Whallon, the method is applicable to only a limited range of circumstances concordant with certain constraining assumptions. These assumptions are: (1) clusters in a scatter are all of the same average density; (2) clusters are fairly homogeneous, internally, in their artifact densities; and (3) clusters are not nested or surrounded by a low density scatter of isolated items.

Finally, the approach specifies how to define only single-type clusters; it does not detail how to construct multiple-types clusters composed of artifact types that are co-arranged, that is, use-areas.

MORE APPROPRIATE METHODS FOR INTRASITE SPATIAL ANALYSIS

None of the mathematical methods of spatial analysis available today are totally free of logical inconsistencies with the nature of organization of intrasite archaeological records. There are, however, techniques that minimize inconsistencies and that are more appropriate than the ones just described. These techniques are discussed in this section.

Methods using both grid-cell count data and item-point location data are presented, despite the obvious preferability of the latter in avoiding the problems associated with grids of set sizes, shapes, placements, and orientations (pages 175–180). Archaeological data often are recorded in only gridded form, and techniques must be offered to handle such data. For some tasks, alternative methods of analysis are presented, the different methods having different strengths and weaknesses.

Methods for Assessing Whether Artifacts Cluster in Space

Nth-Order Nearest Neighbor Analysis

First-order nearest neighbor analysis (pages 154–161) is a relatively unconstrained approach to assessing the form of arrangement of artifacts within some natural study area. It fails, however, to provide evaluation of the possible hierarchical organization of items and the size(s) of clusters (grain of patterning).

Other methods belonging to the same family of geographic distance approaches as first-order nearest neighbor analysis also allow evaluation of form of spatial patterning but do not have these same drawbacks. Most of the techniques require at least two of the following classes of data: (1) an estimate of regional item density; (2) item-to-neighboring-item distances; and (3) randomly located point-to-item distances (Pielou 1959:607). The various methods and the aspects of arrangement (intensity, grain, hierarchical arrangement) that they are capable of evaluating are summarized in Table 3.9.

Two of the techniques—those derived by Thompson (1956) and Pielou (1959)—seem most useful to archaeologists, for they: (1) provide tests of signifi-

TABLE 3.9

Geographic Distance Methods Allowing Evaluation of Various Aspects of the Form of Arrangement of Artifact Scatters, and Their Data Requirements

Statistic for evaluating arrangement	Reference	Data required[a]	Aspect of spatial patterning measured
R	Clark and Evans (1954)	a, b	Intensity
$2\lambda_0 \sum_{i=1}^{N} r_n^2$	Thompson (1956)	a, b	Intensity, grain, hierarchy
a	Pielou (1959)	a, c	Intensity, grain
a	Mountford (1961)	a, c	Intensity, grain
z_{st}, ρ_{st}	Holgate (1965)	c	Intensity, grain
A	Hopkins and Skellum (1954)	b, c	Intensity, grain

[a] a = an estimate of regional density of items; b = item-to-neighboring item distances, or a sample of these; c = randomly located point-to-item distances, or a sample of these.

cance of departure from random arrangement in the direction of alignment as well as clustering; (2) allow estimation of the size of clusters; and/or (3) evaluate arrangement at all levels of order (individually or as a whole) in a hierarchically organized scatter of items. Thompson's method, nth-order nearest neighbor analysis, is summarized in this section.

Nth-order nearest neighbor statistics allow evaluation of the form of patterning of items at each of a number of scales larger than the most detailed (the average nearest neighbor distance) by examining measurements from items to their second, third, . . . , nth-order nearest neighbors. The statistics generated by the method are logical analogs of those derived by Clark and Evans (1954) for first-order nearest neighbor analysis. If N is the number of items in a scatter, A the area of the scatter, m the density of items in the scatter, $\bar{r}_{0_n}$ the observed average nearest neighbor distance to nth-order nearest neighbors, and $\bar{r}_{e_n}$ the expected average nth-order nearest neighbor distance under the null hypothesis of random arrangement, then,

$$m = \frac{N}{A} \tag{3.27}$$

$$\lambda_0 = \pi m \tag{3.28}$$

$$\bar{r}_{0_n} = \sum_{i=1}^{N} r_{i_n}/N \tag{3.29}$$

$$\bar{r}_{e_n} = \frac{.5642}{\sqrt{n/m}} \tag{3.30}$$

$$\sigma_{\bar{r}_{e_n}} = \frac{.2821}{\sqrt{m}} \tag{3.31}$$

The equations for determining $\bar{r}_{e_n}$ and $\sigma_{\bar{r}_{e_n}}$ hold for only large n, when the distribution of $\bar{r}_{e_n}$ approaches normality. For $n \leqq 4$, Thompson (1956:392, Table I) provides more accurate formulae.

As in first-order nearest neighbor analysis, an nth-order nearest neighbor statistic R_n can be calculated for each scale examined.

$$R_n = \frac{\bar{r}_{0_n}}{\bar{r}_{e_n}} \tag{3.32}$$

R_n will be approximately equal to 1 if items or *clusters*, depending on the scale of analysis, are arranged randomly within the scatter. It will tend toward 0 if items or clusters aggregate in space, and will range greater than 1 if items or clusters tend to be aligned. The maximum value of R is not determined by Thompson.

The significance of departure of a scatter of items or clusters from a random arrangement at a given scale can be tested most accurately with a χ^2 test similar to that used in first-order nearest neighbor analysis. The χ^2 statistic to be calculated is

$$\chi^2 - \text{stat} = 2\lambda_0 \sum_{i=1}^{N} r_{i_n}{}^2 \qquad (3.33)$$

The form of the test is the same as that given in the section on first-order nearest neighbor statistics (see page 156), with the degrees of freedom equal to $2Nn$. Thompson also provides normal statistics for testing the significance of patterning, but these provide a more approximate solution than the χ^2 approach.

By graphing the average neighbor distances $\bar{r}_{0_n}$ against neighbor orders n, it is possible to determine a number of aspects of patterning: whether items are arranged in a nonhierarchical (uniformly random, aligned) or hierarchical (clustered) manner (including reflexive pairing); whether hierarchically organized clusters exhibit nesting; the form of arrangement of clusters at a given level of a cluster hierarchy (random, clustered, aligned); and the size of clusters. Figure 3.19 shows various aspects of such curves for nonhierarchical, hierarchical–unnested, and hierarchical–nested arrangements when the simplifying assumption of equal numbers of items in clusters at the same hierarchical level is made for illustrative purposes. Note that a nonhierarchical arrangement is characterized by a slowly rising graph, indicating measurement to increasingly distant neighbors as n increases. In contrast, the graph of a hierarchical (clustered) arrangement exhibits a "jut," one neighbor order in range, indicating a change from measurement to nth-nearest neighbors *within* clusters to measurement to nth-nearest neighbors in *different* clusters, much farther away. The size of clusters, in number of items, can be determined from the neighbor order at which the jut occurs. The approximate area of the clusters can be found by graphic construction knowing the number of items that the clusters contain and the average distance between items ($\bar{r}_{0_n}$ for that n immediately before the jut), and assuming some shape for the clusters. The form of arrangement of items within clusters can be determined by calculating an nth-order nearest neighbor statistic, R_n, for some midrange neighbor order *below* the jut and by applying a χ^2 test to the neighbor distances of that order. The form of arrangement of clusters (second level patterning) can be evaluated using the same methods for some midrange neighbor order *above* the jut.

Unnested and nested clustered patterns are distinguishable (see Figure 7.19b, c) by the form of the graph below the jut. For an unnested arrangement, this segment of the graph will be a gently rising line of one slope (with some random variation). For a nested arrangement, this segment, will have multiple slopes, one for each nested level. At lower neighbor orders, the slope will be low, indicating measurement to increasingly distant neighbors within the *same hier-*

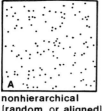

nonhierarchical
(random or aligned)

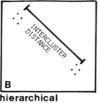

hierarchical
unnested clusters

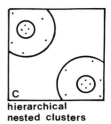

hierarchical
nested clusters

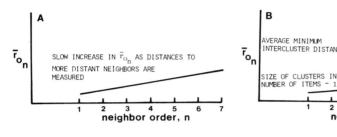

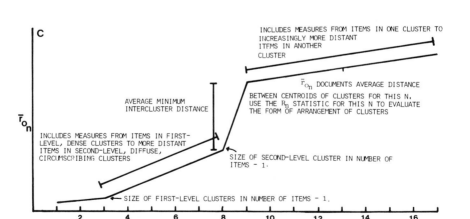

Figure 3.19.   (A) Nonhierarchical arrangements (uniformly random, aligned), (B) hierarchical unnested clustered arrangements, and (C) hierarchical nested clustered arrangements have characteristically different curves of $\bar{r}_0$ against N. For both kinds of clustered distributions, it is possible to determine the size of clusters in number of items and the form of arrangement of clusters (second-level organization within a hierarchical pattern). It is assumed here, for simplicity, that clusters at a given hierarchical level include the same number of items and have similar densities.

archy level, of *similar density.* At higher neighbor orders, the slope will be greater, indicating the average condition of measurement to more distant neighbors in *other, less dense* (surrounding) levels of the cluster hierarchy.

The multiple slopes may manifest themselves simply as an upsweeping curve, depending on the degree of variation in interitem distances within hierarchical levels of the clusters, the intensity of the density differences between levels, the sharpness of the density gradient between levels, and whether all clusters have the same number of levels and items per level. In most archaeological circumstances, where the number of items per cluster at a given level varies from cluster to cluster, an upsweeping curve can be expected. Figure 3.20 shows generalized curves for unnested and nested clustered arrangements where clusters *vary in their number of items.* The two graphs and arrangement of types are distinguishable by the presence or absence of an upsweeping curve before the intercluster jut.

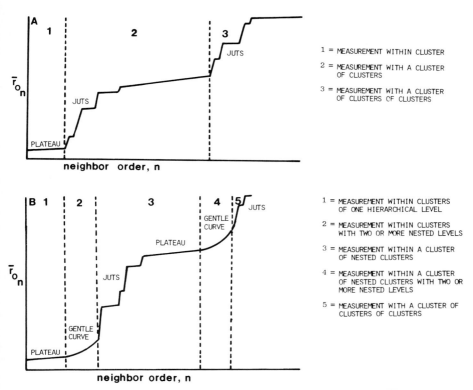

Figure 3.20. (A) Unnested and (B) nested clusters have characteristically different curves of $\bar{r}_{0_n}$ against *N*, even when the number of items per cluster at a given hierarchical level varies from cluster to cluster. Generalized curves are shown. The numbered segments of each curve pertain to the different hierarchical levels of clustering illustrated in Figure 3.5.

Finally, note that when the number of items per cluster varies, in either a nested or unnested arrangement, multiple juts occur in place of a single jut. One jut will occur for each cluster having a different number of items, reflecting the change from measurement to nth nearest neighbors within clusters to measurement to nth nearest neighbors in different clusters, *at different orders for the different sized clusters*. The juts will vary in magnitude in accordance with the different distances between clusters. Gentle slopes may precede each jut if the arrangement is a hierarchical–nested one.

Nth-order nearest neighbor analysis is nearly consistent with the nature of organization of the archaeological record, but has several drawbacks (Table 3.4).

Problems 1 and 2. It restrictively assumes that clusters of a given hierarchical level are of similar size. It also assumes that if clusters are nested, each cluster has the same number of nested levels. As archaeological reality deviates from these conditions, the nearest neighbor statistics $\bar{r}_{O_n}$ and R_n and the χ^2 test of significance reflect mixed information on arrangement from more than one hierarchical level (e.g., within-cluster distances and between-cluster distances, simultaneously) and become less meaningful. Similarly, the graph of $\bar{r}_{O_n}$ against n becomes increasingly more complex and its diagnostic characteristics may become lost.

Problems 3 and 4. Technically, nth-order nearest neighbor analysis is plagued with a framing problem and a boundary problem, just like first-order nearest neighbor analysis. To avoid a framing problem, it is necessary that the area of analysis be a behaviorally meaningful entity. No solutions to the boundary problem have been offered at this time. As a consequence, the nearest neighbor statistic R_n may be inflated and indicate the scatter to be less clustered than it actually is. The χ^2 statistic also will be inflated, making the test for clustering of items more conservative and the test for systematic alignment of items more liberal.

Problem 5. Nth-order nearest neighbor analysis requires much computation time. As the number of items within clusters increases, the amount of calculation that must be done before information on intercluster organization can be extracted rises substantially. Where clusters are large yet spatially discrete, this burden may be reduced by counting the number of items in clusters, beginning the analysis at an order greater than the numerous number of items in a cluster and searching for nth nearest neighbors outside of the cluster to which an item belongs. When clusters cannot be delimited clearly prior to analysis, yet are large, nth-order nearest neighbor analysis may simply be unoperationable.

Pielou's Point-to-Item Distance Statistics

When it is not practial or meaningful to use nth-order nearest neighbor analysis to evaluate the form of arrangement of items in a scatter, as when clusters are large or vary greatly in the number of items or nested hierarchical levels they contain, Pielou's (1959) point-to-item distance statistics may be employed. This approach provides a single measure and test of the form of arrangement of items within a scatter as a whole, considering simultaneously "most if not all" scales of ordering of items (Pielou 1959:608). In its sensitivity to multiple scales of arrangement, it is more informative than first-order nearest neighbor analysis. However, because it mixes information on arrangement from multiple hierarchical levels of patterning into one statistic, it is less satisfactory than nth-order nearest neighbor analysis. The method would be more desirable if it were known what scales of patterning have the greatest and least effect on test results, but this has not been investigated.

Pielou's method begins with the selection of a set of random points within a natural study area. The distance from each random point to the item nearest it then is measured. A measure, a, of the form of arrangement of items within the study area may be calculated by

$$a = \pi D \bar{r}_0^2 \tag{3.34}$$

where D is the density of items in the study area and $\bar{r}_0$ is the average distance from the n random points to their nearest item neighbors

$$\bar{r}_0 = \frac{\sum_{i=1}^{n} r_i}{n}, \tag{3.35}$$

r_i being one point-to-item distance. If the arrangement of items is random at all geographic scales, then a will approximately equal $(n - 1)/n$. Values of a larger than this indicate a tendency toward aggregation, whereas smaller values indicate a tendancy toward alignment.

The significance of deviation of a scatter from a random arrangement can be determined by calculating a χ^2 statistic

$$\chi^2 - \text{stat} = 2n\pi D r_0^2 \tag{3.36}$$

and comparing its value to the χ^2 distribution with $2n$ degrees of freedom. A value of $\chi^2 - \text{stat}$ greater than $\chi^2_{(1-\alpha)}$ (df) indicates significant clustering at the α level, whereas a value less than $\chi^2_{(\alpha)}$ (df) indicates significant alignment at the α level.

When it is operationally impossible to use nth-order nearest neighbor analysis, Pielou's method and first-order nearest neighbor analysis can be used together to give some insight (not obtainable from the methods individually) into the form of arrangement of items at *multiple* scales. If the two techniques produce different results, then it can be concluded that the scatter of items is hierarchically arranged, with one kind of arrangement at the smallest scale and a second or more kinds at larger scales.

Although concordant with the nature of organization of intrasite archaeological records, Pielou's method has two disadvantages.

Problem 1. It does not allow evaluation of the size of clusters.

Problem 2. More seriously, it is not sufficient by itself for assessing form of arrangement. Some aggregated and regular arrangements of items have the same frequency distribution of point-to-item distances as random arrangements (Pielou 1959:613). The results of Pielou's technique must be confirmed by visual inspection of the study area.

Luton and Braun's Contiguity Method

Luton and Braun (1977) have constructed a statistical method for assessing form of arrangement that operates on grid-cell count data. The technique consciously was designed to evaluate the spatial *arrangement* of item-counts among cells, rather than their frequency *distribution*; it consequently avoids all the technical problems of Poisson-based approaches previously discussed (Table 3.4; pages 141–142, Problems 1–5).

To apply the method, the difference in cell counts at each border between all adjacent cells is calculated. The direction in which differences are calculated (left to right versus right to left; up versus down) must remain constant over the whole grid system. The mean and variance of these differences then is determined.

A relative index of arrangement of cell counts can be constructed by finding the ratio of the observed variance of cell count differences to that expected, assuming the random arrangement of cell counts. For a large number of cells, this expected variance is equal to twice the observed variance of the cell counts. The ratio will take the value 1 for a random arrangement, becoming less than 1 as the arrangement becomes more clustered and more than 1 as the arrangement becomes more dispersed.

An absolute assessment of form of arrangement can be made by applying a χ^2/df test to Luton and Braun's index of arrangement. An arrangement clustered significantly for a given α level will produce an index value less than $\chi^2/df_{(\alpha)}$; a significantly dispersed arrangement will yield an index value greater than $\chi^2/df_{(1 - \alpha)}$, where df is the number of differences in counts minus one.

The theoretical basis for the method is the Central Limit Theorem applied to a convoluted function: the difference between two independent random variables. The theorem states that, for large N, this difference is, itself, a random variable with an approximately normal distribution having known moments, regardless of the form of the distribution of the two original variables. The mean of the convolved variate is equal to the difference of the means of the two original variables, and its variance is equal to the sum of their variances (Strackee and van der Gon 1962). In the context of Luton and Braun's method, the two original random variables are (1) the counts of items in a set of grid cells, where counts have a Poisson distribution and are arranged randomly, and (2) the counts of items in neighboring cells in the defined directions, also having a Poisson distribution and being arranged randomly.

Luton and Braun's method can be extended in several ways, given its robust theoretical basis. First, aggregation at specified scales larger than the area encompassed by two neighboring grid cells can be assessed simply by calculating differences between the counts of cells separated by a larger, set distance. Second, patterns of association between pairs of artifact types can be found using the differences in counts of items of different types within cells. Finally, patterns of mutual aggregation of pairs of types can be discerned using between-cell differences of the within-cell differences in their counts. The details of the latter two methods for assessing whether artifact types are co-arranged are not summarized here because they appear less appropriate to this task than does the procedure, polythetic association, which is introduced in the next section. Luton and Braun's methods assume the monothetic organization of depositional sets.

Luton and Braun's contiguity method for assessing form of arrangement is free from the technical problems of Poisson-based methods (see pages 141–142, Problems 1–5). Nevertheless, as a grid-based technique, it still is discordant with the nature of the archaeological record in most ways already discussed for Poisson methods (see pages 143–144, Problems 6–14; Table 3.4). Many of these constraints could be removed partially by applying the technique several times, using grids of different meshes, in a dimensional analytic strategy.

A Method for Assessing Whether Artifact Types Are Co-Arranged

Polythetic Association

The model of intrasite archaeological records described previously (pages 117–121), as well as the problems enumerated in using the measures of covariation, association, and segregation to assess the degree of co-arrangement of artifact types (pages 161–179), suggest some basic technical properties that an accurate measure of co-arrangement probably must have.

Property 1. The measure should use point-location data and be within the realm of nearest neighbor or item-to-point approaches, rather than use grid-cell counts. This is necessary to avoid the many restrictions on analysis posed by the methods using grids of set meshes, shapes, orientations, and placements.

Property 2. The measure should be concerned with the co-occurence *of artifacts of different types within each other's neighborhoods rather than the* covariation *of their densities.* This is necessary to avoid methodological assumptions that are inconsistent with those behavioral and archaeological formation processes that cause artifact types within the same depositional set not to covary.

Property 3. The measure of co-occurence should not be influenced by whether co-occurring artifact types are co-arranged in a more symmetrical or more asymmetrical manner (Pielou 1964). By a *symmetrical* co-arrangement of two artifact types is meant that wherever one artifact type occurs, the other always occurs, and vice versa. In nearest neighbor terms, it means that whenever one artifact type is a second's nearest neighbor, the second artifact type is always the first's nearest neighbor (Figure 3.21a). A symmetrical co-arrangement of two artifact types can occur only when they have equal densities and items of the two types can always pair. *Asymmetrical* co-arrangements of two types occur when they are scattered over the same locale, but in different densities. The items of the lower density artifact type always have items of the higher density artifact type near them, but items of the higher density type only sometimes have items of the lower density type near them. Nearest neighbor relationships are not reciprocal (Figure 3.21b–d).

A monothetic depositional set ipso facto is characterized by artifact types that are co-arranged in a symmetrical manner. Wherever an item of one type within a monothetic depositional set occurs, items of all other types in the set co-occur in the vicinity, and vice versa. A polythetic depositional set, on the other hand, ipso facto is characterized by artifact types that are co-arranged in an asymmetrical manner. Where an artifact of one type occurs, an artifact of another type in the same depositional set may or may not occur, depending on the archaeological formation processes by which the set was generated. Depositional sets that are more polythetic, as a result of the operation of more archaeological formation and disturbance processes on them, are characterized by artifact types that exhibit greater local density differentials and more asymmetry in their co-arrangement.

As a consequence, a measure of co-arrangement of artifact types, to avoid being influenced by the degree to which depositional sets are polythetic and to measure only co-arrangement, must be insensitive to (not affected in value by) whether co-arranged artifact types pattern themselves in an asymmetrical or symmetrical manner, and to variations in the degree of asymmetry of co-arrangement. Specifically, one artifact type within an activity set might have higher curation rates and lower discard rates than other types within it, causing the type to occur in lower densities, and to be *absent* at some locations where the other types occur. Also, multipurpose tools and compound tools, which participate in several activities during the course of their life histories, will be *absent* from some locations where other members of their activity sets have been deposited. *These forms of absences of an artifact type from the vicinity of other artifact types with which it often was used or deposited and with which we might expect it to occur (asymmetry) do not indicate that the missing type is not part of the depositional set represented by the types.* A measure of co-arrangement of artifact types thus should not be affected in value by such absences and asymmetry.

We may see more clearly, now, how association analysis—as a measure of monothetic, symmetrical co-occurrence of artifact types—is inappropriate for defining most depositional sets. Currently used association coefficients do not distinguish between two possible kinds of absences of a type from the neighbor-

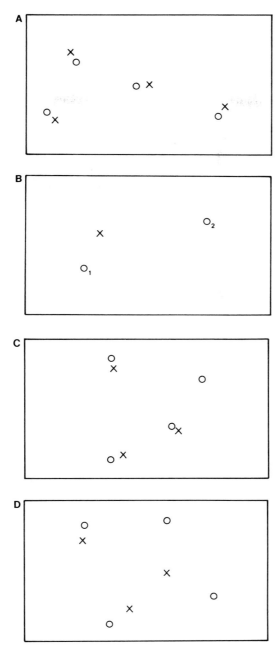

Figure 3.21. (A) A symmetrical co-arrangement of two artifact types, X and O, defining a monothetic set. (B) Asymmetry in nearest neighbors. Artifact X is artifact O_2's nearest neighbor of the opposite kind, but O_2 is not X's nearest neighbor of the opposite kind. Artifact O_1 is artifact X's nearest neighbor of the opposite kind. (C) An asymmetrical co-arrangement of two artifact types, X and O, defining a polythetic depositional set. (D) A more ambiguous asymmetrical co-arrangement of two artifact types, X and O, defining a polythetic depositional set.

hood of other artifact types: (1) absence due to the actual dissociation of the artifact type from a depositional set represented by other types (Figure 3.22), and (2) absence as a result of the polythetic organization of types among depositional sets and their asymmetrical distribution over space (Figure 3.21c–d). Mismatches (counts in the *b* and *c* cells) in fourfold contingency tables *always* are considered a measure of dissociation (Sneath and Sokal 1963:128– 135).

Property 4. The measure of co-arrangement of artifact types should not be influenced by changes over space in the *direction* of asymmetrical relationships between co-arranged types (Figure 3.23). In some neighborhoods, one artifact type within an activity set may be absent because it was not used, deposited, preserved, or recovered, whereas in other neighborhoods, other members of the set may be absent. This circumstance may arise because the factors causing artifact types within a depositional set to be co-arranged in an asymmetrical manner need not have worked uniformly over the whole site, or even within depositional areas. For example, some kinds of artifacts within an activity set may have been ''mined'' and recycled in some parts of a site, whereas elsewhere at the site, other kinds of artifacts within the set may have been collected.

Designing a Coefficient of Polythetic Association. A coefficient of co-arrangement that meets the above criteria and that is consistent with the model of intrasite archaeological records presented earlier in this chapter may be designed. To build it, first consider what a nearest neighbor measure of symmetrical, monothetic co-arrangement might look like, meeting only requisite Properties 1 and 2 just discussed.

A simple statistic comparing the arrangement of items of two artifact types is the average absolute distance between items of one type and their nearest neighbors of the second type. A *base type* and *reference type* are chosen. For each item of the base type, the Euclidean distances at which surrounding items of the reference type occur are compared until the nearest neighbor of the reference

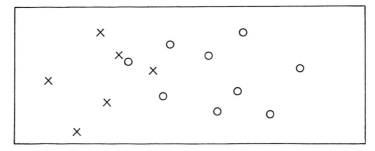

Figure 3.22. Two artifact types, X and O, that belong to different depositional sets but overlap spatially to a slight degree. Other artifact types included in the depositional sets are not shown.

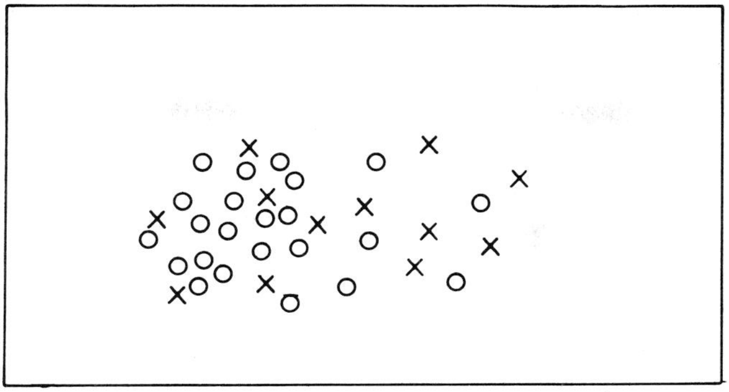

Figure 3.23. A cluster of two artifact types, X and O, that is internally inhomogeneous in the relative densities and direction of asymmetrical co-arrangement of the two types.

type is found. The same procedure then is repeated, this time using the items of the reference type as base points and the items of the base type as the satellite reference points. The average intertype distance can be computed by

$$AVDISTM_{AB} = \frac{\sum_1^n \overline{AB} + \sum_1^m \overline{BA}}{n + m} \qquad (3.37)$$

where n is the number of items of type A, m is the number of items of type B, $\overline{AB}$ is the distance from a given base point of type A to its nearest neighbor of type B, and $\overline{BA}$ is the distance from a given base point of type B to its nearest neighbor of type A. Note that the number of $\overline{AB}$ distances, n, and their sum, need not be equivalent to the number of $\overline{BA}$ distances, m, and their sum. This is so because the number of items of type A and B over a site may not be equal, and the pattern of co-arrangement of the types may be asymmetrical (Figure 3.21a).

The above statistic provides a measure of symmetric, monothetic association of two different types. If two artifact types are co-arranged in a symmetrical manner, such that items of one type are usually close to items of the second type and *vice versa*, defining a monothetic depositional set, both of the sums of distances, $\Sigma \overline{AB}$ and $\Sigma \overline{BA}$, will be small. The value of AVDISTM will be small, indicating that the two types are co-arranged. However, if two artifact types are co-arranged in an asymmetrical manner (similar distributions, different densities; Figure 3.21c–d), such that sometimes the less dense type is not proximate to the more dense type, defining a polythetic depositional set, then one of the sums of distances, $\Sigma \overline{AB}$ or $\Sigma \overline{BA}$, will be large—whichever represents the sum of distances from items of the more dense type to items of the less dense type. The value of AVDISTM, consequently, will be inflated. The coefficient will erroneously indicate that the two types are less *co-arranged* than they really are because its value is influenced by the *asymmetric relationship* between the types as well as their co-arrangement.

To remove the influence of asymmetry on the statistic, it is necessary to consider only those distances from items of the more dense type to items of the less dense type. These distances truly indicate the degree of similar arrangement of the two artifact types and are not inflated by the asymmetrical nature of co-arrangement of the types. The distances from items of the more dense type to items of the less dense type, which reflect the *absence* of items of the less dense type from the neighborhood of some items of the more dense type due to asymmetry, should be ignored. This may be achieved by calculating two average interitem distances

$$\text{AVDIST1} = \frac{\sum_1^n \overline{AB}}{n} \text{, and AVDIST2} = \frac{\sum_1^m \overline{BA}}{m} \qquad (3.38)$$

and choosing the *minimum* of the two as the measure of association of the two types

$$\text{AVDIST} = \min(\text{AVDIST1, AVDIST2}). \qquad (3.39)$$

For example, in Figure 3.21c, the average distance from type X to type O is small, because pairing between the two types is complete from the perspective of type X. The average distance from type O to type X, however, is larger, because pairing is incomplete from the perspective of type O. The smaller average distance would be chosen as the measure of association, *ignoring the effects of those absences* of items of type X from the vicinity of some items of type O that reflect the asymmetric nature of co-arrangement of the two types and that result from the various processes by which the archaeological record was formed, disturbed, and collected.

Higher values of AVDIST, indicating dissociation of two artifact types, are found only when the types tend to not pair in a *symmetrical* manner—when both types are distant from each other and most likely belong to different depositional sets (Figure 3.22).

By defining the strength of association between two artifact types in this manner, then, two *causes* for the absence of an artifact in the proximity of another are separated: (1) the *actual dissociation* of the types belonging to different depositional sets and possibly different activity sets, and (2) the numerous *archaeological formation processes* that cause activity sets and depositional sets to be polythetic in organization and that cause artifact types within a depositional set to be co-arranged in an asymmetrical manner. Only the first factor affects the value of the statistic AVDIST, as should be. The statistic AVDIST then, is a measure of the degree of *polythetic association* of artifact types.

Once a matrix of AVDIST coefficients for all possible pair-wise combinations of types has been calculated, overlapping polythetic depositional sets may be defined by using an *overlapping,* polythetic hierarchical clustering algorithm (Cole and Wishart 1970; Jardine and Sibson 1968) and *multiple* threshold distances specifying the different levels at which different portions of the generated tree may be broken into significant groupings of artifact types. An overlapping clustering algorithm must be used to allow the definition of depositional sets that may be overlapping, as specified by the model of the archaeological record presented early in this chapter. Multiple average nearest neighbor distance thresholds for defining groups of artifact types must be used because different depositional sets may occupy depositional areas of different sizes and densities. The values of the distance thresholds used in defining groups of artifact types in different portions of the tree should be less than the expectable scales or equivalent to the expectable artifact densities of *potential* depositional areas of different kinds that are *suggested* by the relationships among artifact types in the unbroken tree. Some examples of factors that should be considered in defining the expectable nature of depositional areas and appropriate distance thresholds are: the kinds of activities suggested by the potential groupings of artifact types and their space requirements, whether sweeping and cleaning of activity areas probably occurred, and whether depositional sets have been smeared by contemporary farming (in the case of surface collections).

The process of defining groups of artifact thus is an iterative one that involves examining the unbroken tree for potentially meaningful groups of artifact types; postulating expectable distance thresholds for such groups; checking to see whether the potential groups are defined by the postulated thresholds; and reexamining the unbroken tree for other potential groupings, should the first groupings not be defined by the postulated thresholds, etc. Standard procedures for defining a single, tree-wide threshold for defining clusters, although more systematic, are less concordant with the nature of the data.

If the number of artifact types to be clustered is greater than approximately 16, it may not be feasible to use overlapping polythetic clustering algorithms to define depositional sets. The computation time required on a computer may be too large (Cole and Wishart 1970:162). In these cases, multidimensional scaling techniques may be used as an alternative to represent the relationships between types in a few dimensions, and to define overlapping polythetic clusters of types.

Further Considerations of Design. The coefficient, ADVIST, satisfies the first three criteria described above as required for accurate measurement of the co-arrangement of artifact types. It does not fulfill the fourth; it is influenced by changes over space in the direction of asymmetrical relationships between co-arranged artifact types. The coefficient requires the assumption that if two artifact types are co-arranged and co-arranged asymmetrically, the direction of asymmetry is uniform across the whole area of analysis.

For pairs of artifact types having random or aligned arrangements, this assumption poses no problems. If two artifact types have random or aligned arrangements and are co-arranged asymmetrically as well, the direction of asymmetry ipso facto is uniform across the study area. However, if two artifact types have clustered arrangements and are co-arranged asymmetrically, the assumption of uniform asymmetrical co-arrangement, where asymmetry occurs, may be overly constraining. The direction of asymmetry may vary from cluster to cluster: in some clusters one type of artifact may be more plentiful, whereas in other clusters another type may be more plentiful. Direction of asymmetry also may vary within a cluster (Figure 3.23). In these circumstances, the coefficient, AVDIST, will be inflated by the effects of changes in the direction of asymmetry.

To circumvent this problem, for each pair of artifact types exhibiting clustered arrangements, it is necessary to partitioned the study region into areas that *potentially* might differ from each other in the direction of asymmetrical co-arrangement of the types (should they be co-arranged) and that are internally homogeneous for this characteristic. Then, within each uniform stratum, the coefficient AVDIST may be calculated without bias, and the average of all AVDIST statistics from all strata, weighted by the numbers of distances used in calculating them, may be used as an accurate measure of co-arrangement of the artifact types across the study area:

$$\text{AVDISTP} = \frac{\sum_{i=1}^{k} x_i(\text{AVDIST}_i)}{\sum_{i=1}^{k} x_i} \tag{3.40}$$

where AVDIST_i is that AVDIST coefficient found in the ith uniform stratum and x_i is the number of interitem distances (n or m in equation 3.38) used to calculate the AVDIST coefficient in stratum i, and k is the number of strata.

The unbiased AVDISTP coefficients for all pairs of artifact types where both types exhibit clustered arrangements, along with the AVDIST coefficients for all other possible pairs of types, then can be grouped by cluster analysis or multidimensional scaling, as previously described, to define polythetic, overlapping depositional sets not influenced by changes in the direction of asymmetrical co-arrangement over the site.

Partitioning the study area into uniform strata for a particular pair of clustered artifact types can be achieved by the following method. First, the limits of single-type clusters for both artifact types are defined, using one of the methods to be described later (pages 202–207). Second, the study area is partitioned into broad "potential zones of analysis" containing one or more single-type clusters of *both kinds* but no more than one pair of single-type clusters different in kind *that overlap spatially* (a potential use-area) (Figure 3.24). Each potential zone of

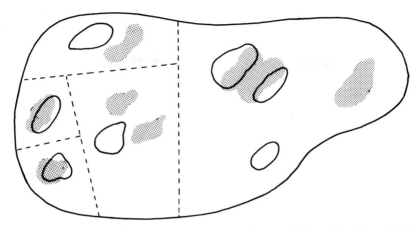

Figure 3.24. A site may be partitioned into broad zones within which different kinds of single-type clusters of artifacts are closer to one another than they are to similar single-type clusters, and within which asymmetry of co-arrangement of artifact types is uniform at the scale of the cluster.

analysis, which contains at most one co-arrangement of two types (one multitype cluster), is, by definition, uniform in the asymmetrical co-arrangement of types within it (if the types are co-arranged at all), assuming the multitype cluster is internally homogeneous in its direction of asymmetrical co-arrangement of types. Third, to insure homogeneity *within* each multitype cluster, the following remaining steps must be taken.

For the multitype cluster in question, the local densities of items of each type within the neighborhood of each item of both types is calculated. The radius of the neighborhood used to calculate local densities should be much less than the radius of the multitype cluster, but large enough to include several items of either type. Next, the multitype cluster is divided into areas of contiguous neighborhoods that similarly have greater densities of one artifact type than the other. These areas are homogeneous in the direction of asymmetry of the two types and may serve as strata within which unbiased AVDIST coefficients may be calculated. If single-type clusters also occur in the "potential zone of analysis," they must be combined with those homogeneous areas within the multitype cluster that are closest to them and that predominate in the artifact type they contain, to define the appropriate strata.

Extension of the Method to Data in the Form of Grid-Cell Counts. The method just summarized requires item point location data for the computation of geographic distances. For some data sets, however, it may be feasible to convert grid count data into a form consistent with the proposed methodology. If the archaeological site from which the data are taken is large enough, compared to the size of the collection units, and if the collection units are not larger than the expectable *minimal* dimensions of depositional areas, the centers of collection units may be used to approximate the actual provenience of the artifacts within them. This approach has been used on two data sets (Carr 1977, 1979, 1984a), giving reasonable results and allowing the investigation of polythetic patterning that otherwise would not have been possible.

Data Screening Required by the Method. Artifact types occurring *ubiquitously* across a site in *high densities* must be handled in a special way if they are not to cause analytical misrepresentations of the data. The manner in which they are handled should be consistent with their form of arrangement and with one's understanding ôf the activities and depositional processes by which the arrangement was produced.

Two circumstances are possible. First, the items of the ubiquitously, densely distributed artifact type might also exhibit significant *clustering*. This arrangement could result from either of two different sets of processes. It could represent the deposition of debris from an activity that produced much waste and that could be and was performed anywhere within the site, but that more often occurred in the vicinity of some preferred social gathering places (e.g., hearths) or some preferred physically attractive work areas. Whittling and knapping are examples of such activities. The arrangement also could reflect an artifact type: (1) that was disposed of at high rates; (2) that had multiple purposes, such that it was deposited at numerous locations of work or discard, producing clusters of the type; and (3) that then was "smeared" (Ascher 1968) by natural or human processes (e.g., soil creep or plowing) partially obscuring the discreteness of the clusters. Raw materials such as igneous rock, sandstone, and limestone, as well as pottery, in some Archaic and Woodland sites in the Eastern United States have spatial arrangements fitting this description.

As a second possible circumstance, the items of the ubiquitously, densely distributed artifact type might be scattered in a fairly *even density* over the whole site (a uniform or random arrangement). This arrangement could reflect either of the above two sets of formation processes, followed by *intensive* smearing of the artifact type so as to obscure most evidence of clustering. It might also represent debris from an activity that could be and was performed anywhere within the site, with preferred areas of performance being located differently and randomly at different times over the course of many reoccupations of the site.

Artifact types arranged in the second manner can be analyzed together, using the method of polythetic association to determine their degree of co-arrangement. They cannot, however, be analyzed with nonubiquitously distributed types without distorting the relationships between these types in the clustering routine. The ubiquitously scattered types will associate polythetically, strongly, and approximately equally with all nonubiquitously distributed types, masking the relationships between the latter (Carr 1979). Thus, two separate analyses—one for evenly, ubiquitously scattered artifact types and one for nonubiquitously scattered artifact types—must be performed. This requirement is not undesirable because the two different kinds of artifacts have different depositional patterns and can be expected to belong to different depositional sets.

Ubiquitious, clustered artifact types, too, might be analyzed with the ubiquitious, evenly scattered types and segregated in analysis from nonubiquitously scattered types to avoid distortion of relationships between the nonubiquitously scattered types. This, however, would bypass the opportunity for investigating relationships between locations where the ubiquitous types tend to cluster and locations where nonubiquitous types cluster. To investigate such patterns with accuracy, it is necessary to partition the arrangement of each ubiquitous, clustered type into its two dimensions—ubiquitous and clustered—and to analyze these dimensions separately. The clustered dimension of each type can be analyzed with artifact types that are nonubiquitously distributed. The ubiquitous dimension of each type can be analyzed with types having a ubiquitous, even arrangement.

This procedure is satisfying because it acknowledges that the arrangement of a ubiquitously clustered type is a compound result—a palimpsest—of two distinct depositional processes (e.g., the deposition of an artifact in a clustered distribution, followed by smearing) (Carr 1982).

To partition a ubiquitous, clustered arrangement of artifacts into its two dimensions, the techniques of spatial filtering or Fourier analysis (Carr 1982, 1983, 1984a; Davis 1973) can be applied. These techniques allow the construction of a smoothed surface of broad-scale spatial trends in artifact density variation (representing the ubiquitous dimension) and the calculation of small-scale, local deviations in artifact density from the trend (representing the clustered dimension). A complete detailing of the procedures of spatial filtering using grid-count and item-point location data is beyond the scope of this chapter. However, specific procedures for isolating items belonging to the clustered dimension of a compound artifact arrangement using point location data are discussed in the next section on delimiting clusters.

Evaluation of Polythetic Association. The technique of polythetic association is consistent with the organization of intrasite archaeological records with one exception (Table 3.4). The method is capable of determining the degree of co-arrangement of artifact types at only the most local scale of analysis, represented by interitem distances; it leaves broader-scale co-arrangements uninvestigated. Thus, although the approach is adequate for defining sets of artifact types that repeatedly occur in *close proximity* to each other and represent depositional sets, broader scale, hierarchical relationships between depositional sets and between clusters, describing patterns of activity organization and community structure, cannot be assessed. This limitation might be overcome by seeking relationships among *n*th-order nearest neighbors, a route of analysis that remains to be investigated.

A trial application of *some* of the aspects of polythetic association previously described is given by Carr (1979). The depositional sets defined by its application were intuitively meaningful. More rigorous testing of the full set of procedures is under way (Carr 1984a).

Methods for Delimiting Spatial Clusters of Artifacts

Modified Radius Approach I

Two techniques for defining single-types clusters and multiple-type clusters (depositional areas) can be designed by modifying Whallon's (1974) "radius approach" (see pages 181–182). Both require data in the form of item point locations.

The first method begins with a series of histograms of interitem nearest neighbor distances, one histogram for each artifact type showing significant clustering by one of the methods previously described (see pages 183–189). If the histograms exhibit large outliers, these must be eliminated, to prevent their inordinate effect on the statistics to be calculated in later steps. This screening process is acceptable because isolated single items corresponding to such large nearest neighbor distances are not of consequence in defining clusters of items. If the histograms are multimodal, they should be partitioned into their component modes by visual, graphic, or numerical methods (e.g., Bhattacharya 1967). The different modes of nearest neighbor distances in a histogram hopefully pertain to items within *different clusters of different densities,* there being minimal dispersal of the interitem distances of items in *one* cluster among several modes. This may be checked for each individual mode by plotting on a map all the item-pairs to which the nearest neighbor distances within that mode pertain. Most of the item-pairs should cluster spatially into one cluster or several clusters of similar density, for a given mode. If the histogram of nearest neighbor distances for an artifact type is multimodal but does not show this correspondence between the items to which a mode pertains and spatial clusters of those items, the method outlined here is inappropriate.

Next, the mean and standard deviation of the nearest neighbor distances in each frequency distribution, if it is unimodal (or each mode, if it is multimodal), is determined. A cutoff distance of 1.65 σ above the mean is defined for each unimodal distribution and mode, encompassing those 95% of all nearest neighbor connections that are more likely to occur within rather than between clusters. For each artifact type, a map is then made, showing the locations of all items of that type. Circles are drawn around each item, the radius of the circle being equivalent to the cutoff distance of the mode and type to which the item belongs. The intersecting circles for items of the same type and mode should define one or more clusters of items of the same type and of similar density. Types having histograms of nearest neighbor distances with multiple modes will have multiple clusters of different densities, at least one cluster for each mode.

Once spatial clusters for each type have been delimited on the maps of items of single types, the maps can be overlaid to define depositional areas. Depositional areas will be indicated by the similar placement of clusters of items of *those types that previously have been shown to form depositional sets.* Clusters of items that overlap but contain types that do not form depositional sets simply reflect different depositional areas that happen to overlap in *some* cases. The *exact* perimeter of a depositional area should be defined by the *union* of the areas ocurring within the clusters having similar placement and having types within the same depositional set, as opposed to the *intersection* of such areas (Figure 3.25). *This procedure accommodates the polythetic arrangement, within and between depositional areas, of items of different types in the same depositional set* (e.g., artifact types with different discard rates and densities).

 THAT PORTION OF THE PERIMETER OF THE DEPOSITIONAL AREA DEFINED BY CIRCLES SURROUNDING ITEMS OF TYPE ".″ WITH A SMALL CUTOFF RADIUS

 THAT PORTION OF THE PERIMETER OF THE DEPOSITIONAL AREA DEFINED BY CIRCLES SURROUNDING ITEMS OF TYPE "X″ WITH A LARGER CUTOFF RADIUS

Figure 3.25.   Depositional areas can be defined by the *union* of areas within clusters containing artifacts of types previously shown to form depositional sets.

The modified radius approach is concordant with the nature of organization of the archaeological record with two exceptions (Table 3.4). (1) Clusters must be fairly homogeneous internally in local artifact density, to the extent that clusters of different average densities do not share a large proportion of subareas with similar local density. (2) Clusters may not be hierarchically nested to the extent that they are internally heterogenous in artifact density and that the first condition holds. Either condition may cause items associated with nearest neighbor distances in single modes of a multimodal histogram not to cluster spatially, prohibiting the definition of meaningful cutoff distances. For these situations, the second modified radius approach may be used to delimit depositional areas.

Modified Radius Approach II

The second approach for defining depositional areas, modified from Whallon's (1974) method, again involves the definition of single-type clusters, followed by the overlaying of clusters of two or more types.

To begin, for each artifact type showing significant spatial clustering by some method, a data matrix is assembled. Each data matrix lists the two dimensional coordinates of each item of the type in question and the distances of the items from their nearest neighbors of the same type. The information contained in each matrix defines a surface of nearest neighbor distance values, which also may be interpreted as a surface of local item density values. Each matrix then is analyzed using digital spatial filtering techniques (Gonzalez and Wintz 1977; Carr 1982) to isolate: (1) large-scale geographic trends in the values of nearest neighbor distances—trends in item density—and (2) local deviations of nearest neighbor distance values and item density from the broader trends. The latter, if negative in value, may be interpreted as locations of significant artifact density/clustering.

Spatial filtering of a surface represented by irregularly spaced nearest neighbor distance values at the locations of items first requires the rediscription of the surface as a regular, fine-meshed grid of distance values. The values of each such grid point can be determined by interpolation from the values of the original observations surrounding it (Davis 1973:310–317).

A smoothed surface of nearest neighbor distance values representing large-scale density trends then is obtained by replacing each grid value with a weighted average of the grid values surrounding it. The particular smoothing *operator* or *filter function* used to accomplish this task can vary in the weighting scheme used and the distance (*filtering interval, search radius*) over which averaging occurs (Davis 1973:225–227). A generalized filter of the form specified by Zurflueh (1967) is preferable over other generalized operators in most cases where the specific structure of the data is not known, and is recommended. The filtering interval used in generating the smoothed surface should be slightly greater than the *maximum* expectable size of artifact clusters, in order to define trends sufficiently broad that they do not include local variations in density attributable to the clustering of artifacts. Different artifact types may be analyzed with filters having different interval widths, according to the expectable maximum size of their clusters.

Local deviations of nearest-neighbor distances and item density from broader density trends can be found with two steps. First, a smoothed value at each of the original, irregularly spaced item locations is found by interpolation from the smoothed values of adjacent grid points. Second, the smoothed value at each item location is subtracted from its original value. The resulting residual values define a map of locations where nearest-neighbor distance values are less than the expectable local norm (item density is anomalously high) and greater than the expectable local norm (item density is anomalously low). The former, *negative* nearest-neighbor distance anomalies are of interest as locations of significantly high artifact density that comprise single-type artifact clusters.

To define the perimeter of such clusters, a map is constructed with circles drawn around those items having anomalously low nearest-neighbor distances, the radius of each circle equal to the smoothed nearest neighbor distance of the item it is drawn around. Intersecting circles in the map should define one or more clusters having items of the same type but in variable average densities that are greater than the local norm.

The same filtering and mapping operations are repeated for each artifact type showing significant clustering. The perimeters of multitype depositional areas may be defined, as before, by the union of areas within those clusters containing artifacts of types previously shown to be co-arranged.

Those steps of this method involving the use of spatial filtering techniques to define a smoothed surface and a surface of local deviations can also be achieved using Fourier analysis (Carr 1982, 1983, 1984a; Gonzalez and Winz 1977). Although more complex, Fourier analysis can provide a technically cleaner definition and separation of large-scale trends and local deviations when filter functions are carefully designed.

The method just outlined is very nearly concordant with the nature of organization of intrasite archaeological data (Table 3.4). Its primary drawback is that it requires, prior to analysis, an estimate of the maximum expectable size of artifact clusters of each type, in order to generate the smoothed surface of nearest neighbor values for each artifact type. The estimate may be made on the basis of visual inspection of the spatial data prior to analysis or a priori behavioral considerations, including ethnographic documentation of the sizes of use-areas of kinds expected to be found.

The method also does not allow objective analysis of the hierarchical organization of depositional areas. Although it is possible to delimit different levels of a cluster hierarchy using different filters with smoothing intervals of different widths, choice of the widths requires a priori knowledge of the scales of the different levels of the cluster hierarchy. This knowledge usually is obtainable only through visual inspection of the data, in which case analytical results represent only technical verification of what already has been subjectively observed.

The Contiguity-Anomaly Method

The contiguity-anomaly (CA) method was designed by Gladfelter and Tiedemann (1980, 1984), with aid from B. Hole (Tiedmann *et al.* 1981). Like the modified radius approach II, it evaluates local variability in some measure independent of regional trends, using a running operator function. However, this method additionally provides an assessment of the *significance* of local variability, which the radius approach does not.

The CA method uses grid-count data. It aims at locating "interesting" grid cells—cells having values (e.g., artifact densities) that are significantly different from or similar to the values in adjacent cells, compared to expectation. Using the numerator of Geary's C statistic of auto-correlation (Geary 1968) as a basis, the difference of a cell from its k neighboring cells for some variable is defined as

$$SSD = \sum_{i=1}^{k} (x_i - x_0)^2 \qquad (3.41)$$

where x_0 is the value of the variable in the cell of concern, and the x_i are the values in the k surrounding cells. This deviation then is used in either of two ways to determine whether the value in a particular cell, relative to those in surrounding cells, is expectable, significantly different, or significantly similar. (1) The mean and variance of all deviations in the study area is determined. A particular cell value is classified significant if its deviation is greater than some number of standard deviations above the mean or less than some number of standard deviations below the mean. (2) Through Monte Carlo simulation, the cells within the study area can be rearranged a number of times, and the cumulative distribution of deviations estimated. A given cell value then is classified as significant if its deviation is greater or less than that associated with a pre-specified percentage of cells in the cumulative distribution.

To enhance the sensitivity of the method to more subtle local deviations, it is necessary to identify extreme outliers in the histogram of cell values and remove them from consideration. This can be done with a number of standard statistical or graphic methods.

Once interesting cells have been identified, they may be classified along two dimensions: (1) by whether they represent significantly large or small local deviations, and (2) by the value of their observations (high, medium, low, etc.) compared to the mean of cell observations in the study area. Using this classification, the study area can be mapped for areas having significant localized maxima and minima; for planar surfaces composed of cells with significantly similar values; and for significant slopes between planar surfaces of different average value.

The CA method is intended by its designers to be used with grid cells of the size of the phenomenon of interest, to allow definition of the locations of the phenomenon. In the case of the analysis of intra-site artifact distributions, grid cells of artifact counts would be constructed to the expected size of depositional areas. This approach allows the locations of clusters of artifacts and areas of very low artifact density (e.g., cleaned work areas) to be pinpointed, as Gladfelter and Tiedemann (1984) illustrate. It does not, however, lead to a precise delimitation of the boundaries of depositional areas.

It is possible to modify the approach slightly, in order to define the borders of depositional areas, by using grid cells much smaller than the areas. When this is done, cells within the interior of a depositional area will have significantly similar artifact counts (high or low, depending on whether the area is a location of artifact clustering or vacancy), provided the area is relatively homogeneous in artifact density. The borders of the depositional areas, where artifact counts change most rapidly from cell to adjacent cell, will be composed of cells classi-fied as significant slopes, provided the area has artifact densities sufficiently anomalous compared to background artifact densities.

Upon defining the limits of single-type artifact clusters and voids, multitype clusters and voids representing depositional areas may be defined by the union of such areas having similar placements and having types within the same deposi-tional set, as discussed previously (page 203).

The CA method, as adapted here to the problem of delimiting depositional areas, is discordant with the organization of the archaeological record in three ways.

Discordance 1. It assumes that each artifact cluster or void is either (1) relatively homogeneous internally in its artifact densities compared to other zones within the study unit, or (2) is fairly anomalous in its average artifact density such that artifact densities change rapidly at its borders. If neither of these conditions occurs, the deviations of cells comprising the area and its boundary will not be classified as significantly interesting (similar and different, respectively). Although the CA method provides some control over these prob-lems by allowing the threshold values defining the significance of local devia-tions to be varied, the response of the method has limits.

Discordance 2. Closely related to the first discordance, the CA method as-sumes that all depositional areas are similar in their degree of internal homogene-ity of artifact densities and in their density changes at their borders. Also, background artifact density variation is assumed uniform over the density area. These assumptions derive from the fact that the significance of local deviations is defined using *one* frequency distribution or cumulative frequency distribution of deviations pertaining to the whole study area.

Discordance 3. The CA method, as all spatial techniques using grid-cell count data for one grid system, may produce variable results, depending on the mesh of the grid in relation to the scale of archaeological anomalies.

The modified radius approach II is not encumbered by any of these problems or erroneous assumptions.

The contiguity-anomaly approach has several advantages over the modified radius approach II. (1) It allows patterns of local anomalies to be assessed objectively for their significance in addition to being discovered. (2) It does not require a continuous area of study. A number of discontinuous neighboring areas (e.g., a series of block excavations), each with multiple grid cells of equal mesh, may be examined as a unit. (3) The CA method allows the definition of nested cluster perimeters of a cluster hierarchy, so long as levels of the hierarchy are relatively internally homogeneous in density and have crisp boundaries.

Unconstrained Clustering

Unconstrained clustering is a method designed by Whallon (1979, 1984) explicitly to delimit multitype clusters (depositional areas) without violating their nature. The approach is best viewed as a *general strategy* that may involve a number of alternative algorithms and indices at the different stages of analysis, rather than a specific technique. Consequently, in discussing and evaluating it, it is necessary to keep separate those comments pertinent to the general strategy from those relevant to the way Whallon has operationalized it.

The method accomodates either grid-count or item-point location data. In either case, the first step in analysis is to represent the distributional data for each artifact type as a generalized pattern that does not restrict the size and shape of zones of different artifact density. The use of a contour map of each artifact type for such a representation is suggested. It can be constructed using any of a number of interpolation and data-smoothing methods (Cole and King 1968; Davis 1973), such as a running operator function defining the local density of artifacts of a given type within a stated search radius, or a two-dimensional running mean. The constructed surface is theoretically continuous, but in practice is represented by a fine-meshed grid of smoothed artifact densities.

Next, the smoothed densities of artifacts of each type at the *original* item locations or grid points (or some arbitrary grid of points) are determined. For a given type, its density at a data location is obtained by interpolation from its smoothed artifact densities at the nearest four grid points among the many representing its contour surface.

The similarity of each pair of original item or grid locations to each other with respect to their local artifact inventories then is measured using some similarity coefficient (e.g., a Euclidean distance or a Jaccard coefficient), operating on some measure of the artifact inventory of each data location (e.g., relative artiface type densities, the presence/absence states of types). Data locations then are grouped according to their similarity into sets using some unweighted, poly-thetic agglomerative clustering algorithm (e.g., average linkage, Ward's meth-od). Sets of similar locations, defined by some similarity threshold, are plotted on a map, their distribution indicating the spatial arrangement of localities of similar artifact composition. If clusters that are internally homogeneous in their artifact composition occur within the study area, locations similar in their artifact inventories will aggregate spatially, defining the limits of the clusters. Clusters similar in artifact composition will be allocated to the same set of data locations, indicating their like nature.

Unconstrained clustering, as a *general* strategy, has several problems but also offers an advantage over the modified radius approach II (Table 3.4).

Problem 1. The method is based on the unwarranted assumption that deposi-tional areas are fairly homogeneous, internally, in their artifact compositions. In particular, variation in composition within an area deriving from the polythetic arrangement of items of different types is not accomodated. To the extent that subsectors of a depositional area vary in their artifact inventories as a result of polythetic-causing formation processes, recovery methods, or artifact classifica-tion (Figure 3.23), data locations within different subareas may be characterized as dissimilar and allocated to different sets by the clustering routine, obscuring the integrity or altering the boundary of the depositional area.

The aspect of unconstrained clustering responsible for this circumstance is the nature of the similarity coefficients available for defining the degree of similarity in the artifact composition of two localities. As was discussed previously (see pages 192–196), such coefficients assume monothetic organization; the max-imum degree of similarity they can specify between observations *attenuates* as the attributes they operate on (here, artifact types within locales) become more polythetically distributed.

This problem is somewhat alleviated by clustering *smoothed* estimates of local artifact densities rather than local artifact densities, themselves. Local occur-rences of an artifact type in frequencies less than expectable, or unexpected absences of it, resulting from polythetic causing factors, are subdued within depositional areas by the smoothing operation.

Problem 2. In a similar manner, different clusters that are polythetically alike in their artifact compositions may be misrepresented as dissimilar, composi-tionally, by the monothetic similarity coefficients used in the clustering pro-cedure. This problem is not diminished by the preclustering smoothing operation.

Problem 3. The artifact inventories characterizing data locations and the pat-tern of similarity found between pairs of data locations will vary with the width of the running operator function used to construct the contour maps of each type and the degree to which the original data thus are smoothed. No criterion is offered to suggest the appropriate scale at which patterning should be sought. This is the same problem that dimensional analytic techniques were devised to circumvent (see pages 145–147, 151–153).

Problem 4. As Whallon (1979:12) points out, the strategy does not admit overlap among spatial clusters. Overlapping clusters are represented by a series of discrete sets of locations defining a gradational change in artifact composition. This results because the clustering algorithms used to define sets of similar points do not allow the construction of overlapping sets. Although overlapping clustering routines do exist (Jardine and Sibson 1968), they are too limited in the number of observations they can process to be useful to this method. This circumstance is not a problem to the extent that overlapping areas can be identified by inspection of the maps produced by the method.

To the good, unconstrained clustering allows the investigation of the potentially multilevel, hierarchically nested organization of depositional areas within sites. To delimit clusters at various levels of a cluster hierarchy, it is only necessary to vary the criterion of how similar two data locations must be to be considered members of the same set of similar locations. This is achievable by adjusting the threshold similarity coefficient value used to define sets of similar locations within the dendrogram of locations. The multiple, appropriate thresholds will be evident in the dendrogram or the plot of dissimilarity values against fusion step generated by the clustering procedure. In contrast, using the modified radius approach II, hierarchically nested organization of clusters can be defined only with iterative procedures (repeated adjustment of filter widths).

Finally, at the level of *specific operationalization* of unconstrained clustering, there is one problem with Whallon's application of the strategy. As a measure of the artifact inventories of each datum location to be clustered, Whallon used the relative frequencies (proportional densities) of artifact types. This, coupled with the requirement of internal homogeneity of clusters dictated by his use of a monothetic Euclidean distance coefficient, implies the assumption that within clusters, and between clusters of a similar nature, the *ratios* of artifact types remain constant. He also states this assumption as likely (Whallon 1984). As shown previously (pages 162–165), such an assumption is discordant with the expectable nature of the archaeological record, implying monothetic organization of depositional sets, expedient artifact deposition, and a number of the other problems discussed for correlation analysis. To circumvent these problematic assumptions, it is necessary to use (1) some other measure of the artifact inventories of data locations, and/or (2) some nonstandard similarity coefficient unaffected in value by the polythetic distribution of artifact types within and between clusters.

Unconstrained clustering is a very flexible strategy for defining depositional areas. It is likely that with further experimentation with the approach, reasonable solutions to its problems will be found.

CONCLUSION

The scientific process by which method and theory are advanced so as to improve our understanding of complex phenomena is a stepwise one. It involves repeated comparison between data, pattern-searching techniques, and interpretive models for their degree of logical consistency, and repeated alteration of model and techniques to bring them closer in line with data structure.

Our understanding of the structure of archaeological deposits and archaeological spatial data has improved over the past 10 years as the nature of human behavior and archaeological formation processes has been investigated and become apparent. The mathematical search techniques that we use to define the spatial organization of artifacts and facilities within sites, however, have not changed much during this time; they are logically inconsistent in various ways with the understanding we now have of the organization of the archaeological record and its causes. It is hoped that the proposed model of archaeological deposits and the evaluations of currently used spatial analytic techniques reviewed in this chapter will make archaeologists aware of these inconsistencies and suggest means by which they may be overcome. The alternative techniques presented here are a step in the right direction of eliminating discordance between data structure and method, but much more work is needed.

ACKNOWLEDGMENTS

This chapter owes much of its form to Robert Whallon, who taught me as a graduate student to question actively the appropriateness of applying particular techniques in analyzing particular kinds of data structures—to ask what assumptions about the data the techniques make, and whether those assumptions are justifiable in light of the nature of the phenomenon of interest. To him I am most indebted and very thankful. Michael Schiffer and a number of anonymous reviewers provided very constructive comments that helped me rephrase or add to certain critical arguments I have made in the paper. These I greatly appreciate, and have incorporated. P. Greig-Smith graciously read the manuscript for mathematical errors and currency. I am thankful for the heavy time commitment he undertook and his careful screening, though I remain responsible for the chapter's content.

REFERENCES

Adams, R. McC., and H. J. Nissen
    1972   *The Uruk countryside.* Chicago: University of Chicago Press.
Ahler, S. A.
    1971   Projectile point form and function at Rodgers Shelter, Missouri. *Missouri Archaeological Society, Research Series* 8.
Ammerman, A. J., and M. W. Feldman
    1974   On the making of an assemblage of stone tools. *American Antiquity* **39**(4, Pt. 1):610–616.

Anderberg, M. R.
    1973   *Cluster analysis for applications.* New York: Academic Press.
Anderson, D. C., and R. Shutler
    1977   Interpreting the major cultural horizons at the Cherokee sewer site (13CK405): A preliminary assessment. Paper presented at the 35th Plains Conference, Lincoln, Nebraska.
Ascher, R.
    1968   Time's arrow and the archaeology of a contemporary community. In *Settlement Archaeology,* edited by K. C. Chang. Palo Alto: National Press Books. Pp. 47–79.
Balout, L.
    1967   Procedes d'analyse et questions de terminologie dans l'etude des ensembles industrials du Paleolithique Inferieur en Afrique du Nord. In *Background to evolution in Africa,* edited by W. W. Bishop and J. D. Clark. Chicago: University of Chicago Press.
Battle, H. B.
    1922   The domestic use of oil among southern Aborigines. *American Anthropologist* **24**:171–182.
Behrensmeyer, A. K.
    1975   The taphonomy and paleoecology of Plio-Pleistocene vertebrate assemblages east of Lake Rudolf, Kenya. *Museum of Comparative Zoology* Bulletin 146(1).
Bhattacharya, C. G.
    1967   A simple method of resolution of a distribution into Gaussian components. *Biometrics* **23**:115–135.
Binford, L. R.
    1972   Directionality in archaeological sequences. In *An archaeological perspective,* by L. R. Binford. New York: Seminar Press. Pp. 314–326.
    1976   Forty–seven trips. *In* Contributions to anthropology: The interior peoples of northern Alaska, edited by E. S. Hall, Jr. National Museum of Man, Mercury Series, Archaeological Survey of Canada Paper 49.
    1978   *Nunamiut archaeology.* New York: Academic Press.
Binford, L. R., and S. R. Binford
    1966   A preliminary analysis of functional variability in the Mousterian of Levallois facies. *American Anthropologist* **68**(2):238–295.
Binford, L. R., et al.
    1970   Archaeology at Hatchery West. Society for American Archaeology, *Memoirs* 24.
Bordes, F.
    1961   *Typologie du Paleolithique Ancien et Moyen.* Bordeaux: Imprimeries Delmas.
    1968   *The Old Stone Age.* New York: McGraw–Hill.
Brown, J. A.
    1971   Dimensions of status in the burials at Spiro. *In* Approaches to the social dimensions of mortuary practices edited by J. A. Brown. Society for American Archaeology, *Memoirs* 25.
Brown, J. A., and L. Freeman
    1964   A UNIVAC analysis of sherd frequencies from the Carter Ranch pueblo, eastern Arizona. *American Antiquity* **31**:203–210.
Brose, D. S., and J. F. Scarry
    1976   The Boston Ledges shelter: comparative spatial analysis of early Late Woodland occupations in Summit county, Ohio. *Midcontinental Journal of Archaeology* **1**(2):179–228.
Carr, C.
    1977   The internal structure of a Middle Woodland site and the nature of the archaeological

record. Preliminary examination paper, Department of Anthropology, University of Michigan.

1979   Interpretation of resistivity survey data from earthen archaeological sites. Unpublished Ph.D. dissertation, Department of Anthropology, University of Michigan.

1981   The polythetic organization of archaeological tool kits and an algorithm for defining them. Unpublished paper presented at the annual meetings of the Society for American Archaeology, San Diego.

1982   Dissecting intra-site artifact distributions as palimpsests. Paper presented at the annual meetings of the Society for American Archaeology, Minneapolis.

1983   A design for intrasite research. Unpublished paper presented at the National Park Service Research Seminar in Archaeology. Fort Collins, CO.

1984a   Alternative models, alternative techniques: variable approaches to intra-site spatial analysis. In *Analysis of archaeological data structures,* edited by C. Carr. New York: Academic Press, (In press.)

1984b   Getting into data: philosophies on the analysis of complex data structures. In *Analysis of archaeological data structures,* edited by C. Carr. New York: Academic Press. (In press.)

Christensen, A. L. and D. W. Read

1977   Numerical taxonomy, R-mode factor analysis, and archaeological classification. *American Antiquity* **42**:163–179.

Clark, J. G. D., and M. W. Thompson

1954   The groove and splinter technique of working antler in the Upper Paleolithic and Mesolithic, with special reference to the material from Star Carr. *Prehistoric Society, Proceedings* **19**:148–160.

Clark, P. J., and F. C. Evans

1954   Distance to nearest neighbor as a measure of spatial relationships in populations. *Ecology* **35**:445–453.

Clarke, D. L.

1968   *Analytical archaeology.* London: Methuen.

Cole, A. J., and D. Wishart

1970   An improved algorithm for the Jardine–Sibson method of generating overlapping clusters. *Computer Journal* **13**(2):156–163.

Cole, J. P., and C.A.M. King

1968   *Quantitative Geography.* New York: John Wiley.

Cole, L. C.

1949   The measurement of interspecific association. *Ecology* **30**:411–424.

Collins, M. B.

1975   The sources of bias in processual data: an appraisal. In *Sampling in archaeology,* edited by J. W. Mueller. Tucson: University of Arizona Press. Pp. 26–32.

Cook, T. G.

1973   Koster: a lithic analysis of two Archaic phases in west-central Illinois. Unpublished Ph.D. dissertation draft, Department of Anthropology, Indiana University.

1976   Koster: an artifact analysis of two Archaic phases in westcentral Illinois. Northwestern University Archaeological Program *Prehistoric Records* 1, Evanston.

Cowgill, G. L.

1972   Models, methods, and technique for seriation. In *Models in archaeology,* edited by D. L. Clarke. London: Methuen. Pp. 381–424.

Crabtree, D. E.

1967   Notes on experiments in flintknapping, 3. The flintknapper's raw materials. *Tebiwa* **10**:8–25.

1968   Mesoamerican polyhedral cores and prismatic blades. *American Antiquity* **33**: 446–478.

1972   An introduction to flintworking. Idaho State University Museum *Occational Papers* 28.

Crabtree, D. E., and E. H. Swanson

1968   Edge–ground cobbles and blade making in the Northwest. *Tebiwa* 11:50–58.

Craytor, W. B., and L. R. Johnson, Jr.

1968   Refinements in computerized item seriation. *University of Oregon Museum of Natural History*, Bulletin 10.

Dacey, M. F.

1968   Order neighbor statistics for a class of random patterns in multidimensional space. *Annals of the Association of American Geographers* 53:505–515.

1973   Statistical tests of spatial association in the locations of tool types. *American Antiquity* **38**:320–328.

David, F. N., and P. G. Moore

1954   Notes on contagious distributions in plant populations. *Annals of Botany* (London, N. S.) **18**:47–53.

Davis, J. C.

1973   *Statistics and data analysis in geology.* New York: Wiley.

de Heinzelin de Braucourt, J.

1962   *Manuel de typologie des industries lithique.* Bruxelles: L'Institute Royal Des Sciences Naturelles De Belgique.

Driver, H. E.

1961   *Indians of North America.* Chicago: University of Chicago Press.

Earle, T. K.

1976   A nearest neighbor analysis of two Formative settlement systems. In *The early Mesoamerican village,* edited by K. V. Flannery. New York: Academic Press, Pp. 196–223.

Ebdon, D.

1976   On the underestimation inherent in the commonly used formulae. *Area* **8**:165–169.

Ellis, H. H.

1940   *Flint working techniques of the American Indians: an experimental study.* Columbus: Ohio State University Bureau of Business Research.

Evans, F. C.

1952   The influence of size of quadrat on the distributional patterns of plant populations. University of Michigan, *Cont. Lab. Vert. Biol.* **54**:1–15.

Freeman, L., and K. W. Butzer

1966   The Acheulean station of Torralba (Spain). A progress report. *Quarternaria* **8**:9–21.

Gardin, J. C.

1965   On a possible interpretation of componential analysis in archaeology. *In* Formal semantic analysis, edited by E. A. Hammel. *American Anthropologist, Special Publication* 67:9–22.

Geary, R.

1968   The contiguity ratio and statistical mapping. In *Spatial analysis: a reader in statistical geography,* edited by B. Berry and D. Marble. Englewood Cliffs, New Jersey: Prentice–Hall.

Getis, Q.

1964   Temporal land-use pattern analysis with the use of nearest neighbor and quadrat methods. *Annals of the Association of American Geographers* **54**:391–399.

Gifford, D. P.
    1978   Ethnoarchaeological observations of natural processes affecting cultural materials. In *Explorations in ethnoarchaeology,* edited by R. A. Gould. Alburquerque: University of New Mexico Press. Pp. 77–101.
    1981   Taphonomy and paleoecology: a critical review of archaeology's sister disciplines. In *Advances in archaeological method and theory,* (Vol. 4), edited by M. B. Schiffer. New York: Academic Press. Pp. 365–438.
Gladfelter, B. G., and C. E. Tiedemann
    1980   A computer program for evaluating archaeological spatial data. Paper presented at the annual meetings of the Society for American Archaeology, Philadelphia.
    1984   The contiguity–anomaly technique of spatial autocorrelation. In *Analysis of archaeological data structures,* edited by C. Carr. New York: Academic Press. (In press.)
Gonzalez, R. C., and P. Wintz
    1977   *Digital image processing.* Reading, Massachusetts: Addison–Wesley.
Goodall, D. W.
    1974   A new method for the analysis of spatial pattern by random pairing of quadrats. *Vegetatio* 29:135–146.
Goodyear, A.
    1974   The Brand site: a techno–functional study of a Dalton site in northeast Arkansas. Arkansas Archaeological Survey, *Research Series* 7.
Gould, R. A.
    1971   The archaeologists as ethnographer: a case from the Western Desert of Australia. *World Archaeology* 3(2):143–178.
    1978   *Explorations in ethnoarchaeology.* Albuquerque: University of New Mexico Press.
Gould, R. A., D. A. Koster,and A. H. L. Sontz
    1971   The lithic assemblage of the western desert Aborigines of Australia. *American Antiquity* 36(2):149–169.
Graybill, D. A.
    1976   New analytical strategies for spatial analysis. Paper presented at the Annual Meetings of the Society for American Archaeology, St. Louis.
Greig-Smith, P.
    1952a   Ecological observations on degraded and secondary forest in Trinidad, British West Indies. II. Structure of the communities. *Journal of Ecology* 40:316–330.
    1952b   The use of random and contiguous quadrats in the study of the structure of plant communities. *Annals of Botany* (London, N. S.) 16:293–316.
    1961   Data on pattern within plant communities. *Journal of Ecology* 49:695–702.
    1964   *Quantitative plant ecology.* London: Methuen.
Haggett, P.
    1965   *Locational analysis in human geography.* London: Arnold.
Hartigan, J. A.
    1975   *Clustering algorithms.* New York: Wiley.
Hempel, C. G.
    1966   *The philosophy of natural science.* Englewood Cliffs New Jersey: Prentice–Hall.
Hietala, H. J., and R. E. Larson
    1980   Intrasite and intersite spatial analyses at Bir Tarfawi. In *Prehistory of the eastern Sahara,* edited by F. Wendorf and R. Schild. Pp. 379–388. New York: Academic Press.
Hietala, H. J. and D. S. Stevens
    1977   Spatial analysis: multiple procedures in pattern recognition. *American Antiquity* 42(4):539–559.

Hill, A. P.
    1975   Taphonomy of contemporary and late Cenozoic East African vertebrates. Unpublished Ph.D. dissertation, Department of Anthropology, University of London.
Hill, J. N.
    1970   Broken K. pueblo: prehistoric social organization in the American Southwest. University of Arizona, *Anthropological Papers* 18.
Hodder, I. R.
    1972   Locational models and the study of Romano–British settlement. In *Models in archaeology,* edited by D. L. Clarke. London: Methuen. Pp. 887–909.
Hodder, I. R., and M. Hassal
    1971   The non-random spacing in Romano–British walled towns. *Man* **6**:391–407.
Hodder, I. R., and C. Orton
    1976   *Spatial analysis in archaeology.* Cambridge: Cambridge University Press.
Hole, F., and M. Shaw
    1967   Computer analysis of chronological seriation. *Rice University Studies, Monograph in Archaeology* **53(4).**
Holgate, P.
    1964   Some new tests of randomness. *Ecology* **53**:261–266.
Hopkins, B., and J. G. Skellam
    1954   A new method for determining the type of distribution of plant individuals. *Annals of Botany,* **18**:213–227.
Hsu, S., and C. E. Tiedemann
    1968   A rational method of delimiting study areas for unevenly distributed point phenomena. *Professional Geographer* **20**:376–381.
Jardine, N., and R. Sibson
    1968   The construction of hierarchic and non-hierarchic classifications. *Computer Journal* **11**(2):177–184.
Jones, E. W.
    1955   Ecological studies on the rain forest of southern Nigeria, IV. The plateau forest of the Okomu Forest reserve. *Journal of Ecology* **43**:564–594.
    1956   Ecological studies on the rain forest of southern Nigeria, IV. The plateau forest of the Okomu Forest reserve, (continued). *Journal of Ecology* **44**:83–117.
Joslin-Jeske, R.
    1981   The effects of curation on the archaeological record. Paper presented at the 46th annual meetings of the Society for American Archaeology, San Diego.
Kay, M.
    1980   Features and factors: activity area definition at Rodgers shelter. *In* Holocene adaptations within the lower Pomme de Terre river valley, Missouri, edited by M. Kay. Pp. 561–622. Unpublished report to the U. S. Army Corps of Engineers, Kansas City district, contract DACW41-76-C-0011. Springfield: Illinois State Museum.
Keeley, L. H.
    1977   The functions of Paleolithique flint tools. *Scientific American* **237**:108–126.
Kendall, M. G.
    1948   *Rank correlation methods.* London: Griffin.
Kershaw, K. Q.
    1957   The use of cover and frequency in the detection of pattern in plant communities. *Ecology* **38**:291–299.
    1964   *Quantitative and dynamic ecology,* Chapter 6, the Poisson series and the detection of non-randomness. New York: American Elsevier. Pp. 96–113.
Kimball, R., R. N. Shepard, and S. B. Nerlov (editors)
    1972   *Multidimensional scaling,* (Vol. 1 and 2). New York: Seminar Press.

Kraybill, N.
  1977   Pre-agricultural tools for the preparation of foods in the Old World. In *Origins of agriculture,* edited by C. A. Reed. The Hague: Mouton. Pp. 485–522.
Kruskal, J. B., and M. Wish
  1978   *Multidimensional Scaling.* Sage University.
Kullback, S. M., M. Kupperman, and H. H. Ku
  1962   An application of information theory to the analysis of contingency tables. *Journal of Research, National Bureau of Standards—B., Mathematics and Physics.* **66**B(4): 217–228.
Lange, F. W., and C. R. Rydberg
  1972   Abandonment and post-abandonment behavior at a rural central American house-site. *American Antiquity* **37**:419–432.
Leechman, D.
  1951   Bone grease. *American Antiquity* **16**:355–356.
Lewarch, D. E., and M. J. O'Brien
  1981   Effects of short term tillage on aggregate provenience surface pattern. *In* Plowzone archaeology: contributions to theory and technique, edited by M. J. O'Brien and D. E. Lewarch. Vanderbilt University, *Papers in Anthropology.*
Lieberman, G. J., and D. B. Owen
  1961   *Tables of the hypergeometric probability distribution.* Stanford: Stanford University Press.
Luton, Robert M., and David P. Braun
  1977   A method for testing the significance of aggregation and association in archaeological grid cell counts. Unpublished paper presented at the annual meetings of the Society for American Archaeology.
Marquardt, W. H.
  1978   Advances in archaeological seriation. In *Advances in archaeological method and theory,* (Vol. 1), edited by M. B. Schiffer. New York: Academic Press. Pp. 257–314.
Mason, O. T.
  1889   Aboriginal skin–dressing: a study based on material in the U.S. National Museum. United States National Museum, *Annual Report* 553–590.
  1895   *The origins of invention.* London: Walle Scott.
  1899   The man's knife among the North American Indians: a study in the collections of the United States National Museum. Smithsonian Institution, *Annual Report for the Year* 1897:727–742.
McCarthy, F. D.
  1967   *Australian Aboriginal stone implements.* Sidney: V. C. N. Blight, Government Printer, New South Wales.
McKellar, J.
  1973   *Correlations and the explanation of distributions.* Manuscript on file, Arizona State Museum Library, Tucson.
McNutt, C. M.
  1981   Nearest neighbors, boundary effect, and the old flag trick: a general solution. *American Antiquity* **46**(3):571–591.
Miles, C.
  1973   *Indian and Eskimo artifacts of North America.* New York: Bonanza Books.
Moorehead, W. K.
  1912   Hematite implements of the United States together with chemical analyses of various hematites. *Phillips Academy, Bulletin* 6. Andover.
Morisita, M.
  1959   Measuring the dispersion of individuals and analysis of the distributional patterns.

Kyushu University, *Memoires of the Faculty of Science, Series E (Biology)* 2:215–235.

1962 I_δ-index, a measure of dispersion of individuals. *Research in Population Ecology* 4:1–7. Fukuoka: Kyushu University.

Mountford, M. D.
1961   On E. C. Pielou's index of non-randomness. *Journal of Ecology* 49:271–276.

Nero, Robert W.
1957   A "graver" site in Wisconsin. *American Antiquity* 22(3):300–304.

O'Connell, J. E.
1977   Room to move: contemporary Alyawara settlement patterns and their implications for Aboriginal housing policy. Manuscript on file, Australian Institute of Aboriginal Studies, Canberra.

1979   Site structures and dynamics among modern Alyawara hunters. Paper presented at the Annual Meetings of the Society for American Archaeology, Vancouver.

Odell, G. H.
1977   The application of micro-wear analysis to the lithic component of an entire prehistoric settlement: methods, problems, and functional reconstructions. Unpublished Ph.D. dissertation, Department of Anthropology, Harvard University, Cambirdge, Massachusetts.

Odell, G. H., and F. Odell-Vereecken
1980   Verifying the reliability of lithic use-wear assessments by 'blind tests': The low power approach. *Journal of Field Archaeology* 7(1):87–121.

Osborne, C. M.
1964   The preparation of Yucca fibers: an experimental study. In *Contributions of the Wetherill Mesa archaeological project,* assembled by D. Osborne. Society for American Archaeology, *Memoirs* 19:45–50.

Paynter, R., G. W. Stanton, and H. M. Wobst
1974   Spatial clustering: Techniques of discrimination. Paper presented at the annual meetings of the Society for American Archaeology.

Peale, T. R.
1871   On the use of the brain and marrow of animals among the Indians of North America. *Smithsonian Institution, Annual Report for* 1870:390–391.

Peebles, C. S.
1971   Moundville and the surrounding sites: some structural considerations of mortuary practices, II. *In* Approaches to the social dimensions of mortuary practices, edited by J. A. Brown. Society for American Archaeology, *Memoirs* 25.

Pielou, E. C.
1959   The use of point-to-plant distances in the study of pattern of plant populations. *Journal of Ecology* 47:607–613.

1960   A single mechanism to account for regular, random, and aggregated populations. *Journal of Ecology* 48:575–584.

1964   Segregation and symmetry in two-species populations as studied by nearest neighbor relationships. In *Quantitative and dynamic ecology,* edited by K. A. Kershaw. New York: American Elsevier. Pp. 255–269.

1969   *An Introduction to mathematical ecology.* London: Methuen.

1975   *Ecological diversity.* New York: Wiley.

1977   *Mathematical ecology.* New York: Wiley.

Pinder, D. A.
1971   The spatial development of the Luton Hat Industry in the early twentieth century. *Southampton Research Series in Geography* 6. University of Southampton, England.

Pinder, D., I. Shimada, and D. Gregory
    1979   The nearest neighbor statistic: archaeological application and new developments. *American Antiquity* **44**:430–445.

Plog, F.
    1974   Settlement patterns and social history. In *Frontiers of anthropology,* edited by M. J. Leaf. New York: Van Nostrand. Pp. 68–91.

Price, T. D. II
    1975   Mesolithic settlement systems in the Netherlands. Unpublished Ph.D. dissertation, Department of Anthropology, University of Michigan, East Lansing.

Reid, J. J.
    1973   Growth and response to stress at Grasshopper pueblo, Arizona. Unpublished Ph.D. dissertation, Department of Anthropology, University of Arizona.

Riddell, F., and W. Pritchard
    1971   Archaeology of the Rainbow Point site (4–Plu–594), Bucks Lake, Pumas County, California. *In* Great Basin Anthropological conference 1970: selected papers, edited by C. M. Aikens. University of Oregon, *Anthropological Papers* 1:59–102.

Roper, D. C.
    1976   Lateral displacement of artifacts due to plowing. *American Antiquity* **41**(3):372–375.

Rummel, R. J.
    1970   *Applied factor analysis.* Evanston: Northwestern University Press.

Saunders, J. J.
    1977   Late Pleistocene vertebrates of the western Ozark highland, Missouri. Illinois State Museum, *Reports of Investigation* 33. Illinois State Museum, Springfield.

Saxe, A. A.
    1970   *Social dimensions of mortuary practices.* Unpublished Ph.D. dissertation, Department of Anthropology, University of Michigan, East Lansing.

Schiffer, M. B.
    1972   Archaeological context and systemic context. *American Antiquity* **37**:156–165.

    1973   Cultural formation processes of the archaeological record: applications at the Joint site, east central Arizona. Unpublished Ph.D. dissertation, Department of Anthropology, University of Arizona, Tucson.

    1975a   Behavioral chain analysis: activities, organization, and the use of space. *Fieldiana: Anthropology* **65**:103–120.

    1975b   The effects of occupation span on site content. *In* The Cache River archeological project, assembled by M. B. Schiffer, and J. H. House. Arkansas Archeological Survey, *Research Series* 8:265–269.

    1975c   Factors and "tool kits": evaluating multivariate analysis in archaeology. *Plains Anthropologist* **20**:61–70.

    1976   *Behavioral archeology.* New York: Academic Press.

    1977   Toward a unified science of the cultural past. *In* Research strategies in historical archeology, edited by S. South. New York: Academic Press. Pp. 13–40.

    1982   Identifying the formation processes of archaeological sites. Manuscript on file, Department of Anthropology, Arizona State Museum Library, Tucson.

Schiffer, M. B., and W. L. Rathje
    1973   Efficient exploitation of the archaeological record: penetrating problems. In *Research and theory in current archeology,* edited by C. L. Redman. New York: Wiley. Pp. 169–179.

Semenov, S. A.
    1964   *Prehistoric technology: an experimental study of the oldest tools and artifacts from traces of manufacture and wear.* London: Cory, Adams, and MacKay.

Shipman, P.
  1981   *Life history of a fossil: introduction to taphonomy and Paleoecology.* Cambridge: Harvard University Press.
Simpson, E. H.
  1949   Measurement of diversity. *Nature* **163**:688.
Sneath, P. H., and R. R. Sokal
  1973   *Numerical Taxonomy.* San Francisco: Freeman.
Sollberger, J. B.
  1969   The basic tool kit required to make and notch arrow shafts for stone points. *Texas Archaeological Society, Bulletin* 40:231–240.
Speth, J. D.
  1972   Mechanical basis of percussion flaking. *American Antiquity* **37**:34–60.
Speth, J. D., and G. A. Johnson
  1976   Problems in the use of correlation for investigation of tool kits and activity areas. In *Cultural change and continuity,* edited by C. Cleland. New York: Academic Press, Pp. 35–75.
Stein, J.
  1983   Earthworm activity: a source of potential disturbance of archaeological sediments. *American Antiquity* **48**(2):277–289.
Stiteler, W. M., and G. P. Patil
  1971   Variance-to-mean ratio and Morisita's index as measures of spatial patterns in ecological populations. In *Statistical ecology, (Vol. 1): spatial patterns and statistical distributions,* edited by G. P. Patil, E. C. Pielou, and W. E. Waters. University Park: Pennsylvania State University Press. Pp. 423–452.
Strackee, J., and J. J. D. van der Gon
  1962   The frequency distribution of the difference between two Poisson variates. *Statistica Neerlandica* **16**:17–23.
Svedberg, T.
  1922   Ett bidrag till de statistika metodernas användning inom vaxbiologien. *Svensk bto. Tidskr.* **16**:1–8.
Swanton, J. R.
  1946   Indians of the southeastern United States. *Bureau of American Ethnology* Bulletin 137.
Thomas, D. H., and R. Bettinger
  1973   Notions to numbers: Great Basin settlements as polythetic sets. In *Research and theory in current archeology,* edited by C. L. Redman. New York: Wiley. Pp. 215–237.
Thompson, H. R.
  1956   Distribution of distance to nth neighbor in a population of randomnly distributed individuals. *Ecology* **37**:391–394.
  1958   The statistical study of plant distribution patterns using a grid of quadrats. *Australian Journal of Botany* **6**:322–342.
Tiedemann, C. E., B. G. Gladfelter, and B. Hole
  1981   The contiguity–anomaly method: a nonstandard approach to spatial autocorrelation. Paper presented at the annual meetings of the Society for American Archaeology, San Diego.
Tixier, J.
  1963   *Typologie de l'Epipaleolithique du Maghref.* Paris: Arts et Metiers Graphiques.
Trubowitz, Neal
  1978   The persistence of settlement pattern in a cultivated field. In *Essays in northeastern anthropology in memory of Marian White,* edited by W. Engelbrech, and D. Grayson. Rindge, New Hampshire: Franklin Pierce College.

1981   Settlement pattern survival on plowed northeastern sites. Paper presented at the annual meetings of the Society for American Archaeology, San Diego.

Voorhies, M. R.
1969a   Sampling difficulties in reconstructing late Tertiary mammalian communities. *Proceedings of the North American Paleontological Convention*, September 1969, Part E:454–468.
1969b   Taphonomy and population dynamics of an early Pliocene vertebrate fauna, Knox County, Nebraska. University of Wyoming. *Contributions to Geology, Special Paper* 1.

Wandsnider, L. A., and L. R. Binford
1982   Discerning and interpreting the structure of Lazaret cave. Paper presented at the annual meetings of the Society for American Archaeology, Minneapolis.

Washburn, D. K.
1974   Nearest neighbor analysis of Pueblo I–III Settlement patterns along the Rio Puerco of the east, New Mexico. *American Antiquity* **39**:16–34.

Watanabe, H.
1972   *The Ainu ecosystem.* Seattle: University of Washington Press.

Wahugh, F. W.
1916   Iroquois foods and food preparation. Canada Department of Mines, *Geological Survey Memoir* 86, Anthropological Series 12.

Whallon, R.
1973   Spatial analysis of occupation floors I: application of dimensional analysis of variance. *American Antiquity* **38**:320–328.
1974   Spatial analysis of occupation floors II: the application of nearest neighbor analysis. *American Antiquity* **39**:16–34.
1979   Unconstrained clustering in the analysis of spatial distributions on occupation floors. Paper presented at the 44th Annual Meetings of the Society for American Archaeology, Vancouver.
1984   Unconstrained clustering for the analysis of spatial distributions in archaeology. In *Intrasite Spatial Analysis*, edited by H. J. Hietala. Cambridge: Cambridge University Press. (In press.)

Wheat, Joe Ben
1972   The Olsen–Chubbuck site: a Paleo-Indian bison kill. Society for American Archaeology, *Memoirs* 26.

Wilmsen, E. N.
1970   Lithic analysis and cultural inference: A Paleo–Indian case. University of Arizona, *Anthropological Papers* 16.

Winters, H. D.
1969   *The Riverton culture.* Illinois State Museum (Springfield) and Illinois Archaeological Survey (Urbana).

Wood, R. W., and D. L. Johnson
1978   A survey of disturbance processes in archaeological site formation. In *Advances in archaeological method and theory*, vol. 4, edited by M. B. Schiffer. New York: Academic Press. Pp. 315–381.

Yellen, J. E.
1974   The !Kung settlement pattern: an archaeological perspective. Unpublished Ph.D. dissertation, Department of Anthropology, Harvard University, Cambridge, Massachusetts.
1977   *Archaeological approaches to the present.* New York: Academic Press.

Zubrow, Ezra
    1971   Carrying capacity and dynamic equilibrium in the prehistoric Southwest. *American Antiquity* **36**:127–138.

Zurflueh,
    1967   Applications of two dimensional linear wavelength filtering. Geophysics 32:1015–1035.

Discovering Sites Unseen

FRANCIS P. MCMANAMON

INTRODUCTION

Growing concern exists among archaeologists about the methods and techniques used to discover archaeological sites, reflecting increasing interest in regional analysis and archaeological resource management. Newly explicit attention to site discovery owes much to the requirements of contemporary archaeological resource management, which has as one of its general goals an understanding of the full range of archaeological resources, not simply those most easily found or already known (King *et al.* 1977:105ff.; Schiffer and Gumerman 1977:211ff.). The attention, however, is not limited to resource management concerns or to archaeology in the United States (e.g., Dyson 1978:253–255, 1982; Ammerman 1981:64–5, 81). Archaeological research of any sort that uses survey data from regions where site discovery is difficult must confront and resolve, or at least acknowledge, discovery problems.

Recent articles discuss site discovery problems generally and provide both a widely applicable framework for deriving solutions to specific discovery problems and specialized concepts and a vocabulary for discussing such problems (S. Plog *et al.* 1978; Schiffer *et al.* 1978). Two of these concepts, *visibility* and *obtrusiveness*, are central to the identification and solution of discovery prob-

ADVANCES IN ARCHAEOLOGICAL
METHOD AND THEORY, VOL. 7

lems. *Visibility* is a characteristic of the modern environment in which a site is located. It refers to the extent to which a site has been buried or covered by soil aggradation and vegetation since its last occupation (Schiffer *et al.* 1978:6–7). Visibility, for example, is high in a region where vegetation is sparse and soil aggradation has been minimal. In such regions, sites on the present ground surface will be visible. Visibility is low in densely vegetated areas or where soil aggradation has been common, such as an uncultivated meadow, a forest, or a floodplain. In regions with these characteristics, sites will be buried and generally undetectable on the modern surface by the naked eye.

A site's *obtrusiveness,* on the other hand, depends upon its contents and the discovery technique used to detect it (Schiffer *et al.* 1978:6). Consider first the effect of site contents upon obtrusiveness. Large sites with dense and widespread contents or architectural remains are relatively obtrusive. When they are on or near the surface, such sites are highly obtrusive. They can be detected by many techniques so the easiest and the least-expensive technique can be chosen to discover them. Highly obtrusive sites, such as Midwestern mound complexes, thick eroding shell middens in coastal areas, Iroquois village sites in plowed fields, or large Southwestern habitation sites with architectural remains, are hard to miss. Simple intensive pedestrain survey using only visual inspection probably will discover sites with such characteristics. Many, probably most, sites are not highly obtrusive, however. Nor does the inclusion of a few highly obtrusive remains guarantee that a site will be discovered. Even a site with some obtrusive contents might go undiscovered because of poor visibility or an insufficiently intensive application of a discovery technique. Where visibility is hindered by vegetation and soil aggradation, the discovery of sites or portions of sites with relatively unobtrusive contents requires more complicated, time-consuming, and expensive techniques. The goal of using these special techniques is to increase the obtrusiveness of the sites so that they can be discovered.

A wide range of techniques has been or could be used to discover sites, though not all techniques are equally effective for all kinds of archaeological remains. Nor are all techniques suited for the full range of study-area sizes, environmental conditions, or project budgets. Confronted by the variety of possible techniques, each with varied capabilities and limitations, archaeologists must choose carefully when designing a discovery investigation.

The aim of this chapter is to provide some guidance for this decision making, either directly or by directing readers to appropriate references. In the following sections a number of techniques are described and their effectiveness, considering the kinds of remains they can detect and their logistical limitations, is discussed. As readers will see, my research and interest in the archaeology of Northeastern North America, where sites tend to be unobtrusive and visibility low, clearly pervades this article. The emphasis here is upon the effectiveness of a variety of techniques for the discovery of sites with unobtrusive contents in environments where visibility is poor and subsurface testing frequently necessary. Nevertheless, the effectiveness of technique given other remains and circumstances also is touched upon.

The identification of one or two discovery techniques that can be applied universally is not the goal of this study. On the contrary, it is recognized from the start that project goals, schedules, budgets, and environmental constraints, in addition to the variety of discovery techniques and methods of deploying them, tend to make each project's discovery problems and their solutions unique. It would be inappropriate to suggest a discovery technique for use in all situations. On the other hand, it is important to point out the strengths, weaknesses, assumptions, and constraints embodied in different techniques so that they can be considered accurately for use in specific situations.

The focus here is upon site discovery, not site examination or excavation. The latter two activities are site-specific and occur only after a site has been discovered. Their goals are to determine the size, shape, structure, and contents of a site. A number of recent articles that address various concerns for site-specific investigations of subsurface sites can be consulted regarding this topic (e.g., Asch 1975; Brooks *et al.* 1980; Brown 1975; Carr 1982; Chartkoff 1978; Chatters 1981; Dekin 1976, 1980; Knoerl 1980; Nance 1981; Newell and Dekin 1978; Rice *et al.* 1980; Versaggi 1981). Site discovery, on the other hand, focuses on a study area with the goal of locating all or a sample of sites within it. Often a technique applicable for discovery will be inappropriate for examination, and vice versa. By analyzing a number of techniques I hope to suggest whether they are useful for site discovery, examination, or both, as well as the general vegetation and topographic conditions under which each will be effective. Many of the techniques considered in this chapter are of limited effectiveness for the discovery of sites. In some cases this is due to the types of remains that the techniques are able to detect; in others it is caused by logistical or visibility problems.

A related aim of this chapter is to assemble a bibliography, albeit far from comprehensive, referencing useful but often obscure or limited-distribution reports and papers that throw light on the topic of site discovery. The bibliography serves also to point readers to fuller descriptions of the techniques. This is especially so for the more technically sophisticated techniques, many of which are not effective for the discovery of sites lacking either structural remains, or dense and abundant features, or anthropic soil horizons.

This article is, to my knowledge, the first extensive comparative study of site-discovery problems and specific techniques. Although many archaeologists have confronted the problem in specific situations, they have not faced the problem of general comparisons of techniques. For this reason there is little comparative information about different techniques and no existing framework for evaluating the effectiveness of different techniques. Where the former exist I have incorporated them here. To serve as a framework for evaluating effectiveness, I have developed a crude model of the abundance and intrasite distribution of the constituents of archaeological sites. As with all modeling, this involves both generalizations and some speculation.

The ability of each technique to detect various site constituents is a measure of its effectiveness for discovering different kinds of sites. If a technique cannot detect or is a poor detector of some constituents, sites with these constituents will be unobtrusive; they ordinarily will not be discovered using this technique. The effectiveness of any technique as a means of site discovery depends upon its ability to detect at least one of the constituents held in common among the sites being sought. The capability of the technique, however, is only one requirement for effective site-discovery. The detectable constituent(s) must occur commonly among the sites sought as well as be abundant and widespread enough within these sites to be intercepted and identified, given the specific application of the technique.

The next section considers these latter aspects of site obtrusiveness: intersite frequencies of site constituents and their intrasite and abundance distribution. Subsequent sections describe various techniques that have been or might be used to discover sites. The usefulness of each technique for site discovery is evaluated considering the constituent(s) it can detect as well as its logistical requirements.

THE CONSTITUENTS OF SITES

The archaeological record can be thought of as a more or less continuous spatial distribution of artifacts, facilities, organic remains, chemical residues, and other less-obvious modifications produced by past human activities (Dancey 1981:17–28; Dincauze et al. 1980:63–70). The distribution is far from even, with large areas where archaeological remains are infrequent and widely dispersed (e.g., Thomas 1975). There are other areas, however, where materials and other remains are abundant and clustered. It is these peaks of abundance and clustering in the archaeological record that commonly are referred to as *sites* (Dancey 1981:20).

For heuristic purposes and cultural or behavioral interpretations, archaeologists frequently describe sites as the loci of past human activities (e.g., Hester et al. 1975:13; Hole and Heizer 1969:59ff.). From other analytical perspectives, however, this facile, general definition is inadequate. For one thing, activities occur in systemic contexts and do not consistently result in remains deposited in archaeological contexts. Some kinds of activities had loci but did not result in the deposition of artifacts or residues into archaeological contexts. Other kinds of activities, for example, transporting goods or traveling, simply are not fixed to one location.

From a practical perspective, for problems of site discovery, the activity-oriented definition of *site* is not operational enough to be useful. When considering problems of discovery, sites are more properly defined operationally as the loci of archaeological materials and residue (Schiffer and Gumerman 1977: 183–184). Here, archaeological remains are divided into several categories referred to collectively as *site constituents*. Site constituents include, but are not necessarily limited to: artifacts, features, anthropic soil horizons, and human-generated anomalies of soil chemistry, resistivity, magnetism, or other soil characteristics. Several of these constituents are described and discussed in more detail below. The types, frequency, and intrasite spatial distribution of different constituents within a site strongly affect the likelihood of its detection.

Discovery itself requires only the detection of one or more site constituents. This is sufficient to suggest that a site might be present. The criteria that are used subsequently to determine whether a ''site'' actually exists (see Dancey 1981: 20–21) are immaterial to the prior issue of discovery. The important points of the preceding discussion for the perspective in this chapter are (1) that archaeological sites are physical and chemical phenomena, (2) that there are different kinds of site constituents, and (3) that the abundance and spatial distribution of different constituents vary both among sites and within individual sites.

It is important to consider the extent to which different types of site constituents occur among archaeological sites when evaluating the effectiveness of various techniques for site discovery. If, for example, a technique will detect only a site constituent that is expected to occur in a small fraction of the sites within a study area, then that technique is hardly likely to be the best choice if a project goal is to obtain a sample of sites that represent the total variation among sites. On the other hand, if a project goal is to identify only sites with a constituent that is relatively rare, then a technique that will detect that constituent is ideal, even if it detects no others.

It is important to consider the abundance and spatial distribution of various constituents within sites when considering the effectiveness of the techniques for site discovery. A constituent that occurs in many sites, but in only small amounts or in very small areas of sites, is likely to require a discovery technique that can be applied economically at very close intervals within a study area in order to ensure the detection of the rare or highly clustered constituent. If no such technique is available, a constituent with these intrasite characteristics is not a good candidate to focus discovery efforts on, despite its common occurrence among the population of archaeological sites.

Despite the fundamental relationship between discovery, the intersite frequency of site constituents, and their intrasite abundance and distribution, archaeologists have not examined and described the occurrence of site constituents systematically. This is because archaeological site analysis aims mainly to interpret site contents and structure culturally or behaviorally. It also reflects the traditional emphasis on the investigation of easily located sites, that is, obtrusive sites in areas where visibility is high and discovery was and is no problem. Recent concern among some archaeologists for the physical and chemical characteristics of archaeological sites indicates that this lacuna of archaeological information will begin to be filled in soon (Carr 1982; Nance 1980b, 1981; Rice *et al.* 1980; Scott *et al.* 1978; Stone 1981a, 1981b). The past lack of attention, however, means that there is no consolidated data base for reference regarding information about the intersite abundance or the intrasite frequency and distributions of site constituents in sites of various types, time periods, and different regions. Yet this sort of information would be extremely useful for determining the effectiveness of different techniques for discovering sites with particular frequencies and distributions of various constituents.

The following discussion about various site constituents, therefore, contains no empirically confirmed general statements. Lacking a comprehensive or core data-set for reference, examples of the abundance and distribution of different constituents are drawn from my experience and familiar sources rather than a more generally representative sample. The examples are not offered as "typical" sites; however, most sites contain one or more of the constituents discussed here. As will be noted instantly by historical archaeologists, the discussion and examples derive from my experience with and research interest in prehistoric remains. I hope that insights regarding historic-period remains also can be derived from this presentation but no one should infer that it is intended to do so directly.

Five of the most-common site constituents are considered in this chapter: (1) artifacts, (2) features (i.e., former facilities or parts of facilities), (3) anthropic soil horizons, (4) chemical anomalies, and (5) instrument anomalies, including magnetic, resistivity, and subsurface radar anomalies, as well as anomalies affecting surface vegetation or soil. These are what I perceive as the most commonly recognized and discussed constituents, not a comprehensive listing of all possible fractions of the archaeological record.

Artifact, Feature, and Anthropic Soil Horizon Distributions

The intrasite distributions of artifacts, features, and anthropic soil horizons are not isomorphic; nor are they invariably found, individually or as a group, at all sites. For this discussion, however, they are combined because the examples used here permit direct comparisons of their respective intrasite frequencies and distributions. Before proceeding, the terms must be defined. The term *artifacts* is used here to refer to the portable products and byproducts of human activities. Included are tools and manufacturing debris of stone (lithics), ceramics, wood, bone, antler, and other raw materials, along with fire-cracked rock and faunal and floral remains. Artifacts can be isolated or part of a dense cluster. They can be found within features and anthropic soil horizons, but it is the frequency and distribution of artifacts outside these other constituents that is of interest here. By *feature* is meant a sharply delimited concentration of organic matter, structural remains, soil discoloration, or a mixture of these and artifacts. Features typically are small relative to total site area; examples include trash or storage pits, hearths, house floors, building foundations, and postmolds. *Anthropic soil horizon,* on the other hand, refers to an extensive deposit that might be sharply or diffusely delimited. Such soil horizons typically result from deposition of large amounts of organic remains in a roughly delimited, relatively large (compared to features) area. They frequently have artifacts and features embedded in their matrices. Anthropic soil horizons sometimes are termed *middens.* A well-known example of such horizons is *shell middens,* dense deposits of shellfish and other remains found along some coasts and rivers. *Trash middens,* that is, dense, consolidated deposits of secondary refuse found in or adjacent to some sedentary settlement sites, are another frequently reported type of anthropic soil horizon. In other cases, such horizons are merely bands of distinct and anomalously colored soil in which sufficient organic material was deposited by human activities to alter the color of the natural soil profile. Anthropic horizons are the principal constituent used for the detection of deeply buried sites, as is discussed below.

For the comparisons in this section, the abundance or frequency of the individual types of constituents are measured by their average occurrence per excavation unit. The extent of the spatial distribution is measured by the number or percentage of excavation units in which the constituent occurs. The latter measure is not an ideal one for measuring the spatial arrangement of a constituent. Given the limited comparative data available, however, it is the measure that allows the most direct comparison of the extent of spatial distribution of the different constituents.

The difficulty of finding reports that include descriptions of the intrasite abundance and the spatial distribution of artifacts (as defined above), features, and anthropic soil horizons was surprising initially. Upon reflection, however, it is a logical expectation of the lack of attention by archaeologists to the strictly physical characteristics of sites and the lack of concern about discovery. Three examples are offered here, although even these require some extrapolation to derive comparative information about the intrasite abundance and horizontal distribution of artifacts, features, and anthropic soil horizons.

One source that includes sufficient data is the report on the Hatchery West site (Binford *et al.* 1970), an Archaic through Late Woodland village site in Illinois. The report describes the surface distribution of several kinds of common artifacts—chert chippage, ceramic sherds, and fire-cracked rock—as well as the distribution of subplowzone features within a large area from which the plowzone was stripped mechanically. By focusing upon the area where plowzone stripping occurred, distributions of artifacts and features can be compared to one

FRANCIS P. MCMANAMON

another directly. Apparently no anthropic soil horizon was found at Hatchery West, so this constituent is not included in the comparison. It is possible, however, to compare the abundance and spatial distribution of surface-collected artifacts, specifically ceramic sherds and chert chippage, with those of sub-plowzone features.

Ninety-six 6×6 m surface collection units were located within the area subsequently stripped. Judging from the artifact distribution maps in the report (Binford *et al.* 1970:5, Figure 2), 90% of the area was covered by a surface distribution of 1 to 5 ceramic sherds per 6×6 m collection unit (Table 4.1). Certainly sherd frequency per unit would have been higher and their spatial spread wider if the entire plowzone had been excavated and screened rather than only the surface artifacts collected. The surface distribution of chert chippage at a frequency of 10 or more per 36 m² at least partially covered 79% of the collection units; overall it covered approximately 59% of the stripped area (Binford *et al.* 1970:10–11, Figures 3 and 4). As with the sherds, recovery of chert chippage

TABLE 4.1

Comparisons of Abundance and Spatial Distributions of Artifacts, Features, and Anthropic Soil Horizons

Site/reference	Artifacts	Features	Anthropic soil horizons
Hatchery West, plowzone stripped area (Binford, *et al.* 1970: Figs. 2 and 3, pp. 7–13).	1. Ceramics (≥ 1 sherd/36 m²) cover 90% of the area. 2. Chert chippage (≥ 10 pieces/36 m²) occurs in 79% of the 6×6 m units, or approximately 59% of the area.	1. Occur in 53% of the 6×6 m units. 2. Cover 15% of the area	None recorded
Bacon Bend Site (40MR25) Stratum 7 (Chapman 1981: Figs. 7 and 12, pp. 12–29).	1. Occur in 94% of the $5 \times 5'$ excavation units. 2. $\bar{X}$/unit = 61.[a]	1. Occur in 61% of the $5 \times 5'$ excavation units. 2. $\bar{X}$/unit = 1.1	Widespread in the excavated area.
Iddins Site (40LD38) Stratum III (Chapman 1981: Figs. 48, 57 and 59, pp. 48–60)	1. Occur in 95% of the $5 \times 5'$ excavation units. 2. $\bar{X}$/unit = 145.[a]	1. Occur in 67% of the $5 \times 5'$ excavation units. 2. $\bar{X}$/unit − 1.4	Widespread in the excavated area.

[a] Average is for most frequent artifact type reported for site. Bacon Bend = "general excavation debitage"; Iddins = "bifacial thinning flakes $> \frac{1}{4}$ inch."

from all of the plowzone surely would have increased the inferred frequency and spread of chert chippage.

None of the 6 × 6 m grid units were filled completely by features that occur in at least a part of 51 collection units, or 59% of the total number. These 51 units included many that contained only a small section of feature, and features commonly overlapped the boundary between two or more units. Features covered only about 15% of the subplowzone surface of the stripped area.

As the data are described in the report, it is not possible to derive the frequencies of ceramics or chert chippage for each 6 × 6 m unit, nor can the exact area covered by artifacts be estimated as it can for features. Despite this, the overall spatial distributions of artifacts can be described and clearly are much more widespread than that of the features at Hatchery West.

A second example, one that includes consideration of an anthropic soil horizon, comes from a survey and two excavations by Chapman (1977, 1978, 1981) in the Little Tennessee River Valley. Chapman conducted a survey to locate deeply buried sites, and discovered a large number of them. Among the sites he partially excavated after their discovery are the Bacon Bend and Iddins sites. The report on these sites (Chapman 1981) contains data that allow a direct comparison of the intrasite abundance and spatial distribution of artifacts, features, and anthropic soil horizons.

Chapman (1978:3) selected for excavation portions of sites where anthropic soil horizons were prominent, so these data are biased in their favor. Judging from the photographs and excavation wall profiles in the site reports, the anthropic horizons are spread widely throughout the excavated areas (Chapman 1981:9–11, 50–55). These excavated areas are only a part of each site area, however, as demonstrated by the trenching done to delimit the anthropic soil horizon at the Iddins site. At Iddins, the anthropic soil horizon referred to by Chapman as a *midden* was identified in Trenches 2, 4, 5, and 7, which are distributed over a linear distance of about 100 m (300 feet). Artifacts, on the other hand, seem to be distributed more widely. In each of the trenches at least a few artifacts or pieces of fire-cracked rock were found. Artifacts or fire-cracked rock were also found in other trenches on either side of the main group. The distances between the main group of trenches (2, 4, 5, 6, 7) and the outliers (1, 3) are substantial, 190 m (625 feet) and 270 m (900 feet) respectively, and the continuous distribution of artifacts throughout the intervening areas is an inference that might not appeal to everyone. Even the spread of artifacts into part of this area, however, means that their spatial distribution is wider than that of the anthropic soil horizon. Furthermore, sites with artifacts but no anthropic soil horizons were not uncommon throughout the Little Tennessee survey area. In summarizing his results, Chapman (1978:3, 143) notes that many sites he discovered did not include thick, definite anthropic soil horizons like those at Bacon Bend and Iddens, although artifacts were found.

The spread of artifacts, of course, differs from their frequency in any given area and they must occur frequently enough to be discovered. For the excavated portions of the Bacon Bend and Iddins sites, data are available to estimate the average frequency per 5 × 5 ft excavation unit for both artifacts and features (Table 4.1). Artifacts occur in about 30% more excavation units than features and are much more frequent per unit. Most features, of course, are much larger than most artifacts; however, it is likely that within individual excavation units artifacts are more widely distributed than features and cover more space than the feature(s) within the unit. The large number of artifacts per unit, unless they are tighly clustered, suggests a wider distribution than does the small number of features, most of which are circular with diameters of about 60 cm (2 feet) (Chapman 1981:Figures 12 and 59). Data about the specific locations of artifacts within the excavation units are unavailable to pursue this question further.

The frequencies and spatial distributions of artifacts and features from these two excavation areas probably is not representative of the entire site areas. The areas excavated were chosen because they seemed to have the densest distribution of organic and artifactual remains (Chapman 1981:3). Other sections of the sites, within a boundary drawn according to a low frequency of artifacts or features, would not have such frequent and dense remains.

A third example provides data from entire site areas. These data come from four sites investigated as part of the Cape Cod National Seashore Archeological Survey (McManamon 1981b, 1981c, 1982). Sites were examined by shovel tests (ca. 40 cm diameter) and small excavation units (50 × 50 cm, to 150 × 150 cm). The tests and excavation units were distributed over the site areas, which were defined as the areas inside a 1-lithic-artifact-per-shovel-test contour line. A few of the tests and excavation units are adjacent to one another; most are spaced at 10 to 25 m intervals. The number of tests and units at the sites ranges from 34 to 86. The average frequencies of site constituents for tests and units in which they occur is given per .25 m^3 so that excavations with different volumes can be compared directly (Table 4.2). Artifacts are represented directly by the remains of chipped stone, but some extrapolation is required to infer the frequency and distribution of features and anthropic soil horizons. Features are represented by the occurrence of dense remains of fire-cracked rock or of distinctly delimited anomalies of soil color, texture, or contents. Anthropic soil horizons are represented most frequently by dense shellfish remains, a relatively common, but not ubiquitous, type of anthropic soil horizon in coastal archaeological sites.

As in the other examples, artifacts are dispersed much more widely than either of the other constituents—in 79–82% of the excavations (Table 4.2). Features occur in 2 to 19% and anthropic soil horizons in 6 to 28%. In addition to occurring in less of the area of these sites, the variation in occurrence is far more pronounced in the latter two types of constituents.

These three examples support the impression of many archaeologists about the

TABLE 4.2

Relative Frequency of Occurrence of Artifacts, Features, and Anthropic Soil Horizons in Excavation Squares and Shovel Tests at Four Sites on Outer Cape Cod, Massachusetts

Site (N units at site)	Occurrence	Chipped stone	Dense fire-cracked rock[a]	Dense shell-fish remains[a]
19BN274/339	% of units	79	17	17
(70)	$\bar{X}$ per unit	30/.25m³	2258g/.25m³	973g/.25m³
19BN341	% of units	81	19	28
(86)	$\bar{X}$ per unit	104/.25m³	305g/.25m³	439g/.25m³
19BN273/275	% of units	79	2	17
(53)	$\bar{X}$ per unit	29/.25m³	461g/.25m³	412g/.25m³
19BN340	% of units	82	6	6
(34)	$\bar{X}$ per unit	24/.25m³	445g/.25m³	319g/.25m³

[a] Dense deposits are those of 100 g or more. The percentages also include units that have features or anthropic soil horizons without dense fire-cracked rock or dense shellfish remains, respectively.

relative intrasite abundance and spatial distribution of these three site constituents. Artifacts commonly are the most widespread and abundant of site constituents. Features and anthropic soil horizons do not commonly approach the extended spatial distribution of artifacts and in some cases might not even exist in a site area or large portions of it.

Regarding the intersite abundance of these three types of site constituents, it might be sufficient to note that it is easy to conceive of archaeological sites that contain neither features nor anthropic soil horizons, but not so easy to imagine one without artifacts. This is so for two reasons. First, artifacts are made and used in more, and more widely distributed, activities than the other two constituents. In general, features result from activities that involve the construction, maintenance, and use of facilities such as storage pits, hearths, and structures. Anthropic soil horizons result from the relatively large-scale processing or dumping of organic materials. Both of these kinds of general activities are likely also to involve artifacts, some of which frequently end up in archaeological contexts along with the remains of the facility; that is, the feature(s) or the organic remains (the anthropic soil horizon). In addition, artifacts that are used in systemic contexts independent of facilities or large amounts of organic materials also are deposited in archaeological contexts through discard, loss, or abandonment.

The second reason that artifacts are more frequent and widespread in the archaeological record than are features and anthropic soil horizons is their relative durability. Lithic artifacts, for example, can persist for millions of years, withstanding weathering by natural agents and postdeposition disruptions by fauna or human agents. Not all types of artifacts are as durable as lithics, of course. Ceramics, metal, and bone artifacts, for example, break down rapidly in some depositional environments. In general, however, artifacts in archaeological contexts are less likely to be destroyed by natural soil processes or unnatural disruption (e.g., agricultural plowing) than either features or anthropic soil horizons.

In summary, all other things equal, techniques that detect artifacts will be more effective at discovery than those that detect only features or anthropic soil horizons. This general point is elaborated in a later section and consideration is given to the levels of intrasite artifact frequencies and spread that facilitate site discovery.

Chemical and Instrument Site Constituents

Like the first three constituents described, the last two are grouped for discussion, but for a different reason. It is argued here that these types of site constituents are of limited value for site discovery for at least one out of the following three reasons: (1) they have a low frequency among sites, (2) they are infrequent and/or highly clustered within sites, or (3) their detection requires extensive, detailed background information that is difficult to obtain for large study areas. On the other hand, for intrasite examination following discovery, the investigation of these types of constituents can be extremely useful both for planning excavations and behavioral interpretation (e.g., see Tite 1972; Carr 1977, 1982).

As with the previous section, this one is not a comprehensive description of the characteristics of chemical and instrument site constituents. A detailed presentation of the genesis, development, and interpretation of such constituents requires substantially more space than is available here, as demonstrated by Carr's (1982) thorough and illuminating examination of the chemical and resistivity constituents at the Crane site. Here my aim is merely to draw upon the detailed work that has been done and to argue for the position outlined above.

Chemical anomalies within sites usually are caused by the deposition of organic waste in the soil through the disposal of garbage, urination, and excretion (Cook and Heizer 1965:12–14; Provan 1971:39). Carr (1982:449–467) provides very detailed estimates of the proportions of various chemical elements in different kinds of refuse material. A variety of chemical elements within archaeological sites have been investigated, including calcium, carbon, magnesium, nitrogen, potassium, sodium, sulfur, and especially phosphorus in the form of soil phosphate (e.g., Carr 1982; Cook and Heizer 1965; Eidt 1973, 1977; Heidenreich and Konrad 1973; Heidenreich and Navratil 1973; Proudfoot 1976; Provan 1971; Valentine *et al.* 1980; Woods 1977).

Cook and Heizer's (1965:29–61) analysis of the chemical constituents of two groups of sites in California contains the largest number of archaeological sites (73) compared chemically. A recent but less-extensive study of Eidt (1977: 1330–1332) compares a smaller number of sites for soil phosphate fractions. The sites analyzed by Cook and Heizer were divided by them into two groups. The first group included 48 sites from northern California. One sample from each of these was analyzed for percentage of total phosphorus. The results were compared to the percentage of total phosphorus expected in natural soil, based upon 193 samples from locations in central and northern California.

Cook and Heizer (1965:40) considered values greater than the mean for the natural soils by two standard errors to indicate significant cultural modification of the site soil chemistry. They found significantly high scores in all but 8 of the 48 sites. Of the 8 with low scores, they dismiss 2 as from sterile portions of the sites and the others as from sites that were not substantially occupied (e.g., a temporary camp or cemeteries [1965:41–44]).

The first series data, however, have several serious problems. First, only a single sample is available from each site. Usually a single sample is insufficient for characterizing the abundance and distribution of phosphorus throughout the site. Proudfoot (1976:104–109) provides a thorough discussion and examples of soil phosphate variation and sampling concerns. Second, because the archaeological site soil tests are single values rather than averages, the appropriate comparison would have been with a score two standard *deviations* from the mean value for natural soil instead of the two standard *errors* of the mean value used. The standard deviation describes the spread of actual scores, such as those available from each archaeological site. The standard error of the mean is an estimate of the sampling distribution of the mean and usually is substantially smaller than the standard deviation. Third, the archaeological site samples are biased toward high phosphorus content because most of them "contained actual site midden, or matrix" (1965:40). Finally, the in-site values are compared with average natural soil values for a large area rather than with samples from natural soils adjacent to the site, making it is impossible to know how frequently naturally high phosphorus in the parent material of the site soil caused anomalously high scores in the site areas. The large percentage of sites with significantly high scores, therefore, is not necessarily an indication that such scores are abundant among all sites.

Data from the second series of sites examined by Cook and Heizer are more detailed and avoid these problems. Scores for a series of tests are given and areas adjacent to sites were tested for comparisons. For this example a separate analysis of two other California sites by Cook and Heizer (1965:29–39), which provides similar data, is included with the second series of sites. Like the first, the second series of sites is from the northern or central parts of the state. From among this group of 15, the results of chemical tests from six are described in

TABLE 4.3

Variation in Chemical Constituents among Six California Sites and Adjacent Off-Site Areas[a]

Site (N samples)	Carbon (%)				Nitrogen (%)				Phosphorus (%)				Calcium (%)			
	$\bar{X}$	s	-2s	+2s	$\bar{X}$	s	-2s	+2s	$\bar{X}$	s	-2s	+2s	$\bar{X}$	s	-2s	+2s
NAP-1 (3)	5.61	.70	4.21	—	.352	.066	.220	—	1.12	.03	1.06	—	14.80	1.53	11.74	—
NAP-1, off site (4)	4.60	2.86	—	10.32	.239	.105	—	.449	.19	.19	—	.57	.16	.07	—	.30
NAP-131 (15)	1.80	.81	.18	—	.128	.044	.04	—	.12	.04	.08	—	.15	.06	.03	—
NAP-131, off site (2)	1.16	0	—	1.16	.100	.012	—	.124	.08	.01	—	.10	.06	0	—	.06
Elam (13)	33.62	9.35	14.92	—	.741	.195	.351	—	3.36	1.17	1.02	—	9.10	4.32	.46	—
Elam, off site (4)	*	*	—	*	.703	.130	—	.963	.24	.11	—	.46	1.54	.85	—	3.24
Haki (11)	11.80	2.56	6.68	—	.319	*	*	—	.136	.050	.036	—	.421	.150	.121	—
Haki, off site (5)	8.75	6.48	—	21.71	.182	.107	—	.396	.114	.035	—	.184	1.017	.590	.150	2.197
Alnuiki (9)	11.84	7.35	0	—	.205	.057	.91	—	.107	.04	.99	—	.189	.160	.157	—
Alnuiki, off site (8)	4.61	*	—	*	.121	*	—	*	.078	*	—	*	.118	*	—	*
Kicil (9)	11.58	8.52	0	—	.217	.085	.47	—	.116	.059	0	—	.493	.455	0	—
Kicil, off site (6)	9.99	*	—	*	.253	*	—	*	.080	*	—	*	.263	*	—	*

[a] Data from Cook and Heizer (1965:29–61); *, value not available.

enough detail for sample statistics ($\bar{X}$ and s) to be derived, and in four cases for the same statistics to be generated for adjacent off-site areas (Table 4.3).

Analysis of the four cases for which the mean and standard deviation for site and off-site tests are available follows in more detail below. Before proceeding, however, in is interesting to examine more closely the range of mean values for different elements among the sites and off-site areas (Table 4.4). The site and off-site ranges partially overlap for all elements; for nitrogen and carbon they are practically the same. Carbon shows a wide range of values both on and off sites, as does calcium. These figures point out the need for detailed background information on the natural soil level of chemical elements in any area where chemical testing is used, and for careful, extensive sampling as part of such a testing program (Carr 1982; Proudfoot 1976). The California data demonstrate that no widely applicable single value exists for any of these elements that conclusively indicates the presence or absence of a site.

The comparison of specific sites versus off-site areas sheds further light on the likelihood that unnaturally high chemical values will be found within site areas. Cook and Heizer included individual test scores for four off-site areas. They do not provide a general statement about how they drew boundaries separating the site from its natural soil setting. However, the specific descriptions they provide for each of the second series of sites indicate that they used observed surface distributions of artifacts and middens, historical and ethnographic accounts, or, for some sites, partially buried but visible structural remains. Using the same statistics generated from the site and off-site test scores, Table 4.5a shows the percentages of scores within sites that are below the upper 95% confidence interval for natural soil scores. Within some sites some elements have substantial percentages of low scores. Examining the lower end of the expected distribution of scores for site areas (Table 4.5b), it is clear that many of the actual scores from off-site areas overlap with it. In other words, whereas some sites contain sections where element scores are anomalously high, other substantial sections have scores not significantly different (at least at the 95% confidence level) from the scores found in adjacent off-site areas.

TABLE 4.4

Range of Mean Values for Percentage of Chemical Elements among Six California Sites and Adjacent Off-Site Areas

Elements	Sites	Off-site areas
Carbon	1.80–11.84	1.16–9.99
Nitrogen	.128–.741	.100–.703
Phosphorus	.12–3.36	.078–.24
Calcium	.15–14.80	.06–1.54

[a] Data from Cook and Heizer (1965:29–61).

TABLE 4.5

Chemical Constituent Scores within Four California Sites and in Adjacent Off-Site Areas[a]

Site (N samples)	Carbon (%)	Nitrogen (%)	Phosphorus (%)	Calcium (%)
Low scores within sites (%)[b]				
NAP-1 (3)	100	100	0	0
NAP-13 (15)	6	67	33	0
Elam (13)	*	92	0	8
Haki (11)	100	91	91	100
High scores in off-site areas (%)[c]				
NAP-1 (4)	50	75	0	0
NAP-131 (2)	100	100	50	100
Elam (4)	*	100	100	100
Haki (5)	60	*	100	100

[a] Data from Cook and Heizer (1965). *, value not available.
[b] Scores within sites less than two standard deviations above the mean for the adjacent off site tests.
[c] Scores in off-site areas less than two standard deviations below the mean for the adjacent site.

Similar results come from a detailed chemical survey of the Robitalle site (a Huron village in Ontario) and the adjacent off-site area (Table 4.6). The reports about this site (Heidenreich and Konrad 1973; Heidenreich and Navratil 1973) distinguish only the village area of the site rather than a site boundary. Some of the area outside the inferred village area undoubtedly contains trash deposits, chemical anomalies, and so forth associated with the village, and is properly considered part of the site area. The distinction in Table 4.6 between village and nonvillage areas, therefore, is not strictly a site–off-site dichotomy. Despite this, the variation in scores (Table 4.6) suggests the discontinuous distribution of anomalously high chemical scores inside sites in which they occur.

TABLE 4.6

Chemical Constituent Values (%) at the Robitalle Site, Ontario, Canada[a]

Element	Village area (N = 42 samples)		Outside village area (N = 98 samples)	
	High scores	Low scores	High scores	Low scores
Phosphorus	69	31	23	77
Magnesium	21	79	3	97
Calcium	83	17	17	83

[a] Data from Heidenreich and Navratil (1973) and Heidenreich and Konrad (1973). All samples with scores above the 95% confidence interval for natural soils are considered high. Those with scores at or below this value are counted as low.

A third example from a multicomponent site in Northern Ireland (Proudfoot 1976) shows a similar pattern. There the analysis of phosphate content in over 80 samples showed wide ranges of values across the site area. Proudfoot (1976:110) in fact interpreted many of the scores as the result of natural conditions, such as natural phosphate-rich igneous rocks and soil development. He does note, however, that at least some of the Neolithic pits seem to have been partially filled with phosphate-rich material from human activities.

The first two examples of intrasite scores and site–off-site comparisons used the 95% confidence limits of the inferred distributions. There is nothing magical about this level of significance (Cowgill 1977). It is used here because Cook and Heizer and Heidenreich, Konrad, and Navratil, from whose work most of the examples or data are drawn, use the 95% limit in one way or another. Obviously a less-stringent confidence limit would alter the percentages in Tables 4.5a, 4.5b, and 4.6.

From these examples three generalizations relevant to site discovery can be derived about the chemical constituents of archaeological sites. First, a hefty percentage of all sites might contain no anomalous chemical constituents. In their most-detailed analysis of California sites (the second group of sites discussed above), Cook and Heizer (1965:40–61) found that 38% (5/13) showed no significant deviation from the chemical characteristics of adjacent natural soils.

Second, these examples of the intersite abundance of significantly high anomalous scores suggest that it varies widely among sites and among elements within sites. The mere occurrence of a significantly high score within a site in no way ensures that anomalously high scores will be obtained from all of the site area. These points are confirmed by a very detailed example and analysis of intersite variation among chemical site constituents by Carr (1982:387–551).

Finally, it ought to be clear that the accurate identification of anomalously high chemical scores that were generated by prehistoric human behavior requires very detailed and extensive information from both off-site and site areas. To emphasize this, consider the Crane site, a 2.6 ha (6.5 acre) multicomponent Woodland site in Illinois. Carr (1982:467) notes the large number of distinct spatial strata into which the site area could be divided based upon differences in the texture and chemical composition of the natural soil parent material, variation in the degree of soil profile development, and the chemical effects of differential historic period land-use. For accurate interpretation of soil chemical test scores, background information about these natural and historic phenomena should be available. Although Carr (1982) skillfully demonstrates that this kind and detail of background information can be assembled, organized, and interpreted within a relatively small area—for example, the Crane site—a similar level of analysis over wider study areas would be extremely difficult.

Site constituents that are detectable using various instrument techniques, such as resistivity, subsurface radar, and remote sensing, are considered as a group for two reasons. First, the anthropic anomalies that the different instruments detect are caused by the same general kind of archaeological remains. These site constituents are anomalous localized patterns of electric resistance, magnetism, radar reflection, surface vegetation—for example, cropmarks or soil reflection. The clearest anomalies are caused by remains that distinctly and strongly differ in material and texture from the surrounding soil matrix; examples include filled ditches, walls, roads, kilns, pits, and house floors. Second, the overall frequency of such constituents as well as their intrasite abundance and distribution are expected to be similar because the anomalous patterns that are the constituents are caused by similar kinds of remains.

Unfortunately, except for two examples regarding remotely sensed constituents, I have not uncovered data amenable to multisite comparisons. The two examples discussed below, however, do give a notion of the frequency of these types of site constituents among all sites.

For a recent survey of Ninety-Six National Historic site, located in the meadows and woods of the South Carolina piedmont, documentary research and archaeological fieldwork identified 22 sites within the approximately 200 ha (500-acre) study area (Ehrenhard and Wills 1980). Of these, five (23%) were detected through aerial photograph interpretation using black-and-white and infrared images plus a photogrammetric topographic map with a 2-foot contour interval (Table 4.7).

Within the five sites that were identified by remotely sensed constituents, the remains generating the anomalies were linear or rectangular, usually the remains of a historic period structure or structural feature. All five sites were in areas cleared of most vegetation (Ehrenhard and Wills 1980:264–285). Table 4.7 shows that recent disturbances were the most easily detected with fewer than half of the historic and none of the prehistoric sites detected. The undetected sites either lacked the necessary constituents to cause the recognizable anomalies or were in locations lacking the visibility requirements of black-and-white and infrared imagery.

The second example demonstrates the same requirement of structural archaeological remains and low-lying vegetation or a lack of vegetation for the successful identification of archaeological sites, in this instance using color infrared

TABLE 4.7

Detection of Known Sites at Ninety-Six National Historic Site, South Carolina[a]

	Prehistoric	Historic	Recent historic
Known sites (22)	8 (36)	9 (41)	5 (23)
Anomalies caused by sites and observed (5)	0 (0)	3 (60)	2 (40)

[a] Data from Ehrenhard and Willis (1980). Values in parentheses are percentages.

aerial photographs in the Tehuacan Valley in Mexico (Gumerman and Neely 1972). The types of sites visible on the imagery, either directly by an anomalous reflectance pattern or indirectly through crop marks included platform mounds, canals, subsurface foundations, former water and soil control ditches or dams, courtyards, plaza areas, and ball courts. On the other hand, small sites without the remains of structures were not detected by the imagery analysis (Gumerman and Neely 1972:522–523).

Vegetation patterns also strongly affected the ability to detect the full range of site types. In most of the Tehuacan study area the ground surface was "almost barren limestone or travertine with little or no soil cover . . . the dominant vegetation comprises short grasses" (Gumerman and Neely 1972:525). Forest canopy vegetation, however, obscured all sites in the areas where it occurred. The forest canopy in this instance was a "thorn-forest" with a canopy 1–2 m above the surface. Although the canopy was not uniformly dense, it did effectively conceal even sites with otherwise detectable constituents so that they could not be distinguished from natural features (Gumerman and Neely 1972:526).

These briefly described examples indicate that anomalous patterns of soil reflection or vegetation are characteristic of some kinds of archaeological sites; more precisely, of some portions of some sites. Typically, former structures or structural facilities, for example, ditches and dams, cause these anomalies. This type of site constituent will exist among archaeological sites to the extent that such distinct and different remains are close enough to the surface to affect soil or vegetation. Beyond the question of how frequently this constituent occurs, its detection requires stringent conditions of visibility. Obtrusiveness, in this instance, is affected strongly by visibility. Low-lying vegetation, such as particular grasses or crops, is essential for crop marks to be detected and the absence of vegetation is a prerequisite for soil mark detection. Forests or shrub cover ordinarily prevent the detection of either.

Considering the relative rarity of the remains that cause them, most instrument site constituents seem unlikely to be widespread or abundant enough in the archaeological record to be the targets of *general* site discovery surveys. Readers will recognize that these types of constituents have been considered here superficially at best. This is so because the focus of this chapter is upon the discovery of sites, especially sites within which the remains necessary to cause instrument site constituents are rare. The next section identifies a variety of logistical constraints on instrument techniques that, like the points brought out here, argue for their use in intrasite rather than discovery applications.

At the beginning of this section on site constituents I argued that archaeologists should pay more attention to the physical and chemical characteristics of archaeological sites, and that the evaluation of discovery techniques required this kind of a perspective. The information about site constituents presented here and conclusions derived from it are based upon a strictly inductive approach. I have looked at specific examples and drawn general conclusions based upon them. To a large extent this approach was born of expediency.

A different, more difficult, but ultimately more useful approach to describing site constituents could be developed using a deductive framework; that is, by beginning with a series of activities that one expected to occur and predicting the types and distributions of site constituents that would be generated by them. This approach holds the promise of great progress for the evaluation of discovery techniques as it already has demonstrated its usefulness in methodological and behavioral analysis applications (Carr 1982; Cook 1976; Schiffer 1975).

TECHNIQUES FOR DISCOVERING SITES

A goal of this chapter is to identify the advantages and disadvantages of different techniques for site discovery, not to select one technique that will solve all site-discovery problems. In practice, several techniques often are joined in concert as parts of a single investigation. Different techniques are appropriate, for example, during various parts of a multistage sampling design, or in parts of an investigation area that present different discovery problems because of variation in soil aggradation, vegetation, access, or other conditions.

Furthermore, the main intent of this chapter is to consider the techniques appropriate to discover unobtrusive sites in places where visibility is poor. Therefore, not every discovery technique used by archaeologists is mentioned, and not all those mentioned are discussed in equal detail. Techniques useful only where visibility is good or only for the discovery or examination of relatively obtrusive sites are not described or evaluated comprehensively. Situations for which such techniques are useful are mentioned briefly.

Surface Inspection

The most commonly employed discovery technique is surface inspection of lightly vegetated areas, eroding soil profiles, and plowed fields. Surface inspection has been applied with a wide range of approaches from opportunistic and spotty checks to very careful, intensive inspection of all (or an explicitly defined sample) of a study area. In the colorful terminology of House and Schiffer (1975:40), the approaches have ranged, with increasing intensity of inspection and, not surprisingly, greater numbers of site discoveries, from "whistle stop" to "hunt-and-peck" to "gladhand" to "gumshoe."

Surface inspection is a relatively quick and inexpensive discovery technique that is effective under two conditions. First, at least a portion of the archaeological sites of interest must be on the surface. Sites that were once buried but have been brought to the surface by plowing or erosion are included among these. The second condition is that the ground surface be cleared enough for sites' contents to be recognized visually. These conditions are met in large expanses of arid, lightly vegetated parts of the world. There, surface inspection, if intensive and rigorously applied, probably is effective for discovering most, though not all, sites (Hirth 1978; Judge 1981; Kirkby and Kirkby 1976:241–246; Schiffer and Gumerman 1977:214–215; Tolstoy and Fish 1975). In many regions, however, soil aggradation, natural disturbances within soil profiles (Wood and Johnson 1978), and vegetation have buried or obscured archaeological remains. Where this has occurred, sites without structural remains at or near the surface are very unobtrusive and difficult to discover. In these contexts, if surface inspection is the discovery technique, its effectiveness is limited to such windows of visibility as eroding shorelines, wind blowouts, roadway cuts, and plowed fields; and only those sites being eroded or within reach of the plow are susceptible to detection.

Where extensive modern agriculture and seasonal plowing occur, such as the American Midwest, surface inspection remains the most common discovery technique. Even with plowing, however, the problem of poor visibility some-times remains, caused by the adhesion of soil to artifacts, making them difficult to see. Careful scheduling of surface inspections to take advantage of low amounts of ground cover, recent plowing, and recent heavy natural precipitation that washes soil off artifacts can reduce this concern but not eliminate it (Ammerman and Feldman 1978; Hirth 1978:130; Roper 1979:21–23). Although probably not preventing the discovery of some sites, this visibility problem is likely to cause a bias toward the discovery of sites with large numbers and dense concentrations of artifacts or highly obtrusive remains. The discovery of shell middens in coastal areas provides an example. In Cape Cod National Seashore, Massachusetts, the estimated frequency per acre of shell middens based upon an intensive probability sample drawn using a rigorous subsurface testing technique is similar to the frequency per acre based upon all previously known and reported prehistoric sites, most of which are shell middens. Based upon the intensive probability sample, however, the estimated frequency per acre for *all* prehistoric sites is 3–5 times the estimated shell-midden frequency (McManamon 1981b, 1981c). The previously known sites were reported over the years by avocational archaeologists who discovered them haphazardly in eroded cliffs, plowed fields, or construction areas. The collectors were not searching intensively or testing for subsurface remains and the most obtrusive remains, that is, shell middens, in locations where visibility was good were the ones detected.

A number of archaeologists have tried to improve visibility in regions with dense plant cover so that surface inspection could be used as a primary discovery technique. One method is to plow areas not currently cultivated (Binford *et al*. 1970; Davis 1980; Ives and Evans 1980; Keel 1976; Kimball 1980; Snethkamp 1976; Trubowitz 1981). Purposeful plowing markedly increases the amount of surface area that can be inspected; however, the difficulty of artifact visibility if the plowing is not followed by heavy precipitation also must be considered and the plowing and surface collecting scheduled accordingly. Plowing can present a variety of logistical problems as well (Trubowitz 1981). Forests are too dense for use of plows. Thick shrubbery or brush must be cleared before a plow can be used (Davis 1980; Kimball 1980). Where land parcels are small, and especially where they are used residentially, obtaining permission to plow is likely to be difficult or even impossible.

Archaeologists have utilized a variety of other means of increasing surface visibility by removing surface cover. Techniques used include raking or blowing away leaf litter (Bergman 1980; Forney 1980; Lafferty 1979, personal communitation 1982; Otinger *et al.* 1982; Scott *et al.* 1978; Taylor *et al.* 1980) and the use of heavy equipment, specifically a small bulldozer, to clear surface vegetation (Lafferty 1979). Although possibly appropriate to overcome some discovery problems, these additional techniques of increasing surface visibility have a major drawback. They result in the inspection of only the soil surface rather than a volume of soil. This differs from plowing, which draws artifacts from throughout the soil volume. Wood and Johnson (1978), using work by Darwin (1881), Atkinson (1957), and others, have described in some detail how in many areas natural soil movement processes bury archaeological remains deposited originally on the surface (see also Lewarch and O'Brien 1981:299–311). Hughes and Lampert (1977) argue that in loose sandy soils human treading around an occupations or activity areas has buried remains deposited on the surface. Therefore, surface vegetation clearing, even where geomorphic soil aggradation has not occurred, might not reach far enough beneath the modern surface to scratch up and detect archaeological sites.

Discovery techniques that aim to increase surface visibility can be effective. They are relatively inexpensive and will be useful under the following three conditions. First, the sites of interest must be detectable visually on or near the surface once the vegetation is removed or the soil plowed. This condition applies to all the techniques mentioned above whereas the last two conditions mainly relate to the equipment techniques, plowing, and other heavy machine clearing. The second, condition regards natural constraints; vegetation must not be too dense or substantial, for example, and topography not too steep or irregular for equipment access and performance. Finally, legal access to the investigation area must be obtainable. This might be particularly difficult for equipment clearing, which is unlikely to be acceptable to landowners in developed commercial, residential, or recreational areas.

Subsurface Techniques for Site Discovery

Other techniques increasingly are being developed and applied where surface inspection has been recognized as ineffective. The techniques described below are termed *subsurface* because each detects one or more kinds of subsurface anomaly. For ease of discussion and evaluation, the techniques are divided into four general classes: instrument techniques, chemical tests, remote sensing techniques, and subsurface probes. The first two classes are described rather briefly because their principal use has been intrasite examination rather than site discovery. Considering the kinds of site constituents these two types of techniques detect, the detailed background data required for accurate interpretation of their results, and their logistical requirements, they are likely to remain useful primarily for intrasite investigations. The third class of techniques—remote sensing techniques—have proved to be effective for the discovery of sites with certain kinds of constituents when such sites are located in areas where visibility is good. Although these conditions limit the instances for which remote sensing is an effective discovery technique, when such conditions are met by a project's goals and the study area, remote sensing techniques will prove quick, accurate, and relatively inexpensive.

None of these first three types of techniques is described or evaluated comprehensively in this chapter; interested readers should consult specialist references for complete details. The description and evaluation in this chapter are limited to the consideration of the techniques as tools for site discovery. In keeping with the emphasis of the earlier sections on the discovery of unobtrusive sites in environments with poor visibility, subsurface probes—the final technique considered here—are described and evaluated comprehensively. Before discussing the probes, however, the other techniques are dealt with.

Instruments

The major instrument techniques used in archaeological field investigations have been magnetometry, resistivity, and subsurface radar. Magnetometers detect slight variations in the earth's magnetic field. Some kinds of buried archaeological features, especially pits and structures that have been burned, and hearths, produce such variations (Aitken 1970:681; Steponaitis and Brain 1976:455; Tite 1972:7–57). Magnetometers have been used since the late 1950s "for specific problems in connection with particular excavations" (Scollar 1969:77; see also examples in Aitken 1970; Breiner 1965; Leehan and Hackenberger 1976; Tite 1972:43–52). Given appropriate soil and magnetic background conditions they can be very successful, such as in an examination of sites partially buried by a sand dune at Oraibi Wash in Arizona (Rice *et al.* 1980:7) where a proton magnetometer detected and delimited areas that contained large numbers of hearths, pits, and structures. Additional examples of the kinds of subsurface features detectable are prehistoric stockade ditches (Black and Johnston 1962; Johnston 1964:128) and large storage pits (Gramley 1970). Clark (1975) reports the use in England of portable magnetometers for surveying relatively large areas, such as rights-of-way for proposed highways. He notes their successful detection of pits, hearths, ditches, and kilns.

Although they obviously can detect some kinds of features or anthropic soil horizons successfully and are relatively portable, wide-scale use of magnetometry for site discovery is unlikely to be effective for three reasons. First, the large, distinct anomalies they detect are a relatively rare in the archaeological record. Large, distinct features or anthropic soil horizons seem to be relatively infrequent and spatially clustered constituents of sites in which they occur and they are expected to be absent in many other sites. Second, magnetometers are hindered or even made useless by substantial magnetic background such as is common within most modern developed areas. Third, natural magnetic properties of some soils or small variations in topography, soil horizon depths, and surface geological anomalies also can mask the magnetic contrast of otherwise detectable archaeological features unless the raw magnetic readings are filtered through sophisticated statistical computerized procedures to eliminate the natural magnetic noise (Scollar 1969). Thus, substantial amounts of information about the natural magnetic background are required. These detailed data can be collected for a site area or a portion of a site, but usually it is impossible to obtain the necessary data from an entire large study area.

Resistivity surveying measures the resistance to an electric current of soil and possible archaeological anomalies embedded in the soil matrix (Clark 1970; Tite 1972:7–57). Typically, large distinct features and anthropic soil horizons that differ substantially in consistency from the surrounding soil matrix can be detected as either anomalously high or low resistivity scores. Carr (1977:162; 1982:1–45) refers to dozens of American or European examples of the successful detection of individual abode, masonry, or hollow subsurface remains using resistivity. As with magnetometry, the focus of resistivity testing has been intrasite, and mainly the detection of individual features such as trenches, walls, house depressions, and large distinct filled pits (e.g., Clark 1970:696; Ford 1964; Ford and Keslin 1969; Goodman 1971; Klasner and Calengas 1981). Overall intrasite structure also can be detected using resistivity even in sites where features are small and earthen, if appropriate statistical procedures are applied (Carr 1977, 1982; Lieth *et al.* 1976).

Reservations similar to those regarding the applicability of magnetometry for site discovery can be raised for resistivity surveying. It detects a range of archaeological site constituents similar to that for magnetometry, thus having similar limitations for site discovery. In addition, a series of potential logistical problems make resistivity surveying undesirable for site discovery, or even for intrasite investigations, in areas with stony soil or dense vegetation. The probes through which the electric charge is sent and resistance to it detected must be inserted into the soil in a careful alignment. These requirements can be deterred by stony soil or dense vegetation. Also, as with magnetometry, the collection and interpretation of natural background data is important but time-consuming in large survey areas.

Ground-penetrating radar is a technique with a short history of archaeological applications. Developed for geologic and engineering studies (e.g., Morey 1974), it has been applied by archaeologists in a variety of contexts including prehistoric (Roberts 1981a, 1981b; Vickers and Dolphin 1975; Vickers *et al.* 1976) and historic period sites (Kenyon and Bevan 1977; Parrington 1979:198–199; Weston Geophysical 1980). Ground-penetrating radar detects subsurface discontinuities as echoes of radar pulses that it transmits. The characteristics of the echo allow the determination not only of anomaly presence but of its depth, shape, and position in the soil profile. Soil characteristics, such as moisture content, can affect radar readings strongly, so detailed soils data are required for accurate interpretation (see Roberts 1981a, 1981b). Like resistivity, substantial and distinct features or anthropic soil horizons are the most likely to be detected by ground-penetrating radar. The radar equipment usually is housed in a small, low cart that is rolled over the area investigated. The area must be relatively smooth and without vegetation or with only low grassy cover for the cart to move freely. Problems similar to those outlined for the other two techniques apply for subsurface radar as well. In addition, subsurface radar equipment is much more expensive to purchase or lease than equipment for magnetometry or resistivity survey.

In summary, these three instrument techniques are likely to remain primarily as intrasite examination techniques. In sites with the appropriate constituents, one or more of these techniques can be very effective and efficient for the exploration of site structure or the location of areas for excavation. Their use for site discovery, however, would require three rare and stringent conditions: (1) that the sites sought contain substantial and distinct features or anthropic soil horizons; (2) that the area to be investigated be small with regular topography, a soil type compatible with the technique, and blanketed by only a low grassy ground cover, and (3) that the necessary expertise be available to conduct appropriate data-filtering techniques, collect the necessary background data, and interpret the resultant scores. In most cases, the kinds of sites for which these instrument techniques are useful can be discovered using quicker, less-expensive techniques with fewer logistical constraints. Once they are discovered, far more detailed investigation of their structure and contents using one or more of the instruments can be done effectively and efficiently within the site areas.

Chemical Tests

The earlier section on chemical anomalies within site areas indicated the substantial use of chemical tests for intrasite investigations to determine site structure, prehistoric activities, and the best locations for large excavations (Ahler 1973; Carr 1982; Cook and Heizer 1965; Eidt 1977; F. Goodyear 1971:202–222; Heidenreich and Konrad 1973; Heidenreich and Navratil 1973; Limbrey 1975:326–330; Overstreet 1974; Proudfoot 1977; Provan 1971; Valentine *et al.* 1980). Among the elements used for these analyses, phosphorus in the form of fixed phosphate compounds has been especially and most widely used. Whereas the other elements have been limited to intrasite investigations, phosphate testing has had a rather long history of use for site discovery as well. In northwestern Europe, Arrhenius in the 1930s and later Lorch used it as a means of discovery as well as to identify areas within sites for excavation (see bibliography in Provan 1971; Sjoberg 1976:447). More recent attempts to use this technique for site discovery have occurred (Eidt 1973, 1977; Provan 1971:44–46; Sjoberg 1976). Eidt's (1973) first article describing a simple rapid field technique for the qualitative or semiquantitative estimation of phosphate content seems to have provoked several of the recent attempts to use the technique for discovery as well as intrasite studies. Eidt himself (1977), however, recognized the uncertainty and limitations of the rapid field technique. Phosphate intensities could not be compared rigorously due to uncertainty about the effects of sample size, unequal extraction of phosphate types, and other conditions under which the sample was collected and analyzed (Eidt 1977:1329). Furthermore, the rapid technique could not distinguish between high scores resulting from large amounts of naturally occurring phosphates and those derived from culturally deposited phosphorus (Eidt 1977:1329).

More quantitative analytic techniques have been applied recently (Carr 1982; Eidt 1977; Hassan 1981; Sjoberg 1976). These increase the amount of time required to analyze each sample, but they permit more rigorous comparison among the samples and more definite interpretations of the scores. The new analytic techniques, however, are not necessarily intended for discovery studies. Eidt (1977:1332) summarizes his article describing the new analysis by proposing a two-part method for chemical examination of archaeological sites. The initial part would be the old ''rapid qualitative field test'' for locating sites with a second stage of quantitative analysis to verify and analyze further if a site has been discovered. A two-stage approach to discovery, with the second stage requiring laboratory analysis before results are available to interpret, might work in some situations, but the amount of time needed to accomplish all the steps is likely to limit its applications.

For discovery investigations, Hassan's (1981) method of analysis seems more promising. He has developed a quantitative analysis that can be done in the field, with the laboratory preparation of each sample requiring between 8 and 18 minutes (Hassan 1981:385). The value of this method is that it can be accomplished in a single stage with quantitative analysis of each sample. Time requirements are less than those expected for Eidt's two-stage approach, but still substantial. In addition to the sample preparation, time is necessary for establishing the grid for sample collection, collecting the samples, and analyzing the results. The time requirements per sample might restrict Hassan's technique mainly to intrasite investigations; and the fact that the two examples he uses to illustrate the technique are intrasite studies probably is more than coincidental.

Ahler (1973:129–130), Eidt (1977), and Proudfoot (1976) discuss the useful-ness of various levels of different kinds of phosphorus and phosphate compounds for the identification of subsurface archaeological sites. Proudfoot (1976) in particular describes the difficulties of interpreting scores considering different phosphate compounds, variation in natural phosphate levels, and the number of samples taken in a given area. On balance, the identification and interpretation of variation in soil phosphorus or phosphate levels throughout large survey areas requires substantial detailed background data. The logistical problems of estab-lishing a close-interval grid system and extracting, analyzing, and interpreting thousands of samples for a large study area probably limits the efficiency of this technique for site discovery in most cases.

Sjoberg (1976:447–448) has made the most direct assertion in the recent literature that phosphate analysis is an uncomplicated and inexpensive discovery technique. He bases this assertion on what he interprets as the complete success of phosphate analysis as a major means of site discovery in northwestern Europe, specifically Sweden. Provan (1971:44–46), however, relates one example in which phosphate tests failed to discover expected sites in a 2.8-km^2 study area in Norway.

As Sjoberg describes his method, there are two main drawbacks to its wide-spread use for site discovery. First, he proposes a 25-m-interval systematic grid in a study area for the collection of samples. He acknowledges that this is a large interval and that phosphate-rich features and anthropic soil horizons can easily be missed by it, thereby leaving undetected sites without abundant and widespread amounts of these constituents. The problem with so large an interval for discov-ery is emphasized by Sjoberg's strong recommendation that for intrasite exam-ination a grid interval of 1 m is the maximum.

The time requirements of Sjoberg's procedure (1977:449–450) are the second major difficulty. His data indicate that the collection of each sample requires about 9 minutes. If the lab procedure, which Sjoberg recommends instead of Eidt's rapid field technique, is as time-consuming as Hassan's procedure, each sample will require between 17 and 27 minutes. Those are substantial time requirements for sample collection and lab analysis, and do not include addi-tional time costs for transportation or analysis of the scores. The time required per sample, rather than theoretical questions about its widespread effectiveness, might limit the application of this technique to intrasite examination or discovery investigations covering relatively small areas. In fact, the detailed examples that Sjoberg (1976:452–453) presents are intrasite examinations for which he empha-sizes in his conclusion (1976:454) the usefulness of phosphate analysis.

In summary, chemical tests have not been used for discovery investigations and probably are of limited use for discovery. The exceptions are tests for various phosphorous compounds that are stable and relatively widespread in archaeological features and anthropic soil horizons. Phosphate tests might be useful for site discovery when the area to be searched is relatively small. Successful applications also will require a short interval between tests, ample testing of natural chemical background values, and quantitative lab or field chemical analysis of the samples collected.

Remote Sensing Techniques

The techniques included under the term *remote sensing* include high- and low-level aerial photography and satellite imagery (Avery and Lyons 1981; Lyons and Avery 1977; Lyons *et al.* 1980). A variety of films and other sensor imagery types, imagery angles, and scales of measurement are associated with the techniques (Morain and Budge 1978). Remotely sensed imagery has two direct archaeological applications: (1) providing data for planning fieldwork logistics and stratifying investigation areas for sampling and (2) identifying specific site locations. Satellite photography and sensor imagery usually are limited to the former (e.g., Brown and Ebert 1980; Ebert *et al.*, 1980; McCauley *et al.* 1982; Wells *et al.* 1981). Because the focus here is on site discovery, satellite remote sensing is not discussed further. Discussions of its equipment and uses for archaeologists as well as more detailed bibliographies are available in Lyons and Avery (1977), Lyons *et al.* (1980), Morain and Budge (1978), and Baker and Gumerman (1981:29–37). The substantial usefulness of aerial photographs for planning fieldwork logistics and sample stratification are not discussed either except in passing. The bibliographies of the works cited above include references to such applications, of which, Aikens *et al.* (1980) and Ebert and Gutierrez (1979, 1981) are specific examples.

Aerial photography has long been used for archaeological investigations, frequently as a site-discovery tool (Crawford 1924; Reeves 1936; see also many references in Lyons *et al.* 1980). The discovery of archaeological sites using aerial photography involves the detection of one of three possible archaeological anomalies (Lyons and Avery 1977:56–62): (1) above-surface features, especially structures, or anthropic soil horizons, (2) shadow marks caused by above-surface structural remains, (3) plant or soil marks caused by subsurface features or anthropic soil horizons. Discovery of the first two kinds of anomalies requires that that archaeological remains be above or on the surface and visible from the air. This means that vegetation must be sparse or low enough to allow the direct view of surface remains, their low relief, or the subtle shadows they cast. In some regions favorable conditions have combined to make remote sensing an important, widely useful discovery technique. The successes of direct or shadow observation have been mainly in arid, sparsely vegetated sections of the American Southwest (Berlin *et al.* 1977; Schaber and Gumerman 1969; see many of the articles in Lyons 1976; Lyons and Ebert 1978; Lyons and Hitchcock 1977; Lyons and Mathien 1980). Less expected has been its occasional successful use in more densely vegetated regions, for example Harp's (1974, 1977) discovery of sod-wall remains of semisubterranean prehistoric structures in the Canadian subarctic by studying magnified 15,000:1-scale photographs stereoscopically. Surface-exposed shell middens in California have been detected directly using infrared aerial photography. Surface shell in the middens appeared as a bright white on the infrared imagery, making them stand out from their surroundings (Tartaglia 1977:45). In the heavily vegetated American Midwest also one type of archaeological site—earthen mounds—has been discovered through direct observation of aerial photographs (Baker and Gumerman 1981:9–10; Black 1967; Fowler 1977). In another case, stone fish-weirs were discovered in the Potomac River using aerial photographs (Strandberg and Timlinson 1969).

Where dense vegetation and buried sites are the rule, the detection of plant and soil marks are the typical ways in which sites are discovered through the analysis of aerial photographs. The former are caused by differential plant growth of either natural or cultivated species due to variation in topography, soil moisture, or organic content caused by buried archaeological features, structures, or an anthropic soil horizon. Crop marks, a widely known type of differential plant growth, have been recognized and described, if not always correctly interpreted, for centuries (Fagan 1959). Soil marks occur at sites where substantial near-surface midden deposits have high organic-refuse content. Sharp contrast in soil color and reflection between the near-surface anthropic soil horizon and the surrounding natural soil matrix make the marks discernible (Baker and Gumerman 1981:12). In order for plant marks to be discovered, vegetation must be low-lying (Evans and Jones 1977; Munson 1967). Forest canopy is unaffected by most archaeological sites into or through which individual trees might grow, and even intermittent canopy cover can mask sites, preventing their discovery (Baker and Gumerman 1981:12; Gumerman and Neely 1972:526). Of course soil marks will be invisible whenever any vegetation is present.

In rare cases abrupt changes in the type of vegetation actually might point out site locations. Three examples are known from extensive marsh or swamp areas in Veracruz (Mexico), Florida, and Louisiana (Bruder et al. 1975; J. Ehrenhard 1980; Newman and Byrd 1980). In each case archaeological site locations correlate strongly and positively with slight elevations within the wetlands resulting in markedly different vegetation on the elevated areas. The vegetation differences are detected easily using aerial photographs. Topographic change independent of the archaeological sites themselves cause the vegetation difference in the Florida and Louisiana cases but the strong and steady correlation of sites with slightly elevated areas makes site discovery by association possible. In the Veracruz example, at least some of the extra elevation of site areas is caused by mounds constructed as part of prehistoric occupation areas.

Europeans, particularly in Great Britain and West Germany, have used oblique as well as vertical aerial photographs to detect plant marks caused by structural archaeological features at Iron Age and Roman period sites (Evans and

Jones 1977; Martin 1971; see also many references in Lyons *et al.* 1980). Oblique photos have been used occasionally but far less frequently in the United States (Baker and Gumerman 1981; Black 1967; Fowler 1977; Lafferty 1977) where vertical photographs at a variety of scales have been the standard imagery. Imagery scale has varied, but usally 1:20,000 has been the smallest scale usable for the detection of plant or soil marks (Baker and Gumerman 1981:36; Strandberg 1967). In many areas this scale might be too small but can be enlarged to suit the discovery need (Baker and Gumerman 1981:29–31). Imagery at the 1:20,000 and larger scales also are useful for logistical and sample design purposes.

Like scale, variation in the type of film used for aerial photographs affects detection of plant and soil marks. Put simply, there are four general kinds of film: black and white, color, black-and-white infrared, and color infrared (Avery and Lyons 1981:7–11; Lyons and Avery 1977). Each type has its own strengths and weaknesses that usually are specific to particular discovery applications. No single film serves all purposes; different types provide complementary information and for diverse kinds of information several types of imagery covering the same area should be studied simultaneously (Avery and Lyons 1981:9). Matheny (1962) presents a detailed comparison of black and white, color, and color infrared films for one heavily vegetated area. In general, black and white is a useful film for a variety of purposes (Avery and Lyons 1981:7; Fowler 1977), color for the identification of plant marks, land-cover types, and landforms (Baker and Gumerman 1981:32), and color infrared for distinguishing vegetation types (Baker and Gumerman 1981:32; Gumerman and Neeley 1972; Lyons and Avery 1977). For any particular situation, however, the usefulness or superiority of any film type might vary. For situations in which vegetation variation is important for discovery, color or color infrared can simplify and speed up interpretation (Strandberg 1967). In other instances, such as the direct detection of visible, obtrusive sites, these much more expensive films frequently are no more information than normal black and white.

Some of the conditions necessary for aerial photograph interpretation to be effective for site discovery, such as vegetation, have been mentioned already. It also should be clear that to be discovered sites must be near the surface and contain distinct structural features such as house walls, foundations, or trenches, or prominent cultural soil horizons, such as dense shell or organic middens. Another important consideration for the successful detection of plant or soil marks is scheduling when the imagery is taken (Baker and Gumerman 1981: 34–35; Martin 1971). The prominence of soil marks, for example, is affected by plowing and soil moisture; they are most prominent 2–3 days after a heavy rain (Lyons and Avery 1977:61). In some regions during certain seasons cloud cover regularly interferes with obtaining clear imagery (Baker and Gumerman 1981:35; Lyons and Avery 1977:85). Other considerations also should be taken into account. Plant marks, for example, are more or less prominent, therefore easier or more difficult to detect, depending upon the texture and composition of the soil (Lyons and Avery 1977:61).

In summary, for near-surface sites with abundant and widespread or at least prominent structural features or anthropic soil horizons, remote sensing is a very useful discovery technique given appropriate visibility conditions, imagery, and scheduling. Because of the scale of photographs, large areas can be examined relatively thoroughly and quickly, although the consistency of analysis and detection will vary with the visibility conditions at the time the imagery was taken.

The three types of techniques presented so far are likely to be effective mainly for the discovery of sites with abundant and widespread features, especially structural ones, and anthropic soil horizons. The more prominent, distinct, and larger the individual features or horizons, the more likely they are to produce an anomaly that is detectable by an instrument, a chemical test, or on an aerial photograph. If, however, an investigation aims in whole or in part to discover sites with less obtrusive, and in some cases positively unobtrusive, constituents, techniques discussed in the following sections will be needed. This is especially so where visibility is poor in part or all of the study area.

Subsurface Probes

Among the discovery techniques considered in this chapter, subsurface probes are discussed in the most detailed because of their widespread applicability, use, and potential effectiveness for site discovery. As archaeologists increasingly have undertaken surveys in areas with poor surface visibility, they have turned to subsurface probes as a discovery technique (Brose 1981; Casjens *et al.* 1978, 1980; Chatters 1981; Claassen and Spears 1975; Custer 1979; Feder 1977; Gatus 1980; Ives and Evans 1980; Lovis 1976; Lynch 1980; McManamon 1981a, 1981b, 1981c, 1982; Nance 1980a, 1980b; Otinger *et al.* 1982; F. Plog *et al.* 1977; Scott *et al.* 1978; Spurling 1980; Stone 1981a; Thorbahn 1977, 1980, n.d.; Weide 1976).

A wide range of probes has been used to discover sites. Although they more or less form a continuum in terms of size, shape, and volume, probes are described here as four distinct categories for ease of presentation. The dimensions given for each type of probe are generalizations rounded off for convenience; nevertheless they convey the magnitude of difference in size among the probes. Usually probe sizes are not measured precisely during discovery investigations. The aim typically is to complete a large number of similarly sized probes rather than a few carefully measured ones. The different kinds of probes discussed here are:

1. Soil cores: 2–3 cm (about 1 inch) diameter cylinders 50–100 cm (20–36 inches) long.

2. Auger holes: 1–15 cm (4–6 inches) diameter cylinders of soil dug to various depths, depending upon the soil and expected depth of sites.
3. "Divots": 30 × 30 × 8 cm (about 12 × 12 × 3 inches) volumes cut out of the mat of surface vegetation, overturned, and inspected.
4. Shovel tests: roughly shaped cylinders or rectangular volumes with a relatively wide range of dimensions: diameters 25–75 cm (10–30 inches) or surface dimensions of 25 × 25 cm (about 10 × 10 inches) to 100 × 100 cm (about 40 × 40 inches) with depths up to 150 cm (about 60 inches) depending upon soil type and expected depth of sites.

Subsurface tests are hardly a new discovery technique. Shovel tests have been used by archaeologists to discover sites since at least the early twentieth century (e.g., Moorehead 1918, 1931). The difference is that these early tests were sporadic and linked to informant information or hunches. Although this kind of traditional application continues, many contemporary applications are more rigorous in the placement of probes and coverage of study areas and are part of an explicit sampling strategy.

Before continuing with the consideration of subsurface probes' one special problem, the particular discovery problems related to deeply buried sites are touched on. With few exceptions, usually intrasite examinations (e.g., Chatters 1981; Gordon 1978; Muto and Gunn n.d.; Price *et al.* 1964; Reed *et al.* 1968), the depth of subsurface probes has been limited to about 1 m. More deeply buried sites are missed by most probes. When an investigation has as a goal the discovery of deeply buried sites, other subsurface techniques must be used. One technique already has been alluded to in a previous section—trenching, using a backhoe (Chapman 1976, 1977, 1978, 1981). Others also have used this technique successfully (Collins 1979; Reidhead n.d.).

The size and depth of trenches have been limited by the capability of the backhoe. Chapman (1977:3) describes trenches 13 feet long at the top tapering to 3 to 4 feet at the bottom. Depths range between 12 to 14 feet (Chapman 1978:3) and 1 to 13 feet (Reidhead n.d.:6). In all these cases, toothless backhoe buckets were used. Sites typically were identified by inspecting trench sidewalls for artifacts, features, and cultural soil horizons.

The massive volume excavated by each deep trench requires large amounts of time and limits strictly the number of trenches that can be excavated. Intensive coverage of large areas is impossible without substantial amounts of money. For this reason all the investigators cited here were forced to leave large intervals between trenches. Each acknowledges the difficulties this causes for site discovery and site delimitation as well as for the accuracy of the sample of sites discovered and the precision of estimates based upon it (Chapman 1977:9–11, 1978:91; Reidhead n.d.:8).

The problems for the discovery of deeply buried sites have been merely introduced here, not discussed in detail and by no means resolved. The areas where this technique is relevant usually can be identified using existing geomorphic data. All archaeologists should be cognizant of the potential problem whenever they work in areas where substantial aggradation might have occurred. For further discussion and detail readers are referred to the works cited and to investigators pursuing the problems.

Soil Cores

Soil cores initially seem an attractive technique. They are collected using soil tube samplers such as those made by the Oakfield Company (Forestry Suppliers 1980:144–145). Their small diameter makes them relatively easy to use in some soil types and they can be quickly recorded (Casjens et al. 1980:10). In southeastern Massachusetts, Thorbahn (1977, 1980, n.d.) supervised a survey of the I-495 highway corridor (21 km × 120 m) that used as a discovery technique soil cores with follow up shovel tests where anomalies occurred. Based upon this work, Thorbahn (1980:16) considers soil cores "the most efficient means for preliminary subsurface testing over a large survey area." The anomalies detected usually were "flecks of charcoal or thin bands of oxidized soils (Thorbahn n.d.:6)." Thorbahn mentions that during excavations at the 13 I-495 sites for which he presents data "scatters of charcoal flecks and patches of discolored soil were observed throughout" (n.d.:6) each site. Such a frequency and widespread distribution of anthropic soil horizons is not expected based upon the models of archaeological site constituents developed above.

Others who have used soil cores have not detected, or perhaps have detected but not recognized, the anomalies described by Thorbahn. For a survey of a 25 ha area in Washington, Chatters (1981) used 2.5-cm diameter soil cores in a systematic grid with a 50-m interval. He discovered two anthropic soil horizons, both "middens," one historic and the other prehistoric. Casjens et al. (1980:10) describes soil cores as effective for discovering dense shell deposits but not other sites or parts of sites. Luedtke (1980:38) concurs with these conclusions, noting that soil cores "may miss sites with sparse shell and will be least useful where shell is not found at all." None of these investigators confirms the occurrence of the type of anomaly detected in the I-495 study.

If soil cores detect only features or anthropic soil horizons, which are not widely distributed or frequent within many sites and are absent from others, the interval between individual cores must be relatively small. Because cores can be collected and recorded quickly, small intervals are possible; but the shorter interval seems not to make up for the limitations of the site constituents they detect. In a review of discovery investigations using soil cores in Rhode Island between 1977 and 1979, Robinson (1981:49) noted an overall lack of efficiency in the use of cores for discovery. Fewer than half (9 out of 19) of the anomalies detected by soil cores in these studies proved to be archaeological sites after intensive subsurface testing. Because discovery of sites using cores requires verification with larger subsurface units and might be accurate less than 50% of the time, the efficiency of the preliminary core testing is more apparent than real.

It seems clear that soil cores will be effective for discovering only those sites with abundant and widespread features or anthropic soil horizons (Robinson 1981:49). In a controlled comparison of discovery techniques at eight sites undertaken as part of the Cape Cod National Seashore Archeological Survey, only 1 of 100 soil cores taken within site areas detected a site constituent and that was a piece of plaster extracted along with the soil (McManamon 1981a; 1981c:202–220). The soil core profiles within known site areas did not show clearly anomalous color or texture patterns indicative of features or cultural soil horizons.

The comparison mentioned in the last paragraph tested three discovery techniques: cores, augers, and shovel tests. Transects of various lengths, typically 100–200 m long, were placed so that they fell partially within and partially outside site boundaries. Cores, auger holes, and shovel tests were placed adjacent to each other 1–2 m apart along each transect. Spacing along the transect varied; cores and augers were placed every 5 m, shovel tests every 12.5 or 25 m. Placement of the probes was designed to give each technique as equal as possible a chance to discover archaeological remains in any particular location. Shovel tests were not "confined only to site areas with high artifact densities," as mistakenly reported by Nance (1983:327–328) based upon incorrect information in Thorbahn (n.d.:13).

Soil cores present some technical problems as well. In dry, sandy soils, the cylinder of soil often fell out of the tube sampler as it was extracted. In clayey or gravelly soils, insertion of the sampler is difficult or impossible (Chatters 1981; Thorbahn n.d.:9; Trubowitz 1973:7–8) Thorbahn (n.d.:9) notes also that the subtle anomalies detected in the I-495 sites were obscured by deep plowzones or waterlogged soils.

Soil cores have been useful for the intrasite examination of some kinds of sites. They can "aid in defining the spatial distribution of known sites" (Trubowitz 1973:7–8). At two sites in Washington state, Chatters (1981) successfully used close-interval (5 and 2 m) coring to (1) determine the depth, horizontal extent, and stratification, (2) monitor overburden stripping, (3) delimit small activity areas, and (4) assist the stratigraphic excavation of particular excavation units.

Overall, it appears that soil cores are a technique less attuned to site discovery than to the examination of known sites, or portions of them, with relatively dense features or anthropic soil horizons. As a discovery technique it will effectively and efficiently discover sites with large numbers and high densities of these kinds of site constituents. Many sites, however, do not contain such constituents, or contain few of them. The inability of cores to detect artifacts, the most common and widespread archaeological anomaly, makes soil coring a discovery technique for specialized applications rather than general purposes.

Auger Holes

Like soil cores, auger holes are cylinders of soil, but they are larger, with diameters ranging from 10 to 15 cm (about 4 to 6 inches). The auger hole contents are inspected to check for artifacts or feature fill and the profile of the hole is inspected for features or anthropic soil horizons. Auger holes, therefore, can detect three principal site constituents: artifacts, features, and anthropic soil horizons. Because of the hole's narrow diameter, however, profile inspection and therefore feature or soil horizon detection can be difficult. Several investigators have noted that auger holes are too narrow or that the profile cannot be cleaned sufficiently, especially in its deeper parts (Casjens et al. 1980:11; Claassen and Spears 1975:126). Auger holes have been dug with a variety of tools, including standard posthole diggers, bucket augers, and hand or motorized twist augers (Forestry Suppliers 1980:26–30, 143–145). Wood (1975:2) describes the technique: "we found that a pair of manually operated post-hole diggers were an inexpensive, portable, and effective tool for locating buried or obscured sites. With some practice a person can dig a small shaft as deep as 1.5 meters and bring out 10 cm core sections which in turn can be inspected for evidence of human occupation." Bucket augers are used similarly, except that the soil is held by friction alone and lifted out in a wide tube. As described below, dry and loose soils present a problem for bucket augers. Ferguson and Widmer (1976:23–29) used a mechanical screw auger mounted on a four-wheel-drive truck; the soil brought to the surface by the auger was screened to recover artifacts. Percy (1976:31) used a Sears' smaller power screw auger. Auger holes have been used in the eastern (Casjen et al. 1980; Ferguson and Widmer 1976; Percy 1976; South and Widmer 1977; Wood 1975) and middle United States (Claassen and Spears 1975; Leehan and Hackenberger 1976; Scott et al. 1978) and in Mesoamerica (Fry 1972) for examination of known sites as well as for discovery investigations.

Ferguson and Widmer (1976) report that the 6-inch-diameter screw auger they used discovered artifacts 80% of the time within site boundaries during a survey in the Middle Savannah River Valley in Georgia. The sites at which the auger holes detected artifacts, however, contained dense artifact scatters covering wide areas. They cautioned that "smaller sites with different types of debris might not prove so obvious when sampled by [auger holes]" (Ferguson and Widmer 1976:28). Wood (1975:10), despite an enthusiastic endorsement of the technique, cautions about its unreliability when artifact density is low. At Tikal, Guatemala, Fry (1972:261) reports the effective use of auger holes for discovering artifact clusters and related structures. At another Maya site, Chalchuapa in El Salvador, however, the same technique was unsuccessful, at least partially because of a lower artifact density (Fry 1972). For New England, Casjens *et al.* (1980:11) note that "prehistoric sites with smaller amounts of cultural material might not be found" using auger holes.

In a controlled comparison of discovery techniques done as part of the Cape Cod National Seashore Archeological Survey, bucket augers used within eight known sites recovered artifacts only 45% of the time (54 recoveries/119 holes) (McManamon 1981a; 1981c:202–205). This rate, which is well below that for shovel tests, probably is due partially to the problem of extracting loose dry sand from the auger hole. Nevertheless, it is far below the 80% success rate of Ferguson and Widmer cited above and, along with the other examples, raises questions about the effectiveness of auger holes as a general discovery technique.

The effectiveness of auger holes for site discovery seems to be affected strongly by the intrasite distribution of artifacts. They can detect artifacts when the artifacts are abundant and widely distributed. Auger holes are less likely to discover artifacts when the artifacts are either scarce though widely distributed or plentiful but spatially clustered. The relatively small volume of soil extracted and inspected by auger holes seems to be the reason for their peculiar pattern of effectiveness. The effect that variation in probe volume has upon the likelihood of recovering artifacts is considered below. Readers should note that none of the examples of auger use cited above reported frequent or consistent discovery of features or anthropic soil horizons. The technique certainly is capable of detecting them and it is unlikely that all the investigators cited would have ignored or failed to notice features and anthropic soil horizons if they had occurred. The failure to detect these site constituents, therefore, supports the hypothesis that features and anthropic soil horizons are infrequent or, if abundant, are highly clustered and difficult to detect in most cases.

Several investigators report technical problems using the tools available to extract the soil from auger holes. In Arkansas, Claassen and Spears (1975:126) tested the usefulness of a 7-cm-diameter auger. They termed it "awkward and inefficient"; root and rocks in the soil prevented completion of three out of six tests. The single completed test took 40 minutes. The other two were abandoned without completing them after 40 minutes had been spent digging each. Casjens *et al.* (1980:11) agree partially: "post hole diggers work well in sand; they cut roots efficiently but do not work well in rocky soil." They add that digging an auger hole is back-breaking work. Loose dry sand is another problem for posthole diggers (South and Widmer 1977:129). The sand cannot be held between the digger blades to remove it from the hole. Bucket augers rely on friction and a rigid soil structure to hold sections of soil in the bucket while they are lifted out of the auger hole. For this tool even wet sand can be difficult to extract. This was a major problem with bucket augers tested in sandy soil on Outer Cape Cod, Massachusetts (McManamon 1981:202–205). Soils with some clay, wet silt, or organic material were much less trouble to extract; however, dry sandy soil was the most common type along a number of the transects tested. In many cases the soil had to be dug from the auger hole with a garden hand shovel or trowel after the bucket auger failed to remove it. Similar problems forced the abandonment of bucket augers as a site examination technique in an investigation of a historic period site in Lincoln, Massachusetts (Pratt 1981:6).

In summary, auger holes can be an effective, efficient technique of site discovery. The increase in diameter from soil cores allows the auger holes to detect a wide range of site constituents. They should be able to detect three principal site constituents: artifacts, features, and authropic soil horizons. However, sites without abundant, widespread artifact deposits seem to be missed by auger holes. Because they can be dug and recorded quickly, given appropriate soil conditions (that is, a nonsandy soil without dense rocks, gravel or roots), auger holes can be used for discovery investigations covering large areas if sites with abundant and widespread artifact deposits, features, or authropic soil horizons are the target population.

Divoting

William Lovis brought national prominence to the problem of site discovery in densely vegetated environments with his 1977 *American Antiquity* article. Lovis used a discovery technique termed *divoting*. Divots are 25–30 cm (10–12 inch) squares cut into the forest floor or vegetation mat. The mat and adhering topsoil then are flipped over and inspected visually for artifacts. The exposed soil below the mat is inspected for features. Depending upon the soil profile, either topsoil or the topsoil and subsoil are inspected. In northern Michigan, where topsoil is thin, Lovis (1976:367) was able to inspect the interface between the topsoil and subsoil. The topsoil adhered to the vegetation mat and the top of the subsoil was exposed in the cut. In regions with thicker topsoil, a divot would not penetrate to the subsoil; only one possible horizon of the soil would be exposed and inspected in the cut, although all the topsoil above the cut level can be scraped off the bottom of the mat and inspected visually in the process (Williams 1976:5–6).

The relatively small volume inspected by divots suggests that they might be subject to constraints regarding the kind of sites they discover similar to those that seem to affect auger holes. The volume of a divot is slightly larger than the volume of an auger hole: a $30 \times 30 \times 10$ cm divot has approximately a 9000-cm^3 volume and a 15-cm diameter, and a 50-cm-deep auger hole has approximately 8800 cm^3. In a careful critique of Lovis's article, Nance (1979) pointed out just this problem of using such a small-sized unit for discovery.

All in all, divoting does not have much to recommend it as a discovery technique. Like surface clearing, divots inspect a surface rather than a soil volume. Divots share with auger holes the unfortunate likelihood of missing sites without dense and widespread constituents. Unlike auger holes, however, the depth below surface that divots can test is very shallow. Sites buried by practically any soil aggradation will be missed as a matter of course. Furthermore, inspection is exclusively visual. Other subsurface probes can, and often do, involve screening the contents to recover artifacts. This is important because the artifacts by which a site is detected are typically small and often are dirt-coated or embedded in clumps of soil. Quick visual inspections of divots probably are insufficient to detect dirty embedded artifacts, especially the tiny nondistinctive ones that compose the bulk of most site assemblages. All in all, divots have a very limited application for site discovery because of their small volume, shallow excavation, and inability to incorporate screening for inspection.

Shovel Tests

Shovel tests are the largest-volume subsurface probes. At the surface their dimensions range from 25- to 75-cm diameters for circular tests and 25 to 100 cm on a side for square ones. Depths usually vary according to the depth of archaeological deposits or their expected depth, but depths over 100 cm are physically difficult to excavate and therefore rare. Tests with a circular surface shape usually are cylinders, although below 50 cm their shape tends to become more conical because of physical constraints. Similarly, square units are less cubic and more pyramidal as their depth increases. These slight changes can be accounted for as necessary for comparisons among shovel tests during data analysis. Because tests must be dug quickly, field supervisors must continually monitor testing to maintain as much consistency in shovel test size and shape as possible.

Shovel tests like postholes discover artifacts, features, and anthropic soil horizons. Unlike postholes, shovel test dimensions are large enough for eacy inspection of the complete profile on all walls of the unit for its complete depth. Artifacts are recovered from the shovel test fill. Frequently all contents of each test are screened to facilitate the recovery of small artifacts (Bergman 1980:37; Casjens *et al.* 1980; McManamon 1981a, 1981c; Nance 1980b:172; Spurling 1980:32ff; Weide 1976), although some investigators have relied upon visual inspection of the test fill (A. Goodyear 1978:9; House and Ballenger 1977:46). Smaller shovel tests have surface dimensions similar to those of divots, however, they are dug much deeper and therefore inspect a larger volume; in addition, shovel tests that are screened have their contents inspected much more carefully than divots. These additional characteristics of shovel tests make them more likely to detect one or more site constituents.

Large volume seems to be the most important factor increasing the effectiveness of shovel tests over other techniques. In a controlled comparison of auger holes versus shovel tests (40-cm diameter) within site areas on outer Cape Cod, Massachusetts, test pits were over 70% more effective than auger holes (78% of the shovel tests recovered artifacts, only 45% of postholes) although the soil from both types of tests was screened (McManamon 1981a, 1981c, 1982). This is not to suggest that screening is unimportant. The available data suggest that discovery effectiveness is far greater when the soil from tests is screened rather than inspected visually. The two examples suggest, however, that screening alone does not increase the effectiveness of postholes or divots to the level of test pits. The greater volume of the latter is a crucial factor in its effectiveness as a discovery technique.

The price of the increased likelihood of site discovery when larger-volume tests are used is time, which, as Henry Ford and a host of others since have stressed, is money. Larger-volume tests require longer to dig, screen, collect from, and record so they result in higher labor cost per test. For this reason shovel tests usually are spaced more widely apart within quadrat or transect sample units than are soil cores or auger holes. Larger spaces between test units complicate the logistics necessary for precise unit location. Investigators aiming to discover sites cannot afford to locate test pits as precisely as if site examination or excavation were the activity at hand. Each pit must be located precisely enough to ensure adequate coverage of the transect or quadrat, but quickly enough to allow the field workers to cover as much ground as possible during a workday. Controled pacing and compasses, rather than long tapes and transits, are the appropriate means of arranging test-pit grids in quadrats or along transects. As with consistency in test-pit size and shape, care by field crew and supervisors is an essential ingredient for success.

Shovel tests, when their contents are screened to retrieve artifacts, seem likely overall to be the most effective of the subsurface techniques that have been used for site discovery. They have an important combination of advantages. First, they will detect the most common and widespread site constituent—artifacts— plus two others—features, and cultural soil horizons. Second, their relatively large volume gives them a greater likelihood of including one or more artifacts or remains from features or anthropic soil horizons within a site area. Screening is a crucial part of the shovel test technique. It overcomes visibility problems caused by soil adhering to artifacts and permits the recovery of small artifacts that could be missed easily, even by careful troweling. In general, larger shovel tests are likely to be more effective at discovery than are smaller ones. The general case, however, might be reversed because of specific circumstances or project goals. In some situations, for example, it might be desirable to excavate a larger number of smaller tests than a small number of larger ones.

Each site discovery investigation requires individual attention and perhaps a unique solution to the problems confronted. When subsurface probes appear to be the answer, it is crucial that the variety of available probes be considered in light of the problem at hand. Two concerns must be balanced in deciding among subsurface probes: (1) the artifact, feature, and authropic soil horizon frequencies and distributions expected within the sites being sought, plus the size of the sites, all of which affect the effectiveness of different kinds of probes, and (2) the cost of different types of probes. For convenience of presentation the costs are discussed first.

The Cost of Subsurface Probes

Information about the cost of using different subsurface probes is neither widely available nor easily compared when it is found. Total project costs are not good measures for comparison because they vary according to a variety of factors independent of discovery technique costs, such as remoteness of the study area, amount of travel to and from portions of the area being tested, the ease or difficulty of movement due to vegetation or topography, and the ease or difficulty or excavation due to soil conditions. The combination of these kinds of factors makes total project costs unique to the specific conditions encountered and the manner with which they were dealt. Cost in dollars is not the easiest way to compare techniques either. Dollar costs depend upon the cost of labor, which can vary independently of the discovery technique used. Instead, in the examples below, cost is figured indirectly in the time required to complete individual tests or for test coverage of standard-sized areas. Time estimates then can be used with the standard cost of labor for the project to compute dollar costs if they are desired.

Two ways of comparing the time requirements of different subsurface probes are possible. One is to calculate only the time required for excavating, inspecting, recording, and backfilling individual probes of different sizes. This is a basic cost that can be multiplied by the number of probes planned, and added to related costs such as the costs of setting up a test grid, moving between tests, and traveling between areas to be tested to calculate total cost of tests. A few examples of individual test time requirements are available. More commonly, the time needed to test a particular-size area is reported. Area coverage time estimates combine the time required for all the activities just listed above and are associated with a particular number and alignment or system of aligning the probes. Being linked to specific applications, these statements of time requirements are less easily compared than those for individual probes.

The time requirements of individual probes is available from a few reports, but for shovel tests only. Nevertheless, the available information is useful, if not comprehensive. Data from the 1979 season of the Cape Cod National Seashore Archeological Survey (McManamon 1981b, 1982) indicate the time required simply to excavate, sift through, record, and backfill moderate-size shovel tests (Table 4.8). These data have two principal implications. First, there is substantial variation between the time required within and outside site areas. Some of the additional time within site areas is due to more careful recording of soil data and the increased time needed to collect artifacts. Undoubtedly some is due to a

TABLE 4.8

Time Required for Shovel Tests[a]

| Sample unit-site | Time per test (minutes) | | Comments |
	X̄	Range	
2 19BN285	16	—	
2 19BN286	13	10–20	
5 19BN289	15	8–18	
6 19BN287	9	5–10	
7 19BN288	35	10–85	only 2 > 20 minutes
10 19BN273	15	7–19	
10 19BN274	24	15–70	only 1 > 25 minutes
10 19BN275	32	15–75	only 1 > 20 minutes
19 19BN276	—	5–32	only 3 > 20 minutes
Outside site areas[c]			
2	11	10–12	
3	12	7–24	
4	6	5–10	
5	9	7–12	
6	9	5–15	
7	10	9–10	
8	7	5–18	
9	10	10–10	
10	14	7–30	
11	9	5–20	
12	5	2–7	
13	7	5–11	
14	10	5–28	
15	9	4–14	
16	5	3–10	
17	9	5–15	
19	7	4–12	
20	9	5–13	
21	6	3–11	
22	5	2–12	
23	6	3–10	
25	5	2–8	
26	11	5–25	

[a] Shovel tests 40 cm in diameter, dug into glacial soil horizon, usually 25–75 cm deep. Data from 1979 field season, Cape Cod National Seashore Archaeological Survey. Within sites averages are based upon 5 to 10 tests. Outside site areas averages and based upon 10 to 30 tests.

[b] Overall average about 20 minutes.

[c] Overall average about 8 minutes.

heightened expectation of finding artifacts within a site area that makes crew members unconsciously increase their attention to the inspection of screens for small artifacts and test profiles for features or anthropic soil horizons. Investigations that plan to use shovel tests for examination within site areas will require more time for each test than those that limit their activities to discovery alone.

The second noteworthy point about the time requirements is the relative rapidity with which shovel tests can be done. The rough average of 8 minutes per probe outside site areas, for example, is at the low end of the 8–18 minutes per sample needed for the chemical analysis alone in Hassan's quantitative field chemical test (Hassan 1981:385). Even within site areas only seven shovel tests required more than 20 minutes to complete. The overall average of roughly 20 minutes per test is misleadingly high because of these few extreme cases.

Comparable data on the time requirement for individual shovel tests are very sparse. House and Ballenger (1976:52) estimated that each 1 m × 1 m × 10–15 cm test they excavated required 15–20 minutes to dig, examine carefully (but not screen), and backfill. By comparing these figures with those for the data from the Cape study the extra time required for screening can be estimated (Table 4.9). These estimates assume that apart from the screening all other activities done for each shovel test were similar. Because this is not certain, the estimated time requirements are only approximate. More accurately, they are approximations rather than specific estimates of time requirements. The figures suggest, however, substantial overlap in the rates at which soil is inspected for shovel tests that were screened and those that were not. The decrease in the rate of soil inspection due to screening might well be acceptable given the more reliable artifact identification afforded by screening.

Those archaeological reports that include information about time requirements for subsurface probes typically provide them in terms of the time required to test a standard-size area using particular probe sizes and spatial arrangements. Thus, Thorbahn (n.d.) reports that in the forests and fields of southeastern New England an average of 40 soil cores/hectare using random walk transects, plus the shovel tests necessary to confirm core anomalies as actual archaeological sites, required 1.5 person days. Also using soil cores but on the floodplain of the former Black River near Seattle in western Washington, Chatters (1981:Table 1)

TABLE 4.9

Estimated Approximate Time Requirement of Screening

Estimated time required without screening[a]
  100 × 100 × 10–15 cm shovel tests
  Approximate volumes = 150,000–100,000 cm^3
  Approximate time required = 10–15 minutes
  Approximate rate = 6600–15,000 cm^3/minute

Estimated time required with screening[b]
  40-cm diameter × 25–75 cm shovel tests
  Approximate volumes = 31,000–94,000 cm^3
  Approximate time required = 8–20 minutes[c]
  Approximate rate = 1600–11,800 cm^3/minute

---

[a] House and Ballenger (1976:52).
[b] Cape Cod National Seashore Archaeological Survey, 1979 data.
[c] For overall average, see Table 4.8.

records that 80 hours (10 person days) were needed to test a 25-ha area using a systematic grid with a 50-m interval. He also reports the time required for two other soil core grids, one with a 5-m interval and the other with a 2-m interval. Spurling (1980:45 ff.) records that 500 × 500 m square quadrats (25 ha) with 100 1 × 1 m tests in a systematic unaligned arrangement required 12–16 person days in the Upper Peace River Valley of eastern British Columbia. Another survey in a different, but similar, part of the Peace River drainage required only 12–14 person days/quadrat. Spurling (1980:48) accounts for the difference by variation in travel time among quadrats, the time required to locate quadrats, and crew size.

Together these three examples provide some comparisons between shovel tests and soil cores as well as between a single linear array of probes and systematic grid arrays (Table 4.10). Comparison of the estimated number of soil cores versus 1 × 1 m shovel tests per person day gives a hint of the substantial differences in time requirements. Missing from this comparison, however, is any consideration of the depth of the different probes or variation in soils into which the different probes were made. A soil core sunk 2 m or more into floodplain silts might require more time than a 1 × 1 m unit dug to a relatively shallow 25 cm. More detailed data comparing soil cores, augers, and shovel tests with consistent depths and soil conditions are presented below.

The other interesting comparison exists between the transect alignment (Thor-

TABLE 4.10

Comparisons of Time Requirements: Soil Cores versus Shovel Tests and Transects versus Grids

Investigation	Probe type and array	Probe interval (m)	Reported rate (No. probes/ tested area/ person-days)	Estimated rate for 1 ha (probes/ person-days)	Estimated probes/ person-day[a]
Chatters (1981: Table 1)	soil core, systematic grid	50	105/25 ha/10	4.2/2.5	2
		5	47/.15 ha/4	313.3/26.6	12
		2	107/.025 ha/6	4280/240	18
Thorbahn (n.d.)	soil core, linear, random walk transect	10	40/1 ha/1.5[b]	40/1.5	27[b]
Spurling (1980: 32–37)	1 × 1 m shovel test, stratified, systematic, unaligned grid	50[c]	100/25 ha/12–16	4/1.6–2.0	2–3

[a] Values are rounded to nearest integer.
[b] Includes time needed for shovel tests to confirm anomalies in soil cores.
[c] Approximate.

bahn n.d.) and the systematic grids (Chatters 1981). The logistical requirements of laying out a formal grid might be a contributing factor for lower rates that Chatters reports. Movement between soil core locations might also account for the lower rates because, as the interval between cores decreases, the rate increases. Formally established systematic grids require substantial commitments of time and consequently reduce the rate at which probes can be completed.

On the other hand, probes arranged in systematic grid patterns can provide for more even coverage of quadrat sample units than can narrow transects, and site frequency estimates based upon data from systematically tested quadrats are less biased by boundary effects than are transect-derived ones (S. Plog 1976; S. Plog *et al.* 1978:395–400). Successful use of grids for discovery investigations requires a careful mix of speed and precision. To paraphrase George Cowgill (1968:367), do not use a transit and tape when a pocket compass and pacing will do.

The final set of data presented in this section provides more details on the different time requirements of soil cores, augers, and shovel tests. Again, these data come from the 1979 field season of the Cape Cod Archeological Survey (Table 4.11). Shovel tests were arrayed systematically at 25-m intervals within 100 × 200 m survey units. Each unit contained 32 tests. If artifacts were discovered in a shovel test, additional shovel tests were placed around it. As an experiment, soil cores and augers were excavated at 5-m intervals along a number of transects coinciding with shovel test lines within 11 survey units. The shovel tests were generally 40 cm in diameter and 25–75 cm deep, depending upon the depth of postglacial deposits. The summary statistics in Table 4.11 indicate that soil cores and augers can be completed, on the average, about 2.5 times as quickly as 40-cm-diameter shovel tests. A substantial overlap (24–40) exists in the ranges of soil core, auger, and shovel test rates, however. These data contradict the lopsided comparison of 1 × 1 m shovel tests versus most of the soil core examples in Table 4.10 and probably more accurately indicate the magnitude of difference in time required by these different probe techniques.

Two other noteworthy points are suggested by these data. First, the rate of shovel tests/person days increased as the season progressed and crews became more familiar with the technique and method. Second shovel tests inspect volumes of soil more efficiently than do cores or augers. Cores and augers on the average can be done about 2.5 times faster than shovel tests, but whereas a shovel test 40 cm in diameter and 50 cm deep inspects about 63,000 cm³ of soil, an auger 10 cm in diameter and 50 cm deep inspects only about 3900 cm³. The shovel test inspects over 16 times the soil volume of the auger for less than 3 times the cost. Enough augers to equal the volume of a given-size shovel test cannot be done as quickly as the shovel test. The question of which technique is more effective and cost-efficient then revolves around the size, artifact frequencies, and intrasite artifact distribution of the sites that are to be sought by an investigation.

TABLE 4.11

Rates of Shovel Test, Auger, and Soil Core Completion[a]

	Shovel test[b]			Auger and soil core[c]	
Survey units	Test date	Tests/person-day[d]	Survey unit	Test date	Tests/person-day[d]
12,16,22	9 July 79	19	40	24 July 79	30
14	9 July 79	8	48	27 July 79	50
25,31,33	10 July 79	14	35,38	30 July 79	28
15,21	10 July 79	11	4,33,52	31 July 79	72
31	12 July 79	15	1,5,44	1 August 79	72
47	12 July 79	11	3	2 August 79	24
31,37,48	16 July 79	13			
36,43	16 July 79	12			
48,49	17 July 79	14			
35,44	L& July 79	13			
40,49	18 July 79	16			
34,35,42	18 July 79	17			
29,38,40	19 July 79	20			
52	20 July 79	22			
23,28	23 July 79	15			
20,32	24 July 79	15			
27,32,51	25 July 79	12			
51	26 July 79	10			
35,38	30 July 79	14			
39	30 July 79	15			
33,39	31 July 79	13			
33	1 August 79	28			
33	2 August 79	28			
39,97	6 August 79	30			
60	7 August 79	12			
59	7 August 79	14			
58,59	8 August 79	15			
57,58,59	9 August 79	17			
57.56	13 August 79	20			
56,129	14 August 79	14			
76,75,89	14 August 79	19			
150,128,149	15 August 79	24			
67,68	15 August 79	13			
75,68	16 August 79	17			
93,94	16 August 79	21			
70	17 August 79	21			
79	20 August 79	17			
95	20 August 79	21			
77,80	21 August 79	22			
96,97	21 August 79	18			
80,87	22 August 79	23			
97,151	22 August 79	21			
87,86	23 August 79	16			
88,143,123	23 August 79	20			
125	24 August 79	16			
123	24 August 79	24			
91,113	28 August 79	40			
141,101,100	28 August 79	24			
134,136	29 August 79	37			
118,121	30 August 79	20			

[a] Cape Cod National Seashore Archaeological Survey, 1979 season.
[b] $\overline{X} = 18$; $Md = 17$; range = 8–40. 25-m interval.
[c] $\overline{X} = 46$; $Md = 40$; range = 24–72. 5-m interval.
[d] Approximate rate.

Armed with this kind of cost information, it is possible to estimate the numbers of different probes that can be done within specific time periods and project budgets. But the information is useful for more than predicting budgets and time requirements. It can be used to choose the appropriate probe size for specific discovery problems. Consider, for example, a situation in which the size, artifact density, and artifact distribution of the sites of interest for a discovery investigation can be predicted reliably. As is discussed in the next section, the probability of probes of different sizes discovering such sites can be estimated roughly, as can the probability of discovery using differing numbers of different size probes. These sets of probabilities then can be evaluated in light of the rate at which different-size probes can be completed. A decision upon the discovery technique to be used made with such comparative information in hand would be truly informed regarding the cost-effectiveness of a larger number of smaller probes versus a smaller number of larger ones. In the next section ideas of how discovery probabilities are affected by site size and artifact abundance and density are explored.

FACTORS THAT AFFECT SITE DISCOVERY USING SUBSURFACE PROBES

The detection of a site using a type of subsurface probe depends upon four factors: (1) site size, (2) the frequency and intrasite distribution of artifacts, (3) the size of the probe, and (4) the number and spacing of probes. This section specifically considers subsurface probes; however, the four factors, with some modification, also influence the likelihood of site discovery using other techniques that detect site constituents other than artifacts. The frequency, spatial distribution, and size of features and anthropic soil horizons, for example, have important effects upon the likelihood of site discovery using soil cores, chemical tests, or instrument techniques, as do the number of cores or spacing of chemical or instrument readings. Therefore, although these constituents and techniques are not discussed explicitly here, insights drawn from this section might be relevant for them.

Archaeologists have begun to examine some of these factors in order to assess directly their effect upon archaeological data sets. Regarding site discovery, Krakker *et al.* (n.d.), Lovis (1976), Lynch (1980, 1981), Nance (1979, 1980a, 1980b, 1983), Scott *et al.* (1978), Stone (1981a, 1981b), and Thorbahn (n.d.) are directly applicable. In addition, several papers on site examination include discussions relevant for discovery with minor modifications only (Chartkoff 1978; Nance 1981:153–160; Nance and Ball 1981).

The first two factors—site size and artifact frequency and distribution—can be regarded as independent variables. The former were discussed generally in the earlier section on site constituents. Both are among the given characteristics of the archaeological record. The other factors—probe size and number and spacing of probes used—are controlled to some extent by the investigator who decides the size of probe to be used and the number of probes to be placed within the study area. Abstract models of relevant site characteristics as well as specific archaeological sites data have been used to examine the effect of variation in probe size or number upon discovery likelihood. The examples described below involve more or less simple versions of the archaeological record and site discovery investigations. They should not be generalized widely or uncritically; rather they provide ideas or guidance for the analysis of more complex specific situations. Remember also that successful *discovery* using subsurface probes requires the recovery of only one artifact to indicate the presence of a site (Nance 1981:153ff.; Stone 1981a:45–49, 1981b).

Probe Size

Parts of the preceding section suggested the importance of probe size for successful site discovery. Soil cores, which have the narrowest diameter among subsurface probes, appear to be relatively ineffective for the discovery of sites without abundant and widespread features or cultural soil horizons because their small diameter nearly always prevents them from discovering artifacts. Although that particular problem is skirted by subsurface probes with slightly larger dimensions, the smaller of these probes appear less likely to discover sites without abundant and widespread amounts of artifacts than are probes with larger dimensions. Once more, an example comparing augers and shovel tests comes from a test of discovery techniques conducted as part of the Cape Cod National Seashore Archeological Survey (McManamon 1981b:204–205). The overall results indicate that augers with diameters of about 10 cm are only 58% as effective as shovel tests with 40-cm diameters at discovering artifacts within site areas. This is so despite the fact that augers outnumber shovel tests by approximately 4 to 1 in this experiment. Considering only the results from the prehistoric sites tested, the augers do slightly better but still are only 67% as effective as the shovel tests. The prehistoric sites where the tests were done have estimated artifact densities of 45 to $50/m^2$ of the surface area, which is roughly the average for all prehistoric sites discovered by the survey.

A more abstract model using a variety of values for artifact abundance and density permits comparisons among a wider range of probe sizes (Table 4.12). Imagine an archaeological site, or a portion of a site, 10 m square and 50 cm deep. Within this volume envision artifacts spaced evenly, vertically as well as horizontally, throughout the volume of the site. With this kind of even distribution the probability that different-size probes will discover artifacts is a function of the number of artifacts in the site matrix and the size of the probe. The greater

TABLE 4.12

Probabilities of Single Subsurface Probe Discovering Site[a]

Probe diameter (cm)[b]	Number of probes (per 10m²)[c]	Number of artifacts in site				
		10,000 (100/m²)	5,000 (50/m²)	1,000 (10/m²)	100 (1/m²)	10 (.1/m²)
Auger (10)	10,000	1.00[d]	.50	.10	.01	.001
Auger (20)	2,500	1.00	1.00	.40	.04	.004
Shovel test (25)	1,600	1.00	1.00	.63	.06	.006
Shovel test (50)	400	1.00	1.00	1.00	.25	.025
Shovel test (100)	100	1.00	1.00	1.00	1.00	.100

[a] Site dimensions: 10 × 10 × .5 m.

[b] Depth of each probe except divot is 50 cm.

[c] The potential probe locations are packed evenly within the 10 m²; spaces between potential probe locations are devoid of artifacts.

[d] Probabilities are calculated as the number of artifacts divided by the number of probes per 10 × 10 m area.

the number of artifacts and the larger the probe size, the greater the probability that a probe will contain an artifact, thus discovering the site. As the number of artifacts decreases, the probability that small probes will be successful decreases much sooner than the probability of success using larger ones (Table 4.12). Because they encompass more volume, the larger units have a greater likelihood of containing one or more artifacts when artifact frequency and density fall. Table 4.12 shows, for example, that when the model site contains 1000 artifacts (10/m² of surface area), a randomly placed auger 20 cm in diameter has a probability of .4 of containing an artifact. This is because only 1000 of the 2500 possible 20-cm-diameter augers in the site area contain artifacts. The other 1500 would be located in sterile soil between artifacts. Under the same site conditions, however, a 50-cm-diameter shovel test is certain to include more than one artifact ($p = 1.0$), because there are only 400 possible shovel tests in the area that also contains 1000 evenly distributed artifacts. Two suggestions are derived from Table 4.12. First, for sites with very low-average artifact densities, relatively large shovel tests might be the only effective subsurface probe. Second, and more important, the probabilities in Table 4.12 suggest that for sites or portions of sites with artifact frequencies of 50/m² or above, subsurface probes of relatively modest dimensions will be as effective as larger ones. Because the smaller probes can be dug, inspected, and recorded more quickly, they will be more efficient and a better choice of discovery technique for sites with sufficiently high artifact frequencies.

It is quite clear, unfortunately, that this model is burdened with two unrealistic assumptions. Artifacts within sites are neither uniformly distributed nor abundant. Table 4.13 shows typical variation in spatial distribution both within site

TABLE 4.13

Intrasite Variation in the Spatial Distribution of Lithic Artifacts[a]

Site (N shovel tests)	Shovel tests with N artifacts (%)				
	$N = 0$	1	2	3	≥ 4
19BN273/275 (48)	23	19	13	8	35
19BN274/339 (47)	32	26	9	9	26
19BN281 (75)	12	19	11	12	47
19BN282/283/284 (82)	22	13	15	9	41
19BN323 (44)	27	34	11	5	23
19BN333/336/337 (39)	26	28	10	13	21
19BN340 (27)	22	7	22	15	33
19BN341 (67)	28	19	9	9	34
19BN355 (22)	41	23	9	9	14
19BN356 (19)	42	39	16	5	0

[a] Shovel tests systematically arrayed at intervals of approximately 6, 12, or 25 m. Data from 1980–1981 field seasons Cape Cod National Seashore Archeological Survey.

areas and among sites. These data suggest, for example, that between 12 and 42% of the areas of these sites are devoid of artifacts. Variations in artifact abundance also are substantial (Table 4.14), with the variances in artifact frequency among equal-size test units commonly exceeding the mean by a factor of 2 or more. The sites' values of the variance/mean ratio and the negative binomial parameter k (Table 4.14) also suggest substantial spatial clumping of lithic artifacts. Values greater than 1.0 for the variance/mean ratio suggest an aggregated spatial pattern. For k, low values indicate pronounced spatial clumping (Pielou 1977:124–128).

These data reveal the gap between the simple site model described above and archaeological reality. Nonetheless, the model points out the relationship between artifact density and probe size. This can be explored further, along with the relationship between site size and discovery using another set of archaeological site data, this time from southeastern Massachusetts (Tables 4.15 and 4.16). The site data display a wide range of values for site area, average artifact frequency, and percentage of site area with relatively high artifact frequency (i.e., ≥ 16 artifacts/m², a value chosen for convenience of computing). The

TABLE 4.14

Intrasite Variation in the Abundance of Lithic Artifacts[a]

Site (N of shovel tests)	Lithic artifacts per shovel tests		Variance/mean[b]	k[c]
	$\bar{X}$	s^2		
19BN273/275 (48)	2.9	8.6	2.96	1.48
19BN274/339 (47)	2.1	5.7	2.71	1.23
19BN282/283/284 (82)	4.3	22.8	5.30	.99
19BN323 (44)	2.8	20.9	7.46	.43
19BN333/336/337 (39)	3.0	16.2	5.40	.68
19BN340 (27)	3.3	12.6	3.82	1.17
19BN355 (22)	1.6	5.4	3.38	.67
19BN356 (19)	.8	.8	1.00	0.00

[a] Shovel tests with diameters of approximately 40 cm. Data from 1980–1981 field seasons Cape Cod National Seashore Archeological Survey.

[b] $s^2/\bar{X}$ (Pielou 1977:124–126)

[c] $k = \bar{X}^2/(s^2 - \bar{X})$ (Pielou 1977:128–134; Nance 1983).

TABLE 4.15

Effects of Site Size, Artifact Abundance, and Shovel Test Size on Discovery[a]

Site number	Site area (hectares)	Average artifacts/m²	% of site area with artifacts >16/m²	Estimated number of successful shovel tests[b] (10/hectare)	
				25-cm diam.	50-cm diam.
7AP	1.594	64.6	58.3	10.1	11.2
7CP	1.086	7.1	8.3	2.3	3.9
7DDP	.789	71.7	64.2	5.5	5.9
7GP	.112	35.0	64.5	.8	.8
7HHP	.829	60.3	60.	5.4	6.0
7KP	2.054	72.4	65.3	14.4	15.5
7MP	1.297	28.5	26.7	4.8	6.5
7PP	.285	14.5	14.5	.8	1.2
7RP	.167	22.8	48.9	1.0	2.0
7SP	.176	101.3	71.4	1.4	1.4
7TP	.188	12.1	9.1	.4	.7
7UP	1.647	7.2	10.2	3.7	6.1
9DP	.029	128.9	67.7	.2	.2

[a] Data from I-495 Archaeological Project, Public Archaeology Laboratory, Brown University (Thorbahn n.d.:Tables 2 and 3).

[b] Estimates based upon number of tests that would be placed randomly within a site area, multiplied by the probability that the test would contain at least one artifact. Ten shovel tests randomly placed within each hectare.

TABLE 4.16

Correlation Matrix of Table 4.15 Variables

	Site area	Artifacts/m²	% Area with ≥16 artifacts/m²	Number of successful tests 25 cm	50 cm
Site area	—	—	—	—	—
Artifacts/m²	−.14	—	—	—	—
% Area with ≥16 artifacts/m²	−.12	.83	—	—	—
Successful tests(25 cm, 10/ha)	.85	.19	.30	—	—
Successful tests(50 cm, 10/ha)	.92	.09	.19	.99	—

estimated number of successful shovel tests takes account of the intrasite spatial variation in artifact abundance. In deriving the estimates Thorbahn (n.d.:17–24) properly assigned lower probabilities of successful discovery to the percentage of shovel tests expected to be placed within the portions of sites containing few or no artifacts. The estimated number of successful tests is based upon 10 shovel tests placed randomly in each hectare of the study area.

The correlations between variables (Table 4.16) indicate that site area is highly and positively correlated with the number of shovel tests that recover artifacts— .85 for 25-cm-diameter tests and .92 for tests 50 cm in diameter. Neither average artifact frequency nor percentage of site area with relatively high artifact density are correlated substantially with the number of successful tests. This suggests that it is the area over which a site extends rather than the density of artifacts within it that most strongly influences the probability of discovery. A closer look at this particular data set confirms this. Four of the 13 sites would not be detected by shovel tests with 25-cm diameters; that is, these 4 have estimated numbers of successful tests that are less than 1.0. Among these 4, the ranges of values for average artifacts per m² and percentage of site area with relatively high artifact density are 12.1–128.9 and 9.1–67.7 respectively. These are not out of line with the value ranges of these variables for all 13 sites: 7.1–128.9 artifact/m² and 8.3–71.4% of the site area. On the other hand, the 4 sites are among the smallest in area of the 13. All 4 are below .3 ha in area, whereas only 3 of the remaining 9 sites have such small areas.

In only one case, Site 7PP, does increasing the shovel test size to a 50-cm diameter increase the estimated number of successful shovel tests to above 1.0. It is interesting that Site 7PP has relatively low values for average artifacts per m² and percentage of site area with relatively high artifact density. Analysis of the abstract model-site data above (Table 4.12) indicates that sites with such characteristics would have better chances for discovery using larger shovel tests.

The Number and Spacing of Probes

The site data presented above (Tables 4.13–4.15) demonstrate on a larger scale the problem of discovering relatively rare items that Nance (1981:153–160; see also Nance 1983) has discussed in detail on the intrasite level. A site such as 9DP (Table 4.15), which occupies under 3% of a hectare, would be difficult to find, given the constraints of the survey design, despite its abundance of artifacts and high artifact density. Because archaeologists have no control over site size, they can only improve their ability to discover small sites by increasing the number of shovel tests. Increasing the size of individual tests might help in some cases, such as with Site 7PP (Table 4.15). In general, however, more tests, whether by using shorter intervals in a systematic array or a larger number of randomly placed tests per unit of area, are the key to improving the likelihood of discovering the small sites. Furthermore, the intensity of effort might have to be substantially increased. In the case at hand, a doubling of the number of tests per hectare from 10 to 20 would result in all but two of the sites, 7TP and 9DP (Table 4.15), having estimates of greater than 1.0 for the number of successful shovel tests (25-cm diameter). Another doubling to 40 tests/hectare would give 7TP a value of 1.6 estimated successful tests, but a value of only .79 for 9DP. The latter site would still have a value less than 1.0 for estimated number of successful tests if the intensity were 50 tests/hectare. The value finally tops 1.0, specifically 1.17, for a test intensity of 60 shovel tests/hectare. For easier comprehension of the effort necessary for comparable systematic and simple random shovel test arrays, Table 4.17 shows the approximate interval between systematically placed tests at the levels of test intensity referred to above.

Little has been said here directly about the effect of the spatial arrangement of probes upon site discovery. The effectiveness of specific arrangements of probes depends upon the specific distribution of the site constituent being sought in particular situations. Therefore, I concentrate here on how variations in the

TABLE 4.17

Test Intervals for Comparable Numbers of Tests/Hectare

Tests/hectare	Number of m² for which test is centroid	Interval between tests (m)[a]
10	1000	32
16	625	25
20	500	22
25	400	20
40	250	16
50	200	14
60	167	13

[a] Approximate.

number of probes affects the likelihood of site discovery. There are, however, several general considerations about the arrangement of probes presented below. The choice of whether to use an arrangement that is systematic, simple random, or some combination of these should be guided by the project's goals, the expected distribution of the constituent being sought, and logistics. No particular type of arrangement has a monopoly on effectiveness.

A systematic arrangement will provide the most even coverage of a given area or sample unit (McManamon 1981a, 1981c), although, as Tables 4.15 and 4.17 and the preceding discussion have shown, the interval among probes might have to be very small to discover rare or highly clustered constituents. A danger of using systematic arrangements is that the interval among probes might inadvertently match a set interval between archaeological remains, resulting in the probes consistently missing their targets. This seems more likely to be a potential problem when features are the target constituent because several types of features (e.g., hearths, house floors, postmolds) might have intrasite distributions that are at least roughly systematic. Artifact intrasite distributions, on the other hand, seem less likely to be arranged systematically and probably present no such problem for the use of a systematic grid.

A systematic grid with adjacent lines of probes offset or staggered has a more economical packing of probes (Krakker *et al.* n.d.). The offset grid evenly and equivalently covers an area or sample unit with fewer probes than would be required by a more traditional grid with evenly aligned probes.

With proper planning, an arrangement of randomly located probes can provide data suitable for estimation of the overall frequencies and distribution of archaeological remains in a study area. Simple random arrangements of probes usually should be used only when data are to be used for estimation and the probes are themselves the sample units (Nance 1980b, 1983). A simple random arrangement frequently covers an area very unevenly. Sites in portions of the area not covered by the probe arrangement go undiscovered. This will cause problems for estimation of site frequencies when the sample units are the areas to be covered by the probe grids rather than the probes themselves (McManamon 1981c, 1982). When a site constituent that is believed to have a systematic arrangement is being sought, yet roughly even coverage of an area or sample unit is desired, an arrangement with random and systematic aspects, such as a stratified, unaligned random grid may be the answer (Spurling 1980).

Returning again to the relationship between the number of probes and site discovery, obviously substantial effort would be necessary to ensure the discovery of all the types of sites represented in Table 4.15. Unless a complete inventory of sites is required, however, less time-consuming means are available in many instances to estimate the frequencies of sites too small to be discovered consistenty.

The estimated numbers of successful shovel tests discussed above are, after all, only approximations that should hold over the long term. Some small sites will be discovered even though the test interval or intensity is not adequate to discover all of them (Krakker *et al.* n.d.:6; Lovis 1976; McManamon 1981c: 195–204; Nance 1979). The characteristics of these sites (e.g., site size and artifact density) combined with the frequency with which they actually were identified can be used to estimate the numbers of such sites still undetected.

If for some reason no sites below the size expected to be discovered have been detected, it still is possible to determine the likelihood that sites of a certain size and artifact density do exist but have been missed by the discovery technique used. Stone (1981a:45–49) has demonstrated the use of the Poisson distribution for evaluating this type of negative evidence. He also has applied the Poisson distribution for the more general case of evaluating the probability of success of individual shovel tests and the estimation of necessary sample sizes for different levels of discovery probability (Stone 1981b; see also, Krakker *et al.* n.d.;).

This section has identified and discussed factors that affect the probability that sites will be discovered by subsurface probes. Although some insights have been noted, there have been no comprehensive revelations. This is dictated by the nature of the problem. Whether or not a site of certain size and artifact density is discovered depends upon the specific technique used and the method in which it is applied. Happily, ways of conceptualizing and resolving this problem are receiving more prominent, extended, and sophisticated attention within the discipline. Such study can only improve the ability of archaeologists to interpret the explain the past.

SUMMARY AND PROGNOSIS

There is no general resolution to the problem of site discovery, but the fact that it is increasingly recognized as a problem to be dealt with explicitly is an improvement (e.g., Carr 1982; Lynch 1980, 1981; Nance 1980b, 1981, 1983; Rice *et al.* 1980; Schiffer *et al.* 1978; Stone 1981a,b). This chapter is, I hope, a clear introduction to the problem, to some of the approaches and perspectives about it, and to the methods and techniques that individually or in combination can solve it.

The concept of site obtrusiveness (Schiffer *et al.* 1978:6) was introduced at the beginning of this chapter. It has two aspects: (1) the ease with which site contents are detectable, and (2) the type of technique(s) necessary to discover the site or sites of interest. The first principal section of this chapter considered the intersite frequency, intrasite abundance, and intrasite spatial distribution of the physical and chemical constituents believed to be most common among archaeological sites. The suitability of different site constituents as targets for discovery efforts depends upon their frequency among and within sites, and their intrasite spatial distribution. Constituents that are abundant and widespread, in most cases, will be more easily discovered than those that are not.

Accessible and clear descriptions of archaeological remains in the terms necessary for judging the obtrusiveness of different constituents are surprisingly rare, but some generalizations have been gleaned from those that are available. Artifacts, the portable products and by-products of human activities, are the most common type of constituent among sites. Within most archaeological sites, artifacts are the most abundant and widespread type of constituent. Other constituents are features, anthropic soil horizons, and human-induced anomalies that can be detected by chemical or instrument tests and analysis. In many cases, the anomalies are related to features or soil horizons. Features and anthropic soil horizons with large amounts of organic remains, for example, cause anomalously high chemical scores. Other features and horizons that are distinctly different in composition from the surrounding soil matrix of the site can cause anomalies that are detectable using resistivity magnetometry, subsurface radar, and remote sensing analysis. Not all features or soil horizons, however, cause anomalies, at least easily detectable anomalies (Carr 1982). Easily detectable chemical or instrument anomalies are expected to occur in a relatively small portion of the total number of sites in the archaeological record. In a smaller portion of sites, for example, than contain features or anthropic soil horizons because it is subsets of the total number of features and horizons that cause the chemical and instrument anomalies. In general, then, artifacts are found in most sites, features, and anthropic soil horizons in a smaller proportion of sites, and chemical and instrument anomalies in a yet smaller proportion.

Regarding intrasite abundance and distribution, artifacts again top the list with features, followed by anthropic soil horizons. The multisite examples of the other two types of site constituents considered in the first section did not permit comparisons with the first three types or each other. The examples did point out, however, an additional drawback of aiming discovery efforts at chemical and instrument anomalies. The detection of most humanly induced archaeological chemical or instrument anomalies requires substantial, detailed data about the natural chemical, textural, and moisture characteristics of the soil throughout a study area. The collection of these detailed data for intrasite analysis is far more feasible (Carr 1977, 1982) than for discovery investigations in large study areas. Site constituents that can be detected using remove sensing analysis usually do not require this extensive background data; however, they typically require very good visibility conditions. Even a slight forest or shrub canopy can hide the anomalies from sight, preventing discovery.

All other things equal, artifacts should be the site constituent that discovery efforts aim to detect. All other things often are unequal, of course, and archaeologists quite properly have aimed discovery efforts at other site constituents to overcome special constraints or focus on particular types of sites (Bruder *et al.*

1975; Chapman 1977, 1978; Ehrenhard 1980; Harp 1974, 1977; papers in Lyons 1976, Lyons and Ebert 1978, and Lyons and Hitchcock 1977). To emphasize a point made at the beginning of this article, project goals and limitations ultimately should determine the discovery technique or techniques used. The process and reasons for reaching the decision should be explicit because the choice of technique affects so strongly the types of sites that will be discovered.

More data about site constituents, presented clearly and quantitatively, are needed. As the preceeding section of this chapter showed, a host of questions about the effectiveness and efficiency of different discovery techniques cannot be answered in detail without such data. The probabilities of successful discovery presented in the preceding consideration of the effectiveness of subsurface probes required assumptions about the size, artifact density, and artifact distribution within sites. The accuracy of the assumptions that were used to represent sites in the archaeological record is unclear. Archaeologists' ability to resolve questions about method and technique will improve substantially as clear and reliable data describing the physical and chemical characteristics of the record become better known. The progress being made along these lines is encouraging but much more attention is necessary.

The second major section of this chapter described and evaluated a variety of archaeological field techniques for their effectiveness in site discovery investigations. Subsurface probe techniques received the most attention. Chemical tests and instrument techniques such as resistivity, magnetometry, and subsurface radar are more likely to be useful for intrasite analysis, given the detailed background data necessary for their accurate analysis, the logistical problems their application to large survey areas would involve, and the kinds of anomalies they can detect. Remote sensing techniques in general can be effective for site discovery in areas of good surface visibility when the sites are on or near the surface and contain large, distinct features, preferably former structures or anthropic soil horizons. Several exceptions were noted in which surface visibility was poor, that is, the study areas had dense vegetation but slight elevations of site areas caused differences in vegetation or vegetation growth that were easily detected by aerial photographic analysis (Bruder et al. 1975; Ehrenhard 1980; Newman and Byrd 1980).

As a group, subsurface probes seem most widely applicable for site discovery because, in general, they can detect the most-common site constituents: features, anthropic soil horizons, and, especially, artifacts. Among subsurface probes, shovel tests probably are the most effective overall for site discovery. Their effectiveness varies, however, according to (1) the size and intrasite artifact abundance and distribution of the target sites and (2) the volume, (3) number, and (4) arrangement of the shovel tests. If the size and intrasite artifact abundance and distribution of target sites is known or can be estimated, the likelihood of site discovery given various sizes and numbers of tests is predictable. Considering the small size or intrasite clustering of some sites, however, the total discovery of all types of sites for even relatively small study areas where subsurface probes are necessary will require substantial dilegence, effort, and funding.

This fact raises the issue of archaeological sampling. Many of the discovery techniques discussed here are very time consuming and, therefore, very costly to apply intensively over large areas. One solution, usually a poor one, is to apply a technique extensively; that is, to increase intervals between tests, reducing the number of tests per unit area. This will result in the discovery of only sites with very large areas.

A solution that is likely to provide more accurate and ultimately more useful results is to examine a portion, or sample, of the study area intensively, then use the sample data to estimate the characteristics of the archaeological record in the entire area. If probability sampling is used, the precision of estimates usually can be calculated objectively, but even informed, explicit judgment sampling can derive estimates that can be qualitatively evaluated. The discovery of rare sites, in any case, probably will require informed judgment sampling (Schiffer *et al.* 1978:4–6). Study areas can be stratified to accommodate combinations of probability and nonprobability sampling. Strata with high expected site-densities can be sampled using a probability design with other strata sampled judgmentally. Furthermore, explicit sampling designs, probability or otherwise, need not be limited to arid environments with clear surface visibility, as recent successful applications in the thick brush, shrubs, and forests of Kentucky and Massachusetts illustrate (McManamon 1981b, 1981c, 1982; Nance 1980a, 1980b, 1983).

As archaeologists undertake more site discovery investigations in regions where discovery is difficult, seeking sites that are hard to find, they must grapple with a variety of concerns. Among these are the goals of their investigations, the characteristics of the sites they seek, the effectiveness for site discovery and logistical requirements of field techniques available to them, and the appropriate sampling method for applying the chosen technique. The heartening increase in the numbers of archaeologists involved in such deliberations and the quality of the recent grappling make site discovery an exciting frontier of contemporary archaeological theory, method, and technique.

ACKNOWLEDGMENTS

Several major revisions ago this chapter was a paper entitled "Site discovery: past and future directions" that was presented at the 43rd Annual Meeting of the Society for American Archaeology in 1978. Many colleagues have helped me with the various revisions by providing copies of articles or papers as well as comments. My thanks to all who have done so, particularly those who helped on the present version: A. Ammerman, K. Anderson, V. Carbone, J. Chapman, J. Chatters, A. Dekin, J. Ebert, B. Graham, R. Ice, J. Jacobson, R. Lafferty, M. Lynott, J. Nance, S. Plog, K. Quilty, K.

Schneider, M. Shott, and P. Thorbahn. In addition, several anonymous reviewers provided detailed and thoughtful comments on earlier drafts. I thank Michael Schiffer for his careful summation of the reviews, as well as his own comments. I appreciate his encouragement throughout the course of this chapter's development. Kent Schneider deserves both my thanks and my vengeful wrath for suggesting this revision in 1981. I have not always heeded the comments that others have generously provided, but I hope they will agree with me that the article has improved because of their efforts.

A host of individuals were instrumental in the careful collection and preparation of data that are presented here from the Cape Cod National Seashore Archeological Survey. All those who have worked for the survey have my sincere thanks, but I owe special debts to Elena Filios, Terry Childs, and Dave Lacy for the 1979 data on the effectiveness and costs of various discovery techniques. Others associated with the supervision of this project also have my thanks, especially Chris Borstel, Jim Bradley, Helen Delano, Joyce Fitzgerald, and Mary Hancock for the data used in this chapter. Irene Duff once again skillfully and cheerfully typed innumerable drafts of pages, sections, tables, and bibliography, and managed to accomplish her other substantial duties as well. Finally, Carol, Adalie, Kate, and Daisy have been supportive of this effort, divertive when diversion was called for, and tolerant about the time away from them that this work has caused. This article is for them, especially Daisy whose life spanned its inception, growth, and completion.

REFERENCES

Ahler, Stanley A.
  1973   Chemical analysis of deposits at Rodgers Shelter, Missouri. *Plains Anthropologist*
         18:116–131.
Aikens, C. Melvin, L. G. Loy, M. D. Southard and R. C. Haines
  1980   *Remote sensing: a handbook for archeologists and cultural resource managers, basic
         manual supplement:Oregon.* Cultural Resources Management Division, National Park
         Service, Washington, D.C.
Aitken, M. J.
  1970   Magnetic location. In *Science in archaeology,* edited by D. Brothwell and E. S. Higgs.
         New York:Praeger. Pp. 681–694.
Ammerman, Albert J.
  1981   Surveys and archaeological research. *Annual Review of Anthropology* **10**:63–88.
Ammerman, Albert J. and M. W. Feldman
  1978   Replicated collection of site surfaces. *American Antiquity* **43**:734–740.
Asch, David L.
  1975   On sample size problems and the uses of nonprobabilistic sampling. In *Sampling in
         archaeology,* edited by W. Mueller. Tucson:University of Arizona Press. Pp.
         170–191.
Atkinson, R. J. C.
  1957   Worms and weathering. *Antiquity* **31**:217–233.
Avery, Thomas E. and Thomas R. Lyons
  1981   *Remote sensing: aerial and terrestrial photography for archeologists.* Cultural Re-
         sources Management Division, National Park Service, Washington, D.C.
Baker, Craig and George J. Gumerman
  1981   *Remote sensing: archeological applications of remote sensing in the north central
         lowlands.* Cultural Resource Management Division, National Park Service, Wash-
         ington, D. C.

Bergman, Marcey P.
  1980   Muddles in the puddles: archeological survey in Virginia. M.A. thesis on file. Depart-
          ment of Anthropology, University of Virginia, Charlottesville.
Berlin, G. Dennis, J. R. Ambler, R. H. Hevly and G. G. Schaber
  1977   Identification of a Sinagua agricultural field by aerial thermography, soil chemistry,
          pollen/plant analysis and archaeology. *American Antiquity* **42**:588–600.
Binford, Lewis R., S. R. Binford, R. Whallon and M. A. Hardin
  1970   Archaeology at Hatchery West. *Memoirs of the Society for American Archaeology,*
          No. 24.
Black, Glenn
  1967   *Angel site: an archaeological, historical, and ethnological study,* Vol. 1 Indi-
          anapolis:Indiana Historical Society.
Black, Glenn A. and Richard B. Johnston
  1962   A test of magnetometry as an aid to archaeology. *American Antiquity* **28**(2):199–205.
Breiner, Sheldon
  1965   The rubidium magnetometer in archeological exploration. *Science* **150**:185–193.
Brooks, Mark J., S. W. Green and S. M. Perlman
  1980   A strategy for determining the extent and variability of archeological sites in temperate
          forest locales. In Discovering and examining archeological sites: strategies for areas
          with dense ground cover, F. P. McManamon and D. J. Ives (assemblers). *American
          Archaeological Reports,* #14, American Archaeology Division, University of Mis-
          souri, Columbia.
Brose, David S.
  1981   Archaeological investigations in the Cuyahoga Valley National Recreation Area. *Ar-
          chaeology Research Reports* #30. Cleveland Museum of Natural History, Cleveland,
          Ohio.
Brown, Galen N. and James I. Ebert
  1980   Correlations between cover type and lithology in the Teshekpuk Lake Area, Alaska: a
          remote sensing analysis. In *Cultural resources remote sensing,* edited by T. R. Lyons
          and F. J. Mathien. Cultural Resource Management Division, National Park Service,
          Washington, D.C. Pp. 51–78.
Brown, James A.
  1975   Deep-site excavation strategy as a sampling problem. In *Sampling in archaeology,*
          edited by J. W. Mueller. Tucson: University of Arizona Press. Pp. 155–169.
Bruder, J. Simon, Elinor G. Large and Barbara L. Stark
  1975   A test of aerial photography in an esturine mangrove swamp in Veracruz, Mexico.
          American Antiquity **40**:330–337.
Carr, Christopher
  1977   A new role and analytical design for the use of resistivity surveying in archaeology.
          Midcontinental Journal of Archaeology **2**:161–193.
  1982   *Handbook on soil resistivity surveying: interpretation of data from earthen archeologi-
          cal sites.* Evanston, Illinois:Center for American Archeology Press.
Casjens, L., G. Bawden, M. Roberts and V. Talmage
  1978   Field methods in New England cultural resource management. In Conservation archae-
          ology in the Northeast: toward a research orientation, edited by A. E. Spiess. *Peabody
          Museum Bulletin* #3. Cambridge, Massachusetts. Harvard University.
Casjens, L., R. Barber, G. Bawden, M. Roberts and F. Turchon
  1980   Approaches to Site Discovery in New England Forests. In Discovering and examining
          archeological sites: strategies for areas with dense ground cover, F. P. McManamon

and D. J. Ives (assemblers). *American Archaeological Reports* #14. American Archaeology Division, University of Missouri, Columbia.

Chapman, Jefferson
1976 Early Archaic site location and excavation in the Little Tennessee River Valley. *Southeastern Archaeological Conference Bulletin* **19**:31–36.
1977 Archaic period research in the lower Little Tennessee River Valley. *Reports of Investigations* 18. Department of Anthropology, The University of Tennessee, Knoxville.
1978 The Bacon Farm Site and a buried site reconnaissance. *Report of Investigation*, No. 23. Department of Anthropology, The University of Tennessee, Knoxville.
1981 The Bacon Bend and Iddins Sites: the Late Archaic period in the lower Little Tennessee River Valley. *Report of Investigation*, No. 31. Department of Anthropology, The University of Tennessee, Knoxville.

Chartkoff, Joseph L.
1978 Transect interval sampling in forests. *American Antiquity* **43**:46–53.

Chatters, James C.
1981 The application of coring techniques in inventory, assessment and the formulation of excavation strategy. Paper presented at the 46th Annual Meeting, Society for American Archaeology, San Diego, California.

Clark, Anthony
1970 Resistivity surveying. In *Science in Archaeology*, edited by D. Brothwell and E. S. Higgs. New York:Praeger. Pp. 695–707.
1975 Archaeological prospecting: a progress report. *Journal of Archaeological Sciences* **2**(4):297–314.

Claassen, Cheryl P. and Carol S. Spears
1975 An assessment of ambulatory site surveying, shovel testing and augering. In Arkansas Eastman Archeological Project, edited by Charles M. Baker *Arkansas Archeological Survey Report* #6. Fayetteville Arkansas. Pp. 123–27.

Collins, M. B. (editor)
1979 Excavations at four Archaic sites in the Lower Ohio Valley. *Occasional Papers in Anthropology* 1, Department of Anthropology, University of Kentucky, Lexington.

Cook, S. F. and R. F. Heizer.
1965 Studies on the chemical analysis of archeological sites. *University of California Publications in Anthropology* **2**:1–102.

Cook, Thomas Genn
1976 Koster:an artifact analysis of the Archiac phases in west central Illinois. In *Prehistoric Records*, No. 3. Northwestern University Archaeological Program, Evanston, Illinois.

Cowgill, George
1968 Archaeological applications of factor, cluster and proximity analysis. *American Antiquity* **33**:367–375.
1977 The trouble with significance tests and what we can do about it. *American Antiquity* **42**:350–368.

Crawford, O. G. S.
1924 Archaeology from the air. *Nature* **114**:580–582.

Custer, Jay F.
1979 An evaluation of sampling techniques for cultural resources reconnaissance in the Middle Atlantic area of the United States. Unpublished Ph.D. dissertation, Department of Anthropology, The Catholic University of America, Washington.

Dancey, William S.
1981 *Archaeological field methods: an introduction.* Minneapolis, Minnesota: Burgess Publishing Co.

Darwin, Charles
1881   *The formation of vegetable mould through the actions of worms with observations on their habits.* London:Murray.
Davis, R. P. Stephen, Jr.
1980   A summary report of probabilistic "non-site" sampling in Tellico Reservoir, 1979. In The 1979 archaeological and geological investigations of Tellico Reservoir, edited by Jefferson Chapman. *Reports of Investigations* #29. Department of Anthropology, University of Tennessee, Knoxville. Pp. 59–90.
Dekin, Albert A.
1976   Elliptical analysis: an heuristic technique for the analysis of artifact clusters. In Eastern Arctic prehistory: Paleoeskimo problems, edited by M. S. Maxwell. *Memoirs of the Society for American Archaeology,* No. 31. Pp. 79–88.
1980   Spatial theory and the effectiveness of site examination in the Northeast. In Discovering and examining archeological sites: strategies for areas with dense ground cover, F. P. McManamon and D. J. Ives (assemblers). *American Archaeological Reports* #14. American Archaeology Division, University of Missouri, Columbia, Missouri.
Dincauze, Dena F., H. M. Wobst, R. Hasenstab, D. M. Lacy
1980   *Retrospective assessment of archaeological survey contracts in Massachusetts, 1970–1979.* Manuscript on file, Massachusetts Historical Commission, Boston, Massachusetts.
Dyson, Stephen L.
1978   Settlement patterns in the *Ager Cosanus*:the Wesleyan University survey, 1974–1976. *Journal of Field Archaeology* 5:251–268.
1982   Archaeological survey in the Mediterranean Basin:a review of recent research. *American Antiquity* 47:87–98.
Ebert, James I. and Alberto A. Gutierrez
1979   Cultural resources remote sensing in the eastern deciduous woodland: experiments at Shenandoah National Park. Paper presented at the 2nd Conference on Scientific Research in the National Parks, San Francisco.
1981   Remote sensing of geomorphical factors affecting the visibility of archaeological materials. Paper delivered at the Annual Meeting of the American Society of Photogrammetry. Washington, D.C.
Ebert, J. I., G. N. Brown, D. L. Drager, D. P. Hsu and T. R. Lyons
1980   Remote Sensing in Large-scale Cultural Resources Survey: A Case study from the Arctic. In *Cultural Resources Remote Sensing,* edited by T. R. Lyons and F. J. Mathien. Cultural Resources Management Division, National Park Service, Washington, D.C. Pp. 7–54.
Eidt, R. C.
1973   A rapid chemical field test for archeological site surveying. *American Antiquity* 38:206–10.
1977   Detection and examination of anthrosols by phosphate analysis. *Science* 197:1327–33.
Ehrenhard, E. B. and W. H. Wills
1980   Ninety-Six National Historic Site South Carolina. In *Cultural Resources Remote Sensing,* edited by T. R. Lyons and F. J. Mathien. Cultural Resources Management Division, National Park Service, Washington, D.C. Pp. 229–291.
Ehrenhard, John E.
1980   Cultural resource inventory of the Big Cypress Swamp: an experiment in remote sensing. In *Cultural Resources Remote Sensing,* edited by T. R. Lyons and F. J. Mathien. Cultural Resources Management Division, National Park Service, Washington, D.C. Pp. 105–117.

Evans, R. and Jones R. J. A.
  1977   Crop marks and soils at two archaeological sites in Britain. *Journal of Archaeological Science* **4**:63–76.
Fagan, Brian M.
  1959   Cropmarks in antiquity. *Antiquity* **33**:279–81.
Feder, Kenneth L.
  1977   Are we failing our test pits?: a comment on sub-surface sampling procedures. Paper presented at the Eastern States Archaeological Federation Annual Meeting, Hartford, Connecticut.
Ferguson, Leland G. and Randolph J. Widmer
  1976   Archeological examination of a transect through the Middle Savannah River Valley: The Bobby Jones Expressway, Richmond County, Georgia. *Research Manuscript Series* #89. Institute of Archaeology and Anthropology, University of South Carolina, Columbia.
Ford, Richard I.
  1964   A preliminary report of the 1964 resistivity survey at the Schultz Site (20 SA 2). *Michigan Archaeologist* **10** (3):54–58.
Ford, Richard I. and Richard O. Keslin
  1969   A resistivity survey at the Norton Mound Group, 20 Ktl, Kent County, Michigan. *Michigan Archaeologist* **15**(3):86–92.
Forestry Suppliers
  1980   *Forestry Suppliers, Inc. Catalog 30 (Spring 1980 to Spring 1981).* Jackson, Mississippi.
Forney, Sandra Jo
  1980   An evaluation of cultural resources locational strategies in the North Florida flatlands. Paper presented at the 45th Annual Meeting, Society for American Archaeology, Philadelphia.
Fowler, Melvin L.
  1977   Aerial archeology at the Cahokia site. In Aerial remote sensing techniques in archeology, edited by Thomas R. Lyons and Robert K. Hitchcock. *Reports of the Chaco Center 2*. The Chaco Center, National Park Service and the University of New Mexico, Albuquerque. Pp. 65–80.
Fry, Robert E.
  1972   Manually operated post-hole diggers as sampling instruments. *American Antiquity* **37**:259–60.
Gatus, Thomas W.
  1980   A review and comments on surface and subsurface survey methodologies operationalized in Kentucky. *Southeastern Archeological Conference Bulletin* **28**:141–145.
Goodman, Kenneth C.
  1971   The McGraw garden site: an earth resistivity survey experiment. *Ohio Archaeologist* **21**(4):8–13.
Goodyear, Albert C.
  1978   An archeological survey of the primary connector from Laurens to Anderson, South Carolina. *Research Manuscript Series* #122. Institute of Archeology and Anthropology, University of South Carolina, Columbia.
Goodyear, F. H.
  1971   *Archaeological site science.* New York:American Elsevier.
Gordon, Bryon C.
  1978   Chemical and pedological delimiting of deeply stratified archaeological sites in frozen ground. *Journal of Field Archaeology* **5**:331–8.

Gramly, Richard M.
    1970   Use of magnetic balance to detect pits and postmolds. *American Antiquity* **35**:217–20.
Gumerman, George J. and James A. Neely
    1972   An archaeological survey of the Tehuacan Valley, Mexico: a test of color infrared photography. *American Antiquity* **37**:520–27.
Harp, Elmer, Jr.
    1974   Threshold indicators of culture in air photo archaeology: a case study in the Arctic. In *Aerial photography in anthropological field research,* edited by E. Vogt. Cambridge, Massachusetts:Harvard University Press. Pp. 14–27.
    1977   Aerial photography for the Arctic archeologist. In Aerial remote sensing techniques in archeology, edited by Thomas R. Lyons and Robert K. Hitchcock. *Reports of the Chaco Center* 2. The Chaco Center, National Park Service and the University of New Mexico, Alburquerque. Pp. 51–64.
Hassen, F. A.
    1981   Rapid quantitative determination of phosphate in archaeological sediments. *Journal of Field Archaeology* **8**:384–387.
Heidenreich, C. E. and S. Navratil
    1973   Soil analysis at the Robitaille site, part I: determining the perimeter of the village. *Ontario Archaeology* **20**:25–32.
Heidenreich, C. E. and V. A. Konrad
    1973   Soil analysis at the Robitaille Site, part II: a method useful in determining the location of longhouse patterns. *Ontario Archaeology* **20**:33–62.
Hester, Thomas, R., R. F. Heizer and J. A. Graham
    1975   *Field methods in archaeology.* (6th ed.). Palo Alto, California: Mayfield Publishing Company.
Hirth, Kenneth G.
    1978   Problems in data recovery and measurement in settlement archaeology. *Journal of Field Archaeology* **5**(2):125–132.
Hole, Frank and Robert F. Heizer
    1969   *An introduction to prehistoric archeology.* (2nd edition). New York:Holt, Rinehart and Winston.
House, John H. and Michael B. Schiffer
    1975   Archeological survey in the Cache River basin. In The Cache River Archeological Project: an experiment in contract archeology, M. B. Schiffer and J. H. House (Assemblers). *Arkansas Archeological Survey, Research Series* 8. University of Arkansas, Fayetteville, Arkansas. Pp. 37–54.
House, John H. and David L. Ballenger
    1976   An archeological survey of the Interstate 77 route in the South Carolina Piedmont. *Research Manuscript Series* 104. Institute of Archeology and Anthropology, University of South Carolina, Columbia.
Hughes, P. J. and R. J. Lampert
    1977   Occupational disturbance and types of archeological deposit. *Journal of Archaeological Science* **4**:135–140.
Ives, David J. and David R. Evans
    1980   Locating sites in east-central Missouri: problems and solutions. In Discovering and examining archeological sites: strategies for areas with dense ground cover, F. P. McManamon and D. J. Ives (assemblers). *American Archaeological Reports* 14. American Archaeology Division, University of Missouri, Columbia.
Johnston, Richard B.
    1964   Proton magnetometry and its application to archaeology: an evaluation at Angel Site. *Indiana Historical Society, Prehistory Research Series* **4**(2):45–140.

Judge, W. James
    1981   Transect sampling in Chaco Canyon—evaluation of a survey technique. In *Archeologi-cal Surveys of Chaco Canyon, New Mexico,* Alden C. Hayes, David M. Brugge and W. James Judge. Cultural Resource Management Division, National Park Serivce, Washington, D.C. Pp. 107–143.
Keel, Bennie C.
    1976   An archaeological reconnaissance of East Pork Lake, Ohio. *Reports in Anthropology* 5. Laboratory of Anthropology, Wright State University, Dayton, Ohio.
Kenyon, Jeff L. and Bruce Bevan
    1977   Ground-penetrating radar and its application to a historical archaeological site. *Histor-ical Archaeology* **11**:48–55.
Kimball, Larry R.
    1980   A summary report of probabilistic sampling of select excavated sites in Tellico Reser-voir, 1979. In the 1979 archaeological and geological investigations in the Tellico Reservoir, edited by J. Chapman. *Report of Investigations* 29. Department of An-thropology, University of Tennessee, Knoxville. Pp. 91–109.
King, Thomas F., P. P. Hickman and G. Berg
    1977   *Anthropology in historic preservation: caring for culture's clutter.* New York:Aca-demic Press.
Kirkby, A. and M. J. Kirkby
    1976   Geomorphic processes and the surface survey of archaeological sites in semi-arid areas. In *Geoarchaeology,* edited by D. A. Davidson and M. L. Schackley. Boulder, Colorado:Westview Press. Pp. 229–238.
Klasner, J. C. and P. Calengas
    1981   Electrical resistivity and soils studies at Orendorf archaeological site, Illinois: a case study. *Journal of Field Archaeology* **8**:167–174.
Knoerl, John J.
    1980   Site resolution and intra-site variability. In Discovering and examining archeological sites: strategies for areas with dense ground cover, F. P. McManamon and D. J. Ives (assemblers). *American Archaeological Reports,* No. 14, American Archaeology Di-vision, University of Missouri, Columbia.
Krakker, James J., M. J. Shott and P. D. Welch
    n.d.   Design and evaluation of shovel test sampling in regional archeological survey. Manu-script submitted to *Journal of Field Archaeology,* March 1982.
Lafferty, Robert H.
    1977   The evolution of the Mississippian settlement pattern and exploitative technology in the Black Bottom of Southern Illinois. Unpublished Ph.D. dissertation, Department of Anthropology, Southern Illinois University, Carbondale.
    1979   An application of heavy equipment to site location survey. Paper presented at the 36th Southeastern Archaeological Conference, Atlanta, Georgia.
Leehan, Kevin and Steven Hackenberger
    1976   The use of a proton magnetometer and auger sampling in an archaeological setting. Paper presented at the 41st Annual Meeting of the Society for American Archaeology. St. Louis, Missouri.
Leith, C. J., K. A. Schneider and C. Carr
    1976   Geophysical investigation of archeological sites. *Bulletin of the International Associa-tion of Engineering Geology.* **14**:123–128.
Lewarch, Dennis E. and Michael J. O'Brien
    1981   The expanding role of surface assemblages in archaeological research. In *Advances in archaeological method and theory,* Vol. 4, edited by M. B. Schiffer. New York:Aca-demic Press. Pp. 297–342.

Limbrey, Susan
    1975   *Soil science and archaeology*. London: Academic Press.

Lovis, William A.
    1976   Quarter sections and forests: an example of probability sampling in the Northeastern woodlands. *American Antiquity* **41**:364–372.

Luedtke, Barbara
    1980   Survey of the University of Massachusetts Nantucket Field Station. In *Widening Horizons*, edited by C. Hoffman. Attleboro, Massachusetts:Massachusetts Archaeological Society. Pp. 95–129.

Lynch, B. Mark
    1980   Site artifact density and the effectiveness of shovel probes. *Current Anthropology* **21**:516–17.
    1981   More on shovel probes. *Current Anthropology* **22**:438.

Lyons, Thomas R. (assembler)
    1976   Remote sensing experiments in cultural resource studies: nondestructive methods of archeological exploration, survey, and analysis. *Reports of the Chaco Center*, No. 1. The Chaco Center, National Park Service and the University of New Mexico, Albuquerque.

Lyons, Thomas R. and Thomas E. Avery
    1977   *Remote sensing: a handbook for archeologists and cultural resource managers*. Cultural Resources Management Division, National Park Service, Washington, D.C.

Lyons, Thomas R. and James E. Ebert (editors).
    1978   *Remote Sensing and Non-Destructive Archeology*. Remote Sensing Division, Southwest Cultural Resources Center, National Park Service and the University of New Mexico, Albuquerque.

Lyons, Thomas R. and Robert K. Hitchcock (editors).
    1977   Aerial remote sensing techniques in archeology. *Reports of the Chaco Center*, No. 2. The Chaco Center, National Park Service and the University of New Mexico, Albuquerque.

Lyons, Thomas R., Robert K. Hitchcock and Wirth H. Wills
    1980   *Aerial anthropological perspectives: a bibliography of remote sensing in cultural resource studies*. Cultural Resource Management Division, National Park Service, Washington, D.C.

Lyons, Thomas R. and F. J. Mathien (editor).
    1980   *Cultural Resources Remote Sensing*. Cultural Resources Management Division, National Park Service, Washington, D.C.

Martin, Anne-Marie
    1971   Archaeological sites—soils and climate. *Photogrammetric Engineering*. **37**:353–57.

Matheny, R. T.
    1962   Value of aerial photography in surveying archaeological sites in coastal jungle regions. *American Antiquity* **28**:226–230.

McCauley, J. F., G. G. Schaber, C. S. Breed, M. J. Groller, C. V. Haynes, B. Issawl, C. Elachi and R. Blom
    1982   Subsurface valleys and geoarcheology of the eastern Sahara revealed by shuttle radar. *Science* **218**:1004–1020.

McManamon, Francis P.
    1981a Parameter estimation and site discovery in the Northeast. *Contract Abstracts and CRM Archeology* **1**(3):43–48.
    1981b The Cape Cod National Seashore Archeological Survey: a summary of the 1979–1980 results. *Man in the Northeast* **22**:101–130.
    1981c Probability sampling and archaeological survey in the Northeast: an estimation ap-

proach. In *Foundations of Northeast Archaeology,* edited by D. R. Snow. New York:Academic Press. Pp. 195–227.

1982   Prehistoric land use on outer Cape Cod. *Journal of Field Archaeology* **9**:1–20.

Moorehead, W. K.

1918   Susquehanna archaeological expedition. *Pennsylvania Historical Commission Report* 2:117–26.

1931   The Merrimack archaeological survey, a preliminary paper. *Phillips Academy Department of Archaeology Papers,* Vol. 4. Andover, Maryland.

Morain, Stanley A. and Thomas K. Budge

1978   *Instrumentation for remote sensing in archeology.* Cultural Resource Management Division, National Park Service, Washington, D.C.

Morey, Rexford M.

1974   Continuous subsurface profiling by impulse radar. *Proceedings of Engineering Foundation Conference on Subsurface Exploration for Underground Excavation and Heavy Construction.* American Society of Civil Engineers.

Munson, Patrick J.

1967   A Hopewellian enclosure earthwork in the Illinois River Valley. *American Antiquity* **32**:391–393.

Muto, Guy R. and Joel Gunn

n.d.   *A study of late-Quaternary environments and early man along the Tombibbee River, Alabama and Mississippi, Phase I Final Report (draft).* Report on file Interagency Archeological Services, National Park Service, Atlanta.

Nance, Jack D.

1979   Regional subsampling and statistical inference in forested habitats. *American Antiquity* **44**:172–176.

1980a   Lower Cumberland archaeological project 1978. *Southeast Archaeological Conference Bulletin* **22**:123–135.

1980b   Non-site sampling in the lower Cumberland River Valley, Kentucky. *Mid-Continental Journal of Archaeology* **5**:169–191.

1981   Statistical fact and archaeological faith: two models in small sites sampling. *Journal of Field Archaeology* **8**:151–65.

1983   Regional sampling in archaeological survey: the statistical perspective. *Advances in archaeological method and theory* (vol. 6), edited by M. B. Schiffer. New York:Academic Press.

Nance, Jack D. and Bruce Ball

1981   The influence of sampling unit size on statistical estimates in site sampling. In Plowzone archeology:contributions to theory and technique, edited by M. J. O'Brien and D. E. Lewarch. *Publications in Anthropology* 27. Vanderbilt University, Nashville. Pp. 51–70.

Newman, Robert W. and Kathleen M. Byrd

1980   Aerial imagry in locating and managing archaeological resources along the Louisiana coast. *Louisiana Archaeology* **7**:101–108.

Newell, Raymond R. and Albert A. Dekin

1978   An integrative strategy for the definition of behaviorally meaningful archaeological units. *Paleohistoria* **20**:7–38.

Otinger, Jeffrey L., Robert H. Lafferty III and Robert D. Jones

1982   Field tactics and laboratory methods. In Settlement predictions in Sparta. *Arkansas Archeological Survey Research Series* 14. University of Arkansas, Fayetteville. Pp. 101–116.

Overstreet, David F.
  1974   A rapid chemical test for archaeological surveying: an application and evaluation. *Wisconsin Archaeologist* **55**:252–70.
Parrington, Michael
  1979   Geophysical and aerial prospecting techniques at Valley Forge National Historical Park, Pennsylvania. *Journal of Field Archaeology* **5**:193–197.
Percy, George
  1976   Use of a mechanical earth auger as a substitute for exploratory excavation at the Torreya Site (8 Li/8), Liberty County, Florida. *Florida Archaeologist* **29**:24–32.
Pielou, E. C.
  1977   *Mathematical ecology.* New York:John Wiley and Sons.
Plog, Fred, Margaret Weide and Marilyn Stewart
  1977   Research design in the SUNY-Binghamton contract program. In *Conservation archaeology:a guide for cultural resource management studies,* edited by Michael B. Schiffer and George J. Gumerman. New York:Academic Press. Pp. 107–120.
Plog, Stephen
  1976   Relative efficiencies of sampling techniques for archeological surveys. In *The early Mesoamerican village,* edited by Kent V. Flannery. New York:Academic Press. Pp. 136–158.
Plog, Stephen, Fred Plog and Walter Wait
  1978   Decision making in modern survey. *Advances in archaeological method and theory,* Vol. 1, edited by M. B. Schiffer. New York:Academic Press. Pp. 384–420.
Pratt, Marjorie K.
  1981   *Archaeological survey at the Hartwell Tavern Site, Minute Man National Historical Park, Lincoln, Massachusetts.* Final report on file Division of Cultural Resources, North Atlantic Regional Office, National Park Service, Boston.
Price, John C., Richard Hunter and Edward V. McMichael
  1964   Core drilling in an archaeological site. *American Antiquity* **30**:219–211.
Proudfoot, B.
  1976   The analysis and interpretation of soil phosphorus in archaeological contexts. In *Geoarchaeology:earth science and the past,* edited by D. A. Davidson and M. L. Shackley. Boulder, Colorado:Westview. Pp. 93–113.
Provan, Donald M.
  1971   Soil phosphate analysis as a tool in archaeology. *Norwegian Archaeological Review* 4(1):37–50.
Reed, Nelson A., John W. Bennett and James W. Porter
  1968   Solid core drillings of Monk's Mound: techniques and findings. *American Antiquity* **33**:137–148.
Reeves, Dache M.
  1936   Aerial photography and archaeology. *American Antiquity* **2**:102–107.
Reidhead, Van A.
  n.d.   *Prehistoric cultural resources in the Clark Maritime Center, Clark County, Indiana: test excavations.* Report on file, Glenn A. Black Laboratory of Archaeology, Indiana University, Bloomington.
Rice, Glen, D. Jacobs, S. Upham, G. Feinman and J. Daddario
  1980   Test investigations of buried sites along Oraibi Wash. *Arizona State University Office of Cultural Resource Management Report 49.* Arizona State University, Tempe, Arizona.
Roberts, Michael E.
  1981a Subsurface radar and Hohokam archaeology. In *Salt-Gila Aqueduct Central Arizona*

project archaeological data collection studies and supplemental class 3 survey, 1980–1981 annual report, compiled by Lynn S. Teague and Patricia Crown. Cultural Resource Management Division, Arizona State Museum, Tucson. Pp. 62–70.

1981b   Radar survey at Las Colinas, Phoenix, Arizona: final report. Institute for Conservation Archaeology, Peabody Museum, Harvard University, Cambridge, Massachusetts.

Robinson, Paul A.
1981   The need for comparability in discovering and examining prehistoric sites in contract archeology: an example from Rhode Island. *Contract Abstracts and CRM Archeology* **1**(3):48–50.

Roper, Donna C.
1979   Archaeological survey and settlement pattern models in central Illinois. *Illinois State Museum, Scientific Papers,* (Vol. 16). Springfield.

Schaber, G. G. and G. J. Gumerman
1969   Infrared scanning images—an archaeological application. *Science* **164**:712–713

Schiffer, Michael B.
1975   Behavioral chain analysis:activities, organization and the use of space. In Chapters in the prehistory of eastern Arizona, 4 *Fieldiana:Anthropology* **65**:103–119.

Schiffer, Michael B. and George J. Gumerman (editors).
1977   *Conservation archaeology: a guide for cultural resource management studies.* New York:Academic Press.

Schiffer, Michael B., Alan P. Sullivan and Timothy C. Klinger
1978   The design of archaeological survey. *World Archaeology* **10**(1):1–29.

Scollar, Irwin
1969   Some techniques for the evaluation of archaeological magnetometer surveys. *World Archaeology* **1**:77–89.

Scott, Thomas T., M. McCarthy and M. A. Grady
1978   Archaeological survey in Cherokee, Smith and Rusk Counties, Texas: a lesson in survey methods. *Archaeological Research Program, Research Report* 116. Southern Methodist University, Dallas, Texas.

Sjoberg, Alf
1976   Phosphate analysis of anthropic soils. *Journal of Field Archaeology* **3**:447–456.

Snethkamp, Pandora E.
1976   Chapter 5:P.I.N. 9357.12. In *The I-88 Archaeological Project: 1975 summer season,* edited by Margaret L. Weide. Public Archaeology Facility, State University of New York, Binghamton.

South, Stanley and Randolph Widmer
1977   A subsurface sampling strategy for archeological reconnaissance. In *Research strategies in historical archeology,* edited by Stanley South. New York:Academic Press. Pp. 119–150.

Spurling, Brian E.
1980   Site discovery and assessment techniques for mixed cover regimes. *Saskatchewan Archaeology* **1**:25–56.

Steponaitis, V. P. and J. P. Brain
1976   A portable differential proton magnetometer. *Journal of Field Archaeology* **3**:455–463.

Stone, Glen D.
1981a   The interpretation of negative evidence in archaeology. In *Atlatl: Occasional Papers Number Two,* edited by E. Staski and J. Anderson. Department of Anthropology, University of Arizona, Tucson, AZ. Pp. 41–53.

1981b   On artifact density and shovel probes. *Current Anthropology* **22**:182–183.

Strandberg, Carl H.
    1967   Photoarchaeology. *Photogrammetric Engineering* **33**:1152–57.
Strandberg, Carl H. and Ray Timlinson
    1969   Photoarchaeological analysis of Potomac River fish traps. *American Antiquity* **34**:312–9.
Tartaglia, Louis James
    1977   Infrared archeological reconnaissance. In *Aerial remote sensing techniques in archeology,* edited by Thomas R. Lyons and Robert K. Hitchcock. *Reports of the Chaco Center,* No. 2. The Chaco Center, National Park Service and The University of New Mexico, Albuquerque. Pp. 35–50.
Taylor, R. L., M. F. Smith, R. D. Brooks, and G. T. Hanson
    1980   The Russell Archeological Project: a survey of forested lands in the south Applachian Piedmont. In Discovering and examining archeological sites: strategies for areas with dense ground cover, F. P. McManamon and D. J. Ives (assemblers). *American Archaeological Reports* 14, American Archaeology Division, University of Missouri, Columbia, MO.
Thomas, David H.
    1975   Nonsite sampling in archaeology: up the creek without a site. In *Sampling in archaeology,* edited by J. W. Mueller. Tucson:University of Arizona Press. Pp. 45–60.
Thorbahn, Peter
    1977   *Archeological reconnaissance survey of Interstate I-495 and relocated Route 140: interim report.* Public Archaeology Laboratory, Brown University, Providence, Rhode Island.
    1980   Site survey in New England: a field experiment in sampling theory and research design. In Discovering and examining archeological sites: strategies for areas with dense ground cover, F. P. McManamon and D. J. Ives (assemblers). *American Archaeological Reports,* 14, American Archaeology Division, University of Missouri, Columbia.
    n.d.   Sampling bias and regional settlement systems: a case study from southern New England. Manuscript on file, Public Archaeology Laboratory, Inc., Providence, Rhode Island.
Tite, M. S.
    1972   *Methods of physical examination in archaeology.* London:Seminar Press.
Tolstoy, Paul and Suzanne K. Fish
    1975   Surface and subsurface evidence for community size at Coapexco, Mexico. *Journal of Field Archaeology* **2**:97–104.
Trubowitz, Neal L.
    1973   Instrumental and chemical methods of site survey and testing in the Allegheny and Gennessee River valleys. Paper presented at the annual meeting of the Eastern States Archaeological Federation, Dover, Delaware.
    1981   The use of the plow in archaeological survey: an experimental example from western New York. *American Society for Conservation Archaeology Report* **8**(5 and 6):16–22.
Valentine, K. W. G., K. R. Fladmark and B. E. Spurling
    1980   The description, chronology, and correlation of buried soils and cultural layers in a terrace section, Peace River Valley, British Columbia. *Canadian Journal of Soil Science* **60**:185–197.
Versaggi, Nina
    1981   The analysis of intra-site variability. *Contract Abstracts and CRM Archeology* **1**(3):31–39.

Vickers, R. S. and L. T. Dolphin
    1975   A communication on the archaeological radar experiment at Chaco Canyon, New Mexico. *MASCA Newsletter* **11**(1).

Vickers, Roger, L. Dolphin and D. Johnson
    1976   Archeological investigations at Chaco Canyon using a subsurface radar. In Remote sensing experiments in cultural resource studies, T. R. Lyons (assembler). *Reports of the Chaco Center* 1. National Park Service and University of New Mexico, Albuquerque. Pp. 81–101.

Weide, Margaret L. (editor)
    1976   *I-88 Archaeological Project:1975 summer season.* Public Archaeology Facility, State University of New York, Binghamton.

Wells, Ian, Jay Custer and Vic Klemas
    1981   Locating prehistoric archaeological sites using LANDSAT. Paper presented at the 15th International Symposium on Remote Sensing of the Environment, Ann Arbor, Michigan.

Weston Geophysical Corporation
    1980   Geophysical surveys at the Adams Birthplaces National Historic Site. Report on file, Division of Cultural Resources, North Atlantic Regional Office, National Park Service, Boston, Massachusetts.

Williams, Kenneth R.
    1976   A preliminary assessment of techniques applied in the FAI-255 Survey. Paper presented at the 41st Annual Meeting, Society for American Archaeology, St. Louis, Missouri.

Wood, W. Dean
    1975   A sampling scheme for sub-surface archaeological survey. Paper presented at the 1975 Southeastern Archeological Conference, Gainesville, Florida.

Wood, W. Raymond and Donald Lee Johnson
    1978   A survey of disturbance processes in archaeological site formation. *Advances in archaeological method and theory,* Vol. 1, edited by M. B. Schiffer. New York:Academic Press. Pp. 315–381.

Woods, William I.
    1977   The quantitative analysis of soil phosphate. *American Antiquity* **42**(2):248–252.

Remote Sensing Applications in Archaeology

JAMES I. EBERT

INTRODUCTION

Aerial and other photography have been an integral part of the methodology of archaeology for more than a century. Not until recently, however, has *remote sensing* begun to be mentioned more and more often in the literature of our field. Remote sensing is a term that was born in the past two decades of advances in space and electronic technology, and encompasses a wide array of techniques directed toward the collection, analysis and use of data derived "remotely"— that is, from a distance. The remote sensing of the outer planets of the solar system is obviously done from afar. Remote sensing of interest and use to the archaeologist, however, is often but not always undertaken from much closer to the subject, so simple distance between the phenomena being measured and the sensing device does not offer a full description of remote sensing. More important than distances are the ways in which things in the real world are measured. For the purposes of this chapter, *remote sensing* is the science and technology of obtaining information or data about physical objects and the environment through the process of recording, measuring and interpreting photographic images and patterns of electromagnetic radiant energy.

ADVANCES IN ARCHAEOLOGICAL
METHOD AND THEORY, VOL. 7

Summarizing those remote sensing techniques and methods of relevance to the archaeologist is not easy because of the diverse amalgam of devices, data types, analytical equipment, products, and applications that are lumped together under this rubric. Some remote sensing, such as that which falls under the heading of site photography, is universally employed by archaeologists. Other techniques, for instance photogrammetry using stereometric photographs, are more complex approaches that offer vast increases in the accuracy of recording and monitoring changes in archaeological sites, structures, and materials. Still other areas of archaeological remote sensing—most of these presently still being explored and proven—may have profound implications for archaeological theory in that they change the way we look at the archaeological record and its relationships to the rest of the world. One example of this is the use of remote sensor data, especially those collected from space platforms, as a basis for designing archaeological samples and predictive modeling. Projecting distributions of archaeological sites and their characteristics on the basis of explicit and planned samples, necessitated by current approaches to cultural resources management, requires the measurement of environmental variables in consistent ways across large areas or even regions, a task ideally suited to remote sensing. The large-scale, low-resolution perspective offered the archaeologist from space by using remote sensor imagery for such sample stratification underlines the importance of environmental activity loci, and deemphasizes any total reliance on intrasite patterning for explanation of the past.

RECORDING THE ELECTROMAGNETIC SPECTRUM

Electromagnetic radiation is emitted from all materials above absolute zero ($0°$ Kelvin [K]); wavelengths of the electromagnetic radiation emitted are related to the temperature of the material (Colwell *et al.* 1963; Siegal and Gillespie 1980). In practice, only very hot objects such as the sun emit enough radiation to be useful for most remote sensing purposes; for this reason, most remote sensing is based upon the detection and measurement of electromagnetic radiation, reflected from the surface of objects, and emitted primarily by the sun. Various wavelengths of electromagnetic radiation interact in strikingly different ways with the surface of the earth and materials on it. For this reason discussions of remote sensing recording techniques are best couched in terms of the wavelength band in which they operate; commonly recorded wavelengths appear in Figure 5.1.

The most familiar portion of the electromagnetic spectrum is, for humans, the optical wavelengths, commonly used for photography. Three subbands within the optical wavelengths are the ultraviolet (0.3–0.4 m), the visible wavelengths (0.4–0.725 m), and the near-infrared (0.725–1.1 m). All the optical wave-

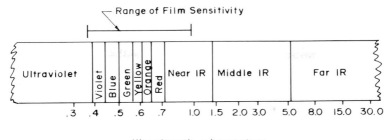

Figure 5.1.   A portion of the electromagnetic spectrum ranging from the ultraviolet to the far infrared (IR) bands, and comprising those wavelengths most commonly used for remote sensing. The range of the optical–chemical sensitivity of photographic films is also shown. From Avery and Lyons (1981).

lengths cause changes in certain kinds of materials such as the emulsions of photographic films, and are thus easily recorded with cameras. Black-and-white and color photography of the visible wavelengths has long been a mainstay for field recording of archaeological evidence. Other films are sensitive to the ultraviolet and near-infrared wavelengths. A common emulsion for recording near-infrared radiation is false-color infrared (CIR) or "camouflage detection" film (Reeves 1975). In this film, the color response of the emulsion layers sensitive to blue, green, and red visible light is shifted so that green, red, and near-infrared light are recorded in their place. Objects reflecting near-infrared radiation (not to be confused with infrared or heat radiation) appear in a wide range of reds and pinks in such films, a trait especially valuable because subtle variation in vegetation types and vigor of growth can be detected.

Infrared wavelengths are not easily recorded by optical/chemical film and camera systems, but both middle-infrared (1.1–5.5 m) and far-infrared or heat radiation (5.5–15.0 m) can be detected by electromechanical or electronic scanning devices. Infrared scanners are complex and difficult to operate, and are extremely expensive because relatively few have been manufactured, although they do have archaeological applications that are touched upon later in this chapter.

Microwave radiation consists of very short radio waves, from 1 mm to 1 m in length, and these cannot be recorded on photographic film either. These wavelengths are recorded using specialized scanning radar receivers.

Photographic detector systems (camera–film combination) that react to optical-wavelength electromagnetic radiation, then, have been and continue to be the sources of the most widely available and archaeologically useful remote sensor data. Another data-collection system, the multispectral scanner, also records optical wavelengths as well as infrared radiation. *Multispectral scanners* are so named because they record patterns and intensities of radiation in a number of narrow wavelength bands over a target area simultaneously. Because materials reflect or emit and absorb electromagnetic radiation differently in each of these wavelength bands, multispectral scanners can be used to make relatively fine distinctions between different substances and conditions on the ground (see Figure 5.2). Like thermal scanners, multispectral scanners are extremely complicated and enormously expensive to maintain and operate, and their data are very difficult to analyze. Most airborne multispectral scanner data are, for this reason, beyond the range of consideration for realistic archaeological appliations. The exception to this is multispectral data collected by the Landsat series of satellites, a subject that is discussed at length later in this chapter.

The wavelength of electromagnetic radiation reflected or emitted from an object depends upon the source of the electromagnetic radiation, the path through which that radiation is transmitted, and the material from which the radiation is reflected. Most electromagnetic radiation recorded in archaeological remote sensing comes from the sun, which emits vast amounts of infrared and optical-band radiation. Sunlight is filtered through the atmosphere, during which certain wavelengths are attenuated and then reflected or absorbed by the Earth's surface and the materials on it. Reflected optical-band and near-infrared light is recorded when it strikes a photographic emulsion or multispectral scanner detector; heat from absorbed light, retained at depth in the ground and radiated when surface temperatures cool, can cause an increase in the temperature of materials, which can be measured using a thermal scanner. The patterns of reflection and absorption thus recorded contain information about the distribution and nature of archaeological sites and materials, soils and landforms, vegetation, and a host of other phenomena of interest to archaeologists.

LIMITATIONS OF ARCHAEOLOGICAL REMOTE SENSING

Prior to any discussion of applications of remote sensing to archaeology and cultural resource management, it is necessary to consider the ways in which remote sensing might *not* be applicable in these areas. Of course, there are

---

Figure 5.2. Representation of the spectral resolutions of a number of multispectral scanner systems, as well as the photographic emulsions used in Skylab missions. The ERIM (Bendix), Texas Instruments RS18, and Daedalus DS 1260 MSS systems are all airborne, and at least one (ERIM/Bendix) has been used for experiments in the detection of cultural resources (Moraine et al. 1981). The use of Landsat MSS imagery is discussed later in this chapter. The Skylab photographic spectral resolutions represent, in general, the resolutions of most common types of aerial photographic film. The graph line running through the various MSS and photographic resolution ranges in this figure is the reflectance curve of a hypothetical surface; the best sensor or combinations of sensors for this surface can be deduced from study of the figure. From Moraine et al. (1981:63).

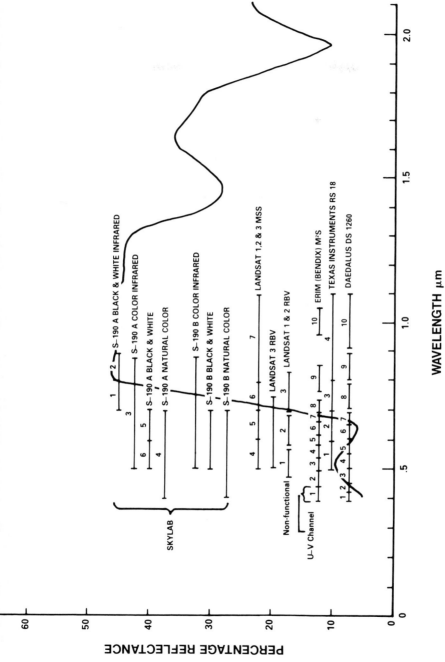

WAVELENGTH μm

Figure 5.2.

limitations to any measurement technique applied to any science or field of work. Under certain conditions even methods that have proven to be useful and efficient in dozens of other similar cases may not help in solving what seems to be a nearly identical problem. In the case of remote sensing applications to archaeology, however, it is doubly important to discuss the circumstances in which this methodology might not work entirely satisfactorily, for it has been suggested that some enthusiasts have "oversold" archaeological remote sensing (see, for instance, Dunnell 1980).

Limitations of archaeological remote sensing can be of several types or causes. First, and most obviously, there are inherent limitations in remote sensing devices or systems themselves. The scale and thus the resolution of any image product depends partially upon the altitude of the platform on which the remote sensing device rests, imposing certain restrictions in virtually any mission. For instance, extremely large-scale photographs are difficult to take from most commercial aircraft because they cannot safely fly slowly at low altitudes. The spatial resolution of an image also depends on other factors, such as lenses, film grain, shutter speed, and scanning rate—all of which are physically determined and none of which may offer optimum resolution for all problems. To provide maximum resolution, a system must generally image a small area; it therefore requires more images to cover a study area at high resolution. There is an obvious tradeoff between resolution and cost of remote sensor data.

Spectral resolution is another important sensor system limitation. Different sensors measure different portions of the electromagnetic spectrum. Before a wise determination of the optimal sensor system for any problem application can be made, it is necessary to decide which wavelength bands will be most useful—a process which may take long and expensive experimentation. Photography covers only a small portion of the electromagnetic spectrum but provides high spatial resolution; scanning systems, which can cover many more spectral bands, generally offer lower spatial resolution, depending on aircraft speed and altitude.

Remote sensor systems offer various levels of accuracy and precision, and a system that offers quite enough for one sort of task or problem may be insufficient for another. Accuracy and precision are especially important in photogrammetry, which employs special metric cameras compatible with sophisticated plotting equipment. Normal cameras, even the more expensive off-the-shelf models, are simply not capable of high photogrammetric accuracy or precision.

Finally, another class of inherent instrumental limitations in any remote sensing project is imposed by those instruments available for laboratory analysis. The least expensive and most commonly available tool for the interpretation of aerial photographs is a stereoscope; these range in sophistication from plastic pocket models to precision roll-film stereoscopes costing $20,000 or more. Monoscopic viewing methods (such as Variscan viewers, for instance) are generally not as useful as stereoscopic viewing. If proper analytic laboratory equipment is not available because of cost or any other factor, results of applications of remote sensing to problems may not be satisfactory.

Another broad class of limitations in archaeological remote sensing is due to environmental factors. Many sensor systems are greatly affected by weather conditions such as clouds, mist, or haze. If it is necessary to "see" the surface of the ground using remote sensor data, heavy ground cover obviously presents a problem, as will snow or water cover. The hour of the day, and day of the year, on which remote sensor imagery is collected affects the sun angle and thus light intensity and shadows. Some systems, in particular thermal scanners, record phenomena that are very transient and are detectable for only a few hours or even less, at very rare times when soil moisture, the state of vegetative cover, and the difference between ground and air temperatures are exactly right (Perisset and Tabbagh 1981; Tabbagh 1977).

Individual human limitations may cause a remote sensing application to be less than satisfactory. The experience of a photointerpreter, both in looking at stereophotos and in having a knowledge of the area being inspected, is often of great importance. Some individuals are unable to perceive stereo even through stereoscopes, and so are prevented from interpreting aerial photographs in the most useful manner. Some people are simply better as prolonged photointerpretation than others, due to "patience" or some other intangible qualities. An important factor affecting the individual's ability to make useful interpretations of photographic data is the availability of supplementary or preliminary information on a study area. Prior to formulating recognition patterns, one must have some sort of idea about what to expect on the ground. Most individuals can interpret aerial photographs showing visible light patterns easily, but require more practice with infrared photographs and extensive experience before they can interpret many sorts of scanner or radar data.

Finally, there is a class of "cultural" limitations imposed on remote sensing applications to archaeological problems that stem from the ways we do archaeology. It is vitally important to know what needs to be measured—that is, to have a problem orientation and to translate it into measurable variables—before doing any sort of measurement. Data collection and analysis must be properly specified for the problem at hand; if they are not, results may be of limited usefulness. Another cultural limitation is imposed by project planning and execution time. Acquistion of aerial photographs or space imagery collected previously by government or other agencies may take literally months from the time an order is placed; because it is advantageous to have such data even when other project activities are in the planning stages, it is necessary to order such data far in advance. Economic limitations imposed by project budgets may make it impossible to obtain and utilize the optimal remote sensor data for a specific problem.

The enumeration of all the above limitations of remote sensing in archaeology and cultural resource management may at first seem discouraging, suggesting that one might never find worthwhile applications of remote sensing to any problem. With imagination and perseverance, however, archaeologists can generally adapt to their needs at least a small part of the wide range of versatile techniques that comprise remote sensing. The point is that all potential limitations of any measurement technology must be contemplated, understood, and controlled for in order to assure useful data collection for any purpose.

THE DEVELOPMENT OF AERIAL ARCHAEOLOGY AND CULTURAL RESOURCES REMOTE SENSING

A short survey of the development of applications of aerial photography and remote sensing to archaeology and cultural resources management is necessary for a number of reasons. First, it should be appreciated that the use of aerial photography in archaeology is neither novel nor untested, having been an integral part of fieldwork and the literature since the early 1900s in both Europe and the Americas. A historic overview is necessary, in addition, to point up the parallels and differences between archaeological remote sensing in Europe and Great Britain, on the one hand, and the Americas (primarily the United States) on the other. This very real dichotomy between *aerial archaeology,* as it is called across the Atlantic, and *cultural resources remote sensing* here, could potentially be confusing to students of archaeology and archaeological applications of aerial photography and other remote sensing techniques. Finally, due to both environmental and historical or academic differences in the development of archaeological remote sensing in England and Europe versus that in the United States, there are gaps and deficiencies, at least at the present, in both approaches. Discussion of these can perhaps foster greater understanding and integration of elements from both sides of the Atlantic into a more coherent subfield of archaeology.

Interestingly, serious archaeological uses of aerial photographs began on both sides of the Atlantic at about the same time. It is true that the first archaeological aerial phtography was taken over Stonehenge in 1906 from a balloon, and that a number of aerial photos of archaeological sites taken prior to 1920 can be found in European archives, but serious and systematic aerial archaeology was born with the exploits of Colonel G. A. Beazeley (1919, 1920) in Mesopotamia and the aerial photography of the Cahokia Mounds in Illinois in 1921 (Avery and Lyons 1981). In the early years of the 1920s, the major impetus to archaeological aerial photography was in Europe, with pioneers and advocates of the technique publishing methods and results profusely. O. G. S. Crawford can probably be thought of as the father of aerial archaeological surveys (Crawford 1923, 1924a, 1924b, 1929); in France, Poidebard (1929, 1931, 1932) was also experimenting with aerial archaeology. The European technique at this time was to fly systematically across the countryside in an aircraft, looking for traces of archaeological sites such as Roman fort foundations, medieval field boundaries, and large-scale traces of past cultural habitation or use. When found, such traces were photographed with hand-held cameras (Piggott and Piggott 1939).

In the United States and Central America, aerial archaeology was also being developed along much the same lines as in Europe. In 1929 and 1930, Charles Lindbergh and his wife flew over and photographed archaeological sites in Mexico and the Southwestern United States (Figure 5.3) with the help of A. V. Kidder (Kidder 1929, 1930a, 1930b; Lindbergh 1929), while U.S. Army fliers, under the direction of Neil Judd, photographed prehistoric canals in the Gila and Salt river basins of Arizona (Judd 1930, 1931). Elsewhere in the Americas, aerial photography was employed extensively by the Shippee–Johnson Expedition, resulting in the discovery of the ''Great Wall of Peru'' and a number of other sites there (Shippee 1932a, 1932b, 1933, 1934).

The Second World War in Europe, rather than slowing the pace of aerial archaeology, resulted in advances in aircraft and aerial photographic techniques, and many military fliers adopted aerial archaeology as a hobby that they pursued and perfected. In Switzerland (Bandi 1942) and Germany (Buttler *et al.* 1938), notable work in aerial archaeology was undertaken, whereas on the other side of the lines two of the most influential aerial archaeologists of all time surveyed England aerially. It was during this time that many of the interpretive principles still used today in site discovery from aerial photographs were described by Derrick Riley (Riley 1943, 1944), and that J. K. S. St. Joseph, honored in 1982 at an international meeting of aerial archaeologists as central to the field, began flying and writing (St. Joseph 1945, 1949, 1950). Immediately following the war, the pace of aerial archaeology in continental Europe was quickened by Bradford (1947a, 1947b, 1949, 1952) in Italy and Chombard de Lauwe (1948a, 1948b) in France.

During and after the war, aerial archaeology in the United States was nearly dormant, with notable exceptions (Bascom 1941, for instance). This may have been due to a shift of ''aerial concern'' from this country to Europe for military reasons, but more probably was because archaeology had begun to change in this country, to diverge from the classical–historical emphasis of European archaeology into a more environmentally directed, anthropological field. This may in part be due to the fact that the environment of much of the United States has been less changed during recent prehistory than that of Europe, but there is a theoretical basis to this shift as well. When archaeological aerial studies commenced again in the Americas in the 1950s, it was with a direction decidedly different than in Europe. Stanley Stubbs (1950) employed aerial photographs of the extant Indian Pueblos in what would later be thought of as ethnoarchaeology; aerial imagery was also used to study village sites along the Missouri River (Solecki 1952, 1957, 1958; Wedel 1953). Gordon Willey, in the prototype of modern regional archaeological studies, employed aerial photography to gain a regional geo-

Figure 5.3.   Some of the earliest aerial photography of archaeological sites in the United States was taken by Col. Charles Lindbergh and his wife. This aerial oblique photograph of Pueblo Pintado, at what is now Chaco Culture National Historical Site in northwestern New Mexico, was taken by the Lindberghs in 1929. It may be more blurred than photos from modern aerial cameras, but it contains structural data not available today; compare this with the Pueblo Pintado photograph in Figure 5.4. Photograph courtesy of the School of American Research, Santa Fe, New Mexico.

graphic perspective and analyze the environment in the Virú Valley of Peru (Willey 1953, 1959).

The late 1950s and 1960s saw a virtual continuation, in Europe, of aerial surveys aimed at the production of oblique photographs of many spectacular archaeological sites, with emphasis on their architectural aspects (Agache 1962, 1964, 1966, 1967; Carbonnel 1965; Chevallier 1962, 1963, 1964, 1965; Martin 1966, 1968; St. Joseph 1966; Scollar 1963, 1965). These aerial surveys were often very intensive, resulting in the discovery of many thousands of archaeological sites, unlike the American aerial exploration of the time. In the United States, a totally new field of applications to archaeology and anthropology was emerging, resulting in a virtual explosion of aerial archaeology directed toward the analysis of subsistence practices (Denevan 1966, 1970; Harp 1966, 1967, 1968; Strandberg 1962; Strandberg and Tomlinson 1965), the search for undiscovered archaeological remains (Matheny 1962; Rainey 1960, 1966; Solecki *et al.* 1960), site mapping and spatial analysis (Millon 1964, 1970; Millon [ed.] 1973), and the development of devices for intrasite mapping (Whittlesey 1966a, 1966b, 1967, 1969). The use of aerial photography and other remote sensing techniques for regional, anthropologically oriented archaeology continued with equal or even greater impetus into the 1970s (Coe 1974; Gumerman 1971a, 1971b, 1971c; Gumerman and Lyons 1971; Gumerman and Neely 1972; Vogt 1974a, 1974b).

The differences that evolved since the early 1900s between European and British aerial archaeology and cultural resources remote sensing in the United States persist to this day. In Europe and England there are a large number of professionals devoted almost entirely to aerial archaeological pursuits. By and large, their activities consist of flying as systematically as possible across the countryside in airplanes, searching for unknown sites or vegetative and soil patterning that emphasize previously known ones. When such phenomena are found, they are photographed in oblique view with hand-held aerial cameras to obtain the optimal sun and view angle. For use in site-location files, the geometry and placement of the sites as recorded on oblique photographs must be transformed manually (Ebert *et al.* 1979; Scollar 1968) or digitally (Palmer 1977, 1978) to a horizontal coordinate system. A pioneering effort at making digital transformation of this sort possible is discussed in detail below.

American cultural resources remote sensing has diverged from using oblique aerial photographs in this way since at least the later 1940s. It is true that in the United States we have very different archaeological sites and materials than in Europe but, more important, American archaeologists have had different theoretical directions and goals, being anthropologically oriented toward the analysis of past behavior and particularly toward regional subsistence and other resource procurement strategies. It is in this context that remote sensing offers the greatest advantages to archaeology because aerial photographs and other remote sensor data allow the measurement and correlation of many aspects of the physical and cultural environment over space.

FINDING AND ACQUIRING AERIAL PHOTOGRAPHS

Obviously, the first step in applying aerial photography to any problem, cultural or otherwise, is to obtain aerial photographs. There are basically three ways in which the archaeologist can do this. For certain types of applications, using existing aerial photographs taken at some time in the past and available from a number of federal and state agencies or engineering firms can be economical and rewarding. Another alternative is to take one's own aerial photographs with a hand-held camera from an aircraft. Finally, there are many aerial photographic or engineering firms that can be hired to fly systematic coverage of an area using metric, large format (generally 9 × 9″) cameras.

The choice between using extant aerial imagery or flying one's own to specifications depends upon a number of factors, including the existence and nature of previously flown imagery, its availability for copying and the costs involved. In addition, other factors will influence the utility of extant aerial photographs in archaeological applications. One universal problem with using aerial photographs taken for engineering and mapping purposes is that they are usually flown with the sun high overhead, at midday, to minimize shadows that are not used as cues by a photogrammetric mapping plotter operator. Unfortunately, shadows provide some of the most useful cues to the photointerpreter for locating buried or subtle archaeological remains on the ground. Mapping and engineering photographs are also often flown during the winter in areas of deciduous tree cover so that the contours of the ground rather than of the treetops can be mapped; some archaeological uses of aerial photographs, such as the characterization of vegetation in an area for sample stratification or explanatory purposes, could require leaves-on photography. It is unlikely that *any* aerial photographs flown at an earlier time for nonarchaeological purposes will be totally suitable for any archaeologist's application, and for this reason perhaps the best solution is to collect and inspect available photographs *and* to fly additional imagery suited specifically to the task at hand. Because the kinds of imagery that will be required will differ with each problem orientation, it is not possible to formulate any one set of rules or guidelines as to just what will be required; the individual researcher will have to determine this through careful inspection of existing photographs and, in many cases, experimentation.

Almost all the United States has been photographed from the air, using large-format metric cameras, at least once and often many times in the past. The earliest systematic aerial photographic coverage of this country was undertaken by the U.S. Department of Agriculture's Soil Conservation Service for soils mapping; later, beginning in the mid-1940s, the U.S. Geological Survey began a program of systematic black-and-white aerial photography for topographic mapping purposes. In addition, NASA aircraft have photographed many parts of this country from various altitudes and in many emulsions. Recently, the U.S. Geological Survey initiated its current High Altitude Photography (HAP) project aimed at the creation of metric scale maps, and is rephotographing the entire country at 1:80,000 scales in both black and white and color. In every state, highway departments, natural resource departments, and other offices have photographed at least part of the surface area at various times. The U.S. Army Corps of Engineers takes aerial photograph of rivers, dams, and reservoir areas, as does the Bureau of Reclamation and the Tennessee Valley Authority. Private engineering firms have been hired through time by mining, engineering, utility, and other concerns to take aerial photographs of building and project areas, and these may be available to the archaeologist. Finally, for any land-disturbing cultural resource management project, it is almost certain that aerial photographs have been flown and used for estimating cuts and fills, for placing access roads, and in general for engineering planning—and these should be available to the archaeologist as well.

Finding existing aerial photographs often takes a bit of detective work. Some agencies, such as the U.S. Geological Survey's EROS Data Center, maintain efficient computer indexing systems and can determine what imagery they hold for an area quickly and at little or no charge. Other agencies have more cumbersome indexing systems, and some have none at all. Some likely national sources at which to inquire about existing aerial photographs are listed in Table 5.1. The most comprehensive guide available listing state and local sources of remote sensor imagery is John R. May's (1978) "Guidance for Application of Remote Sensing to Environmental Management (Appendixes A and B)," published by the Mobility and Environmental Systems Laboratory, U.S. Army Engineer Waterways Experiment Station, P.O. Box 631, Vicksburg, MS 39180. Most government sources of existing aerial photographs will make prints available at relatively low cost, from about $2.99 to $7.00 per frame.

If aerial photographs are available for a study area, they may be perfectly sufficient for application to a specific archaeological problem. Most blanket-flown, government (Soil Conservation Service, U.S. Geological Survey) aerial photographs are taken at scales between 1:20,000 and 1:40,000, and these might for instance be quite suitable for mapping vegetation zones or surface hydrology in an area of interest. Such photographs can also be used for pinpointing site locations, as is discussed later. On the other hand, they may not be sufficient for some other purposes, such as seeing physical evidence of structural sites. When using existing aerial imagery, one must accept what is available or turn to another source of aerial photographs.

TABLE 5.1

Some National Sources of Existing Aerial Photographs and Remote Sensor Data

Source	Imagery types and scales	Address
Agricultural Stabilization and Conservation Service	Black-and-white and color infrared photos, scales 1:10,000 to 1:120,000 of about 80% of land surface of USA	ASCS Aerial Photography Field Office PO Box 30010 Salt Lake City, UT 84130
Soil Conservation Service	Black-and-white photo of all 50 states (not all states completely covered), averages about 1:40,000 scale	Soil Conservation Service (SCS) Cartographic Division Federal Building Hyattsville, MD 20782
US Department of Agriculture Forest Service	Black-and-white, black-and-white infrared, color, and color infrared photos at 1:6000 to 1:80,000 scales covering National Forest Service areas	US Forest Service Division of Engineering Washington, DC 20250 (write for the address of the regional office in your area)
Bureau of Land Mangement	Federal lands in AZ, CA, CO, ID, MN, NV, NM, OR, UT, and WY in black-and-white and color, scales 1:12,000 to 1:125,000 (mostly 1:31,360)	Bureau of Land Management Denver Service Center Denver Federal Center, Bldg. 50 Denver, CO 80225
Bureau of Reclamation	Scattered federal lands in the western US at 1:600 to 1:24,000 scales. Black-and-white, color, and color infrared coverage.	US Bureau of Reclamation Engineering and Research Ctr. Building 67, Denver Federal Center Denver, CO 80225
US Geological Survey	USGS mapping photography (black-and-white, scales 1:20,000 to 1:80,000), NASA high altitude photos (black-and-white, color, color infrared at scales of 1:40,000 to 1:180,000), and manned and unmanned satellite data for entire country and much of the world	US Geological Survey EROS Data Center User Services Division Sioux Falls, SD 57198
National Archives	Black-and-white photo at scales of 1:15,840 to 1:56,600 of about 85% of the USA (some flammable nitrate base film and not currently available in copy form)	National Archives and Records Service Cartographic Archives Division Washington, DC 20408
National Ocean Survey	Black-and-white, color photos at scales of 1:10,000 to 1:30,000 of shorelines of Great Lakes and connecting waterways	NOS Lakes Survey Center 630 Federal Building Detroit, MI 48226
	Panchromatic black-and-white, color, and color infrared at scales of 1:5000 to 1:60,000, of most coastal areas in the US and most civil airports	NOS Coastal Mapping Division C-3415 Rockville, MD 20852

Flying one's own aerial photographs (Figure 5.4) may be a very workable solution to many archaeological problems (Grady 1982). Most aerial photographs taken by the archaeologist will differ from conventional aerial photographs in a number of ways. Aerial photographs intended for mapping purposes are normally taken with the camera lens axis vertical, whereas hand-held aerial photographs will be oblique, showing the site or area at an angle. This is often quite desirable for illustrative purposes and can be used for reconnaissance of vegetation patterns and shadow marks, but oblique photos are a very difficult medium from which to create maps. The archaeologist's personal or project camera will probably be a single-lens reflex with a 35-mm or slightly larger film format; aerial cameras are far more accurate devices designed specifically for aerial photography with, most commonly, 9 × 9 inch formats. "Do-it-yourself" aerial photos are taken from light airplanes, balloons, kites, or other varieties of camera platforms—imagination is the only limit.

The most satisfactory aircraft for small-format oblique aerial photographs are light, high-wing craft such as the Cessna 150/152 or Cessna 172. Almost any 35-

Figure 5.4. Aerial oblique photograph of Pueblo Pintado, at Chaco Culture National Historical Site, taken in 1979 with a Hasselblad EL200 camera and black-and-white film. This photograph is typical of the sort of aerial imaging that can be done by the archaeologist without recourse to aerial photographic firms. Compare the long, back wall of the Pueblo as depicted in this photograph with the same wall segment in Figure 5.3. Sequential rephotography of cultural sites can provide the means of monitoring structural changes and other impacts to which archaeological sites are continually subjected. Aerial photography by Alberto A. Gutierrez.

mm, single-lens reflex camera with a normal 50-mm lens is suitable for such photography, although it should be noted that if digital processing to remove geometric distortions or image blur is to be undertaken, a between-the-lens shutter is essential because focal plane shutters introduce uncontrollable distortion at high shutter speeds. Automatic light metering and power film winding capabilities can be helpful in the air. Telephoto lenses are difficult to hold steady during flight. Blurring caused by vibration and motion of the aircraft can be minimized by use of a fast film and shutter speed. Films that can be used advantageously include black-and-white panchromatic films for general photography, black-and-white and color infrared film for definition for vegetation patterns, and color or color transparency film for site area view. The use of various filters with these films can increase their usefulness for certain problem applications; a lengthy discussion of film–filter combinations can be found in Bevan (1975). Careful records of the location of each exposure should be made or marked on a map during flight because it can be very difficult to determine the exact locations of photographs after a flight. An overview from a higher altitude or with a wider angle lens is often extremely helpful in detecting and correcting erroneous map entries that somtimes occur.

Aerial photographs made with small-format cameras mounted below tethered balloons have also proven useful in some archaeological applications (Whittlesey 1970, 1971). Unfortunately, tethered balloons are difficult to orient exactly, making much trial-and-error photography necessary. In addition, they are relatively costly to fill with helium and are probably practically applicable only to long-term, repeated photography of excavation units. Kites have been experimented with as well for archaeological site photography, with little success (although see Anderson 1979). Light aircraft will probably remain the staple platform for the archaeologist wishing to do his or her own aerial photography; an interesting variation on this is the recent use of ultralight aircraft (Walker 1981) for archaeological site photography. Ultralight aircraft have low stall (minimum) airspeeds and can fly safely at much lower altitudes than can larger airplanes, reducing image blur and increasing the scale of photography possible with normal focal-length lenses.

The source of the highest-quality and, for many cultural resources applications, most-useful aerial photography is the photogrammetric engineer or professional aerial photographic firm. Using specially modified aircraft and precision metric aerial cameras, these experienced personnel can fly blanket coverage of a study or project area to rigid specifications. Nine by 9 inch format aerial photographs are generally flown with 60% endlap and 30% sidelap (Figure 5.5) to ensure stereo coverage of all points in the overflight area; this is important not only for stereo viewing, but for photogrammetric mapping, as is discussed later in this chapter. Professionally flown aerial photography can be taken at virtually any scale deemed appropriate to the problem at hand, the only physical con-

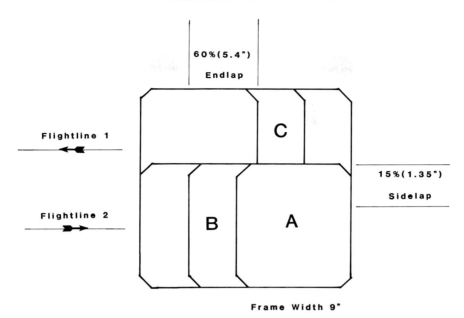

Figure 5.5. Endlap, sidelap, and area coverages of two aerial photographic flight lines of three frames each. The letters on various areas of the flightline mosaic pictured here refer to those in Table 5.2, which lists area coverages of 9″ × 9″ aerial photos for different scales. A, area covered by a whole single frame; B, area gained within a single flightline whenever a subsequent photograph is exposed; C, area gained per exposure when more than one flight line is involved.

straints being the altitude above the ground at which the pilot is willing to fly (practically limiting maximum scales to about 1:500 with standard 6-inch aerial lenses). Scale, as mentioned previously, determines to a large extent the resolution or the size of the smallest details that can be seen in the photograph. It might at first be imagined that the largest possible scale would be optimum for any project, but it must be remembered that at large scales, many more frames are needed to cover an area. This increase in number of frames is geometric: each halving of scale (say, from 1:1000 to 1:500) and thus doubling of resolution results in a *fourfold* (2^2) increase in the number of exposures that must be taken. Because vertical-axis aerial photography is flown at a consistent scale and at a regular spacing, it is fairly easy to estimate the number of frames needed to cover an area of any size at various scales (Table 5.2). The number of frames flown is one of the major determinants of comparative overflight costs, although when very few frames are required, time in the air becomes the major factor. Some attempts have been made at providing guides for the estimation of aerial photographic costs (Aguilar 1967; Jorde and Bertram 1976), but constantly changing

TABLE 5.2

Spatial Characteristics of 9″ × 9″ Vertical Aerial Photographs Taken at Various Scales[a]

Scale		Width of photograph, in feet (and miles)	Area covered by single photograph (A, in Figure 5.5), in acres (and mi²)	Distance gain per exposure, single line, in feet (and miles)	Distance gain per flight line, in feet (and miles)	Area gain per exposure (B, in Figure 5.5), in acres (and mi²)	Net model gain per exposure (C, in Figure 5.5), in acres (and mi²)	Largest map scale[c]	Minimum contour interval[c]
1:600	1″ = 50′	450[b] (.09)	4.6 (.01)	190[b] (.03)	315[b] (.06)	1.6 (.003)	1.2 (.002)	1″ = 7′	.18′
1:1200	1″ = 100′	900 (.17)	18.5 (.03)	380 (.07)	630 (.12)	6.5 (.01)	5 (.008)	1″ = 13′	.35′
1:2400	1″ = 200′	1800 (.34)	74 (.12)	760 (.14)	1260 (.24)	27 (.04)	20 (.03)	1″ = 26′	.7′
1:3600	1″ = 300′	2700 (.51)	167 (.26)	1080 (.20)	1890 (.36)	58 (.09)	46 (.07)	1″ = 40′	1′
1:4800	1″ = 400′	3600 (.68)	297 (.46)	1440 (.27)	2520 (.47)	106 (.16)	83 (.12)	1″ = 53′	1.3′
1:6000	1″ = 500′	4500 (.85)	465 (.73)	1800 (.34)	3150 (.60)	164 (.26)	130 (.20)	1″ = 67′	1.7′
1:7200	1″ = 600′	5400 (1.02)	669 (1.05)	2160 (.41)	3870 (.72)	238 (.37)	187 (.29)	1″ = 80′	2′
1:10,000	1″ = 883′	7497 (1.42)	1290 (2.02)	2990 (.57)	5248 (.99)	460 (.72)	361 (.56)	1″ = 110′	2.8′
1:12,000	1″ = 1000′	9,000 (1.70)	1,860 (2.91)	3,600 (.68)	6,300 (1.19)	659 (1.03)	520 (.81)	1″ = 133′	3.1′
1:24,000	1″ = 2000′	18,000 (3.41)	7,438 (11.62)	7,200 (1.36)	12,600 (2.39)	2,637 (4.12)	2,082 (3.25)	1″ = 267′	6′
1:36,000	1″ = 3000′	27,000 (5.11)	16,735 (26.15)	10,800 (2.05)	18,900 (3.58)	2,909 (4.55)	4,685 (7.32)	1″ = 400′	10′

[a] Table shows the characteristics of maps derived photogrammetrically from these aerial photos using commonly employed plotting systems. This table, which should be used in conjunction with the illustration of stereo endlap and sidelap shown in Figure 5.5, can be used as a general guide to the number of exposures that will be required to cover an area monoscopically ("Area covered by single photograph")and in stereo ("Area Gain Per Exposure")

[b] All distance, area, and gain figures are for 9″ × 9″ aerial photographs, 60% endlap, and 30% sidelap.

[c] Map scale and contour internal figures are for plotting equipment with 7.5× scale of restitution.

prices makes this difficult in practice. The best guide to current prices and alternative scale, film, and other factors for any problem is the professional photogrammetric or aerial photographic engineer. It is likely that several of these can be found in the telephone book in any area (look under "aerial photographs" or "mapping"). If not, the archaeologist might wish to contact the American Society of Photogrammetry, the professional photogrammetric society in this country, at 210 Little Falls Street, Falls Church, VA 22046; telephone (703) 543–6617. The Society's Journal, *Photogrammetric Engineering and Remote Sensing,* also carries a listing of some photogrammetric engineers.

AERIAL PHOTOINTERPRETATION

Photointerpretation involves the extraction of information or data from photographs, generally by looking at those photographs in a number of different ways. Prior to photointerpretation it is necessary to know just what data are sought from the photos—this is another way of saying that one must have a problem orientation, a far more efficient way of undertaking any scientific inquiry than simply "looking to see what is there." A problem orientation will dictate the type of photographs being used as well as permit a preinterpretation recognition pattern—a listing of how the phenomena one is searching for might be measured—to be compiled.

Photointerpretation from vertical aerial coverage is best begun by laying aerial photographs out in flight lines or in a mosaic—that is, by arranging these in an overlapping fashion to show the entire study area (or parts of it, if the entire mosaic is unwieldy because of its size). It is important that all interpretations of the locations of suspected sites or other desired phenomena be cross-referenced on a map that will be useful in the field. This is most easily accomplished by photointerpreting the location of each of the photographic prints onto the map, using such reference points as distinctive topographic features, roads, watercourses, and other features that can be located on a map. A previously compiled base map, such as the USGS topographic map series, can be used for this purpose, or an original base map can be compiled showing the location of each print.

Once a flight line or print location map is completed, photointerpretation can commence. A simple method of defining areas of interest is simply to place a transparent film overlay atop the mosaic and to mark areas of interest on the film, thus creating a photointerpretative map. More detailed and complete photointerpretation can be accomplished with a stereoscope. Stereoscopes are instruments that allow an interpreter to see one of the two prints of a stereo pair (an overlapping pair of aerial photographs) with each eye. Mental overlapping of opposite parallax effect, which is discussed at greater length under the heading of photogrammetry below, allows the interpreter to see a three-dimensional image of the portion of the stereophotographs that coincide (about 60% of their width). Due to an overlap somewhat larger than that seen when viewing a scene with the naked eye, the vertical (or z) dimension appears exaggerated about seven times normal, making subtle topographic details visible. There are three basic types of stereoscope: the pocket stereoscope, which is inexpensive and portable but does not afford the high quality view of other stereoscopes; the mirror stereoscope, which costs between about $300 and $1000, and allows the interpreter to scan the entire overlap area of a stereo pair, using magnification if desired; and sophisticated roll-film stereoscopes costing as much as $20,000 or more. When photointerpreting with a stereoscope, a separate film overlay can be made for each photographic print, and interpretations drawn on this overlay. These data can then be transferred to a map by tracing on a light table, or through the use of a camera obscura type of sketcher or OMI Stereofacet plotter (Hampton and Palmer 1977), or more accurately by creating a control network using conjugate points from adjacent aerial photographs to correct for scale and parallax differences.

A control network is created to compensate for scale differences between adjacent aerial photographs and within each photograph, and for parallax distortions. The geometry of aerial photographs is discussed in technical detail in a later section of this chapter, as are these types of "errors" that occur in single photographs. It will be intuitively obvious to anyone who has used photographs for any purpose, however, that not all objects or relationships in any photograph except one taken of a perfectly flat surface will be at the same photographic scale, and that parallax distortions will exist in the photograph as well. A control net attempts to average these errors through proper orientation of overlapping frames. This is accomplished through triangulation from the aerial photographs through the construction of *templets* (Lattman and Ray 1965:101–126), which are graphic representations of the directions from the vertical photograph's central point or principal point to identifiable terrain features.

Prior to the construction of the templets, each pair of successive overlapping frames is viewed on a stereoscope, and a number of *tie points* are identified and marked. These are points that can be seen on each photograph of the pair and can be identified as the same object—for instance, the base of a tree as visible on both the left and right frames. Enough tie points should be located on each photograph to allow overlapping with consecutive frames in the flight line, and with adjacent flight lines as well, usually requiring about 9 points located for the most part near the edges of the image (Figure 5.6). A templet consisting of a square of transparent film material (acetate or mylar, generally) is then laid over the photograph, and the center and tie points marked. Radials are then drawn from the center point to the tie points. Templets are overlapped so that the radials intersect (Figure 5.7), providing a "best fit" arrangement of the individual

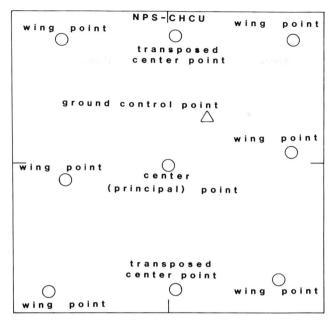

Figure 5.6. A vertical aerial photograph marked with photographic center points and wing or tie points prior to templet construction. Each point marked with a circle corresponds to an "identical" point on the prior or subsequent photograph in the flight line. The triangular ground control point is a point on the ground with known coordinates, used to superimpose the final traced photointerpretive map with other maps.

frames. It is this geometric arrangement of aerial photographs that provides the most planimetric map representation, and that is used during tracing or transfer of interpreted information from the photographs to maps.

One of the most obvious applications of photointerpretation is the discovery and mapping of cultural sites, materials, and modifications of the landscape that might mark the existence of places that should be further investigated on the ground. Indications of the existence of sites and materials can be distinguished on the basis of a number of photographic qualities including tone, texture, color, pattern, shape, and size. Photographic tone is a measure of the relative amount of light reflected by an object on the ground, and is fundamental to all other recognition elements except color (Ray 1960). On a black-and-white photograph, tones range from black to white and the spacing of variations in tone determines the texture of a portion of an image. Texture can be used to separate disturbed soils from undisturbed surface, to discriminate differences in vegetative cover that might signal the presence of buried materials, or to discern areas of disturbed topography. Pattern refers to the arrangement of features seen in a

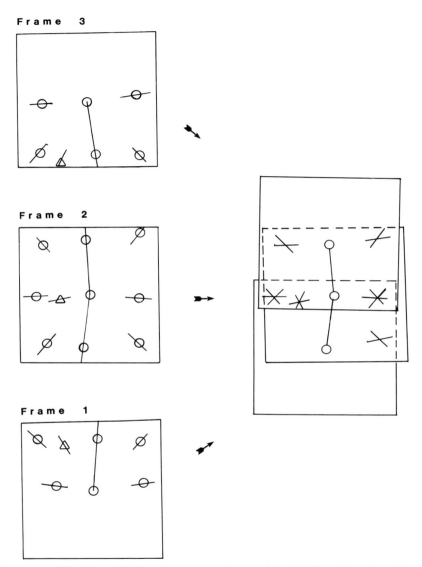

Figure 5.7. The assembly of transparent overlay templets. At left are three templets pre-pared for assembly; at the right these have been assembled into a control net. The radial line intersections show correct relative map positions of the points. The control net in turn serves as a guide for the most planimetric overlay of photointerpreted information. (After Lattman and Ray 1965.)

photograph; it is perhaps the most useful interpretation element for archaeologist, for one of the most common distinctions between cultural and noncultural patterning is the occurrence in the former of straight lines and geometric patterning. It should be noted that some natural features such as jointing of rock and periglacial phenomena can cause patterning that appears strikingly cultural. Shape and size simply refer to the extent of patterning. In color photographs, color becomes an important photointerpretive factor, for the human eye can interpret approximately 1000 times as many tints and shades of color as it can shades of gray (Ray 1960:8). The number of colors that can be distinguished can cause considerable confusion as well, particularly when large-scale photographs are being interpreted. Differences in soil color often result from variations in the amount of organic material contained in soils, sometimes introduced through cultural processes. Color differences in a stand of uniform vegetation can be caused by differential nutrients in the underlying soil, or by mechanical and hydrologic considerations (Avery 1977).

In agricultural areas of the United States, and particularly in Europe, much attention has been give to a very useful class of photointerpretive phenomena referred to as *crop marks* (Riley 1944, 1979), variations caused in crops or sometimes in natural vegetation when these are near a threshold of water or other stress. Cereals and grasses are most prone to exhibit crop marks, and root crops least so. Positive crop marks are areas of better vegetative growth, occurring where the soil is loose or water is retained over such features as filled ditches, or on areas with high amounts of organic nutrients. Negative crop marks, areas of poorer growth, are found over buried wall foundations. In addition, the nature of soils and the hydrologic balance in a specific area may have complex effects on the meaning of crop marks and their appearance, or on whether crop marks will even be found in an area. Recognizing crop marks resulting from buried archaeological remains requires constant vigilance throughout the growing season, for these may appear and disappear very quickly after light rains or during spells of dry heat. The ''European'' style of aerial archaeology discussed earlier is based largely on the recognition and inspection of crop marks, whereas these have been largely ignored by American archaeologists. This may be due to the fact that most British and European aerial archaeologists are pilots as well, and have little difficulty flying day after day to find the optimum instant at which to photograph crop marks. American archaeologists would profit by paying closer attention to the techniques of old-world aerial archaeologists, and might have fun flying their own airplanes as well!

Photointerpretation of vegetative and other natural differences in aerial photographs has been used productively in a number of recent projects in the United States, however. Recently, aerial photointerpretation was employed in the location of traces of the Continental Army encampment of 1777–1778 at Valley Forge by the University of Pennsylvania museum (Nicholas Hartmann, personal communication, 1981), located in an area of extreme subsequent cultural disturbances. Existing vertical aerial photographs of the area were of relatively small scale, so oblique photographs were taken from altitudes of 150 to 610 m above the ground with a hand-held 35-mm camera in a light aircraft, allowing these to be taken when vegetative stress differences were greatest. It was found that such indications were most visible after sudden thunderstorms following long hot periods, at which time traces of eighteenth-century roads and light-colored patches thought to be the remains of hut floors were noted under forest cover.

Similar techniques were employed at Ninety-Six National Historic Site in South Carolina in an attempt to locate General Nathaniel Green's encampment of 1781 (Wills 1980). Black-and-white and color infrared aerial photographs were photointerpreted for this purpose, unfortunately with little success; it was determined, after the fact, that oblique photography might have been a better discovery medium—a valuable lesson to other archaeologists confronted with similar problems.

The locations of archaeological sites in the Big Cypress Swamp, in southern Florida, were the target of National Park Service archaeologists faced with compliance of Section 106 of the Historic Preservation Act of 1966 (Ehrenhard 1980). Due to extreme difficulty of travel over even small distances in such southern swamps, aerial photointerpretation was employed to pinpoint sites, which were then visited, recorded, and analyzed on the ground. Color infrared aerial photographs at a scale of 1:80,000 were stereoscopically inspected to discover high dry hummocks along banks near deep sloughs or marshes. When these were visited on the ground, it was found that 80% were indeed archaeological sites.

Color infrared aerial photographs can be particularly useful in interpreting vegetative differences, as indicated by a photointerpretive experiment at Chalmette National Historic Park in New Orleans (Mathien 1981) where indications of ditches comprising portions of fortifications that were seen only with difficulty on black-and-white imagery were easily discovered using a color infrared transparency emulsion. Color infrared emulsions, sensitive to near infrared radiation, discriminate subtle differences in the vigor of vegetative growth that are difficult to discern when viewed in green light.

Some cultural sites and material, however, are indicated not by vegetative tone, texture, and patterning, but by other physical phenomena on the surface of the ground. Often, the archaeologist's cue to the existence of such materials is geometric patterning or the existence of lines of materials. Such pattern indications are employed by Grady (1981) in the discovery and mapping of stone alignments in Wyoming using black-and-white aerial photographs taken from a light aircraft with a hand-held camera. Some cultural phenomena that are nearly undetectable from the ground because of their scale and subtlety have been discovered from the air due to their geometric patterning. In the San Juan Basin of New Mexico, surrounding Chaco Canyon, an extensive network of what are thought to be prehistoric roadways, dating from approximately A.D. 900–1200, was discovered almost solely through the use of aerial photointerpretation (Camilli 1979; Ebert and Hitchcock 1980). Prior to the analysis of aerial photographs of the area by R. Gwinn Vivian of the University of Arizona and the Remote Sensing Division of the National Park Service in Albuquerque, several kilometers of the most obvious of these features had been found on the ground, where they appear as shallow trenches or swales a decimeter or two deep and uniformly about 9 m wide. Stereo photointerpretation of aerial photographs revealed a network of faint, very straight lines throughout the Chaco Canyon area; subsequent photointerpretive efforts by the Bureau of Land Management have extended the network for at least 160 km in all directions from this apparent center. Interestingly, because of the faintness and the long, linear pattern traced by the roadways, medium-scale aerial photography at about 1:30,000 scale is more useful than larger-scale imagery in their detection. Black-and-white photography shows the features as well as color emulsions because physical relief and shadow and not the sparse vegetation of the San Juan Basin allow the roadways to be seen.

For most archaeological discovery applications, scale is a limiting factor in that as scale becomes smaller, so does the resolution that a photograph is capable of recording. At some scale, it would seem, the resolution of aerial photographs would be such that the largest conceivable archaeological site would be invisible. In this regard, it is interesting that it has even been suggested that archaeological sites can be discovered through the digital processing of Landsat multispectral scanner data (Lade 1982). Landsat multispectral scanner data are discussed later in this chapter in the context of sample stratification based on regional differences in vegetation, soils, and other environmental factors; this imagery provides a resolution of approximately 80×80 m per picture element or pixel. If in fact actual sites can be detected using these data, then future satellite-borne scanners, which will provide much higher resolutions, may be useful sources of data for digital or manual photointerpretation for site-discovery purposes.

Although aerial photointerpretation is a potentially important technique for the discovery of archaeological sites, aerial photographs and their analysis also offer other advantages when applied to archaeology and cultural resource management. Aerial photographs contain all the information available on maps and much more; in fact, most modern maps have been compiled from aerial photographs. Making a topographic map from aerial photographs is a process of abstraction during which much information inherent in the photographs is sorted out and discarded in favor of the sorts of details mapmakers are interested in, and other information not on the photographs is injected (road passability, settlement population, etc.). Although it is possible to find one's location in the field on a map, it is usually much easier to do so using an aerial photograph because such features as individual trees and bushes, boulders, and specific topographic features can be found and pinpointed. If the aerial photographs are accurately referenced to a map using features that were chosen by the mapmaker, then exact locations on the ground can be placed precisely on the map. The combination of aerial photographs and a map with these photographs carefully referenced allows far more accurate mapping of site locations than such methods as triangulation with a compass or attempting to interpret the map by itself through the process of finding specific details on the photograph, such as trees or rocks, and relating these to other details seen on both the photographs and the map (Ebert 1977; Loose and Lyons 1976; Reher 1977). Interpretation of aerial photographs can also yield much logistic information such as the best transport routes to survey areas and the boundaries of sample units in the field, facilitating their location by field crews.

All interpretations made from aerial photographs or for that matter any other remote sensing data source must be checked against other data to determine whether they are in fact correct interpretations. This process has been called *field checking* (Lyons and Avery 1977:65) or *ground truth checking,* but in fact it is not necessary to check all conclusions on the ground. Other remote sensor data sources, such as aerial photographs at a different scale or flown at a different time, can also be used to confirm or negate the results of aerial photointerpretation. Archaeological survey from the surface of the ground, which is really just remote sensing from about 1.5 m altitude, may or may not be a comprehensive method of ground truth checking, depending upon conditions such as vegetative cover and the nature and scale of the phenomena being studied (Ebert and Lyons 1980).

CULTURAL RESOURCES PHOTOGRAMMETRY

Photogrammetry is measurement from photographs or other remote sensor data, and is used to measure physical distances in either two or three dimensions, and to make maps or plans. Such products provide the ideal basis for documentation of the original or at least the present state of cultural resources, including sites, features, and artifacts within sites, and structures of all types. Comparison of two or more sets of physical measurements of the same site or structure, measured photogrammetrically at different times, allows the detection and analysis, or "monitoring," of changes in the physical form of a site that may affect its information content or integrity.

The basics of photogrammetry are much older than airplanes, and in fact the first photogrammetry employed photographs taken on the ground, or terrestrial photographs, in France almost immediately following the invention of practical photography by Louis Daguerre in 1839. Compilation of maps through photogrammetric methods gained popularity in France, Germany, and Italy over the next few decades, and the first photogrammetry in the United States involved photomapping of enemy territory by the Union Army during the Civil War in 1862. The later 1800s and early 1900s saw the widespread use of terrestrial photogrammetry by the U.S. Geological Survey, especially for mapping Alaska. In 1909, Wilbur Wright took the first photographs from an airplane in Italy, and shortly thereafter airplane photographs became the mainstay of photogrammetry (Karara 1979). Both aerial and terrestrial photographs offer the archaeologist opportunities for the accurate, precise, and economical recording of virtually any archaeological data photogrammetrically.

Measurements from photographs depends on a number of basic geometric properties of an imaged scene. These properties are probably best understood through reference to an idealized camera diagram (Figure 5.8). The broken line through the center of the lens and film is the optical axis of the camera, which is vertical with respect to the ground in a vertical aerial photograph. This line passes through the principal point of the photo. Any object on the ground sub-tends an angle, x, at the lens equal to that of the image of that object on the film. The geometry of the similar triangles so formed dictates that the flight height of the aircraft (H), the focal length of the camera (f), and the film image (i) and actual ground object size (O) are related in the following way:

$$\frac{f}{H} = \frac{i}{O}$$

The scale of a photograph is the ratio between the image size and the object size. If the focal length of the lens and altitude of the camera are known, this ratio is easily determined:

$$\text{scale} = \frac{\text{focal length}}{\text{flight height}};$$

units for focal length and flight height must be the same. It would be fortunate in the light of scientific commitment to the metric system if all aerial camera lens focal lengths were measured in metric units, but this is sadly not the case; commonly used aerial lenses are almost universally 6-inch, $8\frac{1}{2}$-inch, or 12-inch focal length.

If the ground were perfectly flat and parallel to the film plane at all times, the scale of all objects on the ground would be the same across the image for any given flying height and focal length. In the real world, of course, this is not the case. The scale given for aerial photographs is a nominal scale measured at the principal point of the image; other scales in the photograph will vary depending on object's plane and that of the principal point. Another photographic distortion introduced by differences in the horizontal plane of objects in a real-world scene being photographed is radial displacement due to relief. The images of objects on

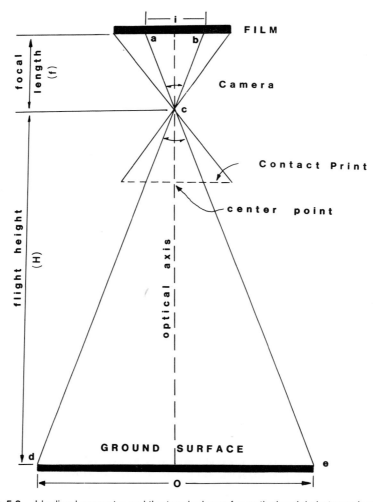

Figure 5.8.   Idealized geometry and the terminology of a vertical aerial photograph and the camera recording it. Triangles *abc* and *cde* subtend similar angles at *c,* which allows the calculation of scale relationships between the image (i) and the object (o) distances as discussed in the text.

a vertical aerial photograph are displaced outward, radially from the principal point of the image in proportion to their distance from that principal point, and their height above or below the horizontal plane of the principal point. This is often striking when viewing a photograph taken vertically downward on a dense stand of tall, straight trees, all of which appear to lean outward from the center (except for the tree exactly at the principal point). Essentially, from the perspective of the photograph, one is "looking" not only at the top but at the side of each tree, or any vertical object (Figure 5.9). For any single photograph, the amount of radial displacement of the top of a standing object with respect to its base can be calculated as

$$m = \frac{rh}{H},$$

where m is the radial displacement from the top on the object to its base, r is the radial distance on the photograph from the principal point to the base of the image, h is the height of the object displaced, and H is the flight height. The same units must be used for h and H, and for m and r, in this equation. This "error" in a single photograph, then, can be used to measure object heights. This relationship also illustrates that radial displacement is more pronounced when photographs are taken at lower heights above the ground, regardless of the focal length of a lens. Therefore, photographs of one scale can exhibit different amounts of radial displacement, with those taken with the shorter focal length lens (from a lower altitude at a give image scale) being more radially distorted. This is important to keep in mind when tracing from a single, monoscopic photograph to map interpreted features. Also, because radial displacement is dependent upon the distance from the center of a photograph, it is best to do one's tracing and mapping using images from as near the principal point of a photograph as possible.

A stereoscopic photograph, or model, has additional geometric properties that make measurement of three-dimensional points possible. One of the most important of these is parallax, which is an apparent shift in the position of an object (in its image) caused by a shift in the point of observation. This shift is apparent on the comparison of two images of the same object taken from different vantage points on an overlapping pair of aerial photographs. Parallax, then, is the difference in radial displacement of the image of an object on different photographs. The calculation of parallax from a stereo pair of photographs is not diagrammed or discussed at length in this chapter, not because the simple trigonometry of the relationship is difficult to understand, but rather because archaeologists will hardly ever find themselves in a position where hand measurements of parallax are necessary or useful. Parallax measurement can be made using parallax bars or wedges and a stereoscope, or even with a ruler and a bit of care (Lattman and Ray 1965; Wolf 1974:143–174), but this is a tedious process at best and it is often difficult to maintain consistency during such hand measurement. Fortunately, highly accurate photogrammetric plotting devices exist to make the archaeologist's job easier, and these are discussed below.

Prior to any discussion of practical photogrammetric mapping using plotters or any other methods, however, it is necessary to touch again on the concept of photogrammetric control. Photogrammetric plotting can be used to determine the three-dimensional relationships between an almost infinite number of points

Figure 5.9. The photograph is approximately the northeast quarter of a 9 × 9″ vertical aerial photograph of Chalmette National Historical Park in Louisiana. The tall monument that appears in the extreme upper right corner of this scene, which is itself vertical, illustrates the effects of radial displacement and appears to lean away from the center of the photograph. The notations on the photo's border show the original scene to be at a scale of 1:1920, or 1 inch = 160 feet; the crown-shaped black markings in the border are fiducial marks and aid in locating the exact center of the print.

contained within a stereo model but to convert these to meaningful units the actual, on-the-ground relationships between a few of these points must be known. For all practical photogrammetry, some sort of control or scale must be determined for the stereo model. There are two ways of accomplishing this used in most aerial photogrammetry. Where practical, the area to be measured or mapped is visited prior to the overflight, and a number of points marked so as to be visible in the subsequent photos using X- or L-shaped panels made from plastic flagging material about 30 cm wide, available at surveying equipment stores. The true horizontal and vertical distances between these points, usually four or more in a scene (Figure 5.10), are measured using surveying equipment. If the premarking of control points is impractical, the photographs can be taken into the field after flying, and specific points such as rocks, trees, or road intersections can be "field identified" and their spatial relationships measured.

Several different photogrammetric products and variations thereof can be derived from stereophotographs. The simplest of these is the planimetric map, a two-dimensional representation of the outlines of objects and features in a scene. All distances in a planimetric map are in correct scaled relationship with one another. Planimetric maps are compiled by radial plotting, a technique also used to map areas using transit or alidade data. In the case of photogrammetric radial plotting, the "transit stations" are represented by the center of each photograph, and outlines thus drawn (Figure 5.11).

Orthophotography is a variation of planimetric plotting in which a planimetric photograph, that is a monoscopic image with scale and displacement variations

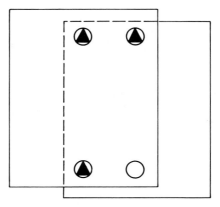

Figure 5.10. To measure and map photogrammetrically the spatial relationships between all visible points in a metric stereo pair, it is only necessary to set minimal field control. Most photogrammetric engineers require four control points within the stereo model, or the area of overlap between two subsequent prints in a flight line. The horizontal distances between three of these points (triangles) and the vertical differences between four of them (circles) must be measured, on the ground, prior to setting up the images in a plotting device.

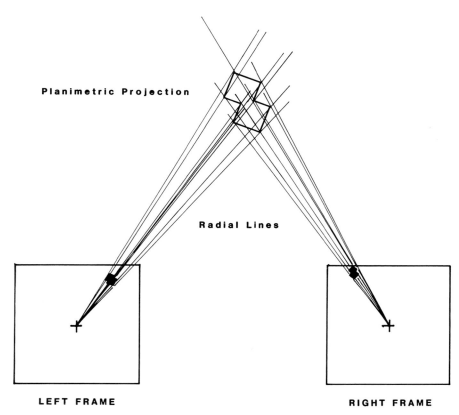

Planimetric Projection

Radial Lines

LEFT FRAME   RIGHT FRAME

Figure 5.11. The principles of radial planimetric plotting from stereo aerial photographs are the same as in radial line plotting with a plane table/alidade or transit Radial lines shot from each "instrument station," the centers of the photograph in this case, are extended beyond coordinates that define the image of the object of interest in the photograph. Where corresponding lines intersect, a point is drawn on a map base and the result is a planimetric map of the area of interest. This sort of plotting can be easily done on a drafting table, using two stereophotos and much caution. In practice, detailed photogrammetric maps are best made using radial line plotting instruments such as those described in the text.

Figure 5.12. Map of Kin Bineola, a Pueblo III period structure at Chaco Culture National Historical Park in northwestern New Mexico, compiled photogrammetrically from a single aerial stereo pair. Field control points were located at the corners of the fence surrounding the structure. The configurations of Kin Bineola's walls as well as contour lines and spot elevations within rooms (X's) have been included in this map. Photogrammetric maps such as this are compiled using sophisticated metric camera–plotter systems and must be contracted for with photogrammetric engineering firms.

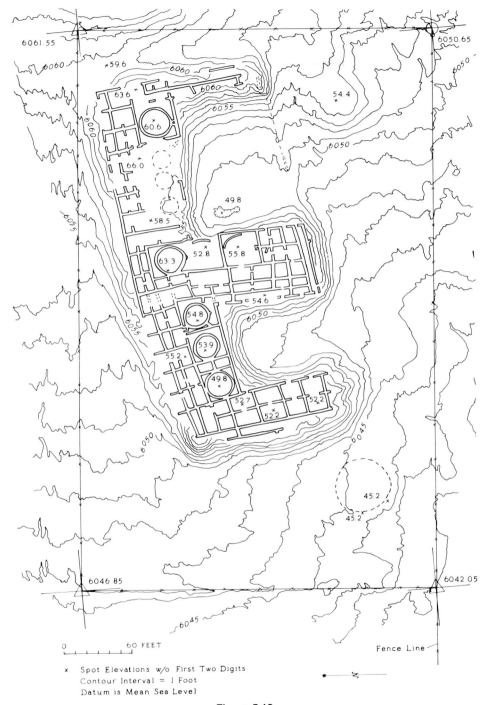

Figure 5.12.

removed, is made. Orthophotographs are equivalent to planimetric maps of a study area, but they are much more than that in that they show not only accurate relationships between objects and features, but also contain photographic detail. Orthophotos are compiled by optical or electronic instruments that scan a stereo terrain model of a scene and simultaneously expose a series of scan lines on photographic film; they can be a versatile and economic aid to many phases of archaeological mapping and fieldwork (Ebert *et al.* 1979; Prewitt and Holz 1976).

Topographic maps are also compiled photogrammetrically, using not only the two-dimensional information that appears in planimetric maps, but also denoting a third "height" dimension as well. Photogrammetric, topographic maps are made by stereoplotters, devices that allow a plotter operator to view a stereo model of a scene and a tiny dot or cursor point with which they can follow the terrain elevations and outline objects in the scene. Photogrammetrically compiled topographic maps can be made at virtually any horizontal scale and contour interval, depending upon the scale of the photographs used and the capabilities of the camera–plotter system available (Table 5.2). Topographic maps of archaeological site areas offer valuable archaeological data, such as structural configurations, and can often be "photointerpreted" to show the locations of otherwise subtle and hidden features (Figure 5.12). In addition, there is even more information on such a map that pertains to the problems of archaeology and cultural resource management today: information about the amounts of dirt that may need to be moved to excavate the site and the nature of influences and everyday impacts on a site. Periodic rephotography and remapping of a site area during excavation can provide a record of actual areas dug and studied, and the other impacts that the archaeologist may have on the area (Figures 5.13 and 5.14). A very useful and versatile map product can also be produced by the photographic superimposition of a photogrammetrically derived topographic map and an orthophotograph of the same area, showing three-dimensional contours as well as the great detail available in a photographic image (Figure 5.15).

Many modern photogrammetric plotting devices are equipped with electronic servomechanisms that automatically draft a manuscript map while the operator views the stereomodel. These plotters can also provide digital data on the three-dimensional coordinates of points recorded on the map. Such data can also be used as the basis of creating "three-dimensional" views of a site or structure (Figure 5.16).

Photogrammetric data can also be digitized directly and automatically from either single or stereo aerial photographs, and these digital data transformed through computer manipulation to fit a vertical coordinate system such as that of a map. Digital coordinate transformation is a complex process, but a program at the Rheinisches Landesmuseum in Bonn, West Germany, is presently pointing the way to what may well become a universal cultural resource management approach in the near future. The Landesmuseum, responsible for protecting the

Rhineland's cultural resources, was faced with the necessity of recording and mapping archaeological and historic sites so these could be avoided by land developers and construction activities, and so that when and if excavation for rescue or mitigation purposes became necessary, the actual sites and features within them could be located and studied with a minimum of difficulty. Planning for cultural resource management purposes is particularly crucial in the Rhineland, which is perhaps the most heavily industrialized region in the world. A large number of oblique aerial photographs are available, having been taken during the past 20 years; these, of course, vary greatly in quality and scale. The Rheinisches Landesmuseum has been doing systematic aerial photography of archaeological sites since 1960 using cameras such as the Kodak K20, Williamson F117, and Fairchild F505 (Scollar 1979).

The data base onto which archaeological site locations and outlines were to be transferred for planning purposes was a series of some 4000 base-map sheets at a scale of 1:5000 depicting the entire Rhineland. Early in the Museum's plotting attempts, hand-computational methods were used to "rectify" measurements taken from oblique aerial photographs for subsequent plotting on maps; later, a telephone line linked with a computer was used to speed computations (Scollar 1975). Such calculations are, however, time consuming and often incomplete because only a few point locations can be measured from the oblique image, transformed by calculations, and transferred to the planimetric map. Such computations are doubly difficult when the terrain is hilly, as it is in much of the Rhineland.

In 1974, the Rheinisches Landesmuseum began to design specifications for an operator-interactive computer system to facilitate the rectification and mapping of measurements from oblique photographs, and to perform a number of additional image manipulation and enhancement tasks on these photographs as well. Acquisition of the computer and software was funded by the Volkswagen Foundation, and it was on-line by September 1976.

Figure 5.13. (*overleaf*) (A) Vertical aerial photograph of Pueblo Alto, at Chaco Culture National Historical Park, and (B) a photogrammetric map compiled from a stereo pair of the same scene. At the time of the overflight (September 12, 1976), Pueblo Alto was in its second season of concentrated excavation. The photograph and map clearly show the extent of excavation units and the precise outlines of visible walls of the structure. The latter data were helpful in planning sampling strategies for different rooms and roomblocks. Note the white, L-shaped field control points set on the ground prior to aerial photography.

Figure 5.14. (*on pages 330–331*) (A) Vertical aerial photograph of Pueblo Alto taken almost exactly 1 year after that shown in Figure 5.13 (September 9, 1977). (B) The map was compiled photogrammetrically from stereophotographs of the same scale and format, and shows the progress of the excavations since the previous aerial photograph. Periodic re-photography and remapping of archaeological sites allows the monitoring not only of natural or inadvertent impacts, but also the compilation of a permanent and highly accurate record of the progress of excavation and other necessary, archaeological disturbance of sites.

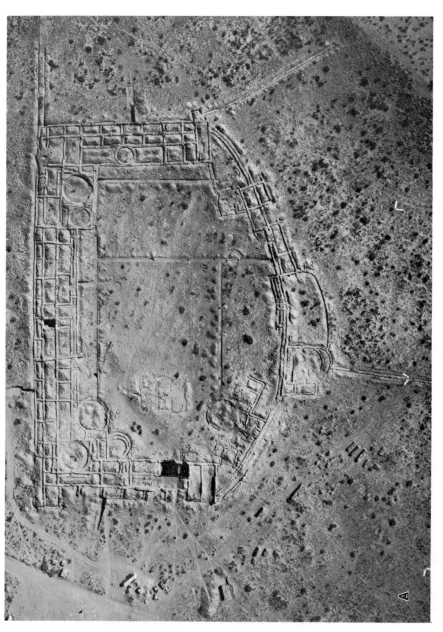

Figure 5.13. (A)

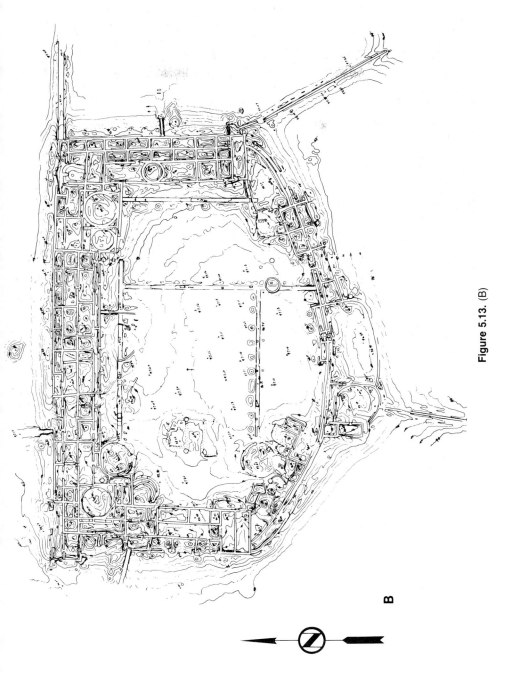

Figure 5.13. (B)

B

Figure 5.14. (A)

B

Figure 5.14. (B)

331

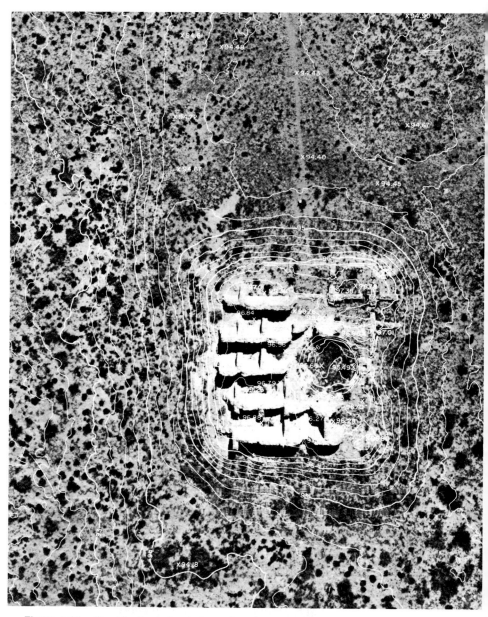

Figure 5.15. Combination orthophotograph and topographic photogrammetric representation of New Alto, a late Pueblo period structure at Chaco Cultural National Historical Park. The base of this product is an orthophotograph, compiled using a stereo pair, which depicts the site photographically in planimetric form—that is, so that all horizontal components of the photograph are in their true scaled positions. Next, a photogrammetric plotter was used to compile topographic contours and some spot elevations in the scene using the same stereo pair of photographs. The two were photographically overlain, thus combining the advantages of spatially corrected photography and topographic mapping. Such a product can be laid on a plane table and used as a base map for alidade mapping of features, artifacts, or analytic units in the field.

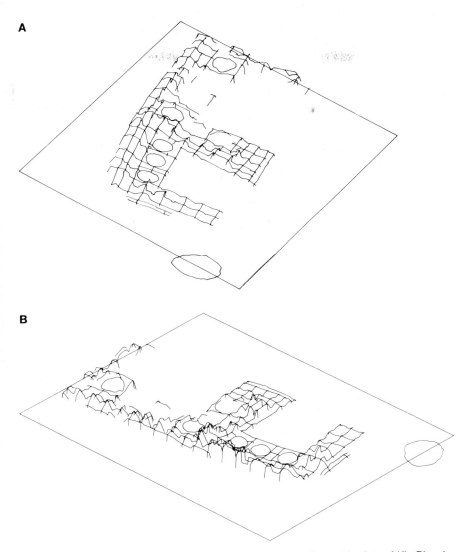

A

B

Figure 5.16. Two computer-constructed "three-dimensional" graphic plots of Kin Bineola Pueblo made with digital data recorded during the plotting of the map shown in Figure 5.12. Computers, working with data such as those that were used to arrive at these graphics, may be useful in determining amounts of dirt to be moved during excavation and in interpretive reconstructions of the possible full extent of sites and structures. Relatively expensive at this time, the costs of such graphic reconstructions will probably decrease dramatically as computers and computer graphics devices become more widely used.

The image processing facility at the Rheinisches Landesmuseum is based on a PDP 11/10 computer for line buffering and control, coupled to a PDP 11/70 computer that performs calculations on image data. The PDP 11/70's capacity is also utilized for storage of collections data for the museum in addition to image processing. Digital image input originates from an Optronics P1000 drum scanner. Color and black-and-white video displays are viewed by the operator, who interactively chooses areas of interest and specified operations to be performed on them. Although aerial photographs comprise the major data source used with this system, it has also been employed to enhance X-rays and specimen photographs and with MSS data. Operations performed by the system can be classed under two major headings: image enhancement and geometric correction–mapping.

Image enhancement is desirable because not all the photographs available to the archaeologist are of consistent quality, contrast, sharpness, or freedom from "noise" (due to scratches, dirt, poor processing, etc.), and lens aberrations. In addition, digital enhancement can add information value to any photographic product by enhancing edges and filtering. The Rheinisches Landesmuseum system performs contrast enhancement, histogram modification or equalization, Fourier transform and nonlinear spatial filtering, spherical lens aberration correction, homomorphic filtering, correction for motion blur, edge enhancement, and nonlinear filtering for removing dust spots and noise (Scollar and Weidner 1979, 1981).

The geometric correction capabilities of the Rheinisches Landesmuseum system provide the solution to mapping archaeological indications and other visible features from oblique aerial photographs. Using ground control data from a limited number of points that appear in a set of photographs, the system creates a "pseudovertical" view of the site. The archaeological area of interest is indicated by the operator from his or her console; for instance, ground outlines of old fields or the walls of an ancient fort. This allows computations to be performed only on areas of interest, rather than rectifying unnecessary modern details or environmental features that may not be of prime importance, thereby speeding computations. Maps (1:1000 scale) are also scanned at 50 micron precision and stored digitally, separately from the digitized cultural resource locations. This allows the revision of cultural resource or map data independently; these can, however, be conjoined and plotted together whenever necessary. In addition, photographic output of rectified views is provided by the system's Optronics P1500 film writer (Scollar 1977).

TERRESTRIAL PHOTOGRAMMETRY

Terrestrial photogrammetry is accomplished using the same basic methods and techniques as is aerial photogrammetry. It nonetheless deserves separate mention because it is very likely that terrestrial photogrammetry will become increasingly popular with and useful to archaeologists in the very near future. The reason for this is that terrestrial photogrammetry allows photogrammetric recording and subsequent mapping from an inexpensive platform—the ground. Aerial photographic site recording is a valuable technique when large sites or areas are to be mapped at moderate scales, but it cannot meet the need for detailed, three-dimensional intrasite plotting of the precise extent of excavation units, or the locations of artifacts and relatively limited and subtle features. Photogrammetry is potentially a more suitable method of intrasite mapping than are most methods of hand plotting because properly collected metric photographs show details and can yield information that is not even realized by the archaeologist during field excavation: differential soil coloration, artifact orientation, physical site disturbances—and all those other classes of data that might be of vital interest to the "archaeologist of the future."

The problem with using photographs for artifact and feature plotting on an intrasite level has always been the lack of a suitable platform. A number of valiant attempts have been made by archaeologists to provide platforms that can yield useful site photographs; these have included the use of cherry-pickers, ladders with long legs, tripods (Nylén 1964), portable bipods (Whittlesey 1966a), and balloons (Whittlesey 1969). The purpose of all these platforms is to provide as nearly vertical-axis photographs of an excavation unit or site as possible; ostensibly, this will allow the tracing of site maps from a mosaic of photos (Boyer 1980; Klausner 1980) or photogrammetry with stereophotos taken from above the site. Photographs taken of archaeological sites from tripods, bipods, and other elevating camera supports, such as ladders with extended legs, are a valuable adjunct to recording the general characteristics of a site quickly and can provide a record of the general orientation of excavations or collection units, features, and the like. It is, unfortunately, difficult to make practical, accurate measurements and maps from photographs taken with nonmetric cameras.

Given a rapidly changing state of the art in photogrammetry today, however, the above statements warrant some discussion. The cameras presently in use for terrestrial photogrammetry, called *metric cameras,* differ in several ways from the normal, nonmetric cameras commonly employed for site photography. Metric cameras have specially corrected lenses, which are carefully collimated to assure perpendicularity of the lens axis and film plane; the center of the lens axis where it intersects the film, or principal point, is marked with fiducial markings.

In general, the radial distortion inherent in metric cameras is less than 5 microns. This is not the case with even expensive nonmetric cameras, and in practice most photogrammetrists today are very reluctant to attempt to make measurements from photographs taken with nonmetric cameras (Muessig 1982:182).

The question, of course, is one of accuracy. Photogrammetric measurements can be made from nonmetric imagery, but with a reduction of accuracy over measurements made from metric photos. A number of recent studies (Karara 1972; Karara and Abdel-Aziz 1974; Faig 1976; Kölbl 1976; van Wijk and Ziemann 1976) have indicated that modified or unmodified nonmetric cameras can produce useful photogrammetric results if proper control and calibration procedures are used. Photogrammetrists engaged in terrestrial photogrammetry usually operate integrated camera-plotter systems, however, and few have made the necessary modifications required to plot from nonmetric photography.

Interestingly for the archaeologist, this picture is changing rapidly today, primarily due to revolutionary electronic advances that soon will make analytic photogrammetric plotting capabilities available at low cost. The great majority of photogrammetric plotting systems in use today, for both aerial and terrestrial photogrammetric purposes, are optical–mechanical systems. Photogrammetry using optical–mechanical systems involves the mounting of overlapping photographs taken perpendicular to a common base line to form a three-dimensional optical model viewed stereoscopically by the plotter operator. The model is scaled using control points visible in the image and previously measured in the field. A small floating dot or mark is optically projected into the scene and seen by the operator, who can cause it to move in three coordinate directions by operator, who can cause it to move in three coordinate directions by operating two hand wheels and a foot treadle. A mechanical linkage transmits the floating mark's movements to a plotting table where a scaled tracing of its movements is created. It is possible to rectify oblique stereophotographs through mechanical and optical adjustments (Turpin *et al.* 1979).

Analytic plotters, on the other hand, operate digitally to create maps and measurements from photographs. Instead of being manipulated in an analog fashion, as in the optical–mechanical plotter, the image is digitized or converted into a matrix of small elements. This is done either by subjectively choosing those points of interest in the scene, and digitizing these (including control points), or by automatically digitizing the gray-scale values present in the photographic image itself. The locations of these points can then be geometrically manipulated, and their altered representations recorded by plotting instruments or by reconstituting the digitized photographic image with a film printer (Doyle 1975:1083–1085). Analytic plotter systems, given the information contained in a single oblique photograph, can transform the location of specified points into a map in any desired plane. In addition, nonlinear corrections in the spacing of the points can be made, allowing the use of nonmetric photographs with comparative ease. Analytic systems can also produce orthophotographs by correcting for obliqueness, image movement, and other errors inherent in nonmetric aerial and terrestrial photographs.

Only a few years ago, the computers necessary to handle analytic photogrammetric calculations were so expensive that only a few such systems were in use worldwide. Today, microprocessors capable of these computations are relatively inexpensive; unfortunately, the peripheral devices required for the input of digitized data and the output of transformed photographic representations are still costly, due for the most part to low demand and production. Only recently, a small analytic photogrammetric system, making use of nonmetric, 35-mm format images and costing less than $75,000, has been advertised as having archaeological applications (HDF/MACO 1982a, 1982b). A simpler yet versatile microprocessor system exhibited at the Archaeological Symposium in Bradford, England, in 1981, which employs a simple digitizer pad and inexpensive plotter for vertical-perspective mapping from oblique photographs, could be duplicated for approximately $5000 (I. Scollar, personal communication, 1980). Possibly within the next few years, analytic photogrammetry should be within the reach of most archaeologists. It is difficult to imagine the full range of archaeological applications of terrestrial site photogrammetry when this happens, and for this reason it is necessary to examine the methods and potential of today's optical–mechanical terrestrial photogrammetry.

Terrestrial photogrammetry, sometimes called close-range photogrammetry (Kobelin 1982:76), has been used for the mapping and plotting of architecture (Figure 5.17) for nearly as long as photography has been practical (Karara 1979), and in fact is increasingly being used for documenting and measuring changes in historic and prehistoric structures (Figure 5.14) (Ebert 1982; Drager 1982; Lyons and Ebert 1982; Ryan 1982). Only quite recently, however, has terrestrial photogrammetry been seriously applied to nonstructural archaeological sites and data. In Australia, it has been used with considerable success on petroglyphs and other rock art (Clouten 1973, 1977; Scogings 1975). Growing from the terrestrial photogrammetric recording of rock art, the technique has also been used recently in the United States for mapping the progress of excavations within and around prehistoric pueblo sites in Arizona (Dennett and Muessig 1980), and for recording rock art, surface artifacts, and site features such as hearths and rock circles in Texas (Turpin *et al.* 1979). The range of site types recorded in the latter study illustrates the general process and potential of modern optical–mechanical terrestrial photogrammetry.

The equipment used in this study, undertaken in 1979 by the Texas Archaeological Survey with the assistance of Dennett and Muessig Associates, Ltd. of Iowa City, consisted of two Wild Heerbrugg wide-angle stereometric camera systems (Turpin *et al.* 1979:330), each with two $6\frac{1}{2} \times 9$ cm format cameras mounted at the ends of base tubes measuring 40 and 120 cm long, respectively. When single metric cameras are used, the exact placement of the instrument at each successive, overlapping exposure must be carefully measured with surveying equipment; the use of dual cameras on a base bar allows identical camera separation and orientation with one setup, reducing field time drastically. The first subject of the Texas Archaeological Survey project was a series of rock paintings on the wall of a rockshelter some 150 m long in Painted Rock Canyon,

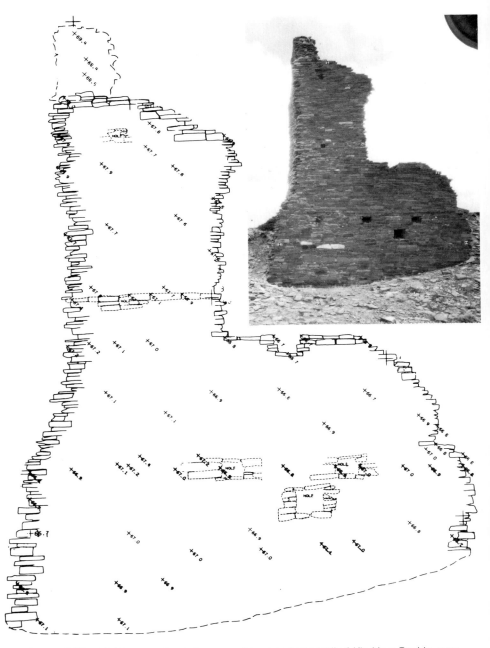

Figure 5.17. Highly accurate photogrammetric plot of one wall of Kin Ya-a Pueblo, near Crownpoint, New Mexico. This plan drawing, produced from metric, terrestrial stereophotographs (one of which is shown in the smaller inset), depicts the outlines of the wall as well as many spot elevations (small x's). These data can be compared with subsequent rephotography and mapping to determine changes in the form, and possible threats to, the structure. In addition, they provide a permanent record of its shape and details.

near the intersection of the Rio Grande and Pecos River. Photography required one pair of exposures with the Wild C-120 (120-cm base) camera, and a second photograph of a smaller section of the panel with the Wild C-40 (40-cm base) camera. A stadia rod was placed against the rear wall of the shelter, providing the only control. Field photography took $2\frac{1}{2}$ hours, although the authors estimate that given their present level of experience it could now be accomplished in an hour or less (Turpin et al. 1979:332). Using these photographs, a vertical 5-cm contour map, a planimetric map, a horizontal cross-section, and two vertical cross-sections of the shelter and its painted figures were produced.

A second site, presenting different problems, was also recorded during the Texas Archaeological Survey experiment. Located near the Painted Rock Shelter, this site consisted of a surface scatter of transported and fire-cracked rock believed to be the remains of hearths and rock ovens. Prior to photography using the Wild C-120 camera system, lithic artifacts scattered within the cracked-rock features were marked with nails and tags so that these could be individually identified and plotted. Three sets of oblique stereopairs were taken from different positions around the rock scatter; this required 1 hour of field time (including tagging of artifacts). A 2-cm contour plot of the site was compiled using a Wild Heerbrugg A40 Autograph plotter. In addition, the planimetric locations and heights of each limestone block and artifact were recorded on another map. Three cross sections of the rock scatter were produced, one from each stereopair. The time required for laboratory plotting of all the rock scatter site maps was $3\frac{1}{2}$ hours. The cameras used in this experiment cost approximately $25,000 each, and the plotter over $100,000—clearly not a "do-it-yourself" proposition for most archaeological projects. Nonetheless, surprisingly little field time was required to photograph these sites. Even at a relatively high cost for rental of equipment and the time of trained photographers, modern optical–mechanical terrestrial photogrammetry may be cost-effective for mapping certain sorts of sites, such as the complex rock art discussed by Turpin et al. (1979).

REMOTE SENSING IN ARCHAEOLOGICAL SURVEY, SAMPLING, AND REGIONAL STUDIES

Some of the most important topics of discussion in archaeology today center about the archaeological survey. Within the past decade or perhaps slightly more there has been a widespread recognition within the profession that much of the data of future archaeologists, as well as the majority of their salaries, may well be the products of systematic surveys of surface remains (Lewarch and O'Brien 1981; Schiffer et al. 1978). There are a number of reasons for this shift in emphasis. The most immediately obvious is that federal laws require surface surveys of areas of potential land disturbance for an assessment of the possible significance of sites and materials that might be affected by construction, inundation, and the like. Another impetus to extensive surface surveys, however, is more theoretical in nature. In order to understand the complex relationships between past human behavior, the utilization of space and resources, and the discard and loss of materials, it may be necessary to examine not only intrasite patterning but the patterning of cultural materials in amalgams of sites as well (Binford 1979, 1982; Isaac 1981). This change in theoretical emphasis has been closely paralleled by shifts in suggested survey methodology, including a "non-site" (Thomas 1975) or "off-site" (Foley 1980, 1981a) sampling and recording strategy. These essentially identical approaches are based on the recognition that human activity and material discard are not, in many cases, strictly confined to spatial clusters designated as *sites* by archaeologists. Instead, materials are distributed throughout the landscape used by past peoples. The distribution of materials recorded by the contemporary archaeologist, of course, results not only from what was discarded in the past, but also from the action of natural postdepositional forces and processes that preserve, hide, expose, or destroy portions of the archaeological record (Foley 1981b; Gifford 1977a, 1977b, 1980; Wood and Johnson 1978). These natural processes as well as past cultural ones must be taken into account by the archaeologists before predictions or projections concerning the past and the distributions of archaeological materials in the present can be made (Plog n.d.a, n.d.b; Plog *et al.* 1978).

The contemporary archaeological directions outlined above are far from solidified, and will undoubtedly be the subject of much controversy within the profession for some time to come. It is clear, however, that shifts in how we think about patterning, and how it will be measured, are afoot today. Understanding the patterning of past behavior and the environmental factors affecting the postdepositional archaeological record involves the measurement and mapping of phenomena over space, a task that virtually requires the application of remote sensing methods and techniques.

To understand present and potential remote sensing applications to survey and regional studies, it might first be best to contemplate some of the goals of the diverse field of archaeology. Three basic types of goals are pursued by archaeologists today: cultural resource management goals, which have to do with our treatment of cultural resources in the present and planning for their treatment in the future; "explanatory" goals, which are directed toward reconstructing or explaining the activities and behaviors in which people took part in the past; and what I call *methodological and theoretical* archaeological goals, those related to linking the present archaeological record with explanations of the past through the consideration of the natural and cultural processes affecting how archaeologists think about what they see. This latter area of archaeological endeavor is the most difficult and complex, for its subject matter ranges from the physical processes that form, preserve, and distort or destroy portions of the archaeological record, through relatively immediate methodological practices affecting fieldwork and its results, to the theoretical frameworks we employ in translating our observations into explanations and testing these. Of course, all archaeologists are involved in pursuing all these goals most of the time (although probably not in the proportions that they might desire!), and other sets of goals that might be more inclusive can be easily imagined. This taxonomy, however, serves here to structure a discussion of remote sensing applications in sampling and regional archaeology.

Three basic categories of remote sensing applications to survey archaeology should also be defined: sampling, projection, and prediction. Definitions to be used for the purposes of this discussion are:

1. *Sampling* is the careful collection of statistics pertaining to parameters of interest from a representative portion of a study area.
2. *Projection* is the formulation of expectations about the distribution and nature of parameters of interest over a region or study area on the basis of statistics collected during sampling.
3. *Prediction* involves the generation of expectations about specific places and circumstances in which certain desired phenomena (e.g., a specific type of site) might be expected to be found most sucessfully.

Remote sensing applications in each of these areas, with respect to each of the abovementioned taxa of archaeological goals, are listed in Table 5.3, and are discussed in detail below. References of published material in which remote sensing techniques are used or are suggested for sampling, projection, or prediction, which is discussed in the following sections, are also given in this table.

These terms are used here in a slightly different manner than in some of the other literature that the reader may encounter. The terms *projection* and *prediction,* in particular, should be further explained. The goal of projection, as defined above, is to arrive at theoretical expectations about patterning in an area. These expectations are based on a sample or samples, and although arguments can be mustered for the accuracy of such a projection, it can never be proven to be strictly "true." A partial sample of cultural materials from an area will not inform the archaeologist of the existence of unique or rare occurrences that the sample missed. Knowing where all resources in an area are through a sample, or in the case of some recent "predictive modeling," knowing where they are not, is neither possible nor is it the desired end-product of projection. Prediction, again as defined here, is a "search technique," used to narrow down the places where certain phenomena might successfully be sought, based on a previous sample as well, and does not provide a means of assessing all the cultural resources in an area and their significance, either. Both have essentially "explanatory" goals. It might be wondered where this leaves the archaeologist hoping to arrive at a blanket assessment, or "100% inventory sample" as required by current federal laws and policy of a Class III survey. This is not an easy question to answer and is certainly not attempted here. The discussion of remote sensing applications in regional survey and sampling which follows suggests that

TABLE 5.3

A Bivariate Taxonomy of Remote Sensing Applications to Survey Archaeology and Regional Studies

Area of remote sensing applications	The present (management)	Archaeological method and theory	The past (explanation, explication)
Sample design	Design of samples to ensure representative coverage and recording of all cultural resource sites, materials, and threats of impacts to these in an area of concern (Brown and Ebert 1978; Drager 1980b; Ebert 1980).	Design of sample to ensure representative coverage of landscape and all factors linking the archaeological record existing in the present with our ideas about the past, deductive testing of inductively derived ideas. (Ebert et al. in press)	Design sample to ensure representative collection of data on settlement system and range of archaeological materials present to allow inductive reasoning concerning past human behavior (Ebert 1978; Ebert and Hitchcock 1977).
Projection	Projections from sample of area of concern to total area to assess amount and nature of resources and impacts to those resources to be dealt with in the future; planning and avoidance (Camilli 1979; Camilli and Seaman 1979; Drager 1980a).	Projection from sample of area to total area of concern or study to assess the effects of postdepositional processes and the methods and procedures used by archaeologists on what we see and how we think about what it means; visibility, natural processes.	Projection from sample of study area to region or larger study area for purposes of explanatory "modeling" (Baker and Sessions 198 ; Haase 1981).
Prediction	Prediction to find specific examples of significant or representative sites or materials to insure preservation or other mitigation; prediction of significant materials most likely to be threatened by impacts (Camilli and Seaman 1979; Ebert and Gutierrez 1980).	Prediction to find sites or materials and processes affecting these illustrative of methodological and theoretical links between the record of the past and our present ideas about its meaning (Ebert and Gutierrez 1981).	Prediction to find specific components of settlement or social system to be studied for purposes of reconstruction and explanation of past activities and behaviors. Site discovery. (McManamon, Chapter 4, this volume; Carstens et al. 1981).

either our laws or our approaches to fulfilling their requirements may be in the early stages of undergoing significant changes.

REMOTE SENSING AND ARCHAEOLOGICAL SAMPLING

Sampling directed toward the discovery and measurement of any phenomena distributed over an area requires the division of a study area into units to be inspected for the phenomena one is interested in. Typically, an area is divided into small grid squares or units of other shapes (transects, circular sample areas, etc.) to be carefully inspected for these phenomena. Once this is done, some methods must be employed to determine which sampling units will be inspected and which will not. A number of methods for accomplishing this have been suggested in the past by geographers, archaeologists, and other scientists concerned with spatial distributions. The simplest scheme is that of random sampling (Hill 1967). Others have suggested various types of stratified systematic samples, designed so that spurious clumps of sample units are not randomly chosen but rather that units are more or less evenly distributed over the study area (Binford 1964; Redman 1973). *Stratified,* in the sense used by these authors, means that the total study area is divided into a number of arbitrary superunits, in the method described by Berry and Baker (1968), from which lesser units are then drawn randomly. Unfortunately, there are at least two major problems with such uninformed sampling schemes. First, there is nothing against which the precision, accuracy, and representativeness of such samples can be tested (although some experimenters have tried—see Judge *et al.* 1975; Plog 1968). Second, sampling using arbitrary stratification schemes assumes that nothing is known about the distribution of archaeological sites in the real world, something that we at least hope is not the case. A goal of any sort of areal sampling is to determine the nature of the nonrandomness of the distribution of parameters of interest and their characteristics through space. The most efficient way to do this is to divide a study area in an a priori way to reflect what one believes to be the cause of nonrandomness of the distribution of phenomena one is interested in (an assumption to be tested later), a method that has been referred to as *informed stratification* (Wood 1955). To achieve maximum sample precision, strata must be chosen so that their respective sampled averages are as different as possible and their variances as small as possible. Clusters within strata, on the other hand, should be as internally homogeneous as possible, thereby minimizing within-stratum variances while maximizing between-stratum variances (Stuart 1962). In this way, a sample stratification can be constructed to "explain" at least some of the variation in the characteristics of parameters of interest within a study area.

Of course, internally homogeneous strata can be constructed on the basis of many sorts of data sources: topographic maps, soils and surface geology maps, hydrologic charts, vegetation or faunal species distribution maps—virtually any sort of information about the distribution of phenomena in the real world that one believes might have affected the distribution of past people and differences in their behavior in the study area. One of the most efficient sources of information on the distribution of natural variables in the world, however, is remote sensor data, and in fact a bit of research will reveal that most maps showing natural distributions have been compiled from aerial photographs or space imagery. The problem with maps compiled by biologists, cartographers, or soils scientists is that their makers had a problem orientation that is probably not totally consistent with that of the archaeologist. In many instances, it is not only more economical but also more appropriate to do one's own interpretation from aerial photographs or space imagery for purposes of archaeological sample stratification.

There are two basic ways of interpreting remote sensor data sources to arrive at a sample stratification: visual and digital. The most available of these, at least to the present-day archaeologist, is visual interpretation of photographic data— either aerial photographs, or prints made photographically from digital Landsat or other satellite data. Basically, a photomosaic or Landsat frame print is overlain with a clear film sheet, and the interpreter begins drawing lines around areas that look the same versus those that look different (see Brown and Ebert 1978; Drager 1980b). The areas so stratified can be regional in scope or may encompass only the immediate area of a site being studied (Dunnell 1980). Some background in the factors that cause areas to look as they do in aerial photographs or satellite data is necessary. The product of such interpretation is ''multivariate'' in that the zones produced define combinations of variables such as soils, landforms, slopes, vegetation, surface hydrology, and geology; these were referred to as ''ecologic/cover-type'' strata or zones in a recent remote sensing stratification directed toward management sampling in the National Petroleum Reserve in Alaska in Alaska's North Slope (Brown and Ebert 1978; Ebert 1980). Such zones may or may not be efficient predictors of differential distributions of sites or their characteristics; the only way to test this is with survey data collected within the strata. The first stage of a multistage sampling design, in which sample units are distributed in proportion to the size of each stratum, is designed as a test of the discrimination of the sampe stratification. If a sample variance is computed for each sample statistic (those measurements that reflect parameters of interest to the archaeologist) within each zone or stratum, these variances can be compared to determine the efficiency of each stratum for each parameter of interest. For instance, if the variance between sample units in one stratum for, say, the sampled size of sites is twice as high as it is in another stratum, the former stratum may need to be further subdivided to provide an efficient sample design. In order to sample better those areas that the stratification tells us less about, the second sample stage can be distributed between strata in proportion to the area of the stratum times the sample variance. Sample stratification of this type has also been used in designing surveys directed toward ensuring a representative sample for explanatory purposes (Ebert 1978; Ebert and Hitchcock 1977), and has been suggested as a method of the a posteriori testing of the usefulness of transect and other sampling designs (Camilli and Cordell, in press; Ebert *et al.*, in press; Judge 1981; Judge *et al.* 1975).

PROJECTION FROM SAMPLES

Projection from a previously collected sample to a larger study area also requires arguments of representativeness to be made, for it must be shown that the natural correlates of the occurrence of a certain site type or other parameter of interest as determined during sampling are also characteristic of the areas to which a sample is to be projected. Data derived from remote sensor imagery interpretation can again be used efficiently in many cases for making arguments of representativeness. It is clear that, until tested, the results of a projection (for instance, estimates of how many sites might be found in an as-yet-unsurveyed area) are only speculative ("theoretical," perhaps) and probably the best justi-fied use of archaeological projections is in the inductive generation of ideas about distributions or dynamics in the past. Vegetation association zones interpreted from aerial photomosaics have been used to estimate probable site densities across Cedar Mesa in southeastern Utah from a relatively small but systematic sample by Haase (1981) in the fulfillment of this type of goal. Baker and Sessions (1981) experimented with the use of digital computer classification of soil zones from Landsat digital tapes in the Bisti–Star Lake region of north-western New Mexico. Using Soil Conservation Service maps and aerial photo-graphs, they selected "training areas" to characterize each soil type; these areas were analyzed using a discriminate function analysis (Stansort II) of Landsat MSS data. Once the computer determines a signature for each soil type, it automatically searches the entire data set (the study area) and classifies areas with similar signatures in that type as well. Correlations between site type occur-rences and soil zones were made within a 2×2 km grid framework, allowing Baker and Sessions to determine which soils zones predicted which types or characteristics of sites. Because more than one soil zone often occurred within each 2×2 km grid square or analytic unit, synthetic variables composed of associations between soil types, 78 "natural" variables in all, were created and used in the correlations with site types as well. Although results of Baker and Sessions's analysis were less edifying than they had expected, their work does illustrate an important point regarding stratifications designed to aid in the for-mulation of sample design or for justifying projections. Because all characteris-tics of archaeological sites or materials cannot be expected to vary directly with all environmental variables that can be measured, a stratification that predicts the distribution of one parameter may not do so for another. It may be that a different stratification is necessary to support arguments of "representativeness" for each variable that the archaeologist may want to sample or explain.

Management applications of archaeological projection have also been sug-gested and undertaken, some using remote sensor data as a basis for the measure-ment of natural variables. It is particularly important to note the speculative nature of untested projections if these are to be used for management purposes, for despite some suggestions to the contrary (for instance, see Plog 1981), it is at least at present against the dictates of federal law and policy (National Park Service 1981) to use anything but a total coverage survey for purposes of deter-mination of significance of the resources of an area (although this is changing, and may soon be subject to interpretation). Projection from the early stages of archaeological sampling of an area (Class I or Class II survey) to the total area of management concern, however, can be useful for planning for the volume of cultural materials that might have to be dealt with during future fieldwork (Camilli 1979; Drager 1980a) and for planning for avoidance, for instance the choice of alternative pipeline or transmission line routes (Camilli and Seaman 1979).

Another area of application of remote sensing–aided archaeological projection, one that will doubtless see more attention in the future, is that of using projections to determine areas of differential postdepositional disturbance, or in which natural factors such as vegetation might cause differential visibility of archaeological materials and thereby necessitate the employment of special field methods or degrees of survey intensity. Such an application has explanatory implications as well, for the distribution of archaeological sites and materials found by a field crew is only partly consequent upon those materials discarded or lost by past peoples. Without considering the factors responsible for differential preservation and/or visibility of cultural sites, it is misleading to begin discussion of past population densities, settlement patterns, and the like (Plog *et al.* 1978; Schiffer *et al.* 1978). Measuring the distribution and nature of natural processes affecting the visibility of archaeological materials using remote sensor data is the goal of an experimental project presently being undertaken at Chaco Culture National Historical Park by Ebert and Gutiérrez (1981). Using 1:6000-scale color transparency aerial photographs, an accurate map of geomorphic units in and around Chaco Canyon was compiled; correlations between these units and more than 2000 recorded archaeological sites there indicates that some of the recorded archaeological distributions are explainable as much in terms of visibility and natural preservation or disturbance as by reference to behavior in the past. Further fieldwork and photointerpretation directed toward the measurement of the dynamics of these geomorphic units and the quantitative determination of their effects over time is being undertaken at the present.

REMOTE SENSING AND ARCHAEOLOGICAL PREDICTION

Prediction of the probable locations of archaeological sites and materials, or the best places to look for these, is often done more unconsciously than explicitly by archaeologists. Armed with extensive experimental knowledge of where certain types of sites are located, some surveyors tend to pick just these places to look carefully for sites, biasing their sample accordingly. Chance ''first discoveries'' in one sort of area, made possible by unusually favorable natural conditions, can cause workers to look more intensively in such areas thenceforward. Using remote sensing for the prediction of the locations of archaeological sites is very similar to this—except that the characteristics of the places in which sites are found are measured using remote sensor imagery instead of depending on the knowledge (usually unquantified and inexplicit) of the surveyor. Prediction of archaeological site occurrence is really a systematic sort of site-discovery technique in which sites that cannot be directly "seen," either on the ground or through technical methods, are sought. McManamon (Chapter 4, this volume) lists a wide range of data sources with the potential of aiding in discovering hidden sites, and remote sensing is one of the most versatile of these.

The goal of predicting the occurrence of sites or cultural materials is simply to find these, for a variety of purposes. In some cases, the archaeologist seeks sites for future study and excavation. In a predictive experiment with such a goal, Carsten *et al.* (1981) isolated the typical landform associations of previously discovered archaeological sites that had been judged "significant" in the Jackson Purchase region of Kentucky. By searching for other unexplored portions of the study area that were similar in landform, they were able efficiently to narrow down areas on the ground that had to be searched to find new sites with potential significance. Similar experiments in Virginia (Lade 1982) have employed digitally enhanced and classified Landsat data rather than photointerpretation to measure landscape variables and predict probable site locations. Digital enhancement may often be a useful addition to photointerpretation because it allows the recognition of details that might not be immediately seen on an unenhanced photograph.

It may be desirable to find specific sorts of archaeological occurrences without undertaking blanket survey or sampling for management purposes, as well. National Park Service areas are good examples of this: archaeological sites are not particularly threatened in the National Parks, at least not over large areas that suffer relatively few cultural impacts. The reason for finding sites in many park areas is to have something to show visitors or to study for scientific, interpretive, or illustrative purposes. A predictive study in Shenandoah National Park in Virginia by Ebert and Gutiérrez (1979, 1980) utilized 1:12,000-scale color aerial transparencies for the measurement of natural correlates of known site occurrence, such as vegetation type and diversity, slope angle and aspect, depth and extent of nearby alluvium, and proximity to geologic faults and contacts (and thus reliable water supplies). Once areas in which sites had been found in the past were characterized, similar but unexplored areas were located by reinterpreting the aerial photographs, and these were marked on maps for checking in the field. These specific and relatively small areas were surveyed, resulting in the discovery of prehistoric and historic sites in 45% of the predictive areas, far better than during random or undirected survey of the area.

Of course, no matter whether archaeological sites occur in National Parks or anywhere else, they are always subject to a greater or lesser degree to natural impacts: erosion, aggradation, periglacial processes, mass wasting, and the effects of biologic agents and chemical weathering. If sites can be found soon enough aided by predictions of where they might be they can often be saved from destruction or damage (Camilli and Seaman 1979; Ebert and Gutiérrez 1981).

VISUAL VERSUS DIGITAL CLASSIFICATION—PROS AND CONS

Both visual interpretation and digital classifications have been used to derive stratifications or zonations for the archaeological purposes of sampling, projection, and prediction. *Visual* interpretations segment or stratify an image into homogeneous areas; a *digital* classification attempts the same thing by using digitally recorded light and dark values rather than the analog image viewed by a human interpreter, and by using a fixed rule or algorithm chosen subjectively. Some remote sensor data, as discussed in earlier parts of this chapter, are recorded in digital form: airborne and satellite scanner data, including that from the Landsat multispectral scanner. Aerial photographs can also be digitized using a scanning microdensitometer or a video digitizer, and the use of filters during scanning color aerial photographs can even produce a kind of ''multispectral'' data. Data recorded in digital form can also be transformed into visual products, such as the color composite prints, approximating color infrared film in their frequency response, that are made from Landsat tapes. Almost any remote sensor data can be interpreted or classified both visually or digitally.

There are, of course, trade-offs between the usefulness, accuracy, and costs of stratifications arrived at visually versus digitally. Human interpreters are internally armed with a vast amount of information about how things in a photograph or other remotely sensed scene should look, and can often correctly identify phenomena they have never seen before. Human interpreters can discriminate between things that look almost identical on the basis of their context, for instance between a cloud and a snowbank, that a machine would classify as the same. The human eye can discriminate minute differences not only in tone but texture. What is more, the human interpreter has a ''built-in'' problem orientation and is able to classify instantly cover types and other phenomena on the surface of the earth in culturally useful ways (Anderson *et al.* 1976).

Human interpreters generalize, too—they average indistinct boundaries between zones, and leave out tiny portions of one zone that may exist within large areas of another. Generalization can be seen as either good or bad depending on one's purpose. At humanly relevant scales, it may be unimportant that a single pear tree lies at the center of a vast expanse of apple trees. When locational data on archaeological sites are being correlated with zones, it may be unimportant that zone boundaries are many meters wide, or only accurate to within 50 m.

Digital classification is different from visual classification in a number of ways. First, it is ''blind'' in that the computer that forms clusters of multispectral reflectance values in an n-dimensional space has no prior knowledge of what things on the ground "look like." This can be remedied, however, by teaching the computer what to expect and by telling it what names to give things. Unless some sort of difficult decision has to be made on the basis of context, like the cloud–snowbank example given above, computers do extremely well when taught. They are faster, more consistent, and more accurate. Digitized data come in small parcels of a fixed and constant size called *pixels* (from "picture elements")—Landsat pixels, for instance, are about 70 m square and each pixel in a digital classification falls within one of the classes formed. Digital classes are, therefore, not generalized like visually interpreted ones are, although a person can interpret the digitally derived classes to arrive at an appropriate level of generalization (Robinove 1979, 1981). What is more, because digital classifications are done numerically, they are quantitative and replicable (Baker and Sessions 1981).

Unfortunately, digital classifications are also expensive. This is the major reason that they have not been universally employed in archaeological remote sensing classifications and stratifications. At the present time, digital image classification and analysis requires sophisticated hardware and software out of the reach of most archaeologists. Given the rapid advances in microcomputer technology today, and the spectacular decreases in the costs of computers and particularly in converting, inputting, and outputting data through peripheral devices, however, it is encouraging to think that doing one's own digital image processing for archaeological purposes may become practical within the very near future.

CONCLUSIONS: ARCHAEOLOGICAL REMOTE SENSING— PAST, PRESENT, AND FUTURE

Remote sensing data sources, methods, and techniques have been at least a peripheral part of archaeology for more than a century. Since the advent of the airplane, the taking and interpreting of aerial photographs has been a much-used adjunct to archaeological exploration and recording around the world; photogrammetry was first used for recording and mapping archaeological structures and sites in the late 1800s. Nonetheless, occasioned by both a rapidly accelerating optical and electronic technology on one hand, and new needs and goals in archaeology on the other, archaeological remote sensing is a still-developing field today. The past decade, or possibly two, has seen widespread experimentation with aerial photographic interpretation, photogrammetric mapping, and the application of remote sensing–derived data to archaeological and cultural resources sampling, projection, and prediction.

Archaeology is a composite and at times convoluted pursuit, requiring a close association between the archaeologist and the record of the past, and much archaeological method and technique has been developed within such a framework. It is imperative in archaeology that, if one cannot "do it oneself," one at least be able to understand what is being done. The purpose of this chapter has been an introduction to this sort of understanding of remote sensing applications in archaeology, and a fuller understanding can, one hopes, be reached by reference to some of the literature cited here and by actual, hands-on attempts at applying remote sensing to archaeological problems. Because archaeological remote sensing is such a young area of endeavor, there are few hard-and-fast rules, and the specific methods worked out for each new need must often be innovative and unique.

Although much of the emphasis of this chapter has been devoted to remote sensing applications that may be performed by the individual archaeologist in pursuance of a cultural resource management or explanatory archaeological problem, some remote sensing approaches involve complicated and often expensive equipment, or the assistance of experienced photointerpreters or remote sensing specialists. Remote sensing has been an integral part of engineering, construction, and geography for many years, and the archaeologist with limited funds or inclination to undertake technical procedures can often find individuals at state and federal government offices, highway departments, and university geography or engineering departments willing to help. In some cases, however, it will be necessary to seek the advice of specialists with experience in actual archaeological applications of remote sensing, in much the same way that dendrochronologists, paleobotanical experts, or geomorphologists are consulted during the course of a project or study. Making precise photogrammetric measurements and maps or performing digital cover-type classifications is as complex as radiocarbon dating. On the other hand, there are many perfectly appropriate and useful remote sensing applications that can be performed by almost anyone anywhere—such is the nature of an archaeological subfield so broadly defined.

There is much to be done in the way of future experimentation with and refinement of archaeological applications of remote sensing. Clearly, the uses of remote sensor imagery and measurements derived from these data in cultural resources sampling and survey are an extremely important subject. Are there classes of natural data that are useful in all geographic areas and cases for sample stratification, and how can they best be measured? What are the best analytic units for survey sampling? Is a "total area survey" really possible, or is all archaeological survey really sampling? These are questions that remote sensing may aid in answering.

Advances in available technology promise to open many avenues of archaeological remote sensing in the future, which will also merit exploration. Soon, both low-cost digital image processing systems and higher-resolution digital data such as that from Landsat-D's thermatic mapper and the "Spot" satellite planned by the French for 1982 should be available, and this may encourage the use of digital analysis for reliable and cost-effective site discovery based on either seeing actual sites, or the rapid classification of site–landform correlations. It may also allow the archaeologist to use digital processing equipment and routines at remote locations or actually in the field, making ''instant field checking'' of site identifications or stratifications possible.

One of the more promising uses of remote sensing in archaeology is the incorporation of remote sensor-derived data, archaeological data on locations and characteristics of sites and materials, and many other classes of locationally organized natural and cultural data into geographic information systems (GISs) that can be cross-referenced almost infinitely at high speed. Such GISs are already being experimented with by natural resources conservation concerns, although to the knowledge of this author they have not included archaeological data to date. When they do, and when such data bases become widespread and available, they will greatly facilitate the incorporation of the insights that can be gained through archaeology into an integrated framework of other natural and cultural data, uniting our science with other spatially oriented fields. This is certainly a goal worth pursuing.

REFERENCES

Agache, R.
  1962 Vues Aériennes de la somme et recherche du passé. *Bulletin Spécial de la Société de Préhistoire du Nord*. Amiens: Musée d'Amiens.
  1964 Archéologie aérienne de la somme. *Bulletin Spécial de la Société de Préhistoire du Nord*. Amiens: Musée d'Amiens.
  1966 Etudes d'archéologie aérienne. Paris: Service d'Édition et de Vente des Publications de l'Éducation Nationale.
  1967 Recherche des moments favorable à la mise en évidence des vestiges archéologiques arases par l'agriculture dans le nord de la france. *Secrétariat de la Commission* **14**:9–18. Paris.
Aguilar, A. M.
  1967 Cost analysis for aerial surveying. *Photogrammetric Engineering* **33**:81–91.
American Society of Photogrammetry
  1980 *Manual of photogrammetry*. 2 Vols. Falls Church, Virginia: American Society of Photogrammetry.
Anderson, James R., Ernest E. Hardy, John T. Roach, and Richard E. Witmer
  1976 A Land use and land cover classification system for use with remote sensor data. *US Geological Survey Professional Paper* 964. Washington, D.C.: US Government Printing Office.
Anderson, R. C.
  1979 A kite supported system for remote aerial photography. *Aerial Archaeology* **4**:4–7.
Avery, T. Eugene
  1977 *Interpretation of aerial photographs*, (3rd. edition), Minneapolis: Burgess Publishing Co.

Avery, T. E. and T. R. Lyons
  1981   Remote sensing: aerial and terrestrial photography for archeologists. Washington, D.C.: National Park Service, Cultural Resources Management Division.
Baker, Craig and Steven Sessions
  1981   Predictive model development and evaluation. In *Archaeological variability within the Bisti-Star Lake region, northwestern New Mexico,* edited by Meade F. Kemrer, Albuquerque, New Mexico: ESCA-Tech Corporation. Pp. 121–173.
Bandi, H-G.
  1942   Luftbild und urgeschichte. 33rd Annuaire: 145–153. Fraunfeld: Société Suisse de Préhistoire.
Bascom, W. R.
  1941   Possible applications of kite photography to archaeology and ethnology. *Transactions of the Illinois Academy of Science* **34**(2):62–63.
Beazeley, G. A.
  1919   Air photography in archaeology. *Geographical Journal* **53**:330–335.
  1920   Surveys in Mesopotamia during the war. *Geographical Journal* **55**:109–127.
Berry, Brian J. and A. M. Baker
  1968   Geographic sampling. In *Spatial Analysis: A Reader in Statistical Geography,* edited by B. J. Berry and D. F. Marble. Englewood Cliffs, New Jersey: Prentice-Hall. Pp. 91–100.
Bevan, Bruce W.
  1975   Aerial photography for the archaeologist. Philadelphia: Museum Applied Science Center for Archaeology, University Museum, University of Pennsylvania. Pp. 126.
Binford, Lewis R.
  1964   A consideration of archaeological research design. *American Antiquity* **19**:425–441.
  1979   Organization and formation processes: looking at curated technologies. *Journal of Anthropological Research* **35**:255–273.
  1982   The archaeology of place. *Journal of Anthropological Archaeology* **1**:5–31.
Boyer, W. Kent
  1980   Bipod photogrammetry. In *Cultural resources remote sensing,* edited by T. R. Lyons and F. J. Mathien. Washington, D.C.: National Park Service. Pp. 327–345.
Bradford, J. S. P.
  1947a   Buried landscapes in southern Italy. *Antiquity* **21**:58–72.
  1947b   Etruria from the air. *Antiquity* **21**:74–83.
  1949   Buried landscapes in southern Italy. *Antiquity* **23**:58–72.
  1952   Progress in air archaeology. *Discovery* **13**(6):177–181.
Brown, Galen N. and James I. Ebert
  1978   Ecological mapping for purposes of sample stratification in large-scale Cultural Resources Assessment: The National Petroleum Reserve in Alaska. *Remote sensing and non-destructive archaeology* edited by Thomas R. Lyons and James I. Ebert. Washington: Cultural Resources Management Division, National Park Service. Pp. 53–63.
Buttler, W., O. G. S. Crawford, and E. Ewald
  1938   Luftbild und vorgeschichte. In *Luftbild und luftbildmessung* 16. Berlin: Hansa Luftbild GmbH.
Camilli, Eileen
  1979   Remote sensing and cultural resources management for the Navajo Indian Irrigation Project (NIIP). In *Report of the cultural resources survey of blocks VI and VII of the N.I.P.P.,* by William Reynolds, Eileen Camilli and David Mayfield. Costa Mesa, California: Earth Sciences Consulting and Technology Corporation.

Camilli, Eileen L. and Linda S. Cordell
in   *The greater southwest: A supplement to the handbook of remote sensing.* Washington,
press   D.C.: National Park Service.
Camilli, Eileen L. and T. Seaman
1979   Preliminary assessment of cultural resources for the crownpoint to Bisti Pipeline route:
        cultural resources management with the aid of remote sensing. In *New Mexico generat-
        ing station environmental assessment.* Albuquerque: Public Service Company of New
        Mexico.
Carbonnel, M.
1965   Les relèves photogrammétriques des monuments de nubie. *Archaéologia* **3**:66–72.
Carstens, Kenneth C., Thomas C. Kind and Neil V. Weber
1981   Using remote sensing in predictive archaeological model: The Jackson Purchase Re-
        gion, Kentucky. In *Proceedings of the Pecora VII Symposium,* edited by B. R. Rich-
        ardson. Falls Church, Virginia: American Society of Photogrammetry. Pp. 494–507.
Chevallier, R.
1962   L'archéologie aérienne en France. *International Archives of Photogrammetry*
        14:401–407.
1963   Ancient and modern colonizations. *Photo Interpretation* **63**:43–49.
1964   *L'avion à la découverte du passé.* Paris: Artheme Fayard.
1965   Photographie aérienne en archéologie. In *Photographie Aérienne: panorama inter-
        technique,* edited by R. Chevallier. Paris: Gauthier-Villars. Pp. 97–105.
Chombart de Lauwe, P.-H.
1948a   Vision Aérienne du Monde. In *La Découverte Aérienne du Monde,* P-H, edited by
        Chombart de Lauwe. Paris: Horizons de France. Pp. 19–56.
1948b   L'évolution des rapports entre l'homme et le milieu. In *La découverte aerienne du
        monde,* P-H, edited by Chombart de Lauwe. Pp. 209–248. Paris: Horizons de France.
Clouten, Neville
1974   The application of photogrammetry to recording rock art: newsletter of the Australian
        Institution of Aboriginal Studies, Canberra, Vol. 1, Pp. 33–39.
1977   Further photogrammetric recordings of Early Man Shelters. Cape York: Newsletter of
        the Australian Institution of Aboriginal Studies. Canberra, Vol. 1, Pp. 54–59.
Coe, M. D.
1974   Photogrammetry and the ecology of the Olmec civilizations. In *Aerial photography in
        anthropological field research,* edited by E. Z. Vogt. Cambridge: Harvard University
        Press. Pp. 1–13.
Colwell, R. N., W. Brewer, G. Landis, P. Langley, J. Morgan, J. Rinker, and A. L. Sorem
1963   Basic matter and energy relationships involved in remote sensing reconnaissance.
        Photogrammetric Engineering **29**(5):761–799.
Crawford, O. G. S.
1923   Air survey and archaeology. *Geographical Journal* **61**:342–366.
1924a   Archaeology from the air. *Nature* **114**:580–582.
1924b   Air survey and archaeology. *Ordnance Survey Professional Papers,* No. 7.
1929   Air photography for archaeologists. *Ordnance Survey Professional Papers,* No. 12.
Denevan, W.
1966   The Aboriginal cultural geography of the Llanos de Mojas. *Ibero-Americana* **48.**
1970   Aboriginal drained field cultivation in the Americas. *Science* **169**:647–654.
Dennett, Sarah and Hans Muessig
1980   Archaeological applications for close-range photography: technical papers of the
        American Society of Photogrammetry, 46th Annual Meeting. Falls Church, Virginia:
        American Society of Photogrammetry. Pp. 335–341.

Doyle, Frederick J., (author–editor)
    1975   Cartographic presentation of remote sensor data. In *Manual of remote sensing,* edited by Robert G. Reeves, *et al.* Pp. 1077–1106. Falls Church, Virginia: American Society of Photogrammetry.

Drager, Dwight L.
    1980a   Projecting archaeological site concentrations from cover-type maps developed from remote sensing data. In *Proceedings of the Conference on Scientific Research in the National Parks* (2nd), Vol. 1. Washington, D.C.: National Park Service. Pp. 151–157.
    1980b   Vegetative stratifications from aerial imagery. In *Cultural resources remote sensing,* edited by T. R. Lyons and F. J. Mathien. Washington, D.C.: National Park Service. Pp. 79–86.
    1982   An experiment to determine the precision of photogrammetric monitoring of archeological structures. In *Technical Papers of the American Society of Photogrammetry, 1982, ASCM-ASP Convention,* Falls Church, Virginia: American Society of Photogrammetry. Pp. 191–193.

Dunnell, Robert C.
    1980   Remote sensing in archaeological sampling design. *Transportation Engineering Journal of the ASCE* 106 (TE3), Procedure Paper 15428. Pp. 349–363.

Ebert, James I.
    1977   Remote sensing within an archaeological research framework: methods, economics and theory. In *aerial remote sensing techniques in archaeology,* edited by T. R. Lyons and R. K. Hitchcock. Reports of the Chaco Center 2, Washington, D.C.: Cultural Resources Management Division, National Park Service. Pp. 169–201.
    1978   Remote sensing and large-scale cultural resources management. In *Remote Sensing and Non-Destructive Archeology*: Thomas R. Lyons and James I. Ebert. Washington: Cultural Resources Management Division. Pp. 21–34.
    1980   Remote sensing in large-scale cultural resources survey: a case study from the Arctic. In Cultural Resources Remote Sensing, edited by T. R. Lyons and F. J. Mathien. Washington, D.C.: National Park Service. Pp. 7–54.
    1982   Photogrammetry: tool for documentation, monitoring, and analysis of cultural resources. In *Technical Papers of the American Society of Photogrammetry, 1982 ACSM-ASP Convention.* Falls Church, Virginia: American Society of Photogrammetry. Pp. 57–61.

Ebert, James I. and Alberto A. Gutiérrez
    1979   Relationships between landscapes and archaeological sites in Shenandoah National Park: a remote sensing approach. *APT (Bulletin of the Association for Preservation Technology)* **XI**(4):69–87.
    1980   Cultural resources remote sensing in the eastern deciduous woodland: experiments at shenandoah national park. In *Proceedings of the Conference on Scientific Research in the National Park (2nd)* Vol. 1. Washington, D.C.: National Park Service. Pp. 118–150.
    1981   Remote sensing of geomorphological factors affecting the visibility of archaeological materials. In Technical Papers of the American Society of Photogrammetry 47th Annual Meeting, Washington, D.C., Falls Church, Virginia: American Society of Photogrammetry. Pp. 226–236.

Ebert, James I. and Robert K. Hitchcock
    1977   The role of remote sensing. In *Settlement and Subsistence Along the Lower Chaco River: The CGP Survey,* edited by Charles A. Reher. Albuquerque: The University of New Mexico Press. Pp. 191–216.

1980   Locational modeling in the analysis of the prehistoric roadway system at and around Chaco Canyon, New Mexico. In *Cultural Resources Remote Sensing,* edited by T. R. Lyons and F. J. Mathien. Washington, D.C.: National Park Service. Pp. 169–208.

Ebert, James I. and Thomas R. Lyons
1980   The Detection, mitigation and analysis of remotely-sensed, "Ephemeral" archeological evidence. In *Cultural Resources Remote Sensing,* edited by T. R. Lyons and F. J. Mathien. Washington, D.C.: National Park Service. Pp. 119–122.

Ebert, James I., Thomas R. Lyons and Dwight L. Drager
1979   Comments of "Application of orthophoto mapping to archaeological problems." *American Antiquity* **44**(2):341–345.

Ebert, James I. and Thomas R. Lyons (author–editors); Bruce W. Bevan, Eileen L. Camilli, Sarah Dennett, Dwight L. Drager, Rosalie Fanale, Nicholas Hartmann, Hans Muessig, and Irwin Scollar (contributing authors)
in   Archaeology, anthropology, and cultural resources management. Chapter 26. To ap-
press   pear in *Manual of Remote Sensing,* 2nd edition. Falls Church, Virginia: American Society of Photogrammetry.

Ehrenhard, John E.
1980   Cultural resource inventory of the Big Cypress Swamp: an experiment in remote sensing. In *Cultural Resources Remote Sensing,* edited by T. R. Lyons and F. J. Mathien. Washington, D.C.: National Park Service. Pp. 105–117.

Faig, Prof. Dr. Ing. Wolfgang
1976   Photogrammetric potentials of non-metric cameras. *Photogrammetric Engineering and Remote Sensing* **42**(1):47–49.

Foley, Robert A.
1980   The spatial component of archaeological data: off-site methods and some preliminary results from the Amboseli Basin Southern Kenya. *Proc. VIII Pan-African Congress in prehistory and Quaternary studies.* Pp. 39–40.
1981a   Off-site archaeology: an alternative approach for the short-sited. In *Patterns of the Past: Essays in Honor of David L. Clarke,* edited by I. Hodder, G. Isaac and N. Hammond. Cambridge: Cambridge University Press. Pp. 157–183.
1981b   A model of regional archaeological structure. *Proceedings of the Prehistoric Society* 47. Pp. 1–17.

Gifford, D. P.
1977a   Observations of modern human settlements as an aid to archaeological interpretation. Ph.D. Dissertation, Department of Anthropology, University of California, Berkeley.
1977b   Ethnoarchaeological observations on natural processes affecting cultural materials. In *Exploration in ethnoarchaeology,* edited by R. A. Gould. Pp. 77–102. Albuquerque: University of New Mexico Press.
1980   Ethnoarchaeological contributions to the taphonomy of human sites. In *Fossils in the Makings,* edited by A. K. Behrensmeyer and A. P. Hill. Pp. 94–107. Berkeley: University of California Press.

Grady, James
1982   Small format aerial photography for the cost-conscious archaeologist. Paper presented at the Annual Meetings of the Society of American Archaeology, Boulder, Colorado. Western Cultural Resources Management.

Gumerman, G. J.
1971a   Archaeology and aerial photography. *Proceedings of the Second ARETS Symposium.* Pp. 206–212. Tucson: University of Arizona.
1971b   The identification of archaeological sites by false color infrared aerial photography. *National Technical Information Service Report* PB2-04540.

1971c   The distribution of prehistoric population aggregates: In Proceedings of the South-western Anthropological Research Group, edited by G. P. Gumerman. *College Anthropological Reports,* No. 1. Prescott, Arizona: Prescott College Press.

Gumerman, G. J. and J. A. Neely

1972   An archaeological survey of the Tehuacan Valley, Mexico: a test of color infrared photography. *American Antiquity* **37**(4):520–527.

Gumerman, G. J. and T. R. Lyons

1971   Archaeological methodology and remote sensing. *Science* 1172:126–132.

Haase, William

1981   Estimates of archaeological site density and distribution on Cedar Mesa, Utah: a study based on photomosaic interpretation and probability sampling. Manuscript on file at Department of Anthropology, Washington State University, Pullman, Washington.

Hampton, J. N. and R. Palmer

1977   Implications of aerial photography for archaeology. The *Archaeological Journal* **134**:157–193.

Harp, E., Jr.

1966   Anthropology and remote sensing. *Proceedings of the Fourth Symposium on Remote Sensing of Environment.* Ann Arbor: University of Michigan. Pp. 727–729.

1967   Experimental air photo interpretation in archaeology. *Photogrammetric Engineering* **33**(6):676.

1968   Anthropological interpretation from color. In *Manual of color aerial photography,* edited by J. T. Smith. Pp. 385.

HDF/MACO

1982a   General description of the MACO 35/70, a miniaturized photogrammetric system based on 35mm and 70mm photography. Preliminary Release. Manuscript on file at HDF/MACO, 2400 Freedom Street, San Antonio, Texas 78217.

1982b   Archaeological photogrammetry. Manuscript on file at HDF/MACO, 2400 Freedom Street, San Antonio, Texas 78217.

Hill, James N.

1967   The problem of sampling. In Chapters in the prehistory of Arizona, 3. *Fieldiana Anthropology* **57**:145–157.

Isaac, G. L1.

1981   Stone Age visiting cards: approaches to the study of early land use patterns. In *Pattern of the Past: Studies in Honor of David Clarke,* edited by I. Hodder, G. Isaac, and N. Hammond. Cambridge: Cambridge University Press. Pp. 131–156.

Jorde, Lynn B. and Jack B. Bertram

1976   Current and future applications of aerospace remote sensing in archeology: a feasibility study. In *Remote Sensing Experiments in Cultural Resource Studies.* T. R. Lyons, assembler. Reports of the Chaco Center Washington, D.C.: Cultural Resources Management Division, National Park Service. Pp. 11–68.

Judd, N. M.

1930   Arizona sacrifces her prehistoric canals. *Explorations and fieldwork of the Smithsonian Institution in 1929.* Washington, D.C.: Smithsonian Institution. Pp. 177–182.

1931   Arizona's prehistoric canals from the air. *Explorations and fieldwork of the Smithsonian Institution in 1930.* Washington, D.C.: Smithsonian Institution. Pp. 157–166.

Judge, William James

1981   Transect sampling in Chaco Canyon—evaluation of a survey technique. In *Archaeological surveys of Chaco Canyon New Mexico,* by Alden W. Hayes, David M. Brugge, and W. James Judge. Washington, D.C.: National Park Service. Pp. 1–68.

Judge, William James, James I. Ebert and Robert K. Hitchcock
    1975   Sampling in regional archaeological survey. In *Sampling in archaeology,* edited by J.
            W. Mueller. Tucson: University of Arizona Press. Pp. 82–123.

Karara, H. M.
    1972   Simple cameras for close-range applications. *Photogrammetric Engineering*
            38:447–451.

Karara, H. M. (editor)
    1979   *Handbook of non-topographic photogrammetry.* Falls Church, Virginia: American
            Society of Photogrammetry.

Karara, H. M. and Y. I. Abdel-Aziz
    1974   Accuracy aspects of non-metric imageries. *Photogrammetric Engineering* 40–
            1107–1117.

Kidder, A. V.
    1929   Air exploration of the Maya country. *Bulletin of the Pan American Union* **63**:1200–
            1205.
    1930a   Colonel and Mrs. Lindbergh aid archaeologists. *Masterkey* 3(6):5–17.
    1930b   Five days over the Maya country. *Scientific Monthly* **30**:193–205.

Klausner, Stephanie
    1980   Bipod photography: procedures for photographic mapping of archaeological sites:
            cultural resources remote sensing, edited by T. R. Lyons and F. J. Mathien, Wash-
            ington, D.C.: National Park Service. Pp. 293–326.

Kobelin, Joel
    1982   Some suggested guidelines for the user in close-range photogrammetry. In *Technical*
            Papers of the American Society of Photogrammetry, 1982 ACSM-ASP Convention.
            Falls Church, Virginia: American Society of Photogrammetry. Pp. 76–79.

Kölbl, Otto R.
    1976   Metric or non-metric cameras. *Photogrammetric Engineering and Remote Sensing*
            42(1):103–113.

Lade, K.-Peter
    1982   The monitoring and detection of archaeological resources in Maryland through the use
            of landsat digitized multispectral data. Paper Presented at the 47th Annual Meeting of
            the Society for American Archaeology, Minneapolis, Minnesota.

Lattman, L. H. and R. G. Ray
    1965   *Aerial photographs in field geology.* New York: Holt, Rinehart and Winston.

Lewarch, Dennis E. and Michael J. O'Brien
    1981   The expanding role of surface assemblages in archaeological research. In *Advances in*
            archaeological method and theory, Vol. 4, edited by M. B. Schiffer. New York:
            Academic Press. Pp. 297–342.

Lindbergh, C. A.
    1929   The discovery of ruined Maya cities. *Science* **70**:12–13.

Loose, Richard W. and Thomas R. Lyons
    1976   The use of aerial photos in archaeological survey along the Lower Chaco River. In
            Remote sensing experiments in cultural resources studies, Association by T. R. Lyons.
            Reports of the Chaco Center 1. Washington, D.C.: Cultural Resources Management
            Division, National Park Service. Pp. 69–71.

Lyons, Thomas R. and Thomas E. Avery
    1977   *Remote sensing: a handbook for archeologists and cultural resource managers.* Wash-
            ington, D.C.: US Government Printing Office.

Lyons, Thomas R. and James I. Ebert
  1982   Photogrammetric measurement and monitoring of historic and prehistoric structures. In *Conservation of Historic Stone Buildings and Monuments.* Washington, D.C.: National Academy Press. Pp. 242–271.
Martin, A-M.
  1966   Geschichte und grundsätzliche Möglichkeiten der luftbild-archäologie in der modernen forschung (includes bibliography). Magister Artium Thesis, Köln University, Bonn.
  1968   Luftbild archäologie in der modernen forschung. *Bildmessung und Luftbildwesen* **3**:178–183.
Matheny, R. T.
  1962   Value of aerial photography in surveying archaeological sites in coastal jungle regions. *American Antiquity* **28**(2):226–230.
Mathien, F. Joan
  1981   Chalmette National Historical Park: a remote sensing project. *Historical Archaeology* **15**(2):69–86.
May, John R.
  1978   Guidance for applications of remote sensing to environmental management, Appendix A: sources of available remote sensor imagery: Appendix B. Sources of new imagery missions. Instruction Report M-78-2. Vicksburg, Mississippi: U.S. Army Waterway Experiment Station.
Millon, R.
  1964   The Teotihuacan mapping project. *American Antiquity* **29**(3):345–352.
  1970   Teotihuacan: completion of map of giant ancient city in the Valley of Mexico. *Science* **170**:1077–1082.
Millon, R. (editor)
  1973   *Urbanization at Teotihuacan, Mexico,* Vol. 1, *The Teotihuacan Map.* Part 1: Text. Austin: University of Texas Press.
Muessig, Hans
  1982   Equipment for close-range photogrammetry. In *Technical Papers of the American Society of Photogrammetry, 1982 ACSM-ASP Convention.* Falls Church, Virginia: American Society of Photogrammetry. Pp. 182–190.
National Park Service
  1981   Cultural resources management guidelines (NPS-28). Release No. 2. Washington, D.C.: Cultural Resources Management Division, National Park Service.
Nylén, E.
  1964   A turret for vertical photography. *Antikvariskt Arkiv* **24**. Stockholm: Swedish Academy of History and Antiquities.
Palmer, R.
  1977   A computer method for transcribing information graphically from oblique aerial photographs to maps. *Journal of Archaeological Science* **4**:283–290.
  1978   Computer transcription from air photographs. *Aerial Archaeology* **2**:5–7.
Perisset, M. C. and A. Tabbagh
  1981   Interpretation of thermal prospection on bare soils. *Archaeometry* **23**: 169–188.
Piggott, S. and C. M. Piggott
  1939   Stone and earth circles in Dorset. *Antiquity* **13**:138–158.
Plog, Fred
  n.d.a   Sampling strategies in the White Mountain planning unit. Albuquerque: *USDA Forest Service, Southwestern Region, Archeological Reports* (in press, M. S., 1977).
  n.d.b   The Little Colorado Planning Unit, Eastern Sector: an analytical approach to cultural

resource management. Albuquerque: *USDA Forest Service, Southwestern Region, Archeological Reports* (in press, M.S. 1977).

1968   Archaeological survey: a new perspective. Unpublished M. A. Thesis, University of Chicago, Chicago, Illinois.

1981   *Managing archeology: a background document for cultural resource management on the Apache-Sitgreaves National Forests, Arizona.* Cultural Resources Management Report 1, USDA Forest Service Southwestern Region.

Plog, S., F. Plog and W. Wait

1978   Decision making in modern surveys In *Advances in Archaeological Method and Theory,* Vol. 1, edited by M. B. Schiffer. New York: Academic Press. Pp. 383–421.

Poidebard, A.

1929   Les révélations archéologiques de la photographie aérienne: une nouvelle mëthode de recherches d'observations en région de steppe. *L'Ilustration,* May 25:660–662.

1931   Sur les traces de rome: exploration archéologique aérienne en syrie. *L'Illustration,* December 19:560–563.

1932   Photographie aérienne et archéologique recherches de Steppe Syrienne, 1925–1931. *Bulletin de Photogrammétrie* **2**:35–49.

Prewitt, Elton R. and Robert K. Holz

1976   Application of orthophoto mapping to archaeological problems. *American Antiquity* **41**(4):493–497.

Rainey, F.

1960   The changing face of archaeology. Expedition **2**(3):14–20.

1966   New techniques in archaeology. American Philosophical Society *Proceedings* **110**:146–152.

Ray, Richard G.

1960   *Aerial photographs in geologic interpretation and mapping.* US Geological Survey Professional Paper 373. Washington, D.C.: US Government Printing Office.

Redman, Charles L.

1973   Multistage fieldwork and analytical techniques. *American Antiquity* **38**:61–97.

Reeves, Robert G. (editor in Chief)

1975   *Manual of remote sensing,* Vols. 1 and 2. Falls Church, Virginia: American Society of Photogrammetry.

Reher, Charles A.

1977   Settlement and subsistence along the Lower Chaco River: The CGP Survey. Albuquerque: The University of New Mexico Press.

Riley, D. N.

1943   Archaeology from the air in the Upper Thames Valley.

1944   The technique of air-archaeology. *Archaeological Journal* **101**:1–16.

1979   Factors in the development of crop marks. *Aerial Archaeology* **4**:28–32.

Robinove, Charles J.

1979   Integrated terrain mapping with digital landsat images in Queensland, Australia. *US Geological Survey Professional Paper* 1102. Washington, D.C.: US Government Printing Office.

1981   The logic of multispectral classification and mapping of land. *Remote Sensing of Environment* **11**:231–244.

Ryan, Robert A.

1982   Close-range photogrammetry and cultural resource management: five case studies. In *Technical Papers of the American Society of Photogrammetry, 1982 ASCM-ASP Convention,* Falls Church, Virginia: American Society of Photogrammetry. Pp. 67–71.

St. Joseph, J. K. S.
  1945   Air photography and archaeology. *Geographical Journal* **105**:47–61.
  1949   Antiquity From the air. *Geographical Magazine* **21**:401–407.
  1950   Air reconnaissance and archaeological discovery. *Nature* **166**:749–750.
St. Joseph, J. K. S. (editor)
  1966   The uses of air photography: nature and man in a new perspective. New York: John
          Day.
Schiffer, M. B., A. P. Sullivan, and T. C. Klinger
  1978   The design of archaeological surveys. *World Archaeology* **10**:1–28.
Scogings, D. A.
  1975   Photogrammetric recording of petroglyphs: *wild reporter* (Heerbrugg, Switzerland),
          No. 9. Pp. 15–16.
Scollar, Irwin
  1963   Einige ergebnisse der archäeologischen liftbildforschung im Rheinland während des
          jahres 1962. *Bonner Jahrbücher* **163**:305–310.
  1965   Archäologie aus der luft: arbeitsergebnisse der flugjahre 1960 und 1961 im Rheinland.
          Düsseldorf: Rheinland-Verlag.
  1968   Computer image processing for archaeological air photographs. *World Archaeology.*
          10(1):71–87.
  1975   Transformation of extreme oblique aerial photographs to maps or plans by conven-
          tional means or by computers. In *Aerial reconnaisance for archaeology,* edited by D.
          R. Wilson. Research Report 12, Council for British Archaeology.
  1977   Image processing via computer in aerial archaeology. *Computers and the Humanities*
          11:347–351. London: Pergamon Press.
  1979   Progress in aerial photography in Germany and computer methods, edited by D. A.
          Edwards and E. A. Horne. *Aerial Archaeology* **2**:8–17. London: The Aerial Archaeol-
          ogy Foundation.
Scollar, I. and B. Weidner
  1979   Computer production of orthophotos from single oblique images or from rotating
          mirror scanners and the mathematics of geometric conversion by computer. *Aerial
          Archaeology* **4**:17–28.
  1981   Computer restitution and enhancement of extreme oblique archaeological air photos
          for archaeological cartography. *Revue d'Archëometrie* **5**:71–80.
Shippee, R.
  1932a   The "Great Wall of Peru" and other aerial photographic studies by the Ship-
          pee–Johnson Peruvian Expedition. *Geographical Review* **22**(1):1–29.
  1932b   Lost valleys of Peru: results of the Shippee–Johnson Peruvian Expedition. *Geographic
          Review* **22**(4):562–581.
  1933   Air adventure in Peru. *National Geographic Magazine* **63**(1):80–120.
  1934   Forgotten valley of Peru. *National Geographic Magazine* **65**(1):111–132.
Siegal, B. S. and A. R. Gillespie
  1980   *Remote sensing in geology.* New York: John Wiley and Sons.
Solecki, R. S.
  1952   Photographing the past. *Missouri River Basin Progress Report, September, 1952.*
          Billings, Montana: United States Department of the Interior, Interior Missouri Basin
          Field Committee.
  1957   Practical aerial photography for archaeologists. *American Antiquity* **22**(4):337–351.
  1958   Considerations in the interpretation of aerial views in archaeology. *Photogrammetric
          Engineering* **24**:798–802.

Solecki, R. S. (author–editor), and J. S. P. Bradford and A. R. Gonzalez (contributors)
  1960   Photo interpretation in archaeology. In *Manual of photographic interpretation,* edited by R. N. Colwell. Pp. 717–733. Washington, D.C.: American Society of Photogrammetry.
Strandberg, C. H.
  1962   Ancient indian fishtraps in the Potamac River. Photogrammetric Engineering **28**(3):476–478.
Strandberg, C. H. and R. Tomlinson
  1965   *Photoarchaeological analysis of Potomac River fish traps.* Alexandria, Virginia: Itek Data Analysis Center.
Stuart, Alan
  1962   Basic ideas of scientific sampling. *Griffin's statistical monographs and courses,* No. 4. London: Charles Griffin and Co., Ltd.
Stubbs, S. A.
  1950   *Brids's eye view of the pueblos.* Norman: University of Oklahoma Press.
Tabbagh, A.
  1977   Sur la determination du moment de mesure favorable et l'interpretation des resultats en prospection thermique archéologique. *Annales de Géophysique* **33**:179–188.
Thomas, D. H.
  1975   Nonsite sampling in archaeology: up the creek without a site? In *Sampling in archaeology,* edited by J. W. Mueller. Tucson: University of Arizona Press. Pp. 61–81.
Turpin, Solveig A., Richard P. Watson, Sarah Dennett, and Hans Muessig
  1979   Stereophotogrammetric documentation of exposed archeological features: *Journal of Field Archaeology* **6**(3):329–337.
van Wijk, M. C. and H. Ziemann
  1976   The use of non-metric cameras in monitoring high speed processes. *Photogrammetric Engineering and Remote Sensing* **42**(1):91–102.
Vogt, E. Z.
  1974a   Aerial photography in Highland Chiapas ethnography. In *Aerial photography in anthropological field research,* edited by E. Z. Vogt. Cambridge: Harvard University Press. Pp. 57–77.
Vogt, E. Z. (editor)
  1974b   *Aerial photography in anthropological field research.* Cambridge: Harvard University Press.
Walker, James
  1981   Improvements in low altitude aerial photography using ultra light aircraft. Report by James Walker, Photo Consultant, Brigham Young University, Provo, Utah.
Wedel, W. R.
  1953   Prehistory and the Missouri Development Program. Summary report on the Missouri River Basin archaeological survey in 1948. River Basin Survey Papers, *No. 1, Bureau of American Ethnology Bulletin* **151**:1–59.
Whittlesey, J. H.
  1966a   Bipod cameras support. *Photogrammetric Engineering* **32**(6):1005–1010.
  1966b   Photogrammetry for the excavator. *Archaeology* **19**:273–276.
  1967   Balloon Over Sardis. *Archaeology* **20**:67–68.
  1969   Balloon and airfoil photography. *MASCA Newsletter* **5**(2). Philadelphia: Museum Applied Science Center for Archaeology, University of Pennsylvania.
  1970   Tethered balloon for archaeological photos. *Photogrammetric Engineering* **36**(2):181–186.
  1971   Aerial photo balloon. *Archaeology* **24**(2):174.

Willey, G. R.
  1953   Prehistoric settlement patterns in the Viru Valley, Peru. *Bureau of American Ethnology Bulletin* **155.**
  1959   Aerial photographic maps as survey aids in Viru Valley. In *The Archaeologist at work,* edited by R. F. Heizer. Pp. 203–207. New York: Harper and Brothers.

Wills, W. H.
  1980   Ninety-Six National Historic Site, South Carolina: Remote Sensing Assessment. In *Cultural Resources Remote Sensing,* edited by T. R. Lyons and F. J. Mathien. Washington, D.C.: Cultural Resources Management Division, National Park Service. Pp. 229–265.

Wolf, Paul
  1974   *Elements of photogrammetry.* New York: McGraw-Hill.

Wood, Walter F.
  1955   Use of stratified random samples in a land-use study. *Annals of the Association of American Geographers* **45**:350–367.

Wood, W. R. and D. L. Johnson
  1978   A survey of disturbance processes in archaeological site formation. In *Advances in archaeological method and theory,* Vol. 1, edited by M. B. Shiffer, New York: Academic Press. Pp. 315–381.

Geomagnetic Dating Methods in Archaeology

DANIEL WOLFMAN

INTRODUCTION

The importance of chronometric studies in archaeology cannot be overstated. Most studies of culture change, which are at the heart of archaeological research, ultimately depend on control of the temporal dimension. Archaeomagnetic direction dating and other geomagnetic dating methods discussed in this chapter can contribute greatly to the solution of many important chronological problems in archaeology.

The impact of the most widely used archaeological dating method, radiocarbon, has been described as revolutionary (Renfrew 1973; Thomas 1978:232). The application of this method, which was an integral part of the transformation of archaeology during the past quarter century, has led to the resolution of many culture-historical problems, thus allowing archaeologists more time to devote to processual studies. However, radiocarbon dating has not solved, nor is it capable of solving, all chronometric problems. In some situations, samples suitable for ^{14}C dating are not available. In addition, this method is not precise enough to resolve many of the processual questions being asked today, including those involving stability and change of settlement patterns and population size. In some cases conflicting radiocarbon results have led to differences of opinion

ADVANCES IN ARCHAEOLOGICAL
METHOD AND THEORY, VOL. 7

about basic chronological sequences. Finally, the radiocarbon method cannot ordinarily date material older than about 40,000 years.

For these reasons and others, the search for additional dating methods has been an important research topic in recent years. Numerous books (e.g., Aitken 1974) and articles (e.g., Taylor 1978) reviewing the various methods have appeared. With the exception of dendrochronology, which existed before ^{14}C but is of limited geographical applicability, and some of those methods restricted to dating very old material (e.g., potassium–argon and fission tracks), none of these has yet fulfilled its expectations. However, while not yet widely used, geomagnetic dating methods have the potential to provide useful chronometric information on material ranging up to several million years in age. In addition, because past geomagnetic direction and intensity are recorded in a variety of materials, the potential areas of application are quite broad. The most important of these methods, archaeomagnetic direction dating, is capable of providing results that are very precise on samples collected from baked archaeological features up to about 10,000 years in age. In some areas this method is beginning to supplement data provided by the radiocarbon method.

The field of study concerned with the application of time-variant geomagnetic phenomena to archaeology and the use of archaeological material in elucidating past behavior of the geomagnetic field is referred to as *archaeomagnetism.* Archaeomagnetism is part of the broad field of *paleomagnetism,* which includes studies of the time variations of the earth's magnetic field, the origins of remanent magnetism, and the application of geomagnetic results to geology and other fields. Paleomagnetism, in turn, is part of a broader field, *geomagnetism,* which also includes studies of the manner in which the earth's magnetic field is generated. In recent years, paleomagnetic studies have virtually revolutionized the field of geology. The many important contributions of paleomagnetism include confirmation of the previously strongly disputed theory of continental drift and the discovery that the geomagnetic field has reversed its polarity many times in the past.

The first of the two basic phenomena that make geomagnetic dating possible is the acquisition of remanent magnetism by fired clay, volcanic rock, and sediment. Fired clay and volcanic rock acquire a magnetism parallel to the direction and proportional to the intensity of the magnetic field in which they cool. Some ocean and lacustrine sediments record the geomagnetic direction at the time of their deposition, perhaps with a magnetic moment proportional to the intensity of the ambient field.

The second basic phenomenon is that the direction and intensity (or strength) of the geomagnetic field vary through time. Change in the direction and intensity of the geomagnetic field with periodicities of hundreds or thousands of years is called *secular variation.* The magnitude of secular variation of direction is on the order of several tens of degrees and that of secular variation of intensity is on the order of 1 oersted (see Appendix 1 for definitions of magnetic units). A change in the polarity of the geomagnetic field is referred to as a *reversal*. A drastic shift of the geomagnetic direction at a point on the earth's surface, away from its alignment toward the polar region followed by a return (probably occurring in less than ca. 2000 years), is referred to as an *excursion*. Reversals and excursions, because they involve such radical changes in the direction of the geomagnetic field, and are relatively rare, serve as time markers against which some very old sites may be approximately dated.

The history of the changes of geomagnetic direction and intensity cannot be determined analytically. The master sequences of secular variation and polarity changes can only be determined by laboratory measurements on samples collected from suitable material. In order to calibrate such sequences, at least some of the samples must be dated by independent methods. Consequently, in the process of establishing the master sequences used in the various geomagnetic dating methods, valuable information about the history of the earth's magnetic field is obtained. These data are particularly important in generating and testing models about the nature of the geomagnetic field. This is one of many instances where archaeological dating methods serve as a focus of interdisciplinary research.

The term *archaeomagnetic dating* is used to refer to those archaeological dating methods based on secular variation of the geomagnetic field. It has also sometimes been used specifically for the dating method based on secular variation of direction using baked clay samples (Wolfman 1979; Eighmy *et al.* 1980). In this chapter to avoid confusion, the more cumbersome term *archaeomagnetic direction dating* is used for the latter. Although the three terms *paleointensity, archaeointensity,* and *archaeomagnitudes* have all been used when referring to intensity measurements made on fired clay from archaeological sites, the first is most widely used and is used here. As indicated above, among the geomagnetic methods it is archaeomagnetic direction dating that is having, and will continue to have, the greatest impact on archaeological research. Reasonably accurate dating with a precision of ±15 to ±60 years at the 95% confidence level can often be obtained on samples of 8 to 10 individually oriented specimens collected from baked archaeological features for most regions and time periods where the past direction of the geomagnetic field is known. The features dated—hearths, kilns, and the floors and walls of burned buildings—are usually of primary cultural importance. Therefore, questions of association that arise in tree-ring, radiocarbon, and some other dating methods are avoided.

Archaeological dating based on past geomagnetic intensity change has yet to be accomplished, but the potential for a useful method appears to be there. Paleointensity measurements can be made on unoriented samples of fired clay, thus avoiding the tedious field procedures necessary for archaeomagnetic direction dating. Of greater importance, a dating method based on this variable has the potential to date pottery, the most common and stylistically diagnostic artifact found in many sites. The rates of change observed in several regions during different time periods and the precision with which the past intensity can be measured on fired clay samples indicate that paleointensity dating may, in some situations, have a precision comparable to that based on secular variation of direction. With both methods, the age of the sample must be approximately known because direction and intensity are not unique functions of time.

Most archaeologists have heard of something called "archaeomagnetic dating"; however, many are unaware of the ways in which the geomagnetic field changes through time and the ways in which baked clay, lava, and sediments acquire a remanent magnetism. These ideas are crucial to understanding the potential of the various geomagnetic methods. They are discussed in detail in geophysics textbooks (e.g., McElhinny 1973) but they have never been summarized for an archaeological audience. Before discussing the dating methods per se and the work thus far accomplished, these topics are reviewed in some detail.

As with any technical subject there are many new terms to be mastered. For the most part they are not difficult to understand. In addition, many of these terms are often replaced with abbreviations of a type that is used with increasing frequency in technical literature (e.g., CRM for chemical remanent magnetism). While these geomagnetic abbreviations are an extra burden when initially encountered, they are no more numerous than those that are found in many other fields. Since they are found throughout the basic literature, it seems advisable to introduce and use them here. The basic terms and their abbreviations are tabulated, with reference to the page on which they are defined, in Appendix 2.

As in other physical sciences, a number of concepts are quantified. For most purposes, archaeologists may regard the various scales of measurement as relative without any loss of comprehension. To make matters a little more confusing, two scales are commonly used in geomagnetic studies. Originally, units were expressed in CGS (centimeter, gram, second) scale but an MKS (meter, kilogram, second) scale is being used with increasing frequency, particularly in some journals. Most paleomagnetists, however, continue to think and talk in the CGS scale; consequently, this scale is used in this review chapter. Magnetic units in both scales are defined in Appendix 1.

THE GEOMAGNETIC FIELD

Description

The configuration of the geomagnetic field, which is generated by motion in the liquid core of the earth, is similar to that of a bar magnet. Such a magnetic field is said to be *dipolar*. The best first-order approximation to the earth's magnetic field at this time is a geocentric dipole inclined at 11.5° to the axis of rotation (Figure 6.1). The axis of this dipole field intersects the earth's surface at 78.5° north latitude, 70° west longitude and 78.5° south latitude, 110° east longitude. These points are called the *north* and *south geomagnetic poles*. Although the earth's magnetic field is essentially dipolar, it has a considerable non-dipole component (comprising about 20% of the total field); consequently, compass readings taken at different points on the surface of the earth do not point to a

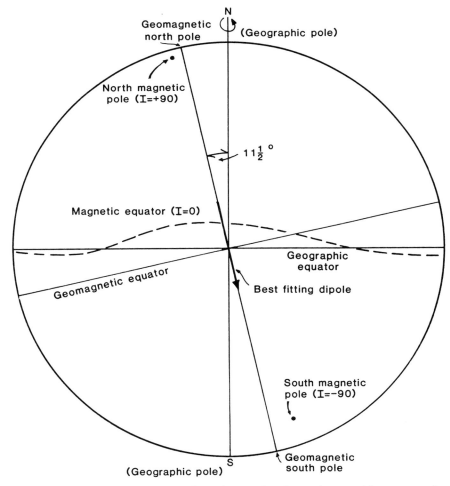

Figure 6.1. Geographic, geomagnetic, and magnetic poles, and geographic, geomagnetic, and magnetic equators. (From McElhinny 1973:5, Figure 3.)

single location. The difference between the field due to the inclined dipole and the total field is referred to as the *non-dipole field*.

At any point on the surface of the earth, the geomagnetic field can be defined by three parameters: declination D, inclination I, and intensity F. The number of degrees variation between true north and the direction that the compass needle points is referred to as *declination*. The northseeking pole of a balanced magnetic needle aligned toward magnetic north and suspended so that it can swing in a vertical plane will point down in most of the northern hemisphere and up in most of the southern hemisphere. The number of degrees between the magnetic direction and horizontal is referred to as *inclination* or *dip*. The intensity, or strength, of the geomagnetic field also varies over the surface of the earth. As with any essentially dipole field, the earth's field is strongest near the geomagnetic poles and weakest near the geomagnetic equator. Inclination also increases with geomagnetic latitude λ and is horizontal at the *magnetic equator* and vertical at the *magnetic* (or *dip*) *poles*. These variables are related in the following way:

$$I = \tan^{-1}(2 \tan \lambda) \tag{1}$$
$$F = Mr^{-3}(1 + 3 \sin^2 \lambda)^{\frac{1}{2}} \tag{2}$$

where F is the intensity at geomagnetic latitude λ, M the moment of the dipole, and r the radius of the earth.

Contour maps of non-dipole intensity (Figure 6.2) show highs and lows as closed roughly concentric loops, referred to as *non-dipole anomalies* or *features*.

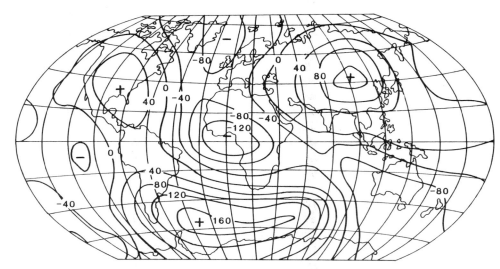

Figure 6.2.   World map showing 40 milligauss contours of the vertical component of the non-dipole field in 1945. (From Tarling 1971:97, Figure 7.3.)

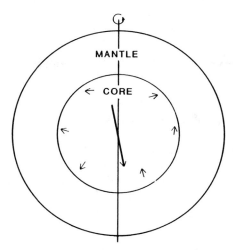

Figure 6.3.   Model of the sources of the geomagnetic field showing a strong central dipole and weaker eccentric dipoles.

For many years it has been common practice to model the geomagnetic field with a large dipole at the center of the earth with smaller eccentric dipoles responsible for the anomalies (Figure 6.3).

In addition to expressing the direction of the geomagnetic field at a point on the earth's surface in terms of declination and inclination, it is often useful to represent these data as a *virtual geomagnetic pole* (VGP). This is defined as the north geomagnetic pole of a geocentric dipole that would generate the declination and inclination values measured at the particular location. The formulas for calculating VGPs from declination and inclination can be found in any basic paleomagnetism text (e.g., McElhinny 1973:23–25).

Polar plots (see Figure 6.4) on which VGPs are plotted are read in the following way: the center of the figure where the perpendicular lines cross is the geographic north pole. The concentric circles are lines of latitude. (On most of the figures they mark 5° intervals, however, on Figure 6.4 they are at 10° intervals. The line marked "0" is the 0° longitude line. Longitudes west are measured in a clockwise direction and are denoted as negative, whereas longitudes east are measured counterclockwise and are denoted using positive numbers.

Analogously, it is often useful to represent geomagnetic intensity in terms of a fictitious central dipole. Because intensity F is a function of both the moment of the geomagnetic field and its inclination (see Equations 1 and 2), it is sometimes desirable to eliminate the effects of the latter. If the inclination is known, its effect can be eliminated by calculating the virtual dipole moment (VDM) using the following formula:

$$\text{VDM} = \frac{Fr^3}{[1 + 3\sin^2(\tan^{-1}(\frac{1}{2}\tan I))]^{\frac{1}{2}}} \tag{3}$$

As is discussed below, when past intensity is measured using pottery samples the inclination is not known. In such situations the intensity value is often converted to a *virtual axial dipole moment* (VADM) that assumes, for want of further information, that the past dipole is oriented along the axis of the earth. Consequently, it usually contains a considerable contribution due to the inclination of the geomagnetic field. It has been estimated that the portion of the inclination variation due to change in direction of the central dipole (*dipole wobble*) alone contributes on the average about 21 to 43% of the intensity variation at 45° latitude (Barton *et al.* 1979:101). Additional variation in intensity values is due to changes in direction of the non-dipole anomalies. (The VADM can be calculated directly by solving for *M* in Equation 2 with λ equal to the *geographic* latitude.)

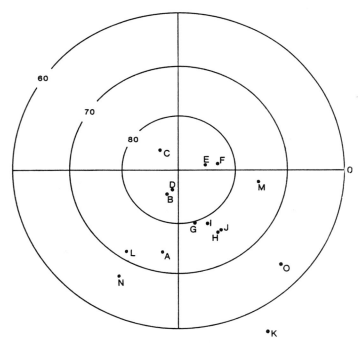

Figure 6.4. 1975 virtual geomagnetic poles for 15 major cities around the world: A, New York; B, London; C, Moscow; D, New Delhi; E, Peiping; F, Tokyo; G, Honolulu; H, San Francisco; I, Mexico City; J, Lima; K, Santiago; L, Rio de Janeiro; M, Salisbury; N, Capetown; O, Canberra. (VGPs calculated from declination and inclination data on Defense Mapping Agency Hydrographic Center 1975a,b)

Since magnetic intensity is inversely proportional to the cube of the distance from the source, the strengths of VDMs and VADMs due to a fictitious geocentric dipole are enormous (on the order of 10^{26} gauss cm^3).

Another procedure for partially normalizing past geomagnetic field strength is to divide the measured paleointensity F by the modern intensity F_0 at the site. However, because the current dipole field is inclined at $11.5°$ and because F_0 values reflect modern non-dipole anomalies, VADMs provide a better indication of intensity variation.

Since, as noted above, the modern geomagnetic field has a significant nondipole component, the locations of contemporaneous VGPs measured from different places on the surface of the earth vary considerably (Figure 6.4). In the same manner, contemporary VDMs and VADMs also vary. However, in a reasonably small region, usually on the order of 800 to 1600 km (ca. 500 to 1000 miles) in diameter, contemporaneous VGPs, VDMs, or VADMs are almost identical and, therefore, are more useful in regional studies of past changes in the geomagnetic field than are the measured values of D, I, and F.

Secular Variation

The declination, inclination, and intensity measured at any point on the surface of the earth are constantly changing. There are minor short-term fluctuations referred to as *transient variation* and, as mentioned above, larger long-term fluctuations with periods of hundreds or thousands of years, referred to as *secular variation*. Transient variations are due to sources external to the earth and are not discussed further. Secular variation of geomagnetic direction within a region is best depicted by a temporally sequential series of VGPs. The best line fit to such a series of points is called a *polar curve* (see Figure 6.7; p. 401).

Changes in the location, intensity, and direction of the anomalies mentioned above, in combination with changes in intensity and direction of the dipole field, are responsible for secular variation of declination, inclination, and intensity. Using high-quality observatory data collected during this century, Bullard *et al.* (1950) demonstrated that the average movement of the nondipole anomalies between A.D. 1905 and 1944 was about .18° of longitude per year to the west. The general tendency for the anomalies to move to the west is referred to as *westward drift*. Using poorer and spotty geomagnetic data recorded between 1600 and 1900, Yukutake and Tachinaka (1968a,b) and Barraclough (1974) have extended the work of Bullard *et al.* (1950) to earlier time periods. Yukutake and Tachinaka (1968a:1059–1062) found that during the past 400 years some of these anomalies of the geomagnetic field appear to be drifting whereas others (sometimes referred to as *standing anomalies*) are stationary. In addition, they found that some of the anomalies flucturated in intensity whereas some of the standing anomalies were fairly stable. It is generally believed that those anomalies which fluctuate in intensity form and decay with periods on the order of hundreds to thousands of years (Bullard *et al.* 1950; Yukutake 1979).

Until recently, primarily because of slow dipole movement during the past 150 years (McDonald and Gunst 1967) and erroneous interpretations of secular variation data recorded in Hawaiian lavas (e.g., Doell and Cox 1971; see Coe *et al.* [1978] for a recent discussion of these data), it was widely believed that dipole wobble did not contribute significantly to short-term secular variation. However, recent analyses of sparse direction data recorded between A.D. 1550 and 1830 suggest that dipole wobble was considerably more rapid during that time period (Barraclough 1974:510; Yukutake 1979:84–85). In addition, archaeomagnetic data (Kawai *et al.* 1965; Barbetti 1977; Lin *et al.* 1979; Champion 1980:134–138) indicate that there has been considerable dipole wobble (perhaps a full period or more) during the past 2000 years.

Recent statistical analysis of paleointensity data from around the world suggests that the dipole field has varied sinusoidally through one complete period during the past 8000 years (Barton *et al.* 1979). Although there has been a tendency to extrapolate the apparent 8000-year period of sinusoidal variation in intensity back in time (e.g., Cox 1968), the few intensity values obtained from earlier time periods (Barbetti and Flude 1979) do not vary in this regular manner.

Reversals and Excursions

Reversals

One of the most interesting features of the geomagnetic field is its occasional reversal of polarity. So surprising was this concept that not so many years ago the possibility was considered that all rocks magnetized in the direction opposite to the direction of the modern geomagnetic field had the property (referred to as *self-reversing*) of becoming magnetized in the direction opposed to the ambient field when they cool (see Cox *et al.* 1964 and Wilson 1967 for a discussion of competing arguments in the mid-1960s). The development of potassium–argon dating and the extensive paleomagnetic sampling programs carried out on volcanic rocks in the 1960s (e.g., Chamalaun and McDougall 1966; Cox *et al.* 1964, 1967) demonstrated conclusively that contemporaneous rocks around the world have the same polarity. This work, which confirmed earlier studies (Mercanton 1926a,b; Matuyama 1929) based on less-secure data, led to the universal acceptance of the phenomenon of geomagnetic field reversal. It should be noted that although self-reversing rocks do occur naturally (Nagata *et al.* 1952), and their existence at one time was the strongest part of the argument against geomagnetic field reversals, they are apparently very rare.

In the past 20 years, evidence from several sources has provided detailed data on the polarity stratigraphy for the past billion years. Measurements made on igneous rocks independently dated by the potassium–argon method were particu-

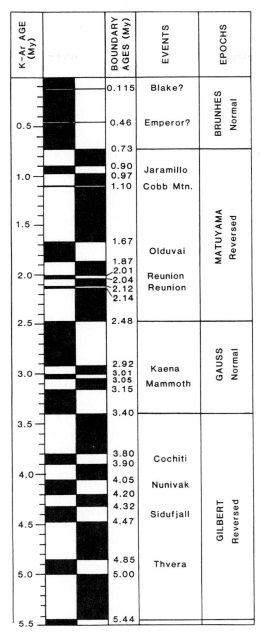

Figure 6.5. Polarity time scale: 5.5 million years B.P. to present. (After Mankinen and Dalrymple 1979:624, Figure 3, with additions from McDougall 1979 and Champion et al. 1981.)

larly important in defining the most recent 5 million years of the polarity scale with great precision and accuracy (Mankinen and Dalrymple 1979; see Figure 6.5). Magnetic measurements on sediments cored from the ocean bottom and on sedimentary rocks greatly extended the polarity record. Another source of information is from basalts that rise in molten form in the middle of the ocean during the process referred to as *sea-floor spreading*. When the basalts are cooled by ocean water they become magnetized in the direction of the ambient magnetic field. As new basalt rises, the older material spreads out from the source and parallel strips of magnetized basalt on the ocean floor then record the sequence of geomagnetic polarity (Vine and Matthews 1963). Data from all four sources have been used to define the polarity scale with somewhat less precision and accuracy for time periods greater than 5 million years. Detailed studies of these data have demonstrated a worldwide sequence of long periods (on the order of 1 million years or longer) of *normal* (what we have today) and *reversed* polarity, referred to as *epochs,* with occasional short periods (ca. 10^5 years or less) of opposite polarity, referred to as *events*. The four most recent epochs were named for important individuals in the history of geomagnetic studies.

The current epoch of normal polarity, called the Brunhes, began about 700,000 years ago. It was preceded by the Matuyama reversed epoch of about 1.8 million years in length. The Gauss (normal; 3.4–2.5 million years B.P.) and the Gilbert (reversed; 5.2–3.4 million years B.P.) are the only other named epochs. The earlier epochs are numbered. Events within the four latest epochs have received names referring to the localities where they were first discovered. Although the polarity sequence presented in Figure 6.5 is based on a recent synthesis of all available data, there are some data (Champion *et al.* 1981; Liddicoat *et al.* 1980) as well as theoretical arguments (Cox 1972) for additional very short events.

The paleomagnetic record not only provides the basis for the polarity scale but also provides data on the reversal process itself. Based on several studies (e.g., Opdyke *et al.* 1973), it appears that a reversal is not a rapid flip but rather a process that usually takes about 4500 years (Fuller *et al.* 1979). The process usually starts with the intensity of the field dropping by as much as an order of magnitude and then building up with an opposite polarity.

Excursions

Excursions, which bear some superficial similarities to reversals, involve rapid (probably less than ca. 2000 years) drastic changes in geomagnetic field direction, during which the VGP shifts more than 45° from the geographic pole and then returns to the same polar region it was in before the excursion began. Most of the available data suggest that during an excursion the VGP does not pass beyond the equatorial region, but the possibility exists that during some excursions the VGP could follow a path through the opposing polar region.

There may be more than one geomagnetic mechanism responsible for excursions. It certainly is conceivable that a strong nondipole feature (or perhaps two acting together) could cause an excursion that would be recorded only on a portion of the surface of the earth (Harrison and Ramirez 1975; Coe 1977). Such a large feature(s) drifting (westward) might cause a series of excursions. These possibilities are particularly plausible during a time when the dipole field is of relatively low intensity, thus enhancing any non-dipole field effects (Liddicoat and Coe 1979). It is even conceivable that at a time of low dipole intensity separate anomalies might cause independent but contemporaneous excursions. Because reversals begin with a drop in dipole field strength, the occurrence of such excursions might, in some situations, be due to a reversal that did not "lock-in" (Cox 1975). An alternate, although perhaps less likely, explanation for excursions is a radical shift of the entire dipole field. Differing interpretations of data suggesting that such a shift of the dipole field might have occurred at circa 30,000 B.P. have been discussed by Freed and Healy (1974) and Barbetti and McElhinny (1976).

Although there is good evidence for pre-Brunhes epoch excursions, particularly in data obtained from Icelandic lavas (Doell 1972; Watkins and Walker 1977), much of the data in the recent literature on late Brunhes epoch excursions is suspect. Until recently it was thought (Noel and Tarling 1975) that there was considerable evidence for a worldwide excursion at about 12,000 B.P., but this is now generally discounted. At least one of the lavas that provided data for an excursion at this time is self-reversing (Heller 1980) and was incorrectly dated (Gillot et al. 1979). Although by no means universally accepted, there is increasing evidence for one or more excursions at about 30,000 B.P. (Barbetti and McElhinny 1976; Freed and Healy 1974; Gillot et al. 1979; Liddicoat and Coe 1979).

THE ACQUISITION OF REMANENT MAGNETISM BY FIRED CLAY AND SEDIMENTS

The magnetism in fired clay, rocks, and sediments is due to small grains of iron-rich magnetic minerals (said to be *ferromagnetic*), dilutely dispersed in a matrix consisting of silicates and other nonmagnetic material. At ambient temperatures these ferromagnetic minerals retain their magnetism in the absence of an applied field. There is, however, a crucial temperature for each ferromagnetic mineral, called the *Curie temperature*, above which it loses its magnetism in the absence of an applied field. The Curie temperatures of what are apparently the two most common magnetic minerals found in fired clay, magnetite (Fe_3O_4) and hematite ($\alpha\text{-}Fe_2O_3$), are 578 and 680° C respectively. Impure forms of magnetite and hematite, particularly with titanium replacing some of the iron, are also important and may behave quite differently than the pure iron oxide. Other magnetic minerals that are of interest in archaeomagnetic studies include goethite (α-FeOOH), lepidocrocite (γ-FeOOH), and maghemite (γ-Fe$_2$O$_3$).

The naturally occurring magnetism of fired clay, rocks, and sediments is referred to as *natural remanent magnetism* (NRM). NRM consists of two types of components: a primary component acquired when the material is heated and cooled or deposited, and secondary components acquired at a later time. An important step in archaeomagnetic direction dating is the elimination of secondary components.

The basic ideas on the acquisition of remanence presented in this section are discussed at much greater length in many books and articles. The texts by Nagata (1961) and McElhinny (1973:32–67), a collection of papers (Dunlop 1977), and a recent review article (Day 1979) will provide the interested reader with a more rigorous introduction to this topic. Theoretical and experimental support for many of the statements made in this section as well as references to the vast rock magnetism literature can also be found in these publications.

Remanent Magnetism in Fired Clay and the Neel Theory

Thermal remanent magnetism (TRM) due solely to heat and *chemical remanent magnetism* (CRM) due to chemical or crystallographic changes below the Curie temperature are responsible for the portion of the natural remanent magnetism of fired clay and igneous rocks acquired when the material is heated and cooled in the earth's magnetic field.

The major portion of the remanent magnetism in most igneous rocks (Evans and McElhinny 1969; McElhinny 1973:48–49) and fired clay is due to very small ferromagnetic particles, each of which acts like a little magnet. Such particles are called *single-domain* or *pseudosingle-domain* grains, depending on their size. The remanent magnetism in each grain is ordinarily oriented along its long axis, which is referred to as the *easy axis*. Larger grains of ferromagnetic material consist of several or many domains (and hence are referred to as *multidomain grains*), which are generally much more weakly magnetized than the single-domain grains and apparently in most but perhaps not all situations do not contribute greatly to the remanence of fired clay. Fired clay is often oxidized with a characteristic red, orange, or yellow color indicating that it has a significant hematite content (magnetite is black). However, because single-domain magnetite is about 100 times more strongly magnetized per unit volume than hematite, a small amount of this material will dominate the more abundant hematite magnetically. A variety of experimental data (e.g., Baumgartner 1973) suggest that in many situations magnetite is the principal magnetic carrier in fired clay. Among these is the strength of fired clay, which usually varies between

10^{-5} and 10^{-3} emu/cc, and occasionally is as high as 10^{-2} emu/cc (see Appendix I for definition of *emu*). More research is certainly needed on the important topic of the magnetic properties of fired clay.

Neel Single-Domain Theory

The following simplified version of a theory developed by Neel (1949, 1955) gives a general idea of the way in which remanent magnetism is acquired in single-domain grains in fired clay.

As noted above, each single-domain grain can be thought of as a tiny magnet with an easy axis of magnetization along which it is magnetized. The magnetization along the easy axis can be reversed if there is enough energy due either to a sufficiently strong applied magnetic field with a component perpendicular to the easy axis and/or to heat. The field strength applied perpendicularly to the direction of magnetism in a particular single-domain grain at 20° C that is required to reverse it is referred to as the *coercive force* or *coercivity* H_c. Coercive force is a function of the mineralogy of the grain and its size and shape. The field strength required to reverse the magnetic direction in a grain is inversely proportional to temperature and is directly proportional to grain size. Magnetic components with low coercivity are said to be *soft*, whereas high coercivity components are called *hard*. Hematite is generally much harder than magnetite.

In the absence of a magnetic field the magnetic directions of domains in an ideal material, consisting of identical single-domain grains, will become randomly remagnetized whenever they are heated above a critical temperature (referred to as the *blocking temperature*) for a short period of time and then cooled. The blocking temperature of most of the remanent magnetism in most igneous rocks and fired clays is between the Curie temperature of magnetite and 100°C below it. The temperature of any material is a function of the average rate of vibration of its constituent atoms. At ambient temperature the atoms in some domains (usually a very small percentage of the total number) at any point in time are sufficiently agitated so that they can acquire a new magnetic direction. This will cause the remanence to decay at ambient temperature in the absence of a magnetic field according to the following equation:

$$M_r = M_0 \exp(-t/\tau) \tag{4}$$

where M_0 is the initial remanence, M_r the remanence after time t, and τ is called the *relaxation time,* which is the mean lifetime of these domains (the half-life of the remanence is .693τ) (In the rock magnetism literature M is used for the total magnetic moment whereas J is used for moment per unit volume.)

In the presence of a magnetic field, domains with a short relaxation time will tend to become magnetized in the direction along the easy axis closest to the field direction.

Ferromagnetic material, if exposed to an increasingly strong magnetic field, will acquire, up to a point, an increasingly strong magnetic moment. The maximum moment per unit volume that can be acquired, which is dependent on grain mineralogy, shape, and volume, is called *saturation magnetization* J_s.

Finally, relaxation time τ is related to coercive force H_c, grain volume v, temperature T, and saturation magnetization J_s in the following way:

$$\tau \sim \exp\left(\frac{vH_cJ_s}{T}\right) \tag{5}$$

Thermal Remanent Magnetism.   Thermal remanent magnetism (TRM) is acquired as heated material cools below the blocking temperatures of its constituent domains. The crucial facts about TRM include the following:

1. It is acquired in a direction parallel (or nearly so) to the direction of the ambient field. Each domain, of course, is not magnetized in the direction of the ambient field, but rather the randomly oriented grains are each magnetized along the easy axis in the direction nearest the ambient field. It is the average direction of all these grains that is parallel to the ambient field.

2. The great stability of TRM follows immediately from Equation 5. For example, grains that have a relaxation time of 100 seconds at a blocking temperature of 500° C will have a relaxation time of about 10^{14} years at 20° C. However, because a typical archaeomagnetic specimen (ca. 10 cc) contains a very large number of ferromagnetic grains, some grains throughout the blocking temperature spectrum will reverse their magnetic directions in any finite length of time giving rise to a (usually small) secondary viscous component.

3. Material consisting of randomly oriented ferromagnetic grains, such as are found in clay, will acquire a remanence linearly proportional to the ambient field up to about 1 gauss (Nagata 1943:88–91), and in some situations somewhat higher, when it is cooled from the Curie temperature.

4. The strength of TRM is directly proportional to cooling time (Neel 1949:131; Coe 1967b:169).

5. The strength of TRM is directly proportional to coercive force (Nagata 1961:158), and also (from Equation 5) to relaxation time.

6. The portion of the remanence acquired on cooling through any temperature interval (from T_2 down to T_1) is called *partial thermal remanent magnetism* (PTRM). It will be lost when the sample is heated in a zero field from T_1 to T_2 and further the sum of the PTRMs is equal to the total TRM. This law of additivity, which was first demonstrated experimentally by Thellier (1938) and derived theoretically by Neel (1949), is one of the most basic and

important in rock magnetism. Although the blocking temperature spectrum in typical fired clay extends down to room temperature and even below, usually only a small portion of the remanence is acquired below 200° C.

Chemical Remanent Magnetism. Chemical remanent magnetism (CRM) occurs when a chemical change in a ferromagnetic mineral takes place below the Curie temperature. The remanence is acquired as the crystal of the newly formed ferromagnetic mineral grows above a crucial size (referred to as the *blocking diameter*) where the relaxation time increases rapidly (see Equation 5). This is analogous to the rapid increase in relaxation time in the vicinity of the blocking temperature. Experimental studies (e.g., Kobayashi 1959) have shown that CRM behaves in some respects like TRM and cannot be fully erased unless the material is heated to its Curie temperature even though it is generally acquired at a much lower temperature. Based on experiments carried out by Kobayashi (1959) on pure hematite reduced to magnetite at 300° C, it has often been stated (e.g., Irving 1964:28–29) that the strength of CRM is much less, (ca. one-tenth) the TRM acquired in the same field. However, some recent experimental data suggest that other magnetic minerals may acquire a CRM much closer in strength to the thermal remanence (D. E. Champion, personal communication, 1982).

Viscous Remanent Magnetism. As an immediate consequence of Equations 4 and 5, rocks, sediments, and fired clay that contain ferromagnetic material in a wide range of grain sizes will acquire a secondary remanence referred to as *viscous remanent magnetism* (VRM). Some grains (said to be *superparamagnetic*) may be so small (below ca. .05 microns in diameter for magnetite and hematite) that a change in field direction can bring about an almost instantaneous reversal in the direction of magnetism in the grain. From Point 5 in the subsection on thermal remanent magnetism and Equation 5, it follows that the stronger its TRM the more resistant a material is to the acquisition of VRM. In addition, because relaxation time is inversely proportional to temperature, what is called a *high temperature viscous remanent magnetism* can be acquired when a ferromagnetic material is heated for a sufficient length of time to somewhat below the highest blocking temperature of its constituent grains. This accounts for the relation between cooling time and TRM intensity mentioned above.

Isothermal Remanent Magnetism. A magnetic field with a component perpendicular to the domain direction stronger than the coercive force can reverse the direction of magnetism in a domain at ambient temperature. A remanence of this type, which can be caused naturally by lightning, is called *isothermal remanent magnetism* (IRM) and can add a significant secondary component in a direction quite different from that of the primary magnetism.

Anhysteretic Remanent Magnetism. An additional type of remanence, *anhysteretic remanent magnetism* (ARM), may be acquired either intentionally or unintentionally in the laboratory. It is due to a steady field in conjunction with a decreasing alternating field. This type of remanence is acquired by those domains whose coercive forces are overcome by the alternating field. As the alternating field attenuates, these domains are magnetized in the direction along their easy axes closest to the direction of the steady field. Although not yet well studied, ARM can be acquired naturally due to alternating fields sometimes associated with lightning (Aitken 1974:148–149).

Rotational Remanent Magnetism. A number of years ago, Doell and Cox (1967) noticed that a remanence was induced in a specimen rotated about an axis perpendicular to an alternating magnetic field generated in a solenoid. Subsequently, Wilson and Lomax (1972) pointed out that such a remanence, which they called *rotational remanent magnetism* (RRM), can arise as long as the angle between the axis of rotation and the alternating field is greater than zero and reaches a maximum when they are perpendicular. Not all material is susceptible to RRM; it has been found in sediments (Hillhouse and Cox 1976:55) but thus far it has not been reported in fire clay. For many years it was generally believed that the best way to eliminate certain types of secondary components was to tumble (i.e., rotate simultaneously about two or more axes) the specimens during alternating field demagnetization (Collinson 1975:669–671). Since the discovery of RRM, alternating field demagnetizers without tumblers have become popular.

Anisotropy

One of the most important facts that makes archaeomagnetic direction dating possible is that fired clay usually acquires a TRM that is parallel to the direction of the field in which it cools. Materials with this property are said to be *isotropic;* those that do not have it are *anisotropic.* Although individual grains are severely anisotropic, if they are dispersed in random orientation, as they usually are in soil and clay, and if the remanent magnetism of the fired clay is not too strong, the material will be isotropic. Unfortunately, these conditions are not always met. When anisotropy occurs in fired clay it is due to either nonrandom alignment of the constituent ferromagnetic grains (*fabric anisotropy*) or distortion of the geomagnetic field due to the magnetism acquired by the fired clay as it cools (*shape anisotropy*).

Fabric Anisotropy. When the easy axes of the constituent ferromagnetic grains are not randomly oriented, what is called *fabric anisotropy* will occur in fired clay. Limited laboratory experimentation (Baumgartner 1973) found no indication of fabric anisotropy in fired clay collected from baked archaeological features. In addition, the success of archaeomagnetic direction dating on such features and the very good agreement of direction measurements made on samples collected from modern and historic baked features with direct observation (Wolfman 1978; Krause 1980) suggests that fabric anisotropy is not a problem with such material. However, Rogers *et al.* (1979:645) have found significant fabric anisotropy in wheel-made pottery. This effect is presumably, in some manner, due to preferential grain alignment during the spinning of the vessel during construction. Fabric anisotropy has also been noted in some pottery manufactured using other techniques (Rogers *et al.* 1979; Sternberg 1982:142).

Shape Anisotropy.   Due to the configuration of a dipole field, magnetized material will have what is called a *demagnetizing field* opposite in direction to its remanent magnetism. As a piece of fired clay cools, if the remanence acquired at high temperatures is sufficiently strong, the demagnetizing field may significantly distort the local geomagnetic field. If this occurs, the direction of the PTRM acquired by those domains with lower blocking temperatures may vary somewhat from the direction of the ambient geomagnetic field. The strength (Stoner 1945) and direction of the distortion depends on the shape of the fired clay object, hence the term *shape* anisotropy. This phenomenon has been observed both in kilns (Aitken and Hawley 1971; Dunlop and Zinn 1980; Hoye 1982) and in pottery (Fox and Aitken 1978). Although a number of variables need to be considered, calculations by Aitken and Hawley (1971:84) suggest that remanences in excess of 4×10^{-3} emu/cc are needed to cause significant shape anisotropy.

Remanent Magnetism in Sediments

The possibility of using the remanent magnetic directions of sediments that have settled through reasonably quiet water as records of past geomagnetic field direction was first recognized more than 40 years ago (Ising 1942; McNish and Johnson 1938). Since the pioneering efforts of Ising and of Johnson, McNish, and their associates, considerable research has been undertaken on sediments from varved and unvarved lacustrine deposits and marginal and deep-sea sediments. There has also been some work on the remanent magnetism acquired by sediments in caves (Creer and Kopper 1976; Schmidt 1982).

Although most work in recent years has been undertaken on wet sediments obtained with coring devices from the bottom of existing lakes and oceans, there have been some very promising results obtained from sediments collected from profiles cut in dry lake beds.

Deep-sea sediments that are deposited very slowly (on the order of a few millimeters to a few centimeters per 1000 years) have been used with considerable success in helping to establish the reversal record during the past 9 million years. Sediments from sources deposited much more rapidly may in some situations provide valuable information about past secular variation of geomagnetic direction. Such sediments offer the possibility of long, continuous secular variation records. Unfortunately, the data thus far obtained are rarely comparable in quality to that obtained from fired clay.

The relatively poor secular variation records obtained from sediments is in a large part due to the complex manner in which many sediments acquire remanent magnetism. Three distinct processes are generally recognized. The alignment of magnetic particles as they settle through water and come to rest on the basin floor is called *depositional detrital remanent magnetism* (DRM) whereas alignment due to rotation after deposition in the wet sediment is termed *postdepositional detrital remanent magnetism* (PDRM) (Verosub 1977a:129). This latter effect is enhanced in many situations by bioturbation. An excellent review of detrital remanent magnetism by Verosub (1977a) is highly recommended to those who wish to pursue the topic further. In addition to depositional and postdepositional detrital remanent magentism, in some cases a significant portion of the remanence in sediments may be due to chemical remanent magnetism (CRM) that can come about by several different processes including oxidation, reduction, and hydration long after deposition.

Experimental work has identified the roles of some of the variables (including field strength and grain size and shape) involved in the acquisition of DRM and PDRM (Barton *et al.* 1980) and some useful discussions of the acquisition of CRM by sediments have also been published (Kent and Lowrie 1974; Johnson *et al.* 1975). However, in specific cases it is rarely clear how the remanent magnetism was acquired, how faithfully the past direction is recorded, and what portion of the remanence is contemporaneous with deposition. Thompson (1977:58) has pointed out that in some situations CRM may be acquired several hundred years after the deposition of lacustrine sediments. The time lag in specific situations due to bioturbation is usually impossible to determine. An additional problem caused by the acquisition of a portion or all of the remanence in sediments after deposition is the smoothing effect it has on the secular variation record. Turner and Thompson (1982) have recently discussed "detransformation" procedures that in some situations will reduce, or possibly eliminate, this smoothing effect.

Recently, Games (1977) has called attention to the remanent magnetism of adobe bricks which he suggests is not acquired due to DRM or PDRM but rather to some unspecified mechanism resulting from squeezing of mud as it is forced into a mold. Consequently, he refers to this mechanism as *shear remanent magnetism* (SRM). Stupavsky *et al.* (1979:271), when discussing this type of remanence, refer to it as *thixotropic* (TxRM), thereby suggesting that the mud is liquefied when it is thrown into a mold. If this is the case, the remanence is a type of PDRM. They also point out the TxRM can occur in sediments due to seismic shock or possibly even when plastic tubing is hammered into relatively dry sediments to collect specimens.

LABORATORY EQUIPMENT AND PROCEDURES

Introduction

Accurate measurements of remanent intensity and direction, which are important in all paleomagnetic studies, are particularly crucial in archaeomagnetic studies where small variations sometimes indicate large differences in age. Remanent magnetism can be measured either directly or by the electric current it induces. Several different types of instruments, all called *magnetometers,* have been developed to make such measurements.

In order to determine the direction of the primary magnetism, acquired at the time the clay was fired or the sediment deposited, secondary components, if present, must be eliminated. This process, called *magnetic cleaning* or *demagnetization,* is accomplished using *thermal* or *alternating field demagnetizers.* The details of the construction and operation of both magnetometers and demagnetizers have been discussed in a variety of sources including an excellent lengthy review by Collinson (1975).

Magnetic Shielding

The magnetic field in a laboratory is due to a combination of fields from the earth, ferromagnetic materials in buildings and office furniture, and electric currents. Because the ambient field is much stronger than the remanence in the specimens and because it changes considerably during the day, laboratory instruments need to be magnetically shielded from the surrounding environment. For many years, a set of Helmholtz coils (consisting of three pairs of mutually perpendicular circular or square electrical coils that can be adjusted to generate a magnetic field equal and opposite to the ambient field) was the standard magnetic shielding used in paleomagnetism laboratories. A more effective shield, which is commonly used today around the sensitive parts of magnetometers and demagnetizers, is an alloy commonly known as *mu metal.* Mu metal shields range in size from single-layer small boxes to an 8-foot cubical room surrounded by two layers of mu metal in which fields as low as one gamma can be maintained. Recently some shielded rooms have been constructed using transformer steel in place of the increasingly expensive mu metal.

Magnetometers

Four different types of magnetometers are commonly used to measure the remanent magnetism in fired clay, rock, and sediment specimens.

The simplest type of magnetometer, first used in the last century, is the *astatic magnetometer.* In its simplest configuration, it consists of little more than a pair of magnets of equal strength and opposite orientation at either end of a short rod suspended from a fine fiber. An alternate configuration, referred to as a *parastatic magnetometer,* eliminates the effects of extraneous horizontal magnetism with a uniform vertical gradient. This system consists of three evenly spaced magnets. The top and bottom magnets are of equal strength and are oriented in the same direction. The central magnet, which has twice the strength of the other two, is oriented in the opposite direction. As with an astatic magnetometer the cubic specimen is placed on a stage below the lowest magnet. It is aligned so that the axis of the magnets is above the center of the specimen and is parallel to two edges of its upper face. The specimen exerts greatest torque on the lowest magnet, thus deflecting the suspension a small amount proportional to the strength of the magnetism perpendicular to the alignment of the magnets in the horizontal plane. The small deflection of the suspended magnet system can be measured in the following way. A small mirror with a vertical line through its center is adhered to the rod connecting the magnets. A light reflected from the mirror onto a scale at a reasonable distance (as much as 5 m) greatly amplifies the deflection of the suspended magnets and allows the strengths of the mutually perpendicular components to be compared. A minimum of three measurements is needed to determine the remanent direction. To reduce the errors due to magnetic inhomogeneity as much as possible, measurements with the specimen in as many as 24 different positions can be made. The direction of the remanent magnetism is computed by vector addition from the average deflection in the three mutually perpendicular directions defined by the edge of the cube.

Carefully constructed parastatic magnetometers are capable of great sensitivity. Under unusual circumstances readings lower than 10^{-9} emu might be obtained (Roy 1963). However, measurements proceed slowly and to achieve great sensitivity the influence of changing magnetic fields must be eliminated and great mechanical stability is needed. Consequently, most laboratories have abandoned astatic magnetometers for cryogenic or spinner magnetometers, but some (including a few doing archaeomagnetic work) are in use in Europe, Japan, and Canada.

For many years *spinner magnetometers* have measured most of the specimens in paleomagnetism laboratories. The name of these instruments derives from the fact that the specimens are spun in a holder on the end of a shaft. The early models were based on the principle (which is used in large power plants) that a spinning magnet will induce a current in a nearby wire coil. In later models, the pick-up coils have been replaced by fluxgates that directly detect the sinusoidal magnetic signal as the specimen spins. Several different types of fluxgates have been used in spinner magnetometers. A ring configuration (Molyneaux 1971) which encircles the spinning specimen seems to give the most accurate readings, particularly on inhomogeneously magnetized specimens. The results from fluxgate spinners have also been improved by interfacing a small computer with the magnetometer to smooth the sinusoidal signal using Fourier analysis. Many pickup coil spinner magnetometers with sensitivity on the order of 10^{-5} emu have been built. With great care in construction and long measuring times sensitivities on the order of 10^{-7} emu are obtainable (McElhinny 1973:77). Fluxgate spinners with sensitivities on this order are available commercially (Molyneaux 1971).

In recent years, very sensitive *cryogenic magnetometers* with SQUID (superconducting quantum interference device) sensors have become increasingly important in paleomagnetic work (Goree and Fuller 1976). These instruments operate near the temperature of liquid helium ($-269°$ C), where there is no electrical resistance, by measuring the weak current induced in a coil when a specimen is placed within it. The great sensitivity (10^{-8} emu) and speed of operation (almost instantaneous) of this type of magnetometer has led to an explosion of studies on weakly magnetized sediments in recent years.

The details of the principles of operation of the spinner and cryogenic magnetometers are a bit technical and, consequently, are not described here. Interested readers are referred to the articles by Collinson (1975) and Goree and Fuller (1976) and the references cited in them.

Comparison of Magnetometers

The performance of magnetometers is limited by their sensitivity, speed of operation, and ability to measure accurately inhomogeneously magnetized material. Because fired clay is usually quite strongly magnetized by rock magnetism standards, most magnetometers have adequate sensitivity for archaeomagnetic work. Baumgartner (1973:22–30) and Thellier (1938:172–173; 1977:242–244) have noted that the magnetism in fired clay may be quite inhomogeneous due to variations in oxidation and temperature when they are baked. Thellier (1938: 172–173), Collinson (1977), and others have discussed measurement problems related to inhomogeneity in fired clay and other ferromagnetic material. Magnetometers with pick-up coils (superconducting and spinning) are usually less prone to errors due to inhomogeneity than are those that measure magnetism directly (i.e., astatic and fluxgate types) (Collinson 1977; Thellier 1938:172). By spinning the specimen (Shaw et al. 1978) or using an off-center configuration (Creer 1967), the effects of inhomogeneity can be reduced when using an astatic magnetometer. Fluxgate magnetometers with ring-shaped fluxgates give somewhat more accurate measurements than others of this type (Collinson 1977; Molyneaux 1971). When using fluxgate magnetometers, errors due to specimen inhomogeneity can be further reduced by smoothing the signal using Fourier analysis. It should be noted that ordinarily when using a properly constructed magnetometer, if six measurements are made on each specimen, the errors due to inhomogeneity should be random and, therefore, if a reasonable number of specimens from a particular baked feature, igneous rock, or sedimentary horizon are measured, the *average* direction should be accurate (Collinson 1977). The main advantage in using an instrument with pick-up coils would then be a reduction in dispersion. Limited comparisons I have made using a cryogenic magnetometer and commercial fluxgate spinners have shown only negligible differences for baked clay specimens encased in plaster cubes $1\frac{1}{16}$ inches on an edge.

Measuring time on all three types of magnetometers has been greatly reduced in recent years due to the interfacing of computers to automatically record, transform, and statistically analyze the raw data.

Magnetic Cleaning

The purpose of magnetic cleaning is to remove secondary magnetism while preserving the primary remanent direction. Secondary isothermal (IRM) and/or viscous (VRM) remanent magnetism can usually be eliminated by applying heat or a decreasing alternating magnetic field to the specimen in a field free space, which randomizes their domain directions. These two procedures are called *thermal* and *alternating field* (or *AF*) *demagnetization,* respectively. The initial field which is then reduced in the AF procedure is referred to as the *peak field.* The rationale for using these procedures is provided by the Neel single-domain theory discussed in the preceding section, particularly as embodied in Equations 4 and 5. In AF demagnetization the magnetic directions of the domains affected by secondary magnetism are randomized by overcoming the coercive forces of such domains. In thermal demagnetization this is accomplished by greatly reducing their relaxation times. Fortunately, in most situations, the secondary components due to IRM and VRM are much more easily erased by one or the other of these two procedures than the primary component. As indicated by Equations 4 and 5, VRM is most effectively erased by thermal demagnetization. However, because there is a direct relation between relaxation time and coercive force (see Equation 5), AF demagnetization is often effective in eliminating VRM. Since magnetite, which is fairly soft, is apparently the dominant magnetic mineral in most fired clay, the use of AF demagnetization in archaeomagnetic direction dating seems justified. It should be noted that IRM, which can be effectively erased using AF demagnetization, will ordinarily not be eliminated by thermal cleaning. Thermal demagnetization may reduce or eliminate the effects due to shape anisotropy that are sometimes found in large strongly magnetized baked features (Dunlop and Zinn 1980). There may be situations in which a combination of AF and thermal demagnetization (sequentially or simultaneously) will be more effective than one or the other, but I know of no work where this has been tried on archaeomagnetic samples.

The primary component will usually include a small contribution from low coercive force and short relaxation time domains. Therefore, the process of demagnetization will weaken this component. In addition, if magnetic shielding is not perfect, a secondary component may be added during the demagnetization procedure. These secondary components become increasingly stronger as the peak field or temperature is increased. Rotational remanent magnetism also increases proportionally to peak field strength. Consequently, elimination of secondary components should be undertaken at the minimum peak field or at the minimum temperature necessary to eliminate secondary components.

The problems related to secondary anhysteretic (ARM) and chemical (CRM) components and the frequency of their occurrence in fired clay have not been thoroughly studied. Sediments can have a considerable secondary chemical remanence, but secondary CRM in fired clay apparently is ordinarily too weak to affect significantly the primary remanent direction. However, Barbetti *et al.* (1977) have discussed potential problems due to secondary CRM when determining paleointensity of baked clay. Most important, secondary components due to CRM and ARM behave in many respects like TRM and are therefore difficult if not impossible to remove using thermal or AF demagnetization.

Early archaeomagnetic studies took place prior to and during the development of thermal and alternating field demagnetization techniques. In these early studies, attempts were made to select suitable samples and sometimes to correct for viscous components by measuring the specimens twice following storage for several weeks in opposite directions. Because a viscous component grows logarithmically through time, such a procedure (sometimes referred to as a *storage test*) gives an indication of a specimen's viscosity. It seems to be a good method for recognizing samples with low viscosity. Material with a hard remanence that acquires an IRM, however, may escape detection with this procedure. In addition, in most situations it probably is not an effective method for making corrections when viscosity is present.

Experiments involving leaching out minerals carrying secondary CRM components have been undertaken on sedimentary material with some success (Collinson 1967a; Kirshvink 1981). This procedure is referred to as *chemical demagnetization*. It would be difficult or impossible to carry out on archaeomagnetic direction specimens because they are usually encased in plaster. However, it might have some success in eliminating secondary CRM from potsherds and other paleointensity specimens.

THE EARLY HISTORY OF ARCHAEOMAGNETISM AND RELATED DEVELOPMENTS IN OTHER AREAS OF PALEOMAGNETISM

The basic phenomena that make archaeomagnetic direction dating possible were discovered before the end of the seventeenth century. Boyle (1691), who is well known in the physical sciences for the gas laws that bear his name, observed that a brick when heated and cooled acquires a magnetism parallel to the direction of the magnetic field. Halley (1692) not only discussed secular variation of geomagnetic direction but made the important observation that a portion of the magnetic field of the earth at that time was drifting westward. In addition, he developed a model, which has some surprisingly modern features, to account for this phenomenon. Yet it was many years before the implication of these ideas for archaeological dating was realized.

The earliest studies on the remanent magnetism of lavas were not undertaken until the middle of the nineteenth century (Delasse 1849; Melloni 1853). The earliest work of which I am aware, on the magnetic properties of archaeological materials was undertaken by Gheradi (1862). Near the end of the century Giuseppe Folgheraiter published a series of papers (e.g., Folgheraiter 1896; 1897a,b; 1899) in which he discussed the possibility of determining past declination and inclination from baked-clay features that have not moved since the time of firing and of using these data for an archaeological dating method. He also made some magnetic measurements on ceramic vessels in an attempt to determine past inclination. It is unfortunate that Folgheraiter's and later Mercanton's (1907, 1918a,b) experimental studies were primarily devoted to this type of work because, in addition to the fact that assumptions about the position of the pot during firing must be made, it is now known that ceramic vessels (particularly those made on a wheel) may be severely anisotropic (Fox and Aitken 1978; Rogers *et al.* 1979). These difficulties may explain the strange results obtained by Folgheraiter (1899:15–16) which suggested the occurrence of an excursion during the first millennium B.C.

The first extensive study of the ability of remanent magnetism to record past secular variation was undertaken by Chevallier (1925) on seven historically dated lavas dating between 1284 and 1911 from Mount Etna in Sicily. Chevallier noted that the average declination values he obtained on the four latest lavas were consistent with observatory data from Rome. However, the measured inclination values were a bit shallow. This was due to shape anisotropy caused by the strong remanence ($10^{-3}-10^{-2}$ emu/g) of the Etna lavas (Tanguy 1970:116). A recent restudy of the Mount Etna lavas (Tanguy 1970) that utilized magnetic cleaning has validated Chevallier's pioneering research. Fortunately, because magnetic cleaning methods had not yet been developed in 1925, the remanent magnetism in these lavas was quite stable.

Although this early work was certainly of great importance, the methodological advances made between about 1930 and 1960 mark the beginning of modern studies not only in archaeomagnetism but in the broader field of paleomagnetism as well. Most of the methodological research in archaeomagnetism during these years was carried out under the guidance of one scholar, Emile Thellier. Thellier and his students discovered basic magnetic properties of fired clay (Thellier 1951; Roquet 1954), developed collecting techniques (Thellier 1936), laboratory equipment (Thellier 1933; 1938:163–216; Pozzi and Thellier 1963), alternating field (Thellier and Rimbert 1954, 1955; Rimbert 1959) and thermal (Thellier and Thellier 1959:318–320) cleaning procedures to eliminate secondary components, and the most widely used method of determining paleointensity (Thellier and Thellier 1959).

Pioneering research in paleomagnetism beginning in the late 1930s was also carried out in Japan by Nagata and his students. Most of it, some of which overlapped that undertaken in France, was carried out on rocks rather than fired clay. Much of the work is summarized in a monograph (Nagata 1943) and

Nagata's (1961) text *Rock Magnetism*. It was in Nagata's laboratory that the first major archaeomagnetic direction study was carried out by the anthropologist Watanabe (1959). Other important early paleomagnetic studies on rocks were carried out by Koenigsburger (e.g., 1938) in Germany. The first studies of secular variation of geomagnetic direction recorded in sediments were begun in the late 1920s by Ising (1942) in Sweden, followed soon after by McNish and Johnson (1938, 1940) at the Carnegie Institution of Washington in the United States.

More than 30 years after the pioneering work of Chevallier, another very important paleosecular variation study on lavas was undertaken (Brynjolfsson 1957). Brynjolfsson's work on a series of superimposed lavas from Iceland was important not only for the data obtained but also for a number of methodological advances, including the following: (1) He investigated secular variation in the lavas using an advanced pick-up coil spinner magnetometer. (2) For the first time in the history of paleomagnetic studies, many of the specimens were cleaned using AF demagnetization. (3) Also for the first time, secular variation data were represented in terms of VGPs and a polar curve from A.D. 960 to 1950 was constructed. (4) He discussed the rock magnetic properties of the lavas; and (5) suggested that dipole wobble is a major component of secular variation. On the negative side he did not tabulate the measurements of magnetic direction nor discuss how the lavas were dated.

The first fairly reliable archaeomagnetic direction and paleointensity data were published during the 1950s. Since that time there has been a steady increase in data, much of which is discussed in some detail in the following sections. The basic work on polarity stratigraphy was begun in the mid-1960s. Research to extend and refine the sequence continues today. The increased production of data during these years was due, at least in part, to the availability of commercially produced instruments and high-speed computers.

Since the early 1970s there has been tremendous interest in using wet sediments cored from lake bottoms to reconstruct past secular variation of direction. Some of the drawbacks of results obtained from these sediments compared to those obtained from fired clay were mentioned in the section above on the acquisition of remanent magnetism. Others are discussed in a later section devoted to this topic. On the positive side, cores containing sediments deposited over thousands of years can be collected rapidly. In addition, the data obtained from sediments are, in part, responsible for current increased interest on the part of geophysicists in the more reliable data obtainable from baked clay.

Most of the archaeomagnetic and other paleomagnetic research of archeological interest thus far published has been devoted to methodological questions and the development of regional reference curves and a worldwide polarity sequence. Thus far there have been rather limited archaeological applications. Archaeomagnetic direction dating has been applied in a few regions in the western hemisphere and polarity stratigraphy has assisted in the dating of fossil remains in several parts of the Old World. The details of the development of these methods, recent applications, and their historic context are discussed in the appropriate sections below. We are, I believe, on the threshhold of a new period when the various geomagnetic methods will be routinely used in archaeological dating.

ARCHAEOMAGNETIC DATING USING SECULAR VARIATION OF DIRECTION RECORDED IN BAKED CLAY

Archaeomagnetic direction dating is, in many instances, capable of providing very precise and accurate chronometric results. As noted above, the method is based on secular variation of geomagnetic direction and the fact that clay when it is fired becomes magnetized in the direction of the ambient magnetic field. When the past history of secular variation is established for an area 800–1600 km in diameter, it is then possible to date a baked feature of unknown age on the basis of its remanent direction. Unfortunately, records of direct measurement of declination and inclination only go back several hundred years for a few locations in Europe. They are available for most of the remaining parts of the world for less than 100 years. The past history of secular variation of geomagnetic direction in an area for earlier time periods can be accurately reconstructed only by collecting fired clay samples from baked features that have not moved since the time of firing, and then measuring the TRM direction in them. The polar curve resulting from such work can be accurately calibrated only if a reasonable number of the samples are independently dated. In some cases, measurements on lava and sediment samples might also provide important data. Archaeomagnetic direction work thus far accomplished has been primarily directed toward establishing calibrated reference curves. A few accurate regional curves have been developed and dates are now being reported in portions of the western hemisphere.

VGPs and Polar Curves

Archaeomagnetic direction data are commonly presented in two different ways. VGPs and polar curves (originally introduced into archaeomagnetic studies by Kawai *et al.* [1965] and Aitken and Weaver [1965]) were discussed above. Alternatively, the data can be depicted by plotting declination and inclination against time and declination against inclination. Since declination and inclination usually vary by several degrees across an area 800 km in diameter, it is necessary to reduce the data to declination and inclination values at a central location. The most satisfactory way of handling the problem (Shuey *et al.* 1970) is to determine the VGP for the sample and from it calculate the declination and inclination values for the base location (Irving 1964:69). This, of course, gives essentially the same results as using VGPs but involves more computation. Before the widespread availability of digital computers, less-satisfactory methods of data reduction involving less computation but requiring questionable assumptions about the configuration of the field were commonly used (Aitken and Weaver 1962; Watanabe 1959:39). Although the virtual dipole approach is clearly better than the alternatives, it should be noted that even in areas as small as 800 km in diameter there is some nondipole variation. Consequently, a small error is introduced when using the VGP (or the analogous dipole method of reducing declination and inclination data) to represent archaeomagnetic data for the entire region. For this reason, a polar curve is actually more accurately depicted as a thin band (on the order of 1° in width) rather than a line.

Since there is some inherent error in both the VGPs used to construct polar curves and the dating method used in calibration, construction of an accurate polar curve takes many samples.

All the curves discussed later in this section and shown on Figures 6.7–6.11 were drawn as the best visual fit to the data points without the aid of statistical techniques. This seems to be an acceptable procedure if all the VGPs used in curve construction are precisely determined. Since in studies where optimal procedures are used such data are almost always highly accurate, only minimal attention need be paid to the ages of the samples to determine the configuration of the curve. Too much reliance on preliminary age estimates based on presumed cultural context and/or a few radiocarbon dates can sometimes cause spurious difficulties during this stage of the analysis. Accurate calibration of a curve, of course, depends heavily on independent dating. Sternberg (1982:59–76) has recently made the first attempt at fitting a polar curve to the data statistically. His approach seems to lose some of the detail that is apparent in the graph of the data points. Undoubtedly, further research in this area will be undertaken.

Since precise and accurate dating is central to their studies, archaeologists are justifiably concerned with the length of time needed to construct a curve in an area. It is dependent on several variables, most importantly the number of baked features available for sampling, the amount of time available for collecting and lab work (ultimately dependent on funding), and the time span of the baked features, each of which may adversely affect the rate at which the research proceeds. In addition, the development of the archaeomagnetic direction dating method has also proceeded slowly because there have been few specialists and laboratories devoted to this type of work. The lack of specialists is, in part, due to the need for expertise in two very different disciplines. However, the length of time prior to publication of some results or the lack of publication of others that has occurred in the past need not be typical. With adequate funding, reasonably accurate curves over 1000 years in length can be developed in many areas in 2 to 4 years and more rapid progress is possible. Although there are still few specialists in this field, results are appearing more rapidly and it is anticipated that the method will be much more widely used in the near future.

Once a polar curve is constructed and calibrated with a reasonable number of independently dated samples, an archaeomagnetic date can be obtained by comparing the sample VGP and its oval of confidence (see below) with the curve (Figure 6.6). Because polar curves cross over themselves and sections of different age pass close together (FIgures 6.7–6.11), the approximate age of the sample must be known. This can often be obtained by another dating method. For time periods since the invention of pottery, stylistic changes will usually provide sufficient chronological information to eliminate ambiguity. In such situations paleointensity data might occasionally be used to assist in age determination.

Collection Procedures

In order to obtain archaeomagnetic direction dates, the individual specimens (usually ca. 6 to 10 per feature) must be accurately oriented with respect to both the horizontal plane and geographic north. (In this article and many others on archaeomagnetism the individually oriented piece of fired clay encased in a plaster cube is called a *specimen*. The group of specimens from a single baked feature is referred to as a *sample*. However, the reader should be aware that many paleomagnetists, when working with rocks and sediments, refer to an individually oriented piece of material as a sample.)

The basic procedure of encasing the fired material in plaster cubes varying in size from 2.5 to 10 cm on an edge has been used for many years, and with minor variation in technique has been discussed many times (Watanabe 1959:27–30; Aitken 1961:133–135; Thellier 1967; Wolfman 1978; Eighmy 1980). Specimens are collected by placing a nonmagnetic (brass or aluminum) cubic mold over a column of fired clay surrounded by modeling clay. The mold is pressed into the modeling clay until it is level, and the volume between the mold and the column is filled with plaster. For baked features that are not very strongly magnetized, a Brunton compass provides a rapid method of orientation with respect to magnetic north. Geographic north can then be determined using declination charts (Fabiano 1975). When the local geomagnetic field is distorted either due to the magnetism of modern buildings, machinery, or to the baked feature itself, a sun compass can be used. Alternatively, a line oriented with respect to landmarks, magnetic north, or the sun can be shot in with a transit or theodolite.

Archaeologists and others often ask what types of material give satisfactory results. The terms *baked* or *fired clay* have been used throughout this chapter to refer to the material sampled because it is within the clay fraction of the baked feature that the remanent magnetism is found. However, baked material with coarse constituents in addition to clay often provide good results. Some authors (e.g., Watanabe 1959) have used the term *baked earth* when referring to the material sampled and, generally, well-baked earth free from large pebbles gives useful results. Although good archaeomagnetic direction specimens may contain a considerable amount of sand, paleointensity specimens, because they are re-fired during the laboratory procedure, must be durable with a high clay content. In addition, as a general rule the strength of magnetism varies directly with the percentage of clay. With respect to baking, it has been found that well-oxidized (red, yellow, or orange in color) material at least 0.75 cm thick will usually provide good results. Good results can also be obtained from well-baked reduced (black) material but not from soil merely blackened due to burning of organic constituents. As with many field procedures, decisions about what to sample improve with experience.

Specific Laboratory Procedures

The purpose of the work carried out in the laboratory is to determine the direction of the magnetic field at the time the fired clay sample was baked. This generally involves eliminating secondary components and accurately measuring the primary magnetic component in each of the specimens. The techniques that have been used to accomplish these two tasks in previous archaeomagnetic direction studies have apparently been reasonably successful. However, more experimental work is needed to determine optimum procedures. Those that have been used and suggestions for improvements are briefly discussed below.

Magnetic Cleaning

The magnitude of secondary components in fired clay is quite variable. Due to the relatively short time (in geological terms) since the primary remanence was acquired, and due to the magnetic properties of fired clay, secondary components resulting from viscous remanent magnetism (VRM) are usually not very great. Often they change primary directions on the order of a few degrees and some-times changes are negligible. However, because a few degrees difference in direction can indicate a considerably different age, even small secondary compo-nents must be eliminated. Large secondary components, which change the pri-mary direction by as much as 90°, have been observed but are not very common. Such large secondary components are apparently due to IRM caused by lightning strikes.

As noted above, a secondary component may be added during the cleaning process. In addition, the strength of the primary component is reduced during the demagnetization. Therefore, the general procedure utilized in magnetic cleaning involves determining the lowest temperature or lowest peak field that eliminates all (or nearly all) the secondary components of the NRM. It is standard procedure to expose the specimens to increasingly high temperatures or increasingly strong peak alternating fields, which are then reduced to zero in a field-free area. Each specimen is measured after each demagnetization step. This procedure is referred to as *progressive* or *stepwise* demagnetization. Although it is not possible in an absolute sense to determine at what level secondary magnetism is fully erased, criteria such as least dispersion of specimen directions in a sample (Irving *et al.* 1961) and/or the level at which direction change ceases (As and Zijderveldt 1958) are often used to determine what is sometimes euphemistically called the "best" level. In order to save time a pilot group of about three specimens are often progressively demagnetized and then the rest of the specimens in the sample are demagnetized and remeasured at the "best" level as determined from the pilot group. The "best" level of AF demagnetization usually occurs between 50 and 300 oersteds (Wolfman 1982a:289). Thermal demagnetization at 100 and 200° C has been found to be effective in removing VRM (Aitken 1974:154).

There has been a strong tendency to rely on one method of demagnetization in archaeomagnetic direction studies (thermal cleaning in Europe [e.g., Aitken and Weaver 1962:7; Burlatskaya *et al.* 1969; Kovacheva and Veljovich 1977] and Australia [Barbetti 1977] and AF cleaning in the United States [Eighmy *et al.* 1980; Wolfman 1973, 1979, 1982a]). It seems that the "best" demagnetization procedure varies from sample to sample and occasionally might vary for individual specimens within a sample. Comparison of results of both AF and thermal demagnetization on large numbers of specimens from a single feature is probably too time consuming for routine processing. However, storage in a zero field for as long as a week prior to AF demagnetization will add some of the benefits of thermal demagnetization with minimal effort. So that the benefits of this storage not be lost, because a significant portion of the remanence of some fired clays is due to domains with relaxation times on the order of seconds or minutes, a specimen should not be exposed to the earth's field when moved between the storage area, demagnetizer, and magnetometer. Controlled experiments to determine the severity of not following this suggestion for fired clay specimens have yet to be undertaken. Ordinarily the effects do not appear to be very serious. Urrutia-Fucugauchi (1981) has discussed the problem for certain rock types.

Statistical Analysis of the Data

A probability density function, with the specimen vectors distributed symmetrically about the mean with their density decreasing normally in all directions (Fisher 1953; McElhinny 1973:77–83), is used in virtually all paleomagnetic direction studies. *Alpha-95* (α_{95}) is the half angle of a circular cone around the mean direction such that there is 95% chance that the population mean direction lies within that cone. This is analogous to approximately two standard errors of the mean in linear statistics and is commonly used as a measure of the precision of an average direction. Since alpha-95 is inversely proportional to the square root of sample size, in order to reduce it by half the sample size would have to be increased by a factor of four. Because (1) it takes 3–4 hours to collect about eight specimens, (2) for sample sizes larger than about six, significant improvement in precision would involve a considerable amount of work, and (3) the alpha-95 values obtained (usually 1 to 4°) when there are this many specimens are sufficiently precise to be useful in archaeomagnetic direction dating, samples of eight specimens (to allow for one or even two outliers) are often collected.

Outliers are generally defined as those specimens whose directions have less than a 5% chance of belonging to the population of specimen directions. They are due to a variety of factors including poorly fired specimens, magnetic inclusions, collecting error, and laboratory error, and usually are not included in calculating the mean direction of the sample. The proper procedure for eliminating outliers, analogous to using a *t* test in linear statistics, has recently been discussed by McFadden (1980).

The dipole formula (McElhinny 1973:23–25) tranforms the average declination and inclination for a sample into a VGP latitude and longitude. This formula also transforms a circle of confidence around the mean direction into an oval about the VGP with its minor axis along the great circle between the site and the VGP (see Figure 6.6). The size of the oval is a function of the size of the circle of confidence (usually alpha-95) and the distance between the site and the VGP, the so-called *colatitude* p.

Precision and Accuracy of Archaeomagnetic Direction Dating

Unfortunately, the distinct terms *precision* and *accuracy* are often used interchangeably or lumped in a single category called *error*. *Precision* refers to the repeatability of the result and *accuracy* to its "truth." The precision and accuracy of archaeomagnetic dates depend on several factors, some of which usually cannot be exactly determined. Generally, random errors reduce precision whereas consistent errors reduce accuracy. Some errors may reduce either precision or accuracy depending on the particular situation. In a single-specimen measurement there is ordinarily some error in accuracy, but if the error is due to a random effect it will be averaged when several specimens are measured. The most important factors that may reduce precision and/or accuracy of direction measurement are collecting error, measurement error, specimen shape or inhomogeneity, secondary components, physical movement, local magnetic anomalies, and anisotropy. As suggested above, criteria for accuracy are rarely clear cut and it should be emphasized that *precision does not necessarily imply accuracy*. However, experience with samples of known age indicates that if (1) there is no obvious movement of the material sampled, (2) secondary components have been eliminated using the criteria discussed above, and (3) if alpha-95 is less than 4°, then there is a high probability that archaeomagnetic direction results on baked clay samples are accurate. it should be emphasized that occasionally these criteria are met but an inaccurate result is obtained. In individual situations it is not clear why this occurs. A lightning strike very close to the baked clay which generates such a high magnetic field that the material becomes saturated with an IRM is, perhaps, the most likely cause. Other possibilities are secondary components due to ARM or CRM.

For most samples of about eight fired-clay specimens, alpha-95 values in the 1–4° range can be obtained. Such consistent high precision is rare in paleomagnetic studies. This characteristic of samples collected from baked features at archaeological sites is probably due to several factors. The relatively young age of the material means that VRM, which is logarithmically related to time, and CRM, due to weathering, will be low. Secondly, baked features at archaeological sites cool very rapidly and, therefore, record an instant in time, whereas lavas and sediments may acquire their remanence over a long period of time. Furthermore, lavas are often quite strongly magnetized and, therefore, may exhibit shape anisotropy.

Although the precision of the direction is determined by the dispersion of the specimen directions, the precision of the *archaeomagnetic date* depends not only on this factor but also on the rate of change of the VGP, the size of the oval of confidence, the spatial relation of the oval to the polar curve, and non-dipole variation in the region.

The rate of change in VGP position in the time periods studied in the Southwest (A.D. 600–1500; DuBois and Wolfman 1970a; DuBois 1975; Hathaway *et al.* 1983), Mesoamerica (A.D. 1–1075; Wolfman 1973), and Arkansas (A.D. 1200–1500; Wolfman 1982a) was somewhat more than 1°/10 years. The major semiaxis of the 95% oval of confidence in these time periods was never more than $1.5 \times \alpha_{95}$. Consequently, if the geomagnetic field was perfectly dipolar in these regions, the precision of the dates at the 95% confidence level would be approximately ±10–15 times the α_{95} value. Because errors are properly added by taking the square root of the sum of their squares, it seems safe to say that even when uncertainties due to nondipole distortion are included in the region and time periods mentioned above, dates with a precision of ±15–60 years at the 95% confidence level can *usually* be obtained (Figure 6.6A, 6.6B). But, there

---

Figure 6.6. Polar curves and ovals of confidence indicating the precision of archaeomagnetic dates that can be obtained in various situations. (A, B) Arkansas polar curve with ovals of confidence of various sizes. (From Wolfman 1982a:281–282, Figures 11–2, 11–3.) (C) (*overleaf*) Arkansas polar curve with an oval of confidence that includes a lengthy section of curve. (From Wolfman 1982a:283, Figure 11–4.) (D) (*overleaf*) Southwestern United States polar curve A.D. 1851–1975 showing the effect of slowly changing geomagnetic field directions on the precision of an archaeomagnetic date (compare with Figures 6.6A,B,C) (After Wolfman 1978:5, Figure 1.)

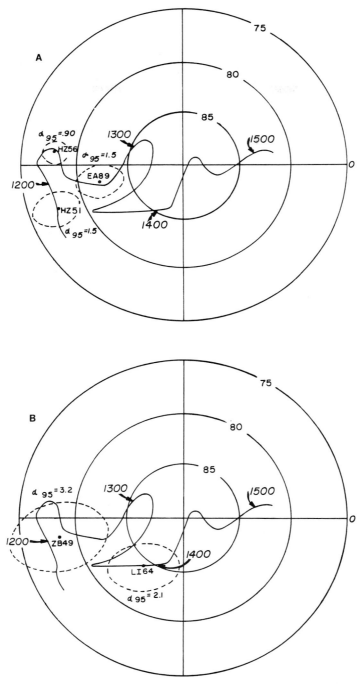

Figure 6.6. (A and B)

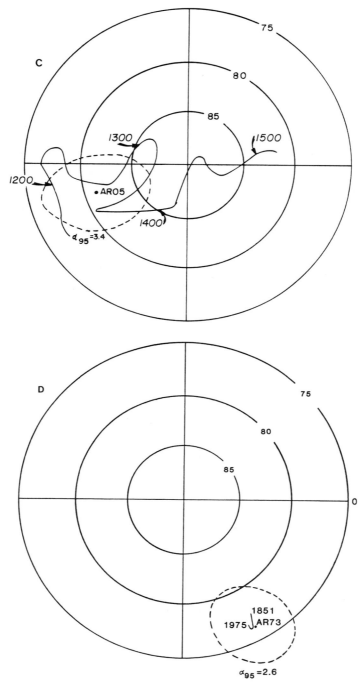

Figure 6.6. (C and D)

are situations in which a sinuous curve configuration can considerably decrease the precision of an archaeological date (Figure 6.6C). Additional difficulties may be encountered where sections of a polar curve of different age cross or pass close together (see Figures 6.7, 6.8, 6.9, and 6.11). However, it is usually possible to resolve such potential problems based on other chronometric information.

When the VGP is changing slowly, it becomes more difficult to construct and calibrate a polar curve and a typical oval of confidence takes in a considerably longer time period. When this happens there are considerably larger errors in both precision and accuracy. Rates of change as slow as 1° every 40 years, based on direct observations, occurred in the southwestern United States between A.D. 1851 and the present. The VGP and its oval of confidence for a sample collected in the Southwest that is believed to date between about A.D. 1810 and 1878, along with the polar curve for A.D. 1851 and 1975 for the region, are plotted on Figure 6.6D. As can be seen, the precision and accuracy in such a situation are poor.

The accuracy of an archaeomagnetic direction date depends on the accuracy with which the VGP is determined (and its attendant problems as discussed above) as well as the accuracy with which the polar curve is drawn and calibrated. Experience suggests that in many situations, even when radiocarbon is the only independent dating method available in an area, polar curves can be calibrated with errors of accuracy of less than 50 years (and in some situations perhaps considerably less). It should be emphasized that even if a calibration is somewhat erroneous, the quantitative relative dating of the samples will in most situations be of very high reliability.

MODERN STUDIES OF SECULAR VARIATION OF DIRECTION RECORDED IN BAKED CLAY

In the past 30 years a number of important studies utilizing samples collected from baked-clay features at archaeological sites have revealed detailed patterns of secular variation of geomagnetic direction for much of the past 2000 years at many locations in the northern hemisphere. Unfortunately, comparable work has not been accomplished in the southern hemisphere. The details of this work, which provides the basic data on which future archaeomagnetic dating can be based, are reviewed in the following sections.

Western Europe

The basic work on secular variation of direction in western Europe was begun by Emile Thellier more than 40 years ago, but a comprehensive report on this research has only recently been published (Theillier 1981).

The earliest direction results were obtained by Thellier (1938:269–276) as a by-product of his work on paleointensity. Because geomagnetic intensity measured on the surface of the earth is a function of both the magnetic moment and inclination of the geomagnetic field (see Equations 1 and 2), independent information about secular variation of one of the components of geomagnetic direction must be obtained. In Thellier's initial work and in a later, more comprehensive study, undertaken in conjunction with his wife, most of the samples were cut from unoriented bricks and tiles fired in France and Switzerland between A.D. 25 and 1750 (Thellier 1938:269–276; Thellier and Thellier 1959:333–355). They were able to obtain an approximate value for the inclination at the time of firing by assuming that bricks and tiles were stacked in kilns roughly perpendicular to the earth's surface as they are in many modern kilns. By measuring the inclination on several bricks or tiles, small variations were averaged and occasional anomalous results discarded. During the course of paleointensity measurements on these samples, thermal cleaning was undertaken and the inclination values reported on unoriented specimens are apparently quite accurate. Later, using the measurements he had made on the remanent magnetism of 60 hearths, ovens, kilns, bricks, and tiles fired prior to 1800, Thellier (1971:322) constructed an inclination versus time curve for Europe for the time periods A.D. 1–950 and 1150–present.

In addition to working with unoriented samples, the Thelliers reported the first results of declination obtained from oriented specimens collected from *in situ* baked clay from three kilns at Carthage in North Africa (Thellier and Thellier 1951) and one kiln near Treves in western Germany (Thellier and Thellier 1952).

In his comprehensive article on archaeomagnetic direction, Thellier (1981) reported declination and inclination values obtained for samples collected from 137 baked features throughout western Europe dating between about A.D. 1–1800. In this extensive study, the directions in 1277 specimens were utilized for an average of more than nine per sample. Although some specimens were AF or thermally demagnetized, apparently the majority were not. Storage tests were used to select only those that were stable for use in constructing the curve. Dispersion within the samples selected is quite small (only two have α_{95} values greater than 4°). However, there were some direction errors as indicated by variation in the average remanent direction values. These errors presumably resulted from shape anisotropy in the large kilns sampled by Thellier but perhaps some were also due to secondary components. Despite this problem, Thellier (1981:118) was able to define a reasonably accurate declination versus inclination curve for most of the time period A.D. 50–present (converted to a polar curve in Figure 6.7).

A few years after the Thelliers published their initial results from kilns (Thellier and Thellier 1951; 1952), Cook, an archaeologist, and Belshé, a geophysicist (1958) working at Cambridge, obtained the first results for samples

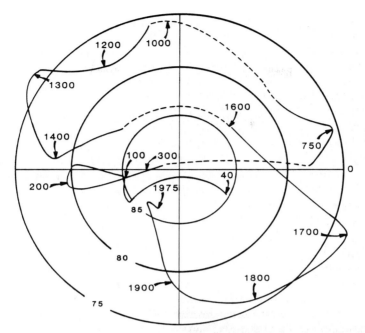

Figure 6.7. West European polar curve A.D. 40–1975. (VGPs calculated from declination and inclination data in Thellier 1979:118, Figure 1, and Defense Mapping Agency Hydrographic Center 1975a, 1975b)

collected in England. A short time later, Aitken and his associates at the Oxford University Research Laboratory for Archaeology and the History of Art began publishing their results (Aitken and Weaver 1962; Aitken *et al.* 1963; Aitken *et al.* 1964; Aitken and Hawley 1966, 1967).

Cook and Belshé (1958) reported on the results from 51 samples that consisted of only 143 specimens for a very low average of 2.8 specimens per sample. More than half the samples (28) consisted of only one specimen. In addition, they did not undertake magnetic cleaning. Not surprisingly, many of their results (particularly for those samples with few specimens) are not in agreement with the more recent and thorough work of Aitken and his associates.

Aitken and his associates collected and measured 164 samples consisting of 2746 specimens in England, for an average of 16.7 specimens per sample. Most of the samples were collected from baked features that date to the past 2000 years. These data have been used to construct a declination versus inclination curve for A.D. 100–300 and A.D. 1000–present (Aitken 1974:157), which is quite similar to Thellier's (1981) independently developed curve for all of western Europe. As with previous studies, extensive magnetic cleaning of the samples was not undertaken. Storage tests were used to identify "suitable" specimens and to make corrections on those with a large viscous component. In addition, errors due to shape anisotropy were noted in some of the large well-baked kilns that were sampled (Aitken and Hawley 1971). In evaluating the results, Hurst (1966:199), an archaeologist, noted, "So in the main, although some of the recent results are worrying, many of them still fit into a logical sequence in the curve. It may well be that only a limited number of types of burnt archaeological structures will give satisfactory results." Quite possibly some of these aberrant results could have been avoided with more extensive magnetic cleaning.

Presumably at least in part due to these problems, work on archaeomagnetic direction at the Research Laboratory for Archaeology and the History of Art ceased in the late 1960s. At about that time, the main emphasis in archaeological dating there shifted to thermoluminescence (e.g., Aitken 1974:85–134). Recently, however, a considerable amount of important paleointensity research on archaeological material, which is discussed in a following section, has been undertaken in that laboratory.

Eastern Europe

Archaeomagnetic research has been carried out in the Soviet Union and elsewhere in eastern Europe for more than 20 years. The early work was carried out by Burlatskaya and Petrova at the Geophysics Institute in Moscow (Burlatskaya and Petrova 1961a,b,c,d; Burlatskaya, Nechaeva, and Petrova 1968, 1969; Burlatskaya et al. 1970), followed by the work of Kovacheva (1968, 1969) in Bulgaria. This early research was similar to that of the Thelliers in France, with emphasis on determining the changes in the intensity of the geomagnetic field. Studies of change in the direction of the field focused on determination of inclination values because they are necessary to normalize the intensity values from different areas. Only a few declination results obtained from samples collected from *in situ* baked-clay features were reported in these early studies.

In recent studies in this area (Rusakov and Zagniy 1973a,b; Kovacheva and Veljovich 1977; Kovacheva 1980), all three components of the geomagnetic field (declination, inclination, and intensity) on specimens collected from the same baked features have often been measured. The direction results obtained by Rusakov and Zagniy (1973a) on 39 samples collected in the Ukraine and Moldavia, most dating between A.D. 1 and 1450, are of high quality with large samples and small α_{95} values.

Kovacheva and Veljovich (1977; Kovacheva 1980) have reported some archaeomagnetic direction results from baked features in southwestern Europe covering the past 8000 years. While their results give an indication of the trends of geomagnetic direction change during portions of this long period, the number of samples thus far collected and processed are not sufficient to determine secular variation of direction in great detail. In the most recent article (Kovacheva 1980), which summarized all previous as well as some new results, the data are presented as average values for each century for which samples have been collected and processed. Unfortunately, for many centuries no baked features have been sampled and for others the results from only one feature are reported.

The Middle East

The Middle East, with its abundant village and urban sites, beautifully stratified tells, and calendrical dating with great time depth, is an area where well-calibrated secular variation curves for each of several regions can be developed. The existence of village sites as old as about 10,000 B.P. (Perrot 1966) containing roasting pits suggest the possibility of developing exceptionally long regional curves. Eventually, archaeomagnetic direction dating should provide precise and accurate archaeological temporal control. Although the great potential in this vast area has been recognized for many years, archaeomagnetic studies are still in their early stages. However, it is encouraging to note that workers from three different countries, Japan, France, and Germany, began collecting samples in the area in the 1970s (Becker 1979; Dollfus and Hesse 1977; Hesse and Lacaille 1974, 1975; Kawai et al. 1972). The limited variable quality data which have thus far been presented are difficult to evaluate.

China

The recent collection of samples from kilns, ovens, and bricks in the Loyang region in the Yellow River Valley has led to the tentative construction of an inclination versus time curve for 500 B.C. to the present and a declination versus inclination curve from 100 B.C. to A.D. 1040 (Wei et al. 1981). The number of the samples collected is still rather low: 10 from bricks (which only provide inclination data) and 7 from kilns and ovens. However, the precision of the results is high. The results are of geophysical interest due to central China's intermediate location between eastern Europe and Japan where more extensive archaomagnetic direction studies have been undertaken. Due to the long sequence of settled village life in the Yellow River Valley with the appearance of civilization by about 2000 B.C., further development of the secular variation curve in this area will ultimately be of considerable archaeological importance.

Japan

An ambitious program to determine remanent direction from baked features at archaeological sites was undertaken by the Japanese anthropologist, Watanabe

(1959), during the 1950s in his native country. Working in close association with Nagata and other Japanese geophysicists, he collected and measured samples from 178 baked-clay features at 55 archaeological sites from as early as 4000 B.C. to as late as about A.D. 1475. The 178 samples collected from hearths, ovens, and kilns consisted of 1378 specimens for an average of 7.7 specimens per sample.

Despite the ambitious nature of the program, there were a number of serious problems. Magnetic cleaning techniques, which were not widely used at that time, were not employed. Had this been done, aberrant results might have been eliminated and greater confidence could have been placed on all the results. However, as noted above, fired clay is often magnetically stable and many of Watanabe's results appear consistent. Unfortunately, many of the samples were concentrated at several points in time. For this reason they provide good data only for the time periods A.D. 250–600 and A.D. 850–1475.

The lack of absolute dates for almost all the samples collected further compli- cated Watanabe's analysis. The radiocarbon dating method was in its infancy and historical dating of most archaeological sites in Japan was very uncertain. De- spite these problems, Watanabe did attempt to plot declination versus time, inclination versus time, and declination versus inclination curves for his data for the past 1700 years. Absolute temporal control was obtained from paleomagnetic results on historically dated lava flows extending back to the eruption of Fu- jiyama in A.D. 864 and a pair of hearths thought, due to historic evidence, to date about A.D. 1300. Smooth sinusoidal curves were then fit to the declination versus time and inclination versus time data points. Such an approach can be no more than a first-order approximation and Watanabe (1959:120–128) noted a number of inconsistencies in the results obtained in this manner.

Following the publication of Watanabe's monograph (1959), additional stud- ies on fired clay, lavas, and ash-fall tuffs (Yukutake 1961; Yukutake, Nakamura, and Horai 1964; Yukutake, Sawada, and Yabu 1964; Mamose et al. 1964; Kawai et al. 1964, 1965; Kawai et al. 1967; Hirooka 1971; Asami et al. 1972; Shibuya and Nakajima 1979) confirmed the general pattern of secular variation suggested by Watanabe but also revealed some significant variations between A.D. 600 and 850. Hirooka's (1971) publication of the results from 152 baked features dating between A.D. 1 and 1750 was particularly important. In examining Watanabe's (1959: Figure 15, Plate III) data, it can be seen that he obtained no samples in what he believed to be the A.D. 700–850 time period. The curves in this interval are determined by fitting a sinusoidal curve to the data with very poor indepen- dent temporal control for the points earlier than A.D. 864. If it is assumed that the samples Watanabe placed in the time period A.D. 600–700 dated somewhat later, Watanabe's curves would be almost identical to those obtained in later archaeo- magnetic studies in Japan.

Very limited magnetic cleaning has been undertaken on the samples collected

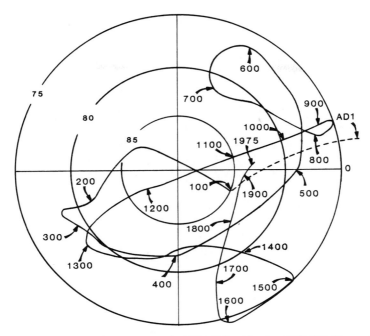

Figure 6.8. Japanese polar curve A.D. 1–1975. (After Hirooka 1971:190, Figure 16; with additions from declination and inclination data in Hirooka 1971:186–187, Figures 13 and 14, and Defense Mapping Agency Hydrographic Center 1975a, 1975b)

in Japan and little attention has been paid to the possibility of magnetic distortion around the kilns and lavas where the samples were collected. Although the average results obtained seem to be very consistent (summarized in the polar curve shown in Figure 6.8), individual results vary somewhat. While the geophysical objectives of the research have been achieved, a thorough review of the results from an archaeological perspective is needed.

Southwestern United States

Undoubtedly the most precise and accurate prehistoric archaeological chronology anywhere in the world has been developed in parts of the southwestern United States for the time period about A.D. 1–1600 using dendrochronology. This area, consisting of Arizona, southern Utah, western New Mexico, and southwestern Colorado, is often referred to as the *Southwest*. Since baked hearths are abundant in sites throughout the area, it has been possible to develop what is believed to be a fairly accurate, well-calibrated polar curve for the time period A.D. 600–1500 (Figure 6.9; see DuBois and Wolfman 1970a; DuBois 1975).

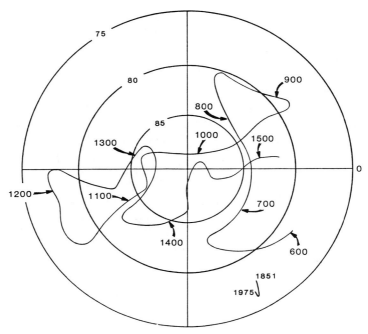

Figure 6.9. Southwestern United States polar curve A.D. 600–1500 and 1851–1975. (After DuBois and Wolfman 1970a and DuBois 1975:138–139, Figures 1 and 2, with additions from declination and inclination data in Vestine *et al.* 1947:232 and from the Tucson Geomagnetic Observatory.)

Work on archaeomagnetic dating in the Southwest began during the summer of 1963 when Norman Watkins, a British geophysicist who was spending a year at Stanford University, left some molds and instructions (Watkins 1963) with several archaeologists working in the area. Unfortunately, although he went on to a distinguished career in many aspects of paleomagnetic studies, he did not continue this work. Another geophysicist, Robert L. DuBois, then at the University of Arizona, also traveled around the Southwest that summer and began making collections. DuBois has continued his work in this and other areas in the western hemisphere since that time and more than 2000 samples (most consisting of 8 to 10 specimens) have been measured in his laboratories at the University of Arizona and later at the University of Oklahoma, where he moved in 1967. This is considerably more than the number of direction samples collected and processed by all other workers in the entire history of archaeomagnetism.

In the 1964–1965 academic year, Naotune Watanabe, the Japanese anthropologist who pioneered this type of work in Japan, worked with DuBois at the University of Arizona where he was a visiting scientist. Unfortunately, after a short report on the work undertaken with Watanabe was published (Watanabe and DuBois 1965) virtually nothing about Dubois's work in the Southwest has appeared in print. A preliminary version of the Southwest polar curve was included in a popular article on archaeomagnetic dating (Weaver 1967) and a refined version of the curve for the time period A.D. 900–1500 appeared in a short article (DuBois 1975) without supporting data. Although thermal demagnetization was undertaken on some of the earliest samples processed (Watanabe and DuBois 1965), most of the samples used in the construction of the current version of the polar curve from A.D. 600–1500 (first presented at the Society for American Archaeology Meetings in Mexico City [DuBois and Wolfman 1970a]) were not cleaned. Interestingly, there were no changes in the A.D. 900–1500 portion of the curve which was published in 1975 (DuBois 1975) following a program of AF cleaning and remeasuring many of the samples.

Despite the lack of publication, DuBois has informed many archaeologists in the Southwest in letters, phone calls, and unpublished lists (e.g., DuBois n.d.a, n.d.b) of the age of their samples determined by comparing the remanent direction with the polar curve. Consequently, many archaeomagnetic "dates" have appeared in publications on Southwest archaeology, but since DuBois has not released pole positions and since the results from many samples have never been reported even in this unsatisfactory form, it is impossible to evaluate the results comprehensively.

It is encouraging that many archaeologists (e.g., Hammack and Sullivan 1981:36–37; Schwartz and Lang 1973) report that the dates given to them are generally in agreement with their estimates based on other dating methods and cultural cross-dating. However, there are some problems. A large group of DuBois's archaeomagnetic dates reported for Chaco Canyon (Windes 1980) are not in agreement with those obtained by other chronometric methods. Since the archaeomagnetic data are not available, it is not possible to more than guess at the causes of these apparently aberrant results.

A smaller number of pole positions measured at other laboratories on samples collected from the Southwest have been published (Shuey and Reed 1972; Shuey 1974; Wolfman 1977, 1978; Eighmy *et al.* 1980; Hathaway *et al.* 1982; Sternberg 1982).

The recent completion of a dissertation by Sternberg (1982) marked the first time that a large body of archaeomagnetic direction data for the Southwest was available. This study contains the results from 158 samples (97 with alpha-95 values less than 4°) ranging in age from about A.D. 650 to 1400. One sample dating between 1906 and 1910 was also included. Sternberg and McGuire (1981; Sternberg 1982) reported that the results from a large number of samples dating between A.D. 900 and 1200, measured in the University of Arizona paleomagnetism laboratory, suggest that although the configuration of the curve published by DuBois (1975) for this time period is essentially correct, his calibration is about

100 years too early. This new calibration would bring the "archaeomagnetic dates" for Chaco Canyon reported by DuBois more into line with evidence based on other dating methods. In addition, the calibration would help explain the surprisingly late dates which I (Wolfman 1977) reported for samples collected in southeastern Arizona using the DuBois (1975) calibration.

In another study of considerable importance, Hathaway *et al.* (1983) summarized the results of independently dated samples collected in southwestern Colorado dating between A.D. 700 and 900. They contend that their data suggest that the configuration of the curve in this time period was considerably different than that originally reported by DuBois and Wolfman (1970a).

On the positive side, the latest portion of this curve seems correct. On the basis of 15 independently dated samples dating between 1150 and 1400, Eighmy *et al.* (1980:516; see also Sternberg 1982) found that there were no major discrepancies with the Southwest curve depicted by DuBois (1975).

It is not surprising that the version of the curve presented in 1970 (DuBois and Wolfman 1970a) was in need of some revision. At that time, very few of the samples had been demagnetized and much of the chronometric data used in the calibration was supplied by archaeologists in the field, prior to detailed analysis of the excavated material.

These recent findings underscore the need to publish pole positions (and/or directions) as well as dates. It is to be expected that in many instances refinements in the configuration and/or calibration of curves will occur as more data become available. Correction in the dates can be made only if all of the original data are available.

While clearly more published data are needed before some of these discrepancies can be resolved, it is very encouraging that some data from this part of the world are being published.

Southcentral United States

In contrast to the Southwest, archaeological dating in the rest of the United States is based on the radiocarbon method. Consequently, some disagreements about local chronologies exist. Archaeomagnetic direction results from the southcentral and southeastern United States would not only provide the basis for more precise archaeological dating, but also could be compared with the data from the Southwest to determine the relative effects of dipole wobble and westward drift during different time periods.

Recently, (Wolfman 1979, 1982a) the results from 52 samples collected in Arkansas and the border areas of the adjacent states have been reported. The polar curve developed for the approximate time period A.D. 1200–1500 (Figure 6.10) is almost identical to the well-calibrated Southwest curve for this time period. Archaeomagnetic dates were reported for 34 samples, out of a total of 50,

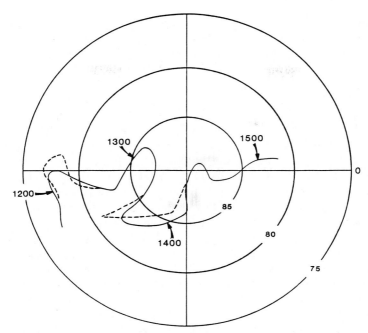

Figure 6.10. Arkansas (dotted line) and Southwestern United States (solid line) polar curves A.D. 1200–1500. (From Wolfman 1982a:280, Figure 11-1.)

dating in this time period. Dates were not reported for those samples with α_{95} values greater than 4° nor for the two that have good precision but anomalous VGPs.

The Arkansas curve was calibrated using radiocarbon dating (based on the Damon *et al.* [1974] calibration), ceramic cross dating, and stratigraphy. These results suggest that the geomagnetic field was dipolar from the Southwest to Arkansas (a distance of over 1600 km during this time period and that westward drift did not significantly contribute to secular variation in the southern United States during this 300-year period.

Due to the proximity of Arkansas to the Southwest (ca. 1600 km and the average rate of westward drift during this century (ca. 0.2°/year) more accurate independent dating of the archaeological sequence in the former area is desirable to confirm or deny these tentative conclusions. It is conceivable that tree-ring dating may eventually provide this (Stahle and Wolfman 1977, n.d.).

Although the opportunities for collecting samples from well-dated baked features are certainly greater in village and urban sites, they can also be collected from sites predating settled life. A current archaeological project at the Modoc Rock Shelter in southern Illinois has led to the collection of samples from 28 well-baked hearths in two stratigraphic units. The results from these samples provide a fairly complete record of secular variation of direction for most of the time period 9000–7000 B.P. (Wolfman, Kean, and Fowler 1982).

Mesoamerica

Mesoamerica is defined as the area in central and southern Mexico, Guatemala, Belize, El Salvador, and western Honduras where civilization arose between 2000 B.C. and A.D. 1521. Earlier hunting and gathering and incipient agricultural sites date as far back as 10,000 B.C., with some evidence of occupation perhaps as early as about 25,000 B.P. (MacNeish 1976:319). This is an area in which the overall archaeological chronology has only recently become relatively clear, and numerous fine-scale chronological problems remain to be resolved. For many years there were sharp disagreements about the age of Classic period cultures that revolved around the problem of the correlation of the Mayan and Christian calendars (Andrews 1965; Lowe 1978). Currently, the radiocarbon evidence very strongly favors the later of the two major contending correlations (the Goodman–Martinez–Thompson, or GMT, correlation), which places the time of the Mayan long count dates between about A.D. 300 and 900. There is, however, some astronomical evidence, that suggests that it may not be correct (Kelley and Kerr 1973).

More than 200 archaeomagnetic samples from Mesoamerica have been collected and measured since 1968. Most of the laboratory work (and all prior to 1979) was undertaken at the University of Oklahoma archaeomagnetism laboratory. The results obtained on samples ranging in age from about A.D. 1 to 1075 collected prior to 1973 have been reported and discussed in my dissertation (Wolfman 1973:177–252). Only a limited amount of demagnetization work was undertaken at the time the dissertation was completed (two specimens from most of the samples were cleaned using progressive AF demagnetization). The results suggest that with the exception of several samples from one mound (C-II-14 at Kaminaljuyú, which presumably was struck by lightning), virtually no secondary components were present in those samples with α_{95} values less than 4°. This is not very surprising. Due to the volcanic origin of the soil in many parts of Mesoamerica, much of the baked clay in this area is quite strongly magnetized (10^{-3} emu/cc and even a bit higher is common). It is, therefore, to be expected that VRM would be minimal. The archaeomagnetic results obtained were internally consistent and in agreement with the reconstruction of Mesoamerican chronology presented in the dissertation based on all other lines of evidence. On the basis of the samples collected prior to 1973, a preliminary polar curve for the time period A.D. 1–1050 was developed (Wolfman 1973:23, 244, and 247) using the VGPs obtained from the 53 samples (out of a total of 93 in this time period) that had α_{95} values less than 4°.

Complete demagnetization of these samples was undertaken at the Oklahoma laboratory between 1973 and 1975. Aside from some information on the results of the demagnetization work on samples from Kaminaljuyú, including those from mound C-II-14 (Charles Cheek, personal communication, 1975), these data have not been provided despite several requests. The directions obtained on fully demagnetized samples from Mound C-II-14 have led to a slight revision of the polar curve for this area (Wolfman n.d.; see Figure 6.11). Using this revised curve, archaeomagnetic dates from Copán in Honduras and San Andrés in El Salvador have recently been reported (Wolfman 1981a, n.d.).

The results obtained earlier (Wolfman 1973:237, 243, and 248) have been used by other archaeologists (e.g., Cheek 1977; Sorenson 1977:43) and provide valuable chronometric information that could not have been obtained otherwise. In addition, Grove *et al.* (1976:120), Carlson (1977:73), and Aveni (1980: 119–120) have discussed the importance of these archaeomagnetic data in testing hypotheses about astronomical alignments of structures and the use of the compass in Precolumbian Mesoamerica.

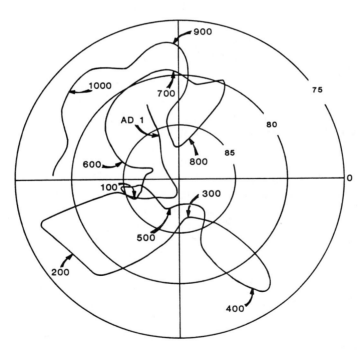

Figure 6.11. Mesoamerican polar curve A.D. 1–1075. (After Wolfman 1973: 238, 244, and 247, Figures 3, 4, and 5.)

Southern Hemisphere

Unfortunately, there has been very little work on secular variation of direction using fired clay in the southern hemisphere. This void in the data is not due to a lack of opportunities. South America, Africa, and the Indian subcontinent have ample archaeological material which could be sampled. Thus far, in this half of the world, there has been only a limited amount of work in Peru and Australia.

Watanabe (1964), whose pioneering archaeomagnetic work in Japan has been discussed above, was the first to collect samples in Peru. The two samples he collected and processed were, of course, insufficient even to begin to construct a curve. In 1969, 1970, and 1973, a total of 49 samples in Peru and an adjacent portion of Bolivia were collected. Preliminary reports were presented in papers at meetings (DuBois and Wolfman 1970b; Wolfman and DuBois 1971) but the results have not been published.

Numerous aboriginal baked-clay features have eroded from sand dunes in the Willander Lakes region of New South Wales. A number of them, dated between about 25,000 and 30,000 years ago by the radiocarbon method, provide evidence for two rapid excursions of the geomagnetic field (Barbetti and McElhinny 1972, 1976). In addition, the results for 17 Holocene baked-clay samples, dated by the radiocarbon method between 6140 and 220 B.P., from 14 ovens, one hearth, and the baked soil around two burned tree stumps have been reported by Barbetti (1977). These results are not sufficient to construct a curve for any portion of this time period.

SECULAR VARIATION OF DIRECTION RECORDED IN SEDIMENTS OF ARCHAEOLOGICAL INTEREST

As discussed in an earlier section of this chapter, due to the complex mechanisms involved in the acquisition of remanent magnetism in sediments, the magnetic data obtained from such material often does not provide a good indication of the direction of the geomagnetic field at the time of deposition.

Other problems involved in obtaining an accurate record of past geomagnetic direction from marine and lacustrine sediments include highly variable sedimentation rates, seismically induced liquefaction long after deposition, difficulties in collecting cores from the bottoms of lakes, including problems related to orientation and rotation of the core in the coring tube, and the weak remanence of many sediments. In most situations it is impossible to obtain exactly contemporaneous specimens from cores extracted from the same lake. Consequently, standard statistical analyses cannot be undertaken and, as can be seen on Figure 6.12, there is quite a bit of random variation in most data obtained from parallel cores. Due to these many limitations, comparisons are usually made on the basis of

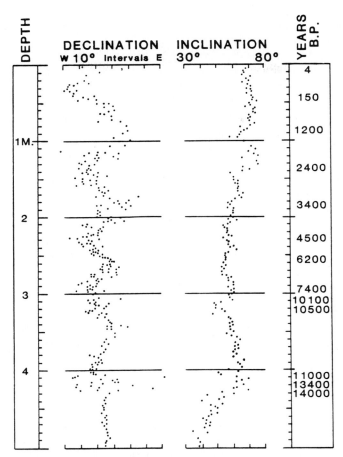

Figure 6.12.   Composite plot of declination and inclination versus depth from several cores from Lake Windermere. (After Thompson 1977:54, Figure 2.)

patterns of long sequences of declination and inclination changes rather than the results of a single sample with a master curve. Even then, much of the lake-sediment data is not refined enough to provide very accurate dating. Finally, physical movement and slumping of deposits in lakes and ocean bottoms are an ever-present problem. This may be the source of many of the large directional changes that have been interpreted by some investigators as evidence for geomagnetic excursions.

The variable nature of remanent magnetic direction records obtained from wet sediments collected in adjacent lake basins and even within the same basin has led some to despair of ever obtaining reliable secular variation records from this source. However, recently obtained consistent results on contemporaneous cores collected in neighboring lake basins (e.g., Banerjee *et al.* 1979; Turner and Thompson 1981) suggest that *in some situations* secular variation may be recorded by sediments with reasonable accuracy. In addition, Turner and Thompson (1982) have recently discussed a promising procedure for "detransforming" results obtained from sediments. This procedure should, in some situations, provide reasonably accurate information about past geomagnetic direction. It is also very encouraging to note that in multispecimen samples collected from some dry sediments (Liddicoat and Coe 1979) a very high degree of agreement between widely separated material has been obtained. Consequently, in the future some carefully selected results from sediments may be of considerable importance in archaeomagnetic studies.

The early history of such work on dry-varved sediments through the recent explosion of studies on cores extracted from the bottom of existing lakes has been reviewed by Lund and Banerjee (1979). Their article also discusses the development of field, laboratory, and statistical techniques. Consequently, only those studies of direct archaeological interest are summarized here.

Cave Sediments in Europe

The most extensive work on the remanent magnetism of sediments in archaeological sites has been undertaken by Kopper and Creer (1973, 1976; also see Creer and Kopper 1974, 1976) on material collected in caves in Europe. Although the authors claim some success in matching maxima and minima in repetitive quasisinusoidal declination and inclination versus time graphs with those obtained from radiocarbon-dated lake and marginal sea-cores, it is conceivable that entire periods of declination and/or inclination could be absent due to erosion or lack of sedimentation for a period of time. Such a missing cycle would, of course, greatly affect age estimation. In addition, Creer and Kopper (1976:48–49) mention that the remanence in many cave sediments is chemical in origin, due to the action of aerobic or anaerobic bacteria that alter ferromagnetic minerals in the sediments. This usually causes an averaging of the change in geomagnetic direction, with at least some of the remanence recording geomagnetic direction at a time later (and perhaps significantly later) than the time of deposition.

In contrast to the situation with archaeomagnetic direction dating of baked-clay features, the association of cave sediments with cultural activity is not always clear. In Tito Bustillo Cave, Creer and Kopper (1974) assume a rather shallow deposit is contemporaneous with Magdalenian paintings in the cave and then claim that the paintings have been dated using the secular variation record. In Jeita Cave in Lebanon (Creer and Kopper 1976), where there are no cultural deposits, it is suggested that the presence of layers of red and black sediments is due to intentional prehistoric slash-and-burn practices, perhaps for animal drives or to clear land for incipient agriculture.

Finally, Kopper and Creer (1976:3) note that "interpretation is an art and the accuracy of the findings will depend on the experience of the interpreter." Consequently, the results thus far obtained must be considered suggestive rather than proven.

Lacustrine Sediments

The occurrence of artifacts discarded from shoreline settlements in lake sediments or lacustrine sediments interspersed with archaeological deposits due to expanding and contracting lake boundaries provide other situations where secular variation might be used for direct archaeological dating. Preliminary studies of this type have thus far been undertaken on sediments collected at Hoxne, Suffolk in England (Thompson *et al.* 1974) and Tlapacoya in central Mexico (Liddicoat 1976:172–205). In both studies, dry sediments were sampled long after the lakes had receded or disappeared. Consequently, it was possible to collect multiple contemporaneous specimens.

In the Hoxne study, specimens were collected from two parallel columns. Although there are a few striking differences, the declination and inclination variation in the two columns had a fairly similar pattern (Thompson *et al.* 1974:234). However, because independently dated secular variation records for this time period (presumably, second interglacial) have yet to be established, no chronometric dates were obtained.

During the course of his dissertation research, Liddicoat (1976) collected samples, consisting of about six specimens each, from dry lacustrine sediments at four early archaeological sites. Unfortunately, the remanences of the specimens collected at three of the sites—Murray Springs and Cerros Negros in Arizona, and Tule Springs in Nevada—were very weak and it was not possible to measure them adequately with the equipment Liddicoat had at his disposal. The results obtained from the fourth site, Tlapacoya, in the Valley of Mexico (Liddicoat 1976:1972–205) were very poor and are in no way comparable to the excellent results Liddicoat (1976; Liddicoat and Coe 1979) obtained from samples collected from dry sediments at Mono and Searles lakes in California and Lakes Lahontan and Bonneville in Utah. In part, this may have been due to the lakeshore or near-shore location of the deposits, which consisted of lacustrine mud, peat, beach gravel, and reworked volcanic ash and pumice, and the fact that the sediments were deposited in shallow water. Since laboratory deposition experiments also gave very inconsistent results, a major portion of the problem may have been due to the material itself. (Liddicoat 1976:312).

The preservation of pollen in lacustrine sediments provides an opportunity to obtain valuable information about climatic change. The dating of this material, consequently, is of considerable archaeological interest. Several attempts to accomplish this using secular variation of geomagnetic direction have been made (e.g., Dickson *et al.* 1978).

Rapidly Deposited Sediments at Chaco Canyon

Nichols (1975) studied the remanent magnetic direction in rapidly deposited sediments in an arid region. He collected the sediments, which probably accumulated during the past 1000 years, at Chaco Canyon, a region of considerable archaeological interest in northwest New Mexico. His results suggest that such material may, in some situations, provide very important data.

Samples, each consisting of eight individually oriented specimens, were collected from sediments in three features: a garden plot, a meander scar, and a canal. Measurements on stratigraphic samples collected from the meander scar provided a sequence of high-precision VGPs. They closely followed, in almost perfect stratigraphic order, an unpublished polar curve developed from samples collected from independently dated baked-clay features for the A.D. 1500–1850 time period (Nichols 1975:44–46). These excellent results were probably obtained because the sediments were deposited rapidly in an arid region. Consequently, any PDRM was acquired shortly after deposition, CRM was negligible, and the sediment in each specimen was deposited in a short period of time. The results for the garden field and the canal were not nearly as good. Nonetheless, more work in similar sedimentary environments certainly needs to be undertaken.

PALEOINTENSITY

The direct dating of pottery, if possible, would be of tremendous importance in archaeological research. Consequently, the possibility of a dating method based on changes of the past intensity of the geomagnetic field, which in theory can be determined from unoriented pieces of fired clay, has excited considerable interest in recent years. The term paleointensity is usually used to refer to studies of this type. The advantages of a dating method based on paleointensity (as compared with archaeomagnetic direction dating) include the ease and speed with which samples can be collected and the abundant opportunities to date material from previously excavated sites. As with archaeomagnetic direction dating, it is dependent on the development of well-calibrated regional reference curves.

Secular variation of intensity is due to the same causes as secular variation of direction: intensity and direction changes in the anomalies that make up the non-dipole field, longitudinal drift of the anomalies, and variation in the strength and direction of the dipole field. As discussed above, of the three parameters used as a measure paleointensity on unoriented samples—F, F/F_0, and VADM—the last provides the best indication of intensity variation. Consequently, on the paleointensity reference curves in this chapter (Figures 6.13, 6.15B, 6.15C, and 6.16B), values originally presented as F or F/F_0 have been converted to virtual axial dipole moments (VADMs).

Consideration of existing curves and the precision obtainable on repeat measurements suggests that when the age of the fired clay is known within ±150 years, with a great deal of work (ca. six to eight specimens in a sample), a date with a precision of ± about 30 years at the 95% confidence level might be obtained in some situations. On the negative side, the sinusoidal configuration of the intensity versus time curves (Figures 6.13, 6.15B, 6.15C, and 6.16B) means that many samples of significantly different ages, which cannot be separated chronologically by other methods, have the same intensity values.

Since time is one of the variables in the reference curves, very accurate independent dating of the samples is essential in their establishment. In this regard, because archaeomagnetic direction dating is capable of independently placing samples in their correct chronological order with great precision, determination of paleointensity on samples taken from baked features may greatly assist in the establishment of an intensity versus time curve. Reciprocally, in some situations, paleointensity measurements can assist in dating samples from baked features of different ages that have identical or similar remanent directions. Of much greater importance, recent work (Fox and Aitken 1978, 1980; Rogers et al. 1979; Walton 1980) has isolated several previously uncontrolled variables that can significantly affect the results obtained. It is still not clear if it will be possible to control all the variables influencing paleointensity determination and how severely this will affect the results. Consequently, at this time the accuracy with which paleointensity determinations might be made is difficult to assess, but the consistent results obtained by different workers in the Southwest and Mesoamerica (Bucha et al. 1970; Lee 1975; Sternberg and Butler 1978) and on such radically different materials as pottery and adobe bricks in Egypt (Games 1980) are encouraging.

Almost all paleointensity work has been directed toward establishing curves and developing methods of determining past intensity. Although a few chronometric inferences have been drawn from such data (Barbetti 1976; Shaw 1979), no paleointensity dates have been reported in the literature. However, a result of considerable archaeological interest emanating from this work is the evidence that atmospheric ^{14}C variation is, in a large part, due to fluctuations in the intensity of the geomagnetic field (Elsasser et al. 1956; Sternberg and Damon 1979).

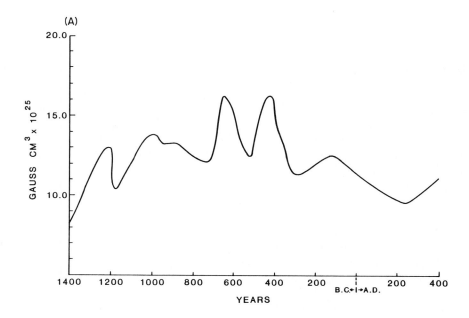

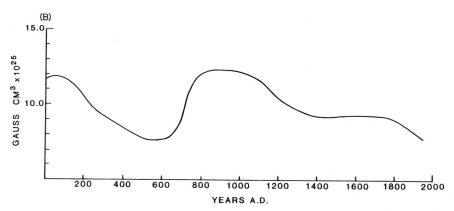

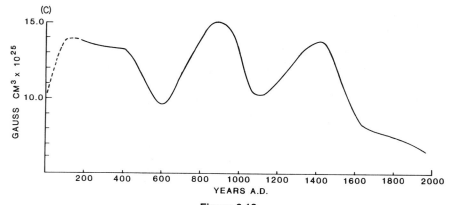

Figure 6.13.

Measurement of Past Intensity

Experimental work by Nagata (1943:88–91) and others has demonstrated that the magnetic moment due to TRM acquired by igneous rock is (nearly) linearly proportional to the intensity of the magnetic field in which the rock is fired up to about 1 gauss. Where this linear relation holds between the NRM of a fired-clay archaeological specimen and the TRM it acquires when heated to about 700° C in a laboratory field F_L, the ancient (or paleo) intensity F_A can then be determined by the simple relationship:

$$F_A = F_L \frac{\text{NRM}}{\text{TRM}} \tag{6}$$

However, heating fired clay to 700° C will often cause mineralogical and/or chemical change in the constituent ferromagnetic minerals, and when this happens, Equation 6 will not be true. In addition, the NRM of an ancient piece of fired clay often consists not only of the original TRM but also may include significant secondary components due to VRM, IRM, and possibly CRM. In this case the NRM is not the magnetic moment acquired when the sample was originally baked and once again Equation 6 will not be true. Additional sources of error are discussed below.

This basic approach to determining paleointensity (using Equation 6) was suggested by Folgheraiter (1899:16) before the turn of the century. Not surprisingly, he could not obtain consistent results when reheating the same pieces several times in the laboratory and discontinued his work on paleointensity.

The Thellier Double Heating Method

A procedure proposed and developed by Thellier and Thellier (1942, 1946, 1959), often referred to as the *Thellier double heating method,* in which the partial NRM lost and the partial TRM acquired in a series of temperature intervals between ambient and about 700° C are determined. This provides a means by which errors due to chemical change and secondary components can, in most instances, he recognized and often eliminated.

The Thellier double heating method of determining the ancient field intensity proceeds as follows:

1. The NRM of the specimen is measured.
2. The specimen is heated to 100° C and cooled in a laboratory field (F_L,

Figure 6.13. Virtual axial dipole moment versus time curves. (A) Athens, Greece: 1400 B.C.–A.D. 400. (After Walton 1979: 644, Figure 1; VADMs calculated from data on the figure.) (b) The Ukraine and Moldavia: A.D. 1–present. (After Rusakov and Zagniy 1973b:276, Figure 1; VADMs calculated from data in Rusakov and Zagniy 1973b:277–284; Table 1.) (C) Peru A.D. 1–present. (After Gunn and Murray 1980:363; Figure 1; VADMs calculated from data in Gunn and Murray 1980: 359–360, Table 2.)

usually on the order of 0.5 oersteds) and the remanent magnetism is measured.
3. The specimen is rotated 180° and Step 2 is repeated.
4. Steps 2 and 3 are repeated a number of times increasing the temperature by 50 or 100° C each time up to 700° C.
5. Using vector addition, the NRM remaining (RNRM) and the PTRM at each temperature are computed and plotted against each other (Figure 6.14). Statistical methods for eliminating noncolinear points and estimating the slope and its standard error have been discussed by Sternberg and Butler (1978) and Coe *et al.* (1978).

If the (RNRM vs PTRM) points are colinear (here referred to as the *straight line criterion*) and if several other criteria are satisfied, the absolute value of the slope of the line will be the ratio of NRM to TRM. Equation 6 can then be used to determine the ancient intensity (F_A). As shown on Figure 6.14, low and high temperature points (the first one or two and last one or two) are often not colinear with the others, due to VRM and chemical (and/or mineralogical) change respectively. However, assuming that the other criteria mentioned below are satisfied, the absolute value of the slope of the line drawn through the colinear intermediate temperature points is equal to NRM/TRM and the ancient intensity can still be determined using Equation 6. Herein lies the great beauty of the Thellier procedure and its superiority over other methods discussed below that depend on a

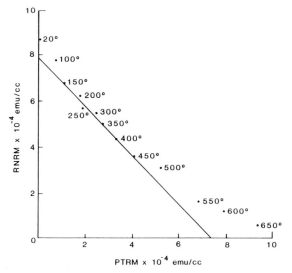

Figure 6.14. RNRM versus PTRM diagram, suggesting presence of mineralogical or chemical change above 450° C and VRM.

single heating to the Curie temperature; that is, even if heating to 700° C changes the material chemically or mineralogically, good results can often be obtained if heating to a lower temperature (500° C, for example) does not bring about such a change.

Colinearity of a reasonable portion of the RNRM versus PTRM points has often been interpreted as an indication that the results are accurate. It should be emphasized that it is not a sufficient condition for accurate results to be obtained using the Thellier double heating procedure.

Variables That Affect Paleointensity Data

In recent years, there has been considerable discussion of the variables that might affect paleointensity determination. Among these are fabric anisotropy, shape anisotropy, cooling rate, stress effects during drilling, mineralogical and chemical change during laboratory heating, weathering, nonlinearity of TRM versus field intensity, multidomain grains, and multiple aboriginal firings. An additional variable of considerable importance is geomagnetic inclination.

Thellier was aware of most of them. Consequently, he included a series of criteria and procedures to improve the accuracy of his paleointensity results (Thellier and Thellier 1959:309–333; Thellier 1977:242–243). The most important of these are the following: (1) choosing weakly magnetized samples to avoid shape anisotropy due to self-demagnetization effects; (2) undertaking preliminary magnetic studies on the material to check for mineralogical or chemical change during heating; (3) an additional check for mineralogical change by reheating to 300° C and remeasuring of the remanence after the complete double heating procedure; (4) rejecting samples that have a VRM in excess of 2% of the total NRM; (5) measuring multiple specimens and multiple contemporaneous samples; (6) rejecting specimens in which the remanent direction changed more than a small amount after the first or second heating; (7) selecting only those samples for which inclination can be determined. Although such painstaking, time-consuming work was essential in the early stages of research on the past intensity of the geomagnetic field, Thellier rejected many samples and he reported very few paleointensity results. The final report based upon many years of work by the Thelliers included only seven paleointensity results (Thellier and Thellier 1959:354). Not surprisingly, later workers have not used all the exhaustive procedures prescribed by Thellier, resulting in the publication of much questionable data. Particularly disturbing is the low number of specimens (sometimes as few as one) in many samples.

Recent research has concentrated on attempts to determine and control some of the variables that might affect the results, including the following:

Anisotropy. Both fabric (Rogers *et al.* 1979) and shape anisotropy (Fox and Aitken 1978) can occur in pottery. The effects of fabric anisotropy can be avoided if care is taken to magnetize the specimen in the same direction in the laboratory as in antiquity. This precaution may eliminate or at least reduce the effects of shape anisotropy. But because the configuration and strength of the self-demagnetizing field of an entire pot may vary somewhat from that of an individual specimen cut from it, it may not be possible in all cases to completely correct for this effect (Games 1979). Consequently, as was suggested by Thellier and Thellier (1959:312), it is probably best to avoid very strongly magnetized material.

Cooling Rate Dependence.   Since remanent moment is inversely proportional to rate of cooling, if the laboratory cooling rate is more rapid than the ancient cooling rate, the Thellier double heating procedure will overestimate the ancient field.

In experiments undertaken by Fox and Aitken (1980:463), in which pottery fired in the lab cooled over 7 hours and the cooling time during the Thellier paleointensity procedure was 30 minutes, errors on the order of 6 to 12% were found. Kiln-fired pottery, bricks, and tiles may take a couple days to cool (Roberts 1961). Consequently, for kiln-fired material, rapid laboratory cooling times (5–30 minutes) can cause errors on the order of 10 to 20% (Fox and Aitken 1980:463). This is in good agreement with theoretical calculations made by Walton (1980). Although correction for this effect in some instances may be difficult, in others reasonable estimates may be possible.

Due to the absence of kilns in Precolumbian America, pottery was usually cooled for only slightly longer time periods (Shepard 1956:81–91) than is customary in routine laboratory processing. There are other places in the world where, for at least part of the time, pottery was not fired in kilns.

Stress and Vibration Effects.   Several investigators (Kuster 1969; Rainbow, Fuller, and Schmidt 1972; Burmester 1977) have noted that coring some rocks adds a remanence in the direction of the ambient field. The problem has been studied in some detail by Burmester (1977), who has used the term *drilling induced remanence* (DIR) for magnetism from this source. He attributes the effect to VRM due to vibration and stress effects.

Gunn and Murray (1980:351) report that, when some potsherds were ground with an abrasive wheel, the sherds were demagnetized across the coercivity spectrum by 10% or more. Although the effect seems different from DIR, the authors suggest that it may be related. In order to avoid this effect, Gunn and Murray broke rather than cut or cored the sherds they sampled. Since cutting and coring are common methods of removing a paleointensity specimen from its matrix, further investigation of this previously unsuspected source of error is clearly needed.

Mineralogical and Chemical Change During Laboratory Heating. Mineralogical and chemical change during heating has long been recognized as one of the most severe problems in determining paleointensity. As discussed above, it is precisely because these changes often occur only at higher temperatures that the Thellier procedure is so useful.

All material that undergoes chemical changes during heating need not be discarded. Such changes may be reduced or eliminated by heating in a vacuum or nitrogen. Experiments on the effect of baking clay in gases other than air were first undertaken by Thellier (1938:223–262) many years ago. More recently, Khodair and Coe (1975) have shown that considerable improvements in paleointensity determinations for some lavas can be made if they are heated in a vacuum. For some material prolonged heating, even well below the Curie temperature, may cause chemical and mineralogical change. In this case, the Thellier procedure will usually not provide useful results. Single heating methods that in some situations may avoid this source of error are discussed in the following section.

A potentially more serious problem is that mineralogical and chemical changes can begin at low temperature and continue during further heating in such a way that the straight line criterion can be satisfied, thus leading to a false result (e.g., U.S.–Japan Cooperation Program in Micronesia 1975). It is likely that thus far most such occurrences have gone undetected. It is therefore not known whether they are common. Preliminary studies and heating in a vacuum should keep them at a minimum. The additional step of heating to 300° and remeasuring the remanence after the complete double heating procedure will probably identify such material after the fact. This step, proposed by Thellier (1977:243), is not very time consuming.

Weathering.   As briefly discussed above, during the burial of fired clay in the ground a variety of oxidation and hydration reactions may chemically alter some of its ferromagnetic minerals. The effect of this alteration on paleointensity determination will depend on the strength of the CRM of the new minerals and further transitions when they are heated in the laboratory. Barbetti and McElhinny (1976:532–536) and Barbetti *et al.* (1977) have studied the consequences of such changes including the hydration of hematite (α-Fe_2O_3) to lepidocrocite (γ-$FeOOH$). Leaching such altered minerals out of the clay in the laboratory (i.e., chemical demagnetization) may reduce their disturbing effects on paleointensity determination.

Multidomain Grains.   Although rarely stated explicitly, the theoretical justification for the Thellier double heating procedure strictly applies only to single-domain grains. Recent experimental and theoretical work has demonstrated that the data points in the Thellier double heating experiment will follow a concave upward line if a significant portion of the remanence is carried by multidomain grains (Banerjee and Butler 1977; Levi 1977).

Nonlinearity of Remanence and Field Strength.   It is generally assumed that the TRM and NRM in Equation 6 are linearly dependent on field strength. Significant departures from linearity in fields above 1 gauss have been noted. To a lesser extent in some material this can occur at lower fields as well (Coe 1967b:169–171). For optimum results the lab field should therefore be as close as possible to the ancient field. This can be accomplished by making a preliminary determination of the ancient field strength using an arbitrary laboratory field.

Geomagnetic Inclination.   An additional factor of considerable importance should be mentioned before briefly discussing some of the data. Almost all of the paleointensity data reported in the literature is past intensity F, past intensity divided by modern intensity F/F_0 or VADMs, all of which are functions of both geomagnetic inclination and intensity. This is significant because the dipole wobble contribution to VADM variation at 45° latitude has been estimated at 21–43% (Barton *et al.* 1979:101). In addition, there is some influence of change in direction of the non-dipole anomalies. Due to the significant dipole wobble contribution, marked similarities may exist in the intensity versus time curves in adjacent areas or even in areas separated by great distances in a north–south direction. Consequently, in order to learn as much as possible about geomagnetic field behavior in the past, it is highly desirable to make as many paleointensity measurements as possible on samples for which paleodirection (or at least inclination) can be determined. Due to the ease of obtaining sherds from archaeological excavations as compared with the great deal of time that must be devoted to collecting oriented samples in the field, the independent variables— intensity and inclination—remain confounded in most studies. It seems likely that some of the rapid changes in paleointensity are primarily due to inclination variation. Interestingly, the confounding of these variables, in some situations, provides opportunities for more precise and accurate archaeological dating.

New Methods

In order to reduce the time needed to measure paleointensity, and in some cases to try to improve the results, a series of other methods for comparing portions of the NRM (acquired in antiquity) and the TRM (acquired in the lab) have been tried.

Some of these newer methods (e.g., Shaw 1974; Smith 1967; Van Zijl *et al.* 1962) involve a single rapid heating to about 700° C. Since for some materials chemical changes are less likely to occur in a single rapid heating than in a series of heatings and coolings, they may have some advantages. Although these methods are effective in eliminating the effects of VRM, there is, of course, no guarantee that a single heating will not cause mineralogical and/or chemical change. Consequently, with the possible exception of the Shaw (1974) method, they lack the most important feature of the Thellier method, the possibility of providing an accurate result even when such changes take place at high temperature.

Van Zijl *et al.* (1962) proposed AF demagnetization (in their work at 219 oersteds) before measuring the NRM and TRM. This approach eliminates the effects of some, but not necessarily all, of the VRM and, of course, high temperature changes, if present, can affect the result.

Paleointensity methods that add progressive thermal (Wilson 1961) or progressive AF demagnetization (Smith 1967) to the basic approach originally tried by Folgheraiter have also been proposed and used. In these methods the slope of the best-line fit to the points determined by demagnetized NRM moments plotted against their corresponding demagnetized TRM moments is used as an estimate of the ratio of the ancient to the lab field. Doell and Smith (1969) went one step further and added AF demagnetization prior to the progressive thermal demagnetization of both the NRM and TRM. Despite some apparent advantages, none of these methods has been widely used and comparisons of the results suggests that in most cases it is better to follow the original Thellier procedure (Coe and Grommé 1973).

An increasingly popular modified AF method has been proposed by John Shaw (1974). A revised version for hard samples has also been used (Shaw 1979). It is considerably faster than the Thellier method and apparently in most situations provides an indication of when chemical change has taken place. As with the Thellier procedure, it may allow results to be obtained even if such a change has occurred. Reliable results have been obtained the few times it has been tested on samples originally fired in a field of known intensity. In addition, in some cases results have been obtained when they could not be using the Thellier method (Shaw 1974). The Shaw method differs from the AF method proposed by Smith (1967) by the addition of two ARMs, the first after the NRM has been demagnetized and the second after the TRM has been demagnetized. The ARMs are then (AF) demagnetized in steps and compared at each level to determine the portion of the coercive force spectrum unaffected by heating in the laboratory (see Shaw 1974 for details of the procedure.) It should be noted that while alteration of the coercive force spectrum suggests chemical change, lack of change does not necessarily indicate that no chemical or mineralogical change has taken place.

As discussed above, an adobe brick apparently acquires a remanence when the mud is liquefied due to strain as it is forced into the mold (Games 1977; Stupavsky *et al.* 1979:271). Games (1977, 1980) has proposed a method for determining paleointensity from such bricks that is virtually identical to the Shaw (1974) method with laboratory heating replaced by dissolving the specimen cut from an adobe brick (generally a cylindrical core) and forming a new specimen of identical dimensions under pressure. This method seems to give good results.

Improved Equipment

The extremely laborious procedures involved in the Thellier method is the principal reason that only a limited amount of paleointensity data is available and that the additional criteria and procedures proposed by Thellier are not carried out very often. Greater speed in the Thellier and other paleointensity methods has recently been achieved using cryogenic magnetometers and microprocessors

(Rogers *et al.* 1979, 1980; Walton 1977). In the latest system (Rogers *et al.* 1980) a cryogenic magnetometer, an oven, and an AF demagnetizer are all inside the same mu metal shield and the steps in the Thellier or Shaw paleointensity procedures are carried out automatically.

Paleointensity Data

Since the publication of the classic paper by Thellier and Thellier (1959) new data have been reported regularly but rather slowly. Most of these have been obtained using the Thellier double heating procedure. Other methods, particularly in recent years, have also been used. Among those studies on large numbers of samples that have led to the construction of what appear to be fairly accurate intensity versus time curves are the following: Sasajima 1965 (Japan), Bucha *et al.* 1970 (U.S. Southwest and Mesoamerica), Rusakov and Zagniy 1973 (Ukraine and Moldavia), Lee 1975 (Mesoamerica), Walton 1979 (Greece), Gunn and Murray 1980 (Peru), Games 1980 (Egypt), and Sternberg 1982 (U.S. Southwest). All the paleointensity studies using archaeological baked-clay samples of which I am aware are listed on Table 6.1. Some typical VADM versus time curves are shown in Figures 6.13, 6.15B, 6.15C, and 6.16B. As is the case for archaeomagnetic direction data, paleointensity data are far more abundant for the northern hemisphere.

Due to the recent studies concerning the problems of paleointensity determination and the recognition of numerous possible sources of error, the question arises whether any of the previously obtained results can be considered valid. While there is, of course, no easy answer to this question, some results are particularly encouraging.

Games (1980) found that paleointensity results obtained on sherds and adobe bricks from Egypt, which are due to very different types of remanent magnetism, are in close agreement. In addition, fairly consistent paleointensity results have been obtained by several different investigators on sherds from the southwestern United States and Mesoamerica. These results may, in part, be due to the absence of wheel-made pottery and kilns in these areas in prehistoric times. Finally, the fact that most of these curves have similar periods and amplitudes suggests that, despite the many potential errors much of the data thus far obtained is at least qualitatively good. Patterns are emerging from these data that are of both geophysical and archaeological interest. A few examples are discussed in the following sections.

Mesoamerica

The intensity F/F_0 versus time curve for Mesoamerica developed by Lee (1975:159) (converted to a VADM versus time curve in Figure 6.15B) is very similar to the inclination versus time curve (Figure 6.15A; Wolfman 1973, 1981)

TABLE 6.1

Paleointensity Studies on Archaeological Baked-Clay Samples

Reference	Sample location(s)
Thellier (1938)	France
Thellier and Thellier (1942)	France
Thellier and Thellier (1946)	France
Thellier and Thellier (1959)	Europe and North Africa
Nagata et al. (1963)	Japan
Nagata et al. (1965)	Mexico, Peru, Bolivia
Hsing-Huei and Tung-Chieh (1965)	China
DuBois and Watanabe (1965)	Southwestern United States
Sasajima (1965)	Japan
Weaver (1966)	Great Britain
Sasajima and Maenaka (1966)	Japan
Athavale (1966)	India
Bucha (1967)	Czechoslovakia
Bucha and Mellaart (1967)	Anatolia
Schwarz and Christie (1967)	Ontario, Canada
Kitazawa and Kobayashi (1968)	Bolivia and Ecuador
Burlatskaya et al. (1969)	East Europe
Athavale (1969)	Egypt
Bucha et al. (1970)	West Mexico and Southwestern United States
Nachasova (1972)	Moscow area, Soviet Union
Rusakov and Zagniy (1973b)	Ukraine and Moldavia
Shaw (1974)	England
Lee (1975)	Mexico and Guatemala, Peru and Bolivia
Barbetti and McElhinny (1976)	Australia
Barbetti (1976)	France
Kovacheva and Veljovich (1977)	Bulgaria and Yugoslavia
Games (1977)	Peru and Egypt
Sternberg and Butler (1978)	Southwestern United States
Walton (1979)	Greece
Shaw (1979)	France
Gunn and Murray (1980)	Peru
Barbetti et al. (1980)	France
Games (1980)	Egypt
Liritzis and Thomas (1980)	Crete
Games and Baker (1981)	England
Arbour and Schwarz (1982)	Quebec, Canada
Sternberg (1982)	Southwestern United States

for this area. The inclination curve has peaks at A.D. 200 and 400 and minima at A.D. 700 and 900. Lee (1975:159) shows an intensity peak at A.D. 475 and a minimum at A.D. 800. This indicates (not very surprisingly) that intensity variation was not entirely a reflection of inclination change at this time. A critical analysis of the available data suggests that intensity values may have been low from A.D. 700 to 900 but it is not clear whether intensity values rose (as did the inclination values for a short time at ca A.D. 800). There are not enough samples nor is the independent dating refined enough to indicate whether the inclination

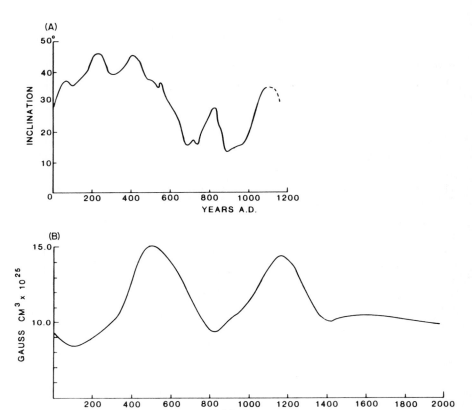

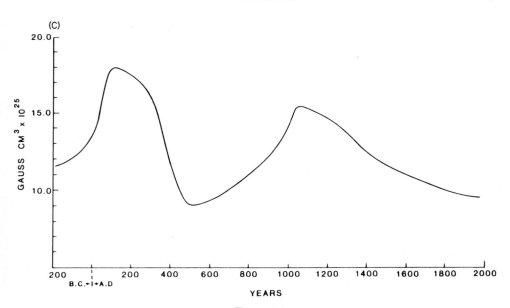

Figure 6.15.

peak at about A.D. 200 also occurred in intensity. Lee's data also indicate an intensity maximum at sometime between A.D. 1050 and 1200, which is in good agreement with the inclination maximum in Mesoamerica at about A.D. 1100–1150.

Bucha *et al.* (1970) constructed an intensity curve based on samples from the northwest edge of Mesoamerica (Figure 6.15C). The configuration of this curve is very similar to the one presented by Lee (1975:159), but the ages of the maxima and minima on Bucha *et al.*'s curve are 100 to nearly 400 years earlier. The dating of the samples used by Lee (1975) to develop his paleointensity curve is supported by many radiocarbon measurements, archaeomagnetic direction results, cross-dating, and native calendars (Wolfman 1973). In contrast, the calibration of the Bucha *et al.* curve seems to be on less-secure footing. It is based on fewer ^{14}C dates, many of which were not obtained from wood charcoal (Taylor *et al.* 1969). This, as well as the inclination curve for Mesoamerica suggests that Bucha *et al.*'s curve should be shifted in time to place one maximum at about A.D. 475, another at about 1100 and a minimum at about A.D. 800. Some inclination and intensity data from the Southwest (ca. 2000 km to the northwest), which are discussed below, also support this dating of the Mesoamerican intensity variations.

The Southwestern United States

Paleointensity data have also been obtained in the southwestern United States, most of it on pottery samples from the Snaketown site in southern Arizona. Values obtained by Bucha *et al.* (1970) on pottery from this site led to the construction of an intensity versus time curve (Figure 6.16B) similar in configuration and calibration to their curve for Mesoamerica with intensity maxima at A.D. 100 and 1100 and a minimum at A.D. 800.

Intensity data obtained on potsherds from Snaketown have also been reported by Sternberg and Butler (1978; Sternberg 1982). Although the general configuration of the intensity curve is similar, the absolute values of the readings originally reported by Sternberg and Butler (1978) are in some cases significantly lower. The apparent source of the discrepancy is fabric anisotropy accompanied by consistently differing orientation of the specimens in each laboratory during heating and cooling (Sternberg 1982:148–151). One particularly interesting result among those recently reported by Sternberg (1982:183–205) suggests the

---

Figure 6.15. Comparison of inclination versus time and virtual axial dipole moment versus time curves for Mesoamerica. (A) Inclination versus time for Mesoamerica: A.D. 1–1075. (Inclination values calculated from data on Figure 6.11 and from additional unpublished data.) (B) Virtual axial dipole moment versus time for Mesoamerica: A.D. 1–present. (After Lee 1975:159, Figure 71; VADMs calculated from data in Lee 1975:176–200, Table 9.) (C) Virtual axial dipole moment versus time for northwest Mesoamerica; 200 B.C.–present. (After Bucha *et al.* 1970:113, Figure 71; VADMs calculated from Bucha *et al.* 1970:111, Table 1.)

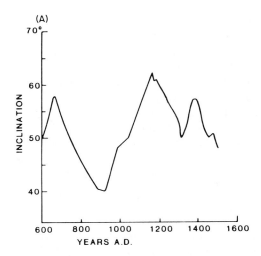

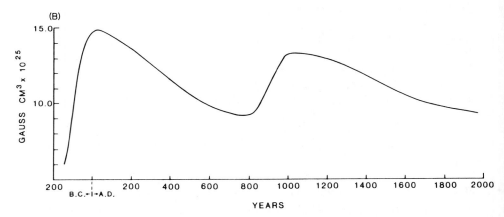

Figure 6.16. Comparison of inclination versus time and virtual axial dipole moment versus time curves for the Southwestern United States. (A) Inclination versus time for the Southwestern United States: A.D. 600–1500. (After DuBois and Wolfman 1971 and DuBois 1975:141, Figure 3.) (B) Virtual axial dipole moment versus time for southern Arizona: 150 B.C.–present. (After Bucha *et al.* 1970:113, Figure 2a; VADMs calculated from Bucha *et al.* 1970:111, Table 1.)

possibility that the peak Bucha *et al.* (1970) placed at A.D. 100 might be earlier in the sequence (i.e., the Vahki phase).

Due to the proximity of the Southwest to Mesoamerica we should expect similar effects of both dipole and probably some nondipole variation to be seen in the inclination and intensity curves for both areas. The intensity minimum at A.D. 800 and maximum sometime between A.D. 900 and 1200 obtained by

Bucha *et al.* are in general agreement with the other directional and intensity data from both the Southwest (Figure 6.16A) and Mesoamerica (Figure 6.15). On the basis of the above discussion it is very tempting to suggest that the intensity maximum at A.D. 100 on the Bucha *et al.* southern Arizona curve should be shifted to sometime between A.D. 400 and 500. The archaeological implications of such a shift are considerable and must be placed in their proper context.

The dating of the early portion of the archaeological sequence at Snaketown is one of the most disputed chronologies in the entire western hemisphere (see Gladwin *et al.* 1937; Gladwin 1942; Wheat 1955; Di Peso 1956; Haury 1976: 325–340; Bullard 1962:53–95; Plog 1978; Schiffer 1982). Gladwin *et al.* (1937), Haury (1976), and Wheat (1955) favor a "long chronology," with the earliest phase, the Vahki, beginning about 300 B.C. and the Sacaton phase (late in the sequence) ending at A.D. 1100. Gladwin (1942), Bullard (1962), Plog (1978), and Schiffer (1982) favor variant versions of a "short chronology" with the Vahki phase beginning somewhere between A.D. 350 and 600 and the Sacaton phase ending at about the traditional A.D. 1100 (Plog) or a little earlier (Bullard) or somewhat later (Schiffer).

The dates of the samples used by Bucha *et al.* (1970) in calibrating their intensity curve are those favored by Haury (one of the coauthors). However, if the peak in intensity were placed at about A.D. 475 rather than 100 on this curve, the paleointensity data would support a variant of the short chronology in which the Estrella phase, the second in the sequence immediately following Vahki, includes this date. This placement of the Estrella phase is a bit earlier than in most, but not all, versions of the short chronology. Plog (1978), primarily on the basis of his analysis of the ^{14}C results, dates this phase between A.D. 350 and 550. If this peak occurred during the Vahki phase, as suggested by some of Sternberg's data, shifting it to about A.D. 475 would put the Estrella phase a bit later in time in better agreement with most versions of the short chronology. At the time most of the paleointensity measurements were made, the effects of several variables were not appreciated; consequently, these inferences must be regarded as tentative. The above discussion is presented to show how such data can be used in chronometric analysis, but clearly more paleointensity measurements and other chronometric data are needed before firm conclusions about this major chronometric problem can be drawn.

The Glozel Controversy

The only case where paleointensity has been used in an attempt to resolve a chronological problem in the Old World involved the archaeological finds from Glozel in central France. This material has been the source of much controversy in recent years.

The excavations at Glozel uncovered pottery and fired-clay artifacts engraved with animal figures and what appears to be writing in a previously unknown script. This material, first reported in 1924 (McKerrell *et al.* 1974:265), was unique then and remains so today. Consequently, many archaeologists (e.g., Renfrew 1975) have argued that they are modern forgeries.

Thermoluminescence studies on the fired-clay objects (McKerrell *et al.* 1974) indicated that they were fired between 700 B.C. and A.D. 100, and microscopic examination indicated that the "writing" was inscribed prior to firing (McKerrell *et al.* 1974:270). Renfrew (1975) and others who have argued that the objects are modern fakes refuse to accept the thermoluminescence results. Because many paleointensity measurements had been made on fired-clay material from western Europe dating between 500 B.C. and the present, the possibility of comparing them with intensity values determined from the Glozel objects existed. Barbetti (1976) undertook such a study and concluded that the intensity of the field in which the Glozel objects were fired was about .45 oersteds, which is about the same as the modern field in that region. Since previously made paleointensity measurements on fired-clay objects from western Europe dating between about 1500 B.C. and A.D. 1500 were almost all considerably higher than the modern intensity, the results obtained by Barbetti (1976:148–149) seemed to indicate that the objects were fired fairly recently.

This apparent contradiction led to a second study by Shaw (1979), who determined paleointensity values for six Samian-ware vessels excavated not far from Glozel, ranging in age from about 50 B.C. to A.D. 200. This study, as well as Walton's (1979) recent paleointensity study on Greek pottery dating between 2000 B.C. and A.D. 400 (see Figure 6.13a), suggest that there was a short departure from the prevailing high intensity between 1500 B.C. and A.D. 1500 in Europe during the first and/or second century A.D., with values nearly as low as those found in the area today.

The intensity minimum based on the results from the Samian-ware samples is placed by Shaw (1974:114) at A.D. 50. The minimum based on results obtained from Greek pottery is thought by Walton (1979:644) to occur at about A.D. 200, which is in good agreement with an inclination minimum at about this time (Thellier 1981:115).

There is then a possibility that the Glozel objects *could* have been fired during the first century A.D. It should be noted that Shaw's (1979) results were obtained on wheel-made Samian ware that Rogers *et al.* (1979) found to be extremely anisotropic. Since Shaw did not fire the Samian-ware specimens (nor the Glozel specimens) in the lab in the same direction as they were fired in antiquity, it is possible that some (or all) of his results are erroneous. Fortunately, in his study of Greek pottery Walton took this precaution. So apparently, there was a short period (ca. A.D. 100) when geomagnetic intensity in Europe was comparable to what it is today. Consequently, paleointensity measurements alone will never be able to resolve this longstanding problem.

REVERSALS AND EXCURSIONS

Reversals

Polarity stratigraphy offers the paleoanthropologist a powerful tool to assist in the chronological placement of deposits containing hominid fossils.

Although methods such as potassium–argon (K–Ar) and fission tracks can provide absolute dates for certain materials such as volcanic rocks and tuff, they usually cannot directly date sediments. Consequently, polarity data obtained on samples of sediment in which fossils have been found can often assist in dating deposits on a much finer scale than would be possible otherwise.

This method, however, is not entirely free from difficulties. Since sequences of normal and reversed polarity repeat many times, stratigraphic, faunal, radiometric, and other evidence often must be considered before meaningful chronological information can be obtained. The many problems that may be encountered in this type of situation are illustrated by the attempts to apply reversal stratigraphy to the fossil-bearing Koobi Fora (Brock and Isaac 1974, 1976; Hillhouse *et al.* 1977) and Shungura (Brown and Shuey 1976; Brown *et al.* 1978) formations in east Africa. They revolved around the correct dating of the KBS tuff that lies in the mid-Koobi Fora formation where many hominid fossils have been excavated. It now appears that K–Ar and fission-track dating both support a date of about 1.88 million years for the KBS tuff (Gleadow 1980; McDougall *et al.* 1980) and reversal stratigraphy now aligns various fossils in the Koobi Fora and Shungura formations with those found at Olduvai Gorge. Such data have also been used to date ''Lucy'' and other hominids found in the sediments of the Hadar formation of Ethiopia (Johanson and Taieb 1976).

While the magnetic stratigraphy in the Lake Turkana–Omo Valley region now seems clear, all the problems of magnetic stratigraphy at the major African hominid sites have not yet been resolved. McFadden *et al.* (1979), for example, recently discussed two alternatives for the paleomagnetic data they obtained at the Makapansgat site where several hominid fossils have been recovered.

Elsewhere in the world, reversal stratigraphy has assisted in the temporal placement of the *Ramapithecus* and *Sivapithecus* fossils found in the Nagri formation in Pakistan (Barndt *et al.* 1978). Davis *et al.* (1980) have used the Brunhes–Matuyama boundary as a horizon marker in their excavations in Tadzhikestan, and reversed magnetic polarity data accompanied by K–Ar dates suggest that the Lower Paleolithic site of Isernia La Pineta in Italy was occupied late in the Matuyama epoch (Coltorti *et al.* 1982).

Although not yet found at an archaeological site, there is increasing evidence (e.g., Creer *et al.* 1980; Denham 1976; Liddicoat *et al.* 1980) that the Blake event was a worldwide, short-lived, reversal at about 110,000 B.P. There are also good data suggesting that there were other very short events in the Brunhes and Matuyama epochs (e.g., Champion *et al.* 1981; Liddicoat *et al.* 1980; Mankinen *et al.* 1978). Perhaps some of these will eventually serve as horizon markers in archaeological contexts.

Excursions

The potential for using late Brunhes epoch excursions for archaeological dating needs to be investigated in greater detail. Due to their short duration, excursions, if they exist in this time period, could be used for fine-scale relative dating.

The existence of occasional excursions in pre-Brunhes epochs seems to be well established on the basis of measurements of samples collected from Icelandic lavas (Doell 1972; Watkins and Walker 1977). However, as noted above, there has been considerable discussion about the reliability of those data suggesting the possibility of late Pleistocene excursions that, if they exist, would be of great interest to archaeologists. Most of the evidence for a reputed excursion(s) at about 12,000 B.P. is now considered suspect. Although the data for an excursion (or perhaps several) in the 25,000–40,000 B.P. range (Denham and Cox 1971; Barbetti and McElhinny 1976; Gillot *et al.* 1979; Liddicoat and Coe 1979) are fairly convincing, some doubts about their validity have been expressed as well (Verosub 1977b). Even if one or more of these excursions did in fact occur, since apparently most excursions are rapid localized (rather than worldwide) phenomena, the chances of a particular hearth recording an excursion is quite low. Consequently, the process of using excursions for archaeological dating may be something like "looking for a needle in a haystack when the needle may not be there" (Wolfman 1981b).

As might be expected, archaeologists have rarely attempted to use this potential dating method. The only attempt of which I am aware to use an excursion to assist in archaeological dating was at the Lewisville site in Texas (Wolfman 1981b, 1982b). While there is some evidence that the site might date somewhere in the 40,000–25,000 B.P. range, measurements made on samples collected from two hearths at the site indicated VGPs within about 20° of the geographic north pole at the time(s) they were in use.

Clearly, the existence and accurate dating of excursions must be established before archaeologists will expend much effort on this potential dating method.

CONCLUDING REMARKS

It has been almost 300 years since the basic principles of archaeomagnetic direction dating were first discovered (Boyle 1691; Halley 1692), but it is only recently that geomagnetic dating methods have begun to have an impact on archaeology. Although there has been a relative paucity of studies in which geomagnetic data have been directly utilized for archaeological dating, the work that has been accomplished clearly indicates its great potential. In the preceding pages the phenomena that make the four dating methods possible, the laboratory procedures, the reference curves which have been developed, and the existing data have been discussed in some detail. The great precision which has been obtained using archaeomagnetic direction dating can help provide solutions to many chronometric problems that often cannot be resolved using other methods except dendrochronology. Such precision, in some situations, might also be obtained using paleointensity dating. It should be noted that in contrast to radiometric methods the precision of the results does not decrease with increasing age.

While all geomagnetic dating methods must be calibrated with other methods, this need not be a severe drawback. Since archaeomagnetic direction data are usually very precise and accurate, they provide a unique opportunity to compare independently obtained radiocarbon and thermoluminescence dates from several different locations within a large area. In this manner, accurate calibrations of the reference curves (far beyond the error limits of individual dates obtained with the chronometric methods used for calibration) can often be obtained.

The accuracy of dating objects and cultural events using geomagnetic methods is greatly enhanced because often it is the object or deposit of primary interest that is dated rather than something merely associated with it. Perhaps of greatest importance, high-precision archaeomagnetic direction results seem to be consistently more accurate and less subject to error during routine processing than those obtained by the radiocarbon and thermoluminescence methods.

Paleointensity dating, which can be applied to unoriented pieces of fired clay, is subject to several potential sources of serious error and in the past was very time consuming. However, a great amount of research in recent years has been directed toward understanding all the mechanisms that affect the paleointensity determination process and the development of regional reference curves. In addition, there have been significant advances in instrumentation that have automated the laboratory procedures. Consequently, I would expect that this method will be more widely used to directly attack chronometric problems in coming years.

In some situations, limitations are imposed due to the fact that geomagnetic direction and intensity are not unique functions of time. But usually with the assistance of stylistic, stratigraphic, and other chronometric data ambiguities, when they occur, can be resolved.

More precise and accurate dating is needed everywhere. It is, therefore, difficult to single out specific areas and/or time periods for further development of archaeomagnetic direction and paleointensity secular variation curves. A few, however, demand attention. For geophysical as well as archaeological reasons the paucity of data from the southern hemisphere is deplorable. The limited amount of data available from areas in the eastern hemisphere where civilizations developed thousands of years ago is particularly disappointing. The Near East, where civilization developed by 3000 B.C., and where earlier village sites with well-baked hearths and ovens exist in profusion in beautifully stratified tells, is an ideal area for developing a 10,000-year direction sequence. In addition, there are excellent opportunities for developing a long paleodirection sequence in northwest India where large cities appeared before 2000 B.C. Unfortunately, no work in this region has yet been accomplished. It is encouraging to note that direction and intensity studies have begun in China where civilization began in the Yellow River Valley about 4000 years ago and Neolithic villages appeared at least 2000 years earlier.

Those areas where village life evolved early provide good opportunities for developing long sequences. But it should not be forgotten that archaeomagnetic baked-clay direction and to a lesser extent paleointensity samples can be collected from sites predating settled life. Eventually, it should be possible to develop archaeomagnetic direction sequences for large portions of the world and perhaps, for a few locations, paleointensity sequences since the beginning of the Holocene. In some cases, it may be possible to obtain good secular variation data from archaeological sites occupied during the Pleistocene as well.

Due to the speed with which sediments deposited over thousands of years can be collected and the availability of very sensitive cryogenic magnetometers, in recent years there has been tremendous interest in using this material to determine past secular variation of geomagnetic direction. Such data will never be as reliable as those obtained from baked clays. However, by working only with sediments that appear to be reliable recorders of past direction, studying their magnetic properties, comparing the results from several basins, and using detransformation procedures, data from this source can assist in the development of secular variation curves. In addition, in some carefully selected situations dating of climatological sequences and archaeological deposits may be possible.

Reversal stratigraphy provides rather unique opportunities to date some ancient materials, including sediments, that are particularly difficult to date using other methods. It is expected that studies of this type, when undertaken in conjunction with other dating methods, will continue to provide chronometric information of great interest to archaeologists and paleoanthropologists. In addition, excursions, may eventually assist in the dating of a few archaeological deposits.

It is only through understanding the mechanisms involved in the acquisition of magnetism by fired clay, rocks, and sediments, and through rigorous application of the methods discussed that optimum results can be obtained. Unfortunately, this has not always been the case in the past. Further refinements of the geomagnetic dating methods will be dependent, at least in part, on continuing research on the mechanisms of the acquisition of remanent magnetism.

In the near future the geomagnetic dating methods should be used with much greater frequency. The development and refinement of secular variation curves (for which there is currently a great need), the tremendous increase in the use of microcomputers to significantly reduce laboratory processing time, the greater appreciation by geophysicists in recent years of the importance of archaeomagnetic data in their discipline, the expanding awareness of archaeologists about the potential of these methods, and, most important, the need for greater precision in modern archaeological studies will considerably increase their application.

Finally, it should not be forgotten that archaeologists have control over a variety of data dealing with the past several thousand and past tens of thousands of years. Interdisciplinary studies, of which those relating to the time-variant characteristics of the geomagnetic field are just a small part, provide data for the benefit of other disciplines as well as archaeology.

APPENDIX 1: MAGNETIC UNITS

Currently, two systems of magnetic units are in use: a centimeter, gram, second (CGS) system, commonly used in everyday conversations, and a meter, kilogram, second (MKS) system, increasingly used in journal articles. Both are defined below.

In the CGS system, the basic unit of magnetic field strength H is the *oersted* (Oe). It is defined as the magnetic field strength in a vacuum at a distance of 1 m from a wire carrying a current of $1000/4\pi$ (ca. 79.6) amperes. Therefore:

$$1 \text{ oersted} = 79.6 \text{ amperes per meter (A/m)}.$$

For some studies it is convenient to speak of another type of magnetic field strength, called the *magnetic induction B*, which is the magnetic flux in a magnetized material. B is defined as follows:

$$B = H + 4\pi J$$

where J is the magnetization of the material in which the measurement is made.

The basic unit of magnetic induction is the *gauss*. Because the magnetization of air is negligible, for all practical purposes in paleomagnetic studies, B and H are the same and sometimes the basic units, gauss and oested, are used interchangeably. For instance, magnetic charts indicate the strength of the geomagnetic field in *gammas* (10^{-5} gauss) but in paleomagnetic studies the term *oersted* is commonly used for the strength of the earth's magnetic field. Conversions to the MKS system in which the *tesla* (T) is the basic unit of magnetic induction are made as follows:

$$1 \text{ gauss} = 10^{-4} \text{ tesla}$$
$$1 \text{ gamma} = 10^{-9} \text{ tesla (or one nanotesla)}$$
The term *microtesla* (μT) $= 10^{-6}$T is also commonly used.

The *magnetization* (*J*) or *magnetic moment* (*M*) per unit volume is dimensionally the same as field strength. The basic unit of magnetic moment is the emu (pronounced "e", "m", "u"). In both systems

$$1 \text{ emu/cc} = 10^3 \text{ A/m}$$

Unfortunately, in the CGS system 1 emu/cc is called a *gauss*. This can be confusing because it is different from the gauss that is the unit of magnetic induction. To avoid this confusion, the term *J gauss* is sometimes used for 1 emu/cc.

In some situations, magnetic moment per unit volume, emu/g (i.e., emu per gram), is used in place of magnetization.

For large magnetic moments (such as the earth's dipole moment) in the CGS system, the term *gauss cm³* is commonly used, whereas in the MKS system *Am²* is used, which is 1000 times larger.

APPENDIX 2: INDEX OF DEFINITIONS OF TECHNICAL TERMS

(continued)

APPENDIX 2: *Continued*

Term	Defined on page number	Term	Defined on page number
magnetic moment (M)	438	sample	392
magnetization (J)	438	saturation magnetization (J_s)	378
magnetic pole	368	secular variation	364
measured paleointensity (F)	370	self-reversing	372
mu metal	383	shape anisotropy	381
natural remanent magnetism (NRM)	376	shear remanent magnetism (SRM)	382
non-dipole anomalies	368	single domain	376
non-dipole field	368	soft	377
normal polarity	374	specimen	392
oersted (Oe)	437	spinner magnetometer	384
paleointensity	365	storage test	387
paleomagnetism	364	tesla (T)	437
partial thermal remanent magnetism (PTRM)	378	thermal demagnetization	386
		thermal remanent magnetism (TRM)	376
peak field	386		
polar curve	371	thixatropic remanent magnetism (TxRM)	382
postdepositional detrital remanent magnetism (PDRM)	382	transient variation	371
		virtual axial dipole moment (VADM)	370
progressive or stepwise demagnetization	394	virtual dipole moment (VDM)	370
pseudosingle domain	376	virtual geomagnetic pole (VGP)	369
relaxation time (τ)	377	viscous remanent magnetism (VRM)	379
reversal	365		
rotational remanent magnetism (RRM)	380	westward drift	371

ACKNOWLEDGMENTS

It is a pleasure to acknowledge the contributions of those who helped me to shape this review article over the past several years. Particularly important were Charles Barton, Richard Dodson, J. Robert Dunn, Duane Champion, Michael Fuller, and Victor Schmidt, who discussed a number of technical points with me. Martin Aitken, Duane Champion, Michael Fuller, Marvin Jeter, Joseph Michels, Michael Schiffer, Gary Scott, Robert Sternberg, John Weymouth, Thomas Windes, and four anonymous reviewers read and commented on one or more drafts of the manuscript. Mary Lynn Kennedy and Marvin Jeter improved my prose with their extensive editorial comments. Jane Kellett drafted the many figures. Finally, I especially thank Michael Schiffer, who asked me to write this review, and my secretary, Mrs. G. G. Williams, who typed several drafts of the manuscript

REFERENCES

Aitken, M. J.
 1961 *Physics and Archaeology* (first edition). Interscience Publishers, New York.
 1974 *Physics and Archaeology* (second edition). Clarendon Press, Oxford.
Aitken, M. J. and H. N. Hawley
 1966 Magnetic Dating—III: Further archaeomagnetic measurements in Britain. *Archaeometry* 9:187–197.

1967   Archaeomagnetic measurements in Britain—IV. *Archaeometry* 10:129–135.

1971   Archaeomagnetism: Evidence for magnetic refraction in kiln structures. *Archaeometry* 13:83–85.

Aitken, M. J., H. N. Hawley, and G. H. Weaver
1963   Magnetic dating: Further archaeomagnetic measurements in Britain. *Archaeometry* 6:76–80.

Aitken, M. J., M. R. Harold, and G. H. Weaver
1964   Some archaeomagnetic evidence concerning the secular variation in Britain. *Nature* 201:659–660.

Aitken, M. J. and G. H. Weaver
1962   Magnetic dating: Some archaeomagnetic measurements in Britain. *Archaeometry* 5:4–22.

1965   Recent archaeomagnetic results in England. *Journal of Geomagnetism and Geoelectricity* 17:391–394.

Andrews, E. W.
1965   Archaeology and prehistory in the northern Maya Lowlands: An introduction. In *Handbook of Middle American Indians*, Vol. 2, edited by G. R. Willey, pp. 288–330. University of Texas Press. Austin.

Arbour, G. and E. J. Schwarz
1982   Archeomagnetic intensity study of Indian potsherds from Quebec, Canada. *Journal of Geomagnetism and Geoelectricity* 34:129–136.

As, J. A. and J. D. A. Zijderveld
1958   Magnetic cleaning of rocks in paleomagnetic research. *Geophysical Journal of the Royal Astronomical Society* 1:308–319.

Asami, E., K. Tokieda, and T. Kishi
1972   Archeomagnetic study of kilns in San-in and Kyushu, Japan. *Memoirs of the Faculty of Literature and Science, Shimane University, Natural Sciences* 5:18–22.

Athavale, R. N.
1966   Intensity of the geomagnetic field in India over the past 4,000 Years. *Nature* 210:1310–1312.

1969   Intensity of the geomagnetic field in prehistoric Egypt. *Earth and Planetary Science Letters* 6:221–224.

Aveni, A. F.
1980   *Skywatchers of Ancient Mexico*. University of Texas Press. Austin.

Banerjee, S. K. and R. F. Butler
1977   Theoretical grain-size thresholds and their application to accurate methods for paleointensity determination. In Palaeomagnetic Field Intensity, Its Measurement in Theory and Practice, edited by Charles M. Carmichael. *Physics of the Earth and Planetary Interiors* 13:268–271.

Banerjee, S. K., S. P. Lund, and S. Levi
1979   Geomagnetic record in Minnesota lake sediments—Absence of the Gothenburg and Erieau excursions. *Geology* 7:588–591.

Barbetti, M.
1976   Archaeomagnetic analyses of six Glozelian ceramic artifacts. *Journal of Archaeological Sciences* 3:137–151.

1977   Measurements of recent geomagnetic secular variation in southeastern Australia and the question of dipole wobble. *Earth and Planetary Science Letters* 36:207–218.

Barbetti, M. and K. Flude
1979   Geomagnetic variation during the late Pleistocene period and changes in the radiocarbon time scale. *Nature* 279:202–205.

Barbetti, M. F. and M. W. McElhinny
    1972   Evidence of a geomagnetic excursion 30,000 yr BP. *Nature* 239:327–330.
    1976   The Lake Mungo geomagnetic excursion. *Philosophical Transactions of the Royal Society of London* 281:515–542.
Barbetti, M. F., M. W. McElhinny, D. J. Edwards, and P. W. Schmidt
    1977   Weathering processes in baked sediments and their effects on archaeomagnetic field-intensity measurements. In Paleomagnetic Field Intensity, Its Measurement in Theory and Practice, edited by Charles M. Carmichael. *Physics of the Earth and Planetary Interiors* 13:346–354.
Barbetti, M., Y. Taborin, B. Schmider, and K. Flude
    1980   Archaeomagnetic results from late pleistocene hearths at Etiolles and Marsangy, France. *Archaeometry* 22:25–46.
Barndt, J., N. M. Johnson, G. D. Johnson, N. D. Opdyke, E. H. Lindsay, D. Pilbeam, and R. A. H. Tahirkheli
    1978   The magnetic polarity stratigraphy and age of the Siwalik Group near Dhok Pathan Village, Potwar Plateau, Pakistan. *Earth and Planetary Science Letters* 41:355–364.
Barraclough, D. R.
    1974   Spherical harmonic analyses of the geomagnetic field for eight epochs between 1600 and 1910. *Geophysical Journal of the Royal Astronomical Society* 36:497–513.
Barton, C. E., M. W. McElhinny, and D. J. Edwards
    1980   Laboratory studies of depositional DRM. *Geophysical Journal of the Royal Astronomical Society* 36:497–513.
Barton, C. E., R. T. Merrill, and M. Barbetti
    1979   Intensity of the earth's magnetic field over the last 10,000 years. *Physics of the Earth and Planetary Interiors* 20:96–110.
Baumgartner, E. P.
    1973   *Magnetic properties of archeomagnetic materials.* Unpublished M.S. thesis, School of Geology and Geophysics, University of Oklahoma.
Becker, H.
    1979   Archaeomagnetic investigations in Anatolia from prehistoric and Hittite sites (first preliminary results). *In* Proceedings of the 18th International Symposium on Archaeometry and Archaeological Prospection. *Archaeo-Physika* 10:382–387.
Belshe, J. C., K. Cook and R. M. Cook
    1963   Some archaeomagnetic results from Greece. *Annual of the British School at Athens* 58:8–13.
Boyle, R.
    1691   *Experimenta & Observationes Physicae.* Printed for J. Taylor and J. Wyat, London.
Brock, A. and G. Isaac
    1976   Reversal stratigraphy and its application at East Rudolf. In *Earliest Man and Environments in the Lake Rudolf Basin,* edited by Yves Coppens, F. Clark Howell, Glynn Ll. Isaac, and Richard E. F. Leakey, pp. 148–162. University of Chicago Press, Chicago.
    1974   Palaeomagnetic stratigraphy and chronology of hominid-bearing sediments east of Lake Rudolf, Kenya. *Nature* 247:344–348.
Brown, F. H. and R. T. Shuey
    1976   Magnetostratigraphy of the Shungura and Usno formations, Lower Omo Valley, Ethiopia. In *Earliest Man and Environments in the Lake Rudolf Basin,* edited by Y. Coppens, F. C. Howell, G. Isaac, and R. E. F. Leakey, pp. 64–68. University of Chicago Press, Chicago.
Brown, F. H., R. T. Shuey, and M. K. Croes
    1978   Magnetostratigraphy of the Shungura and Usno formations, southwestern Ethiopia:

New data and comprehensive re-analysis. *Geophysical Journal of the Royal Astronomical Society* 54:519–538.

Brynjolfsson, A.
  1957 Studies of remanent magnetism and viscous magnetism in the basalts of Iceland. *Advances in Physics* 6:247–254.

Bucha, V.
  1967 Intensity of the earth's magnetic field during archaeological times in Czechoslovakia. *Archaeometry* 10:12–22.

Bucha, V. and J. Mellaart
  1967 Archaeomagnetic intensity measurements on some neolithic samples from Catal Huyuk (Anatolia). *Archaeometry* 10:23–25.

Bucha, V., R. E. Taylor, R. Berger, and E. W. Haury
  1970 Geomagnetic intensity: Changes during the past 3000 years in the western hemisphere. *Science* 168:111–114.

Bullard, E. C., C. Freedman, H. Gellman, and J. Nixon
  1950 The westward drift of the earth's magnetic field. *Philosophical Transactions of the Royal Society of London* A 243:67–92.

Bullard, W. R., Jr.
  1962 The Cerro Colorado site and Pithouse architecture in the southwestern United States prior to A.D. 900. *Papers of the Peabody Museum of American Archaeology and Ethnology*, Vol. 44, No. 2.

Burlatskaya, S. P. and G. N. Petrova
  1961a The archaeomagnetic method of studying changes of the geomagnetic field of the past. *Geomagnetism and Aeronomy* 1:104–112.
  1961b First results from an archaeomagnetic study of the past geomagnetic field. *Geomagnetism and Aeronomy* 1:262–267. English edition translated and produced by Scripta Tecnica Inc. for the American Geophysical Union. Washington.
  1961c First results of a study of the geomagnetic field in the past by the "archeomagnetic" method. *Geomagnetism and Aeronomy* 1:233–236.
  1961d Restoration of the past secular variations of the geomagnetic field by the archeomagnetic method. *Geomagnetism and Aeronomy* 1:383–386.

Burlatskaya, S. P., I. E. Nachasova, T. B. Nechaeva, O. M. Rusakov, G. F. Zagniy, E. N. Tarhov, and Z. A. Tchelidze
  1970 Archaeomagnetic research in the USSR: Recent results and spectral analysis. *Archaeometry* 12:73–85.

Burlatskaya, S. P., T. B. Nechayeva, and G. N. Petrova
  1968 Characteristics of secular variations of the geomagnetic field as indicated by world archeomagnetic data. *Izvestiya, Academy of Sciences, U.S.S.R., Physics of the Solid Earth*, No. 12, pp. 754–759. English edition translated and published by the American Geophysical Union. Washington.
  1969 Some archaeomagnetic data indicative of the westward drift of the geomagnetic field. *Archaeometry* 11:115–130.

Burmester, R. F.
  1977 Origin and stability of drilling induced remanence. *Geophysical Journal of the Royal Astronomical Society* 48:1–14.

Carlson, J. B.
  1977 The case for geomagnetic alignments of Pre-Columbian Mesoamerican sites: The Maya. *Katunob* 10(2):67–88.

Chamalaun, F. H. and I. McDougall
  1966 Dating geomagnetic polarity epochs in reunion. *Nature* 210:1212–1214.

Champion, D. E.
  1980   Holocene geomagnetic secular variation in the western United States: Implications for the global geomagnetic field. *United States Geological Survey Open File Report* No. 80–824.
Champion, D. E., G. B. Dalrymple, and M. A. Kuntz
  1981   Radiometric and palaeomagnetic evidence for the emperor reversed polarity event at 0.46 ± 0.05 M.Y. in basalt lava flows from the eastern Snake River Plain, Idaho. *Geophysical Research Letters* 8:1055–1058.
Cheek, C. D.
  1977   The excavations at the Palangana and the Acropolis. In *Teotihuacan and Kaminaljuyu: A study in prehistoric culture contact,* edited by W. T. Sanders and J. W. Michels, pp. 1–204. Pennsylvania State University Press monograph series on Kaminaljuyu.
Chevallier, R.
  1925   L'aimantation des laves de l'Etna et l'orientation du champ terrestre en Sicile du Xiie au XVIIe Siecle. *Annales de Physique* 4:5–162.
Coe, R. S.
  1967a   Paleo-intensities of the earth's magnetic field determined from tertiary and quaternary rocks. *Journal of Geophysical Research* 72:3247–3262.
  1967b   The determination of paleo-intensities of the earth's magnetic field with emphasis on mechanisms which could cause nonideal behavior in Thellier's method. *Journal of Geomagnetism and Geoelectricity* 19:157–179.
  1977   Source models to account for Lake Mungo paleomagnetic excursion and their implications. *Nature* 269:49–51.
Coe, R. S. and C. S. Gromme
  1973   A comparison of three methods of determining geomagnetic paleointensities. *Journal of Geomagnetism and Geoelectricity* 25:415–435.
Coe, R. S., S. Gromme, and E. A. Mankinen
  1978   Geomagnetic paleointensities from radiocarbon-dated lava flows on Hawaii and the question of the Pacific nondipole low. *Journal of Geophysical Research* 83: 1740–1756.
Cohen, D.
  1970   Large-volume conventional magnetic shields. *Revue de Physique Applique* 5:53–58.
Collinson, D. W.
  1967a   Chemical demagnetization. In *Methods in Palaeomagnetism,* edited by D. W. Collinson, K. M. Creer, and S. K. Runcorn, pp. 306–310. Elsevier Publishing Company, Amsterdam.
  1967b   The astatic magnetometers at Newcastle upon Tyne. In *Methods in Palaeomagnetism,* edited by D. W. Collinson, K. M. Creer, and S. K. Runcorn, pp. 60–65. Elsevier Publishing Company, Amsterdam.
  1975   Instruments and techniques in paleomagnetism and rock magnetism. *Reviews of Geophysics and Space Physics* 13:659–686.
  1977   Experiments relating to the measurement of inhomogeneous remanent magnetism in rock samples. *Geophysical Journal of the Royal Astronomical Society* 48:271–275.
Coltorti, M., M. Cremaschi, M. C. Delitala, D. Esu, M. Fornaseri, A. McPherron, M. Nicoletti, R. van Otterloo, C. Peretoo, B. Sala, V. Schmidt, and J. Sevink
  1982   Reversed magnetic polarity at an early Lower Palaeolithic site in Central Italy. *Nature* 300:173–176.
Cook, R. M. and J. C. Belshe
  1958   Archaeomagnetism: A preliminary report on Britain. *Antiquity* 32:167–178.

Cox, A.
  1968   Lengths of geomagnetic polarity intervals. *Journal of Geophysical Research* 73:3247–3260.
  1972   Geomagnetic reversals—their frequency, their origin and some problems of correlation. In *Calibration of Hominid Evolution*, edited by W. W. Bishop and J. A. Miller, pp. 93–105. Scottish University Press, Edinburgh.
  1975   The frequency of geomagnetic reversals and the symmetry of the nondipole field. *Reviews of Geophysics and Space Physics* 13:35–51.
Cox, A., G. B. Dalrymple, and R. R. Doell
  1967   Reversals of the earth's magnetic field. *Scientific American* 216(4):44–54.
Cox, A., R. R. Doell, and G. B. Dalrymple
  1964   Reversals of the earth's magnetic field. *Science* 144:1537–1543.
Creer, K. M.
  1967   Methods of measurement with the astatic magnetometer. In *Methods in Palaeomagnetism*, edited by D. W. Collinson, K. M. Creer, and S. K. Runcorn, pp. 172–191. Elsevier Publishing Co., Amsterdam.
  1977   Geomagnetic secular variations during the last 25,000 years: An interpretation of data obtained from rapidly deposited sediments. *Geophysical Journal of the Royal Astronomical Society* 48:91–109.
Creer, K. M. and J. S. Kopper
  1974   Paleomagnetic dating of cave paintings in Tito Bustillo Cave, Asturias, Spain. *Science* 186:348–350.
  1977   Secular oscillations of the geomagnetic field recorded by sediments deposited in caves in the Mediterranean region. *Geophysical Journal of the Royal Astronomical Society* 45:35–58.
Creer, K. M., P. W. Readman, and A. M. Jacobs
  1980   Paleomagnetic and palaeontological dating of a section at Gioia Tauro, Italy: identification of the Blake Event. *Earth and Planetary Science Letters* 50:289–300.
Creer, K. M., R. Thompson, and L. Molyneux
  1972   Geomagnetic secular variation recorded in the stable magnetic remanence of recent sediments. *Earth and Planetary Science Letters* 14:115–127.
Damon, P. E., C. W. Ferguson, A. Long, and E. I. Wallick
  1974   Dendrochronologic calibration of the radiocarbon time scale. *American Antiquity* 39:350–366.
Davis, R. S., V. A. Ranov, and A. E. Dodnov
  1980   Early man in Soviet Central Asia. *Scientific American* 243(6):130–137.
Day, R.
  1979   Recent advances in rock magnetism. *Reviews of Geophysics and Space Physics* 17:249–256.
Defense Mapping Agency
  1975a Magnetic variation, Epoch 1975.O, Chart 42 (World). Defense Mapping Agency, Hydrographic Center, Washington, D.C.
  1975b Magnetic inclination or dip, Epoch 1975.O, Chart 36 (World). Defense Mapping Agency, Hydrographic Center, Washington, D.C.
Delesse, A.
  1849   Sur le magnetisme polaire dans les mineraux et dans les roches. *Annales de Chimie et de Physique*, Paris, Vol. 25 (3rd series), pp. 194–209.
Denham, C. R.
  1976   Blake polarity episode in two cores from the greater Antilles outer ridge. *Earth and Planetary Science Letters* 29:422–434.

Denham, C. R. and A. Cox
  1971   Evidence that the Laschamp polarity event did not occur 13,300–30,400 years ago. *Earth and Planetary Science Letters* 13:181–190.
Dickson, J. H., D. A. Stewart, R. Thompson, G. Turner, M. S. Baxter, N. D. Drndarsky, and J. Rose
  1978   Palynology, paleomagnetism and radiometric dating of Flandrian marine and freshwater sediments of Loch Lomond. *Nature* 274:548–553.
DiPeso, C. C.
  1956   The upper Pima of San Cayetano del Tumacacori: An archaeohistorical reconstruction of the Ootam of Pimeria Alta. *The Amerind Foundation Papers,* No. 7.
Doell, R. R.
  1972   Palaeomagnetic studies of Icelandic lava flows. *Geophysical Journal of the Royal Astronomical Society* 26:459–479.
Doell, R. R. and A. Cox
  1967   Analysis of spinner magnetometer operation. In *Methods in Palaeomagnetism,* edited by D. W. Collinson, K. M. Creer, and S. K. Runcorn, pp. 196–206. Elsevier Publishing Co., Amsterdam.
  1971   Pacific geomagnetic secular variation. *Science* 171:248–254.
Doell, R. R. and P. J. Smith
  1969   On the use of magnetic cleaning in paleo-intensity studies. *Journal of Geomagnetism and Geoelectricity* 21:579–594.
Dollfus, G. and A. Hesse
  1977   Les structures de combustion du Tepe Djaffarabad, Periodes I A III. *Cahiers de la Delegation Archaeologique Francaise en Iran* 7:11–47.
DuBois, R. L.
  1975   Secular variation in southwestern U.S.A. as suggested by archaeomagnetic results. In *Proceedings of the Takesi Nagata Conference, Magnetic Fields: Past and Present,* edited by R. M. Fisher, M. Fuller, V. A. Schmidt, and P. J. Wasilewski, pp. 133–144. Goddard Space Flight Center, Greenbelt, Maryland.
  n.d.a   *Archeomagnetic Dating of Archeological Sites.* Final report (Contract No. CX-1595-4-0194), 1974–1975. Interagency Archaeological Services, Denver.
  n.d.b   *Dating of Archaeological Sites by Archeomagnetic Methods.* Final report (Contract No. CX-1595-5-0430), 1975–1976. Interagency Archeological Services, Denver.
DuBois, Robert L. and N. Watanabe
  1965   Preliminary results of investigations made to study the use of Indian pottery to determine the palaeointensity of the geomagnetic field for United States 600–1400 A.D. *Journal of Geomagnetism and Geoelectricity* 17:417–423.
DuBois, R. L. and D. Wolfman
  1970a   *Archeomagnetic dating in the New World.* Paper presented at the 35th Annual Meeting of the Society for American Archaeology, April 29–May 3, 1970, Mexico City.
  1970b   *Archaeomagnetic dating in Mesoamerica and Peru.* Paper presented at the 39th International Congress of Americanists, Lima.
  1971   *Recent archeomagnetic results for the United States.* Paper presented at the 36th Annual Meeting of the Society for American Archaeology, Norman, Oklahoma.
Dunlop, D. J. (ed.)
  1977   Symposium on the origin of thermoremanent magnetization. *Journal of Geomagnetism and Geoelectricity* 29:223–439. (Also published as Origin of thermoremanent magnetization. In *Advances in Earth and Planetary Sciences,* Vol. 1, 212 p., Japan Scientific Societies Press)

Dunlop, D. J. and M. B. Zinn
 1980   Archeomagnetism of the 19th century pottery kiln near Jordan, Ontario. *Canadian Journal of Earth Sciences* 17:1275–1285.
Eighmy, J. L.
 1980   Archeomagnetism: A handbook for the archeologist. *HCRS Publication*, No. 58.
Eighmy, J. L., R. S. Sternberg, and R. F. Butler
 1980   Archaeomagnetic dating in the American Southwest. *American Antiquity* 45:507–517.
Elsasser, W., E. P. Ney, and J. R. Winckler
 1956   Cosmic-ray intensity and geomagnetism. *Nature* 178:1226–1227.
Evans, M. E. and M. W. McElhinny
 1969   An investigation of the origin of stable remanence in magnetite-bearing igneous rocks. *Journal of Geomagnetism and Geolectricity* 21:759–773.
Fabiano, E. B.
 1975   *Magnetic declination in the United States—Epoch 1975.0, Map I-911.* U.S. Geological Survey, Reston, Virginia.
Fisher, R.
 1953   Dispersion on a sphere. *Proceedings of the Royal Society of London* A 217:295–305.
Folgheraiter, G.
 1896   Ricerche sull' inclinazione magnetica all' epoca estrusca. *Rendiconti della R. Accademia dei Lincei* V:293–300.
 1897a   Sulla forza coercitiva dei vasi etruschi. *Rendiconti della R. Accademia dei Lincei* VI:64–70.
 1897b   La magnetizzazione dell' argilla colla cottura in relazione colle ipotesi sulla fabbricazione del vasellame nero etrusco. *Rendiconti della R. Accademia dei Lincei* VI:368–376.
 1899   Sur Les variations seculiares de l'inclinaison magnetique dans l'antiquite. *Archives des Sciences Physiques et Naturelles* 8:5–16.
Fox, J. M. W. and M. J. Aitken
 1978   Self-demagnetizing effects in archaeomagnetic intensity determinations. *Geophysical Journal of the Royal Astronomical Society* 53:153.
 1980   Cooling-rate dependence of thermoremanent magnetisation. *Nature* 283:462–463.
Freed, W. K. and N. Healy
 1974   Excursions of the Pleistocene geomagnetic field recorded in Gulf of Mexico sediments. *Earth and Planetary Science Letters* 24:99–104.
Fuller, M., I. Williams, and K. A. Hoffman
 1979   Paleomagnetic records of geomagnetic field reversals and the morphology of the transitional fields. *Reveiws of Geophysics and Space Physics* 17:179–203.
Games, K. P.
 1977   The magnitude of the paleomagnetic field: a new nonthermal, non-detrital method using sun-dried bricks. *Geophysical Journal of the Royal Astronomical Society* 48:315–329.
 1979   Short period fluctuations in the earth's magnetic field. *Nature* 277:600–601.
 1980   The magnitude of the archaeomagnetic field in Egypt between 3000 and O B.C. *Geophysical Journal of the Royal Astronomical Society* 63:45–56.
Games, K. P. and M. E. Baker
 1981   Determination of geomagnetic archaeomagnitudes from clay pipes. *Nature* 289:478–479.
Gheradi, S.
 1862   Sul magnetismo polare de palazzi ed altri edifizi in Torino. *Il Nuovo Cimento* (Rome) 16:384–404.

Gillot, P. Y., J. Labeyrie, C. Laj, G. Valladas, G. Guerin, G. Poupeau, and G. Delibrias
    1979   Age of the Laschamp paleomagnetic excursion revisited. *Earth and Planetary Science Letters* 42:444–450.

Gladwin, H. S.
    1942   Excavations at Snaketown III: Revisions. *Medallion Papers,* No. 30.

Gladwin, H. S., E. W. Haury, E. B. Sayles, and N. Gladwin
    1937   Excavations at Snaketown, material culture. *Medallion Papers,* No. 25.

Gleadow, A. J. W.
    1980   Fission track age of the KBS tuff and associated hominid remains in northern Kenya. *Nature* 284:225–234.

Goree, W. S. and M. Fuller
    1976   Magnetometers using RF-driven squids and their applications in rock magnetism and palaeomagnetism. *Reviews of Geophysics and Space Physics* 14:591–608.

Grove, D. C., K. G. Hirth, D. E. Buge, and A. M. Cyphers
    1976   Settlement and cultural development at Chalcatzingo. *Science* 192:1203–1210.

Gunn, N. M. and A. S. Murray
    1980   Geomagnetic field magnitude variations in Peru derived from archaeological ceramics dated by thermoluminescence. *Geophysical Journal of the Royal Astronomical Society* 62:345–366.

Halley, E.
    1692   An account of the cause of the change of the variation of the magnetical needle; with an hypothesis of the structure of the internal part of the earth. *Philosophical Transactions of the Royal Astronomical Society* 17:563–578.

Hammack, L. C. and A. P. Sullivan (eds).
    1981   The 1968 excavations at Mound 8 Las Colinas ruins group, Phoenix, Arizona. *Cultural Resource Management Section, Arizona State Museum, Archaeological Series* No. 154.

Harrison, C. G. A. and E. Ramirez
    1975   Areal coverage of spurious reversals of the earth's magnetic field. *Journal of Geomagnitism and Geoelectricity* 27:139–151.

Hathaway, J. H., J. L. Eighmy, and A. E. Kane
    1983   Preliminary modification of the Southwest virtual geomagnetic pole path AD 700 to AD 900: Dolores archaeological program results. *Journal of Archaeological Science* 10:51–59.

Haury, E. W.
    1976   *The Hohokam: Desert Farmers and Craftsmen.* University of Arizona Press, Tucson.

Heller, F.
    1980   Self-reversal of natural remanent magnetisation in the Olby–Laschamp lavas. *Nature* 284:334–335.

Hesse, A. and A. Lecaille
    1974   Un programme de recherhes archeomagnetiques pour la periode pre et protohistorique au proche-Orient. *Paleorient* 2(2):502.

    1975   *Les variations du champ magnetique terrestre en Iran au cinquieme millenaire.* Paper presented at the Symposium on Archaeometry and Archaeological Prospection, Oxford.

Hillhouse, J. and A. Cox
    1976   Brunhes–Matuyama polarity transition. *Earth and Planetary Science Letters* 29:51–64.

Hillhouse, J. W., J. W. M. Ndombi, A. Cox, and A. Brock
    1977   Additional results on palaeomagnetic stratigraphy of the Koobi Fora Formation, east of Lake Turkana (Lake Rudolf), Kenya. *Nature* 265:411–415.

Hirooka, K.
   1971   Archaeomagnetic study for the past 2,000 years in southwest Japan. *Memoirs of the Faculty of Science, Kyoto University, Series of Geology and Mineralogy* 38:167–207.
Hoye, G. S.
   1982   A magnetic investigation of kiln wall distortion. *Archaeometry* 24:80–84.
Hsing-Huei, T. and Tung-Chieh, L.
   1965   Geomagnetic field in the Peking region and its secular variation during the last 2000 Years. *Acta Geophysica Sinica* 14:181–195.
Hurst, J. G.
   1966   Post-Roman archaeological dating and its correlation with archaeomagnetic results. *Archaeometry* 9:198–199.
Ising, G.
   1942   On the magnetic properties of varved clay. *Arkiv for Matematik, Astronomi Och Fysik* 29A(5):1–37.
Irving, E.
   1964   *Palaeomagnetism and its application to geological and geophysical problems.* John Wiley and Sons, Inc., New York.
Irving, E., P. M. Stott, and M. A. Ward
   1961   Demagnetization of igneous rocks by alternating magnetic fields. *Philosophical Magazine* 6:225–241.
Johanson, D. C. and M. Taieb
   1976   Plio–Pleistocene hominid discoveries in Hadar, Ethiopia. *Nature* 260:293–297.
Johnson, E. A., T. Murphy, and O. W. Torreson
   1948   Pre-history of the earth's magnetic field. *Terrestrial Magnetism and Atmospheric Electricity* 53:349–372.
Johnson, H. P., H. Kinoshita, and R. T. Merrill
   1975   Rock Magnetism and Paleomagnetism of some North Pacific Deep-Sea Sediments. *Geological Society of America Bulletin* 86:412–420.
Kawai, N., K. Hirooka, and S. Sasajima
   1965   Counterclockwise rotation of the geomagnetic dipole axis revealed in the world-wide archaeo-secular variations. *Proceedings of the Japanese Academy* 41:398–403.
Kawai, N., K. Hirooka, S. Sasajima, K. Yaskawa, H. Ito, and S. Kume
   1964   Archaeomagnetic studies in southwestern Japan. *1964 Annual Progress Report of the Rock Magnetism Research Group in Japan,* pp. 39–43.
   1965   Archaeomagnetic studies in southwestern Japan. *Annales de Geophysique* 21: 574–578.
Kawai, N., K. Hirooka, K. Tokieda, and T. Kishi
   1967   Archaeo-secular variation of the geomagnetic field in Japan. *1967 Annual Progress Report of Palaeogeophysics Research in Japan,* pp. 81–85.
Kawai, N., K. Yaskawa, T. Nakajima, M. Torii, and S. Horie
   1972   Oscillating geomagnetic field with a recurring reversal discovered from Lake Biwa. *Proceedings of the Japanese Academy* 48:186–190.
Kelley, D. H. and K. A. Kerr
   1973   Mayan astronomy and astronomical glyphs. In *Mesoamerican Writing Systems,* edited by E. P. Benson, pp. 179–215. Dumbarton Oaks Research Library and Collections, Trustees for Harvard University, Washington, D.C.
Kent, D. V. and W. Lowrie
   1974   Origin of magnetic instability in sediment cores from the central North Pacific. *Journal of Geophysical Research* 79:2987–3000.

Khodair, A. and R. S. Coe
  1975   Determination of geomagnetic palaeo-intensities in vacuum. *Geophysical Journal of the Royal Astronomical Society* 42:107–115.
Kirschvink, J. L.
  1981   A quick, non-acidic chemical demagnetization technique for dissolving ferric minerals. *EOS, Transactions of the American Geophysical Union* 62:84.
Kitazawa, K. and K. Kobayashi
  1968   Intensity variation of the geomagnetic field during the past 4000 years in South America. *Journal of Geomagnetism and Geoelectricity* 20:7–19.
Kobayashi, K.
  1959   Chemical remanent magnetization of ferro-magnetic minerals and its application to rock magnetism. *Journal of Geomagnetism and Geoelectricity* 10:99–117.
Koenigsberger, J. G.
  1938   Natural residual magnetism of eruptive rocks, (parts I and II). *Terrestrial Magnetism and Atmospheric Electricity* 43:119–127; 299–330.
Kono, M.
  1978   Reliability of paleointensity methods using alternating field demagnetization and anhysteretic remanence. *Geophysical Journal of the Royal Astronomical Society* 54:241–261.
Kopper, J. S. and K. M. Creer
  1973   Cova Dets Alexandres, Majorca paleomagnetic dating and archaeological interpretation of its sediments. *Caves and Karst* 15:13–20.
  1976   Paleomagnetic dating and stratigraphic interpretation in archaeology. *MASCA Newsletter* 12(1):1–3.
Kovacheva, M.
  1968   Ancient magnetic field in Bulgaria. *Comptes Rendus de l'Academie bulgare des Sciences* 21:761–763.
  1969   Inclination of the earth's magnetic field during the last 2000 years in Bulgaria. *Journal of Geomagnetism and Geoelectricity* 21:573–578.
  1980   Summarized results of the archaeomagnetic investigation of the geomagnetic field variation for the last 8000 years in Southeastern Europe. *Geophysical Journal of the Royal Astronomical Society* 61:57–64.
Kovacheva, M. and D. Veljovich
  1977   Geomagnetic field variations in southeastern Europe between 6500 and 100 years B.C. *Earth and Planetary Science Letters* 37:131–138.
Krause, G. J.
  1980   *Archaeomagnetic methods: A comparison between sun compass and magnetic compass measurements.* Paper presented at the 45th Annual Meeting of the Society for American Archaeology, Philadelphia.
Kuster, G.
  1969   Effect of drilling on rock magnetism (abstract). *EOS, Transactions of the American Geophysical Union* 50:134.
Lee, E. W.
  1970   *Magnetism. An Introductory Survey.* Dover Publications, New York.
Lee, S.
  1975   *Secular variation of the intensity of the geomagnetic field during the past 3000 years in North, Central, and South America.* Ph.D. dissertation, University of Oklahoma. University Microfilms, Ann Arbor.
Levi, S.
  1977   The effect of magnetite particle size on paleointensity determinations of the geomagne-

tic field. In *Palaeomagnetic Field Intensity, Its Measurement in Theory and Practice*, edited by Charles M. Carmichael. *Physics of the Earth and Planetary Interiors* 13:245–259.

1979   The additivity of partial thermal remanent magnetization in magnetite. *Geophysical Journal of the Royal Astronomical Society* 59:205–218.

Liddicoat, J. C.
1976   *A paleomagnetic study of late Quaternary dry-lake deposits from the western United States and Basin in Mexico*. Ph.D. dissertation. University of California, Santa Cruz. University Microfilms, Ann Arbor.

Liddicoat, J. C. and R. S. Coe
1979   Mono Lake geomagnetic excursion. *Journal of Geophysical Research* 84:261–271.

Liddicoat, J. C., N. D. Opdyke, and G. I. Smith
1980   Palaeomagnetic polarity in a 930-m core from Searles Valley, California. *Nature* 286:22–25.

Lin J., Wang Q., and Cheng G.
1979   On the wobble of geomagnetic pole for the last 2000 years. *Seismology and Geology* 1:83–85.

Liritzis, Y. and R. Thomas
1980   Palaeointensity and thermoluminescence measurements on Cretan kilns from 1300 to 2000 B.C. *Nature* 283:54–55.

Lowe, G. W.
1978   Eastern Mesoamerica. In *Chronologies in New World Archaeology*, edited by R. E. Taylor and C. W. Meighan, pp. 377–393. Academic Press, New York.

Lund, S. P. and S. K. Banerjee
1979   Paleosecular variations from lake sediments. *Reviews of Geophysics and Space Physics* 17:244–249.

McDonald, K. L. and R. H. Gunst
1967   An analysis of the earth's magnetic field from 1835 to 1965. *Environmental Science Services Administration Technical Report* IER 46-IES 1.

McDougall, I.
1979   The present status of the geomagnetic polarity time scale. In *The Earth: Its Origin, Structure, and Evolution*, edited by M. W. McElhinny, pp. 543–566. Academic Press, London.

McDougall, I., R. Maier, and P. Sutherland-Hawkes
1980   K–Ar age estimate for the KBS Tuff, East Turkana, Kenya. *Nature* 284:230–234.

McElhinny, M. W.
1973   *Palaeomagnetism and Plate Tectonics*. Cambridge University Press, London.

McFadden, P. L.
1980   Determination of the angle in a Fisher distribution which will be exceeded with a given probability. *Geophysical Journal of the Royal Astronomical Society* 60:391–396.

McFadden, P. L., A. Brock, and T. C. Partridge
1979   Palaeomagnetism and the age of the Makapansgat hominid site. *Earth and Planetary Science Letters* 44:373–382.

McKerrell, H., V. Mejdahl, H. Francois, and G. Portal
1974   Thermoluminescence and Glozel. *Antiquity* 48:265–272.

MacNeish, R. S.
1976   Early man in the New World. *American Scientist* 64:316-327.

McNish, A. G. and E. A. Johnson
1938   Magnetization of Unmetamorphosed varves and marine sediments. *Terrestrial Magnetism and Atmospheric Electricity* 43:401–407.

1940   Determination of the secular variation in declination in New England from magnetic polarization of glacial varves. *IUGG* (International Union of Geodesy and Geophysics), *Section of Terrestrial Magnetism and Electricity*, Bulletin II, pp. 339–347.

Mankinen, E. A. and G. B. Dalrymple
  1979   Revised geomagnetic polarity time scale for the Interval 0–5 m.y. B.P. *Journal of Geophysical Research* 84:615–25.

Mankinen, E. A., J. M. Donnelly, and C. S. Gromme
  1978   Geomagnetic polarity event recorded at 1.1 m.y. B.P. on Cobb Mountain, Clear Lake volcanic field, California. *Geology* 6:653–656.

Matuyama, M.
  1929   On the direction of magnetization of basalt in Japan, Tyosen, and Manchuria. *Proceedings of the Imperial Academy of Japan* 5:203–205.

Melloni, M.
  1853   Sur l'aimantation des roches volcaniques. *Comptes Rendus des Seances de l'Academie des Sciences* (Paris) 37:229–231.

Mercanton, P.
  1907   La methode de Folgheraiter et son role en geophysique. *Archives des Sciences Physiques et Naturelles*, Per. 4, XXIII, pp. 467–482.
  1918a   Etat magnetique de quelques terres cuites prehistoriques. *Comptes Rendus des Seances de l'Academie des Sciences* 166:681–685.
  1918b   Etat magnetique de terres cuites prehistòriques. *Bulletin de la Societe Vaudoise des Sciences Naturelles*, Series 5, 52:9–15.
  1926a   Aimantation de Basaltes Groenlandais. *Comptes Rendus des Seances de l'Academie des Sciences* 180:859–860.
  1926b   Inversion de l'inclinaison magnetique terrestre aux ages geologiques. *Archives des Sciences Physiques et Naturelles*, Per. 5, VIII 345–349.

Michels, J. W.
  1973   *Dating Methods in Archaeology*. Seminar Press, New York.

Molyneux, L.
  1971   A complete result magnetometer for measuring the remanent magnetization of rocks. *Geophysical Journal of the Royal Astronomical Society* 24:429–433.

Momose, K. and K. Kobayashi
  1965   Magnetic direction of the baked earth at the earliest Jomon cultural remains in Kita-Aiki Mura, Nagano Prefecture—preliminary report. *1965 Annual Progress Report of the Rock Magnetism Research Group in Japan*, pp. 101–03.

Momose, K., K. Kobayashi, K. Tsuboi, and M. Tanaka
  1964   Archaeomagnetism during the Old Tomb and the Nara Periods. *1964 Annual Progress Report of the Rock Magnetism Research Group in Japan*, pp. 33–38.

Nachasova, I. Y.
  1972   Magnetic field in the Moscow area from 1480 to 1840. *Geomagnetism and Acronomy* 12:277–280.

Nagata, T.
  1943   The Natural remanent magnetism of volcanic rocks. *Bulletin of the Earthquake Research Institute* 21:1–196.
  1961   *Rock Magnetism*. Maruzen Co. Ltd., Tokyo.

Nagata, T., Y. Arai, and K. Momose
  1963   Secular variation of the geomagnetic total force during the last 5000 years. *Journal of Geophysical Research* 68:5277–5281.

Nagata, T., K. Kobayashi, and E. J. Schwarz
  1965   Archaeomagnetic intensity studies of South and Central America. *Journal of Geomagnetism and Geoelectricity* 17:399–405.

Nagata, T., S. Uyeda, and S. Akimoto
  1952 Self-reversal of thermo-remanent magnetism of igneous rocks. *Journal of Geomagnetism and Geoelectricity* 4:22–38.
Neel, L.
  1949 Theorie du trainage magnetique des ferro-magnetiques au grains fins avec applications aux terres cuites. *Annales de Geophysique* 5:99–136.
  1955 Some theoretical aspects of rock magnetism. *Advances in Physics* 4:191–243.
Nichols, R. F.
  1975 *Archeomagnetic Study of Anasazi-related Sediments of Chaco Canyon, New Mexico.* Unpublished M.S. thesis, School of Geology and Geophysics, University of Oklahoma.
Noel, M. and D. H. Tarling
  1975 The Laschamp geomagnetic 'event'. *Nature* 253:705–707.
Opdyke, N. D., D. V. Kent, and W. Lowrie
  1973 Details of magnetic polarity transitions recorded in a high deposition rate deep-sea core. *Earth and Planetary Science Letters* 20:315–324.
Perrot, J.
  1966 Le gisement Natufien de Mallaha (Eynan), Israel. *L'Anthropologie* 70:437–484.
Plog, F.
  1978 *Explaining culture change in the Hohokam Preclassic.* Paper presented at the 43rd Annual Meeting of the Society for American Archaeology, Tucson.
Pozzi, J. P. and E. Thellier
  1963 Sur des perfectionnements recents apportes aux magnetometres a tres haute sensibilite utilises en mineralogie magnetique et en paleomagnetisme. *Comptes Rendus des Seances de l'Academie des Sciences* 257:1037–1040.
Rainbow, R. R., M. Fuller, and V. A. Schmidt
  1972 Paleomagnetic orientation of borehole samples (abstract). *EOS, Transactions of the American Geophysical Union* 53:355.
Renfew, C.
  1973 *Before Civilization.* Alfred A. Knopf, New York.
  1975 Glozel and the two cultures. *Antiquity* 49:219–222.
Rimbert, F.
  1959 Contribution a l'etude de l'action de champs alternates sur les aimentations remanentes des roches, applications geophysiques. *Revue de L'Institut Francais du Petrole* 14:17–54, 123–155.
Roberts, J. P.
  1961 Temperature measurements. *Archaeometry* 4:19–21.
Rogers, J., J. M. W. Fox, and M. J. Aitken
  1979 Magnetic anisotrophy in ancient pottery. *Nature* 277:644–646.
Rogers, J., J. Shaw, and J. A. Share
  1980 An automatic palaeomagnetic measuring and demagnetising system. *Geophysical Journal of the Royal Astronomical Society* 61:214.
Roquet, J.
  1954 Sur les remanences des oxydes de fer et leur intret en geomagnetisme (1st and 2nd parts). *Annales de Geophysique* 10:226–247, 282–325.
Roy, J. L.
  1963 The measurement of the magnetic properties of rock specimens. *Publications of the Dominion Observatory* 27:421–439.
Rusakov, O. M. and G. F. Zagniy
  1973a Archaeomagnetic secular variation study of the Ukraine and Moldavia. *Archaeometry* 15:153–157.

1973b   Intensity of the geomagnetic field in the Ukraine and Moldavia during the past 6000 years. *Archaeometry* 15:275–285.

Sasajima, S.
1965   Geomagnetic secular variation revealed in the baked earths in west Japan (part 2): Change of the field intensity. *Journal of Geomagnetism and Geoelectricity* 17:413–416.

Sasajima, S. and K. Maenaka
1966   Intensity studies of the archaeo-secular variation in west Japan, with special reference to the hypothesis of the dipole axis rotation. *Memoirs of the College of Science, University of Kyoto, Series B, Geology and Mineralogy* 33:53–67.

Schiffer, M. B.
1982   Hohokam chronology: An essay on history and method. *Hohokam and Patayan: An Archaeological Overview of Southwestern Arizona*, edited by R. H. McGuire and M. B. Schiffer, pp. 299–344. Academic Press, New York.

Schmidt, V. A.
1982   Magnetostratigraphy of sediments in Mammoth Cave, Kentucky. *Science* 217: 827–829.

Schwartz, D. W. and R. W. Lang
1973   *Archaeological investigations at the Arroyo Hondo Site. Third Field Report—1972.* School of American Research, Santa Fe.

Schwarz, E. J. and K. W. Christie
1967   Original remanent magnetization of Ontario potsherds. *Journal of Geophysical Research* 72:3263–3269.

Shaw, J.
1974   A new method of determining the magnitude of the palaeomagnetic field application to five archaeological samples. *Geophysical Journal of the Royal Astronomical Society* 39:133–141.

1979   Rapid changes in the magnitude of the archaeomagnetic field. *Geophysical Journal of the Royal Astronomical Society* 58:107–116.

Shaw, J., R. L. Wilson, and R. Murray-Shelley
1978   An inexpensive microprocessor controlled magnetometer for palaeomagnetic research. *Geophysical Journal of the Royal Astronomical Society* 53:154.

Shepard, A. O.
1956   Ceramics for the Archaeologist. *Carnegie Institution of Washington, Publication* 609.

Shibuya, H. and T. Nakajima
1979   Archaeomagnetism of southwestern Japan measured and compiled in Osaka University. *Rock Magnetism and Paleogeophysics* 6:10–13.

Shuey, R. T.
1974   Archaeomagnetic chronology of U-95 sites. In *Highway U-95 Archaeology* (Vol. II), edited by C. J. Wilson, pp. 207–209. University of Utah, Salt Lake City.

Shuey, R. T., E. R. Cole, and M. J. Mikulich
1970   Geographic correction of archeomagnetic data. *Journal of Geomagnetism and Geoelectricity* 22:485–489.

Shuey, R. T. and R. Reed
1972   Archaeomagnetism of Evans Mound. In *The Evans Site*, edited by M. S. Berry, pp. 289–296. University of Utah, Salt Lake City.

Smith, P. J.
1967   The intensity of the ancient geomagnetic field: a review and analysis. *Geophysical Journal of the Royal Astronomical Society* 12:321–362.

Sorenson, J. L.
1977   Mesoamerican C-14 dates revised. *Katunob* 9(4):56–71.

Stacey, F. D.
    1963   The physical theory of rock magnetism. *Advances in Physics* 12:46–133.
Stahle, D. and D. Wolfman
    1977   The potential for tree-ring research in Arkansas. *Field Notes*, No. 146:5–9.
    n.d.   The potential for archaeological tree-ring dating in eastern North America. (Manuscript on file at the Tree-Ring Laboratory, Department of Geography, University of Arkansas, Fayetteville, Arkansas.
Sternberg, R. S.
    1982   *Archaeomagnetic secular variation of direction and palaeointensity in the American Southwest.* Ph.D. dissertation, University of Arizona. University Microfilms, Ann Arbor.
Sternberg, R. S. and R. F. Butler
    1978   An archaeomagnetic paleointensity study of some Hohokam potsherds from Snaketown, Arizona. *Geophysical Research Letters* 5:101–104.
Sternberg, R. S. and P. E. Damon
    1979   Sensitivity of radiocarbon fluctuations and inventory to geomagnetic and reservoir parameters. In *Radiocarbon Dating,* edited by R. Berger and H. E. Suess, pp. 691–717. University of California Press, Berkeley.
Sternberg, R. S. and R. H. McGuire
    1981   Archaeomagnetic secular variation in the American Southwest. *EOS, Transactions of the American Geophysical Union* 62:852.
Stoner, E. C.
    1945   The demagnetizing factors for ellipsoids. *Philosophical Magazine* 36:803–821.
Stupavsky, M., C. P. Gravenor, and D. T. A. Symons
    1979   Paleomagnetic stratigraphy of the Meadowcliffe Till, Scarborough Bluffs, Ontario: A late Pleistocene excursion? *Geophysical Research Letters* 6:269–272.
Tanguy, J. C.
    1970   An archaeomagnetic study of Mount Etna: The magnetic direction recorded in lava flows subsequent to the twelfth century. *Archaeometry* 12:115–128.
Tarling, D. H.
    1971   *Principles and Applications of Palaeomagnetism.* Chapman and Hall, London.
    1975   Archaeomagnetism: The dating of archaeological materials by their magnetic properties. *World of Archaeology* 7:185–197.
Taylor, R. E.
    1978   Dating methods in New World archaeology. In *Chronologies in New World Archaeology,* edited by R. E. Taylor and C. W. Meighan, pp. 1–27. Academic Press, New York.
Taylor, R. E., R. Berger, C. W. Meighan, and H. B. Nicholson
    1969   West Mexican radiocarbon dates of archaeologic significance. *In* The Natalie Wood Collection of Pre-Columbian Ceramics from Chupicuaro, Guanajuato, Mexico at UCLA, edited by J. D. Frierman. *Occasional Papers of the Museum and Laboratories of Ethnic Arts and Technology,* University of California, Los Angeles 1:17–30.
Thellier, E.
    1933   Magnetometre insensible aux champs magnetiques troubles des Grandes Villes. *Comptes Rendus des Seances de l'Academie des Sciences* 197:232–234.
    1936   Aimantation des briques et inclinaison du champ magnetique terrestre. *Annales de l'Institut de Physique du Globe* 14:65–70.
    1938   Sur l'aimantation des terres cuites et ses applications geophysiques. *Annales de l'Institut de Physique due Globe* 16:157–302.
    1941   Sur la verification d'une methode permettant de determiner l'intensite du champ mag-

netique terrestre dans le passe. *Comptes Rendus des Seances de l'Academie des Sciences* 212:281–283.

1951   Proprietes magnetiques des terres cuites et des roches. *Le Journal de Physique et le Radium* 12:205–218.

1967   Methods of sample collection and orientation for archaeomagnetism. In *Methods in Palaeomagnetism,* edited by D. W. Collinson, K. M. Creer, and S. K. Runcorn, pp. 16–20. Elsevier Publishing Co., Amsterdam.

1971   Magnetisme interne. *Encyclopedie de la Pleiade,* pp. 235–376.

1977   Early research on the intensity of the ancient geomagnetic field. *In* Paleomagnetic Field Intensity, Its Measurement in Theory and Practice, edited by C. M. Carmichael. *Physics of the Earth and Planetary Interiors* 13:241–244.

1981   Sur la direction du champ magnetique terrestre, en France, durant les deux derniers millenaries. *Physics of the Earth and Planetary Interiors* 24:89–132.

Thellier, E. and F. Rimbert

1954   Sur l'analyse d'aimantations fossiles par action de champs magnetiques alternatifs. *Comptes Rendus des Seances de l'Academie des Sciences* 239:1399–1401.

1955   Sur l'utilisation en palemagnetisme, de la desaimantation par champs alternatif. *Comptes Rendus des Seances de l'Academie des Sciences* 240:1404–1406.

Thellier, E. and O. Thellier

1942   Sur l'intensite du champ magnetique terrestre, en France, trois siecles avant les premieres mesures directes. Application au probleme de la desaimantation du globe. *Comptes Rendus des Seances de l'Academie des Sciences* 214:382–384.

1946   Sur l'intensite du champ magnetique terrestre, en France, a l'epoque gallo-ramine. *Comptes Rendus des Seances de l'Academie des Sciences* 222:905–907.

1951   Magnetisme terrestre.—Sur la direction du champ magnetique terrestre, retrouvee sur des parois de fours de epoques punique et romaine, a Carthage. *Comptes Rendus des Seances de l'Academie des Sciences* 233:1476–1479.

1952   Magnetisme terrestre.—Sur la direction du champ magnetique terrestre, dans la region de Treves, vers 380 apres J.-C. *Comptes Rendus des Seances de l'Academie des Sciences* 234:1464–1466.

1959   Sur l'intensite de champ magnetique terrestre dans le passe historique et geologique. *Annales de Geophysique* 15:285–376.

Thomas, D. H.

1978   The awful truth about statistics in archaeology. *American Antiquity* 43:231–244.

Thompson, R.

1977   Stratigraphic consequences of palaeomagnetic studies of Pleistocene and recent sediments. *Journal of the Geological Society of London* 133:51–59.

Thompson, R., M. J. Aitken, P. L. Gibbard, and J. J. Wymer

1974   Palaeomagnetic study of Hoxnian lacustrine sediments. *Archaeometry* 16:233–237.

Turner, G. M. and R. Thompson

1981   Lake sediment record of the geomagnetic secular variation in Britain during Holocene times. *Geophysical Journal of the Royal Astronomical Society* 65:703–725.

1982   Detransformation of the British geomagnetic secular variation record for Holocene times. *Geophysical Journal of the Royal Astronomical Society* 70:789–792.

Urrutia-Fucugauchi, J.

1981   Some observations on short-term magnetic viscosity behaviour at room temperature. *Physics of the Earth and Planetary Interiors* 26:1–5.

U.S.–Japan Paleomagnetic Cooperation Program in Micronesia

1975   Paleosecular variation of lavas from the Marianas in the western Pacific Ocean. *Journal of Geomagnetism and Geoelectricity* 27:57–66.

Van Zijl, J. S. V., K. W. T. Graham, and A. L. Hales
  1962   The palaeomagnetism of the Stormberg Lavas, II. The behaviour of the magnetic field during a reversal. *Geophysical Journal of the Royal Astronomical Society* 7:169–182.
Verosub, K. L.
  1977a   Depositional and postdepositional processes in the magnetization of sediments. *Reviews of Geophysics and Space Physics* 15:129–143.
  1977b   The absence of the Mono Lake geomagnetic excursion from the paleomagnetic record of Clear Lake, California. *Earth and Planetary Science Letters* 36:219–230.
Vestine, E. H., L. Laporte, C. Cooper, I. Lange, and W. C. Hendrix
  1947   *Description of the Earth's Main Magnetic Field and its Secular Change, 1905–1945.* Carnegie Institution of Washington Publication 578, Washington, D.C.
Vine, F. J. and D. H. Matthews
  1963   Magnetic anomalies over oceanic ridges. *Nature* 199:947–949.
Walton, D.
  1977   Archaeomagnetic intensity measurements using a squid magnetometer. *Archaeometry* 19:192–200.
  1979   Geomagnetic intensity in Athens between 2000 BC and AD 400. *Nature* 277:643–644.
  1980   Time–temperature relations in the magnetization of assumblies of single domain grains. *Nature* 286:245–247.
Watanabe, N.
  1959   The direction of remanent magnetism of baked earth and its application to chronology for anthropology and archaeology in Japan: An introduction to geomagnetochronology. *Journal of the Faculty Science, University of Tokyo* 2:1–188.
  1964   Some measurements of the direction of remanent magnetism of baked earth from archaeological sites in Peru. *1964 Annual Report of the Rock Magnetism Research Group in Japan:* 30–32.
Watanabe, N. and R. L. DuBois
  1965   Some results of an archaeomagnetic study on the secular variation in the Southwest of North America. *Journal of Geomagnetism and Geoelectricity* 17:395–397.
Watkins, N. D.
  1963   *Magnetic Dating of Archaeological Specimens.* Unpublished manuscript on file at the Arkansas Archeological Survey, Arkansas Tech University, Russellville, Arkansas.
Watkins, N. D. and G. P. L. Walker
  1977   Magnetostratigraphy of eastern Iceland. *American Journal of Science* 277:513–584.
Weaver, G. H.
  1966   Measurement of the Past Intensity of the Earth's magnetic Field. *Archaeometry* 8:174–186.
Weaver, K. F.
  1967   Magnetic clues help date the past. *National Geographic* 131:696–701.
Wei, Q. Y., T. C. Li, G. Y. Chao, W. S. Chang, and S. P. Wang
  1981   Secular variation of the direction of the ancient geomagnetic field for Loyang region, China. *Physics of the Earth and Planetary Interiors* 25:107–112.
Wheat, J. B.
  1955   Mogollon Culture prior to A.D. 1000. *Memoirs of the Society for American Archeology*, No. 10.
Wilson, R. L.
  1961   Palaeomagnetism in Northern Ireland, Part I. The thermal demagnetization of natural magnetic moments in rocks. *Geophysical Journal of the Royal Astronomical Society* 5:45–58.

1961   Paleomagnetism in Northern Ireland, Part II. On the reality of a reversal of the earth's magnetic field. *Geophysical Journal of the Royal Astronomical Society* 5:59–69.

1967   Polarity inverstions of the earth's magnetic field. In *Magnetism and the Cosmos*, edited by W. R. Hindmarsh, F. J. Lowes, P. H. Roberts, and S. K. Runcorn, pp. 79–84. American Elsevier Publishing Co., New York.

Wilson, R. L. and R. Lomax

1972   Magnetic remanence related to slow rotation of ferromagnetic material in alternating magnetic fields. *Geophysical Journal of the Royal Astronomical Society* 30:295–303.

Windes, T. C.

1980   *Archeomagnetic dating: Lessons from Chaco Canyon, New Mexico.* Paper presented at the 45th Annual Meeting of the Society for American Archaeology, Philadelphia.

Wolfman, D.

1973   *A Re-evaluation of Mesoamerican Chronology: A.D. 1–1200.* Ph.D. dissertation, University of Colorado. University Microfilms, Ann Arbor.

1977   Archeomagnetic dates from the Baca Float Sites. *In* Excavations in the Middle Santa Cruz River Valley, Southeastern Arizona, by D. E. Doyel, Appendix G. *Contributions to Highway Salvage Archaeology in Arizona*, No. 44.

1978   An inundated archeomagnetic sample. Appendix I. In *The Mechanical and Chemical Effects of Inundation at Abiquiu Reservoir*, edited by C. F. Schaafsma. School of American Research, Santa Fe.

1979   Archeomagnetic dating in Arkansas. In *Proceedings of the 18th International Symposium on Archaeometry and Archaeological Prospection. Archaeo-Physika* 10:522–533.

1981a   *Recent archeomagnetic dates from the Maya lowlands and the potential for archeomagnetic dating throughout Mesoamerica.* Paper presented at the Unión Internacional de Ciencias Prehistóricas y Protohistóricas, 10th Congress, Mexico.

1981b   *Looking for a needle in a haystack when the neddle may not be there: The possibility of using geomagnetic excursions as a basis for archaeological dating.* Paper presented at the 21st International Archaeometry Symposium, Brookhaven National Laboratory, Upton, New York.

1982a   Archeomagnetic dating in Arkansas and the border areas of adjacent states. In Arkansas Archeology in Review, edited by M. Jeter and N. Trubowitz, pp. 277–300. *Arkansas Archeological Survey Research Series No.* 15, Fayetteville.

1982b   Archeomagnetic results from the Lewisville Site, Denton County, Texas. Report submitted to the U.S. Army Corps of Engineers. Revised version to be published by the Corps of Engineers in a volume on the 1978–1980 excavations at the Lewisville site.

n.d.   Datación por arqueomagnetismo. (To be published in one of the Copán Archeological Project volumes on the 1978 and 1979 field seasons.)

Wolfman, D. and R. L. DuBois

1971   *Recent archeomagnetic results for Mesoamerica and Peru.* Paper presented at the 36th Annual Meeting of the Society for American Archaeology, Norman, Oklahoma.

Wolfman, D., W. Kean, and M. Fowler

1982   *Archeomagnetic results from Modoc Rock Shelter.* Paper presented at the American Geophysical Union Spring Meeting, Philadelphia.

Yukutake, T.

1961   Archaeomagnetic study on volcanic rocks in Oshima Island, Japan. *Bulletin of the Earthquake Research Institute* 39:467–476.

1979   Review of the geomagnetic secular variations on the historical time scale. *Physics of the Earth and Planetary Interiors* 20:83–95.

458   DANIEL WOLFMAN

Yukutake, T., K. Nakamura, and K. Horai
    1964   Magnetization of ash-fall tuffs of Oshima Volcano, Izu II, Application to Archae-
            omagnetism and Volcanology. *Journal of Geomagnetism and Geoelectricity*
            16:183–193.
Yukutake, T. and H. Tachinaka
    1968a   The non-dipole part of the earth's magnetic field. *Bulletin of the Earthquake Research
            Institute* 46:1027–1074.
    1968b   The westward drift of the geomagnetic secular variation. *Bulletin of the Earthquake
            Research Institute* 46:1075–1102.
Yukutake, T., M. Sawada, and T. Yabu
    1964   Magnetization of ash-fall tuffs of Oshima Volcano, Izu, I, Magnetization of Ash-fall
            Tuffs. *Journal of Geomagnetism and Geoelectricity* 16:178–182.

Index